The Norton Book of Interviews

THE NORTON BOOK OF INTERVIEWS

AN ANTHOLOGY FROM 1859 TO THE PRESENT DAY

Edited with an Introduction by
CHRISTOPHER SILVESTER

Preface by
GAY TALESE

W · W · NORTON & COMPANY · NEW YORK · LONDON

First American edition 1996

Originally published in England under the title
THE PENGUIN BOOK OF INTERVIEWS: An Anthology from 1859 to the Present Day

Printed in the United States of America

Library of Congress Cataloguing-in-Publication Data

Penguin book of interviews.
The Norton book of interviews / edited by Christopher Silvester. —
1st American ed.
p.   cm.
"Originally published as The penguin book of interviews: an
anthology from 1859 to the present day"—t.p.
Includes bibliographical references.
1. Celebrities—Interviews.   2. Biography—19th century.
3.   Biography—20th century.   I. Silvester, Christopher.   II. Title.
CT119.P37   1996
920.009'03—dc20   95–5791

ISBN 0-393-03876-9

W. W. Norton & Company, Inc., 500 Fifth Avenue, New York, N.Y. 10110
W. W. Norton & Company Ltd., 10 Coptic Street, London WC1A 1PU

1 2 3 4 5 6 7 8 9 0

To my History teachers –
Peter Read, Robin Reeve, Ted Maidment and Maurice Cowling

'The interview is the worst feature of the new [journalism] – it is degrading to the interviewer, disgusting to the interviewee, and tiresome to the public.'

Le Figaro; translation published in *The Pall Mall Gazette*, 11 May 1886

'I think the interviewer who knows his duty, who really gets at the mind of the person he interviews, who really places him before the public, who is not a mere auctioneer's appraiser of the wretched man's belongings at so much per thousand words – I really do think such a man is a preserver of contemporary history.'

Raymond Blathwayt, interviewed by C. E. Morland, 'The Art of Interviewing: A Chat with Mr Raymond Blathwayt', *Great Thoughts*, 11 June 1892

'Interviewing, in the journalistic sense – the art of extracting personal statements for publication . . . The major interview is a carefully constructed transmitting device, a medium, a mirror.'

Edward Price Bell, *Major Interviewing: Its Principles and its Functions*, 1927

'The interrogative method has certain specific advantages. While unfavourable to the display of background and contextual information, it is a truth-detector of particular sensitivity. It picks up the false, the mendacious and the phoney, but will also register misjudgement, incompetence and plain folly. It is crude to the extent that the knowledge it conveys is limited by the constraints of question and answer, the yes/no type of communication. But this crudeness imposes a wholesome rigour which the more leisurely historical narrative cannot always match.'

George Urban, interviewed by Melvin J. Lasky, 'The Art of the Interview', *Encounter*, March 1989

CONTENTS

ACKNOWLEDGEMENTS

Editing an anthology is usually regarded as a soft option. But if anyone sneeringly suggests this to me I shall have to restrain myself from punching him on the nose. The conventional route of the anthologist, the library catalogue, was helpful only up to a point, since most interviews appeared in ephemeral publications and have never been reprinted. My first clue as to the abiding interest and vivid quality of old interviews was found in the appendix to a book about South African journalism. There I came across Edmund Garrett's interviews with President Paul Kruger of the Transvaal and the British imperialist statesman Cecil Rhodes. One felt as if one were in a room with each of these men, listening to his nostrums and reflections as one would in reading an interview with a modern politician. In addition to this sensation, which must have struck contemporary readers, the modern reader has the advantage of knowing what happened to the interviewee next or even much later. Having embarked on my journey of discovery, my main guides to sources were the indexes and bibliographies in books about famous celebrities and journalists.

For reasons of restricted space I have excluded work by those interviewers who have had some of their work recently published in separate anthologies: Val Hennessy, John Mortimer, Lynn Barber and Naim Attallah have each done work in this genre that I have admired and enjoyed, and I should like to pay tribute to them here. Other British interviewers, as yet unpublished in collected form, who deserve honourable mentions are Maureen Cleave (*Evening Standard*), Valerie Grove (*The Times*), Catherine Bennett (*The Guardian*), Martyn Harris and Megan Tressider (*The Sunday Telegraph*), and Zoë Heller (*The Independent on Sunday* and *Vanity Fair*).

I should like to thank Philip Kerr, himself an anthologist, for encouraging me in this endeavour and for suggesting Caradoc King as my agent and Viking as my publisher. I should also like to thank Clare Alexander, publishing director of Viking and my editor, as well as others associated with the project such as Judith Flanders, Annie Lee, and Hilary Frost.

Richard Ingrams, editor of *The Oldie*, alerted my attention to the interview with G. K. Chesterton, and put me on to George Sylvester Viereck; Christopher Hawtree lent me his copy of Beverley Nichols's *Are They the Same at Home?* and made other helpful suggestions; Michael VerMeulen tipped me off about the left-wing American publication *New Masses*; Rosie Boycott allowed me to rummage among her library of books about journalism; and Valerie Grove put her private collection of cuttings at my disposal, as well as one or two rare books. In addition, the following persons offered me encouragement or suggestions: Lynn Barber, Tom Bower, Chris Carter, Graydon Carter, Terry Coleman, Jonathan Cooper, Liz Elliot, Janine di Giovanni, George Galloway MP, Kenneth Harris, Robert Harris, Stephen Hermer, Mark LeFanu, Christopher Logue, Bruce Palling, Henry Porter, Rex Reed, Paul Spike, and Francis Wheen.

The research for this anthology has proved a massive undertaking and I have been ably assisted in this regard by a team of diligent and enthusiastic researchers who have ploughed through old newspapers and magazines and obtained photocopies for me. In New York I was fortunate to have Maureen Shelly and Sean Griffin to pursue American material, while in London I was able to call upon the skills of Rosanna Greenstreet, Ed Glinert and Victoria Hull. I have calculated that my researchers spent over 500 hours working on this project, eliminating much chaff and many false leads along the way. Having emphasized the hard work involved, however, I should perhaps say how much I have enjoyed charting this largely unexplored territory.

My thanks are also due to the London Library, which is an anthologist's dream because it alone offers the opportunity to browse through the stacks in search of vital clues. The computerized index of the New York Public Library was another source of clues, and this library's efficient and prompt method of retrieving books is a joy for any scholar. The British Library, of course, was indispensable for consulting the more obscure periodicals of the past. Copies of *New Masses* were examined at the Marx Memorial Library, the only library in the United Kingdom to have a set of this periodical; and *The Pall Mall Magazine* was consulted at the National Art Library, in the Victoria and Albert Museum. Most newspapers, except for some of the US provincial press, were to be found at the Newspaper Library, Colindale.

Christopher Silvester
London, May 1993

The editor and publishers wish to thank the following for permission to use copyright material.

Susan Barnes (Susan Crosland) for her interview with Anthony Wedgwood-Benn, *The Spectator*, 17 October 1987; Jean-Pierre Boscq for Georges Belmont's interview with Marilyn Monroe, *Marie-Claire*, 1960; Angela Conner Bulmer, Executor of Penelope Gilliatt's Estate, for her interview with Vladimir Nabokov, *Vogue*, December 1966; Charlotte Chandler for her interview with Mae West in *The Ultimate Seduction*, Doubleday, 1984; Terry Coleman for his interview with Margaret Thatcher, 'Barrister-at-education', *The Guardian*, 2 November 1971; Express Newspapers plc for Montgomery Clift interviewed by Roderick Mann, *The Sunday Express*, 16 August 1959; The Guardian News Service Ltd for 'Mr L. L. George's Appeal for Real War Cabinet' by Harry Boardman, *Manchester Guardian*, 12 April 1940, and Leo Nikolayevich Tolstoy interviewed by Harold Williams, *Manchester Guardian*, 9 February 1905; Duncan Fallowell for his interview with William Burroughs, *Time Out*, September 1982; Eric Glass Ltd on behalf of the author's Estate for 'Sir Edwin Lutyens' in *Are They the Same at Home?* by Beverley Nichols, Jonathan Cape, 1927; Giles Gordon for his interview with Joe Orton, *Transatlantic Review*, Spring 1967; HarperCollins Publishers for material from *Talks with Mussolini* by Emil Ludwig, Allen and Unwin Ltd, 1933; Kenneth Harris for his interview with Lester Piggott, *The Observer*, 1970; David Higham Associates on behalf of Tom Driberg for his interview with Nikita Khrushchev, *Reynold's News*, 16 September 1956; International Creative Management, Inc. for Josh Greenfield's interview with Arthur Miller, *The New York Times*, 13 February 1972. Copyright © 1972 Josh Greenfield; Milton Robert Machlin for his interview with Ernest Hemingway, *Argosy*, September 1958; Thomas B. Morgan for his interview with Alf Landon, *Esquire*, 1963; National Magazine Co. Ltd for Jocelyn Stevens' interview with Harold Macmillan, *Queen*, May 1963; New Republic, Inc. for Edgar Snow's interview with Mao Tse-Tung, *The New Republic*, 27 February 1965. Copyright © 1965 The New Republic, Inc.; *New York Post* for Michel Mok's interview with F. Scott Fitzgerald, 25 September 1936; The New York Times for Robert Van Gelder's interview with Stefan Zweig, 28 July 1940, Harvey Breit's interview with Dylan Thomas, 17 February 1952, Israel Shenker's interview with Samuel Beckett, 6 May 1956, and Mordaunt Hall's interview with Greta Garbo, 24 March 1929. Copyright © 1940/52/56/29 by the New York Times Company; Paris Review for Julian Jebb's interview with Evelyn Waugh, *The Paris Review*, 1962; Peters Fraser & Dunlop Group Ltd on behalf of the author's Estate for 'The Gentle Art of Being Interviewed' from *Complete Essays and Articles of Evelyn Waugh*, edited by Professor Gallagher; Random Century Group Ltd on behalf of the Estate of Marie A. Belloc for her interview with Henri Rochefort, *The Idler*, April 1894; Rex Reed for his interview with Bette Davis, 1975, included in his book *Valentines and Vitriol*, Delacorte Press, 1977; Jerry Stanecki for his interview with Jimmy Hoffa, *Playboy*, December 1975; Richard Stengel for his interview with Paul Johnson, *SPY*, June 1992; Syndication International for F. W. Wilson's interviews with Stanley Baldwin, *The People*, 25 May and 1 June 1924; Times Newspapers Ltd for Robert Robinson's interview with Brendan Behan, *Sunday Graphic*, 15 July 1956; Henry Brandon's interviews with Frank Lloyd Wright, *Sunday Times*, November 1957 and John Kennedy, *Sunday Times*, June 1960; Virago Press Ltd for Djuna Barnes's interview with Frank Harris in *I Could Never be Lonely without a Husband* by Djuna Barnes, 1987. Copyright © 1985 Sun and Moon Press.

Every effort has been made to trace all copyright holders. If any have been overlooked inadvertently the publishers will be pleased to hear from them.

PREFACE

by Gay Talese

Journalism is a voyeuristic vocation that attracts to its employment many people who are often naturally shy and insatiably curious, and each day they are assigned to view the world with a critical eye and a detached sense of intimacy. To become personally or emotionally involved is considered contrary to objective journalism; and yet a press card is a license to pry, to invade privacy if necessary, even to charm and flatter if it will lead to unlocked doors, deeper insights, and to what this book suggests is a kind of "erotic" encounter.

While this anthology is confined to literary interaction, its spirit is guided by the body's most erotic organ, the brain. We learn on the following pages how some of the world's smartest, best-known, and most determinedly self-protective people have briefly surrendered themselves to the scrutiny and use of pursuing journalists—and, as is often the case when matters of the heart dominate the head, with painful and disillusioning consequences. Yet the exhibitionistic tendencies of countless individuals who are famous or infamous, and the voyeuristic antennae that draw journalists to their doors, unfailingly produce new candidates for this *pas de deux* that Oriana Fallaci, the Italian journalist and novelist with the interviewing instincts of a temptress, describes as mental "coitus."

In this book of more than eighty interviews, extending back to the 1850s, we relive the adventures of a variety of suitors on assignations (and presumably expense accounts) as they interact with their subjects and objects of interest in various parts of the world. We find them in a Viennese flower garden with Sigmund Freud; in the woodlands of Prussia with Prince Otto von Bismarck; in a small Norwegian hotel with a tight-lipped Henrick Ibsen; in a house parlor in Germany having tea with Adolf Hitler. We see them with an up-and-coming Swedish actress named Greta Garbo not long before she realized that her reputation was better served by saying less; and we find them with a down-and-out forty-year-old novelist, F. Scott Fitzgerald, while he reclines in bed having another drink. Interviewed in this book are two ex-journalists who made headlines in other endeavors: Benito Mussolini as a Fascist dictator and Karl Marx as a philosopher of mass exploitation. We are also privy to the last published interviews of the prematurely dead labor leader Jimmy Hoffa (presumably murdered by the Mafia) and the Hollywood movie star Marilyn Monroe.

"Are you happy?" Ms. Monroe was asked by a French journalist in 1960, a year before she divorced playwright Arthur Miller and during a period when she would become personally involved with both President John F. Kennedy and his brother Robert. "I think so," she replied. "... I'm only thirty-four and have a few years to go yet..." At thirty-six she overdosed on barbiturates.

Much of what was first said long ago and is reprinted in this book could have been said yesterday.
• "Journalism is a bad business."—Leo Tolstoy, 1905
• "Men are afraid of change"—Christabel Pankhurst, English suffragette, 1910
• "Literary parties . . . the back-to-nature, feministic movement [are] choking the life out of art."—Wyndham Lewis, English novelist and artist, 1931

There is also a recounting of history with a different spin: the Cheyenne chief Two Moon's mournful remembrance of the 1876 Battle of Little Big Horn in Montana ("Get your horses; the white man is coming"), and Gertrude Stein's praise of Dr. Samuel Johnson's biographer that journalism professors might find difficult to endorse ("Boswell is the greatest biographer that ever lived . . . because he put into Johnson's mouth words that Johnson probably never uttered, and yet you know when you read it that that is what Johnson would have said under such and such circumstance—and you know all that because Boswell discovered Johnson's real form which Johnson never knew.")

I discovered much in this book that *I* never knew even though I spent my early professional years conducting interviews (I worked for the *New York Times* from 1955 to 1965); and in later life, as an author of books and a veteran of publicity tours, I have been the subject of interviews and, of course, frequently humbled by the experience. I can therefore appreciate the misgivings of Rudyard Kipling who, while he sought and gained an interview with Mark Twain in 1889 that is reprinted in this volume, had no desire himself to cooperate with the Boston press when it sought to track *him* down in 1892—although it ultimately did publish a so-called interview (also reprinted in this volume) that fits Saul Bellow's description of the type of journalism that leaves thumbprints on one's windpipe.

My own worst experience occurred in 1972, while researching a book to be entitled *Thy Neighbor's Wife*—a study of America's sexually liberating tendencies and its desensitivity to nudity—I allowed a journalist who was an old friend (or so I thought) to accompany me to a nudist spa, after which he proceeded to describe me in print with such coarseness that I would never again assume that friendship extends beyond the length of an interview.

Examples of betrayal and deception abound in this book, not only from the direction of interviewer-to-subject but the other way around. The Mormon leader, Brigham Young, lied during his 1859 interview with Horace Greeley, as we learn in Christopher Silvester's comprehensive Introduction; and Mr. Silvester also suggests that Britain's most renowned interviewer during the late nineteenth century, W. T. Stead, tended to make the people he was communicating with seem more eloquent than they actually were, although he was credited with possessing a remarkable memory and he never took notes. Indeed, note-taking was avoided by many of Mr. Stead's journalistic contemporaries, it being deemed a distraction that would inhibit the conversational flow of the other participant involved in the interview. I myself never cultivated anything approximating Mr. Stead's retentivity during my own journalistic days, but I also shied away from note-taking, or I took notes briefly and as unobtrusively as I could on a small folded sheet of paper. Tape recorders were becoming fashionable during the end of my newspaper days; I loathed them instantly, and believe today that their popularity has had a dehumanizing effect on the personalized journalism that I and many others practiced effectively in the 1950s and 1960s.

The tape recorder is to fine interviewing what fast-food is to fine cooking. It permits a journalist to spend a minimum amount of time with a subject while following the question-and-answer path that leads to the undistinguished kind of article-writing that prevails today. The plastic rolls of tape record the first-draft drift of people's responses, and I think it has inspired a laziness on the part of young journalists, and deafened them to the subtle nuances inherent in all exchanges between communicating people. What is being lost, in my opinion, is the art of listening—an art that this volume celebrates most impressively since most of the interviews herein pre-date the popularity of the little plastic box. If listening is seductive, if good listeners make good lovers, then this book might qualify as a nightstand reader.

THE NORTON BOOK OF
INTERVIEWS

INTRODUCTION

I

Since its invention a little over 130 years ago, the interview has become a commonplace of journalism. Today, almost everybody who is literate will have read an interview at some point in their lives, while from the other point of view, several thousand celebrities have been interviewed over the years, some of them repeatedly. So it is hardly surprising that opinions of the interview – of its functions, methods and merits – vary considerably. Some might make quite extravagant claims for it as being, in its highest form, a source of truth, and, in its practice, an art. Others, usually celebrities who see themselves as its victims, might despise the interview as an unwarranted intrusion into their lives, or feel that it somehow diminishes them, just as in some primitive cultures it is believed that if one takes a photographic portrait of somebody then one is stealing that person's soul. V. S. Naipaul 'feels that some people are wounded by interviews and lose a part of themselves'.[1] Lewis Carroll, the creator of *Alice in Wonderland*, was said to have had 'a just horror of the interviewer' and he never consented to be interviewed:

> It was his horror of being lionized which made him thus repel would-be acquaintances, interviewers, and the persistent petitioners for his autograph and he would afterwards relate the stories of his success in silencing all such people with much satisfaction and amusement. Not long ago Mr Dodgson happened to get into correspondence with a man whom he had never seen, on some questions of religious difficulty, and he invited him to come to his rooms and have a talk on the subject. When, therefore, a Mr X was announced to him one morning he advanced to meet him with outstretched hand and smiles of welcome. 'Come in, Mr X, I have been expecting you.' The delighted visitor thought this a promising beginning and immediately pulled out a note-book and pencil, and proceeded to ask 'the usual questions'. Great was Mr Dodgson's disgust! Instead of his expected friend here was another man of the same name, and one of the much-dreaded interviewers, actually sitting in his chair! The mistake was soon explained, and the representative of the press was bowed out as quickly as he had come in.[2]

Rudyard Kipling expressed an even more condemnatory attitude towards the interviewer. His wife, Caroline, writes in her diary for 14 October 1892 that their day was 'wrecked by two reporters from Boston'. She reports her husband as saying to the reporters: 'Why do I refuse to be interviewed? Because it is immoral! It is a crime, just as much of a crime as an offence against my person, as an assault, and just as much merits punishment. It is cowardly and vile. No respectable man would ask it, much less give it.'[3] Yet Kipling had himself perpetrated such an 'assault' on Mark Twain only a few years before. H.G. Wells in an interview in 1894 referred to 'the interviewing ordeal',[4] but was a fairly frequent interviewee and forty years later found himself interviewing Joseph Stalin. Saul Bellow, who has consented to be interviewed on several occasions, nevertheless once described interviews as being like thumbprints on his windpipe.

Distrust of the interview and the interviewer has been a constant theme since the beginning. General Boulanger, the French political leader of the 1880s, told an interviewer from *The Pall Mall Gazette* of his first brush with an English interviewer:

> Did I ever tell you of the first 'interview' I ever had on English soil? No? Well, listen. It was at the Hotel Bristol, the morning after my arrival from Belgium. I was sitting down to breakfast, an individual was shown into the room. His face as unknown to me as his name. Without bidding me bonjour he marched up to the table: 'Are you General Boulanger?' said he. 'Yes,' I answered, somewhat taken aback. 'Then be good enough to answer these questions,' and to my amazement he took a little notebook out of his breast pocket, and began firing off a series of impertinent questions. Mastering the situation, I rose. 'There is the door, be good enough to walk through it, monsieur.' After uttering an ejaculation he disappeared, greatly to my relief, and I sent for the manager of the hotel and told him that no one was in future to be shown in to me until I had seen his card. Imagine my surprise the next day to see two long columns, headed 'Interview with General Boulanger', in the next day's paper.[5]

Several decades later, the film actor Dustin Hoffman recounted (also in an interview) his own, equally disillusioning, first experience of an interviewer. 'They've already decided what you are . . .,' he explained. 'I had just Beacon-waxed my floor and she came in, smelled, and says, "You been smoking pot in here?" And I said, "That's Beacon wax." And she says, "Come on . . . I know what you people do." '[6]

W.L. Alden, writing in 1895, was scathing in his analysis of the whole process of interviewing on the grounds that it had a corrupting effect on the parties involved:

> He [the interviewer] is the most potent force in the manufacture of liars and hypocrites that ever existed. The man who submits to an interview

knows that he is talking for publication. He, therefore, expresses all sorts of nice hypocritical sentiments which he thinks will please the public, and he abstains from expressing his real convictions because the public would not approve of them. In other words, he persistently lies, and it is the Interviewer who instigates him to lie. As for the Interviewer himself, his trade is to lie. He must make an interesting article out of his interview with this or that man, and if the man is dull and uninteresting, as he almost invariably is, the Interviewer feels compelled to put sentences in his victim's mouth which will make the report of the interview readable. That is to say, the report of the interview is always more or less untrue, and the Interviewer depends on the piquancy of his lies for his success with his readers ... The reader of the interview feels confident that the Interviewed lied when he made any definite statement; and further, that the Interviewer lied when he said that the Interviewed made the statement in question.[7]

However, it is as well for those who write interviews for a living, as for those who regard the experience of being interviewed as a wretched business, to keep a sense of proportion. The interview is a broken-backed form of discourse, which is necessarily partial. The interviewer is ultimately in control of what is published, although one nineteenth-century interviewer wrote that the interviewee 'if he wishes it ... must be largely master of its manner',[8] while another wrote that it 'is always in the power of the interviewed to strike the keynote'.[9] The result may be banal or profound, pedestrian or intriguing. It may grant us admittance to the mind of the subject or allow the subject to bamboozle us with his own tendency to self-mythologize. Whatever the case, there is inevitably a trade-off. One modern interviewer, Lynn Barber, has put it like this:

> ... the interview seems to me a perfectly straightforward, if perhaps rather cynical, transaction. As with any commercial transaction, both sides hope to get slightly more than they give, and one side is bound to be disappointed. If the journalist is disappointed, though, he/she can simply dump the interview – a fact sophisticated subjects are aware of, so they try to give good tape. They try to make themselves interesting but in a way that does not give too much of themselves away.[10]

Yet despite the drawbacks of the interview, it is a supremely serviceable medium of communication. 'These days, more than at any other time, our most vivid impressions of our contemporaries are through interviews,' Denis Brian has written. 'Almost everything of moment reaches us through one man asking questions of another. Because of this, the interviewer holds a position of unprecedented power and influence.'[11]

II

The interview can be defined as a 'face to face meeting for the purpose of a
formal conference, between a representative of the press and someone from
whom he wishes to obtain statements for publication',[12] and interviewing has
been called 'the art of extracting personal statements for publication'.[13] The
credit for having invented the interview has been attributed both to Horace
Greeley, editor of the *New-York Tribune*, and to James Gordon Bennett Sr, the
proprietor of *The New York Herald*. Greeley's famous interview in Salt Lake
City with Brigham Young, the leader of the Mormon Church, was published in
August 1859, although Bennett is credited with interviewing the US president
Martin Van Buren in Washington twenty years earlier. Yet the Van Buren
'interview' consists merely of a few paragraphs in which Bennett offers a
description of their meeting, the proximate scope of their conversation and
some tart observations about his subject's appearance, but virtually no reported
speech, either direct or indirect.[14]

Greeley's interview with Brigham Young, by contrast, can lay claim to being
the first fully-fledged interview with a celebrity, much of it in the question-and-
answer format familiar to modern readers. While Bennett's *Herald* published
reports which contained tiny snatches of reported conversation back in the
1830s, these can hardly be counted as interviews in the accepted, modern sense.
For instance, Bennett's 1836 published conversation with Rosina Townsend, a
witness in the Ellen Jewett murder case, has sometimes been described as the
first interview, although one historian has pointed out that 'with its Q and A
form as commonly used then in reports of trials, [*it*] sounds more like an
unofficial deposition (an official was present) ...' Indeed, historians have
suggested that the tendency towards the interview technique grew from the
familiarity of journalists and readers with verbatim court reports and with the
'human interest' element that arose from such reports.[15] However, the emergence
of the interview coincided with several other developments. Mass education and
mass-market publications, for instance, meant that there was a receptive audience
for numerous and various opinions; such was the nature of modern bourgeois
society that there was also an increasing number of persons qualifying as
celebrities, many of whom were not themselves writers; the rise of the realistic
novel meant that readers were increasingly familiar with naturalistic dialogue,
though some interviewers might succumb to the 'temptation to see men and
their settings through the eyes of a fourth-rate period dramatist';[16] but above all
else the ascendancy of the interview was part of a revolution in the perception
of public figures. As the historian J.A. Froude told the interviewer Raymond
Blathwayt in a letter, he had been 'deeply interested' in Blathwayt's interview
with one of his old friends, the eminent biologist Sir Richard Owen: 'You have
hit him off to the life, and I could almost imagine I was sitting in the room and

talking to him.'[17] This was, and has been ever since, the fundamental reason why the interview has such a grip on the reader – the illusion it conveys of intimacy with celebrities and those who are the witnesses of momentous events.

A few months after the Greeley/Young interview, the *New York Herald* sent a reporter to interview Gerrit Smith, a Quaker, about his role in the Harper's Ferry incident, in which John Brown led a rogue band of anti-slavery agitators on a raid against an arsenal. Edwin L. Shuman in his *Practical Journalism* (1903) quotes an American editor, whom he discreetly calls 'Brown', as attributing the first interview to the *New York Herald* in 1859: 'When the John Brown raid occurred at Harper's Ferry the *Herald* sent a reporter to call on Gerrit Smith in his home in Peterborough. Smith discussed the matter freely and the result was an interview in the modern sense. During the civil war it was applied to many men and became a permanent feature of journalism.'[18] Another commentator has described this as 'the first conventional interview'.[19] However, J.B. McCullagh, who later became editor of the St Louis *Globe-Democrat*, was credited with popularizing the interview as a daily journalist in the years following the Civil War, and his example was followed by various writers such as Murat Halstead, Henry Watterson, Joe Howard and George Alfred Townsend. Indeed, McCullagh became the first journalist to interview a US president, when he interviewed Andrew Johnson shortly before Johnson was impeached.[20]

In September 1890 the American journalist Frank A. Burr wrote an article in *Lippincott's Magazine* called 'The Art of Interviewing', in which he looked back with professional pride on the twenty-five years since the invention of the interview: 'Like all other changes in a great industry, the method has been abused both by interviewer and interviewed, fully as often by the latter as the former. But had it not been for the interview much valuable matter relating to the history of this country since 1860 would have been lost, not only to the nation, but to the nation's annals.' Yet back in the 1860s the *Chicago Tribune*, for example, did not appreciate this attribute of the interview and its criticism was reprinted in London, in the *Daily News*: 'A portion of the daily newspapers in New York are bringing the profession of journalism into contempt so far as they can, by a kind of toadyism or flunkeyism, which they call interviewing.'[21] And *The Nation*, the New York liberal journal, declared in 1869 that the interview 'as at present managed is generally the joint product of some humbug of a hack politician and another humbug of a newspaper reporter'.[22] A couple of years later, changing tack only slightly, *The Nation* charged the interview with making 'fools of great men'.[23] Richard Grant White, editor of the magazine *Galaxy*, wrote that the interview was 'the most perfect contrivance yet devised to make journalism an offence, a thing of ill savour in all decent nostrils'.[24] By contrast, Henry W. Grady, the editor of the *Atlanta Constitution*, pointed out that the interview had prestigious antecedents, as 'Socrates, a thoroughly respectable person, introduced the custom on the streets of Athens.'[25]

Few early interviews were on a par with the Socratic dialogues and the highbrows might cavil, but once invented the interview proved irresistible as a means of journalistic inquiry and was soon deemed acceptable, at least as coming from American reporters. Here is an account of what was said when the Emperor of Brazil found himself being interviewed by a representative of *The New York Herald* while on a visit to Cairo, Egypt, in 1871:

CORRESPONDENT: I see a copy of Galignani, containing an interview with Mr Seward, from the *New York Herald*, on your table. Has your majesty read it?

DOM PEDRO: I did, with interest. Mr Seward has been a great traveler [*sic*], and seems to have thoroughly improved his opportunities for observation. I shall not be able to go so far as he has done. By the way, I suppose I am now being 'interviewed', which, I believe, is the term.

CORRESPONDENT: Yes, your majesty; but I will with pleasure submit my manuscript to your secretary if there should be anything you may wish expunged.

DOM PEDRO: Thank you; but perhaps it will not matter. I have been in a constant state of 'interview' all my life, and consequently say nothing I am not willing to have made public. It is rather novel, though, to find a correspondent of the *New York Herald* under the shadow of the Pyramids.

CORRESPONDENT: They are enterprising men, the *Herald* correspondents, and go everywhere.

DOM PEDRO: Well, you are an enterprising people, and deserve the great prosperity you enjoy ... But I must ask you to excuse me now, as I am engaged to receive the Prince Heretier at this hour. I wish you good morning.[26]

The Oxford English Dictionary puts the origin of the word 'interview' as a journalistic term in 1869, and in that year an item in *The Nation* reminded readers that interviewing 'is confined to American journalism'.[27]

However, Henri de Blowitz, the European correspondent of *The Times*, was allowed to interview such public figures as King Alfonso XII of Spain, Maurice Gambetta (architect of France's Third Republic), Prince Bismarck, the Shah of Persia, Pope Leo XIII, and Sultan Abdul Hamid II of Turkey for dispatches he sent to *The Times* (though Bismarck denounced the journalist in the Reichstag for reporting what *he* had understood to be a private conversation). In a curious display of double standards, though, *The Times* was not prepared to countenance the publication of interviews with domestic celebrities. The first interview to be conducted with a public figure in England was with the Liberal politician, W.E. Forster, on his return from a trip to Bulgaria, and the interviewer was W.T. Stead. Forster agreed to be interviewed by Stead but laid down two conditions (the second being somewhat absurd):

I have no objection to be interviewed, for I think the interview affords a public man an invaluable agency for launching his ideas without responsibility, and enabling him to feel the public pulse before formally committing himself on the subject; but there are two provisos. First, no interview should ever be published until the proof or the MS. has been submitted to the person interviewed for his correction; and, secondly, the fact that the interview has been read before its publication by the interviewed should never be revealed to the world, otherwise an interview which was known to have been revised by the person interviewed would be almost as compromising to him as if he had written a signed article or made a public speech.[28]

Stead was responsible for popularizing the interview formula in the Britain of the 1880s. In the first six months of 1884, for example, *The Pall Mall Gazette*, an evening paper edited by Stead, carried no less than seventy-nine interviews.[29] Sir Wemyss Reid in his *Memoirs* argued that Stead's interviews with 'the foremost men of our time' marked the inception of what quickly became known as 'The New Journalism'.[30] Indeed, the interview was regarded with suspicion by many of the traditionalists of the British press, partly because it was new and partly because it was an import from the United States. One commentator wrote sneeringly in 1887 that the interview, long a staple of foreign correspondent work and 'cautiously adopted nearer home in such series as "Celebrities at Home"', was now 'freely resorted to in the case of any politician, religionist, social reformer, man of science, artist, tradesman, rogue, madman, or any one else, who cared to advertise himself or his projects or pursuits, and in whom the public could be expected to take an interest'.[31] The editor and the proprietor of *The Pall Mall Gazette* deserved much of the blame, so this commentator argued, for introducing the phenomenon to daily journalism in Britain and for 'dressing out their interviews with dramatic or melodramatic, minutely accurate or judiciously imagined details.'

These sneers did not worry Stead. He had seen the ultimate justification of what he was doing when his interview with 'Chinese Gordon' about imperial policy in the Sudan actually persuaded the Gladstone government to send Gordon to Khartoum, thus giving rise to Stead's later boast that he ran the empire from Northumberland Street – the site of the *Pall Mall Gazette* offices. Consequently, Stead was a proselytizer for the interview. In an 'Occasional Note' in *The Pall Mall Gazette* on 5 April 1884 he wrote: 'One of the superstitions of the English press – superstitions which are fortunately on the wane – is that interviewing in England is a monstrous departure from the dignity and propriety of journalism. None of our dignified contemporaries hesitates to interview anyone outside the British Isles, but interviewing . . . must not cross the channel.'

A few months later, in August 1884, Stead wrote a leader entitled 'Interviewing versus Bookmaking' in which he commented on the decision by Lord Chief Justice Coleridge to write a book about a recent ten-week visit to the United States. Stead argued that whatever demand existed for Lord Coleridge's reflections to be published it was 'not really a demand for literature, but a demand for conversation . . . It would be absurd to hear Lord Coleridge philosophizing about America. It is very natural to want to hear him talk about it. But for a talk, a book is not the proper form.' Again in August, Stead praised the interview for its essentially demotic quality and its applicability to those unable to write well, yet whose opinions might be of interest. He described the interview as '. . . the most interesting method of extracting the ideas of the few for the instruction and entertainment of the many which has yet been devised by man . . . Many notable men are more or less inarticulate, especially with the pen, and to them the intervention of the interviewer is almost as indispensable as that of an interpreter is to an Englishman in China.'[32] At the end of the year, Stead was able to claim a triumph: 'Among the permanent gains of the year the acclimatization of the "interview" in English journalism certainly should be reckoned. That this form of influencing public opinion supplied, as the phrase goes, a real want, is proved by the fact that it only needed a single example to make most of the newspapers follow suit . . . Before this time next year we confidently expect to see the interview acclimatized in the columns of the "leading" journal.'

The highbrow disdain for the interview as a form was expressed in a searing unsigned comment published in *The Saturday Review* on 6 September 1890. The comment was in response to the article by Frank A. Burr published in that month's edition of *Lippincott's Magazine*. As we have already seen, this looked back over the first twenty-five-odd years of the practice of interviewing in American publications and concluded that the interview had made a valuable contribution to contemporary historical knowledge. Stead leapt to the defence of Burr in the same day's edition of *The Pall Mall Gazette*. Burr's only offence, said Stead, was 'that for a number of years he had earned his living as the medium between men who had something to say and a public which wished to hear it . . .':

> On the face of it, an interview is only the account of a conversation: a means, that is to say, of conveying the views or depicting the personality of a man to which history has always owed at least half its reality and colour . . . In so far as the interviewer is merely a sort of convenient private secretary who gives to the world a signed article by the man of the moment on the subject of the moment without giving him the trouble of literary composition, or the public the expense of spending half-a-crown on a belated review which many of them will neither afford to buy or care to read, we take it that he stands or falls with journalism as a whole . . . And the interviewer has this point of advantage over the reviewer in the

comparison – he does convey the sayings of men who have a right to speak, while the *Saturday Review* conveys the sayings of somebody who is generally, no doubt, a scholar, and, more often than not, a gentleman, but whose credentials in other respects are shrouded behind the veil of anonymity.

Stead conceded that interviewers, particularly those of the 'Celebrity at Home' variety, were sometimes guilty of lapses of taste, but that 'compared to the value of an immense engine of democratic enlightenment, a fault here and there of taste need not stop the world from rubbing round'.

At the same time that Stead was forcing the interview down the throats of British newspaper readers, there was one man in the United States who more than any other was seeking to popularize the interview as a feature of everyday journalism. This was Joseph Pulitzer, perhaps the most famous figure in the annals of American journalism because of the celebrated prizes which bear his name to this day. His newspaper, the New York *World*, carried several ground-breaking interviews, including one with Queen Victoria. Although it consisted largely of a laborious description by the journalist of his delicate approach to the monarch in a Scottish churchyard, one memorable phrase falls from her lips when she exclaims to her equerry that the reporter is 'as audacious as the rest of his nation'.[33] Another interview, with a former US president, General Ulysses S. Grant, in 1884 was significant because Grant used the occasion to announce his endorsement of John Logan for the Republican presidential nomination. The interview put *The World* ahead of the pack on a major news story.[34]

Pulitzer was quite certain of the elements that constituted a proper interview. Perhaps in part because of his blindness, Pulitzer attached great value to detailed physical descriptions of interviewees in his paper. 'Please impress on the men who write our interviews with prominent men,' he wrote in a memo to a senior member of his staff, 'the importance of giving a striking, vivid pen sketch of the subject: also a vivid picture of the domestic environment, his wife, his children, his animal pets, etc. Those are the things that will bring him more clearly home to the average reader than would his most imposing thoughts, purposes or statements.'[35] This aspect of the interviewing art was also a preoccupation for Henri de Blowitz, though, as his biographer has pointed out, 'it is hard to decide how much this was the result of real observation and how much was due to the literary and dramatic conventions of the period, in which men and women were for ever sighing, flushing, contracting their facial muscles or betraying by the light of their eyes some powerful inner emotion'.[36]

Similar conventions to those laid down by Pulitzer were observed by George Newnes when he began to publish a series of 'Illustrated Interviews' in his London monthly *The Strand Magazine* in the early 1890s. As well as containing colourful descriptions, these articles were invariably accompanied by various portraits or photographs of the subject at different stages of his or her life, photographs of his or her residence, and other illustrations (such as samples of the subject's letter-hand). *The Idler*, another illustrated monthly, edited by Jerome K. Jerome, had a similar interview feature called 'Lions in their Dens'. But the anonymous author of a 1900 handbook for aspiring journalists, *How to Write for the Magazines*, ventilated his dislike for too much colour:

> Don't, therefore, talk so much about 'Miss Jennyson's room being a scene in Fairyland!' Don't prate about her lovely old ormolu cabinets; her fine Chippendale furniture; her charmingly-hung brass bedstead! Unless there is something very special why Miss Jennyson's bedstead should be brought in (as, for instance, if it were a gift to her from some royal or very famous person), it is doubtful whether the reading public takes enough interest in the lady herself to care two buttons what sort of bedstead she has! They would resent Miss Jennyson prying into their most sacred private apartments, and so do not let them pry into Miss Jennyson's.[37]

By 1895 the interview, although established as a staple journalistic technique, was still drawing the fire of high-minded critics. In an essay on 'The New Journalism' in the *New Review*, Evelyn March Phillips deplored the cult of banality to which the practice of interviewing had given rise:

> On a journey last week, a friend supplied me with two sixpenny illustrated papers. They contained eight interviews betwen them. Now, time was when the interview was justified upon the plea that it was calculated to gratify intelligent curiosity; that it gave an insight into the individuality of conspicuous people, and allowed them an opportunity of supplementing information already in the hands of the public by informal explanation; or that it placed before us clearly the principles of some interesting discovery or creation. But the important personages have been sucked dry long since; remarkable characters do not crop up in proportion to the demand for them; so a list that has started merrily enough tails off to any mediocrity who o'ertops his fellows by an inch. During that afternoon in a railway carriage I had time to work steadily through those revelations offered for the week's acceptance. The most were concerned with actors and actresses whose names conveyed little to my mind. Here was interviewed a lady who rides a spotted horse at some circus, and there were given two portraits, with intimate details of a she-Parisian whose claim on the public attention consists in being handsome and notorious. Anybody interested in the description of a palm-treed flat with Liberty draperies, or in the not remarkable tastes and the by no means original opinions of second-rate burlesque actresses, would have found plenty to inform and amuse. Interesting suggestion or word of wit there was none.

The opening sentences of one interview did indeed raise brief expectations. 'It is not easy to write an interview,' it began, 'when you have been holding your sides with laughter. So-and-so has never ceased saying quaint things in his own inimitable way.' I glanced forward eagerly, but all the quaint things had been left to the imagination.[38]

Not all interviews were sources of triviality. Indeed, some publications saw the interview form as an opportunity for high-mindedness. *Great Thoughts*, founded in London in 1884, had a Congregationalist deacon, Thomas Smith, for its proprietor and a Wesleyan minister, the Revd Robert P. Downes, for its editor. A weekly magazine, it consisted of essays and book reviews, quotations from authors, serialized novels of an ethically earnest kind, and interviews – with clerics naturally, but also with writers, politicians, philanthropists, explorers, missionaries and social reformers. Smith and Downes believed in the interview as an instrument of moral edification and as a spur to intellectual self-improvement 'which should lend to abstract thought the charm of personal life and example', as Dr Downes put it. 'I was impressed with the idea,' he reflected some years later, 'that it would be a good thing to supply portions of pure and ennobling literature to my fellow-countrymen, at a price which would place them within the reach of all . . . I desired also to provide an antidote to so much offered to the reading public which is trashy, frivolous, and deteriorating.'[39] The magazine's star interviewer, Raymond Blathwayt (who probably had more assignments as a jobbing interviewer over a twenty-five-year period than any of his contemporaries), was the son of an Anglican divine and himself a former curate, and *Great Thoughts*, which had a circulation of 50,000, was 'largely read by the clergy and ministers of all denominations'. Thomas Smith, interviewed by Blathwayt for *Great Thoughts* in 1892, explained that a good weekly should contain everything 'that will uplift' and should be 'based on moral, social, and scientific lines – for science, in my opinion, is part of religion . . .'[40]

By the early 1890s the publication of interviews had reached epidemic proportions. Apart from the accessibility of the form, interviews made good commercial sense. They were the best way of associating a publication with distinguished names from all walks of life, without having to pay such personages the substantial fees as writers that their celebrity would otherwise invite. When Harry Cust became editor of *The Pall Mall Gazette*, one of his journalists, Lincoln Springfield, 'found that the line of least resistance, yielding the most plentiful copy with the smallest output of exertion' was the interview. It helped too that Cust, as heir-presumptive to an earldom, was related to many of the subjects the magazine selected.[41]

In its number for December 1895, *The Idler* published a symposium of 'the Interviewed', discussing the question 'Are Interviewers a Blessing or a Curse?' The participants were Mrs Lynn Linton, Barry Pain, W.T. Stead, John Strange Winter, and W.L. Alden. Mrs Lynton described interviewers as 'about the biggest nuisances and the most futile failures of all at present patronized by this crazy age'. She felt that interviews were 'the purest humbug', that they were 'shallow' and of questionable value as guides to the personalities of their subjects, because two interviewers would be bound to form different impressions of the same person. As we have already seen, another enemy of the interview, W.L. Alden, argued that the interview-subject deliberately presented a bogus front to please the public, while the interviewer, if he felt that the subject was 'dull and uninteresting', would put false words into the subject's mouth in order to spice up the copy. As if to confirm this point, though not disapprovingly, W.T. Stead wrote: 'I have had a pretty extensive experience, both as interviewer and interviewed, as the result of which I should say that those whom you interview are most impressed with the marvellous accuracy of your memory when you make them talk a great deal better than they did.' T.P. O'Connor, the Irish Nationalist MP and a journalist himself as well as a newspaper proprietor, recalled the experience of being interviewed by Stead during another interview with a journalist from the *Sketch*:

> I always dread a chance interviewer like you, because you put my thoughts in your own bright and vigorous language, and the result is sometimes startlingly egotistic in tone. I was interviewed once by Mr Stead, when he was in prison, and the next day I hid myself: I found myself addressing the world after so infallible, cocksure, and lofty a fashion that I blushed at my own image. I was Steadesque, not statuesque; and though I admire Mr Stead, I prefer to speak in my own character. Pray, don't do me the same disfavour.

Stead's reaction to this criticism was sanguine:

> Disfavour indeed! 'Oh wad some power the giftie gie us, to see oursels as ithers see us.' I am not to blame if Mr O'Connor did not like the reflection of his blushing countenance in the mirror of my interview. If Mr O'Connor had not the opportunity of revising the proof of his interview before it appeared, the omission can only be explained on the ground that I was in durance vile and could not see to things. It was the inexorable rule at the *Pall Mall Gazette* not to publish any interview until the proof had been revised by the interviewed one.[42]

Although Stead refers to his interviewing technique as mirroring his subject, he often mirrored himself. One interviewer reckoned that this was peculiar to the English as opposed to the American type of interview:

> The observant reader will notice that I have managed to run in five capital 'I's' in the first few lines of this article. There you have the whole

secret of interviewing as practised AD 1894 in England. The successful interviewer blazons forth as much of his own personality as possible; using his victim as a peg on which to hang his own opinions. If the interviewer could be induced to hang himself as well as his opinions the world would be brighter and better . . .

. . . In America you get the real thing, and even the youngest man there understands how it should be done. An interviewer should be like a clear sheet of plate glass that forms the front window of an attractive shop, through which you can see the articles displayed, scarcely suspecting that anything stands between you and the interesting collection.[43]

Another reason why the interview drew the fire of social commentators was that it was an area of journalistic endeavour where women were allowed to compete equally with men. As Professor John Carey has pointed out in his *The Intellectuals and the Masses*: 'For some male intellectuals, a regrettable aspect of popular newspapers was that they encouraged women . . . popular journalism became, however imperfectly, a channel for awareness, independence and self-reliance among women.'[44] That the interview as conducted by women had taken grip in the United States is attested by Henry James's 1880 novel *The Portrait of a Lady*, which contains a female character called Henrietta Stackpole, a tiresome journalist who writes for a fictitious New York magazine called *The Interviewer*. Elizabeth L. Banks, an American journalist who came to work in London during the 1890s, and who caused a stir by working as a domestic servant for a few months in order to write about her experiences, believed that interviewing was 'the most pleasant, interesting, and edifying branch of journalistic work that can be taken up by a woman' because it 'throws her into contact with the great, the extraordinary, and the interesting people of the world'.[45] Indeed, it offered women a rare chance to meet with public men unchaperoned, and for this reason some public men objected to female interviewers, only assenting on the condition that there should be a third person present. The practice took longer to become established on the Continent, where, according to *Pall Mall Gazette* journalist Hulda Friederichs, the foreign celebrities that she visited seldom 'forgot to be astonished at, and a little curious about, the lady interviewer'.[46] Elizabeth Banks thought that women made 'much better interviewers than men' because they were 'usually more tactful', had a 'far greater amount of adroitness among their natural characteristics', were 'also quicker and more apt at observing and taking account of the little things of life', and were 'more capable of making "much ado about nothing" when they return to their offices after having been in conversation with a prominent person'.[47] One editor praised female interviewers because 'more than once . . . a celebrity who at first had been disinclined to talk yielded to their persuasiveness and droitness.'[48]

III

The burgeoning cult of the celebrity meant that readers of newspapers and magazines developed the appetite for acquainting themselves with the minutest details of the lives of public personalities. It is hardly surprising that some celebrities found the interviewing process wearisome and their own contributions to it repetitive. 'People will think me the biggest gossip in Europe if I allow myself to be interviewed again – for the fiftieth, or is it the hundredth time? – since I have returned to Paris,' explained the French novelist Alphonse Daudet to R.H. Sherard in an interview for the July 1895 edition of *The Humanitarian*. 'And further, *mon fils*, what new things can I say? Have I not emptied my sack? Indeed, I have been made to say more things than I ever did say, greatly to my annoyance. Was I not reported to have spoken with contempt and in misrepresentation of your beautiful English women, whom never did I so criticize, and so on?'

Another who belonged to the ranks of the much-interviewed was the American writer Mark Twain. In 'Mark Twain, A Conglomerate Interview, Personally Conducted by Luke Sharp', in the February 1892 edition of *The Idler*, Twain was quoted as saying: 'If anyone interviews me again, I will send him a bill for five times what I would charge for an article the length of an interview.' Indeed, when Twain reached the age of seventy, in 1900, he 'denied himself to most interviewers' and 'publicly announced that he would never again hold forth on any stated subject unless he had given that subject proper reflection beforehand'. A few years later he visited England and was asked for an interview by a newspaper so that they could 'marconigraph' it to American liners crossing the Atlantic. 'Why that's work,' said Twain, 'and I've retired from work long ago.'[49] In one sense, the interview, for all its educative and entertainment value, has always been a deeply parasitic form. 'My God!' exclaimed Wilson Mizner to the female interviewer Djuna Barnes in 1916, 'am I to be held up for intellectual plunder all the way to my office? The jewels of my speech that I have already lavished on you would make you a pair of suspenders.' Oriana Fallaci, while distinguishing her own interviews from the common or garden variety, admits that interviews 'are much easier to do than writing . . . you take the "flower" of others and you sell it as your own.'[50] In the first couple of decades of the twentieth century, British cricketers became reluctant interviewees. The reason for this was that 'several of them, when engaged to write on the leading matches throughout the season, realized that their special knowledge was of special value; and they became less disposed to talk for publication'.[51]

In 1895 a rather curious libel action arose – as the result of an interview that had never taken place. W.S. Gilbert, the famous librettist of the Savoy operas, found himself being sued for libel by a lady journalist, the Comtesse de Bremont. The Comtesse was an interviewer for *St Paul's* magazine and had written to Gilbert asking for an interview. Gilbert had replied, demanding a fee of twenty guineas for granting an interview (he later explained that he had asked for the fee because the Comtesse had a reputation for indiscretion). She then retorted that she looked forward to writing his obituary notice for nothing. Gilbert sent copies of their correspondence with a covering note to various newspapers, so that their editors would be aware of the lady's spite towards him, and the lady subsequently sued for libel on the grounds that Gilbert's covering note had supposedly contained innuendoes to the effect that she had fraudulently assumed the title of Comtesse and that she was not a woman of good repute. Gilbert successfully defended the action, but the points of interest here are that the celebrity was nervous about being interviewed by a particular journalist and that he regarded his opinions as having a modest commercial value.[52]

When Edward John Hart asked the actress Sarah Bernhardt, at the end of a very long interview for *The Strand Magazine*, whether there was nothing more she could tell him, she gave an answer which expressed frustration at her plight as a professional interviewee:

My friend, it is not possible! one version at least of everything I do or have done is known and written about. Everyone who interviews me asks more or less the same questions. I go over the same ground repeatedly, and what answers I don't give they invent for themselves. The moment I intend producing a new play, all the French papers want to know about it.

You know, I must reserve a few secrets for my memoirs, which I am bringing out shortly. In them I shall simply content myself with telling the story of my life, clearing up what is obscure, and setting right much that has been written and said about me, and which was not worth contradicting in detail or which at the time I had no opportunity of refuting, and so it has become a tradition I have not at this moment the leisure to rectify.[53]

George R. Sims, the playwright and humorous newspaper columnist, explained the perils of celebrity to Arthur H. Lawrence, an interviewer from *The Idler*. The main burden was the vast amount of letters he received:

'Now do you see how interviews damage one? Each interview opens up a fresh lot of correspondence. Why, if it wasn't for a little capital this celebrity business would drive me into the workhouse. People think it's a nice thing to have one's name put about. Personally, I'm seriously thinking of retiring to a cottage, and changing my name – it would pay better. You can take my word for it that if you say anything about the miseries of having a big letter-bag, people will think it a joke. Just look at that!' and Mr Sims handed me a letter in which a lady stated that she suspected her sister's husband of being insane. 'He murders people continually,' I read. 'He is a doctor and in the habit of sending poisons by post.' 'I feel sure you would not mind going to his house as a guest and watching him,' the lady continues, 'you would soon discover the truth, if he did not recognize you.' 'You have seen that specimen letter for yourself,' said Mr Sims, when I had read it. 'You see the idea, I am to go down to Londonderry – at my own expense, and *disguised*!'

Later in the same interview, Sims was asked his opinion of interviewers:

'The only thing I like about interviewing is that it brings a stranger under my roof with whom I can exchange views before I go back to my drudgery,' he replied. 'I can tell you about an experience in interviewing which I did not like. The interviewer knew nothing whatever about me, and told me that he had not had time to read up my history. The conversation went on much in this way: "What is your profession?" he said. "Well, I'm a journalist and dramatist," I replied. "Oh, on *The Referee*? Are you a sporting correspondent or what?" "I write Mustard and Cress." "Dear me! what a curious title," and I found that he afterwards wrote: "it may not be generally known that Mr George R. Sims is the author of *Lights of London*, &c." And he kept on at me like that all the way. "Books? Would you mind giving me the names of one or two of them?" I pointed them out in the bookcase. He looked at the wrong shelf, and entered up the names of several books by Charles Reade and Mayne Reid, as I subsequently found when I corrected the proof.'[54]

The creator of Sherlock Holmes, Arthur Conan Doyle, was another reluctant interviewee, at this stage of his career, as he explained to an anonymous interviewer from *The Idler* in October 1894:

'What has the public got to do with an author's personality?' he asked. 'I vowed more than two years ago that I should never see an interviewer again.'
'But you are going to America –'
'Ah, in America it is a different thing. One should adapt one's self to the ways of a country.'

The Americans themselves recognized the difference. 'The interest in interviews with celebrities which the American public manifests cannot be understood by the average Englishman or Englishwoman,' wrote the interviewer Gertrude Lynch. 'To them interviews are personal things, and against an intrusion upon their personality tradition and habit raise a barbed-wire fence of reticence. To us, on the contrary, the interview, so-called, has been for a long time an expected portion of our omnivorous reading. The great mass of the American public receives its education through the newspaper press.' Not only did the American public have a head start of twenty years over the British public where interviews were concerned, but their sense of cultural inferiority impelled them to seek endorsements of every aspect of their own culture from European visitors. Aside from seeking his views on aesthetic matters, for example, American reporters invited Oscar Wilde during his lecture tours in the early 1880s to comment on American landscape, architecture, mores, etc. This habit could produce some comic results, as when visiting celebrities found themselves being enlisted, usually quite without their knowledge, let alone consent, as partisans in some local dispute. The academic Goldwin Smith complained in a letter to the president of the Toronto Press Club that a 'distinguished friend of mine, being at New York, was surprised at reading some severe comments which he was reported to have made on the fire service of that city, a subject which had not entered his mind'.[55] The English labour agitator George Holyoake gave a witty description of his experience of American interviewers in his memoirs: 'When in America in 1879, I found in some parts a class of Reversible Reporters. After an interview I found next day in the paper sentiments put down to me the very reverse of what I had expressed. Once I tried the experiment of saying the opposite of what I meant, and next day it came out all right.'[56]

The humorist Barry Pain once wrote a fantasy about a sanatorium for the cure of habitual liars at which the staff of professional liars who administered the aversion therapy included an American Interviewer. However, Joyce Kilmer, herself an American interviewer, wrote an article defending this professional type and rejecting the caricature as 'a solar-myth'. The American interviewer, she argued, was most likely a well-read and well-paid university graduate: 'It is his business to be well informed about contemporary literature, and he knows as much as you know about Vorticism and Artzibasheff.' British authors were quite as likely to act dishonourably as American interviewers. Even though they would invariably receive a proof of an interview for correction, they might be told after publication that their remarks had been ill-chosen. For example, an author might have volunteered the opinion that Washington Irving was immoral, but, when told that Americans loved Washington Irving, he might repudiate the interview:

He can get up on the lecture platform and say: 'I am learning the ways of the American Interviewer. Recently I told one of the tribe that I thought Washington Irving was a master of the novel, and he reported me as saying that this great author, whom I have venerated all my life, was immoral.' He can send this repudiation to the newspaper in which the interview appeared, can cause his publisher to multigraph it and send it broadcast. He can, and often does, clear his reputation at the expense of his honour.[57]

G.K. Chesterton, in his 1923 travelogue *What I Saw in America*, described the experience that every European celebrity had to undergo upon arrival in New York Harbour, where reporters, many of whom happened to be Irish-Americans, 'boarded the ship like pirates'. He was impressed by the curiosity of these interviewers about his most banal opinions:

> ... in America the fact of my landing and lecturing was evidently regarded in the same light as a murder or a great fire, or any other terrible but incurable catastrophe, a matter of interest to all pressmen concerned with practical events. One of the first questions I was asked was how I should be disposed to explain the wave of crime in New York. Naturally I replied that it might possibly be due to the number of English lecturers who had recently landed. In the mood of the moment it seemed possible that, if they had all been interviewed, regrettable incidents might possibly have taken place.

However, Chesterton was not hostile to the method of these importunate journalists, recognizing in it evidence of the transatlantic gulf in cultures. 'American interviewing is generally very reasonable, and it is always very rapid ... American interviewing has many of the qualities of American dentistry.' Even so, the practice could give rise to confusion. Chesterton gives as an example his experience on arriving in a particular town where 'there had been some labour troubles'. He volunteered some reflections about capitalism and labour:

> All this moral and even metaphysical generalization was most fairly reproduced by the interviewer, who had actually heard it casually and idly spoken. But on the top of this column of politicial philosophy was the extraordinary announcement in enormous letters, 'Chesterton Takes Sides in Trolley Strike'. This was inaccurate. When I spoke I not only did not know that there was any trolley strike, but I did not know what a trolley strike was. [A trolley is the American term for a tram.] I should have had an indistinct idea that a large number of citizens earned their living by carrying things about in wheel-barrows, and that they had desisted from the beneficent activities. Any one who did not happen to be a journalist, or know a little about journalism, American and English, would have supposed that the same man who wrote the article had suddenly gone mad and written the title.

American interviewers also tended to translate the words of foreign visitors into their domestic idiom, as Chesterton discovered when asked who he thought was the greatest American writer:

> I have forgotten exactly what I said, but after mentioning several names, I said that the greatest natural genius and artistic force was probably Walt Whitman. The printed interview is more precise; and students of my literary and conversational style will be interested to know that I said, 'See here, Walt Whitman was your one real red-blooded man.'

Chesterton's final observation was that American interviewers had a tendency to over-dramatize their encounters when it came to committing them to print:

> The reports are far more rowdy and insolent than the conversations. This is probably a part of the fact that a certain vivacity, which to some seems vitality and to some vulgarity, is not only an ambition but an ideal. It must always be grasped that this vulgarity is an ideal even more than it is a reality. A very quiet and intelligent young man, in a soft black hat and tortoise-shell spectacles, will ask for an interview with unimpeachable politeness, wait for his living subject with unimpeachable patience, talk to him quite sensibly for twenty minutes, and go noiselessly away. Then in the newspaper next morning you will read how he beat the bedroom door in, and pursued his victim on to the roof or dragged him from under the bed, and tore from him replies to all sorts of bald and ruthless questions printed in large black letters. I was often interviewed in the evening, and had no notion of how atrociously I had been insulted till I saw it in the paper next morning. I had no notion I had been on the rack of an inquisitor until I saw it in plain print; and then of course I believed it, with a faith and docility unknown in any previous epoch of history.[58]

The Canadian humorist Stephen Leacock in another travelogue, *My Discovery of England*, described the process of being interviewed after arriving in London and how 'the questions that I had every right to expect after many years of American and Canadian interviews failed to appear'. Again, there was the fact that America and Canada, being younger societies than England, tended to invite opinions about themselves from the visitor:

> I am thinking here especially of the kind of interview that I have given out in Youngstown, Ohio, and Richmond, Indiana, and Peterborough, Ontario. In all these places–for example, in Youngstown, Ohio–the reporter asks as his first question, 'What is your impression of Youngstown?'
>   In London they don't. They seem indifferent to the fate of their city. Perhaps it is only English pride. For all I know they may have been

burning to know this, just as the Youngstown, Ohio, people are, and were too proud to ask. In any case I will insert here the answer I had written out in my pocket-book (one copy for each paper—the way we do it in Youngstown), and which read:

'London strikes me as emphatically a city with a future. Standing as she does in the heart of a rich agricultural district with railroad connection in all directions, and resting, as she must, on a bed of coal and oil, I prophesy that she will one day be a great city.'

The advantage of this is that it enables the reporter to get just the right kind of heading: PROPHESIES BRIGHT FUTURE FOR LONDON. Had that been used my name would have stood higher there than it does today – unless the London people are very different from the people in Youngstown, which I doubt. As it is they don't know whether their future is bright or is as dark as mud. But it's not my fault. The reporters never asked me.

Similarly, no American or Canadian interview would be complete, Leacock suggests, without an inquiry as to the subject's impression of 'our women'. Instead, in London he had to 'keep my impression of London women unused in my pocket while a young man asked me whether I thought modern literature owed more to observation and less to inspiration than some other kind of literature'.[59]

The *New Yorker* profile writer A.J. Liebling declared that 'there is almost no circumstance under which an American doesn't like to be interviewed, an observation which I have had a chance to verify in cracks in the Tunisian rocks, under mortar fire. We are an articulate people, pleased by attention, covetous of being singled out.'[60] Truman Capote agreed with this judgement: 'Anybody can be interviewed if you go about it the right way. If you study the problem, there isn't a single person in the world, from violent prison hermits to chatterbox starlets, that if you really map out the problem you can't get to talk about themselves.' Another commentator has described America as 'the interviewer's paradise. Where else is a murderer's best friend his interviewer?'[61]

America is the natural home, too, of the professional interviewee, and a professional interviewee can be as much of a craftsman as a professional interviewer. Mark Twain was the prototype, and in more recent times there have been stalwarts such as James Thurber, Truman Capote and Norman Mailer. Charles Holmes, in his biography of Thurber, wrote that the famous humorist:

... seldom refused a request [for an interview], partly because he was an old newspaperman and sympathized with reporters, and partly because he was one of the great talkers of his time. He had opinions on everything and liked to express them: he was a superb story-teller and mimic, and he loved an audience. Over the years, he made the interview-monologue into an art-form, the oral equivalent of the autobiographical essay which he had developed to perfection in his prose. It was, perhaps, the form most congenial to him as he grew older. The key to it was the balance between the casual, conventional manner–its spontaneous quality–and the basic structure of ready-made topics, anecdotes and routines which gave it substance and coherence. Depending upon how the particular interview was going, Thurber would rely mostly on his standard anecdotes or introduce fresh material and improvise on it as the spirit moved him.[62]

Some celebrities almost deserve medals for endurance. When asked at a press conference if there was any question he had not been asked, Charlie Chaplin felt obliged to answer, 'I don't think so.'[63]

IV

Isaac F. Marcosson, who was the star interviewer for *The Saturday Evening Post* in the 1910s and 1920s, compared great interviewing to salesmanship: 'Interviewing outstanding personalities is in the last analysis merely a piece of glorified salesmanship . . . The elements that enter into scientific merchandising, whether with safety razors, soap or shoes, are in a larger scale the same elements that contribute to success in handling difficult and inaccessible personalities and persuading them to talk for publication'.[64] Marcosson not only interviewed the men who were fighting the First World War, such as Lloyd George, Sir Douglas Haig, Foch, and Clemenceau, but he also managed what in his own estimation was a more demanding task, namely to 'make the Wall Street sphinxes talk': legendary financiers like E.H. Harriman and Thomas F. Ryan. 'With the flow of speech which I helped to accelerate, began a whole new public attitude toward them. Advertising always pays.'[65]

Another practitioner of the craft of interviewing was Edward Price Bell of the *Chicago Daily News*, who interviewed Benito Mussolini, Ramsay MacDonald, Dr H.W. Evans (the imperial wizard of the Ku Klux Klan), Raymond Poincaré and Mackenzie King, among others. In his pamphlet, *Major Interviewing: Its Principles and its Functions* (1929), he claimed that the interview with a major political figure:

. . . may be made a moral and intellectual force of a high order, accentuating sound principles and ideals, marshaling vital facts and arguments, stimulating men to action, leaving its impress upon history. Evangelic and educative is the great interview, changing moral apathy into moral order, ignorance into knowledge, bridging the gulf between genius and understanding . . . The great interviewer's underlying purpose is to unlock the lips of wisdom – to make the sphinx of judgement speak.[64]

Henri de Blowitz approached the monarchs and senior politicians whom he interviewed almost on equal terms. Because of his wide knowledge he was able 'to ask the pertinent question, to steer the conversation in the desired direction, above all to produce the feeling in the absence of which no dialogue, for publication or otherwise, can hope to prosper: that the person being interviewed was talking to an informed, interested, and interesting man – in other words, that the occasion was one of a two-way exchange of news and views'.[67] Another Victorian interviewer, Frank Banfield, felt that 'an interview is an affair of two. Two brains, two personalities, two points of view come in visible contact, and, just in proportion as this dual play is adequately rendered, is the interview bright and pleasant reading, or dull and lifeless'; and that the interview is 'the temporary alliance of two intelligent men on level terms, for the production of what is an article in more or less dialogue form.'[68] Ideally, the interview should be of benefit to both interviewer and interviewee, as the interviewer George Urban has recently argued: '. . . the interviewee is – voluntarily, but vulnerably – in the hands of the questioner. But the interviewer has a responsibility to the man who has agreed to expose himself to his curiosity. The two should feel (even if they seldom do) that they are engaged in a joint enterprise.'[69]

Joint enterprise was hardly an apt description of the encounter in New York between an English interviewer who worked for the American press in the 1880s, John B. Lane, and King Kalakaua of the Sandwich Islands (which later became Hawaii), who did not have it in mind to converse. Lane was ushered into the King's presence by his chamberlain, who was a German baron, but was unable to ask a single question, so pressing was the King's urge to communicate his opinions:

'Yes, I like New York,' said the dusky potentate; 'and I admire your public buildings and your institutions. I think your ladies are very beautiful; they dress elegantly, and have small feet. What a great country it is! and what a grand man was Washington – first in war, first in peace, first in the hearts of his countrymen! I like your oysters. Glad to see you. Take a cocktail with the baron. Good-bye.'

I was dismissed; I could not very well remain any longer, so I shook the big brown hand which the king extended and left with the baron.

'I taught him that speech expressly for the reporters,' said the Hawaiian Lord High Chamberlain. 'He never says anything else. It is good, *nicht wahr*? Let us drink.'

We drank. Then the baron kissed me on the cheek, and left me, saying, 'And now I must give His Majesty his bath.'

The duties of His Excellency seemed to be various.[70]

Sometimes the interviewee has been so unwilling a subject that the exercise has been rendered futile, as with this unintentionally comic exchange when a New York reporter called on President Grant in 1874.

REPORTER: Your Excellency, I have come to ask you, if the inquiry be deemed pertinent, what your views are on the third-term question. The press —
PRESIDENT GRANT: I have nothing to say on the subject.
REP: Well — I thought, as the subject occupies a large share of public attention —
P.G.: I have nothing to say on the subject.
REP.: At least, I might be pardoned for asking you if, in case —
P.G.: I have nothing to say on the subject.
REP: I was merely going to say that in case you had good reasons for not wishing to commit —
P.G.: I have nothing to say on the subject.
REP.: I trust, your Excellency, that this will not be deemed an intrusion?
P.G.: I have nothing to say on the subject.
REP.: At least nothing could have been further —
P.G.: I have nothing to say on the subject.
REP.: (Going.): Your Excellency, I am, in any event, glad that I have had the pleasure of —
P.G.: I have nothing to say on the subject.
REP: (Pleasantly and politely.): Good morning.
P.G.: I have nothing to say on the subject.[71]

The unwelcoming reaction of Rudyard Kipling when approached by a couple of newspaper journalists from Boston in 1892 is an early instance of an interview in which the reporter makes a virtue out of the non-cooperation of his subject. Kipling refused to grant them an interview, but this made little difference, for the ensuing argument, in which they sought to dissuade him from his refusal and he sought to explain his objections to being interviewed, itself became the matter of their interview articles.[72] US president Rutherford Hayes refused to talk on the subject about which John B. Lane had been sent to interview him, 'but he gave me a lot of interesting information about various species of domestic fowls and the best ways of breeding them, and presented me with a photograph of a Cochin-China hen of abnormal size.' The resourceful Lane sold the interview to an agricultural weekly.[73]
Kate Carew of the *New-York Tribune* tried to interview the Anglo-Irish novelist George Moore in 1913, but instead of an interview 'what it resolved itself into was an encounter in three rounds'. Carew pitched questions to him about American politics; the comparative aptitudes of the novel or the drama to reflect real life; English politics; Ireland; whether he believed in war; the poetic

spirit in England and America; whether plays had been influenced by the post-impressionist movement; his methods of work, his relaxations, the books he liked; etc. Moore dismissed most of her questions as uninteresting, trivial, absurd, or prying. By the end of her published article, which nonetheless ran to a few thousand words, Carew declared that it 'wasn't an interview . . . only the true tale of the lively Artistic Temperament of a serious Man of Letters'.[74]

In 1943, the Hollywood correspondent of the *New York Herald Tribune*, Thornton Delehanty, interviewed Tallulah Bankhead about the making of the film *Lifeboat*. Try as he might, Delehanty was unable to fix her on the subject he had in mind. 'I had two interviews with Tallulah Bankhead,' he explained. 'In the first I learned all about her home in Bedford Village and about early American furniture. In the second, I learned about her Sealyham pup. I know more about that pup than Ray Stannard Baker knows about Woodrow Wilson.'[75] In James Thurber's 1927 short story called 'The Interview', a reporter visits a bibulous and curmudgeonly novelist. He passes several hours in the novelist's company but is unable to obtain any material that is suitable for publication.[76] The novelist 'has obviously been driven to cover by too much success, too many interviews, and too much marriage, and he no longer communicates with the world in the usual ways'.[77]

The *story* of the interview, in some cases the adventure of the interview, may be all that the writer has at the end of the assignment. One journalism guide, published in 1913, suggested that 'the narrator may still present a good story by narrating his foiled efforts or by quoting the questions which the great man refused to answer'.[78] Perhaps the best example of this sub-genre of the interview, sometimes called 'the foiled interview', is a piece written by Jack Richardson for *Esquire* (published in December 1963) called 'Mr Fisher is Open'. It tells the story of Richardson's forlorn attempts to obtain an interview with Eddie Fisher, the American popular singer who was then enjoying a show-business comeback. At the outset Richardson's editor tells him that 'Eddie is very open right now.' This ominous phrase is echoed by Fisher's PR woman who tells him that 'right now he's rather open.' Fisher then 'interviews' Richardson to find out what kind of story the journalist wants to write about him. It later transpires that Fisher has heard that *Esquire* is planning a series of stories about public personalities under the general heading 'The Losers' and suspects that he is slated for a spot in this ignominious series. Richardson meets with Fisher's press agent, Bob Abrahms, and the following exchange takes place:

> 'You see,' Abrahms began in a semi-apologetic voice, 'Eddie right now is rather – well, he's rather . . .'
> 'Open?' I volunteered.
> 'Right. If we could only have some idea what you're going to write about.'

Richardson has one further meeting with Fisher during which the singer explains that 'there's an area in the past that I just don't want to go into' – namely, Fisher's failed marriage with Elizabeth Taylor. Fisher seeks to stave off the reporter's curiosity about him by declaring that there are a hundred Eddie Fishers. Richardson says he'll settle for one, but he has already realized that the exercise is pointless. Even so, the adventure has been worthwhile: a few thousand words of sharp observation, gentle satire, and the revelation that, despite the protestations of his handlers that he is 'very open right now', Fisher is in fact profoundly insecure and uncommunicative.

So how does the interviewer 'unlock the lips of wisdom' and 'make the sphinx of judgement speak'? Henri de Blowitz, who tended to interview monarchs and senior politicians, was said to do 'all the talking in a conversation *à deux*'[79] and Blowitz's biographer has written that such an approach 'may, with a difficult subject such as Abdul Hamid, be necessary in order to release the waters of loquacity, but on the whole a journalist who goes in for this persistently becomes someone whom busy men justifiably shun'.[80] When interviewed by Mrs Maud Churton Braby in 1904, W.T. Stead complimented her on her loquaciousness: 'That's the whole secret of successful interviewing – for the interviewer to talk all the time.'[81] Pete Martin of *The Saturday Evening Post*, interviewed by Bing Crosby a few decades later, disagreed. He preferred to use silence rather than talk as his method of extraction: 'There's a trick to interviewing. If you sit there and don't open your trap, it makes the other fellow nervous, and he'll talk. A sound vacuum worries people.'[82] A.J. Liebling agreed with this approach: 'The worst thing an interviewer can do is talk a lot himself. Just listening to reporters in a bar-room, you can tell the ones who go out and impress their powerful personalities on their subject and then come back and make up what they think he would have said if he had had a chance to say anything.'[83] Indeed, Stead was sometimes guilty of this offence. His interviews with Tsar Nicholas II of Russia and Sultan Mehmed V of Turkey consist largely of his own long and opinionated statements, barely disguised as questions, interspersed with polite and non-committal, almost meek, responses from the bemused monarchs. As one writer put it, the interview with Tsar Nicholas II 'represents one of Stead's feats of memory, for it is all conversation in the first person. Stead has, of course, more space than the Tsar.'[84] This was consistent with Stead's self-deluding notion that what he called government by journalism would supersede traditional forms of government; similarly Blowitz in the introduction to his published interview with the Shah of Persia in *The Times* explained with pride that the Shah had contacted him to arrange an interview because he wanted to know 'your impressions of the events that are taking place in Europe, as it is your mission to observe them'.[85]

Isaac F. Marcosson believed that the interviewer's approach necessarily depended on his subject's personality as much as his own. 'Some silent men must be swept irresistibly into conversation on the high tide of talk. You take the initiative. Then too there is the type who begins to speak the moment you see him. All you have to do is guide the current of words. There is also the man who interviews the interviewer.' He gave as examples of each type respectively: the Wall Street financiers, Theodore Roosevelt, and David Lloyd George.[86] Djuna Barnes, in a piece about a New York theatrical impresario entitled 'Interviewing Arthur Voegtlin Is Something Like Having a Nightmare', concluded that 'it had taken me two superb hours to find out, in the end, that he had been mostly interviewing me!'[87]

However, W.T. Stead's opinion that interviewers should do most of the talking was echoed several decades later when *The New Yorker* published Truman Capote's notorious profile of Marlon Brando. As Capote later explained: 'The secret to the art of interviewing – and it is an art – is to let the other person think he's interviewing you ... You tell him about yourself, and slowly spin your web so that he tells you everything. That's how I trapped Marlon.' Brando clearly understood how he had been trapped: 'The little bastard spent half the night telling me all his problems. I figured the least I could do was tell him a few of mine.'[88] Elsewhere, Capote has elaborated:

> If you're having a difficult time with a subject, then you, in effect, change roles. And you, the interviewer, begin by making little confidences of your own that are rather similar to things that you think you will draw out of them. And suddenly they'll be saying: 'Ah yes, my mother ran away with five repairmen, too.' See what I mean? Or: 'Ah, yes, my father robbed a bank and was sent to prison for ten years, too. Isn't it extraordinary we should have those same things happen in our lives?' etc. And then you find you're off to the races.[89]

To some extent, the technique of the interview reflects the model of psychoanalysis with the analyst coaxing his patient into self-revelation. Leonard Probst noted that the film actors he interviewed in the late 1960s were 'more candid and self-knowing than they might have been, say, in the 1940s. A number of those interviewed have been in psychoanalysis, although some mentioned this outside the interview.' Geoffrey Wheatcroft has suggested that the celebrity's desire to submit himself to the interviewer is the result of a deep-seated human need to confess:

> Most of us are both vain and silly enough to think that by exposing ourselves we will make ourselves more attractive and plausible, though not many moments' thought suggests that this isn't likely to be so. We like talking about ourselves, confessing even. The discovery of this side of human nature was, after all, essential for traditional priestcraft, and now for the new priestcraft of journalism.[90]

But subjects often forget that they are in the presence of journalists. 'I am a journalist,' said Henri de Blowitz, 'not a confessor.'[91] When Pete Martin of *The Saturday Evening Post* turned in an interview with Dean Martin, his editor told him, 'You've got a real gutsy piece here, so gutsy we'd better send it to our lawyer. Maybe this guy is libelling himself.'[92] The self-libel was Dean Martin's confession that he was a shoplifter:

> There wasn't much else for a kid to do except a little stealing; neckties, hubcaps – stuff like that. But a little shoplifting never hurt anybody. Every kid has done his share of it in his time. Even today when I go into a haberdashery and spend $500, I steal a necktie or a pair of gloves or a pair of socks. I'm sure that the owners know it, but I'm such a good customer they don't really care. Everyone has a little larceny in him, a little bit of original sin; only some of it's not too original.[93]

Other practitioners prefer to see the interview more in terms of an erotic encounter than an act of confession. Oriana Fallaci, the Italian journalist whose interviews with world leaders were published internationally during the 1960s, 70s and 80s, has described her provocative approach in this way: 'I provoke them because I get involved, because my interviews are never cold, because I fall in love with the person who is in front of me, even if I hate him or her. An interview is a love story for me. It's a fight. It's a coitus.'[94]

Marie Brenner, who wrote interview-profiles for *New York* magazine during the late 1970s and 80s before switching to *Vanity Fair*, has agreed with this judgement: 'Yes, it's a seduction, absolutely. Normally, you want the person you're interviewing to respond to you, because if they respond to you, then you can loosen them up. And if you loosen them up, they'll really let their hair down and talk to you.' Brenner has said that she seeks to put her subject at ease by being 'incredibly sociable, as a good Texas girl'. She first of all admires her subject's house as if she were at a party in her native San Antonio.[95] The longer the interviewer spends with the subject, the stronger the bond that develops. With few exceptions, both parties will be ingratiating. As Janet Malcolm has put it, 'the metaphor of the love affair applies to both sides of the journalist-subject equation'.[96]

Sometimes interviews find their way into print where the sensual element is so strong as to induce embarrassment in the reader. Mrs Eleanor 'Cissy' Patterson, editor of the Washington *Herald*, was overwhelmed by the charisma of Al Capone when she interviewed him. 'Once I looked *at* his eyes,' she wrote. 'Ice-gray, ice-cold eyes. You can't anymore look *into* the eyes of Capone than you can look into the eyes of a tiger . . .' She described his hands: 'Enormous. Powerful enough to tackle – well, almost anything, although superficially soft from lack of exposure.' Her concluding sentence made everything clear: 'It has been said, with truth, that women have a special kind of sympathy for gangsters. If you don't understand why, consult Dr Freud.'[97]

Yet the love affair often turns sour. Rex Reed has recalled: 'Natalie Wood treated me like her long-lost college boyfriend . . . . but she hasn't spoken to me since I wrote a funny description of how she sat on the floor of a New Orleans hotel room eating eggs Benedict off the coffee table, opening a bottle of Dom Perignon with her teeth, and doing Russian imitations in her nightgown.' She thought that Reed had made her seem like a 'gun moll'. [98] Various commentators have noticed how 'the killer interview' (© Geoffrey Wheatcroft) or 'jugular journalism' (© Mark Lawson) is increasingly taking over from blander efforts: 'As in the *corrida*, not only is the interviewer-matador the centre of attention in her suit of lights; this is a blood sport. Fifteen hundred words flash by, a succession of passes with the *muleta*, and then comes the *estocada*, and another carcass is dragged away by the mule-team.'[99] Note, here, the gender of the preposition – '*her* suit of lights'. For this brand of hostile encounter is predominantly the preserve of the female. In Britain, Val Hennessy, Lynn Barber, Catherine Bennett, and Barbara Amiel are its chief proponents. Some have wondered why celebrities offer themselves as sacrificial lambs to these harpies. The demands of publicity are such that, as one writer has wittily put it, the celebrity faces 'the choice between starving and being eaten'.[100] One anonymous celebrity has suggested that most of Lynn Barber's victims 'are middle-aged men and I can only assume that they have this fantasy that they are going to charm her'.[101] Certainly, Barber's approach is essentially psychoanalytical and often incurs the *post facto* resentment of her subjects – she would defend it as an antidote to all the puffing interviews that indulge the vanity of celebrities and promote them on their own terms. However, if taken to extremes, this approach can be overstrained and ugly. 'Another thing I hate,' volunteered Orson Welles in a 1960 *Sight & Sound* interview, 'is these interviews in depth, as they call them, where some public personality is made to look ridiculous. To take some pretty, sexy girl who doesn't pretend to be anything else and make a fool of her – this is horrible . . .'[102]

A key aspect of interviewing technique which can have awkward ethical implications is the problem of actually preserving the words of the subject. In the early days, interviewers tended to work from memory. Before the invention of the tape recorder, even note-taking was regarded by some as vulgar and off-putting. J.B. McCullagh, when interviewing President Johnson, refrained from note-taking because 'it would have frozen the irascible current of his [Johnson's] soul'.[103] 'To use a note-book is to destroy the freedom of expression of the person attacked,' wrote Frank A. Burr. 'This kills the interesting personality which should pervade every interview, if this method of gathering news is to fill its full purpose.'[104] Yes, but how to remember? Henri de Blowitz was hired as the European correspondent of *The Times* when he demonstrated his ability to reproduce from memory the exact words of a long speech given by the French politician Louis Thiers – without a single error and before an official written version was made available to rival journalists. As a child Blowitz had demonstrated prodigious powers of memory, as when his father promised to give him a gold-knobbed cane if he could recite by heart the legend of 'Kosros the Wise' the following day. He won the cane, which he did not keep, though he kept his memory.[105] W.T. Stead never took notes, but straight after an interview he would write or type up the conversation from memory. As a safeguard, the subject would then be invited to read and correct a proof of the article. In the late nineteenth cenury, when persons were bombarded with less information and fewer distractions (such as popular music, cinema or television), it must have been easier to train one's memory to such a task. Djuna Barnes was asked by one interviewee whether she had been taking notes. 'I don't have to,' she replied. 'My memory always makes a paragraph out of a note automatically.'[106] In recent times, Kenneth Harris of the London *Observer* has practised the skill of re-creating entire interviews from memory.

Often, the circumstances in which an interview is given dictate the need for sharp powers of recall. Ernest Foster, editor of *Cassell's Saturday Journal* in the 1890s, recalled that some interviewees 'preferred the open air, and it was while striding across Clapham Common early one morning at such a pace that the journalist could hardly keep up with him that Mr John Burns expounded his views on making London an ideal city . . . An aëronaut had to be accompanied in a balloon ascent; a metropolitan magistrate on an omnibus journey across London.'[107] In 1914 the editor of *The Young Man*, Walter Wynn, tracked down General Bramwell Booth, the Salvation Army leader, to a Turkish bath in the Strand and proceeded to interview him there. Wynn pronounced the result so successful that he resolved to interview great men at their baths in future, because 'they cannot get away quickly, and they must sit it out'.[108] The humid atmosphere, however, presumably ruled out any form of note-taking. When Isaac Marcosson interviewed Woodrow Wilson in 1912, he was hampered by the fact that the interview had to be conducted in an open-top car:

> I have interviewed men on trains, ships, in the air, and under the ground. Yet I doubt if any similar work was done under the handicaps that marked that first talk with Mr Wilson. The car jolted; constituents shouted greetings to him from the roadside. All the while I had to keep up a running fire of questions and remember what was being said. We touched every possible subject from tariff and good government to the personal guilt of corporations. It was impossible to take many notes. I had to remember what I heard.[109]

In 1947, when Earl Wilson obtained his first interview with the New York mobster Frank Costello, he was not allowed to take notes because Costello 'had a fear of note-taking', so he had to keep 'ducking in and out of phone booths and the men's room to write down snatches of his answers'.[110] Rex Reed went one step further when he actually found himself interviewing singer-comedienne

Bette Midler while she was sitting on the toilet in a gay bathhouse. Isaac F. Marcosson believed that men '*always* talk best when they eat', though Oriana Fallaci found that an interview with film director Federico Fellini in a restaurant was beset with too many interruptions and distractions and she later had to conduct the interview over again.[111]

Groucho Marx refused to allow the use of tape recorders in interviews. 'Even for ten thousand dollars, I wouldn't let *Life* magazine use a tape recorder,' he told one interviewer. 'You'll have to write everything down on cards.' Eric Lax, the interviewer from *Life*, said: 'I was more nervous than I'd ever been interviewing anyone before. I wanted to get every word, but he told me I couldn't use a recorder. I listened as hard as I could, drove away a short distance, and scribbled frantically.'[112] A pioneer of the tape-recorded interview was Henry Brandon, who later recalled his experience interviewing Edmund Wilson, the historian and critic: 'He had a real microphone fright, but after twenty-four hours he came to terms with the presence of a tape recorder and the interview technique ... In the end, after two days of talk at his family retreat in Talcottville, NY, I ran out of tape and it was Wilson, who by then had come to enjoy the experience, who was eagerly telephoning the shops in villages nearby to find me more tapes.'[113] An interviewer wielding a tape recorder can produce an extraordinary variety of reactions, as Charles Higham explains:

> Mae West was one who refused to tolerate the recorder, and after she discovered she was being taped had it carefully dismantled and placed in the entrance hall of her apartment until the interview was over. Her cries of 'No, no, *no!* I never do!' are still on the first two minutes of the tape, like the exclamation of a rape victim. Lucille Ball and Ralph Bakshi looked at the machine as though they were staring into the barrels of a shotgun. Paul Anka hugged it to his breast like a child. Roman Polanski insisted on recording the interview separately to make sure I was totally accurate.[114]

Rex Reed once interviewed an anxious Warren Beatty – an exercise he compared to 'asking a haemophiliac for a pint of blood' – and Beatty too wanted a back-up recording for his own purposes:

> There were two tape recorders, a special requirement for the interview, a tiny Norelco that operated on cartridges and a larger Wollensak which had been borrowed from a girl friend. Warren puttered around a few minutes, shaking them, holding them up to his ear. They were both broken. 'Forget the tape recorder. I'll trust you.'

Truman Capote has said that use of a tape recorder is 'a great mistake, because the moment you introduce a mechanical device into the interview technique, you are creating an atmosphere in which the person isn't going to feel really relaxed, because they're watching themselves'.[115] Lynn Barber, on the other hand, has said that she is so dependent on the tape recorder 'that I couldn't have been an interviewer if it hadn't been invented'. She recognizes that some interviewers use shorthand, but believes herself that 'maintaining eye contact is vital'.[116]

The use of the portable tape recorder from the mid-1950s onwards gave a boost to newspaper and magazine interviews of the Q & A type, with Henry Brandon doing them for *The Sunday Times* in London and *Playboy* publishing such interviews on a monthly basis (starting with the jazz musician Miles Davis in September 1962). The confrontational television interview, pioneered by Mike Wallace in the 1950s and 60s, also had an effect on how print journalists approached the interviewee. The broadcast interviewer enjoyed greater latitude than the print journalist, because although there was less opportunity to editorialize, a television interview could be much more of an ordeal (especially if broadcast live). The only option for an interviewee in such circumstances is to refuse to answer questions, which naturally sounds evasive, or simply to walk away from the camera (as Sir James Goldsmith once famously did). Another factor which made for a change in approach was the increasing knowledge of psychoanalysis, or, at least, popular perception of it. The *Saturday Evening Post* profilist Maurice Zolotow has said that before the Second World War the interviewer 'kept on the acceptable conscious level. He never attempted to penetrate into the unconscious or undesirable phases of his subject's life or personality.'[117] Nowadays, of course, most interviewers are amateur psychoanalysts.

V

Since the very beginning of his historical existence, the interviewer has been regarded as a potential traducer of his subject. Janet Malcolm, in her book *The Journalist and the Murderer*, has suggested that the journalist inevitably presents himself as a false friend in what she calls 'the journalist–subject encounter'. The fact that the subject may be trying to manipulate the journalist does not alter the fact that the journalist will almost inevitably betray the subject, she has argued. It is not because he is committing an immoral act, but rather it is a phenomenological truth.

This is how an interviewer from the *San Francisco Examiner* found Robert Louis Stevenson when he descended upon the author's house at Vailima, in Polynesia, in December 1893:

'Well, no; I'm not particularly fond of reporters, particularly the American variety; but come on in, and I'll have a go with you, anyhow.'

Such was the greeting with which Robert Louis Stevenson received the announcement of my name and business as we met on the broad verandah of his island home, far back in the hills of Upolu, the land of the southern cross and the sacred hen ... I started in to explain that my business was not to misrepresent or garble the statements of earth's greatest living novelist.

'That's all right,' he said laughing. 'Come in and see what there is to be seen, and ask us all sorts of questions. Then run riot with your pen, and when the paper comes, I'll read the article, damn till the air is blue, and everything will be all right.'[118]

When Raymond Blathwayt was commissioned to write a character sketch of Lord Northcliffe, he requested an interview with the newspaper proprietor, who sent back the following reply:

Dear Mr Blathwayt,

I am sorry, but I must ask you to excuse me from acceding to your request. I am like the little boy at a school treat who, when the squire's wife came round to him and asked him if he would like some strawberry jam promptly replied –

No, thank you, marm, I works at the place where they makes it![119]

W.T. Stead's rule about submitting a proof of an interview to the subject for final approval before publication is rarely followed today. The famous *Paris Review* interviews with writers (which have been published since the early 1950s) have adhered to this practice, but then *The Paris Review* has declared itself the home of the 'rewritten interview' – since the aim is to obtain the clearest expression of the author's purpose. An interview with Iris Murdoch, for example, was almost entirely rewritten by her. In most cases, however, a publication does not have such rarefied requirements. Because the interview can be such a seductive experience, subjects often come to regret unguarded remarks. They would perhaps alter them if given the opportunity, and sometimes indeed deny, out of shame or embarrassment, that they uttered their reported words. An 1890 commentator regretted the tendency for American newspapers to assign inexperienced reporters to do major interviews, because misstatements and errors would creep into the published products and give 'public men an easy opportunity to deny their own words, if their statements did not happen to strike the public, when in print, as they expected they would when they uttered them'.[120] One manual for journalists, published in 1917, clearly advised against showing interviewees a draft of the article:

... only under extraordinary circumstances should a reporter agree to submit his copy for criticism before publication. Many a good story has had all the piquancy taken out of it by giving the one interviewed an opportunity to change his mind or to see in cold print just what he said, – a fact that accounts for so many repudiated interviews. In nine cases out of ten the newspaper man has reported the distinguished visitor exactly, but the write-up looks different from what the speaker expected. Then he denies the whole thing, and the reporter is made the scapegoat, because the man quoted is a public personage and the reporter is not.[121]

Having already been in trouble with Bismarck over an interview, Henri de Blowitz went on to cause trouble for Count Münster, the German Ambassador in Paris. In an interview, Münster told Blowitz of the circumstances surrounding Bismarck's resignation from office. When the interview was published he had to backpedal to escape censure at home. He informed Blowitz that while the report of his words had been 'very exact' he had nonetheless instructed the Wolff Telegraph Agency to aNounce that 'there was a certain amount of imagination in the story published'. Blowitz did not object, even when the Count later decided wholly to repudiate the interview.[122]

Nor has the sight of a proof before publication been any guarantee that repudiation will not follow upon publication. An English newspaper, in the wake of Stanley Baldwin's repudiation of an interview with a lobby journalist, wrote that 'politicians have been known to repudiate responsibility for interviews, even when the actual proof of the interview, revised by the politician's own hand, had been in the possession of the publishing journal'.[123] At the suggestion of Edward VII, who wanted his cousin, Kaiser Wilhelm II, to gain greater experience of the British, Colonel Edward Montagu Stuart-Wortley placed his home, Highcliffe Castle, at the disposal of the Kaiser for several weeks in the summer of 1907. During this period, the Colonel and the Kaiser had many discussions about Anglo-German relations. When a friend of W.T. Stead's wrote to Stuart-Wortley asking whether the Kaiser might grant Stead an interview, the Kaiser declined. The following year, when Stuart-Wortley attended the German manoeuvres as the Kaiser's guest, he proposed to write an account of their talks for newspaper publication. The Kaiser agreed on the condition that a proof should be submitted to him and to a German government official. Stuart-Wortley's notes were put into the form of a single interview by J.B. Firth of *The Daily Telegraph* and published in October 1908. Unfortunately, it caused an uproar in Britain and much embarrassment in Germany, where it transpired that government officials had not bothered to read it in advance. Another interview which the Kaiser had given in July 1908 to W.B. Hale of the American *Century Magazine* was suppressed at the insistence of the German Foreign Office because its hostile tone regarding England was so much at variance with the Kaiser's indulgent attitude in the *Daily Telegraph* interview.[124]

In early 1931, Eugene Lyons of the United Press agency became the first Western correspondent to obtain an interview with Joseph Stalin. At the end of the interview Stalin said that although he did not wish to interfere with what Lyons might write, he 'would be interested to see what you make of this interview'. Lyons asked Stalin if he could borrow a Latin script typewriter and proceeded to type up his article in an adjoining office. An interpreter read back the completed article to Stalin who wrote on the typescript: 'More or less correct, J. Stalin.'[125]

In the early days of the *Playboy* interview, during the 1960s, the 'interviewees were shown edited versions of their interviews and given virtual copy approval'; but *Playboy* 'became aware of occasional attempts to sanitize a printed conversation – in effect, to censor it' and after 1974 the policy was changed. Yet it was not just interviewees who tried to sanitize their reported words. Bob Dylan was furious when he read the proofs of Nat Hentoff's interview with him for *Playboy*, because the article's editors had put unfamiliar words into his mouth. Dylan later told his biographer about the incident:

> I read the proofs and I said: 'Where in the fuck did you get these words?' Hentoff told me that the man from *Playboy* wrote in things to make it sound a little better . . . And they were downright fucking, silly-ass, you know, geech-like phrases. Peacock phrases. Just dumb bullshit, asinine things that . . . anybody that has ever met me and heard me talk knows I would not say. I said: 'You're not getting this article, man.' I called the lawyers right away . . . and the lawyers sent *Playboy* a letter and they got frightened. So they called back and I said: 'Could I have the article rewritten . . .?' I answered the questions. I did it very bad, man. I should have done it much better.[126]

In 1956 William Faulkner was interviewed by Russell Warren Howe, the New York correspondent of *The Sunday Times* (London), but a longer version, which appeared in an American publication, *The Reporter*, stirred up controversy in the American press because of Faulkner's remarks about the South being 'armed for revolt' and ready to fight again for secession. Faulkner repudiated this second version as inaccurate and softened the blow to Howe by implying that he, Faulkner, had been drunk. He wrote to *The Reporter* to say that its version 'contained statements that no sober man would make, nor, it seems to me, any sane man believe'. Howe responded that 'all the statements attributed to Mr Faulkner were directly transcribed by me from verbatim shorthand notes . . .'[127]

It has been a perennial complaint of interviewees that they have been, if not actually misquoted, then misrepresented: that the published version of the interview gives a quite different impression than the one they recall. Truman Capote has explained it thus: 'No one likes to see himself as he is or cares to see exactly set down what he said or did. I don't like to myself when I am the sitter and not the portraitist. And the more accurate the strokes, the greater the resentment.'[128] Few interviews have ever been literal recordings of the words exchanged between journalist and subject. The constraints of space have often dictated that such conversations be edited, and the process of editing means that some aspects of such conversations will be pointed up. Harvey Breit, who interviewed many authors for *The New York Times Book Review* in the 1940s and 50s, would distil a conversation conducted over an hour or so, usually at lunchtime, into 850 words. The Q & A format is no guarantor of absolute authenticity. The *Playboy* interviews, for example, were invariably done as Q & As. They ran to several thousand words, but virtually none of them had been performances delivered at a single sitting. The interviewer often met his subject for several encounters and tape-recorded many hours of conversation. Since the interview is a journalistic or literary form – we consume it as such and not as mere oral testimony – it has always been permissible to demand that life should imitate art rather than the other way around. Harvey Breit has compared it to the 'creative process':

> Often the right words had to be located (and the search went into the sounds of syllables and the weights of words); and yet had to be accurate just as a word has to be accurate in a poem or story. Even at times the form had to be thought out or 'felt' for: one had to know *how* to begin and *where* to end. This form seldom if ever followed the sequence of the oral talk. It was created, whether for good or evil. Disparate parts were juxtaposed. A phrase carelessly buried in the middle was unearthed to make a grand finale ... Manipulation was not only consonant with scrupulousness, it was essential to it. One had to condense and heighten, one had to try to find the figure in the carpet, one had to sacrifice detail to gain impact. In short, a good deal of the job had to be symbolic; to try to be naturalistic in so tight a frame would have meant, I am convinced, to be quite unjust. Obviously, one stayed within the circumference of the talk and put forward precisely the ideas articulated in question. But there was invariably an inflection to be sought for, an atmosphere to be insinuated, an exit to be summoned (summed up). I don't wish to exaggerate the problem, but these Talks did not write themselves. In a small, exacting way, 'creative' problems arose, and one had to deal with them.[129]

Nor has the problem of the published interview being but one partial version of the interview-encounter been solved by the now almost universal use of the tape recorder. Today most newspapers and magazines insist on the journalist recording the interview for legal reasons in case of a libel action, whether the journalist wishes to do so or not. Kenneth Harris felt that the tape recorder inhibited his subjects, but he too eventually succumbed to its blandishments. Consequently, his prodigious powers of recollection declined. ('Memory is like a muscle,' he has told this author.)

Janet Malcolm has reminded us that before 'the invention of the tape recorder, no quotation could be verbatim – what Boswell quotes Dr Johnson as saying was obviously not precisely what Johnson said; we will never know what that was – and many journalists continue to work without benefit of this double-edged technological aid, doing their work of editing or paraphrasing on the spot, as they scribble in their notebooks'.[130] Just as W.T. Stead made his subjects 'talk a great deal better than they did',[131] so Janet Malcolm believes that it is a duty of the interviewer to be charitable:

> When a journalist undertakes to quote a subject he has interviewed on tape, he owes it to the subject, no less than to the reader, to translate his speech into prose. Only the most uncharitable (or inept) journalist will hold a subject to his literal utterances and fail to perform the sort of editing and rewriting that, in life, our ear automatically and instantane-ously performs . . . Fidelity to the subject's thought and his characteristic way of expressing himself is the sine qua non of journalistic quotation – one under which all stylistic considerations are subsumed. Fortunately for reader and subject alike, the relatively minor task of translating tape-recorderese into English and the major responsibility of trustworthy quotation are in no way inimical; in fact, as I have proposed (and over and over again discovered for myself), they are fundamentally and decisively complementary.[132]

Malcolm has demonstrated how she compressed passages of transcript in order to avoid repetitions and *longueurs*, and Penelope Gilliatt has described her interview-profiles, mostly published in *The New Yorker*, as 'records of real-life lines that are, in spirit, more like fictional lines of dialogue because, when they come to be quoted they are compressed'.[133]

Similarly, the technique of the *Playboy* interview, as established by the supervisor of the earlier efforts, Murray Fisher, was:

> . . . to sift and refine the raw verbiage of a tape transcript into a linear, continuous conversation . . . This meant there was always a process of distillation and condensation, of reshuffling and rearranging, but with sufficient faithfulness to the original that the material had the verisimilitude of natural, spoken conversation. It was never a matter of 'improving' a person's language, but of squeezing out the repetitions and meanderings, the pauses and false starts, which are mentally edited out by listeners but not by readers. That the technique is successful is supported by the fact that many of the interviewees have volunteered publicly that

the published interviews reported *exactly* what they said – even though no interview has been published verbatim.[134]

Yet it is one thing to compress transcribed material in a responsible fashion and another to compress it in such a way that the subject's intended meaning is transformed. When Maureen Orth interviewed Margaret Thatcher for a *Vanity Fair* profile in May 1991, the former British prime minister made her own tape recording of the conversation for her archives. The published profile, which painted a picture of Mrs Thatcher as a bewildered and lost figure now that she was out of office, carried a quote from her in which she appeared to denigrate the value of domestic life – 'home is where you come to when you have nothing better to do'. Within days, a row had erupted, with Mrs Thatcher's office releasing a verbatim transcript to *The Times*. This showed that her original words had been compressed and that the remark quoted in *Vanity Fair* had actually been spoken in the context of a reference to her grown-up children. 'Home is where you come when you haven't anything better to do. We are always there' – a quotation within a quotation, something she had imagined herself saying to either Mark or Carol Thatcher rather than a description of her own attitude towards domestic life. On this reading, Mrs Thatcher is transformed from a heartless career woman into an affectionate mother resigned to the realization that her chicks have long since flown the nest. The editor of *Vanity Fair*, Tina Brown, leapt to the defence of the profilist Maureen Orth, arguing that she was the only person fit to interpret Mrs Thatcher's remarks, as there had been no one else present. 'We've listened to the tape several times since in the office,' she wrote in a letter to *The Times*, 'and it's quite clear that it's quite unclear. Mrs Thatcher may be speaking as a character addressing her children, or she may be speaking as herself. Without being there, watching her and detecting the nuance, it's impossible to tell.' Orth's compression of her subject's words had the effect, though doubtless unintended, of making some innocuous remarks sound rather sinister.[135]

The debate about the relative merits of the Q & A and the written-up interview is another constant theme in the history of the genre. The Q & A can turn out to be rather wooden, hence this advice in a 1917 journalism manual:

The report may be livened up greatly with bits of description portraying the speaker and his surroundings, particularly when they harmonize or contrast with his character or the ideas expressed. An excellent device for presenting the spirit of an interview – giving an atmosphere, as it were – is to interpolate at intervals in the story personal eccentricities or little mannerisms of speech of the one interviewed. Mention of pet phrases, characteristic gestures, sudden display of anger, unexplainable reticence in answering questions, etc., will sometimes be more effective than columns of what the speaker actually said. Indeed, it is often of as much importance to pay attention to the incidentals as to the remarks of the one talking.[136]

A different approach has been advocated by Digby Diehl, whose interviews appeared in the *Los Angeles Times* during the 1970s. He prefers the Q & A:

> The Q & A, written well, is easily as structured and artificially shaped by a writer as the profile. But from the inception there is a different methodology to the writing process. Initially, the writer does not sally forth in search of some 'hook', 'angle', or 'personal viewpoint'; he just wants to evoke from his subject the most coherent and valuable statements he can stimulate. Thus, during an interview, the writer actually listens to and responds to his subject – as opposed to noting the wallpaper, the consistency of their sandwiches, or the nervous twitches of his prey. But most significantly, during the writing process, a writer utilizing the Q & A form experiences that peculiar loss of ego involvement that can only come from a sense that the responsibility for the statements in the article rests with the subject and not with himself.[137]

At his best, the Q & A interviewer is something akin to a performance artist and while some have managed to efface themselves in this way, one of the most accomplished performers in this field, Oriana Fallaci, has managed to make the Q & A seem more, rather than less, egotistical than the written-up interview. Another commentator, however, balances the pros and cons of the two traditions:

> A fairly large number of interviews employ the essay-interview format. This kind of report can provide an otherwise stark occasion with a warmer and more familiar 'world' of discourse. Its drawback, of course, is that we may hear the subject's voice less frequently and that his words may be subordinated to the interviewer's 'fiction'.[138]

Allegations of falsehood are never far away where interviews are concerned, but deception travels in both directions. The first ever interview between Brigham Young and Horace Greeley was an instance of an interviewee lying to his inquisitor. Young denied certain allegations about the Mormons – that they murdered and robbed migrants passing through the Utah Territory – which have since been proved by historians (along with the fact of Young's knowledge of such acts); and he also claimed to have only fifteen wives when he actually had at least seventy. Frank Sinatra was apparently too restless and fidgety to allow someone to interview him at the considerable length that *Playboy* requires from its subjects, so Mike Shore, the executive in charge of advertising at Sinatra's recording company, Reprise Records, took it upon himself to compose an entire interview, questions *and* answers, which Sinatra approved and which appeared in the February 1963 edition of *Playboy*. In this, 'Sinatra' made all the right liberal noises about religion, civilization and the need for global disarmament, but Shore took care to ensure that these opinions were delivered in the style of a tough-talking, hard-drinking, gambling man:

> I believe in you and me. I'm like Albert Schweitzer and Bertrand Russell and Albert Einstein in that I have a respect for life in any form. I believe in nature, in the birds, the sea, the sky, in everything I can see or that there is *real* evidence for. If these things are what you mean by God, then I believe in God, but I don't believe in a personal God to whom I look for comfort or for a natural on the next roll of the dice. I'm not unmindful of man's seeming need for faith; I'm for *anything* that gets you through the night, be it prayer, tranquilizers, or a bottle of Jack Daniels. But to me religion is a deeply personal thing in which man and God go it alone together, without the witch doctor in the middle.[139]

'Self-creation and self-concealment', according to Wilfrid Sheed, were the twin motives of those writers who have submitted themselves to the *Paris Review* 'rewritten interview' approach. 'Having been given the chance to revise their words and to erase the banalities of spontaneity,' Sheed has explained, 'they are free to invent not only themselves but their way of presenting themselves.'[140] Truman Capote 'exaggerated the facts and created untrue stories about himself', the compiler of a book of Capote interviews has said. 'The extent of the exaggeration was sometimes a reflection of the way he responded to the interviewers and their gullibility.'[141] Francine du Plessix Gray has said that a book promotion tour 'mostly consists of lying our way across the United States to protect our privacy and powers'.[142] When Young Boswell asked Dorothy Parker whether she played golf, she replied: 'Only in interviews. You see, I live for my public.'[143] The poet W.H. Auden's 'interviewing self' has been described as 'an extra person, like the Holy Ghost, generated by self-contemplation';[144] while Thomas Morgan, who wrote interviews and profiles for American magazines in the 1950s and 60s, devised his own term for the phenomenon of the 'interviewing self' that celebrities tend to adopt:

> Over time, deliberately, they create a public self for the likes of me to interview, observe, and double-check. This self is a tested consumer item of proven value, a sophisticated invention refined, polished, distilled, and certified OK in scores, perhaps hundreds of engagements with journalists, audiences, friends, family, and lovers. It is not really them, but curiously it is not *not* them either. It is the commingling of an image and a personality, or what I've decided to call an Impersonality.[145]

The writer William Faulkner was inclined to play with the curiosity of interviewers about his private personality, as is demonstrated in a 1931 interview with

Marshall Smith of the *Memphis Scimitar*: 'I was born male and single at an early age in Mississippi, I am still alive but not single. I was born of a Negro slave and an alligator, both named Gladys Rock. I have two brothers, one Dr Walter E. Traprock and the other Eagle Rock, an airplane . . .'[146]

The interview is an uneasy and ambiguous ingredient in the self-mythologizing process that all public personalities engage in at one time or another. Sometimes, of course, an interviewer can get completely the wrong end of the stick. Evelyn Waugh, in one of his funniest essays, described the ordeal of being interviewed by a formidable Scandinavian lady who was evidently under the erroneous impression that he was a satirical proletarian writer. Waugh enjoyed the joke too much to want to enlighten his interrogator.[147] The French film director Jean-Luc Godard was formerly a film critic and interviewer for *Cahiers du Cinéma*. In 1975 he told James Conaway, an interviewer from *The New York Times Magazine*, 'to make up this article. He claimed to have invented whole interviews with Jean Renoir and Roberto Rossellini and "they contained no more lies than truth" . . .'[148]

Yet there is an even more fundamental problem for the interview as a form and that is the notion that the interviewer is complicit with the celebrity in the perpetration of some immense exercise in deception – not so much that the interviewer is destined to deceive his readers but that he is destined to be deceived, to be a willing patsy in the celebrity's agenda of hype. While the journalist is trying to break down the interviewee's barriers with the twin weapons of flattery and charm, Minette Marrin has written, 'any experienced interviewee will be doing his or her best to charm or flatter' the journalist.

> American show-business subjects seem to have been taught to compliment you ecstatically on what you're wearing and ask you where you can get it: perhaps somebody should point out to them that this one has been rumbled in London . . . if you do eat the biscuit, accept the compliment, apply flattery yourself or even like the subject, you find yourself in a kind of complicity. You are, to some extent, compromised . . . Behind almost every interview in print, I suspect, there is the shadow of the piece the journalist really wanted to write . . . most journalists suffer, I suspect, from the widespread human weakness of longing to be loved; the risk here is that writing profiles becomes simply an extension of one's social life.[149]

Naturally, this tendency is less marked where the interview encounter is perfunctory, although powerful persons will often overawe their interviewers by their presence alone. Merely by agreeing to find precious moments in their overburdened schedules, such persons are flattering their interviewers. Cornelius Vanderbilt Jr was given over three and a half hours by Stalin, Tom Driberg was granted a four-and-a-half-hour interview by Khrushchev (without interruption), while after two and a half hours Oriana Fallaci was asked whether she would honour Deng Xiao-ping with a second interview. 'At that point,' she has said, 'I lost my mind. I jumped, I fell on him, I kissed him.'[150] After his initial interview with Stalin, Eugene Lyons later recalled, 'I did not change my mind about my essential reaction to Stalin's personality. Even at moments when the behaviour of his regime seemed most hateful, I retained that liking for Stalin as a human being . . . In the simplicity which impressed me more than any other element in his make-up, there was nothing of make-believe, nowhere a note of falseness or affectation.'[151] In recent times, few examples of the sycophantic interview could compare to that of Saddam Hussein by a plainly spellbound Andrea Reynolds: 'His nails were beautifully manicured and his hands were strong and gracefully expressive. His gestures were slow, but his eyes were in perpetual movement . . . Saddam said goodbye charmingly. As if he were a movie star wanting me to be his fan. He took my hand, put his other hand over it and shook it warmly.'[152]

The development of the interview in this century has proceeded by fits and starts. In the 1930s it was Hollywood fan magazines such as *Motion Picture* that carried the concept of the celebrity interview forward by delving into marital and romantic relationships (some of which were dreamed up by publicists). In the 1950s it was Pete Martin of *The Saturday Evening Post* and the interview-profilists of *Esquire*, such as Helen Lawrenson and Thomas B. Morgan who carried on the tradition. In the 1960s it was magazines like *Mademoiselle* and *Playboy* (which published in-depth encounters with politicians and intellectuals as well as with show-business personalities). In the 1970s it was *Rolling Stone* and Andy Warhol's *Interview* in the United States, and *New Musical Express* in Britain.

During the last three decades a new type of interviewee has held sway, as ubiquitous and as prey to the curiosity of readers as churchmen were in the late nineteenth century. Few phenomena in the history of the interview can compare to the intense interest shown in popular music celebrities since the 1960s. Rock stars have generated more interest than film stars because their artistic activity has exercised a more powerful effect on popular culture. The breakthrough, according to one commentator, came in 1959 when Gloria Stavers, editor of *16 Magazine*, conducted an interview with Paul Anka, the first in a regular series conducted on the basis of her Forty Very Intimate Questions that she thought readers wished to have answered. 'It seems strange today that this charming and inane call-and-response interview was at one time an important journalistic innovation,' says *Rolling Stone* interviewer Jonathan Cott. 'It eliminated once and for all the press agent/record company barrier between the reader and the star.' The *Rolling Stone* interview sought to get inside the heads of those artists whose work was 'transforming the popular culture and art of the nation' and to stand as 'the most authoritative nonmusical communication between a performer and his audience'. Jann Wenner's 1971 interview with John Lennon was 30,000 words long and was spread over two consecutive issues of *Rolling Stone*. The message of this and other such *Rolling Stone* interviews was an echo of the Romantic concept of the artist: 'To commit to a life in rock & roll . . . is to be extraordinary.'[153]

Film actors, too, are conscious of their extraordinariness. According to Leonard Probst, they have 'an intense fascination with themselves, with their origins, experiences, anxieties, in each thing that happens to them. This is not narcissistic, self-loving, but pragmatic. The more clearly they know themselves, the better they function. Commitment to work is total.' He observed that such actors compete not with their rivals but with their own ideal selves – hence the importance of the interview as a means of defining their roles.[154] Writers see self-expression as an imperative: 'Being interviewed,' Tennessee Williams once told Charlotte Chandler, 'does have the advantage of self-revelation. I must articulate my feelings, and I may learn something about myself. It makes me more self-aware, more aware of my own unhappiness.'[155]

There has, though, been a disturbing development in recent years pertaining to interviews with film actors. As Emma Soames has written: 'The star system, led by Hollywood, has hijacked the interview, tied it up and all but killed it stone dead. Its heartbeat is so faint as to be almost imperceptible – even while the space it occupies grows . . . Interviewees – admittedly only if they are rich and famous – now control the interview.'[156] Lynn Barber's first interviewing assignment for *Vanity Fair* was spiked because the interviewee, film actor Nick Nolte, disliked her attitude and instructed his press agent to refuse to provide exclusive pictures to *Vanity Fair* if they were to go ahead and publish. The Hollywood press agents, of whom there are only half a dozen of any significance, now operate a cartel. Unless the writer's treatment of their client meets with their approval, they are likely to refuse not only future access to the client in question but also future access to any of their other clients. However, the interview has demonstrated its resilience as a genre and will no doubt withstand these current prohibitions.

As the rich and varied opinions of both practitioners and victims of the interview, and the wide-ranging contents of this volume, demonstrate, there are no fixed rules about how to conduct an interview encounter or how to fashion an interview for publication. The only requirement for this anthology has been that each interview must be an encounter between two persons, where one party by and large does the questioning and the other the answering and where both parties are aware that the result is intended for publication. These are what distinguish the interview from the recollected conversations which have peppered countless memoirs, biographies and autobiographies since Boswell's *Life of Johnson*. Beyond that, my criteria for selection have been threefold. Some interviews have been chosen for their craftsmanship as pieces of journalism, others for their historical significance *qua* their subjects or subject-matter, others still for their sheer delight and entertainment value. There is to my mind no better description of the multifarious approaches to interviewing than this one given by Frank Banfield in 1895. 'Sometimes,' he wrote, 'it may take the shape of an article interspersed with dialogue, sometimes, of an adroitly directed monologue. One can lay down no fixed rules. Each real interview must have its own colour, as varying as the moods, or characters, of the different interviewees, though the tone of the individual interviewer may, and in my view should, affect the whole.'[157]

Notes

1. Diana Cooper Clark, *Interviews with Contemporary Novelists*, London, Macmillan, 1986, p. 1.
2. 'In Memoriam. Charles Lutwidge Dodgson (Lewis Carroll)', *The Manchester Guardian*, 19 January 1898.
3. Quoted in Rudyard Kipling, *Something of Myself*, ed. Thomas Pinney, Cambridge, Cambridge University Press, 1990, p. 244.
4. H.G. Wells, interviewed by Arthur H. Lawrence, *The Young Man*, August 1897.
5. *The Pall Mall Gazette*, 7 August 1889.
6. Dustin Hoffman, interviewed by Leonard Probst, *Off Camera: Leveling about Themselves*, New York, Stein & Day, 1975, p. 100.
7. 'Are Interviewers a Blessing or a Curse?', *The Idler*, December 1895.
8. Frank Banfield, 'Interviewing in Practice', *The National Review*, November 1895.
9. Gertrude Lynch, 'Interviewed and Interviewer: Certain Celebrities as the Reporter Sees Them', *The Saturday Evening Post*, 18 March 1905.
10. Lynn Barber (in the course of reviewing Janet Malcolm, *The Journalist and the Murderer*), *London Review of Books*, 21 March 1991.
11. Denis Brian, *Murderers and Other Friendly People: The Public and Private Worlds of Interviewers*, New York, McGraw-Hill, 1973.
12. *The Oxford English Dictionary*, Vol. V, Oxford, 1961.
13. Edward Price Bell, *Major Interviewing: Its Principles and its Functions*, Chicago, published as a pamphlet by the Chicago Daily News Co., 15 January 1927.
14. George Turnbull, 'Some Notes on the History of the Interview', *Journalism Quarterly*, September 1936; Nils Gunnar Nilsson, 'The Origins of the Interview', *Journalism Quarterly*, Winter 1971.
15. Nilsson, op. cit.
16. Frank Giles, *A Prince of Journalists: The Life and Times of Henri Stefan Opper de Blowitz*, London, Faber and Faber, 1962, p. 139.
17. Raymond Blathwayt, *Through Life and Round the World, Being the Story of My Life*, London, George Allen & Unwin, 1917, p. 165.
18. Edwin L. Shuman, *Practical Journalism: A Complete Manual of the Best Newspaper Methods*, New York and London, D. Appleton, 1903, pp. 47–8.
19. Marlen Pew, 'Shop Talk at Thirty', *Editor & Publisher*, 13 October 1934.
20. *Cincinnati Daily Commercial*, 13 February 1868.
21. *Daily News*, 17 December 1869.

22. *The Nation*, 28 January 1869.

23. ibid., 17 July 1873.

24. *Galaxy*, New York, December 1874.

25. *Atlanta Constitution*, 16 August 1879.

26. Quoted in John Brady, *The Craft of Interviewing*, Cincinnati, Writer's Digest, 1976, p. 226.

27. *The Nation*, January 1869.

28. Quoted by W.T. Stead in his contribution to the symposium referred to in above, *The Idler*, December 1895.

29. Raymond L. Schults, *Crusader in Babylon: W.T. Stead and the Pall Mall Gazette*, Lincoln, University of Nebraska Press, 1972, p. 83.

30. ibid., p. 61.

31. Henry Fox Bourne, *English Newspapers*, London, Chatto & Windus, 1887, II, p. 343.

32. *The Pall Mall Gazette*, 23 August 1884.

33. Queen Victoria interviewed by the New York *World*, 17 June 1883.

34. Ulysses S. Grant interviewed by T.C. Crawford, the New York *World*, 22 March 1884.

35. Quoted in Don Carlos Seitz, *Joseph Pulitzer, His Life & Letters*, New York, Simon & Schuster, Inc., 1924, p. 422.

36. Giles, op. cit., p. 145.

37. *How to Write for the Magazines* (by '£600 a year from it'), London, Grant Richards, 1900, pp. 103–4.

38. Evelyn March Phillips, 'The New Journalism', *New Review*, August 1895.

39. Raymond Blathwayt, 'The Editor of "Great Thoughts": A Character Sketch and an Interview', *Great Thoughts*, 1909.

40. Raymond Blathwayt, 'The Ethics of the Higher Journalism: An Interview with the Proprietor of "Great Thoughts"', *Great Thoughts*, 17 July 1892.

41. Lincoln Springfield, *Some Piquant People*, London, T. Fisher Unwin, 1924, p. 82.

42. 'Character Sketch: T.P. O'Connor, MP', *The Review of Reviews*, 1902.

43. 'A Chat with Conan Doyle' (by an 'Idler' Interviewer), *The Idler*, October 1894.

44. John Carey, *The Intellectuals and the Masses: Pride and Prejudice among the Literary Intelligentsia, 1880–1939*, London, Faber and Faber, 1992, pp. 7–8.

45. Elizabeth L. Banks, *The Autobiography of a 'Newspaper Girl'*, London, Methuen, 1902, p. 287.

46. Hulda Friederichs, 'Difficulties and Delights of Interviewing', *The English Illustrated Magazine*, Febuaury 1893.

47. Banks, op. cit., p. 287.

48. Ernest Foster, *An Editor's Chair: A Record of Experiences and Happenings*, London, Everett & Co., 1909, p. 193.

49. Revd H.R. Haweis, 'A Prince of Humourists: Interview with "Mark Twain"', *Great Thoughts*, 5 October 1907.

50. Jack Huber and Dean Diggins, *Interviewing America's Top Interviewers: Nineteen Top Interviewees Tell All About What They Do*, New York, Birch Lane Press, 1991, p. 28.

51. Foster, op. cit., p. 194.

52. *The Pall Mall Gazette*, 19 December 1895.

53. Edward John Hart, 'Illustrated Interviews. No. XL. – Sarah Bernhardt', *The Strand Magazine*, 1905.

54. Arthur H. Lawrence, 'Christmas – Then and Now!: Mr George R. Sims at Home', *The Idler*, December 1897.

55. Arnold Haultain (ed.), *A Selection from Goldwin Smith's Correspondence*, London, T. Werner Laurie, 1913, p. 419.

56. George Jacob Holyoake, *Sixty Years of an Agitator's Life*, London, T. F. Unwin, 1893, II, pp. 156–7.

57. Joyce Kilmer, 'The American Interviewer', *The New Witness*, 10 January 1918.

58. G.K. Chesterton, *What I Saw in America*, London, Hodder and Stoughton, 1923, pp. 47ff.

59. Stephen Leacock, *My Discovery of England*, New York, Dodd, Mead, 1922, pp. 21ff.

60. A.J. Liebling, 'Interviewers', *The Best of A.J. Liebling*, London, Methuen, 1965, p. 197.

61. Brian, op. cit., p. vii.

62. Charles Holmes, *The Clocks of Columbus: The Literary Career of James Thurber*, London, Secker and Warburg, 1973, p. 315.

63. R.J. Minney, *The Journalist*, London, Geoffrey Bles, 1931, p. 87.

64. Isaac F. Marcosson, *Adventures in Interviewing*, London, John Lane, The Bodley Head, 1919, p. 68.

65. ibid., p. 71.

66. Price Bell, op. cit.

67. Giles, op. cit., p. 140.

68. Both quotations from Frank Banfield, op. cit.

69. 'The Art of the Interview', Melvin J. Lasky, *Encounter*, March 1989.

70. John B. Lane, 'Confessions of an Interviewer', *The Pall Mall Magazine*, December 1893.

71. A.F. Hill, *Secrets of the Sanctum, an inside view of an editor's life*, Philadelphia; Claxton, Remsen & Haffelfinger, 1875, pp. 59–60.

72. *The Sunday Herald* (Boston) and the *Boston Globe*, 23 October 1892.

73. John B. Lane, 'Confessions of an Interviewer', *The Pall Mall Magazine*, December 1893.

74. George Moore interviewed by Kate Carew, *The New-York Tribune*, 26 January 1913.

75. Quoted in Maurice Zolotow, *It Takes All Kinds*, London, W.H. Allen, 1953, p. 3.

76. First published in *The Thurber Carnival* (1945); revised version in *Thurber Country*, London, Penguin Books, 1962; also, Holmes, op. cit., pp. 283–4.

77. Holmes, op. cit., p. 284.

78. Willard Grosvenor Bleyer, *Newspaper Writing and Editing*, Boston, Houghton Mifflin, 1913, pp. 130–31.

79. Giles, op. cit., p. 140.

80. ibid., p. 154.

81. W.T. Stead interviewed by Mrs Maud Churton Braby, *The World of Dress*, June 1905.

82. Bing Crosby, 'I Call on Pete Martin (Conclusion)', *The Saturday Evening Post*, 12 August 1961.

83. A.J. Liebling, op. cit., p. 197.

84. J.W. Robertson Scott, *The Life and Death of a Newspaper*, London, Methuen & Co., 1952, p. 160; for the interview with Sultan Mehmed V, see *The Review of Reviews*, February 1913.

85. Giles, op. cit., p. 148.

86. Marcosson, op. cit., p. 71.

87. Djuna Barnes, 19 July 1914.

88. Gerald Clarke, *Truman Capote*, London, Hamish Hamilton, 1988, p. 302.

89. Brian, op. cit.; quoted in M. Thomas Inge, *Truman Capote: Conversations*, University Press of Mississippi, 1987, p. 222.

90. 'Home Thoughts: Geoffrey Wheatcroft on the Killer Interview', *The Independent Magazine*, 25 August 1990.

91. Giles, op. cit., p. 160.

92. Bing Crosby, 'I Call on Pete Martin', *The Saturday Evening Post*, 5 August 1961.

93. Pete Martin, 'I Call on Dean Martin', *The Saturday Evening Post*, 29 April 1961.

94. 'An Interview is a Love Story', *Time*, 20 October 1975, p. 31.

95. Huber and Diggins, op. cit., p. 136 and p. 138.

96. Janet Malcolm, *The Journalist and the Murderer*, London, Bloomsbury, 1991 p. 59.

97. John Kobler, *Capone: The Life and World of Al Capone*, London, Michael Joseph, 1971, pp. 311–12.

98. Rex Reed, *Do you Sleep in the Nude?*, London, W.H. Allen, 1969, p.xi.

99. *The Independent Magazine*, 25 August 1990.

100. Francine du Plessix Gray in her introduction to George Plimpton, ed., *The Paris Review Interviews, Fifth Series*, New York, Viking Press, 1981, p. xi.

101. Quoted in 'Jugular Journalism', Mark Lawson, *Mirabella* (UK), November 1990.

102. Derrick Grigs, 'Conversation at Oxford', *Sight & Sound*, Spring 1960.

103. Perry J. Ashley (ed.), *Dictionary of Literary Biography*, Vol. 23, American Newspaper Journalists, 1873–1900, Detroit, Gale Research, 1983, p.204.

104. 'The Art of Interviewing', Frank A. Burr, *Lippincott's Magazine*, September 1890.

105. Henri Stephan de Blowitz, *My Memoirs*, London, Edward Arnold, 1903, p. 7.

106. Alyce Barry (ed.), *Interviews: Djuna Barnes*, Washington, DC, Sun and Moon Press, 1985, p. 258.

107. Foster, op. cit., pp. 177–8.

108. *The Young Man*, September 1914.

109. Marcosson, op. cit., p. 81.

110. Earl Wilson, *The Show Business Nobody Knows*, London and New York, W.H. Allen, 1972, pp. 121–2.

111. Reference to Reed from Brady, op. cit., p. 160 (Brady omits to mention that it was in a gay bathhouse – as told to the author by Reed himself); references to Marcosson and Fallaci from Brady, ibid., pp. 156–7.

112. Both quotations regarding Groucho Marx from Charlotte Chandler, *Hello, I Must Be Going: Groucho & his friends*, New York, Doubleday, 1978, p. 251.

113. Henry Brandon, *Conversations with Henry Brandon*, London, André Deutsch, 1966, p. 9.

114. Charles Higham, *Celebrity Circus*, New York, Delacorte, 1979, p. 7.

115. Brian, op. cit., p. 226.

116. Lynn Barber, *Mostly Men*, London, Viking, 1991, p. xiv.

117. Quoted in Brady, op. cit., p. 230.

118. Quoted in J.A. Hammerton, Stevensoniana, London, Grant Richards, 1902.

119. Blathwayt, op. cit., p. 165.

120. Burr, op. cit.

121. M. Lyle Spencer, News Writing: The Gathering, Handling and Writing of News Stories, New York, D.C. Heath, 1917, pp. 127–8.

122. Giles, op. cit., p. 157.

123. Yorkshire Observer, quoted in The People, 25 May 1924.

124. Lord Burnham, Peterborough Court, London, Cassell & Co., 1955, pp. 149–54; also Lucy Maynard Salmon, The Newspaper and the Historian, New York, Oxford University Press, 1923, pp. 236–7.

125. Eugene Lyons, Assignment in Utopia, London, George G. Harrap & Co., 1937, pp.384–9.

126. Quoted in Robert Shelton, No Direction Home: The Biography of Bob Dylan, New York, William Morrow and Co., p. 287.

127. The two versions appeared in The Sunday Times, 4 March 1956, and The Reporter, 22 March 1956; Faulkner's repudiation in The Reporter, 19 April 1956.

128. Brian, op. cit., p. 226.

129. Harvey Breit, The Writer Observed, London, Alvin Redman, 1957, pp. 15–16 and 23–4.

130. Malcolm, op. cit., p. 157.

131. 'Are Interviewers a Blessing or a Curse?', The Idler, December 1895.

132. Malcolm, op. cit., p. 155 and p. 158.

133. Penelope Gilliatt, Three-Quarter Face: Reports and Reflections, New York, Coward,Mc-Cann & Geoghegan, 1980, p. 13.

134. Barry G. Golson (ed.), The Playboy Interview II, p. x.

135. Diary item by the author, The Independent on Sunday, 2 June 1991.

136. M. Lyle Spencer, op. cit., p. 130.

137. Digby Diehl, Supertalk, Garden City, NY, Doubleday, 1974, p. viii.

138. Albert J. Devlin (ed.), Conversations with Tennessee Williams, Jackson, University Press of Mississippi, 1986, pp. viii–ix.

139. Quoted in Kitty Kelley, His Way: The Unauthorized Biography of Frank Sinatra, New York, Bantam Press, 1986, pp. 334–6.

140. Wilfrid Sheed in his introduction to George Plimpton, ed., Writers at Work: The Paris Review Interviews, Fourth Series, New York, Viking Press, 1976, p. xiv.

141. M.Thomas Inge, op. cit., p. x.

142. George Plimpton (ed.), Writers at Work: The Paris Review Interviews, Fifth Series, p. xiv.

143. Young Boswell (pseud. for Harold Stark), People You Know, New York, Boni and Liveright, 1924, p. 294.

144. Wilfrid Sheed in his introduction to George Plimpton (ed.), Writers at Work: The Paris Review Interviews, Fourth Series, p. xi.

145. Thomas B. Morgan, Self-Creations: Thirteen Impersonalities, New York, Holt & Rinehart, 1969, p. 4.

146. Quoted in James B. Meriwether and Michael Millgate, eds., Lion in the Garden: Interviews with William Faulkner 1926–1962, New York, Random House, 1968, p. x.

147. Evelyn Waugh, 'The Gentle Art of Being Interviewed', *Vogue* (New York), July 1948 (reprinted in this anthology).
148. *The New York Times Magazine*, 24 December 1972.
149. *The Sunday Telegraph*, 14 July 1991.
150. Cornelius Vanderbilt Jr, *Man of the World: My Life on Five Continents*, New York, Crown Publishing, 1959, p. 60; Tom Driberg, *Ruling Passions*, London, Jonathan Cape, 1977, p. 240; Fallaci quoted in Huber and Diggins, op. cit., p. 30.
151. Lyons, op. cit., p. 390.
152. *Tatler*, March 1991.
153. Jann S. Wenner, 'A Letter From the Editor', *Rolling Stone*, 15 October 1992.
154. Leonard Probst, op. cit., p. 11.
155. Charlotte Chandler, *The Ultimate Seduction*, Garden City, NY, Doubleday & Company Inc., 1984, p. 352.
156. *Evening Standard*, 22 April 1993.
157. Banfield, op. cit.

BRIGHAM YOUNG

Interviewed by Horace Greeley
New-York Tribune, 20 August 1859

Brigham Young (1801– 77), the Mormon leader, was born in Vermont and converted to Mormonism in his early thirties. He succeeded the founder of the sect, Joseph Smith, as president in 1844 and led its members on a trek from Illinois, where they had been ousted by the local citizenry, to Utah in 1847. There, he and his followers founded Salt Lake City and declared a free and independent state, but the US Congress created the Utah Territory and made him its governor. Young reigned as an absolute monarch, and 3,000 US troops were required to help install non-Mormon federal officers. He also claimed the prophetic succession from Joseph Smith and, despite the fact that Smith had always been opposed to polygamy, he persuaded his followers that he had received a revelation from Smith sanctioning such a practice after all.

In September 1857 Young made some fiery speeches which encouraged some of his followers to disguise themselves as Indians and attack a rich emigrant train from Missouri and Arkansas, *en route* to California. When the emigrants managed to defend themselves, the Mormons divested themselves of their disguises and, affecting to have arrived to rescue the emigrants, persuaded them to lay down their arms and walk to Salt Lake City under escort. The Mormons then proceeded to massacre 120 emigrants, sparing only seven children. Attempts by the federal government to investigate the Mountain Meadows massacre, as it came to be known, and bring the perpetrators to justice were foiled by the uncooperative attitude of the Mormon community. The US government imposed a new governor, backed with troops, to replace Young with the intention of thereby curbing the practice of polygamy. Nevertheless, Young remained an influential figure in Utah and amassed a fortune of some $2,500,000, which was bequeathed to his seventeen wives and fifty-six daughters. The Saint who had led the massacre, John D. Lee, was rewarded with extra wives and a probate judgeship by Young for keeping 'silent as the grave' about the event. However, in 1875 Lee was tried, convicted and executed for the murders and he excoriated Young as 'the most treacherous, ungrateful villain on earth' for finally withdrawing his protection.

Horace Greeley (1811– 72) was one of the most influential American journalists of the nineteenth century, as well as a politician. He began his career as a printer and in 1841 he launched a daily paper, the *New-York Tribune*, which he edited for the most part until his death. The political allegiances of the paper altered during the period of his editorship, which encompassed the great mid-century debates about slavery and states rights and the Civil War to which they gave rise. Having earlier been an advocate of secession for the Southern states, he emerged as one of Lincoln's keenest supporters. After the Civil War he urged a reconciliation between the North and the South, a stance which was unpopular, and in 1872 he stood without success as a candidate for the presidency.

This interview, which is the first example of the genre (see Introduction), took place in Salt Lake City, Utah, while Greeley was traversing the country from east to west. It was published throughout the world. Interestingly, it contains several lies on the part of the interviewee. He gave a falsely low figure for both the number of his wives and the extent of his personal wealth (he had obtained land, grazing rights, farming monopolies, a wood monopoly, control of water supplies, and the right to award liquor licences). He also denied the existence of the Danites, his secret order of destroying angels, or Shenpips, who preyed on Gentiles and practised 'blood atonement'.

My friend Dr Berhisel, MC, took me this afternoon, by appointment, to meet Brigham Young, President of the Mormon Church, who had expressed a willingness to receive me at 2 p.m. We were very cordially welcomed at the door by the President, who led us into the second-story parlor of the largest of his houses (he has three), where I was introduced to Heber C. Himball, Gen. Wells, Gen. Ferguson, Albert Carrington, Elias Smith, and several other leading men in the Church, with two full-grown sons of the President. After some unimportant conversation on general topics, I stated that I had come in quest of fuller knowledge respecting the doctrines and polity of the Mormon Church, and would like to ask some questions bearing directly on these, if there were no objections. President Young avowed his willingness to respond to all pertinent inquiries, the conversation proceeded substantially as follows:

H.G.: Am I to regard Mormonism (so-called) as a new religion, or as simply a new development of Christianity?

B.Y.: We hold that there can be no true Christian Church without a priesthood directly commissioned by and in immediate communication with the Son of God and Savior of mankind. Such a church is that of the Latter-Day Saints, called by their enemies Mormons: we know no other that even pretends to have present and direct revelations of God's will.

H.G.: Then am I to understand that you regard all other churches professing to be Christian as the Church of Rome regards all other churches not in communion with itself – as schismatic, heretical, and out of the way of salvation?

B.Y.: Yes, substantially.

H.G.: Apart from this, in what respect do your doctrines differ essentially from those of our Orthodox Protestant Churches – the Baptist, or Methodist, for example?

B.Y.: We hold the doctrines of Christianity, as revealed in the Old and New

Testaments – also in the Book of Mormon, which teaches the same cardinal truths, and those only.

H.G.: Do you believe in the doctrine of the Trinity?

B.Y.: We do; but not exactly as it is held by other churches. We believe in the Father, the Son, and the Holy Ghost, as equal, but not identical – not as one person [being]. We believe in all the Bible teaches on the subject.

H.G.: Do you believe in a personal devil – a distinct, conscious, spiritual being, whose nature and acts are essentially malignant and evil?

B.Y.: We do.

H.G.: Do you hold the doctrine of Eternal Punishment?

B.Y.: We do; though perhaps not exactly as other churches do. We believe it as the Bible teaches it.

H.G.: I understand that you regard Baptism by Immersion as essential.

B.Y.: We do.

H.G.: Do you practice infant baptism?

B.Y.: No.

H.G.: Do you make removal to these valleys obligatory on your converts?

B.Y.: They would consider themselves greatly aggrieved if they were not invited hither. We hold to such a gathering together of God's People as the Bible foretells, and that this is the place and now is the time appointed for its consummation.

H.G.: The predictions to which you refer have, usually, I think, been understood to indicate Jerusalem (or Judea) as the place of such gathering.

B.Y.: Yes, for the Jews – not for others.

H.G.: What is the position of your Church with respect to Slavery?

B.Y.: We consider it of Divine institution, and not to be abolished until the curse pronounced on Ham shall have been removed from his descendants.

H.G.: Are there any slaves now held in this Territory?

B.Y.: There are.

H.G.: Do your Territorial laws uphold Slavery?

B.Y.: Those laws are printed – you can read for yourself. If slaves are brought here by those who owned them in the States, we do not favor their escape from the service of those owners.

H.G.: Am I to infer that Utah, if admitted as a member of the Federal Union, will be a Slave State?

B.Y.: No; she will be a Free State. Slavery here would prove useless and unprofitable. I regard it as a curse to the masters. I myself hire many laborers and pay them fair wages; I could not afford to own them. I can do better than subject myself to an obligation to feed and clothe their families, to provide and care for them, in sickness and health. Utah is not adapted to Slave Labor.

H.G.: Let me now be enlightened with regard more especially to your Church polity: I understand that you require each member to pay one-tenth of all he produces or earns to the Church.

B.Y.: That is a requirement of our faith. There is no compulsion as to the payment. Each member acts in the premises according to his pleasure under the dictates of his own conscience.

H.G.: What is done with the proceeds of this tithing?

B.Y.: Part of it is devoted to building temples and other places of worship; part to helping the poor and needy converts on their way to this country; and the largest portion to the support of the poor among the Saints.

H.G.: Is none of it paid to the Bishops and other dignitaries of the Church?

B.Y.: Not one penny. No Bishop, no Elder, no Deacon, or other church officer, receives any compensation for his official services. A Bishop is often required to put his hand in his own pocket and provide therefrom for the poor of his charge; but he never receives anything for his services.

H.G.: How, then, do your ministers live?

B.Y.: By the labor of their own hands, like the first Apostles. Every Bishop, every Elder, may be daily seen at work in the field or the shop, like his neighbors; every minister of the Church has his proper calling by which he earns the bread of his family; he who cannot or will not do the Church's work for nothing is not wanted in her service; even our lawyers (pointing to Gen. Ferguson and another present, who are the regular lawyers of the Church), are paid nothing for their services; I am the only person in the Church who has not a regular calling apart from the Church's service, and I never received one farthing from her treasury; if I obtain anything from the tithing-house, I am charged with and pay for it, just as any one else would; the clerks in the tithing-store are paid like other clerks, but no one is ever paid for any service pertaining to the ministry. We think a man who cannot make his living aside from the Ministry of Christ unsuited to that office. I am called rich, and consider myself worth $250,000; but no dollar of it was ever paid to me by the Church or for any service as a minister of the Everlasting Gospel. I lost nearly all I had when we were broken up in Missouri and driven from that State; I was nearly stripped again when Joseph Smith was murdered and we were driven from Illinois; but nothing was ever made up to me by the Church, nor by any one. I believe I know how to acquire property and how to take care of it.

H.G.: Can you give me any rational explanation of the aversion and hatred with which your people are generally regarded by those among whom they have lived and with whom they have been in contact?

B.Y.: No other explanation than is afforded by the crucifixion of Christ and the kindred treatment of God's ministers, prophets and saints in all ages.

H.G.: I know that a new sect is always decried and traduced – that it is hardly ever deemed respectable to belong to one – that the Baptists, Quakers, Methodists, Universalists, etc., have each in their turn been regarded in the infancy of their sect as the offscouring of the earth; yet I cannot remember that either of them were ever generally represented and regarded by the older sects of their early days as thieves, robbers, murderers.

B.Y.: If you will consult the contemporary Jewish accounts of the life and the acts of Jesus Christ, you will find that he and his disciples were accused of every abominable deed and purpose – robbery and murder included. Such a work is still extant, and may be found by those who seek it.

H.G.: What do you say of the so-called Danites or Destroying Angels, belonging to your Church?

B.Y.: What do *you* say? I know of no such persons or organization. I hear of them only in the slanders of our enemies.

H.G.: With regard, then, to the grave question on which your doctrines and practices are avowedly at war with those of the Christian world – that of a plurality of wives – is the system of your Church acceptable to the majority of its women?

B.Y.: They could not be more averse to it than I was when it was first revealed to us as the Divine will. I think they generally accept it, as I do, as the will of God.

H.G.: How general is polygamy among you?

B.Y.: I could not say. Some of those present [heads of the Church] have each but one wife; others have more: each determines what is his individual duty.

H.G.: What is the largest number of wives belonging to any one man?

B.Y.: I have fifteen; I know no one who has more; but some of those sealed to me are old ladies whom I regard rather as mothers than wives, but whom I have taken home to cherish and support.

H.G.: Does not the Apostle Paul say that a bishop should be 'the husband of one wife'?

B.Y.: So we hold. We do not regard any but a married man as fitted for the office of bishop. But the Apostle does not forbid a bishop having more wives than one.

H.G.: Does not Christ say that he who puts away his wife, or marries one whom another has put away, commits adultery?

B.Y.: Yes; and I hold that no man should ever put away a wife except for adultery – not always even for that. I do not say that wives have never been put away in our Church, but that I do not approve the practice.

H.G.: How do you regard what is commonly termed the Christian Sabbath?

B.Y.: As a divinely appointed day of rest. We enjoin all to rest from secular labor on that day. We would have no man enslaved to the Sabbath, but we enjoin all to respect and enjoy it.

Such is, as nearly as I can recollect, the substance of nearly two hours' conversation, wherein much was said incidentally that would not be worth reporting, even if I could remember and reproduce it, and wherein others bore a part; but, as President Young is the first minister of the Mormon Church, and bore the principal part in the conversation, I have reported his answers alone to my questions and observations. The others appeared uniformly to defer to his views, and to acquiesce fully in his responses and explanations. He spoke readily, not always with grammatical accuracy, but with no apparent desire to conceal anything, nor did he repel any of my questions as impertinent. He was very plainly dressed in thin summer clothing, and with no air of sanctimony or fanaticism. In appearance, he is a portly, frank, good-natured, rather thick-set man of fifty-five, seeming to enjoy life, and be in no particular hurry to get to heaven. His associates are plain men, evidently born and reared to a life of labor, and looking as little like saintly hypocrites or swindlers as any body of men I ever met. The absence of cant and snuffle from their manner was marked and general, yet, I think I may fairly say that their Mormonism has not impoverished them – that they were generally poor men when they embraced it, and are now in very comfortable circumstances – as men averaging three or four wives apiece certainly need to be.

If I hazard any criticisms on Mormonism generally, I reserve them for a separate letter, being determined to make this a fair and full expose of the doctrines and polity, in the very words of its Prophet, so far as I can recall them. I do not believe President Young himself could present them in terms calculated to render them less obnoxious to the Gentile world than the above. But I have a right to add here, because I said it to the assembled chiefs at the close of the above colloquy, that the degradation (or, if you please, the restriction) of Woman to the single office of child-bearing and its accessories, is an inevitable consequence of the system here paramount. I have not observed a sign in the streets, an advertisement in the journals, of this Mormon metropolis, whereby a woman proposes to do anything whatever. No Mormon has ever cited to me his wife's or any woman's opinion on any subject; no Mormon woman has been introduced or has spoken to me; and, though I have been asked to visit Mormons in their houses, no one has spoken of his wife (or wives) desiring to see me, or him desiring me to make her (or their) acquaintance, or voluntarily indicated the existence of such a being or beings. I will not attempt to report our talk on this subject, because, unlike what I have above given, it assumed somewhat the character of a disputation, and I could hardly give it impartially; but one remark made by President Young I think I can give accurately, and it may serve as a sample of all that was offered on that side. It was in these words, I think exactly: 'If I did not consider myself competent to transact a certain business without taking my wife's or any woman's counsel with regard to it, I think I ought to let that business alone.' The spirit with regard to Woman, of the entire Mormon, as of all other polygamic systems, is fairly displayed in this avowal. Let any such system become established and prevalent, and Woman will soon be confined to the harem, and her appearance in the street with unveiled face will be accounted immodest. I joyfully trust that the genius of the Nineteenth Century tends to a solution of the problem of Woman's sphere and destiny radically different from his.

•

KARL MARX

Interviewed by R. Landor
The World, 18 July 1871

Karl Marx (1818–83), the political and social philosopher, began his career as a newspaper editor in Cologne in the early 1840s. When his paper was closed for political reasons, he left for Paris where he edited another newspaper until that too was closed for the same reason. However, he found a home in London, where he wrote his greatest works of philosophy and political economy. He also wrote journalism, serving as a foreign correspondent of the *New York Tribune* from 1851 to 1862. His master-work, *Das Kapital*, was published in 1867.

New York *World* correspondent R. Landor interviewed Marx in London, filing his report on 3 July 1871. The other German gentleman present throughout the interview is thought to have been Engels. Only a couple of months earlier, the Paris Commune, in which Marx had been involved, had been put down with bloodshed.

You have asked me to find out something about the International Association, and I have tried to do so. The enterprise is a difficult one just now. London is indisputably the headquarters of the Association, but the English people have got a scare, and smell International in everything as King James smelt gunpowder after the famous plot. The consciousness of the Association has naturally increased with the suspiciousness of the public; and if those who guide it have a secret to keep, they are of the stamp of men who keep a secret well. I have called on two of their leading members, have talked with one freely, and I here give you the substance of my conversation. I have satisfied myself of one thing, that it is a society of genuine working men, but that these workmen are directed by social and political theorists of another class. One man whom I saw, a leading member of the Council, was sitting at his workman's bench during our interview, and left off talking to me from time to time to receive a complaint, delivered in no courteous tone, from one of the many little masters in the neighbourhood who employed him. I have heard this same man make eloquent speeches in public inspired in every passage with the energy of hate towards the classes that call themselves his rulers. I understood the speeches after this glimpse at the domestic life of the orator. He must have felt that he had brains enough to have organized a working government, and yet here he was obliged to devote his life to the most revolting task work of a mechanical profession. He was proud and sensitive, and yet at every turn he had to return a bow for a grunt and a smile for a command that stood on about the same level in the scale of civility with a huntsman's call to his dog. This man helped me to a glimpse of one side of the nature of the International, the revolt of labour against capital, of the workman who produces against the middleman who enjoys. Here was the hand that would smite hard when the time came, and as to the head that plans, I think I saw that, too, in my interview with Dr Karl Marx.

Dr Karl Marx is a German doctor of Philosophy with a German breadth of knowledge derived both from observation of the living world and from books. I should conclude that he has never been a worker in the ordinary sense of the term. His surroundings and appearance are those of a well-to-do man of the middle class. The drawing-room into which I was ushered on the night of my interview would have formed very comfortable quarters for a thriving stockbroker who had made his competence and was now beginning to make his fortune. It was comfort personified, the apartment of a man of taste and of easy means, but with nothing in it peculiarly characteristic of its owner. A fine album of Rhine views on the table, however, gave a clue to his nationality. I peered cautiously into the vase on the side-table for a bomb. I sniffed for petroleum, but the smell was the smell of roses. I crept back stealthily to my seat, and moodily awaited the worst.

He has entered and greeted me cordially, and we are sitting face to face. Yes, I am *tête-à-tête* with the revolution incarnate, with the real founder and guiding spirit of the International Association, with the author of the address in which capital was told that if it warred on labour it must expect to have its house burned down about its ears – in a word, with the apologist for the Commune of Paris. Do you remember the bust of Socrates, the man who died rather than profess his belief in the gods of the time – the man with the fine sweep of profile for the forehead running meanly at the end into a little snub, curled-up feature like a bisected pothook that formed the nose? Take this bust in your mind's eye, colour the beard black, dashing it here and there with puffs of grey; clap the head thus made on a portly body of the middle height, and the Doctor is before you. Throw a veil over the upper part of the face and you might be in the company of a born vestryman. Reveal the essential feature, the immense brow, and you know at once that you have to deal with that most formidable of all composite forces – a dreamer who thinks, a thinker who dreams.

Another gentleman accompanied Dr Marx, a German too, I believe, though from his great familiarity with our language I cannot be sure of it. Was he a witness on the doctor's side? I think so. The 'Council', hearing of the interview, might hereafter call on the Doctor for his account of it, for the *Revolution* is above all things suspicious of its agents. Here, then, was his evidence in corroboration.

I went straight to my business. The world, I said, seemed to be in the dark about the International, hating it very much, but not able to say clearly what thing it hated. Some, who professed to have peered further into the gloom than their neighbours, declared that they had made out a sort of Janus figure with a fair, honest workman's smile on one of its faces, and on the other a murderous, conspirator's scowl. Would he light up the case of mystery in which the theory dwelt?

The professor laughed, chuckled a little I fancied, at the thought that we were so frightened of him. 'There is no mystery to clear up, dear sir,' he began, in a very polished form of the Hans Breitmann dialect, 'except perhaps the mystery of human stupidity in those who perpetually ignore the fact that our Association is a public one and that the fullest reports of its proceedings are published for all who care to read them. You may buy our rules for a penny, and a shilling laid out in pamphlets will teach you almost as much about us as we know ourselves.

R.: Almost – yes, perhaps so; but will not the something I shall not know constitute the all-important reservation? To be quite frank with you, and to put the case as it strikes an outside observer, this general claim of depreciation of you must mean something more than the ignorant ill-will of the multitude. And it is still pertinent to ask, even after what you have told me, what is the International Association?

DR M.: You have only to look at the individuals of which it is composed – workmen.

R.: Yes, but the soldier need be no exponent of the statecraft that sets him in motion. I know some of your members, and I can believe that they are not of the stuff of which conspirators are made. Besides, a secret shared by a million men would be no secret at all. But what if these were only the instruments in the hands of a bold, and I hope you will forgive me for adding, not over-scrupulous conclave.

DR M.: There is nothing to prove it.

R.: – The last Paris insurrection?

DR M.: I demand firstly the proof that there was any plot at all – that anything happened that was not the legitimate effect of the circumstances of the moment; or, the plot granted, I demand the proofs of the participation in it of the International Association.

R.: The presence in the communal body of so many members of the Association.

DR M.: Then it was a plot of the Freemasons, too, for their share in the work as individuals was by no means a slight one. I should not be surprised, indeed, to find the Pope setting down the whole insurrection to their account. But try another explanation. The insurrection in Paris was made by the workmen of Paris. The ablest of the workmen must necessarily have been its leaders and administrators; but the ablest of the workmen happen also to be members of the International Association. Yet the Association as such may in no way be responsible for their action.

R.: It will still seem otherwise to the world. People talk of secret instructions from London, and even grants of money. Can it be affirmed that the alleged openness of the Association's proceedings precludes all secrecy of communication?

DR M.: What association ever formed carried on its work without private as well as public agencies? But to talk of secret instruction from London, as of decrees in the matter of faith and morals from some centre of Papal domination and intrigue, is wholly to misconceive the nature of the International. This would imply a centralised form of government of the International, whereas the real form is designedly that which gives the greatest play to local energy and independence. In fact the International is not properly a government for the working class at all. It is a bond of union rather than a controlling force.

R.: And of union to what end?

DR M.: The economical emancipation of the working class by the conquest of political power. The use of that political power to the attainment of social ends. It is necessary that our aims should be thus comprehensive to include every form of working-class activity. To have made them of a special character would have been to adapt them to the needs of one section – one nation of workmen alone. But how could all men be asked to unite to further the objects of a few? To have done that the Association must have forfeited its title of International. The Association does not dictate the form of political movements; it only requires a pledge as to their end. It is a network of affiliated societies spreading all over the world of labour. In each part of the world some special aspect of the problem presents itself, and the workmen there address themselves to its consideration in their own way. Combinations among workmen cannot be absolutely identical in detail in Newcastle and in Barcelona, in London and in Berlin. In England, for instance, the way to show political power lies open to the working class. Insurrection would be madness where peaceful agitation would more swiftly and surely do the work. In France a hundred laws of repression and a moral antagonism between classes seem to necessitate the violent solution of social war. The choice of that solution is the affair of the working classes of that country. The International does not presume to dictate in the matter and hardly to advise. But to every movement it accords its sympathy and its aid within the limits assigned by its own laws.

R.: And what is the nature of that aid?

DR M.: To give an example, one of the commonest forms of the movement for emancipation is that of strikes. Formerly, when a strike took place in one country it was defeated by the importation of workmen from another. The International has nearly stopped all that. It receives information of the intended strike, it spreads that information among its members, who at once see that for them the seat of the struggle must be forbidden ground. The masters are thus left alone to reckon with their men. In most cases the men require no other aid than that. Their own subscriptions or those of the societies to which they are more immediately affiliated supply them with funds, but should the pressure upon them become too heavy and the strike be one of which the Association approves, their necessities are supplied out of the common purse. By these means a strike of the cigar-makers of Barcelona was brought to a victorious issue the other day. But the society has no interest in strikes, though it supports them under certain conditions. It cannot possibly gain by them in a pecuniary point of view, but it may easily lose. Let us sum it all up in a word. The working classes remain poor amid the increase of wealth, wretched among the increase of luxury. Their material privation dwarfs their moral as well as their physical stature. They cannot rely on others for a remedy. It has become then with them an imperative necessity to take their own case in hand. They must revise the relations between themselves and the capitalists and landlords, and that means they must transform society. This is the general end of every known workmen's organisation; land and labour leagues, trade and friendly societies, co-operative stores and co-operative production are but means towards it. To establish a perfect solidarity between these organisations is the business of the International Association. Its influence is beginning to be felt everywhere. Two papers spread its views in Spain, three in Germany, the same number in Austria and in Holland, six in Belgium, and six in Switzerland. And now that I have told you what the International is you may, perhaps, be in a position to form your own opinion as to its pretended plots.

R.: I do not quite understand you.

DR M.: Do you not see that the old society, wanting strength to meet it with its own weapons of discussion and combination, is obliged to resort to the fraud of fixing upon it the imputation of conspiracy?

R.: But the French police declare that they are in a position to prove its complicity in the late affair, to say nothing of preceding attempts.

DR M.: But we will say something of those attempts, if you please, because they best serve to test the gravity of all the charges of conspiracy brought against the International. You remember the last 'plot' but one. A plebiscite had been announced. Many of the electors were known to be wavering. They had no longer a keen sense of the value of the imperial rule, having come to disbelieve in those threatened dangers of society from which it was supposed to have saved them. A new bugbear was wanted. The police undertook to find one. All combinations of workmen being hateful to them, they naturally owed the International an ill turn. A happy thought inspired them. What if they should select the International for their bugbear, and thus at once discredit that society and curry favour for the imperial cause? Out of that happy thought came the ridiculous 'plot' against the Emperor's life – as if we wanted to kill the wretched old fellow. They seized the leading members of the International. They manufactured evidence. They prepared their case for trial, and in the meantime they had their plebiscite. But the intended comedy was too obviously but a broad, coarse farce. Intelligent Europe, which witnessed the spectacle, was not deceived for a moment as to its character, and only the French peasant elector was befooled. Your English papers reported the beginning of the miserable affair; they forget to notice the end. The French judges, admitting the existence of the plot by official courtesy, were obliged to declare that there was nothing to show the complicity of the International. Believe me, the second plot is like the first. The French functionary is again in business. He is called in to account for the biggest civil movement the world has ever seen. A hundred signs of the times ought to suggest the right explanation – the growth of intelligence among the workmen, of luxury and incompetence among their rulers, the historical process now going on of that final transfer of power from a class to the people, the apparent fitness of time, place and circumstance for the great movement of emancipation. But to have seen these the functionary must have been a philosopher, and he is only a *mouchard*. By the law of his being, therefore, he has fallen back upon the *mouchard*'s explanation – a 'conspiracy'. His old portfolio of forged documents will supply him with the proofs, and this time Europe in its scare will believe the tale.

R.: Europe can scarcely help itself, seeing that every French newspaper spreads the report.

DR M.: Every French newspaper! See, here is one of them [taking up *La Situation*], and judge for yourself of the value of its evidence as to a matter of fact. [Reads] 'Dr Karl Marx, of the International, has been arrested in Belgium, trying to make his way to France. The police of London have long had their eye on the society with which he is connected, and are now taking active measures for its suppression.' Two sentences and two lies. You can test the evidence of your own senses. You see that instead of being in prison in Belgium I am at home in England. You must also know that the police in England are as powerless to interfere with the International Association as the Association with them. Yet what is most regular in all this is that the report will go the round of the continental press without a contradiction, and could continue to do so if I were to circularize every journal in Europe from this place.

R.: Have you attempted to contradict many of these false reports?

DR M.: I have done so till I have grown weary of the labour. To show the gross carelessness with which they are concocted I may mention that in one of them I saw Félix Pyat set down as a member of the International.

R.: And he is not so?

DR M.: The association could hardly have found room for such a wild man. He was once presumptuous enough to issue a rash proclamation in our name, but it was instantly disavowed, though, to do them justice, the press of course ignored the disavowal.

R.: And Mazzini, is he a member of your body?

DR M.: (*laughing*): Ah, no. We should have made but little progress if we had not got beyond the range of his ideas.

R.: You surprise me. I should certainly have thought that he represented the most advanced views.

DR M.: He represents nothing better than the old idea of a middle-class republic. We seek no part with the middle class. He has fallen far to the rear of the modern movement as the German professors, who, nevertheless, are still considered in Europe as the apostles of the cultured democratism of the future. They were so at one time – before '48, perhaps, when the German middle class, in the English sense, had scarely attained its proper development. But now they have gone over bodily to the reaction, and the proletariat knows them no more.

R.: Some people have thought they saw signs of a positivist element in your organization.

DR M.: No such thing. We have positivists among us, and others not of our body who work as well. But this is not by virtue of their philosophy, which will have nothing to do with popular government, as we understand it, and which seeks only to put a new hierarchy in place of the old one.

R.: It seems to me, then, that the leaders of the new international movement have had to form a philosophy as well as an association for themselves.

DR M.: Precisely. It is hardly likely, for instance, that we could hope to prosper in our war against capital if we derive our tactics, say, from the political economy of Mill. He has traced one kind of relationship between labour and capital. We hope to show that it is possible to establish another.

R.: And as to religion?

DR M.: On that point I cannot speak in the name of the society. I myself am an atheist. It is startling, no doubt, to hear such an avowal in England, but there is some comfort in the thought that it need not be made in a whisper in either Germany or France.

R.: And yet you make your headquarters in this country?

DR M.: For obvious reasons; the right of association is here an established thing. It exists, indeed, in Germany, but it is beset with innumerable difficulties; in France for many years it has not existed at all.

R.: And the United States?

DR M.: The chief centres of our activity are for the present among the old societies of Europe. Many circumstances have hitherto tended to prevent the labour problem from assuming an all-absorbing importance in the United States. But they are rapidly disappearing, and it is rapidly coming to the front there with the growth as in Europe of a labouring class distinct from the rest of the community and divorced from capital.

R.: It would seem that in this country the hoped-for solution, whatever it may be, will be attained without the violent means of revolution. The English system of agitating by platform and press until minorities become converted into majorities is a hopeful sign.

DR M.: I am not so sanguine on that point as you. The English middle class has always shown itself willing enough to accept the verdict of the majority so long as it enjoyed the monopoly of the voting power. But mark me, as soon as it finds itself outvoted on what it considers vital questions we shall see here a new slave owners' war.

I have here given you as well as I can remember them the heads of my conversation with this remarkable man. I shall leave you to form your own conclusions. Whatever may be said for or against the probability of its complicity with the movement of the Commune we may be assured that in the International Association the civilized world has a new power in its midst with which it must soon come to a reckoning for good or ill.

•

'CHINESE GORDON'

Interviewed by W. T. Stead
The Pall Mall Gazette, 9 January 1884

Charles George Gordon (1833–85), the English soldier later known as Gordon of Khartoum, earned the earlier sobriquet of 'Chinese Gordon' because of his leadership of the 'ever-victorious army' which had succeeded in putting down the Taiping rebellion in 1864, after only a year. He had been regarded as a hero by the British public ever since. Gordon was born in Woolwich and entered the Royal Military Academy there in 1847. Joining the Royal Engineers in 1852, he served in the Crimea. After his spell in China he spent five years in England working as an engineer and engaging in charitable work. In 1873 he was engaged by the Khedive of Egypt, Ismail Pasha, to continue the work of rendering the Nile navigable by establishing staging posts along the river and introducing steamboats to its different stretches. In 1877 he was made governor-general of the Sudan, which was a province of Egypt, and during a two-year period he organized the charting of territory, engineering works and general administration, curbing the slave trade that so offended against his Evangelical beliefs. He left this post in 1879 suffering depression and spent a few years travelling and performing short-term colonial duties. After spending the year 1883 in religious contemplation in Palestine, he was about to apply for military leave in order to take up the job of administering the Congo Free State for King Leopold of Belgium. A couple of months earlier, an Egyptian army, 10,000 strong and under the command of a British officer, had been slaughtered in battle by the followers of the Mahdi, a religious-nationalist fanatic who sought self-rule for the Sudanese tribes.

It was in this context that Stead went to interview Gordon on 8 June at Southampton. Stead returned to London that night and dictated the interview to his secretary; and Captain Brocklehurst, who had been present during the interview and had travelled with Stead back to London, later wrote to Stead's daughter Estelle that the published account of the interview had been a 'truly marvellous effort of memory, for Gordon talked very fast and your father did not take a note'. The interview, which was widely reprinted in the London and provincial press and was 'the subject of universal comment', had an astonishing effect. It persuaded the British prime minister, William Gladstone, to send Gordon to the Sudan. Unfortunately, though, Gordon was given an impossible brief. He was supposed to evacuate British garrisons from the provinces where the Mahdi was on the rampage, and his bolder initiatives were scotched by Sir Evelyn Baring (later Lord Cromer), the British governor of Egypt. Stead had hoped that Gordon might be able to 'Sarawak the Soudan': in other words, rally the tribes to accept his military and administrative leadership, as Rajah Brooke had done in Sarawak. Instead, his garrison was cut off and Gordon was killed on 25 January 1885, two days before a relief column arrived. For years afterwards, the martyrdom of Gordon was a source of shame in British public life, as it was widely felt that his death had been brought about by Gladstone's cabinet dithering over the decision to send reinforcements.

William Thomas Stead (1849–1912) was editor of the Darlington *Northern Echo* (1871–80), then assistant editor (to John Morley) of *The Pall Mall Gazette* (1880–83) and its editor (1883–90). One of the most influential figures in nineteenth-century English journalism, he and T. P. O'Connor were the pioneers of 'the New Journalism'. Not only did he introduce the interview to England, he also experimented with typography, layout, headlines, and other aspects of newspaper production. He campaigned to expose the evils of child prostitution by buying one such child himself and then writing an article called 'The Maiden Tribute to a Modern Babylon' in *The Pall Mall Gazette*. He was imprisoned for three months, a martyrdom which he enjoyed, but the campaign resulted in the Criminal Law Amendment Act of 1885. In 1890 he founded *The Review of Reviews*, a monthly digest of articles from all the other monthlies around the world, with additional articles. He edited this magazine until his death in the sinking of the *Titanic*.

Chinese Gordon's arrival in London from Brussels, *en route* for the Congo, having been announced in yesterday's papers, a communication was immediately addressed to him at Southampton, whither he had proceeded, asking him if he would consent to hold a conversation on the subject of the Soudan with a representative of the *Pall Mall Gazette*. With characteristic modesty, General Gordon begged to be excused, as his views were of insufficient importance to warrant a journey to Southampton. Our representative left town by the next train, and found General Gordon at his sister's house in the outskirts of Southampton. He showed considerable disinclination to express his opinions upon the subject, but on its being represented to him very strongly that he of all men now in the country was best acquainted with the Soudan, and therefore was best able to speak with authority on the question of the hour, he consented to enter upon the subject. As soon as he had broken the ice he went on with the greatest animation, and even vehemence, expressing himself with the utmost clearness and emphasis upon all the phases of the question of the hour. No transcript of the notes of that conversation, which lasted over two hours, can convey any idea of the manner in which the late Governor-General of the Soudan discussed in all the minuteness of detail the difficulties to be faced, and indicated with the utmost precision and confidence both the causes of the disaster and the methods by which the crisis should be faced. By eliminating all that is extraneous to the vitals of the subject, and rigidly confining attention to the central point, it is possible to convey some meagre impression of what Chinese Gordon thinks of the Soudan in the following rough transcript of the substance of his remarks:

'So you would abandon the Soudan? But the Eastern Soudan is indispensable to Egypt. It will cost you far more to retain your hold upon Egypt proper if you abandon your hold of the Eastern Soudan to the Mahdi or to the Turk than what it would to retain your hold upon Eastern Soudan by the aid of such material as exists in the provinces. Darfur and Kordofan must be abandoned. That I admit; but the provinces lying to the east of the White Nile should be retained, and north of Senaar. The danger to be feared is not that the Mahdi will march northward through Wadi Halfa; on the contrary, it is very improbable that he will ever go so far north. The danger is altogether of a different nature. It arises from the influence which the spectacle of a conquering Mahommedan Power, established close to your frontiers, will exercise upon the population which you govern. In all the cities in Egypt it will be felt that what the Mahdi has done they may do; and, as he has driven out the intruder and the infidel, they may do the same. Nor is it only England that has to face this danger. The success of the Mahdi has already excited dangerous fermentations in Arabia and Syria. Placards have been posted in Damascus calling upon the population to rise and drive out the Turks. If the whole of the Eastern Soudan is surrendered to the Mahdi, the Arab tribes on both sides the Red Sea will take fire. In self-defence the Turks are bound to do something to cope with so formidable a danger, for it is quite possible that if nothing is done the whole of the Eastern Question may be re-opened by the triumph of the Mahdi. I see it is proposed to fortify Wadi Halfa, and prepare there to resist the Mahdi's attack. You might as well fortify against a fever. Contagion of that kind cannot be kept out of fortifications and garrisons. But that it is real, and that it does exist, will be denied by no one cognisant with Egypt and the East. In self-defence the policy of evacuation cannot possibly be justified.

'There is another aspect of the question. You have 6,000 men in Khartoum. What are you going to do with them? You have garrisons in Darfur, in Bahr Gazelle, and Gondokoro. Are they to be sacrificed? Their only offence is their loyalty to their Sovereign. For their fidelity you are going to abandon them to their fate. You say they are to retire upon Wadi Halfa. But Gondokoro is 1,500 miles from Khartoum, and Khartoum is 350 only from Wadi Halfa. How will you move your 6,000 men from Khartoum – to say nothing of other places – and all the Europeans in that city, through the desert to Wadi Halfa? Where are you going to get the camels to take them away? Will the Mahdi supply them? If they are to escape with their lives, the garrison will not be allowed to leave with a coat on their backs. They will be plundered to the skin, and even then their lives may not be spared. Whatever you may decide about evacuation, you cannot evacuate, because your army cannot be moved. You must either surrender absolutely to the Mahdi or defend Khartoum at all hazards. The latter is the only course which ought to be entertained. There is no serious difficulty about it. The Mahdi's forces will fall to pieces of themselves; but if in a moment of panic orders are issued for the abandonment of the whole of the Eastern Soudan a blow will be struck against the security of Egypt and the peace of the East, which may have fatal consequences.

'The great evil is not at Khartoum, but at Cairo. It is the weakness of Cairo which produces disaster in the Soudan. It is because Hicks was not adequately supported at the first, but was thrust forward upon an impossible enterprise by the men who had refused him supplies when a decisive blow might have been struck, that the Western Soudan has been sacrificed. The Eastern Soudan may, however, be saved if there is a firm hand placed at the helm in Egypt. Everything depends on that.

'What then, you ask, should be done? I reply, Place Nubar in power! Nubar is the one supremely able man among Egyptian Ministers. He is proof against foreign intrigue, and he thoroughly understands the situation. Place him in power: support him through thick and thin: give him a free hand; and let it be distinctly understood that no intrigues either on the part of Tewfik or any of Nubar's rivals will be allowed for a moment to interfere with the execution of his plans. You are sure to find that the energetic support of Nubar will sooner or later bring you into collision with the Khedive; but if that Sovereign really desires, as he says, the welfare of his country, it will be necessary for you to protect Nubar's Administration from any direct or indirect interference on his part. Nubar can be depended upon: that I can guarantee. He will not take office without knowing that he is to have his own way; but if he takes office it is the best security that you can have for the restoration of order to the country. Especially is this the case with the Soudan. Nubar should be left untrammelled by any stipulations concerning the evacuation of Khartoum. There is no hurry. The garrisons can hold their own at present. Let them continue to hold on until disunion and tribal jealousies have worked their natural results in the camp of the Mahdi. Nubar should be free to deal with the Soudan in his own way. How he will deal with the Soudan, of course I cannot profess to say; but I should imagine that he would appoint a Governor-General at Khartoum with full powers, and furnish him with two millions sterling – a large sum, no doubt, but a sum which had much better be spent now than wasted in a vain attempt to avert the consequences of an ill-timed surrender. Sir Samuel Baker, who possesses the essential energy and single tongue requisite for the office, might be appointed Governor-General of the Soudan; and he might take his brother as Commander-in-Chief.

'It should be proclaimed in the hearing of all the Soudanese, and engraved on tablets of brass, that a permanent Constitution was granted to the Soudanese by which no Turk or Circassian would ever be allowed to enter the province to plunder its inhabitants in order to fill his own pockets, and that no immediate emancipation of slaves would be attempted. Immediate emancipation was denounced in 1833 as confiscation in England, and it is no less confiscation in the Soudan to-day. Whatever is done in that direction should be done gradually, and by a process of registration. Mixed tribunals might be established, if Nubar thought fit, in which European judges would co-operate with the natives in the administration of justice. Police inspectors also might be appointed, and adequate measures taken to root out the abuses which prevail in the prisons.

'With regard to Darfur, I should think that Nubar would probably send back the family and the heir of the Sultan of Darfur. If subsidized by the Government and sent back with Sir Samuel Baker, he would not have much difficulty in regaining possession of the kingdom of Darfur, which was formerly one of the best governed of African countries. As regards Abyssinia, the old warning should not be lost sight of – "Put not your trust in princes;" and place no reliance upon the King of Abyssinia, at least outside his own country. Zoula and Bogos might be ceded to him with advantage, and the free right of entry by the port of Massouah might be added; but it would be a mistake to give him possession of Massouah, which he would ruin. A commission might also be sent down with advantage to examine the state of things in Harrar, opposite Aden, and see what iniquities are going on there, as also at Berbera and Zeila. By these means, and by the adoption of a steady, consistent policy at head-quarters, it would be possible – not to say easy – to re-establish the authority of the Khedive between the Red Sea and Sennaar.

'As to the cost of the Soudan, it is a mistake to suppose that it will necessarily be a charge on the Egyptian Exchequer. It will cost two millions to relieve the garrisons and to quell the revolt; but that expenditure must be incurred any way; and in all probability, if the garrisons are handed over to be massacred and the country evacuated, the ultimate expenditure would exceed that sum. At first, until the country is pacified, the Soudan will need a subsidy of £200,000 a year from Egypt. That, however, would be temporary. During the last years of my administration the Soudan involved no charge upon the Egyptian Exchequer. The bad provinces were balanced against the good, and an equilibrium was established. The Soudan will never be a source of revenue to Egypt, but it need not be a source of expense. That deficits have arisen, and that the present disaster has occurred, is entirely attributable to a single cause; and that is the greatest misgovernment.

'The cause of the rising in the Soudan is the cause of all popular risings against Turkish rule wherever they have occurred. No one who has been in a Turkish province and has witnessed the results of the Bashi-Bazouk system, which excited so much indignation some time ago in Bulgaria, will need to be told why the people of the Soudan have risen in revolt against the Khedive. The Turks, the Circassians, and the Bashi-Bazouks have plundered and oppressed the people in the Soudan as they plundered and oppressed them in the Balkan peninsula. Oppression begat discontent; discontent necessitated an increase of the armed force at the disposal of the authorities; this increase of the army force involved an increase of expenditure, which again was attempted to be met by increasing taxation, and that still further increased the discontent. And so things went on in a dismal circle until they culminated, after repeated deficits, in a disastrous rebellion. That the people were justified in rebelling nobody who knows the treatment to which they were subjected will attempt to deny. Their cries were absolutely unheeded at Cairo. In despair they had recourse to the only method by which they could make their wrongs known; and, on the same principle that Absalom fired the corn of Joab, so they rallied round the Mahdi, who exhorted them to revolt against the Turkish yoke. I am convinced that it is an entire mistake to regard the Mahdi as in any sense a religious leader: he personifies popular discontent. All the Soudanese are potential Mahdis, just as all the Egyptians are potential Arabis. The movement is not religious, but an outbreak of despair. Three times over I warned the late Khedive that it would be impossible to govern the Soudan on the old system after my appointment to the Governor-Generalship. During the three years that I wielded full powers in the Soudan I taught the natives that they had a right to exist. I waged war against the Turks and Circassians who had harried the population. I had taught them something of the meaning of liberty and justice, and accustomed them to a higher ideal of government than that with which they had previously been acquainted. As soon as I had gone the Turks and Circassians returned in full force; the old Bashi-Bazouk system was re-established; my old employés were persecuted; and a population which had begun to appreciate something like decent government was flung back to suffer the worst excesses of Turkish rule. The inevitable result followed; and thus it may be said that the egg of the present rebellion was laid in the three years during which I was allowed to govern the Soudan on other than Turkish principles.

'The Soudanese are a very nice people. They deserve the sincere compassion and sympathy of all civilized men. I got on very well with them, and I am sincerely sorry at the prospect of seeing them handed over to be ground down once more by their Turkish and Circassian oppressors. Yet, unless an attempt is made to hold on to the present garrisons, it is inevitable that the Turks, for the sake of self-preservation, must attempt to crush them. They deserve a better fate. It ought not to be impossible to come to terms with them, to grant them a free amnesty for the past, to offer them security for decent government in the future. If this were done, and the government entrusted to a man whose word was truth, all might yet be re-established. So far from believing it impossible to make an arrangement with the Mahdi I strongly suspect that he is a mere puppet put forward by Ilyas, Zebehr's father-in-law, and the largest slave-owner in Obeid, and that he has assumed a religious title to give colour to his defence of the popular rights.

'There is one subject on which I cannot imagine any one can differ about. That is the impolicy of announcing our intention to evacuate Khartoum. Even if we were bound to do so we should have said nothing about it. The moment it is known that we have given up the game every man will go over to the Mahdi. All men worship the rising sun. The difficulties of evacuation will be enormously increased, if, indeed, the withdrawal of our garrison is not rendered impossible.

'The late Khedive, who is one of the ablest and worst used men in Europe, would not have made such a mistake, and under him the condition of Egypt proper was much better than it is to-day. Now with regard to Egypt, the same principle should be observed that must be acted upon in the Soudan. Let your foundations be broad and firm and based upon the contentment and welfare of the people. Hitherto, both in the Soudan and in Egypt, instead of constructing the social edifice like a pyramid, upon its base, we have been rearing an obelisk which a single push may overturn. Our safety in Egypt is to do something for the people. That is to say you must reduce their rent, rescue them from the usurers, and retrench expenditure. Nine-tenths of the European employés might probably be weeded out with advantage. The remaining tenth – thoroughly efficient – should be retained; but whatever you do, do not break up Sir Evelyn Wood's army, which is destined to do good work. Stiffen it as much as you please, but with Englishmen, not with Circassians. Circassians are as much foreigners in Egypt as Englishmen are, and certainly not more popular. As for the European population, let them have charters for the formation of municipal councils, for raising volunteer corps, and for organizing in their own defence. Anything more shameful than the flight from Egypt in 1882 I never read. Let them take an example from Shanghai, where the European settlement provides for its own defence and its own government. I should like to see a competent special Commissioner of the highest standing – such a man, for instance, as Mr W. E. Forster, who is free at once from traditions of the elders and of the Foreign Office, and of the bondholders, sent out to put Nubar in the saddle, sift out unnecessary employés, and warn evil doers in the highest places that they will not be allowed to play any tricks. If that were done it would give confidence everywhere, and I see no reason why the last British soldier should not be withdrawn from Egypt in six months' time.

'I hope,' said General Gordon, in conclusion, 'that you will explain that I did not wish to press my opinions upon the public. I am very reluctant to say anything calculated to embarrass the Government in a very difficult crisis; but when you appealed to me, I did feel moved at the thought of the poor Soudanese, whom I knew so well and loved so much; and I thought that for once I might, for their sake, depart from the resolution which I had formed in my mind to leave these things to be governed by the Higher Power which cannot err, without comment on my part. They are a good people, the poor Soudanese, and if I can do anything for them I shall be only too glad. But although I have spoken to you quite frankly, I should be much obliged if, when you publish these remarks, you would let it be distinctly understood that I do not wish to depart again from the rule which I have mentioned.'

•

THEODORE ROOSEVELT

Interviewed by *The Pall Mall Gazette*, 9 December 1886

Theodore Roosevelt (1858–1919), the American politician, was the twenty-sixth president of the United States (1901–9). Born into a wealthy New York family of Dutch and Scottish descent, he was afflicted with a delicate disposition which he overcame during trips to the West. Having graduated from Harvard in 1880, he became leader of the New York state legislature in 1884. He later served as head of the New York City police board (1895–7) and as assistant secretary of the US Navy (1897–8). After the adventure of fighting in Cuba during the Spanish-American War, he was elected as Republican vice-president under William McKinley, whom he succeeded as president the following year when McKinley was assassinated. His administration was noted for its regulation of monopolies and trusts and its interest in conservation. He was re-elected in 1905 and pursued an interventionist role in Latin America as well as further progressive reforms. He later split from the Republicans, forming his own Progressive Party, but failed to win back the presidency in 1912. This interview took place shortly after Roosevelt had defeated Henry George, the economist who advocated a simple tax on land values, in the contest for the mayoralty of New York.

Two months ago Mr Roosevelt was shooting grizzly bears in the Rocky Mountains. Less than a month ago he was the nominee of the Republican Party for the mayoralty of New York and was fighting night and day to carry out their wishes. A few days ago he was in London greatly enjoying the overwhelming hospitality of his English friends. Since then he has been married, and he is now on the Continent. After this it would seem superfluous to add that Mr

Roosevelt is a typical American. The remark, however, is not the truism it appears, because Mr Roosevelt is typical of a class of Americans least known in English society: the band, namely, of young men of education, position, and means, who, instead of immediately turning, as they have generally done before, to bread-and-butter occupations, are content with the situations in life in which their fathers have left them, and are seeking a career in the hitherto not-too-clean paths of politics. Mr Roosevelt is young; indeed, he looks less than thirty, but as we said during the recent contest, he has already achieved a number of striking successes in American politics, and is distinctly one of the foremost men of his party. Besides these, he is credited with having introduced fox-hunting, or aniseed-bag-hunting which stands for it, into America, and he is probably the most successful Nimrod outside the ranks of professional backwoodsmen. His most conspicuous physical characteristic, as indeed would naturally be expected, is the extraordinary vigour which is evident in every word and every gesture, and he is pre-eminently one of those smart Americans half an hour of whose conversation acts as a physical and intellectual tonic upon us colder-blooded and duller Europeans. The third point in Mr Roosevelt's reputation is that of a teller of stories, and it is characteristic of the man that he is never so serious as when he is in the middle of some side-splitting yarn of Eastern politics or Western adventure, and that as he approaches the crisis of the drollery his square face assumes a solemnity which is little short of religious. Our representative found him at Brown's Hotel in Dover-street, and sends us the following account of his interview:

'First of all,' said Mr Roosevelt when he had learned the object of my visit, 'you must know that two days before I was nominated I had about as much idea of being chosen to contest the mayoralty of New York as I had of filling the throne of Bulgaria. For eight months I had lived entirely out of the world on my ranche in the Far West and among the Rocky Mountains, where I had been shooting grizzlies and elk and mountain sheep and such things. My friends, however, gave me no time for reflection, and I was hardly home before I was in the thick of the political fight.'

'Did you expect to win, Mr Roosevelt, or was the result a surprise to you?'

'Well, I must admit that when the fight began I thought the chances were a hundred to one against me, but they grew rapidly better every day, and before the polling-day I think I may fairly say the odds had dwindled down to three or four to one. I need not tell you that the old party lines broke down in every direction, and the novel considerations introduced by Mr George's candidature rendered it extremely difficult to form any decent forecast.'

'Your contest, Mr Roosevelt, has been watched from England with unparalleled attention, chiefly owing of course to Mr George, but we have all been more or less doubtful whether we fairly understood in any way the conditions of the struggle. To take the candidates one by one, how would you analyse your own following?'

'My own supporters,' replied Mr Roosevelt, 'consisted first of all of the old principals of the Republican party whom no consideration could induce to vote on a Democratic ticket. These were at one end, and at the other were the young men of my own age and kind, almost all of whom are Republicans, and the majority of whom voted for me. I lost, of course, many Republican votes which should have been given to me, because it was believed that my success was impossible and that therefore the only way to keep George out was by putting Hewitt in, but the number of people intending to vote this way fell off day by day, and if the campaign had been carried on for another week, I honestly believe I should have lost very few votes for this reason.'

'And Mr Hewitt?'

'Mr Hewitt, you will hardly be surprised to learn, stands out in strong contrast to his party. Of Mr Hewitt himself, no one can speak except in terms of great respect; but on the other hand neither can anybody who knows the facts doubt that with the exception of the dissentient Republican votes, which I have already mentioned, Mr Hewitt's supporters were drawn from the very worst strata of American politics and constituted in themselves four-fifths of all the political influences which honest men in America are gradually leaguing themselves together to destroy. I can go further, and say that now he is elected Mr Hewitt will find himself in constant and serious conflict with the men who elected him, or else he will have to close his eyes to many of the most unscrupulous movements of the American political machine. Admirable man and gentleman as he is in all respects, these forces will almost inevitably prove too strong for him. We have seen the same thing in Mr Cleveland's case, and what the President has failed to resist the Mayor of New York will hardly be able to escape.'

'And Mr George? In his candidature, as you know, the chief interest for us lay.'

'I quite understand that, and it is perfectly natural, and I will tell you to the best of my ability what Mr George's position actually, as distinguished from sentimentally, was. He was riding an impossible number of horses. First of all, the Socialists.'

'But why do you not begin with the Anarchists?'

'With us in America the Anarchists and Socialists are practically one body. There are of course individual Socialists of the better type, but taken as a whole, and especially with regard to public action, Socialists and Anarchists are synonymous terms in the United States. They have always got along together perfectly except in one instance, when they had a free fight, but their differences of opinion were soon reconciled by the fact that the police took advantage of them to club both sides with an edifying impartiality. By the Anarchist element I mean first the party of public disorder pure and simple, and also people who have vague notions about the desirability of a general division of property in the interests of the many as distinguished from the privileges of the few. The second section of Mr George's supporters were the honest and ignorant working men, who believed in a dull-headed sort of way that George would "do something" for them. Third, came the honest and intelligent working men – the kind of people who think shallow thoughts on deep subjects and who had convinced themselves – no difficult process – that George represented true principles. Fourth and last were the sentimental philanthropists – the men who tell A that B ought to take C's property, and always like to talk about it. This sort of thing goes on very well so long as B only takes C's property, but when B begins to take A's property as well, then no body is so hot as they in their denunciation of poor B. The most conspicuous members of this class are the anti-monopolists, who talk, let us say, about the confiscation of railroads. As soon as the confiscators go a step further and begin to talk about the confiscation of grocery stores, for instance, these anti-monopolists stand upon their rights as American citizens with most indignant emphasis.'

'But is not an ethnological division of votes always made in American elections?'

'Certainly, and it was never more strikingly shown than in the recent election. To begin with, all the Irish of the Land League voted for George, all the priests and the people they control supported Hewitt, all the young Irish-Americans voted for me. Germans, as a rule, half vote Democratic and half Republican. Of these, the Republican half mostly voted for George, and with them all the crude theorists on social subjects who as a rule take little interest in political struggles. The rest of the foreign population, the Polish Jews, Bohemians, and Italians, voted for George. On the other hand, he got an extremely small proportion of native Americans – in fact, I doubt if 7,000 in all voted for him.'

'But we believed at the time that there was a distinct moral enthusiasm in the support which George received.'

'There certainly was, though it was not perhaps a very logical one. He received what one might call the caste vote of the lower class. They thought that at last the time had come when an honest man could be elected who would look after the interests of the poor. Their sufferings are very real, and they believed that George could remove them. What they fail to see is that these sufferings are irremediable in the first place by any law at all, and in the second place by any of the laws which they wish to see executed. Their votes were honest ones and given with moral enthusiasm, but their motive was quite as intelligent as that of the man who should desire to have the law of gravitation abrogated because he slipped on a piece of orange peel. The 'angel vote' – that is the vote of the people really too good to live – was cast for Hewitt.'

'What would have been the result of George's election?'

'That I can tell you without the slightest hesitation. It would have meant the complete smash-up of the George party. One of two things would inevitably have taken place. Either the rough and disorderly section would have gained the mastery, in which case the decent and honest working-men would have been absolutely alienated; or George would have manifested his sympathy publicly for the honest section of his followers, in which case the disorderly element would have thrown him over with unanimous disgust.'

'But the land nationalizers – that is, the "Progress and Poverty" party as such – would assuredly have supported George and stood by him to the end?'

'I have heard a good deal about George having established the party you speak of in England and Scotland, but in America it simply does not exist. There is no such thing as any body of men whose mission is land nationalization. Anybody with us who begins to want things nationalized does not stop at the land . . . We are far too enterprising for any such restrictions.'

'I have forgotten to ask you about the action of the dynamite Irish.'

'I can answer that question best by telling you a story,' and Mr Roosevelt began to look serious. One morning, immediately after his nomination, Mr Roosevelt was busily engaged in his private room arranging the preliminaries of the fight, when no less a person, or rather, we should say, no greater a person, than the redoubtable Mr O'Donovan Rossa was announced. Mr Rossa's object, as no one who knows anything about the methods of such men will be surprised to learn, was to sell his support to Mr Roosevelt at as high a price as possible, and his proposition was this – he claimed to control a very large Irish vote, and was prepared to promise it to Mr Roosevelt in consideration of two cheques: (1) a little one 'for the cause of Ireland', payable to the fund and dated after election day, so that it might be cancelled if Mr Roosevelt were not elected; (2) a big one drawn to his own order and payable immediately. Vigour, as we have said, is on the whole Mr Roosevelt's most distinguishing characteristic, and this was a fine opportunity for its display. 'Mr Rossa,' said he, 'there are very few men engaged in this fight that I can bully if I wish to, but you are one of them. Just walk right out of this room!' and he opened the door, and the gentleman whose name is a terror to most people in England, from Home Secretary to common constable, meekly disappeared.

'One more question, Mr Roosevelt. You know Englishmen are very much interested in American sport, of which you may be taken as an embodiment. What are its condition and prospects?'

'I am not an embodiment, by a good deal, of American sport, but I am intensely interested in it. There is still much large game-hunting for riflemen who go west, but it is decreasing rapidly. In the eastern States sport has to be artificial, as it is in England; and there, I am thankful to say, the growth of interest in athletics, etc., during the last decade or so has been remarkable. Take riding to hounds, for instance. This has taken firm root with us, and we are already turning out first-class horses. Our horses probably could not go over some of your country here, as they would understand nothing about the obstacles; but as high timber jumpers they are absolutely unequalled. At the New York Horse Show, held a month ago, two of the horses from my own hunt club beat the world's record at high jumping; one, Mr Keener's Hempstead, clearing 6ft 8in, and the other, Mr Collier's Majestic, doing 6ft 7½in; both jumps being measured with a spirit level, by a dozen competent judges, in the presence of several thousand spectators.'

●

HENRY STANLEY

Interviewed by *The Pall Mall Gazette*, 17 January 1887

Sir Henry Moreton Stanley (1841–1904), the Welsh explorer and journalist, was born out of wedlock and originally called John Rowlands. At the age of eighteen he sailed to New Orleans as a cabin boy and was adopted by a merchant named Stanley. Having served in the Confederate army and then in the US navy, he took to journalism; in 1867 he joined the staff of the *New York Herald* and became its special correspondent, travelling to Abyssinia and Spain. In 1869 the *Herald*'s publisher, James Gordon Bennett, telegraphed him 'Find Livingstone', but Stanley was in no hurry. After a leisurely tour of the Middle East, he embarked for Tanganyika in March 1871 and found Livingstone at Ujiji in November. Together they established that Lake Tanganyika was not the source of the Nile as many had believed. Stanley returned from Africa the following year and published *How I Found Livingstone*. He made a further expedition to Uganda and Tanganyika and later published a second book, *Through the Dark Continent* (1878). In 1879 he led an expedition to found the Congo Free State, backed by the Belgian king, and in 1886 he led another expedition to relieve Emin Pasha at the mouth of the Congo river.

In a day or two the finder of Livingstone and the founder of the Congo State will once more set sail for the shores of that dark and mysterious continent in which he has done the best of his life's work. As all the world knows, he goes to rescue Emin Bey, who, to use Mr Stanley's graphic phrase, is 'environed by breadths of unknown territories populated by savage tribes'. Emin Bey's headquarters are at Wadelai, on the Nile, about fifty miles north-east of Albert Nyanza, and here he is supposed to have a small army of 5,000 men, equipped with Remingtons and less efficient firearms. In July of last year word came to Dr Junker that he was short of ammunition and that his troops were disaffected. He is hemmed in by the Arab slave traders, whose caravans he has harassed for so long, and at any time the avenging hordes may sweep him and his settlement from the face of the earth, and the vast tract of country over which he has established his rule will once more be given up to the Arabs. Mr Stanley, who sails for Zanzibar in a day or two, was kind enough to receive one of our representatives yesterday afternoon.

Mr Stanley's head-quarters are in Bond-street, a suite of rooms on the first floor which he has made his home for the last two years. The walls of the vestibule are lined with trophies and pictures of Africa, but there is no sign of barbaric mementos in the modern luxury of his spacious sitting-room, whose walls are hung with water-colours, photographs, and sketches. Explorer, nomad, Ulysses, as he is, he does not despise the pleasures of the upholsterer, as was shown by the handsome cabinets, the sumptuous settees, the soft rugs, strewn about the floor. In a minute he came into the room, erect as ever, smoking a cigar, and remarking, 'I have had no sleep for two nights, and only got back from Brussels at five this morning; but I can give you fifteen minutes. My time is short now.

'We have naturally considered the question of the routes very seriously, and discussed it very thoroughly. I will explain to you how matters stand. It is possible to reach Emin either from the Congo or from Zanzibar. Let us take the Zanzibar route. My expedition is 1,000 strong when it leaves Zanzibar. What will it be when we reach the savage-bound circle drawn round Emin? You have marched, say, 1,000 miles under a torrid sun, each man carrying sixty pounds. During this arduous journey your number is gradually decreasing. Some desert, some are fatigued, some die, some are killed, some are weakened by bhang. The rumour goes about that the real danger does not begin until you reach the fringe of the circle. Panic may seize the men; and then – why, they may desert in a body. They have come from Zanzibar, and the way home is open to them. Take the Congo route. The King of the Belgians has given us permission to use the steamer on the Upper River, the journey is comparatively easy, food is plentiful, and you land your men on the edge of the danger circle fresh, active, in good spirits, and in good condition. But most important of all, they cannot desert. If they turn tail they have not Zanzibar behind them, but only the water of the Congo. The advantages of one route over another are obvious. The difficulty now is the transport from Zanzibar to the Congo. I hope to find a steamer ready when we reach Zanzibar.'

Mr Stanley then spread out a well-worn map of Equatorial Africa, on which the mighty Congo and its tributaries were indicated in heavy blue washes, spreading itself out like a monarch of the forest with its thousand limbs. The great Equatorial lakes were shown on a large scale – Tanganyika, Victoria Nyanza, Albert Nyanza, and the Nile winding its way past Wadelai and Khartoum. Mr Stanley then described a rough circle with a lead pencil through which the expedition has to pass before it can reach the beleaguered Emin. By means of a telegraph form and a pair of rusty dividers, he measured off the possible routes, explaining how the dreaded power of M'Wanga of Uganda, son of his old friend M'Tesa, had spread. 'Here,' indicating the stretch of country between the great lakes, 'are some of the best fighting men in all

Africa, 200,000 of them and more. No matter which route the expedition takes, there is the danger, for Uganda's power extends right up to Albert Nyanza.' 'Could you cross Victoria by boats?' 'We take one boat with us for the rivers,' replied the explorer. 'I cannot tell you what I shall do. My secret must remain undivulged. M'Wanga's emissaries are everywhere.

'Whichever way we go I shall send couriers with dispatches until we touch the fringe of the terrible girdle which encloses Emin in its grasp. From the circumference of this circle to its centre is, I estimate, a distance of some 300 to 400 miles. I shall despatch my last couriers from its edge, and before they reach the coast I shall hope to have come up to Emin Bey. You should hear news of us about July.

'Of course Tipoo Tip is an old friend of mine. I remember him as a most agreeable and gentlemanly fellow. He once beat one of my own men in a foot-race and carried off a silver goblet. His story is told in one of my books, but his power and influence have extended enormously since then. His head-quarters are at Kasonge. M'Wanga must have been a child when I was with M'Tesa, his father. He was educated by a Roman Catholic priest, but when he succeeded his father the priests were the first to suffer. One of my difficulties is that if I trouble him, the missionaries he has in his power (Bishop Hannington was one of his victims) will certainly suffer. He is about twenty now, I should think.'

'What is the full strength of the expedition?' 'About a thousand men, all told. Besides myself I have eight Englishmen, the rest of the number is made of Zanzibaris. Already the caravan has grown beyond my original intention. The estimated cost is £20,000. The preparation has been ordered by cable to Zanzibar, and when we reach there all should be ready. Each porter carries sixty pounds weight, and I allow each European 180lb. baggage. We shall depend for our food upon what the villages and our guns supply, taking only such luxuries as tea, coffee, sugar, tobacco, and the things Africa does not supply. The equipment of an expedition such as this is not a difficult matter, though it is an interesting calculation – a rule of three sum. If twenty men require so much, how many will 20,000 want? One has to calculate the currencies among the different tribes. How many days shall we be marching through tract A? So many. The currency is beads: then so many beads. Through tract B? So many. The currency is cloth: then so many thousand yards of it. Through Tract C? So many. The currency is wire: then so much wire. You see, it is not so difficult, given the experience and the knowledge.'

'Supposing you elect the Congo route, will you proceed as far as the Stanley Falls station?' 'That is a matter of detail which I cannot discuss. We may take one of the big rivers which fall into the Congo on its right bank, or we may keep to the main body of the river. Why should I be afraid to go up to the Falls if I have friendly relations with Tipoo? The station was undoubtedly lost by bad management and want of tact. A female slave escapes from the Arabs and seeks refuge in the station. They refuse to give her up. The consequences are fire and devastation. You ask me what I should have done – give her up. It may be against my principles or against those of every Briton to refuse to protect a refugee slave, but have we not every day to sacrifice them? I might have said to the woman, 'I am very sorry for you, but you must return. I will, however, say a good word for you and see what can be done.' I might even have bought her. A little tact, and the station might certainly have been saved. As it is, for this one woman thousands of slaves have been made. The country was healing up; it is now an open sore. As I have said, slavery may be against my principles, but one slave saved has made many. The chief should have seen that his business was to keep the station. And he might have done it. Suppose you were walking on the Embankment, and a thief said, 'I want your money.' You would perhaps reply, 'But with all due deference to you, I prefer to keep it.' 'To your life?' the thief might reply. You have your alternative. I compare the one slave who cost us the station to your money. It is better to sacrifice a part and save the whole.

'It is very simple. I take my place at the head of the caravan. What is my weapon? A stick. Of course I have my escort. A revolver? The surest weapon is the eye. Prevision. There are scouts in front of us, to the right and the left. Am I not afraid of ambuscades? They have not yet caught me asleep. Mind, this is a rush, not an exploring party. The bugle sounds at 4.30; day begins to dawn at 5; at 5.15 you see the pale grey patches on the horizon; at 5.30 there is light enough to see the path; at six o'clock the sun appears on the horizon – it is hot by 9.30. We have been marching at the rate, say, of two and three quarter miles an hour, the column is close up, the men are still fresh and cheery. By eleven the heat beats down upon you, and there are long gaps in the column, which from a quarter of a mile long at starting is now elongated to a mile and a quarter. It is then time to halt. Early in the morning one has a cup of coffee and a piece of native bread, perhaps, or maybe only a handful of ground nuts. At six o'clock we stop for the night, we have dinner, smoke by the fire, and discuss the next day's work; then bed, for seven hours' sleep. No one wants more. Thirteen miles a day is good work. It depends upon the nature of the country, whether it is dense forest or stretching park land.

'If I die,' wrote Emin Bey, 'who will take this work up? I think only of that. I am too much needed here to think of leaving my post. Time is wanted; but from the seed I have tried to sow doubtless good fruit will spring up.' 'Will he return, do you think, Mr Stanley?' 'I cannot say,' replied the explorer, gazing into the fire, and following the trail of smoke from his cigar. 'I cannot say. Livingstone declined, so may Emin. But the object of the expedition is to take him relief, by supplying him with ammunition. Having fulfilled that part of our undertaking we have to bring out with us the fifty women and children of the Cairo Arabs who are with him. I can say nothing about the stores of ivory which he may have accumulated. No, I have never met him.

'Am I of a hopeful temperament? Well, I daresay we all have our despondent hours when everything seems to go wrong. Who has not, if he sees failure staring him in the face through the folly or carelessness of some member of an expedition, in which all the best qualities of a man are put to the test? I should be despondent if, say, I found at a crucial point of my journey my men were seized with panic, and only a handful of white men was left. These might stay or return; to stay would mean death; to return, to fail. The expedition is full of dangers and difficulties which no one can foresee. I do not want to be troubled with fighting. Fighting is folly if it can be avoided. I prefer diplomacy.

'Yes, I am in excellent health. I never allow the luxuries of civilization to demoralize me, and I never was a gourmand. I shall be happy when I set foot once more on African soil, and I fall readily into my old nomadic ways of life. Tea, coffee, milk, tobacco, but stimulants seldom. Yes, here I smoke six cigars a day. In Africa I have my pipe and mild tobacco. I did not begin to smoke until I was twenty-five, and could not grapple with a pipe till I was thirty. Since then I have always found tobacco a solace and an aid to concentration. I remember when on one journey down the Congo, we were just about to enter a most dangerous country. I knew that a fight was inevitable, and told my men to make ready. I took an observation, lighted my pipe, and smoked for five minutes to settle myself for the action. We were fighting for our lives a few minutes afterwards, and the battle went on for hours. Livingstone never smoked.'

And then I bade the explorer good-bye and good luck.

•

ROBERT LOUIS STEVENSON

Interviewed by *The New York Herald*, 8 September 1887

Robert Louis Balfour Stevenson (1850–94), the Scottish writer, was born in Edinburgh. He was the grandson of the famous engineer Robert Stevenson and the son of a lighthouse engineer. Educated at the Edinburgh Academy, he was a sickly child and his family took him abroad to escape the Scottish climate. He briefly studied engineering at Edinburgh University before switching to law. He wrote a few plays, but his first success came with two books about travel in Belgium and France. It was in France in 1876 that Stevenson met an American divorcee, Fanny Osbourne, whom he followed to America. They married in 1880 and returned to Europe with his stepson, Lloyd Osbourne. Stevenson began to write essays and short stories for magazines, and there followed a series of popular adventure novels – *Treasure Island* (1883), *Kidnapped* (1886), *The Master of Ballantrae* (1889) – and the horror story *The Strange Case of Dr Jekyll and Mr Hyde* (1886). In 1889, still troubled by his tuberculosis, he took his family to live in Samoa for the last few years of his life.

*

Stevenson and his party had left London in the steamer SS *Ludgate Hill* in late August 1887. When the ship approached New York harbour it was boarded by two pilots named Mr Hyde and Dr Jekyll, as the stage version of Stevenson's famous novel was shortly to open in New York. The *Herald* reporter described Stevenson as wearing 'a short velvet jacket and a peculiarly cut low hat' and added that 'his hair was black and full over his shoulders, and his clean cut, refined features suggested a Vandyke'.

In answer to the reporter's inquiry, 'What is your object in now visiting America?' Mr Stevenson said: 'Simply on account of my health, which is wretched. I am suffering from catarrhal consumption, but am sanguine that my sojourn here will do much to restore me to my former self. I came round by the *Ludgate Hill* principally because I like the sea, and because I thought the long voyage would do me good. But I certainly did not expect to make the voyage with one hundred horses. These were taken on board at Havre. The company's agent at Havre was most impertinent to us, but the horses behaved themselves exceedingly well. And I feel pleased to add that the ship's officers were particularly nice, and everything was most pleasant after we got used to the stables.'

'Where do you propose to go?'

'Well, the Lord only knows; I don't. I intend to get out of New York just as fast as I can. I like New York exceedingly. It is to me a mixture of Chelsea, Liverpool, and Paris, but I want to get away into the country.'

'There is a great difference of opinion as to what suggested your works, particularly *The Strange Case of Dr Jekyll and Mr Hyde* and *Deacon Brodie?*'

'Well, this has never been properly told. On one occasion I was very hard up for money, and I felt that I had to do something. I thought and thought, and tried hard to find a subject to write about. At night I dreamed the story, not precisely as it is written, for of course there are always stupidities in dreams, but practically it came to me as a gift, and what makes it appear more odd is that I am quite in the habit of dreaming stories. Thus, not long ago, I dreamed the story of "Olalla", which appeared in my volume *The Merry Men*, and I have at the present moment two unwritten stories which I likewise dreamed. The fact is that I am so much in the habit of making them while I sleep quite as hard, apparently, as when I am awake. They sometimes come to me in the form of nightmares, in so far that they make me cry out aloud. But I am never deceived by them. Even when fast asleep I know that it is I who am inventing, and when I cry out it is with gratification to know that the story is so good. So soon as I awake, and it always awakens me when I get on a good thing, I set to work and put it together.

'For instance, all I dreamed about Dr Jekyll was that one man was being pressed into a cabinet, when he swallowed a drug and changed into another being. I awoke and said at once that I had found the missing link for which I had been looking so long, and before I again went to sleep almost every detail of the story, as it stands, was clear to me. Of course, writing it was another thing.

'*Deacon Brodie!*' I certainly didn't dream that, but in the room in which I slept when a child in Edinburgh there was a cabinet – and a very pretty piece of work it was, too – from the hands of the original Deacon Brodie. When I was about nineteen years of age I wrote a sort of hugger-mugger melodrama, which lay by in my coffer until it was fished out by my friend W. E. Henley. He thought he saw something in it, and we started to work together, and after a desperate campaign we turned out the original drama of *Deacon Brodie*, as performed in London, and recently, I believe, successfully in this city. We were both young men when we did that, and I think we had an idea that bad-heartedness was strength. Now the piece has been all overhauled, and although I have no idea whether it will please an audience, I don't think either Mr Henley or I are ashamed of it. We take it now for a good, honest melodrama not so very ill done.'

•

MARK TWAIN

Interviewed by Rudyard Kipling
From Sea to Sea, 1889

Mark Twain was the pen-name of Samuel Langhorn Clemens (1835–1910), the American writer, who was born in Missouri. He worked as a printer, a Mississippi river pilot ('mark twain' was a call of the man sounding river depth and meant 'by the mark two fathoms') and a gold prospector, before editing a newspaper in Nevada. He moved to San Francisco where he began to publish collections of his journalistic sketches. After travelling to Europe and Palestine, he published a humorous travelogue, *Innocents Abroad* (1869), and edited a newspaper in Buffalo, where he found a wealthy wife. He eventually settled in Hartford, Connecticut, and after a brief and unsuccessful stab at being a publisher devoted his energies to lecturing and writing. He wrote two classic novels, *Tom Sawyer* (1876) and *Huckleberry Finn* (1884), both set in the Mississippi Basin, and several lighter works. He was one of the first professional interviewees.

Rudyard Kipling (1865–1936), the English writer, was born in Bombay, India. His father was principal of the art school in Lahore, and it was in Lahore that Kipling, having been educated back in England, started his professional life as a writer in 1880, as a journalist on the Lahore *Civil and Military Gazette*. His first book of poetry, *Departmental Ditties*, was published in 1886 and his first collection of short stories, *Plain Tales from the Hills*, in 1888. *From Sea to Sea* was a collection of articles he had written about a trip across the United States for the *Civil and Military Gazette* and another paper, the *Pioneer*; 1889 was the year when Kipling emerged as a literary celebrity in London.

This encounter between two major literary figures is interesting partly because Kipling later developed a phobia for interviewers (see the Boston *Sunday Herald* interview with him in 1892, which appears later in this anthology).

You are a contemptible lot, over yonder. Some of you are Commissioners, and some Lieutenant-Governors, and some have the VC, and a few are privileged to walk about the Mall arm in arm with the Viceroy; but *I* have seen Mark Twain this golden morning, have shaken his hand, and smoked a cigar – no, two cigars – with him, and talked with him for more than two hours! Understand clearly that I do not despise you; indeed, I don't. I am only very sorry for you, from the Viceroy downward. To soothe your envy and to prove that I still regard you as my equals, I will tell you all about it.

They said in Buffalo that he was in Hartford, Conn., and again they said, 'perchance he is gone upon a journey to Portland'; and a big, fat drummer vowed that he knew the man intimately, and that Mark was spending the summer in Europe – which information so upset me that I embarked upon the wrong train, and was incontinently turned out by the conductor three-quarters of a mile from the station, amid the wilderness of railway tracks. Have you ever, encumbered with great-coat and valise, tried to dodge diversely-minded locomotives when the sun was shining in your eyes? But I forgot that you have not seen Mark Twain, you people of no account!

Saved from the jaws of the cowcatcher, me wandering devious a stranger met.

'Elmira is the place. Elmira in the State of New York – this State, not two-hundred miles away;' and he added, perfectly unnecessarily, 'Slide, Kelley, slide.'

I slid on the West Shore line, I slid till midnight, and they dumped me down at the door of a frowzy hotel in Elmira. Yes, they knew all about 'that man Clemens', but reckoned he was not in town; had gone East somewhere. I had better possess my soul in patience till the morrow, and then dig up the 'man Clemens' brother-in-law, who was interested in coal.

The idea of chasing half a dozen relatives in addition to Mark Twain up and down a city of thirty thousand inhabitants kept me awake. Morning revealed Elmira, whose streets were desolated by railway tracks, and whose suburbs were given up to the manufacture of door-sashes and window-frames. It was surrounded by pleasant, fat, little hills, rimmed with timber and topped with cultivation. The Chenung River flowed generally up and down the town, and had just finished flooding a few of the main streets.

The hotel-man and the telephone-man assured me that the much-desired brother-in-law was out of town, and no one seemed to know where 'the man Clemens' abode. Later on I discovered that he had not summered in that place for more than nineteen seasons, and so was comparatively a new arrival.

A friendly policeman volunteered the news that he had seen Twain or 'some one very like him' driving a buggy the day before. This gave me a delightful sense of nearness. Fancy living in a town where you could see the author of *Tom Sawyer*, or 'some one very like him', jolting over the pavements in a buggy!

'He lives out yonder at East Hill,' said the policeman; 'three miles from here.'

Then the chase began – in a hired hack, up an awful hill, where sunflowers blossomed by the roadside, and crops waved, and *Harper's Magazine* cows stood knee-deep in clover, all ready to be transferred to photogravure. The great man must have been persecuted by outsiders aforetime, and fled up the hill for refuge.

Presently, the driver stopped at a miserable, little, white wood shanty, and demanded 'Mister Clemens'.

'I know he's a big-bug and all that,' he explained, 'but you can never tell what sort of notions these sort of men take into their heads to live in, anyways.'

There rose up a young lady who was sketching thistle-tops and goldenrod, amid a plentiful supply of both, and set the pilgrimage on the right path.

'It's a pretty Gothic house on the left-hand side a little way farther on.'

'Gothic h— ' said the driver. 'Very few of the city hacks take this drive, specially if they know they are coming out here,' and he glared at me savagely.

It was a very pretty house, anything but Gothic, clothed with ivy, standing in a very big compound, and fronted by a verandah full of chairs and hammocks. The roof of the verandah was a trellis-work of creepers, and the sun peeping through moved on the shining boards below.

Decidedly this remote place was an ideal one for work, if a man could work among these soft airs and the murmur of the long-eared crops.

Appeared suddenly a lady used to dealing with rampageous outsiders. 'Mr Clemens has just walked downtown. He is at his brother-in-law's house.'

Then he was within shouting distance, after all, and the chase had not been in vain. With speed I fled, and the driver, skidding the wheel and swearing audibly, arrived at the bottom of that hill without accident. It was in the pause that followed between ringing the brother-in-law's bell and getting an answer that it occurred to me for the first time Mark Twain might possibly have other engagements than the entertainment of escaped lunatics from India, be they never so full of admiration. And in another man's house – anyhow, what had I come to say? Suppose the drawing room should be full of people, – suppose a baby were sick, how was I to explain that I only wanted to shake hands with him?

Then things happened somewhat in this order. A big, darkened drawing room; a huge chair; a man with eyes, a mane of grizzled hair, a brown mustache covering a mouth as delicate as a woman's, a strong, square hand shaking mine, and the slowest, calmest, levellest voice in all the world saying:

'Well, you think you owe me something, and you've come to tell me so. That's what I call squaring a debt handsomely.'

'Piff!' from a cob-pipe (I always said that a Missouri meerschaum was the best smoking in the world), and behold! Mark Twain had curled himself up in the big armchair, and I was smoking reverently, as befits one in the presence of his superior.

The thing that struck me first was that he was an elderly man; yet, after a minute's thought, I perceived that it was otherwise, and in five minutes, the eyes looking at me, I saw that the grey hair was an accident of the most trivial. He was quite young. I was shaking his hand. I was smoking his cigar, and I was hearing him talk – this man I had learned to love and admire fourteen thousand miles away.

Reading his books, I had striven to get an idea of his personality, and all my preconceived notions were wrong and beneath the reality. Blessed is the man who finds no disillusion when he is brought face to face with a revered writer. That was a moment to be remembered; the landing of a twelve-pound salmon was nothing to it. I had hooked Mark Twain, and he was treating me as though under certain circumstances I might be an equal.

About this time I became aware that he was discussing the copyright question. Attend to the words of the oracle through this unworthy medium transmitted. You will never be able to imagine the long, slow surge of the drawl, and the deadly gravity of the countenance, the quaint pucker of the body, one foot thrown over the arm of the chair, the yellow pipe clinched in one corner of the mouth, and the right hand casually caressing the square chin:

'Copyright? Some men have morals, and some men have – other things. I presume a publisher is a man. He is not born. He is created – by circumstances. Some publishers have morals. Mine have. They pay me for the English productions of my books. When you hear men talking of Bret Harte's works and other works and my books being pirated, ask them to be sure of their facts. I think they'll find the books are paid for. It was ever thus.

'I remember an unprincipled and formidable publisher. Perhaps he's dead now. He used to take my short stories – I can't call it steal or pirate them. It was beyond these things altogether. He took my stories one at a time and made a book of it. If I wrote an essay on dentistry or theology or any little thing of that kind – just an essay that long (he indicated half an inch on his finger), any sort of essay – that publisher would amend and improve my essay.

'He would get another man to write some more to it or cut it about exactly as his needs required. Then he would publish a book called *Dentistry by Mark Twain*, that little essay and some other things not mine added. Theology would make another book, and so on. I do not consider that fair. It's an insult. But he's dead now, I think. I didn't kill him.

'There's a great deal of nonsense talked about international copyright. The proper way to treat a copyright is to make it exactly like real-estate in every way.

'It will settle itself under these conditions. If Congress were to bring in a law that a man's life was not to extend over a hundred and sixty years, somebody would laugh. That law wouldn't concern anybody. The man would be out of the jurisdiction of the court. A term in years in copyright comes to exactly the same thing. No law can make a book live or cause it to die before the appointed time.

'Tottletown, Cal., was a new town, with a population of three thousand – banks, fire-brigade, brick buildings, and all the modern improvements. It lived, it flourished, and it disappeared. Today no man can put his foot on any remnant of Tottletown, Cal. It's dead. London continues to exist. Bill Smith, author of a book read for the next year or so, is real-estate in Tottletown. William Shakespeare, whose works are extensively read, is real-estate in London. Let Bill Smith, equally with Mr Shakespeare now deceased, have as complete a control over his copyright as he would over his real-estate. Let him gamble it away, drink it away, or – give it to the church. Let his heirs and assigns treat it in the same manner.

'Every now and again I go up to Washington, sitting on a board to drive that sort of view into Congress. Congress takes its arguments against international copyright delivered ready made, and – Congress isn't very strong. I put the real-estate view of the case before one of the senators.'

I said: 'Suppose a man has written a book that will live forever?'

He said: 'Neither you or I will ever live to see that man's heirs and assigns, working under your theory.'

I said: 'You think that all the world has no commercial sense. The book that will live forever can't be artificially kept up at inflated prices. There will always be very expensive editions of it and cheap ones issuing side by side.'

'Take the case of Sir Walter Scott's novels,' Mark Twain continued, turning to me. 'When the copyright notes protected them, I bought editions as expensive as I could afford, because I like them. At the same time the firm were selling editions that a cat might buy. They had their real estate, and not being fools, recognized that one portion of the plot could be worked as a gold mine, another as a vegetable garden, and another as a marble quarry. Do you see?'

What I saw with the greatest clearness was Mark Twain being forced to fight for the simple proposition that man has as much right to the work of his brains (think of the heresy of it!) as to the labour of his hands. When the old lion roars, the young whelps growl. I growled assentingly, and the talk ran on from books in general to his own in particular.

Growing bold, and feeling that I had a few hundred thousand folk at my back, I demanded whether Tom Sawyer married Judge Thatcher's daughter and whether we were ever going to hear of Tom Sawyer as a man.

'I haven't decided,' quoth Mark Twain, getting up, filling his pipe, and walking up and down the room in his slippers. 'I have a notion of writing the sequel to *Tom Sawyer* in two ways. In one I would make him rise to great honor and go to Congress, and in the other I should hang him. Then the friends and enemies of the book could take their choice.'

Here I lost my reverence completely, and protested against any theory of the sort, because, to me at least, Tom Sawyer was real.

'Oh, he *is* real,' said Mark Twain. 'He's all the boys that I have known or recollect; but that would be a good way of ending the book'; then, turning round, 'because, when you come to think of it, neither religion, training, nor education avails anything against the force of circumstances that drive a man. Suppose we took the next four and twenty years of Tom Sawyer's life, and gave a little joggle to the circumstances that controlled him. He would, logically and according to the joggle, turn out a rip or an angel.'

'Do you believe that, then?'

'I think so; isn't it what you call kismet?'

'Yes; but don't give him two joggles and show the result, because he isn't your property any more. He belongs to us.'

He laughed – a large, wholesome laugh – and this began a dissertation on the rights of a man to do what he liked with his own creations, which being a matter of purely professional interest, I will mercifully omit.

Returning to the big chair, he, speaking of truth and the like in literature, said that an autobiography was the one work in which a man, against his own will and in spite of his utmost striving to the contrary, revealed himself in his true light to the world.

'A good deal of your life on the Mississippi is autobiographical, isn't it?' I asked.

'As near as it can be – when a man is writing to a book and about himself. But in genuine autobiography, I believe it is impossible for a man to tell the truth about himself or to avoid impressing the reader with the truth about himself.

'I made an experiment once. I got a friend of mine – a man painfully given to speak the truth on all occasions – a man who wouldn't dream of telling a lie – and I made him write his autobiography for his own amusement and mine. He did it. The manuscript would have made an octavo volume, but – good, honest man that he was – in every single detail of his life that I knew about he turned out, on paper, a formidable liar. He could not help himself.

'It is not in human nature to write the truth about itself. None the less the reader gets a general impression from an autobiography whether the man is a fraud or a good man. The reader can't give his reasons any more than a man can explain why a woman struck him as being lovely when he doesn't remember her hair, eyes, teeth, or figure. And the impression that the reader gets is a correct one.'

'Do you ever intend to write an autobiography?'

'If I do, it will be as other men have done – with the most earnest desire to make myself out to be the better man in every little business that has been to my discredit; and I shall fail, like the others, to make my readers believe anything except the truth.'

This naturally led to a discussion on conscience. Then said Mark Twain, and his words are mighty and to be remembered: –

'Your conscience is a nuisance. A conscience is like a child. If you pet it and play with it and let it have everything that it wants, it becomes spoiled and intrudes on all your amusements and most of your griefs. Treat your conscience as you would anything else. When it is rebellious, spank it – be severe with it, argue with it, prevent it from coming to play with you at all hours, and you will secure a good conscience; that is to say, a properly trained one. A spoiled one simply destroys all the pleasure in life. I think I have reduced mine to order. At least, I haven't heard from it for some time. Perhaps I have killed it from over-severity. It's wrong to kill a child, but, in spite of all I have said, a conscience differs from a child in many ways. Perhaps it's best when it's dead.'

Here he told me a little – such things as a man might tell a stranger – of his early life and upbringing, and in what manner he had been influenced for good by the example of his parents. He spoke always through his eyes, a light under the heavy eyebrows; anon crossing the room with a step as light as a girl's, to show me some book or other; then resuming his walk up and down the room, puffing at the cob pipe. I would have given much for nerve enough to demand the gift of that pipe – value, five cents when new. I understood why certain savage tribes ardently desire the liver of brave men slain in combat. That pipe would have given me, perhaps, a hint of his keen insight into the souls of men. But he never laid it aside within stealing reach.

Once, indeed, he put his hand on my shoulder. It was an investiture of the Star of India, blue silk, trumpets, and diamond-studded jewel, all complete. If hereafter, in the changes and chances of the mortal life, I fall to cureless ruin, I will tell the superintendent of the workhouse that Mark Twain once put his hand on my shoulder; and he shall give me a room to myself and a double allowance of pauper's tobacco.

'I never read novels myself,' said he, 'except when the popular persecution forces me to – when people plague me to know what I think of the last book that everyone is reading.'

'And how did the latest persecution affect you?'

'Robert?' said he, interrogatively.

I nodded.

'I read it, of course, for the workmanship. That made me think I had neglected novels too long – that there might be a good many books as graceful in style somewhere on the shelves; so I began a course of novel reading. I have dropped it now; it did not amuse me. But as regards Robert, the effect on me was exactly as though a singer of street ballads were to hear excellent music from a church organ. I didn't stop to ask whether the music was legitimate or necessary. I listened, and I liked what I heard. I am speaking of the grace and beauty of the style.'

'You see,' he went on, 'every man has his private opinion about a book. But that is my private opinion. If I had lived in the beginning of things, I should have looked around the township to see what popular opinion thought of the murder of Abel before I openly condemned Cain. I should have had my private opinion, of course, but I shouldn't have expressed it until I had felt the way. You have my private opinion about that book. I don't know what my public ones are exactly. They don't upset the earth.'

He recurled himself into the chair and talked of other things.

'I spend nine months of the year in Hartford. I have long ago satisfied myself that there is no hope of doing much work during those nine months. People come and call. They call at all hours, about everything in the world. One day I thought I would keep a list of interruptions. It began this way:

'A man came and would see no one but Mr Clemens. He was an agent for photogravure reproductions of salon pictures. I very seldom use salon pictures in my books.

'After that man another man, who refused to see any one but Mr Clemens, came to make me write to Washington about something. I saw him. I saw a third man, then a fourth. By this time it was noon. I had grown tired of keeping the list. I wished to rest.

'But the fifth man was the only one of the crowd with a card of his own. He sent up his card. 'Ben Koontz, Hannibal, Mo.' I was raised in Hannibal. Ben was an old schoolmate of mine. Consequently I threw the house wide open and rushed with both hands out at a big, fat, heavy man, who was not the Ben I had ever known – nor anything like him.

'"But *is* it you, Ben?" I said. "You've altered in the last thousand years."

'The fat man said: "Well, I'm not Koontz exactly, but I met him down in Missouri, and he told me to be sure and call on you, and he gave me his card, and"' – here he acted the little scene for my benefit – '"if you can wait a minute till I get the circulars – I'm not Koontz exactly, but I'm traveling with the fullest line of rods you ever saw."'

'And what happened?' I asked breathlessly.

'I shut the door. He was not Ben Koontz – exactly – not my old school-fellow, but I had shaken him by both hands in love, and . . . I had been bearded by a lightning-rod man in my own house.

'As I was saying, I do very little work in Hartford. I come here for three months every year, and I work four or five hours a day in a study down the garden of that little house on the hill. Of course, I do not object to two or three interruptions. When a man is in the full swing of his work these little things do not affect him. Eight or ten or twenty interruptions retard composition.'

I was burning to ask him all manner of impertinent questions, as to which of his works he himself preferred, and so forth; but, standing in awe of his eyes, I dared not. He spoke on, and I listened, grovelling.

It was a question of mental equipment that was on the carpet, and I am still wondering whether he meant what he said.

'Personally I never cared for fiction or story-books. What I like to read about are facts and statistics of any kind. If they are only facts about the raising of radishes, they interest me. Just now, for instance, before you came in' – he pointed to an encyclopedia on the shelves – 'I was reading an article about "Mathematics". Perfectly pure mathematics.

'My own knowledge of mathematics stops at "twelve times twelve", but I enjoyed that article immensely. I didn't understand a word of it; but facts, or what a man believes to be facts, are always delightful. That mathematical fellow believed in his facts. So do I. Get your facts first, and' – the voice dies away to an almost inaudible drone – 'then you can distort 'em as much as you please.'

Bearing this precious advice in my bosom, I left; the great man assuring me with gentle kindness that I had not interrupted him in the least. Once outside the door, I yearned to go back and ask some questions – it was easy enough to think of them now – but his time was his own, though his books belonged to me.

I should have ample time to look back to that meeting across the graves of the days. But it was sad to think of the things he had not spoken about.

In San Francisco the men of *The Call* told me many legends of Mark's apprenticeship in their paper five and twenty years ago; how he was a reporter delightfully incapable of reporting according to the needs of the day. He preferred, so they said, to coil himself into a heap and meditate until the last minute. Then he would produce copy bearing no sort of relationship to his legitimate work – copy that made the editor swear horribly, and the readers of *The Call* ask for more.

I should like to have heard Mark's version of that, with some stories of his joyous and variegated past. He has been journeyman printer (in those days he wandered from the banks of the Missouri even to Philadelphia), pilot cub and full-blown pilot, soldier of the South (that was for three weeks only), private secretary to a Lieutenant-Governor of Nevada (that displeased him), miner, editor, special correspondent in the Sandwich Islands, and Lord only knows what else. If so experienced a man could by any means be made drunk, it would be a glorious thing to fill him up with composite liquors, and, in the language of his own country, 'let him retrospect'. But these eyes will never see that orgy fit for the gods!

●

THOMAS EDISON

Interviewed by R. H. Sherard
The Pall Mall Gazette, 19 August 1889

Thomas Alva Edison (1847–1931), the prolific American inventor, was born in Ohio. He was expelled from school after a mere three months for being backward and became a newsboy on the Grand Trunk Railway. After working as a telegraphic operator during the American Civil War, he began inventing. He sold an early invention, the paper ticker-tape machine which could transmit stock exchange prices, to finance the establishment of a research laboratory in New Jersey, virtually the first of its kind. Among the 1,000-plus patents he took out were those for the carbon microphone (1877), the gramophone (1878), the incandescent light bulb (1879), the electric valve (1883), and the kinetoscope (1891). He also designed the first electricity distribution installation and the first electric light power plant in New York City in the early 1880s. In a later interview with Theodore Dreiser, Edison confessed that once he had completed an invention he hated it: '. . . when it is all done and is a success, I can't bear the sight of it. I haven't used a telephone in ten years, and I would go out of my way any day to miss an incandescent light.'

Robert Harborough Sherard (1861–1943) was the son of a Church of England clergyman and a great-grandson of William Wordsworth. He was educated at Oxford and Bonn universities and became a professional journalist in 1884, writing for English, American and Australian publications. A friend of Oscar Wilde, he wrote the first major biography of the famous aesthete in 1906. He wrote two series of magazine articles about social conditions which were subsequently published as books, *The White Slaves of England* (1897) and *The Child-Slaves of Britain* (1905). Apart from social reportage, he specialized in interviewing celebrities. The ones I have discovered include: Nellie Melba, Gustave Eiffel and Thomas Edison for *The Pall Mall Gazette*; Henrik Ibsen, Hall Caine and Alphonse Daudet for *The Humanitarian*; Jules Verne, Gaston Tissandier (the balloonist), Camille Flammarion (the astronomer), Alphonse Daudet (again) and Émile Zola for *McClure's Magazine*; and Stanley Weyman (the historical novelist) for *The Strand Magazine*. His interviews with Zola and Daudet formed the basis for biographical studies of these novelists. He also wrote a biography of Guy de Maupassant and an autobiography, *Memoirs of a Mug* (1941). He established the Vindex publishing company in Calvi in 1931 and was a *chevalier de la légion d'honneur*.

*

This is what Edison wrote to me when I proposed he should grant me five minutes' talk with him: 'All right, Friday about eleven in morning, I'll be sane by that time. My intellect is now making 275 revolutions a minute.'

I called at the Hôtel du Rhin this morning at eleven o'clock, and was shown up to the handsome drawing-room on the first floor. Edison was standing by the mantelpiece. At a secretaire by the window were Colonel Gouraud, Mr Durer, and others. At the far end the sweet girl-wife, Mrs Edison, surrounded by various persons. It is always difficult to begin, for one who has come to annoy, but I plunged into matters at once . . .

'About this ore-extracting machine,' Edison said; 'it's going to be a great thing. Already we have eighty machines at work in the iron mines. Yes, it is adapted for iron ore only as yet. I am studying the question of a machine for treating both refractory silver ore and gold ore, and shall get them out by and by. Then we shall make more money.'

I was asking for some particulars as to this machine, when one came up who was enthusiastic, and who 'spoke in the name of humanity' to the 'King of Science', and was verbose and gesticulative. I think any one who has seen Edison face to face with a Bore must love him for all his days. He has the sweetest smile and gives apparent attention, which is the courtesy of conversation. Those who know him well say that at such times, a certain deafness aiding, his thoughts are elsewhere, and pray God that they may be.

'The far-seeing machine?' – 'I have heard,' he said, 'that some European inventors claim to have preceded me in this, but I do not know anything about their inventions. My machine is getting on very nicely. I do not think it will ever be useful for very long distances, and it is absurd to say that it will enable one to see another ten thousand miles away. In a city, however, it will be of practical use. I don't look for anything further, at least at present.'

Colonel Gouraud then said, 'I may tell you something which Mr Edison would never tell you. That gentleman who is talking to Mrs Edison is the Cavaliere Copello. He has just come to Paris on a special mission from the King of Italy to Mr Edison, bringing him the insignia of Grand Officer of the Crown of Italy. These insignia are accompanied by a letter of which you may like to take a copy.' This is the letter:

The presentation by Cavaliere Copello to the King, my august Sovereign, of the phonograph invented by your illustrious self (Signoria) produced the deepest impression upon the mind of his Majesty, who has recorded upon the machine itself his greatest admiration. The King, in consequence, wishing to give you a deserved testimonial of honour for the great scientific discoveries associated with your name, so universally known, has been pleased, of his own accord, to confer upon you the rank of Grand Officer of the Crown of Italy. I am happy to present you herewith, on behalf of his Majesty, the insignia of this high honour, and reserve to myself to send you as soon as possible the Royal diploma. – In the meanwhile, deign to accept, &c.,

RATTAZZI

This distinction confers on Edison the title of Count, and on Mrs Edison that of Countess. I could not help wishing that a few representatives of European flunkeydom could have seen Edison, when in pleasantry one addressed him as 'Count'. His laugh then was worth all the revolutions that were ever made by democracy against the aforesaid flunkeydom. 'This must not be known in New York,' he said. 'They would never stop laughing at my illustrious self.'

'The phonograph?' – 'We have got it into practical form. Already 1,800 machines are in use in commercial houses, and our factories are now turning out forty machines per diem. I have also, at last, been able to make a perfectly solid mailable cylinder, which can go through the post for any distance without risk of damage. All this has been very hard work. On the tools for making the big phonograph alone we spent 5,000 dollars. I have also created a small model – a pocket phonograph, if you like to call it so – the cylinder of which will take 300 words, the length of an ordinary letter, and which will be very practicable for ordinary correspondence. I have the model here, and you can see it any day you like. These are not, however, yet ready for sale.'

'What use can newspaper people make of it?' – 'Oh plenty. It is already used in the *World* office. The machine is placed downstairs. The reporters come in and talk into it. The cylinder is taken upstairs to the composing-room and the compositors set up from its dictation. They attain much greater speed, make more ems in an hour than on the old system, and earn more money.'

'You are a great friend of newspapers and newspaper folk?' – 'I am indeed. The New York reporters are the smartest set of fellows in creation, and I am fond of them. Almost every Sunday I have a party of them down at my place, and some of them spend all the day with me. We have great newspapers in America. I take the *Times* and the *World*, and read every word of them. In America we run public affairs by the papers. Yes, the *World* is the biggest paper out there, just as Mr Pulitzer is our smartest newspaper man. He is smart, and has got some good men round him – Colonel Cockrell and the rest – the cleverest men going.'

'How are you impressed with Paris?' – 'Oh, I am dazed. My head's all in a muddle, and I reckon it will take me at least a year to recover my senses. I wish now that I had come over in my laboratory blouse, and could have gone about unknown and have seen something. The Exhibition is immense, larger than our Philadelphian Exhibition. So far, however, I have seen but very little of it. This morning, however, I saw a tool which will save me 6,000 dols, clear a year. It is a chisel worked by hydraulic pressure. I just saw it, passing by; just a glance. I shall order some, and send them out. They will enable us to reduce our labour by eighteen hands.' 'That's a good morning's business,' said Colonel Gouraud.

– 'Yes,' said Edison, and continued: 'What has struck me so far chiefly is the absolute laziness of everybody over here. When do these people work? What do they work at? I have not seen a cartload of goods since I came to Paris. People here seem to have established an elaborate system of loafing. Some of these engineers who come to see me, fashionably dressed, walking-stick in hand, when do they work? I don't understand it at all.'

'Over here we hear wonderful stories of your working. You have the reputation of being able to work twenty-three hours a day for an indefinite period.' – 'Oh! I have often done more than that, haven't I, Gouraud? As a rule, though, I get through twenty hours a day. I find four hours' sleep quite sufficient for all purposes.'

Edison pronounces the words 'work' and 'working' as some do 'prayer', 'religion'. It is also a religion, it is true.

'I see you smoke. It does not harm you?' – 'Not at all. I smoke about twenty cigars a day, and the more I work the more I smoke.' Some one remarked: 'Mr Edison has an iron constitution, and does just everything contrary to the rules of health. Yet he is never ill.'

I asked: 'Beyond the far-seeing machine and the rest, are there projects?' – 'Any number,' said Edison. 'When we make our big exhibition in America, I shall have to have several new things.' It is perfectly useless to ask Edison for information as to ideas. In him everything is so practical that it seems he cannot talk about what is phantom merely. It is the 'what is' with him and not the 'about to be'.

Mrs Edison then asked the Cavaliere to do her the pleasure of lunching with her, *chez* Brebant, on the Eiffel Tower. Colonel Gouraud asked me to be of the party, and together we went on to order breakfast. *En route* the Colonel asked me to contradict a story which has appeared that he brought to Edison a phonographic message from the Queen. 'Mr Edison received messages from the Queen of Italy, from the King, and from the Prince of Naples. I suppose that is what the story was based upon.'

'When on board the ship,' said Edison, as we sat down to *déjeuner* on the terrace of the Eiffel Tower, *première étage*, 'they put rolls and coffee on the table for breakfast. I thought that that was a very poor breakfast for a man to do any work upon. But I suppose one gets used to it. I would like one American meal for a change – plenty of pie for a change.' He then smashed the roll with his fist.

There were six of us, Mr and Mrs Edison, Colonel Gouraud, the Cavaliere, and Mr Durer, the author of a very remarkable brochure on Edison. And we had the world at our feet. There were shrimps amongst the hors d'oeuvres. Edison had never seen any. 'Do they grow larger?' he asked, and added, 'They give a great deal of trouble for small results.'

'This Eiffel tower?' I said. – 'The work of a bridge-builder,' said one. 'No,' said Edison decisively. 'No. It is a great idea. The glory of Eiffel is in the magnitude of the conception and the nerve in the execution. That admitted, and the money found, the rest is, if you like, mere bridge-building. I like the French,' he added. 'They have big conceptions. The English ought to take a leaf out of their books. What Englishman would have had this idea? What Englishman could have conceived the Statue of Liberty?'

'Will you beat the tower in New York?' – 'We'll build one of 2,000 ft. We'll go Eiffel 100 per cent better, without discount.'

As they were removing the hors d'œuvres I asked: 'This system of execution by electricity?' – 'It is Westinghouse's system, and is being used entirely against his will. He is indignant that his studies in electrical science should have been put to such a use. I, too, am against executions of any description. Put them away to work, but don't kill them.'

Over the *soles frites*: 'There was something in the papers about your experimenting on photography with colours.' Edison smiled. 'No. That is not true. That sort of thing is sentimental. I do not go in for sentiment.' Then he said: 'Poor Carnegie has turned sentimental, quite sentimental. When I saw him last I wanted to talk to him about his ironworks. That is what interests me, immense factories going day and night, with the roar of furnaces and clashing hammers, acres and acres of activity – man's fight with metal. But he would not talk about it. He said, "All that is brutal." He is now interested in and will only talk about French art and amateur photography. It is a great pity.'

'Could not,' I asked, 'a machine be made which could be adapted to the head, and which would record one's thoughts, saving the trouble of speaking or writing?' – Edison reflected. 'Such a machine is possible,' he said; 'but just think if it were invented. Every man would flee his neighbour, fly for his life to any shelter.'

As they brought in the filets à la Brébant, I said, and thought of little Dombey, 'What is electricity after all?' – He said, 'It is a mode of motion, a system of vibrations. A certain speed of vibration produces heat; a lower speed, light; still lower, something else.'

'Is there anything in electricity as applied to medicine?' – 'There is a great deal of humbug in all that,' he said. Then as a careful maître d'hôtel brought in the cradled Clos Vougeot, and served it with exaggeration of anxious ceremony, he added, 'There is a great deal of humbug about wine too. And about cigars. Men go by cost. The connoisseurs are few. At home, for fun, I keep a lot of wretched cigars, made up on purpose in elegant wrappers, some with hairs in them, some with cotton wool. I give these to the critical smokers, tell them they cost 35 cents a piece. You should hear them praise them.'

We talked of cooking and of famous chefs. Also of one who recently engaged a French cook at a Bishop's salary. 'Bright's disease of the kidneys is all the dividend that man will draw,' said Edison. He seems to take delight in commercial phrases. It is comfortable to hear him pronounce the words 'make money'. Commerciality with him is dignified and impressive, vulgar as it is with others. The breakfast was *recherché* in the extreme, but Edison barely touched anything. 'A pound of food a day is all I need when I am working, and now I am not working.' One could not help thinking of Chatterton and his crust.

After dessert, there was champagne, and toasts were drunk. The Cavaliere began. Edison said: – 'The Cavaliere is profuse, but not so much so as another Italian gentleman who once proposed my health, and remarked that even the chickens in his country knew my name.' 'It's a regular sanatorium,' he remarked later on, 'so much "health" being distributed.' Again, 'All this is new to me,' alluding to the ceremonial of our festivities. 'If I stay long here I shall too soon be able to get up and make speeches and wave my arms.'

When the coffee and cigars came in his face brightened up. 'Mr Edison is beginning to breakfast,' said the Colonel. 'Yes,' said Edison, taking an Havannah; 'my breakfast begins with this.' Meanwhile the Cavaliere was urging him to come on to Italy, to be presented to the King, most anxious to see him. Science, art, and municipality would unite to do him honour. Edison shakes his head, a more decided negative than all the circles of the Greek artist. 'No,' he said, 'my nerves won't stand it. I shall just go quietly back to the States from Paris. I shan't go to London even, that cheerful place. I am all topsy-turvy in my head, as it is.' The Cavaliere, however, insists and departs with Mr Edison, still urging his point.

A few minutes later, happening to pass the tower, I saw at its foot again the man, with his face boyish almost for its openness, and the grey hairs over the unwrinkled forehead. Then I looked at the Monument first and then at the man. The Monument thus contrasted appeared infinitesimally small.

●

LILLIE LANGTRY

Interviewed by The *Pall Mall Gazette*, 7 September 1889

Lillie Langtry (1853–1929), the English actress, was born on Jersey, in the Channel Islands; hence her sobriquet, 'The Jersey Lily', which came from the title of a portrait of her by Millais. She married Edward Langtry in 1874 and began her stage career in the early 1880s. She was renowned for her great beauty – Edward VII made her his mistress and Oscar Wilde wrote *Lady Windermere's Fan* for her. Later she managed the Imperial Theatre. Edward Langtry died in 1897 and she married again, this time to a Frenchman. She owned racehorses, wrote her memoirs – *The Days I Knew* (1925) – and died in Monte Carlo.

In the comparative seclusion of Albemarle-street, at a point where the road of Piccadilly is pleasantly tempered by distance, which certainly lends as much enchantment to the murmurs of the metropolis as it does to any 'view', in or out of nature, 'The Jersey Lily' has taken up her temporary abode. For a few short weeks she has been resting from her dramatic labours – that is if constant thought for the future and the wear and tear of rehearsals can be called 'rest' – and contemplating fresh fields for conquest in the land which she has deserted for so long. Being anxious to see and hear for myself (writes a representative of *The Pall Mall Gazette*) what America had done for Mrs Langtry and what Mrs Langtry had done for America during her lengthened sojourn in the States, I called at her hotel a few days ago and made known my desires. In a few moments the object of my quest appeared, looking particularly radiant in a soft grey gown – a perfect symphony in slate – but most decidedly in a hurry. 'I am just off to rehearsal now,' she exclaims, with a pleasant smile; 'but if you will come and see me to-morrow at about six I shall be delighted to have a chat. You know I am so *dreadfully* busy.' Accordingly, at six o'clock on the following day I once more make my way to the purlieus of Clubland, and present myself at 'Pulteney's'. 'Mrs Langtry has not returned yet, but she is sure to be in in a few minutes.' I hear the sound of carriage-wheels; the door opens, and in comes 'The Lily' – this time in a loose-fitting costume of blue – looking rather tired, but not a whit less charming than usual. As I gaze at the features which crowds have craned at and photographers have fought for, I am struck with one or two changes which three years absence has wrought. Mrs Langtry's face seems somewhat thinner, but at the same time more intellectual; her smile is tinged with a shade of thoughtfulness which indicates clearly enough a distinct mental development; there is a far-off look in her eyes, and an occasional air of pathetic intensity in her whole bearing, which will forcibly strike English playgoers who remember the actress in her earlier days. One will look forward to finding a great increase in her power of dramatic expression when she appears again on the London stage. But while these thoughts are running riot in my brain, 'The Lily' is already beginning to talk pleasantly of the past, the present, and the future.

'Yes, I have been away three whole seasons, running about every part of the States, east and west. I have even been down to Mexico, and have travelled on all those railways which are such a source of excitement to the British speculator. For forty weeks out of the fifty-two in each of these years I have acted regularly, and that means pretty hard work. You see, my répertoire is not a light one, for it includes such characters as Lady Macbeth, Rosalind, Pauline Deschapelles, Lady Clancarty, and so on.'

'And don't you find American life terribly wearing?' – 'Well, it certainly would be if I didn't take care of myself. The "one night stands" – that is to say, the towns where a theatrical company only acts for one night – give us the greatest trouble. One very often arrives in the place at about eight o'clock in the evening, and has to be off again at half-past ten. How we get through the plays at all on these occasions I cannot understand; the people, however, seem to take it as part of the regular dramatic system, and raise no objections. But for the actors and actresses it is certainly very trying. I don't know how I should be able to go through such terrible rushes if it were not for my car.'

'And what about this wonderful car, Mrs Langtry, of which we have heard so many rumours?' – 'Oh, it's an actual reality, I can assure you – quite the most delightful vehicle ever hung upon wheels. It is seventy-six feet long, and a good deal wider and higher than any of the "Pullmans" in England. As you know, I had it built specially for me. It contains a dining room where I can entertain twelve people, a kitchen, a servants' room, a bath-room, and my own bedroom, which is really lovely. At one end of the car, which, by the way, is all made of oak, I have a sweet little observatory, and underneath the floor there are wine chests and a larder, where I often keep a whole buck from my ranche. You see I frequently live "on board", for days together when I am out of the way of nice hotels. It has been one of my happiest notions, for I couldn't have got through half the work I have done without my little house, which goes wherever I go, for all the American railways are "broad gauge", you know.'

'And is the silver bath also a fact?' – 'Yes; I wanted everything to look nice, and, as china is so brittle, I thought I would try silver. The experiment was most successful.'

'Might one ask the cost of this miniature palace?' – 'Well, roughly speaking, I paid 30,000 dols. for it, and I think it has been worth quite that sum to me.'

'You are a fairly large landed proprietress in the States, are you not?' 'Yes; my solicitor in New York tells me one can't go wrong in buying real estate in certain parts of the country. I have a cattle ranche of nearly 5,000 acres out west in California, with about 800 head of cattle. I am also going in for horse-breeding there, and have secured a "Hermit" stallion. At present my property is about thirty miles from a railway, but I am looking forward to the time when an extension will bring my piece into the market. Why, in a very few years it may become building land. Do you remember the Los Angeles "boom" four or five years ago, when every one in New York who could scrape a dollar or two together rushed to that town to buy land? Men were sitting at tables in the streets selling real estate by the square mile. At the present time when I visit my ranche I have to go out in a coach and six; but the railway will reach it in time!' And Mrs Langtry smiles at the thought of her judicious investment.

'And what is your wonderful recipe for doing all your hard work with impunity?' – 'Well; I get up in good time, go to bed as early as possible, and never eat supper. This last abstention I believe in thoroughly; neither Mrs Bancroft nor Ellen Terry were ever real supper-eaters; it is all a matter of habit. Perhaps, too, a certain soap has had something to do with my well-being.' 'Ah, do you still remain faithful to your transparent specific?' But Mrs Langtry's only answer is a merry laugh.

'And what has become of the little Chinese boy who accompanied you on your last visit to England?' – 'Oh, like all his race, he got tired of too much civilization and made up his mind he would return to the land of his fathers. He was a delightful little fellow. Did you ever hear of his historic fight with a boy of Lord Charles Beresford's in Eaton-square? The battle was a long and furious one, but my small Celestial came off victor in the end. Once in a fit of temper he cut off the greater part of his own pigtail, thus inflicting on himself the deadliest possible insult. However, I punished the boy by having a false tail made and spliced on to the stump of the real one. He objected to that proceeding very much. I have not filled up his place, and I have no pets at all now. I fear my mode of life is too migratory to suit any of the animal world; so I haven't even got a dog with me.'

'Have you brought your own chef over with you, Mrs Langtry? If not, how will you get on in our provincial hotels?' – 'Oh, my tastes always accommodate themselves to surrounding circumstances. I can live happily in the greatest luxury or with perfect plainness. I am looking forward to a large dose of plainness on my tour in England.'

'And when do you start?' – 'Next Monday at Wolverhampton. My principal production will be Mr Grundy's new play, *Esther Sandraz*, in which I was very successful in Chicago. The piece has been called unsympathetic by the London critics, but I don't think Esther is necessarily such a repulsive personage. I have studied the character very carefully in the original novel, *La Femme de Glace*, and I cannot help feeling that she ought to inspire a good deal of sympathy. By the way, Mr Arthur Bourchier, one of the best English amateur actors, has joined my company, and so taken his first step in what is called "the" profession. I am also going to do a new one-act play by Mr Charles Osborne, entitled *After the Rehearsal*, in which I shall appear as the "Pompadour". I think it will be very effective, and I hope to do it in London before long. Baron Ferdinand de Rothschild has kindly allowed me to copy the costume for the part from a lovely little "Boucher" which he has.'

'And your plans for the future, Mrs Langtry?' – 'Well, they are at present in a very undecided state. My tour will last until Christmas, when I hope to come to London, though where I shall pitch my camp I am unable to say just now. What a mass of theatres have arisen in the West-end since I left England! The last one I visited was the Shaftesbury. It is a beautiful house, and I was so delighted with Mr Willard's acting. I remember him, of course, playing nothing but melodramatic villains.'

'Then we may really expect you in town before long?' – 'Oh yes, certainly. Please tell every one you see, by the way, that I am *not* hopelessly disfigured by a facial operation, as some people have been saying. My so-called "nasal trouble" was of the most trivial kind. But I must say good bye, as I have another "interview" to get through – with my dressmaker.' And with a farewell smile and a cordial handshake 'The Jersey Lily' flies to the clutches of Worth's emissary.

●

SIR ARTHUR SULLIVAN

Interviewed by *The Pall Mall Gazette*, 5 December 1889

Sir Arthur Sullivan (1842–1900), the English composer and conductor, wrote the Savoy operas with librettist W. S. Gilbert. These included *Trial by Jury* (1875), *HMS Pinafore* (1878), *The Mikado* (1885), and *Ruddigore* (1887). His other music included 'The Lost Chord' and 'Onward Christian Soldiers'. This interview marked the opening of *The Gondoliers* (1889).

During the last few weeks there has been no busier man in all London than Sir Arthur Sullivan. When he has not been at work upon the score of his new opera he has had to transfer his energies to the stage of the Savoy Theatre, and divide his time between the piano and the baton. Little wonder, then, that his Cerberus in Victoria-street has been more than ordinarily cautious in the selection of those favoured callers whom he graciously allows to pass into the presence of England's most popular composer. By a fortunate combination of circumstances (writes a representative of *The Pall Mall Gazette*) I found myself the other evening on the threshold of No 2, Queen's Mansions, and, being duly armed with the password, was requested to 'step this way'. The mighty melody-maker is sitting in the cosy little room which has witnessed the evolution of so many operas. Books and pictures surround him on all sides. In one corner stands the piano whose resounding wires have given birth to countless tunes. Sir Arthur, who looks quite appropriately Venetian in his flannel shirt and loose open jacket, is pondering over a voluminous bundle of 'score', and occasionally indicating orchestral effects in pencil upon the surface of a blank sheet.

'I am terribly busy, and have only a few minutes to spare,' are his first words, as he greets me with a cordial hand-shake. 'A few minutes', however, is an elastic phrase, and so I instal myself in an available armchair. 'I am just thinking out the overture,' Sir Arthur goes on, 'for, of course, we must have something to play before the curtain goes up. This is the second act' – and he points to the pile of music in front of him – 'from which I am taking a theme or two. We have had our first band rehearsal to-day at Princes' Hall, and correcting the parts is no light task, I can assure you.'

'And do you always leave your overtures to the last moment?' – 'Oh, yes; always. Hamilton Clarke, who is now in Australia, used to help me with them very often when I was pressed for time. Do you remember the *Mikado* overture? He did that for me. I just arranged the order of the piece – the "Mikado's March", then "The sun whose rays", first for the oboe and then for violins and 'cellos, two octaves apart, and finally the *allegro*. He wrote the whole thing in a very few hours: in fact, he made it almost too elaborate, for I had to cut it down a little. The "Iolanthe" overture was a quick bit of work, too. I did that myself, completing it in less than two days. And there was a lot of fresh writing in it too. I dare say you will recollect the "Captain Shaw" motive combined with those florid passages for the wood-wind.'

'And is the new overture to be in strict "form"?' – 'No. As you know, I took the trouble to do that in the case of *The Yeomen of the Guard*, but it went for nothing after the first night.' I venture to dissent from this last statement, but Sir Arthur is inflexible on the subject. 'Naturally,' he says, 'I should prefer to please serious musicians in such a matter, but one must consider the general public.'

'Of course you will have an oboe solo in your introduction?' – 'Ah, that settles it,' laughs the composer. 'I was just considering that point when you came in, but as you have put it in that way I shall not do so this time.' I shudder at the possible mischief I have done, and beg Sir Arthur not to throw over the instrument he always treats so beautifully. 'Well,' he says, 'what is one to use for a solo if not the oboe? The clarinet is not really effective, the flute is out of the question, so is the bassoon; the cornet I hate as a solo instrument, and strings would hardly do. So you see it is a case of *reductio ad* – oboe.'

'Are you a very rapid worker?' – 'Well, that depends. Sometimes I do three or four numbers in a day, and sometimes I take a fortnight over a single song. I commenced my new opera at Weybridge in July, and worked steadily at it most of the autumn. Of course I had a good break for the Leeds Festival. I did all the orchestration, by the way, in about thirteen days.'

'Which of your many Savoy songs gave you most trouble?' – 'I should say that "The Merryman and his Maid" was one of the most difficult to deal with. I know it took me a fortnight, for I set and reset it over and over again. It was the "House that Jack built" character about it which was so awkward. An additional phrase was added in each verse, as no doubt you recollect. There is a precedent for the style of that particular composition, for Gilbert got the idea of it from a song which he heard on board his yacht – a nautical ballad beginning –

I have a song to sing, O.
Sing me your Song, O!

This went on increasing in length as each verse was sung, just as our "Merryman" did. I have got it written out somewhere, and, if I can only find it, you shall see it.' But a search through many bundles of MSS, fails to bring to light the model of Jack Point's quaint 'singing farce'.

'And what about the music of the new opera, Sir Arthur?' – 'Well, I have made it as light and catching as possible. There is a good deal more work in it than there was in the *Yeomen*, for nearly all the numbers are rapid. You will hear very little slow music in it. Of course the result is that there are more pages in the score. Two minutes' *allegro* means perhaps twenty pages, but with an *andante* movement you would only use about six. There is a quantity of concerted music in the piece – duets, trios, quartets, quintets, and so on. Still I have not altogether neglected the interests of the soloists. The tenor has quite a big song in the second act; Miss Ulinar will have some short couplets; Barrington has got a topical song; and Jessie Bond will, I think, be well suited. Denny has two solos, but they are both of them very slight in character. You will like the Cachuca in the second act. It is composed exactly on the lines of the well-known dance which was so popular some years back – in fact, both rhythm and notes go very near the original.' And the composer demonstrates this to me by humming the refrain. 'In the first act I have tried to put a good deal of Italian colour into my music. You will notice this especially at the beginning of the opera, and in the duet for the two gondoliers. The second act will savour of Spain to a certain extent, though of course I have not made it up entirely of boleros and other Spanish measures.'

'And the *finale* of the first act?' – 'Well, that portion of the opera is not quite so extended as usual, but I am very pleased with the way it comes out. I think *Iolanthe* contained the longest *finale* I ever wrote. Goodness knows how many pages of the score it covered.'

'How does the amount of labour which you devote to one of your operas compare with the trouble which a concert work gives you?' – 'Well, really there is no comparison between the two cases. People generally think that I can rattle off one of these Savoy pieces without the least difficulty in a very short space of time. But that is far from being the truth. I can assure you that my comic operas – light and airy as they may seem – give me far more trouble and anxiety than a cantata like the *The Golden Legend*. In this latter case, you see, I am quite irresponsible. I have no one to consider but my band and my singers. There is no stage business to worry about, and I can make sure of my effects, because I know just how all the component parts of my body of executants will be placed. It is all straightforward and simple. But when I do an opera for the Savoy it is very different. A quantity of the music has invariably to be rewritten – very often more than once. Either singers are not quite suited, or else I find that the situation, when it takes shape upon the stage, requires something different to what I had anticipated. For these reasons, too, I am only able to begin the orchestration when the rehearsals of the piece are well advanced. It is then that I find out for the first time what sort of accompaniment is wanted for each number. For instance, I might write a quintet with the lightest possible orchestral support. Perhaps Gilbert arranges his business so that the singers are well down the stage. In that case all goes well. But if he considers it necessary to post the five ladies and gentlemen at some distance from the conductor and band, I have to make my accompaniment far more prominent. Otherwise the singers would not hear the orchestra, and we should all be at sixes and sevens. In this opera, now, I have had to reset eight numbers. No, my *Martyr of Antioch* and *Golden Legend*, strange as it may seem, gave me far less mental anxiety than my *Pinafore* and *Pirates*. Naturally enough, I am getting thoroughly into the right groove for this work by force of long experience. Consequently, I know by now pretty well what the requirements of the theatre and the company are. But then we have reached double figures in our productions – the new opera will be our tenth – and so have had plenty of opportunities of learning our way about. But, if you will excuse me, I must go on with my work, and get this overture off my mind.'

'Goodbye Sir Arthur; and please let us have the oboe solo!'

•

PRINCE BISMARCK

Interviewed by William Beatty-Kingston
The Daily Telegraph, 10 and 11 June 1890

Otto Edward Leopold von Bismarck (1815–98), the Prussian statesman who created a united Germany, came from a family of *Junkers* (German aristocrats) and studied law and agriculture before entering the Prussian parliament in 1847. He was a royalist and a reactionary who resisted liberal constitutional and, later, socialist initiatives. During the 1860s he presided over the territorial aggrandizement of Prussia against Denmark and Austria, and, in 1870–71, against France. He was made a prince and chancellor of the German empire and ruled for the next nineteen years, during which time Germany became a modern industrial power and formed strategic military alliances against Russia and France. He resigned from the chancellorship in March 1890, along with his son Herbert, who was his foreign secretary, after a disagreement over policy with the emperor Wilhelm II.

William Beatty-Kingston (1837–1900) became a junior clerk in an English government office at fifteen and was employed in the service of a friendly, foreign power before turning to journalism at twenty-eight. He became the *Daily Telegraph* special correspondent accredited to Prussia. He was headquartered in Berlin, made frequent visits to Vienna, and was also the paper's roving Central European correspondent. Bismarck respected him, but was not as fond of him as the text here would suggest, resenting how well-informed he was. Beatty-Kingston stood 6ft 4in tall and his self-confidence matched his height. He was an extremely independent-minded journalist (incidentally believing that journalists are 'earth-made' not 'heaven-born'). A fluent German speaker, he had many interviews with Bismarck over the years but they were usually off the record. On one occasion Bismarck attempted to have him expelled from the country, but the chancellor yielded to British government pressure. In the introduction to this interview (which I have abridged somewhat), Beatty-Kingston refers to his first interview with Bismarck back in 1867, when the statesman had received him at his official residence in the Wilhelmstrasse wearing 'the dark undress uniform of a Prussian cuirassier regiment'. Now, receviing Beatty-Kingston at his country estate at Friedrichsruh, Bismarck was 'dressed *en bourgeois*, with all the careless simplicity that characterizes the attire of German country gentlemen while residing on their estates "far from the madding crowd"'. Bismarck's conversation with Beatty-Kingston was 'chiefly carried on in the English language, which he speaks with extraordinary force and purity, and to which he invariably reverted from brief episodical lapses into German and French'.

Beatty-Kingston's publications included *Wilhelm I, German Emperor and King of Prussia: A Biographical Sketch* (1883), *Our Chancellor* (1884), *Monarchs I Have Met* (1887), *Men and Manners: Personal Reminiscences and Sketches of Character* (1887), and *Men, Cities and Events* (1895), in which this interview was republished. He also translated *Tosca* (1900) and some other opera libretti.

Passing through a spacious antechamber lined with oaken bookcases, I entered a long narrow drawing-room, in the centre of which stood his Highness talking to the Princess and another lady, the fourth and fifth members of the group being two fine Danish hounds, one a singularly handsome black dog named Tyras. Tyras I was gathered to his fathers at a good old age some three years ago; he died painlessly in his master's bed-room, conscious of the latter's presence to the very last. To quote the Prince's own words: 'A few minutes before the faithful old dog died I spoke to him. He had not the strength to wag his tail; but he opened his eyes, and as he looked at me an expression came over his face that told me – as plainly as if he had spoken – that he recognized me, and wished me well.' Tyras II was the gift of the present Emperor, and is 'more even-tempered, but of a less strongly marked individuality' than his predecessor. The other stately hound, a glossy slate-coloured female, of great strength and beauty, is own grand-daughter to the famous 'Realm-Dog', to which she bears a striking resemblance.

Both dogs, as soon as they caught sight of me, advanced hurriedly, bent on an investigation, which, I rejoice to say, turned out satisfactorily to me as well as to themselves. The Prince also came forward to meet me, shook hands with me very warmly, and welcomed me to Friedrichsruh, saying, 'I am very glad to see you again; we have not met, I think, since 1872.' The congratulations I hastened to offer him upon the manifestly excellent state of his health, were fully warranted by the magnificent robustness of his appearance.

At the age of seventy-five, Prince Bismarck is as upright as a dart, and as firm of foot as many a strong man forty years his junior. His complexion, which used to be sallow when I first knew him, is clear and ruddy; his eyes sparkle with all their old fire and brightness; his voice is mellow and sonorous; his heavy moustache and bushy eyebrows are no whit greyer than they were twenty years ago. He looks younger than his age by a decade at the very least. As I walked by his side through the long suite of apartments, in the first of which he had received me, I could not help saying that he had manifestly benefited by his recent rest from the fatigues of office. 'Rest!' he exclaimed; 'yes, a definitive rest. Official life, as far as I am concerned, is all over and done with. Now I shall have time for some of the recreations I have foregone throughout thirty years. Repose is good; still better is the certainty that I shall not have to change houses any more. You English have a proverb that says "three removes are as bad as a fire", and it is a true one.' I had heard from one of his old friends in Hamburg, to whom he had paid a recent visit, that he had announced his intention of accepting dinner invitations, and attending theatrical representations, in the grand old Hanse-town during the following winter. Knowing how secluded a life he had been wont to lead when in the zenith of his power, I asked him whether he had spoken in jest or in earnest on the occasion referred to.

'In earnest,' he replied. 'Don't you think it is high time that I should have a little amusement and enjoy a few social pleasures?'

It was just eleven a.m. – the loveliest weather imaginable, I may mention – as we passed the dining-room clock, glancing at which he stopped short, and said, 'Will you walk with me? I am going for a stroll through the woods near the house, to make my daily round.' A minute later we had quitted the Schloss, and were pacing briskly down a gentle declivity, leading to a sort of green, half lawn, half meadow, skirted on the right hand by slowly-running water, neither pond nor river, but broad, still, and clear, the obvious home of carp.

Let me try to describe the outward seeming of my illustrious host, as he strode firmly along. He wore a soft, broad-brimmed hat, a thick white neckerchief knotted in front, a long, dark, loose coat buttoned up to the throat, grey trousers, and strong double-soled boots. In his right hand, ungloved, he carried a black stick with a slightly curved handle, upon which he rarely leaned while walking on level ground. His moustache no longer overhangs his whole mouth, as of yore, but has been trimmed comparatively short, so as to show the under lip. He bears himself in his old martial fashion, with head erect and shoulders well thrown back; the incipient corpulence which made him appear somewhat over-bulky about ten years ago has entirely vanished.

While we were walking along a broad path traversing the lower ground of the vast park, we met with more than one party of manifestly 'out-for-the-day' people, who stood aside, uncovering respectfully to his Highness, and with whom he did not once omit to exchange a few kindly words. After the third *rencontre* of this kind, I asked him if there were any public right of way through his woods. 'No, none at all,' he replied. 'Indeed, to keep up my own prescriptive rights of way, I am obliged to put up many boards of warning to trespassers. But my threats of pains and penalties are seldom if ever enforced, and these good folks don't seem to pay much heed to them. My keepers strongly object to holiday encroachers, who disturb the deer, they say. Pheasants? No, I have no pheasants – my woods are too large. The pheasant is a stupid bird, apt to lose itself in extensive cover. You see, I have about twenty thousand English acres here, only four thousand of which are under farming, the rest being woodland. The estate costs me more than it brings in; but I am very fond of it, for all that. I have no gardens here, not even close to the house – nothing but wood and water. My gardens are at Varzin, where my wife grows roses. This is altogether a simple, old-fashioned place; it was an inn once, and I have had to make many alterations. I haven't finished with them yet, either, for my writing-room is too small for me, so I'm going to have one of its walls knocked down, and build on to it. I'll show you what I mean to do by-and-by.'

Here we turned off to the left from the waterside into a narrow side-path, winding its way upwards (by zigzags, provided at each turn with rustic benches, offering solace to a 'climbing sorrow') to the summit of a grassy, copse-crested knoll. Having reached the top, we sat down on one of these opportune seats for a few minutes, and, while resting, fell to talking about Nihilism and the difficulties of carrying on any sort of government in Russia.

I asked the Prince whether, in his opinion, there was no way of defeating Nihilism by timely and generous concessions? 'No,' he replied, rather severely; 'no concessions can be made to the Nihilists, who are would-be murderers, one and all – assassins by premeditation, if not by deed. The only way to deal with them is to strengthen and sharpen the law, and to bring it to bear upon them with increased stringency. There can be no question of yielding to these wretches: nothing kindly or conciliatory can be offered to people who do not even know what they want, but are perfectly ready at all times to commit any sort and number of hideous crimes. Doubtless there are many amiable, reasonable, intelligent Russians who desire moderate reforms, but somehow they don't seem to come to the front, or to exercise any real influence on the authorities in power. With the masses, too, they count for nothing. Over-education in Germany leads to much disappointment and dissatisfaction; in Russia, to disaffection and conspiracy. Ten times as many young people are educated there for the higher walks of life than there are places to give them, or opportunities for them, in the liberal professions, to earn a decent living, far less wealth and distinction. Perhaps it is not quite the right kind of learning, too. There are too many free scholarships and presentations by half, by appointment to which poor people's children are taught to be unhappy and useless. Priests' children, for instance, most get their high school and university education for nothing. What good does it do them? When they have gone through it, in nine cases out of ten there is nothing for them to do, and their learning is worse than a superfluity to them, for it makes them discontented – nay, miserable. They have been painfully prepared to compete for greater prizes than life really offers, save to a very few, who rarely spring from their class. I have come across street watchmen in Russia who had studied in Universities, and taken bachelors' degrees. Could anything be more cruel, as well as absurd? Such people, filled with envy and hatred of all that is prosperous and high placed, readily take to conspiracy and crime. They are not fit to construct, but know just enough to qualify them for destroying. It is much easier to damage than to redeem; so they do evil, and call it redemption. Their training is scholastic, pedantically administered to them; not political or even practical. Hence the difficulty of admitting them to any share in the management of public affairs. Constitutional parliamentary government is a very high order of régime, based on special and diffused knowledge, as well as on many judicious compromises – what you English neatly call "give and take". To entrust it to the hands of ignorant men, theorists, visionaries, enthusiasts utterly unversed in political history and actualities, is sheer folly, or rather dangerous madness. The only thing for such people is strong authority, which of course should be just, high-minded, and, if possible, benevolent. On the other hand, unrestricted authority and its exercise harden officials, who are but men, after all. Too much red-tapeism is noxious; but neither is it wise to set too narrow limits to the power and dignity of the State. With you I think Parliament has too much faculty of interference with the State authority and of harassing governments. Russia, if you like, is in the other extreme. But you are an old Parliamentary people, accustomed to party life, and familiar with the necessity of mutual concession at the right moment. The Russians, as I said before, don't know what they want, nor when to stand out, nor when to yield. They are extremists in the politics they don't understand, and are the prey of dogmas or of ideas, as the case may be. At present there is nothing for it but to rule them with an iron rod.'

As, at a leisurely pace, we were strolling downhill by another tortuous woodland path, the labour question cropped up, apropos of the recent Miners' Congress in Belgium. After frankly recognizing and praising the moderation of Mr Burt's address to the delegates, Prince Bismarck abruptly broke out with: 'Tell me, did you ever know a banker with a million who was contented? – or a scientist, politician, artist, lawyer, satisfied with his gains and position? I will go further, and ask you, Have you ever known a contented man? I mean, among the rich, the successful, the highly-born, or highly-placed? How then shall the working-man be contented, whose life is necessarily one of few pleasures and many troubles, of frequent privation and rare indulgence? The more operatives get, the more they want. I don't say it is not natural, not that they differ from other men in this respect; but the fact remains. Let what real grievances they still have right themselves by natural processes, as they will gradually and in due time. Above all, let them continue to improve their position without State interference, which can only do them more harm than good, besides inflicting irretrievable injury upon numbers of other people, quite as worthy of consideration as artisans. I call it intrusive and impertinent to dictate to a labourer how many hours he shall or shall not work, and to usurp his rightful authority over his children in respect to bread-earning occupations. It is said that I first set the example of meddling with workmen's affairs in Germany, and took the initiative in introducing a sort of State Socialism. This is by no means correct. What I did was in the direction of benevolence, not of interference. I advocated the making of some provision for workmen enfeebled by old age, or incapacitated for labour by sickness or accident. I felt that if a mechanician were maimed by some engine, or a miner mutilated by a colliery explosion – or if a man broke down through over-work or bodily illness – something should be done to save him from starvation, or even from an extremity of want. I also thought it desirable, in the true interest of the working classes, that the management and control of funds raised for these purposes should be transferred from red-tape officials to self-supporting corporations, like your benevolent societies, and in this way to promote the development of corporate spirit and enterprise among our working men. I wanted to emancipate them from official restraint and surveillance, to foster in them a passion for self-help, and a love of manly independence, and to inspire them with a feeling of security against the utmost calamities that can befall them – infirmity, crippledom, old age, embittered by abject poverty. When I first recommended my scheme to William I he did not at once understand it in all its bearings; but as soon as they became fully and clearly apparent to him he took it up eagerly, and during the latter years of his life it was his favourite project. Nobody was more deeply interested in it, or more fervently anxious for its success, then he. But to make workmen contented by legal regulations is a mere exaggeration of the fancy – a phantom, evading the grasp whenever approached. If human contentment could be attained, it would be a misfortune. What could be more disastrous than a dead-level of well-being, a millennium of universal satisfaction, blighting ambition, paralysing progress, and leading to moral stagnation? There is plenty of useful work to be done, however, in the way of imparting technical instruction to operatives, loosening the hold of bureaucracy upon them, and encouraging them to undertake the intelligent management of their own affairs, and the safeguarding of their interests by lawful and orderly means, instead of making war upon their employers. Capital and labour ought to be the firmest of friends, and would be so, no doubt, but that each desires to take a little advantage of the other. That, of course, is a purely human characteristic, and we cannot hope to change the nature of mankind. The rights of capital are no less real and respectable than those of labour. We must not forget that!'

As we were nearing the schloss Prince Bismarck spoke to me very favourably of his successor in the Chancellorship, General Caprivi, as 'a fine soldier, a man of remarkable intelligence and varied information – above all, *a thorough gentleman*. I am sure,' continued his Highness, 'that Caprivi's appointment as Reichskanzler was an absolute surprise to him, that he accepted it from a lofty and loyal sense of duty, and that he is quite free from any charge of overweening personal ambition. He has a clear head, a good heart, a generous nature, and great working powers. Altogether a first-class man.'

It was nearly one o'clock when our stroll through the home park of Schloss Friedrichsruh ended, and the ex-Chancellor led the way up a steep flight of stone steps, which we ascended to the strains of a sentimental barrel-organ, ground by a swarthy Neapolitan who had effected a lodgment on the carriage drive fronting the main entrance. From a broad flagged terrace, corresponding in length to the dining room, we passed through a lofty glass door into that apartment, in which luncheon was laid out. The Princess, with three friends, was awaiting us in an adjoining drawing-room. Without further delay we took our places at the table, where we were joined a little later by Count Herbert, much sunburnt, and looking the picture of health, strength, and good humour. Against the right-hand wall of the Friedrichsruh 'Speisesaal', exactly behind the seat occupied by the 'Schlossherrin', stood a life-size full-length portrait of Kaiser Wilhelm II, copied from the original oil painting by Professor Angeli, and representing the young Emperor in full uniform, resting his right hand upon a table, on which are displayed his helmet and the Imperial diadem. It is a huge canvas, about ten feet by six, and somewhat dwarfed all the other pictures in the stately room. During luncheon – at which the two noble hounds assisted, with keen but decorously restrained interest – the conversation was general, touching lightly on many topics of interest, and affording to the Prince abundant opportunity for the display of his unrivalled anecdotical powers and inexhaustible mother-wit. As the meal progressed, I observed that he drank nothing with his food, and asked him whether 'eating dry' were a habit of his own choice, or an article in the dietetic code drawn up for him by his famous 'Leibarzt', Dr Schweninger.

'The latter,' he replied. 'I am only allowed to drink thrice a day – a quarter of an hour after each meal, and each time not more than half a bottle of red sparkling Moselle, of a very light and dry character. Burgundy and beer, both of which I am extremely fond of, are strictly forbidden to me; so are all the strong Rhenish and Spanish wines, and even claret! For some years past I have been a total abstainer from all these generous liquors, much to the advantage of my health and my "condition," in the sporting sense of the word. Formerly I used to weigh over seventeen stone. By observing this regimen I brought myself down to under fourteen, and without any loss of strength – indeed, with gain. My normal weight is now 185lb. I am weighed once every day by my doctor's orders, and any excess of that figure I at once set to work to get rid of, by exercise and special regimen. I ride a good deal, as well as walk. Cigar-smoking I have given up altogether, of course under advice. It is debilitating and bad for the nerves. An inveterate smoker, such as I used to be, probably gets through a hundred thousand cigars in his life, if he reaches a fair average age. But he would live longer, and feel better all his time, if he did without them. Nowadays I am restricted to a long pipe, happily with a deep bowl, one after each meal, and I smoke nothing in it but Dutch Knaster tobacco, which is light, mild, and soothing. You will see presently; the pipe comes in with the pint of red Moselwein. It will be a whole bottle today, and you must help me out with it. Water makes me fat, so I must not drink it. However, the present arrangements suit me very well.'

As soon as the reign of tobacco had definitively set in, the ladies left us, and I changed my seat for one near the head of the table, next to that of his Highness.

After some desultory talk, having reference to times long past and to persons with whom we had been acquainted in common more than a score of years previously – à propos of whom he made the remark, 'My memory is fairly tenacious; but I have personal acquaintance with at least thirty thousand men whose names escape me, though they are mostly people of some note' – I casually observed that his retirement had been unexpected in English political circles, and had taken the general British public quite by surprise.

He replied, 'I dare say it seemed rather sudden to you. Even my kind friends here in Germany scarcely expected it – those dear friends who rejoiced over my renouncement of all my offices, who greedily coveted my political succession, and who now wish me to become one of the living dead – to lurk in my retreat, dumb-foundered, silence-stricken, and motionless. It would be somewhat difficult for me, don't you think so, after forty years' incessant occupation and absorption in political study – after such a tremendous spell of activity and responsibility – to play a part the two inviolable conditions of which are speechlessness and immobility? That is what they want me to do – my kind friends who even sedulously forbear from alluding to my past services to Germany, and from referring to what I have done in the world, lest by comparison they should stunt their own pretensions to recognition, distinction, and advancement. But I am not so easily silenced and paralysed. I can continue, in retirement, to serve my country, and I mean to do so to the last. In some respects I have a freer hand than I had when I was in office. Abroad – for instance, in France and Russia, the only countries possibly bearing us a grudge – I can in many ways promote the propaganda of peace, my main object and aim for twenty years past, now that I am unfettered by any official restraints.

'What is the actual state of Germany's relations with France? you ask. Excellent, indeed; all that both countries can wish it to be. The attitude of the French Government is exemplary; the French people are sincerely pacific, alike in views and hopes. I need not to tell you how peaceably disposed the Germans are; no one is more earnest for peace than his Majesty the Emperor, whose attention is eagerly bent upon home affairs, upon national consolidation, internal improvements, and the establishment of a cordial understanding between class and class. We Germans want nothing from our neighbours but fair dealing and civil treatment. We fought two terrible wars to achieve our unity; we have got it, and mean to keep it; we ask no more. All our armament is purely defensive and precautionary; not a bit of it is intended for attack. No idea of aggression or of further frontier extension finds a lodging in the head of any intelligent German.'

I asked him if, in his opinion, there was no possibility of finally extinguishing the French grievance against the Fatherland by some voluntary and spontaneous concession on the part of Germany – some rectification of frontier involving the retrocession to France of the French-speaking populations now unwillingly submitting to German rule – some arrangement, in short, that would satisfy France without imperilling the security of Germany. 'There is none,' he answered, quite decisively. 'We can yield no territory to them, except after a lost battle. Were the cession small or large, it would only stimulate their appetite for more. They have held provinces inhabited by German-speaking populations for centuries – provinces of which they robbed us by force. Let us now have our turn at holding territories peopled by a French-speaking race. Germany has never wilfully or unprovoked entered France. France has invaded Germany in arms between twenty and thirty times. In 1870 the Frenchmen had all but forgotten their "rights" over Cologne and Mayence; but the Rhine-Line cry was revived fiercely enough then, and would be again if we were to show any disposition to restore any part of Lorraine to them. As far as the subsidence of their resentment against us is concerned, we can only trust to time, as you English did in the case of Waterloo. That grievance died thirty years ago. Victor Hugo did his best to resuscitate it; but the pale ghost he raised soon fell flat, and vanished. It is scarcely possible to content the French, because their self-appreciation knows no reasonable limits. I remember that, whilst I was Minister in Paris, one of my best French friends was old Marshal Vaillant, then Governor of the Tuileries. He was a charming old gentleman, and really had a great regard for me. One day, in 1867, he said to me, "See, my friend, I like you; I like the Germans; in particular I like the Prussian; but I know that we shall have to cross bayonets with you one of these days. We other Frenchmen are like a barndoor cock, ruling the roost, and we cannot bear that any other cock should crow audibly in Europe except ourselves." It was through him I found out that the troops of the Paris garrison had had an eye on me. I had been present at a review in Paris, at the Emperor's invitation, and had watched the march-post closely – not more closely, however, than the soldiers had watched me, it seems. The next day old Vaillant came to see me, and gleefully repeated to me some of the professional comments to which I had given rise. One was *En voilà un qui n'a pas froid aux yeux! Voyez-vous, mon cher*, added the Marshal, *j'aurais bien volontiers donné mon bâton et ma plaque pour qu'ils l'eussent dit de moi!* It was very nice of him, and showed that though a Frenchman, he did not overrate himself or his military reputation.

'What are our prospects in connection with Russia? Quite satisfactory; as good in every respect as they are with regard to France. We wish well to Russia, and she will certainly not attack us. The Russian people is as peaceably inclined as our own. The evils that befell them after, and in consequence of, the last war were so much more cruel and terrible than any they had had to endure in time of peace that they conceived a horror of all military enterprises abroad, and this antipathy has lasted, undiminished in force and intensity, until the present day. Russia owes us no real grudge, and we shall not give her the least cause of quarrel. I have been honoured by the regard and confidence of the present Czar. Whilst I was in office he placed implicit trust in my personal assurances, and I am happy to say that Russo-German official relations were of the most friendly character. Czar Alexander III is really an amiable, kindly, well-meaning Sovereign, fond of his home, deeply attached to his wife and children, amicably disposed to Germany, and sincerely averse to conquest. He also extremely dislikes violent physical exertion, and this is a fact by no means without importance to the peace of Europe. As to the look-out in Bulgaria, I can really give no opinion. Bulgaria is of no direct interest at all to us Germans, and we pay very little attention to her, as long as she keeps tolerably quiet. The Triple Alliance is strong enough to make sure that European tranquillity shall not be seriously disturbed on her account.

'How does the Alliance stand just now? As steadfast as ever; firmly founded on a broad basis of mutual trust and common interests. It is no less close in its cohesion than immovable in its resolve to maintain peace. It will endure, because it is for the good of all, and the natural outcome at once of salutary aspirations and of common sense. There are plenty of good reasons why the principle of its being should be "Each for all, and all for each." A strong Austria is not only essential to the preservation of the European balance of power, but is especially necessary to Germany. Were there no such realm, it would have to be created in our interest. Both the leading elements in the Dual Reich – the German and Hungarian – are well disposed towards us; the former for many obvious reasons, the latter because, knowing itself not strong enough to stand alone, it feels the need of a potent foreign friend who will stand by it at a pinch, and does not believe that it could find that friend in Russia – an absorbent Power greatly feared by all its weak neighbours. The friendship, again, binding Germany and Italy together is a perfectly natural one, as they are not *limitrophe* States, and neither desires to deprive the other of aught. Amity between Austria and Italy is equally necessary to both, seeing that their frontiers join – a circumstance which always entails many potentialities of mutual molestation and consequent quarrel. A more sensible and useful League was never formed than the Triple Alliance, a grand mainstay of which, most fortunately, is the sincere, hearty, faithful friendship subsisting between the Sovereigns of Germany, Austria, and Italy, who entertain the highest personal regard for one another, and are all three extremely popular with their respective subjects. In such supreme contracts Ministers are far less important than Monarchs, even in constitutionally-governed countries blessed with Parliamentary institutions.

'Thanks to the Triple Alliance, I am enabled to believe, and to openly declare my belief, that the peace of Europe is soundly guaranteed, and that its continuance is well assured for a long time to come, unless the Almighty should think fit to ordain one of those tremendous accidents that defeat all foresight and reasonable calculation.

'As for England and Germany, I regard it as an impossibility that these two countries should ever be at war, and as singularly unlikely that they should even quarrel seriously. Were that to happen, however, it might lead to a Continental conflict, even if England should abstain from taking any active part against us by sea or land. But this contingency is as wildly improbable as that we should draw the sword against England. Differences, of course, may occur, as in this African colonial matter, still awaiting equitable settlement. Every such difference between yourselves and us, however, can only be of altogether inconsiderable moment compared to the consequences of an appeal to arms. If we growl a little at one another, that is nothing to be alarmed at. Looking this African affair straight in the face, what does it amount to? In your British Company, I believe, about half a million sterling is embarked; in our German Company, something less. Put the two amounts together, and the sum total at stake does not equal one day's expenditure in mere preparation for a great war. For every man drawn into the ranks by the mobilization process we must reckon, on the average, a loss of two shillings a day, his earnings, and an outlay of three shillings a day for his food, clothing, pay, and transport. A general European war means the mobilization of at least four millions of reserve troops, so there you have your waste of a million per diem for two or three weeks, perhaps, before a shot is fired. After hostilities commence, we may take that waste as doubled in daily amount. All this is without counting the cost of commercial standstills, panics, depreciation of securities, which are more ruinous than war expenses. In the case of England and Germany's colonial rivalry, the object to be attained on either part or both parts – if their double success could be estimated – can never, appraise it as high as you will, be anything like equivalent to the certain calamity that would result from a serious Anglo-German encounter with hot lead and cold steel, all about the partition of regions the worth of which is altogether problematical. For few trustworthy Europeans know anything about these mysterious territories – scarcely even their names. No fear that England and Germany will ever come to blows about them. For my part, I feel sure that Lord Salisbury's temperate and statesmanlike utterances are more to the English taste than Mr Stanley's hot exhortations and bitter denunciations. Between Germans and Englishmen it is always easy to come to a righteous and amicable understanding. We are both fair-dealing peoples; we know one another well, and respect one another sincerely. There has been so much arrant nonsense talked and written about this paltry affair that a few plain words, dictated by common reason, can do no harm.'

A little later our conversation turned upon the late Emperor Frederick, of whom Prince Bismarck spoke in terms of deep reverence and warm admiration. 'He was indeed a most remarkable and estimable man, perfectly amiable, exquisitely kind, and yet no less intelligent, clear-sighted, instructed and resolute. He knew his mind thoroughly, and his determinations, once adopted, were immovable. As German Emperor, had he lived, he would have considerably astonished the world at large by the vigour and personality of his rule. His views of his duties to his subjects, and of his subjects' duties to their Sovereign, were accurately defined and quite unchangeable. He was a true Hohenzollern, of the very finest quality and most brilliant capacities. As for his courage, it was heroic. In respect to the gentle courtesy and delicate consideration he showed to his servants, he resembled his noble father.

'Let me give you a pathetic instance of this fine and gracious trait in his character. During the latter days of his illness, in which he could still – sitting up and dressed – receive me, he never once failed, when I took my leave, to accompany me to the door of his room, nor to open it with his own hands in order to let me out. One day, as he was walking by my side across the room for this purpose, I saw him stagger with pain and weakness, and was just raising my arms to catch him – thinking he was about to fall down – when he managed to seize the door-handle, and, by holding on to it, to keep his feet. Opening the door, he leant back so much, in his agony, that his coat-tails were hanging at least six inches distant from his body; but he neither complained nor groaned, and bore his sufferings so bravely, in manly silence, that it was pitiful to see. Yes, to the very last he evinced a lofty sense of Imperial dignity, authority, and fortitude. Nothing could shake his self-command or ruffle his temper; he was every inch a Kaiser, to the hour of his death. To me, all through that dreadful time, he was in every way admirable – I can find no better word. We perfectly understood one another, and I was his true, devoted servant, as I had been his father's for so many years. Since her awful bereavement, by the way, the Empress Victoria's attitude towards Germany has been, and now is, absolutely irreproachable – the complete realization of a high ideal.'

Before permitting me to quit Friedrichsruh, Prince Bismarck took me over all the ground floor rooms, accompanied by Count Herbert, who, as well as his illustrious father, was at great pains to point out to me countless objects of historical and family interest. In a corridor, leading out of the hall, hangs a metal open-work screen, to which are affixed the armorial bearings of all the five branches of the House of Bismarck, as well as the arms of the noble families quartered with those of the Prince – all correctly emblazoned. In the rooms of the reception-suite, my attention was called to two life-like portraits of his Highness, taken, comparatively recently, by Professor Lembach; two masterly busts of the first German Emperor and of Count Wilhelm von

Bismarck, the Prince's second son; to a stirring battle-piece representing the memorable charge of the 1st Guard Dragoons, at Mars-la-Tour, 'in which tussle', observed the Prince, 'Herbert was badly wounded, and Bill had his horse shot under him. You can see Herbert in the picture, charging just behind his captain'; fine portraits of the ex-Chancellor's father, grandfather, great-grandfather, and a few ancestors contemporary with the Spanish Armada and the Thirty Years War respectively, as well as a striking likeness of himself, taken in the year 1850, and well-executed 'counterfeit presentments' of our Queen, of Frederick William IV, of the King of Saxony, Lord Beaconsfield, Cardinal Hohenlohe, and many another exalted personage of past and present times.

Then, having earnestly thanked the stately Schlossherr for all his kindness and graceful hospitality, I shook hands with him once, twice, and thrice, and took my leave, carrying away with me from Friedrichsruh the pleasantest and most interesting of remembrances. Father and son saw me off at the chief entrance, and waved a final adieu to me, as I passed through the park gate into the grey roadway skirting the railway line and leading to the station.

•

GENERAL WILLIAM BOOTH

Interviewed by *The Pall Mall Gazette*, 4 October 1890

William Booth (1829–1912), the English religious leader and philanthropist, was born into poverty in Nottingham. He was converted to Methodism in 1844 and began to preach on Tyneside. Feeling that Methodism was inadequate in its approach to social problems, he founded the 'Christian Mission' in the East End of London in 1865 and in 1878 this became the Salvation Army. At first he was scorned and some of his troops were imprisoned for open-air preaching. He campaigned against sweated labour and child prostitution. In 1890 he published his book *In Darkest England, and the Way Out*, in which he set out his programme for helping the poor. He was later showered with honours, both in England and the United States.

During the last two or three days, *In Darkest England, and the Way Out* has been canvassed in conversation and in print from every conceivable point of view. The clearing air shows one or two objections or interrogations in clear relief; among others, the one which in friendly criticism we have asked ourselves, as to the 'Sanction of the Kick'. On this and other points, a representative has sought light from General Booth himself.

We began on the prospects of the scheme, and its reception by press and public.

'I have had four Agnostics here this morning,' quoth the General, with a merry twinkle – 'one of them, a well-known man, I might rather call an aggressive Atheist – and they are full of the scheme; they are sick of the do-nothing policy. As for the press – I am well enough satisfied, on the whole. There's a good deal, so far as I've read at present, about my egotism and ignorance of previous workers and of those now working in the same field, which I don't think is fair. I did try to read the thing up – I've done a good deal of reading for a busy man. I couldn't have alluded to the others without saying something in the way of criticizing their methods, or explaining their failure. After all, there are the three millions, aren't there? The existence of those three millions shows that other methods haven't got very far. The *Times* article? No, I didn't much like the temper of the *Times* article – a bit grudging, as you say, a bit carping – but there! What does it matter? A gentleman came here to me to-day almost with tears in his eyes, after reading about my scheme in the *Times*. He read it over three times to his wife, he said, and then came right along here from Nottingham. He was tremendously struck with it, even from the sketchy account they gave, and also with their not finding anything better to say against it than they did; and he promised me £1,000.'

'I must mention that, for the edification of the *Times* leader-writer. Have you had many such offers already?'

'Several. I feel quite happy about getting the money. I see the *Standard*, for want of anything better to say, says the scheme ought to support itself. Support itself! Here are we in England spending ten millions every year on our poor-law, and seven millions in private charities, and nobody knows how many millions in public charities, besides all that's spent on law and police and prisons – (did you see that case the other day of a woman who came up before some magistrates, and they said she'd been up – wasn't it some seventy-something times before?) – and in the face of all this the *Standard* calmly tells me to tackle the whole evil, on which all this money is poured forth, root and branch, and do it all without costing anybody a penny! It is a little too early to ask that just yet. When we've got some way forward, though, I see myself saying to some rate-ridden municipality which spends ten thousand a year on its poor, "Here, give me your paupers and £5,000." Thus I shall look to keep extending my area, and running the thing cheaper as I go on.'

'Tell me, General: what have you to say to the *crux* of the whole scheme, the question of "sanctions"? The difficulty in fighting the sweaters, as you know, is the existence of a huge mass of poor creatures, nerveless in mind and body, out of whom no work can be got except by the application of an amount of driving which is the sweater's *raison d'être*. Suppose, after a turn of rations and work, the old feeling of wanting to loaf and chance it about the streets comes on again, will you *make* a man work? Will you enforce discipline? Will you turn him out if he doesn't work? Or will you just pray over him and let him off?'

The moment the words were out of my mouth, the General was emphatic and voluble in answer. 'Pray over him, yes. Let him off, condone a breach of discipline, no! How do you suppose this Army is run, except on the plan of every man and woman in it obeying every order without a moment's question? Tell me I don't know how to keep discipline? Why, in my own family, among my own children, any one of them from the cradle up would as soon think of not shutting that door, say, if I said "Shut the door", as they would think of flying. Discipline!' cried the General again, thumping a large fist into a large palm, with the look of one who was ready to discipline a bargee, 'Why, it's other folk whom I complain of for not having enough of it. A man who cannot rule himself is not only willing to be ruled – he yearns to be ruled. Fellows come out of prison, where they haven't been able to call their souls their own, disgraced, drilled, broken, ready to obey any one and go any one else's way, to God or the devil. They go elsewhere and get a cup of coffee and a slice. They come here and find themselves straight away under a strong hand (here another vigorous gesture) – and it helps them, and they work under it.'

'Yes, yes,' I ventured to object, 'but, as you are sure to have some impossibles to deal with, who will require "the sanction of the kick" in some form or another, will you give it them?'

'Certainly. First offence, caution and record. Second offence, fine – impound the small moneys which will be saving up in our charge. Third offence – out he goes: goes back to the slough, and wallows there again till he gets really sick and comes round again to me. That's the ultimate sanction.' Drunkenness, or bringing drink on to the estate from outside, will be the sort of offence a man will go out on pretty quick. But neither will I have laziness. Of course, we are all the slaves of habit, and a sodden loafer must have easy jobs at first. But if he doesn't show that he is trying to work, if I can neither prick an ambition in him for this world nor for the next, I won't keep him. In the Dutch colonies they very rarely have to expel. But, of course, I'm prepared for a residuum of very poor creatures, whom it will take me all my time to get the four shillings a week out of – the four shillings which they will cost to keep. All I ask is that they shall try. I take it that most people can get on in the world somehow, as long as they keep good. My object will be to make them keep good, and you see there will be the nosebag of something better always before their noses. Even when I punish I'll have the nosebag only an inch or two away. But,' said the General, with an impressiveness which showed clearly what it is that he himself most relies on, 'you forget one thing. You forget the *spirit* that will be among them. You don't know how it gets hold of people. They may care precious little for religion, and yet be glad of bright, cheery companionship, working in a gang under an officer who works shoulder to shoulder and sings with them at the work. Look at what we are doing already in Whitechapel. Go down and look at the hundred fellows whom we have doing eight hours a day, and looking for work and finding it, and giving way to fresh comers. No bad language – no disobedience. I tell you it gets hold of them. Take the work with a class generally regarded as the most hopeless of any – the women in the rescue homes. We lock no doors. We keep no one. We let no one off work. And we lose, we admit, 40 per cent. We allow so much for breakages. But for 60 per cent we get places – they don't always stick to them, of course, but many do, and we have about three hundred now in London alone out in situations. My great difficulty has been hitherto that I have only had domestic service to put them into and that often means in some dull, prim, puritanical maiden lady's household who makes godliness insufferable. Now I shall be able to send them down to help with fruit and flowers and poultry, and all sorts of small industrial occupations. In fact, it isn't the wicked and the degraded that I regard as the problem. It's the idle. I always used to say, "I can do something with any man so long as he isn't idle. With idleness I can do nothing". Now I am going to tackle idleness. And I shall do it like a father with a spoilt child. Heaps of grown-up people, miserable though they be, are only children who have been spoilt, or have spoilt themselves. They will find a firm hand here.'

He looked it, every inch. I couldn't help asking him, on a sudden impulse, a question I had often wished to put to this most absolute of rulers.

'General, you are a monument of Caesarism. I believe you are the very man to deal with the "submerged tenth". But with the Army itself, have you never thought that a more democratic basis would be good for it? Suppose you announced that there would be an election to the Generalship on January 1, and presented yourself for re-election? Why not? You would get in, of course; and the men would feel they were helping to govern themselves' . . .

The General was quiet, but firm. 'Who ever heard of an army having a general election in the field?' he said. 'Don't you see that everything depends on this organization working like an automaton? Parliamentary government would be fatal to it. If A had a say in the arrangements, when I gave him an order he would feel bound to discuss it; B, with the best intentions, would propose an amendment; and nothing would get done. All hangs on their believing that I am what I say I am – an unselfish worker for God. While they believe that, they obey. The minute they ceased to believe it, the whole fabric would crumble away. But stop – this is a big subject, and not strictly business. I hope you're satisfied about the sanction? Good-bye, then. You won't join us, eh? We shall want—'

But at the danger signal I had fled. You interview General Booth with your life in your hand, so to speak. A strong man is General Booth, with the strength of one who is always ready to learn, but who knows exactly what he means.

•

RUDYARD KIPLING

Interviewed by *The Sunday Herald* , 23 October 1892

Kipling had co-written a novel, *The Naulahka*, with his agent Wolcott Balestier, an American whom he had met in London. When Wolcott died in Germany, Kipling married his sister Caroline Balestier and in 1892 the couple came to live in Brattleboro, Vermont, where Caroline's father had maintained a substantial summer home. The Kiplings built a house with a commanding view of the Connecticut valley which they named 'Nauhlahka'. Caroline's brother Beatty, who also lived in the area, was said to have supplied Kipling with the material for a syndicated story about Vermont people, which was published only a short while after Kipling arrived and which aroused the indignation of the locals. They came to regard Kipling as eccentric and cranky, while Beatty Balestier feuded with his brother-in-law following a land dispute. Kipling sued Beatty for threatening him with a deadly assault, and in order to embarrass him Beatty insisted on refusing to seek bail, thus obliging Kipling himself to bail him. Eventually, the embarrassment drove the Kiplings out of Vermont and they settled in England. This interview appeared in the Boston *Sunday Herald*.

'Yes, I am a boor. I am glad of it. I don't care. I want people to know it.'

That's what Mr Rudyard Kipling is. It's so, for 'he himself hath said it', and those were his last words to the writer as he left him the other day, after having had an interview with a man who is probably one of the most peculiar persons in the world.

Mr Kipling was not at home, but he was out walking, so I drove out past his sunny house on Brattleboro's outskirts, and presently saw a figure bounding down a steep hillside above the road. It was unmistakably Kipling, whom I had so often heard described.

A little, short, stocky body stopped at a barbed wire fence. The legs that supported the body were not very stout. They were covered with a pair of old, skin-tight, brownish, trousers. He wore a very faded greenish Norfolk jacket. A neglige shirt collar and black silk four-in-hand, showed at the neck. His face is dark, he has a crisp, dark brown mustache, determined mouth, sharp, rather retreating eyes, covered by double lens gold bowed spectacles, topped by heavy eyebrows, and his full, broad forehead is covered by not very thick brown hair. He wore a huge, light gray slouch hat, which is his invariable headgear, and by which he is known for miles as a landmark, as it were. This hat makes him look too heavy. In his right hand was a tall staff, that he always carries. His strange looks would betoken a strange man. His appearance was consistent with what was expected.

He halted at the fence at my inquiry.

'Mr Kipling?'

'At your service, sir.'

'May I speak with you a few moments? I am a reporter –'

Fatal word! As soon as he heard it a muttered exclamation in violation of the third commandment was heard, and he pushed between the barbed wire strands regardless of clothes or limb.

'Look out, Mr Kipling, for that wire.'

'It's a d—n sight better than such as you are!' and he was through and out upon the road in a jiffy.

This would never do for an interview. The patient steed stood blinking in the sun while I got out of the buggy and followed after the doughty Kipling.

'Mr Kipling, I come to you as one gentle man would accost another in the street. I did not come under guise of a casual caller, as I was advised.' I explained my assignment to him, he standing with his hands on his staff, looking me through with those piercing eyes.

This was his encouraging reply: 'I refuse to be interviewed. It is a crime. I never was. I never will be. You have no more right to stop me for this than to hold me up like a highwayman. It is an outrage to assault a man on the public way. In fact, this is worse. If you have anything to ask, submit it in writing to me at my house.' With this he darted away.

Here was encouragement. He would say something. So I drew up this document, which was handed to Mr Kipling's servant when she answered my ring a little later:

'Mr Kipling: You having declined to submit to an interview, will you kindly state for the benefit of newspaper men your objections.

'I respectfully submit that your treatment of me was rude and boorish when you were approached as one gentleman would approach another. Will you kindly talk with me five minutes, man to man? What you say in that time I will not use unless I have your permission.'

This somewhat succinct and straightforward document I signed. There was a wait of about 10 minutes.

While waiting I noticed the house and surroundings. The Kiplings live in a little cottage on the Bliss farm, owned by the Balestiers, his wife's people. A great clothes reel in the corner made by the L added to the commonplaceness of the scene. But there is a magnificent view down the Connecticut valley. The parlor, as seen through the open door, is a small room, quite plainly furnished with chairs, sofa, table, Kensington rug on the painted floor and some cabinets and curios from far off India.

Presently the only Kipling came out from the dining table where the maid said he was. I heard him inquire for his 'club'. This sounded auspicious, indeed. He didn't bring it out, however.

'Well, what do you want? Why do you invade the privacy of my house? Didn't I say I wouldn't be interviewed?' These in a quick, jerky way.

'Mr Kipling. I did as you asked, and submitted a question or topic in writing at your house, and I desire an answer.'

I got it.

'Why do I refuse to be interviewed? Because it is immoral! It is a crime, just as much a crime as an offence against my person, as an assault, and just as much merits punishment. It is cowardly and vile. No respectable man would ask it, much less give it.'

'Well, Mr Kipling, just as respectable men as you, if not more so – for they were gentlemen – disagree with you. You are the first man I ever heard of who took this view of it. I never heard the words immoral and criminal applied to it before.'

'Then they were fools. I am right. All I say is true. No, I won't give you any reasons, for you fellows, with your American lack of appreciation and understanding of journalism, couldn't comprehend what I mean. We Englishmen abhor it. What good are reporters, anyway? What do you expect to become or get out of it? The American press is dirty and rotten. I know all about it. I went once with a party of Philadelphia newspaper boys out to a little town where a murder had been committed, and they made that town out a perfect little hell. I tell you, all they want is sensationalism, and you won't get it from me.' At this point I registered a mental note that I was getting it. But he kept on.

'There isn't a single respectable paper in this country. The *New York Tribune* is bearable, but that has some beastly thing in it every now and then that damns it, too. I suppose you want to write me up and put me into some obscure place in your old sheet, though I don't know what one it is.'

'No, sir,' I interrupted, 'you are worth top of column, first page, next to pure reading matter. This treatise on the American press is so gratuitous and new it will not be relegated to an out-of-the-way place.

'Mr Kipling,' I went on, 'you are a citizen of the world, and you owe it something and it owes you.'

'Yes, and that little debt has got to be paid me first,' he snapped back, 'and I shall never pay mine.'

'You are an advanced thinker, a man of reputation, and what you would say on any subject would be valuable and interesting.'

'Valuable,' continued he, 'yet that's another reason why I can't afford to be interviewed. I can get more by writing it myself and selling it to some English magazine, and then I suppose your American publishers would steal it, as they have most of my books. My books contain all I want to say, and they have been bought or stolen, as people choose. The American copy right law is damnable.'

Trying him on a new task, I gave him this: 'You were a member of the press, and the profession wants to know what you have to say. You owe it something.'

'Damn little,' said he, in a way that almost removed any sense of profanity from that little word. It is really almost a pleasure to hear Mr Kipling swear. He has a little English brogue, touched with a tinge of the accent of India, that gives the word of the 'big, big D' a really fascinating sound.

'You may be sure the press owes you less, Mr Kipling,' rejoined the *Herald* man, 'for I very much doubt if ever a newspaper man was treated with less courtesy than in the present instance. You were approached as a gentleman, and your reception and remarks led me to give you a straight tip as to what I thought of you, since you so frankly-expressed your opinion.'

'I admire your frankness,' he replied.

From all that is heard of Kipling, it appears that no one ever answers back to his rough and boorish remarks. He was silent a moment. Then he said:

'Your note I shall preserve as priceless among my literacy curiosities, sir,' but he was assured the favor was mine, and I was glad to have done it, for it showed him what a gentleman thought of him.

'I don't care a damn what you think. You have invaded my rights as a private citizen; and if I could reach you by law I would. I never heard the like before. Now what are you going to say about me? I wish you wouldn't say anything, for I don't care to be quoted.'

'You could hardly expect such courtesy as yours to a brother of your former profession to go unacknowledged, could you?'

He said again he should prefer that nothing be said.

He would see no reason or sense in the fact that when an assignment was given it was to be covered as well as it could be. 'Tell your managing editor,' he went on, 'he doesn't know how to run a paper if he orders an interview, and in this case, when you knew I hated it, you should have told him you shouldn't and wouldn't come.'

'Why, Mr Kipling, I wouldn't have missed this interview, to use your favorite word, for anything.' A flashing of his eyes and a heavy scowl was his reply, and then. 'You haven't got anything, anyway.'

'Oh, yes, I have. I've got enough to tell people to keep away from you.'

'That's what I want.'

Mr Kipling made one extravagant statement, in reply in a question. He stood and took me in with his sharp eyes.

'I suppose you are reading me and my characteristics to use in some of your books.' I am taking you in and sizing you up too.

'What do you think?'

'I am not sure it would be so complimentary that you would like to hear it.'

He didn't ask, but denied that he ever put the personal characteristics he observed into his writings. 'It would be discourteous and cowardly and so nasty mean, you know.'

Mr Kipling denied the old story that he was once told by a New York reporter that if he (Kipling) would sign an interview, it would be used, no matter what it was, and that he told the reporter to write any d—d nonsense he pleased and he would sign it.

He wouldn't do it now, either, not even to endorse his revelation to American journalism that interviewing was immoral and a crime.

Mr Kipling said that had a gentleman – 'even you' – accosted him as I had done, and had asked him for a few minutes' chat, he would have been delighted. There was no brigandage in that, but I was a highwayman because I was a reporter. He wouldn't give any credit because he was not deceived in the way he was approached.

'English journalism,' said Mr Kipling, 'is dignified and respectable. There is no dirty business in it. What you Americans call enterprise is cheap sensationalism of the cheapest sort. The English editor does not insult any respectable man by asking his ideas. They are his own, the same as his home is, and no one has a right to invade them.

'The American reporter is a blot on the journalistic escutcheon, and when one perpetrates a crime, as you have done, he ought to be locked up where he couldn't do any harm. There is nothing in American journalism to admire and less to respect. The English reporter is a gentleman and lets people alone.'

Finally, the maid came to remind him that his dinner was still waiting. He must go. He was glad to have seen me, for he had gotten a vast deal of information. So had I. What could I quote him as saying?

'Well, write what you like. Give your imagination full swing. Stick your old space copy in the back columns of your Sunday paper, and folks will wash it down with their breakfast coffee, the same as they do the other trash; that's all that is printed nowadays. Say I am a boor, for I am, and I want people to learn it and let me alone.'

With that he slammed the door and went in.

Mr Kipling had been interviewed.

●

WILLIAM HOWARD RUSSELL

Interviewed by Harry How
The Strand Magazine, December 1892

Sir William Howard Russell (1821–1907), the war correspondent, was born in Ireland and educated at Trinity College, Dublin. He joined *The Times* in 1843 and also qualified as a barrister, although he never practised. His dispatches from the Crimea (1854–5) exposed the appalling plight of the British soldiers and deeply affected public opinion. He covered the Indian Mutiny, the American Civil War, and the Franco-Prussian War. He also served as private secretary to the Prince of Wales (Edward VII) on journeys to Egypt and India.

Harry How's interviews for *The Strand Magazine* were published by the magazine in book form as *Illustrated Interviews* (1893). His subjects included such notables as W. S. Gilbert, H. Rider Haggard, Henry Irving, Ellen Terry, Professor Blackie, Lord Wolseley, George Augustus Sala, and Harry Furniss.

It may be fairly said that Dr Russell is the accredited father of a professional family which, though necessarily limited in the number of its sons, possesses the world as its debtors. The dodging of bullets and shells, the cornering of ourselves in some haven of refuge from the ferocious charging of maddened horses and men – in short, the participation in all 'the pomp and circumstance of glorious war', is not run after by the average man. Dr Russell was the first of our known war correspondents. The remembrance of this – as I ascended in the lift which delivered me at the door of his flat in Victoria Street – was suggestive of the probable unfolding of a life of the deepest interest. Nor was I disappointed. I spent some hours with Dr Russell, and when it came to 'Good-bye,' he asked: 'Have you got what you want?'

I was in earnest when I asked him if he could cut out ten or twenty years of his life, for my load of delightful information was so great that I feared the space at my disposal could not hold it all. His reply was: 'Ah! willingly, willingly – if I could. The burden of my years is heavier than the load of incidents you are carrying away with you.'

Dr Russell is of medium height, strongly built, wearing a white moustache, and possessing a head of wavy, silver hair. He is now lame from injuries received by his horse falling on him in the Transvaal. He took me from room to room, and as he narrated the little incidents associated with his treasures, it was all done quietly, impressively free from any boastfulness. For he wished me to understand that though his life had often been in danger, in scenes where men won great names for heroic deeds and gave up their lives for their country, he was only a camp follower and nothing more in the nine campaigns which he has seen – he chronicled history, he did not make it. I hope this little article will prove a courteous contradiction to this.

You pass by many articles of rarity in the corridor on your way to the dining-room – cabinets of battle-field relics, jade bowls, Indian and Egyptian ware, a great Hindu deity, once the property of Bainee Mahdo, the Oude Tlookdar, an Indian chief; recreation and sport are represented by gun-cases and a huge bundle of fishing rods in the corner. Here on a table are half-a-dozen cigar cases, one of which, with silver clasps, is from the Prince of Wales, as a souvenir of the visit to India in 1875–6, in which Dr Russell acted as Honorary Private Secretary to HRH; some exquisite cups and bowls of bedree work from Lucknow; and over one of the doors is Landseer's *Horseman and Hounds* which, curiously enough, was reproduced in an article I wrote in this Magazine entitled 'Pictures with Histories', in April, 1891. The cosy, small dining room overlooks Victoria Street, and contains some excellent pictures:

one of Dr Russell's mother, another of the artist, J. G. Russell, ARA, who also painted the portrait of Mr Russell's paternal grandfather opposite that of his uncle, and several depicting scenes in the hunting-field. Two big canvases, however, are particularly interesting. One dated Lucknow, March, 1858, is *The Death of Cleopatra*, painted by Beechey.

'Beechey visited India long before the Mutiny, and was entertained by the King of Oude,' explained Dr Russell. 'He painted this portrait, probably of a Circassian, for the King. During the looting of the Kaiserbagh of Lucknow at the time of the Indian Mutiny, when we were leaving the palace, I remarked to an officer that it was a pity to leave it hanging there.

' "Cut it out of the frame," was his advice. I did so, and a soldier wrapped it round his rifle barrel, and so we got it away.'

The other canvas, painted by a native artist, is of the King of Oude himself, surrounded by his Court and attired in all his Oriental splendour.

'That was one of Thackeray's favourite pictures,' said Dr Russell. 'He would look at it for an hour at a time, saying softly, "Poor old thing! poor old dear! how fine and how silly he looks." Dear Thackeray! – he was one of my dearest and warmest friends. He lived in Onslow Square, very near to my house in Sumner Place, for several years. He was very fond of my wife, and I well remember how, when she was laid low with a serious illness and was not expected to live, Thackeray would stand every morning opposite my house, waiting for me to appear at the window. If I nodded, it was a sign that my wife was a little better, and he came in for a few words; if I shook my head, he went quietly and dolefully away. We often dined at the Garrick Club. One night I met him in Pall Mall on my way home to dinner.

' "Let us dine at the Garrick tonight," ' he said.

'I told him I could not, as I had promised to dine at home.

' "Oh!" said he, "I'll write to Mrs Russell, and I know she will excuse you. It is important, you know."

'I consented. I sent a messenger home with the letter of excuse and a request for the latch-key. It came, with this little note in my wife's handwriting attached to it: "Go it, my boy! you are killing poor Thackeray and Johnny Deane!" Thackeray was delighted and put the note in his pocket. Deane was a neighbour of ours.'

You may count the ink-pots and paper-weights made out of shells and bullets on the tables by the score. But examine these two great boards or shields, covered with red cloth, on either side of the fine side-board. Picturesquely arranged are muskets from the Crimean battle-fields, Alma, Inkerman, etc., matchlocks and tulwars from India, spears, Zulu assegais, swords, fencing foils, revolvers, and old-fashioned pistols. Here is a beautiful dagger from the Rajah of Mundi, near it is the key of one of the magazines of the Great Redan at Sebastopol, which the present owner took out himself on 9th September, 1855, the day of the fall of the place. Handle this remnant of a scabbard thoughtfully:

it once belonged to a poor fellow in the Crimea – the remainder of it was driven by a shell splinter into his side. Examine this curious old blunderbuss, and listen to its story.

'It comes from India,' said Dr Russell. 'A pile of arms were brought in to headquarters at Lucknow to be surrendered. I was examining this article, when Lord Clyde – who was standing by my side – asked: "Is it loaded?"

'No,' I answered, immediately pulling the trigger. But it was! The charge tore up the ground at Lord Clyde's feet, and his escape was miraculous. His anger was considerable. No wonder I did not know it was loaded, for the steel ramrod hopped up when I tried it, but the piece was fully charged with telegraph wire cut into small pieces!'

The drawing-room contains objects of great interest. An autographed picture of the Princess of Wales fondling a kitten rests on the mantel-board with other souvenirs. Just near the piano – which is covered with some fine Japanese tapestry – is Meissonier's '1807'. This beautiful plateau and coffee set of Sèvres was bought at Versailles in 1871, when the people were starving, for a trifle. A tiger's skin – a trophy from India – lies in front of a shelf over which rises a fine mirror. The knick-knacks are countless. This exquisite jade vase – once studded with rubies – was given to its present possessor by the Maharajah of Puttiala. It is one of many here. The medals, one 'in memoriam' of the coronation of the Czar at Moscow, 1856, and silver trinkets are numerous – an immense 'turnip' watch, the property of a great-great-grandfather, was said to be 150 years old when he first had it.

An idol from a Japanese temple, and a chobdar of rare beauty, composed of various stones of different lengths, all with some mystic meaning, are here. A hundred photographs of celebrities are set out on a screen near the door – Sir Collingwood Dickson amongst them.

'The bravest and coolest man I ever knew,' said Dr Russell. 'He practically won the battle of Inkerman with his two eighteen-pounders.'

The portrait of Dr Russell's second son – now Vice-Consul at the Dardanelles – reminds him to tell me that he is now the only survivor of the original party who went with Gordon up to Khartoum when he was first appointed Governor. Gordon made him Governor of Farschodah – a bad place for a white man at present.

'I can see Gordon now,' Dr Russell said, quietly, 'fighting in the trenches at Sebastopol. I can just recall a very striking incident I heard one night. There was a sortie, and the Russians got into our parallel. The trench guards were encouraged to drive them out by Gordon, who stood on the parapet, in imminent danger of his life, prepared to meet death with nothing save his stick in his hand.

'"Gordon – Gordon! come down! you'll be killed," they cried. But he paid no heed to them.

'A soldier said, "He's all right. He don't mind being killed. *He's one of those blessed Christians!*"'

A large portrait of Dr Russell is on the wall amongst others, taken in Chili, in all his medals and decorations. These are many, for he is a Knight of the Iron Cross, an Officer of the Legion of Honour, has the Turkish War Medal of 1854–6, the Indian War Medal of 1857–8, with the clasp for Lucknow, the South African War Medal of 1879, the Medjidieh (3rd and 4th class), the Osmanieh (3rd and 4th class), the St Sauveur of Greece. He is a Chevalier of the Order of Franz Josef of Austria – the Redeemer of Portugal – etc.

We looked through a book of literary and pictorial reminiscences of the Crimea. Many of the sketches, the majority by Colonel Colville, now Equerry to the Duke of Edinburgh, are highly humorous. The gallant colonel has certainly depicted the chroniclers of war's alarms under very trying circumstances, and Captain Swaeby of the 41st, who was killed at Inkerman, presents the landing of the famous war correspondent and the total annihilation of the rival pressmen of the *Invalide Russe* and the *Soldaten Freund* in a boldly dramatic way. Here is a photograph by Robertson. It shows Balaclava – 'The Valley of Death'. On the opposite page is a cartoon from *Punch*. A mother and her children are sitting with open ears and excited, tearful faces listening to Paterfamilias by the fireplace, reading a description of the cavalry fight of Balaclava from *The Times*, and flourishing a poker over his head. That account was written by Dr Russell, and there is little reason to doubt that the word-picture penned by him inspired Lord Tennyson to write the 'Charge of the Light Brigade'.

We turn over the pages of the album. This slip of blue paper is a delivery note from the Quartermaster-General for a box from England, which Dr Russell got up with great difficulty at Balaclava. It created great joy, as the label on it of 'Medical Comforts' suggested to the hungry warriors something good from the old country. They gathered round in anxious expectation. Alas! the box contained wooden legs, splints, and such useful supports in life! The letters from generals commanding are numerous – a passport to the interior after the war, a portrait of Catharine of Russia, and one of the Czar Nicholas, torn down from a wall at Buljanak, and many other mementoes. The reading of a letter from the famous French *chef* Soyer reminds Dr Russell of an anecdote.

Soyer was arrested one night in the Crimea as a spy.

'Who and what are you?' asked the officer into whose presence he was brought.

'I am an officer,' was the reply.

'What rank?'

'I am chief of a battery.'

'Of what battery?'

'Of the Batterie de Cuisine de l'Armée Anglaise, monsieur!' was the witty answer.

'M. Soyer,' continued Dr Russell, 'was very eccentric, but very original – as a cook supreme. He erected a handsome monument to his wife's memory at

Kensal Green, and was on the look-out for an inscription. At last he made known his wish to Lord Palmerston.

' "Well," said the great statesman, "I don't think you can do better than put on it: *Soyez tranquille!*" '

From the drawing-room, the carpet of which was a wedding present from the suite of the Prince of Wales on Dr Russell's marriage to Countess Malvezzi in 1884, we went into the study, the writing table in which was a personal present from the Prince of Wales on the same occasion. Boxes, full to their lids with diaries and papers, are scattered about; the portraits on the walls are mostly family ones, though here and there hang a few outside the immediate family circle. Dickens and Thackeray are not forgotten; and the head of a little dog is here, under which Landseer has written 'Brutus'. It was his own dog.

'The most faithful friend I ever had,' the great artist said, as he put the picture in Dr Russell's hands one day.

Over the mantel-board is a picture of the *Serapis*, the vessel in which Dr Russell accompanied the Prince to India, and photos of the Prince's parties in India and Turkey. A huge paper-weight and an inkstand are not without a history. The inkstand is formed from a piece of a shell which is embedded in a stone from the Palais de St Cloud. It was fired by the French from Valérien at their own palace the day it was burned, just as General, then Colonel, Fraser arrived from Versailles. The paper-weight is also a very formidable bit of a shell which was fired from Vanvres at the staff of the Crown Prince on the 19th September, when they obtained their first view of Paris from the heights of Châtillon after the battle of that day. A very few inches nearer, and the probability is that Dr Russell would not have been sitting in his chair in the cosy study at Victoria Street.

William Howard Russell was born at Lilyvale, Co. Dublin, on March 28th, 1821. He really belongs to a Limerick family, and to this day there is just the faintest and happiest tinge of the dear old brogue on the tip of his tongue. He exemplifies in a way the 'distractions' of the 'distressful country' in politics and religion, for he had a great-grand-uncle hanged on Wexford Bridge in 1798, as a rebel during the war; whilst his grandfather was engaged on the side of Government, and was a valiant member of a Yeomanry Corps. He went to the Rev Dr Wall's, who used to flog severely, and to the Rev Dr Geoghegan's, a dear old fellow, who was not so birchingly inclined, both in the same street; but whatever he knows is due to Dr Geoghegan's school, where he was a 'day boy' for six or seven years. Amongst his schoolfellows were General Waddy (Alma, Inkerman, etc.), R.V. Boyle – who defended Arrah in the Mutiny – General Sir Henry de Bathe, Colonel Willans, and Dion Boucicault, who was then called Boursiquot.

'Boucicault was a very cantankerous boy,' said Dr Russell, 'though unquestionably plucky. I remember he fought a big fellow named Barton – who, by-the-bye, became a famous advocate in India, and died not long ago a JP in Essex –

with one arm tied behind his back, and took a licking gallantly. He was always considered a clever fellow; but, oh! how he used to romance! St Stephen's Green was the great battle-field of the schools – Wall's, Huddart's, Geoghegan's, etc. – in those days. Black eyes were as plentiful as blackberries, and I had my share. I was always very fond of soldiering, and used to get up early and set off from our house in Baggot Street to watch the drills in the mornings at the Biggar's Bush Barracks. I used to get cartridges from the soldiers, which caused my people much annoyance. Yet not so much as they did the old watchman in his box at the corner of Baggot Street. We found him asleep one night, discharged a shot or two inside, and pitched him and his box over into the canal. He escaped, but we did not, for we caught it severely, and deserved it. When the Spanish Legion was raised I made frantic appeals to join – officer, private, anything – and was only prevented from running away with De Lacy Evan's heroes by the strong arm of authority.

'I entered Trinity College in 1838 at seventeen. Only the other day I was present at the tercentenary, and found myself in the identical place I used to occupy at examinations when a student. There I again met an old class-fellow – Rawdon Macnamara, President of the College of Physicians, Dublin. There were glorious doings during election times, when the Trinity College students – who were mostly Orangemen – met the Roman Catholics and engaged them in battle; but, alas! they were tyrannous and strong. The coal porters were there – "the descendants of the Irish Kings from the coal quay"; as Dan O'Connell called them, and sometimes we had to seek safety at the college gates. Sometimes we had it all our own way, and made the most of it. Away we would go to King William's statue on College Green, shouting, "Down with the Pope! Down with the Pope!" During one election there was an exhibition in the Arcade of the "wonderful spotted lady" and "the Hungarian giant". We made a charge, overturned the pay box, dismissed the proprietor, made "the Hungarian giant" run for his life, to say nothing of seeing "the spotted lady" going off into hysterics. The Dublin coal porters used to be called in to disperse us. We frequently parted with broken heads. We were often triumphant, though.'

Dr Russell left college for a couple of years, during part of which he was mathematical master at Kensington Grammar School. He returned to Trinity, and with the elections of 1841 came his first real literary effort, though he is very proud of a sketch and account of an *alauda cristata*, or crested lark, which appeared in the *Dublin Penny Journal* when he was fifteen years of age – the bird was of his own shooting. A cousin, Mr R. Russell, employed on *The Times*, came over to 'do' the elections, and suggested the earning of a few guineas to the young collegian by going to the Longford election and writing an account of it. He accepted the suggestion, and not only penned a vivid description of the scene in the hospital where the wounded voters lay with bruised bodies and cracked craniums, but entered heartily into the political campaign, and spoke and fought in it *con amore*. His description delighted the *Times* people. He received bank-notes and praise, both acceptable and novel; he continued to write more descriptive accounts of the meetings of the day, and Delane, the editor, told him to expect constant employment.

O'Connell? Dr Russell knew him well. No orator has impressed him more, before or since.

'O'Connell was really an uncrowned king,' he said. 'He wore a green velvet cap with a gold band round it, and a green coat with brass buttons. Still, we had a crossing of swords occasionally. The *Times* commissioner, Campbell Foster, characterized a village on O'Connell's estate, at Derrynane, in a letter on the state of Ireland, as a squalid, miserable settlement of cabins, not possessing a pane of glass in any of the houses. O'Connell declared this to be a lie. I was requested by *The Times* to repair to the spot with Maurice O'Connell to see for myself, and to deny or corroborate Foster's assertion. I could not but cor- roborate it. On entering a crowded meeting one night at Conciliation Hall, O'Connell rose up and shouted: "So this contemptible Russell says there is not a pane of glass in Derrynane? I wish he had as many pains in his stomach!"

'Yet O'Connell was always personally kind to me. Once my carriage broke down on the road to Dublin from a monster meeting. O'Connell's was passing at the time. He turned out poor Tom Steele, gave me his place, and a good dinner into the bargain. "Honest Tom Steele", as they all called him. He was devoted to O'Connell, and after his death became disconsolate, and eventually threw himself off Waterloo Bridge.'

It was just before the arrest of O'Connell that Dr Russell saw Lord Cardigan for the first time. He was with his regiment of hussars, near Clontarf, where there was a great display of the military who had been sent to prevent the great agitator from holding a meeting, which had been declared illegal by proclama- tion. Cardigan was quite magnificent. The next time Dr Russell met him was in a transport going to Varna. The third time he saw him crestfallen and wounded not quite in front after Balaclava. But O'Connell and his head pacificator, Tom Steele, wore great bunches of shamrock in their coats, and a great posse of priests begged the people to disperse quietly. Then commenced the memorable Irish State trials.

'Both *The Times* – for which I wrote the descriptive portion of the trials – and the *Morning Herald* had chartered special steamers to carry the news and the results of the Government prosecutions to London,' said Dr Russell. 'The great day came. The trial of O'Connell and the traversers lasted long, but at last it was over. It was very late on a Saturday night when the jury retired; the judge waited in court for some time, but went away after an hour's expectancy, and the other newspaper correspondents left to get refreshments. I was sitting outside the court, wondering whether I should go to bed. Suddenly my boy rushed up to me.

'"Jury just coming in," he said.

'And they brought in a verdict of guilty. The moment I heard it I flew from the court, jumped on a car – drove to the station, where I had ordered a special train to be in readiness – got to Kingston – hailed the *Iron Duke*, the steamer chartered by *The Times* – got up steam in half an hour, and left with the consolation that the steamer of the *Morning Herald* was lying peacefully in harbour! Arrived at Holyhead – sped away – special to London – tried to sleep, couldn't – tight boots – took them off. Reached Euston, man waiting with cab, struggled to get on boots, only managed the left foot, and when I reached the *Times* office it was with one boot under my arm.

'As I got out of the cab in Printing House Square, a man in shirt-sleeves – whom I took to be a printer – came up to me.

'"So glad to see you safe over, sir!" he cried. "So they've found him guilty?"

'"Yes – guilty, my friend," I replied.

'The *Morning Herald* came out next day with the news of the fact – the bare fact – as well as *The Times!* The gentleman in the shirt-sleeves was an emissary from their office!'

In 1846 Dr Russell married the daughter of Mr Peter Burrowes, and severed for a short period his connection with *The Times*, in the same year becoming 'Potato Rot Commissioner', as it was termed, to the *Morning Chronicle*, for which he wrote letters from the famine-stricken districts in the West of Ireland. In 1848 he was special constable on the occasion of Fergus O'Connor's abortive Chartist demonstration at Kennington, and in 1849 he accompanied the Queen's flotilla on a visit to Ireland, and described for *The Times* the first review at Spithead by the Queen, as well as the first review of the French fleet at Cherbourg by Napoleon, after the *coup d'état*. He was summoned home from Switzerland in the same year to attend the Duke of Wellington's funeral. At this ceremony Dr Russell saw the late Cardinal Howard, then a cornet, riding at the head of a detachment of the Life Guards.

'I was at his funeral only a week or two ago, at Arundel,' he said. 'A Roman Catholic bishop spoke to me at the Castle, after the ceremony was over. Did I remember him? No, I did not. He introduced himself as Dr Butt, Bishop of Southwark, who thirty-six years ago was Catholic chaplain in the Crimea, and presently I met his venerable colleague, Bishop Virtue, who had also been a chaplain in the Army before Sebastopol. I had not seen either of them since. At lunch I sat next Father Bowden, chief of the Brompton Oratory, who had been in the Guards, and who was a fellow member of the Garrick Club.'

We hurried over events. The first battle he saw was that between the Danes and Prussians at Idstedt in 1852, where he was put in a place of safety, which half an hour afterwards became the centre of action! He was wounded under the arm by a bullet. In February, 1854, he went to Malta with the advanced guard of the army. He scarcely wanted to go. He pleaded his business at the Bar, and other matters, to the editor of *The Times*; besides, how could he leave his young wife and two little ones?

'Nonsense!' said Delane. 'It'll be a pleasant excursion. When the Guards get to Malta, and the Czar hears of it, he won't be mad enough to continue his adventure. You'll be back before Easter term begins, depend on it'; for Dr Russell at this time was in practice in election and Parliamentary cases, having been called to the Bar in 1850.

'Well,' added Dr Russell, smilingly, 'I got back in 1856!'

His descriptive writing from the Crimea of the dreadful winter roused England and turned out the Government.

What terrible pictures his pen was forced to paint! It was one long story of suffering, from the beginning to the end. The war correspondent paid £5 for a ham, 15s. for a small tin of meat, 5s. for a little pot of marmalade, £6 for a pair of common seaman's boots, and £5 for a turkey; and he fattened up that turkey for days. The turkey was kept under a gabion. It wanted three days to Christmas. Dr Russell, accompanied by a friend, went forth to look at the bird that was to be killed for the banquet. They looked through the wickerwork and could see the feathers, but the bird did not move. They raised the gabion. Alas: some villain had stolen the turkey, leaving nothing but the claws, head, and wings!

'That was a very miserable Christmas Day,' added Dr Russell. 'Inkerman had just been fought, the army was practically dying out. Then consider the terrible knowledge we possessed. We spent that Christmas Day knowing that there was no hope of entering Sebastopol for weeks to come.'

Dr Russell wrote his account of the battle of the Alma in the leaves of a dead Russian's note-book upon a plank laid across a couple of barrels, under a scorching sun.

Dr Russell put a little brass eagle in my hand.

'That is from the shako of a Russian soldier,' he said. 'I never saw such gallantry. The fellow rushed out of the column that came down on the Light Division, and which had thrown the Scots Fusiliers into confusion, and made straight for the standard of the Guards. He clutched the staff – swords and bayonets cut and pierced him, but he fought on; and Lindsay and others had to fight for it too. At last he dropped, and I brought this brass eagle, which Norcott's sergeant gave me, as a memento of one of the most persistent examples of hopeless bravery I ever witnessed.'

When peace was declared he returned to England in the spring of 1856. He reached home late at night, and his wife led him quietly upstairs to a bedroom. She opened the door, and there stood his little ones in their night-gowns at the foot of the bed, singing: 'Oh! Willie, we have miss'd you, Welcome! welcome home!'

'I had never heard the song before,' said Dr Russell, 'and I thought it was some little ditty of their mother's teaching for my welcome. Imagine my disgust next morning, when sitting at breakfast, to hear a band of Ethiopian melodists outside strike up – "Oh! Willie, we have miss'd you!"'

Now, Dr Russell's baptismal appellation is William.

He had not long been home ere he was asked to go out again to Russia to describe the Coronation of the Czar, the account of which he considers his best bit of writing.

'Whilst at one of the receptions at Moscow,' he said, 'I met a Russian officer, who spoke excellent English, who had been at Balaclava, and was much interested in the details of the day. In the course of conversation he said: –

'"I laid the first gun of my battery against a troop of your artillery so true, that when the shell burst, it blew the officer who was riding in front into pieces."

'"Pardon me! You are mistaken," I said. "Permit me to tell you that Captain Maude, who was the officer who rode in front of that troop, is now standing close behind you!" Major, now General, Maude was indeed badly wounded by that shell, but he is now alive and well, I hope, and at the head of the Queen's stable.

'Returning home again, Thackeray and others suggested that I should lecture on the war. I did so, with Willert Beale as my impresario. I used to rehearse my lecture before a select audience – Mark Lemon, Shirley Brooks, John Leech, Thackeray, Delane, Douglas Jerrold, and half the Garrick Club, who used to introduce, "Hear! hear! cheers and laughter" at appropriate places. At last the eventful night of the *début* as lecturer came. The scene was Willis's Rooms. I peeped into the vast room. Great Heavens! The hall was filled with Crimean officers. I recognized Lord Lucan, Lord Rokeby, Airey, etc., etc., all grimly expectant in front, and many familiar faces behind.

'I can't go on,' I said.

'"Nonsense," said Thackeray. "I've lectured, so can you."

'"I can't do it, I tell you – go, somebody, and say I'm ill. The money will be returned!"

'Just then Deane came up with a bumper of champagne. I couldn't drink it. I peeped through the doorway again, when suddenly I was seized and run on to the platform by Thackeray and Co. So I unwillingly made my first appearance as a lecturer in rather an undignified manner.

'I visited many towns in England, Scotland, and Ireland, and made money by my tour, but it was distasteful to me; I was glad when my engagements were over, and have never lectured since, though often asked to do so. When the Indian Mutiny broke out I was abroad, but I was sent for, and after a short holiday, I was asked by Delane very urgently to go out and join the army preparing to relieve Lucknow, under Colin Campbell. That was in 1857. The very day I arrived at Calcutta, the news came that Havelock was dead, and that Colin Campbell had got the garrison and the women and children out of Lucknow, but that he was unable to take the place. I went up country to join Sir Colin Campbell's headquarters at Cawnpore, with Pat Stewart.

'Sir Colin said to me: "Now, Mr Russell, you're welcome. You have seen something of war. I am going to tell you everything. But only on one condition. That when dining with headquarters mess you don't blab what you hear. There are native servants behind every chair watching, and what is said inside the tent is known outside five minutes afterwards. I want to show you my plans for attack on Lucknow. Go with Colonel Napier. He will let you see what we are going to do." The officer to whom Sir Colin introduced me, afterwards Field Marshal Lord Napier of Magdala, took me across to his tent. "Now", said he, "here are our plans – ask me anything you please. Mind! You must keep my purdah down."

'Now, though I had not been long in India I knew that a "purdah" meant a curtain. I rose and let down the flap over the entrance of the tent, shutting out all the light.

'Napier smiled.

'"No, no," he cried, "what I mean is, you must keep my plans to yourself!"'

Dr Russell was present at the siege of Lucknow, and also served in the campaigns of Oude, Rohilcund, etc. Whilst on one of the many night marches Sir Colin made in India, he received a kick from a horse which nearly led to the loss of his life.

'A horse broke loose and commenced to attack my little stallion,' he said. 'I went to its assistance, when the brute, which belonged to Donald Stewart, an Indian officer on the staff, let fly at me, catching me on my right thigh. The kick bent the scabbard of a sword I was wearing, and fairly drove it into my right thigh. We were just on the move, hoping to come into action with some Oude rebels, and I was in agony – unable to move a step – so I was placed in a litter and carried along with the sick of the headquarters staff into Rohilcund. Small-pox broke out at Lucknow, and clung to us on the march, and among the sick were Sir W. Peel (he died at Cawnpore), Sir David Baird, and Major Alison. On the 25th March, 1858, the battle of Bareilly was fought. Our coolie bearers had carried the sick litters into a shady tope or grove of trees – the sun was fierce. There I lay, helpless, listening to the sound of battle close at hand. My only clothing consisted of a shirt. Suddenly a cry burst from the camp followers:

'"The Sowars are coming! The Sowars are coming!"

Our Syces ran up with the chargers. How I did it, I do not know. But I hopped out of my litter and scrambled up into the saddle – the flaps felt like molten iron, and the blister on my leg rolled up against the leather roasted by the sun outside the tope – on my horse. My servant – a very brave fellow – held on by the stirrup leather, flogging the horse, for I had only bare feet and bare legs. Suddenly he let go. He saw a Sowar making for us, and he released his hold so as not to impede my flight. He was cut down, I presume, for I never saw him again – and his wages were due. I struggled on, but the sun was more powerful than I. I had only proceeded a few yards when I fell off my horse insensible – with sunstroke.

'Then I heard a voice.

' "Look – a white man!" '

'It was some of our people, thank God! They thought I had been killed, and that the Sowars had stripped off my clothing, for I was naked, all save my shirt, and it was bloody. They bent over me. "He's warm," cried one of the men – it was Tombs' battery that had come up. I got back to camp, but I was very near the point of death; and, indeed, I had the unique and unpleasant trial of listening to my good friends and physicians, Tice and Mackinnon, discussing the question of my burial at the foot of the charpoy, on which I was stretched, apparently dead.'

Such is one of the experiences of Dr Russell during the Indian Mutiny.

Yet another Christmas Day (1858) was spent in India on the borders of Nepaul. The day dawned upon an anxious people, but it *was* Christmas, and the war correspondent, with a party of friends, meant to keep it up. They gathered for dinner in a large mess tent, from the ridge pole of which hung a huge lamp. A well-known Scotch enthusiast's presence suggested a Highland fling as an appropriate finish. The gallant Highlander got on the table, and his tripping was so vigorous that it shook down the lamp. In two minutes the tent was in flames. So ended another Christmas Day.

In 1859 Dr Russell returned to England, and received the Indian War Medal with the Lucknow clasp. In 1860 he started the *Army and Navy Gazette*, of which he is still part proprietor and editor, and in 1861 went to the United States, in time to hear Mr Lincoln deliver the Inaugural Address at Washington, which was accepted as a proclamation of war against their 'domestic institutions' by the Southern States. He was exceedingly well received, and sat down at Lincoln's first official dinner in the White House, being the only person there who was not a Cabinet Minister. He was unfortunately present at the first battle of Bull Run. Dr Russell gave it as his opinion that McDowell, the general commander of the Federal troops, may have lost that battle through eating too much water-melon. He was a confirmed vegetarian, and ate too much of that fruit the morning of the action. At all events, brave and capable as he was, McDowell was beaten. The Federals fled in disorder from the field, and Dr Russell had to describe the flight, which was to him personally a most disagreeable experience. The North, angry and frightened, could not forgive; and when his account of the battle – which the leading journal of New York declared was awaited with as much anxiety as a Presidential message – arrived, the vials of wrath were poured out upon him. Dr Russell was not altogether popular in America. The man who does not fear to speak and write the truth is not always a popular personage. He wrote facts, hard-hitting facts, and the Press nicknamed him 'Bull Run Russell', as if he caused the disaster. However, newspaper abuse did not deprive him of the necessary breath to reach England.

In 1866 he joined the Austrian Army under Benedek, and again, at König-grätz, had to fly before a victorious enemy; but he visited Kuhn's headquarters, Custozza, etc., remaining in Vienna some time after as the *Times* correspondent.

Now comes a memorable year, 1870, which brought the declaration of war between France and Germany. He asked to join the French headquarters, but the Emperor said: 'I should be happy to see Mr Russell at my headquarters, but nothing shall induce me to receive a correspondent of a paper which has shown itself so hostile to me as *The Times*.' The French Government would not allow the presence of any correspondents. Dr Russell heaped coals of fire on their heads, so to speak, when, after the battle of Worth, a little later on he assisted in securing the release of two correspondents of the Paris Press from captivity, who had sought refuge in the clock tower of a church.

Dr Russell proceeded to Berlin and joined the staff of the Crown Prince. Colonel Pemberton, of the Grenadier Guards – a valued friend – burning with a desire to see service, joined him, as did also Lord Ronald Gower, who – when his mother was Mistress of the Robes – had been much with the Queen's children, and who was sure of a warm welcome from the Crown Princess.

'Our reception,' said Dr Russell, 'at the New Palace, Potsdam, was most gracious, but the Crown Princess was in tears. She said: "You have arrived at a dreadful moment. My husband and his father start for the scene of carnage immediately. You have traversed the Palatinate, and you have seen the peaceful towns and villages which will soon be heaps of ashes, and the harvest ripening in the fields will soon be soaked with blood; but I feel assured we shall conquer in the end."

'In the midst of the preparations for war, I was bidden to the christening of a little princess at the Palace. I was presented to the Emperor by Lord Augustus Loftus, our ambassador on the occasion. His Majesty made a very kindly speech and said, "The Press is a new power, and I accept you as its ambassador."

'The day of my arrival at Berlin, Count Bismarck sent to say that he would like to see me early next morning (*Morgen früh*) at the Foreign Office – what "early" meant I knew not. I was in the Wilhelmstrasse before the doorkeeper was awake. It was long after eight o'clock before I was introduced to the Great Chancellor, who offered me a cigar, and as soon as I was seated launched into serious business. I was much impressed with his estimate of the Emperor of the French. "He is a dreamer – a mere dreamer," he said. "I went to see him at Biarritz in order to come to some understanding about our relations, and, if possible, to clear the sky. I had practical questions to propose and settle but I could not get him to grapple with a single one. He wished to entertain me with his theories for the removal of the causes of poverty, and for meeting the dangers of an educated proletariat. I was only anxious to lay the way for peace; but, no! he would have none of it. Now see what we have come to!"

'My interview with Count Bismarck lasted two hours, during which he spoke almost uninterruptedly, with great vivacity, generally in French, frequently breaking out into English, and he quoted Shakespeare at least twice.

'At the close of the interview I asked him to procure me a Legitimation, without which I could not accompany the army. "I am not the man for that.

General von Roon is your man." "But I do not know him, sir." "Well, perhaps he will do it for me – we will see."

'The Legitimation business detained us several days in Berlin. In the meanwhile, the mobilization of the army was rapidly going on. It was almost impossible to obtain horses, and we could get no vehicles. I will tell you how we managed to get one. One day we saw a Berlin egg-cart, a sort of flat van on wheels. An idea struck us. Why not buy an egg-cart, get a light frame to go over the top, and cover it with canvas? Excellent. So we bought a cart and rigged it up. But how to distinguish it? Another happy thought. My crest is a goat, so we painted a big black goat on the canvas. All through the campaign vulgar boys and people would point at it and cry – "Ba-a-a! Ba-a-a!" to the great annoyance of my servant. One curious thing occurred in connection with my waggon. An English officer attached to the French army as one of the Geneva Cross Association saw this cart in the French lines, and inferred that the German army had been defeated and my cart captured. I lost my egg-cart on the march to Versailles.'

At last Dr Russell got away from Berlin with Lord R. Gower and Colonel Pemberton. His military railway ticket – the number of the train and the time-table of the stations were printed on it – was dated some time before war was declared! At Worms they left the train and took a carriage for Landau. Their coachman was not a man to be sought after. At one spot he refused to go any farther with the pair of horses, which had been obtained after much trouble, and they only got to Wissembourg the night after the battle, in rear of the Crown Prince's staff. The result was that Dr Russell and Lord Ronald Gower were arrested as spies, and sentries placed over them, with orders to shoot them if they stirred.

'A false alarm roused the sentries,' the old war correspondent explained. 'They left us. We made good our escape into the inn, where a good Samaritan gave us some delicious hot coffee. Years afterwards I came across the landlord's son who had so befriended us, as a waiter at the Salthill Hotel, Dublin.'

Dr Russell was at the battle of Worth. The Crown Prince's dinner was very simple, consisting of soup served in metal cups, and boiled ration-meat, bread, cheese, and beer. There was silver on the table, however. It belonged to the camp equipment of Frederick the Great, and was, and is always, carried at the Royal headquarters in war time. He spoke of the great anguish of the Crown Prince as he read the names of his fallen officers.

Dr Russell was at the siege and fall of Paris, which he entered with the Crown Prince, and took a cartload of fresh meat and vegetables over the bridge into Paris, the first day it opened, to the British Embassy. There he found Sir Richard Wallace in his shirt-sleeves, serving out horse-flesh to the starving English grooms, tutors, and governesses. He remained in Paris till the massacre by the Communists in the Place Vendôme, and returned the night after the Commune expired in ashes and blood. He looked on at the gay city in flames.

'As I watched millions of fiery tongues leaping up towards the sky,' continued Dr Russell, 'my mind went back to the extravagant splendour of the year in which the Great Exhibition was held, when I served on the jury in the arms department. There, on the grand-stand of the racecourse, I saw the Emperor. With him were two Emperors and several Kings. He was reviewing part of the great army which in a few years was to be swept into captivity. What an inconceivable change! I stood behind the Emperor of Germany on the same grand-stand from which he reviewed the German army previous to its triumphant march into Paris. I could scarcely believe the evidence of my senses when I rode under the Arc de Triomphe in the train of the conqueror down the Avenue of the Champs Elysées. That afternoon, after incurring many dangers – indeed, imminent peril – I managed to get from the Prussian lines, and make my way to the railway station. There a special train arranged to take me to Calais, whence I sent my account to *The Times* of the entry of the German army into Paris.'

Dr Russell took from one of his great despatch boxes a number of volumes. Among them were the diaries of his trip to India when he accompanied the Prince of Wales as honorary private secretary. *The Times* asked Dr Russell to act as their correspondent. Then trouble arose. Other correspondents wanted to go in the *Serapis*, but this was objected to. At last a compromise was arrived at.

'It was,' said Dr Russell, 'to the effect that I could not write letters from the *Serapis* as the *Times* correspondent, and that the other newspaper correspondents might go to India on their own responsibility. Still letters *did* appear in the columns of *The Times* during the voyage out. I used to write to the editor personally, and he would put in my communication with the heading: 'We have received the following from a friend on board the *Serapis*.' It is impossible to describe all the rejoicings and festivities. I saw in Nepaul an army of 900 elephants for the hunting party arranged by Jung Bahadur, surely the biggest elephantine gathering on record! And such sport as there was. The Prince is a very steady rifle shot,' and together we looked through the record of a day's shooting as chronicled in the diary:-

'HRH Prince of Wales: One tiger 7ft 6in; one pig, two hares, one partridge.

'Lord Suffield: One tiger, 7ft 9in; one tiger's cub, three cheetahs.

'Prince Louis of Battenberg: One cheetah.

'Captain Rose: One tiger, 9ft 6in, which charged the Prince of Wales, wounding his elephant.

'Russell: One cheetah.

'Col. Fitz-George: One pig.'

And so forth. 'Ellis. Prinsep, Sam Browne, Fayrer, various heads.'

'One day we killed six tigers,' said Dr Russell, 'of which the Prince shot five. The best work in this direction on the part of the Prince was a couple of tigers shot in an hour – one was killed with the first shot; the other creature took a long time to come out of its lair. We threw every soda-water bottle we had got with us at him until he was roused by one thrown by Jung Bahadur, which burst on a stone near his head. We left Bombay in the March of 1876, bringing home a grand menagerie and an infinite wealth of presents for the Prince. We arrived at Portsmouth on the 11th of May – after visiting many of the principal cities homewards – and the following day made a state entry into London.'

Dr Russell's last campaigning experience was in 1879, when he accompanied Lord Wolseley to South Africa, and was at the taking of Sekukuni's stronghold. The close of the pleasant hours spent with the famous war correspondent was nearing, and lighting up our cigars, he looked back upon that well-remembered day when he met with the regrettable accident which resulted in his lameness.

'We had arrived within ten or twelve miles of Pretoria,' he said, 'and halted for the day. I said I would go on to Pretoria and get my despatches off. I left the camp alone. Sir Baker Russell suggested my taking an orderly. But I wouldn't. Whenever I meet Sir Baker now he always says: "Ah! you should have taken that orderly." I rode six miles from the camp over a sprint, reaching a road which led down a steep hill to a ford. The threatening sky told me to look out for a Cape storm. They rush down upon you with scarcely a warning. I knew the river at the bottom of the road would swell rapidly, so I urged my horse forward down the hill. I got into the middle of the ford just as the storm burst on us in all its fury. A flash of lightning struck the water, my horse reared violently, lost his footing, threw me over his shoulder, and I fell under him. My right leg was caught by the stirrup; my left leg was under the horse's shoulder; his neck lay over my chest, preventing me from rising. There was I on my back, with my right hand on the bottom of the river, and with my left jogging the reins to make the poor beast rise – the water slowly rising with the pouring torrents – I was drowning. I could feel the water getting higher and higher – it reached my neck, my chin – when, with almost a dying effort, as my horse struggled up a little, I made an attempt to move my leg, but down he went again. However, the strap of my spur gave way – my right leg was liberated – I was able to raise myself on it and to pull at the horse's head. My horse got up; I managed to lean on him, and he just carried me to the bank. I tried to get on his back, and down he went again, so with my leg doubled under me I put one hand on his shoulder, and so I crawled on to the house of an old Scotch farmer named Gray. He put me into bed, and rubbed me with "Cape smoke", and I found that I had not only lost my helmet, note-books and despatches, but that my leg was useless, with a chance of being lame for the remainder of my days.

'In the morning the head-quarters staff rode across the ford, amongst them Lord Wolseley. He called at the farm; Gray told him of my plight, and he came to my side.

' "I thought my last day had come, and that my body would never be found," I said to him.

' "My dear fellow," was his characteristic reply, "I would never have left the country until I had found you, and I would have given you a jolly good burial!" '

I knocked the ash off my cigar and rose to go.

'But what, Dr Russell,' I asked, 'do you consider the most unenviable position in which you were ever placed – in what battle?'

'It wasn't in a battle,' he answered, merrily, and laughing happily. 'Oh, no! it wasn't in a battle. It was in a bed! When I was accompanying the Prince to India, we stayed at the Palace at Athens. One night the King said to me, "Do you get up early, Mr Russell?"

'"Yes, sir," I replied; "I generally rise at six o'clock."

'"Very well, we'll say half-past six tomorrow morning. I want to walk with you in the garden and talk over one or two things."

'I went upstairs to bed. I couldn't sleep. The mosquitoes bit me to their hearts' content, particularly about the hands and arms. I happened to have a pair of long white kid gloves in my bag. I got up and put them on.

'I awoke in the morning with the knowledge of having somebody by my bedside. It was the King, accompanied by his big dog. It was half-past six! I sat up in bed.

'"In half an hour, Mr Russell," said the King, smiling, as he left the room, "I shall come back for you."

'At breakfast that morning, during a moment of silence, the King, addressing the Queen, with a sly glance in my direction, said:-

'"Well, I've met a great many dandies in my time, but Mr Russell beats them all. He actually sleeps in white kid gloves!"'

●

SAMUEL SMILES

Interviewed by *The Young Man*, March 1893

Samuel Smiles (1812–1904), the Scottish writer and social commentator, worked in Leeds as a surgeon, newspaper editor and railway company official. His first book was a biography of George Stephenson, the railway engineer, and with his second book his fame and fortune were guaranteed. *Self-Help* (1859) was a manual of self-improvement with many edifying examples from the lives of successful men. It was the great best-seller of the Victorian age and was still being referred to approvingly more than a century later – by Margaret Thatcher.

'What do you want to interview me for? There is nothing particularly interesting in *me!*'

'The young men of today, sir, are of a different opinion.'

Dr Smiles had risen when I entered his study, and that is how he greeted the

representative of *The Young Man*. The author of *Self-Help* lives in an unpretentious house in one of Kensington's quietest 'gardens'. His sanctum is well
stocked with books, and the walls are hung with portraits of eminent men.
Even if I had not noticed the odour of tobacco, a conspicuous assortment of
pipes and pipe-cases would have told me that Dr Smiles is not a member of the
Anti-Narcotic League. Speculating as to the probable age of the lively, good-
humoured old gentleman before me, I mentally put him down at about seventy; but
before the conversation had proceeded very far, he revealed the little secret to me.
He was explaining that he brought me there before eleven o'clock in the morning
because at that hour he always goes out for a walk – 'to keep myself alive. When I
cease to walk I shall cease to exist,' said he; and then added with a chuckle,
    'I shall be eighty-one before your article is published.'
    I could hardly believe this, until I caught sight of the features of Mr
Gladstone, who was beaming down upon us from above the mantelpiece. The
speaker's hair was quite white, but his eyes were keen and penetrating, with an
occasional gleam and flash which reminded me of the Grand Old Man himself.
He afterwards told me his sight was so good that he never wore glasses; and
when he presently wrote an inscription for me, the writing was firm and clear.
Dr Smiles told me that he will shortly celebrate his golden wedding – 'If I live,'
he added merrily; 'but anyway I don't expect to survive it. A golden wedding,'
he went on, more or less seriously, 'usually does for a man – it is the last effort
of expiring nature.' He certainly did not look like expiring at the time of the
interview, and when I mention that so far back as 1872 he had a sharp attack of
paralysis, and wrote, with sombre cheerfulness, that he still hoped to see
Florence and Rome 'before he died,' the reader will feel reassured. That is
twenty years ago, and he is still at work. Only last year he added another to his
eminently practical series of books. They stood in a row in a revolving bookcase beside the author; and being generously asked whether I would like any, I
selected *Self-Help* – an old friend. I remember how the perusal of a borrowed
copy stimulated me years ago when I used to sit three hours at a stretch helping
myself to a knowledge of shorthand. Dr Smiles told me that he has had similar
testimonies from all parts of the world, particularly from America. Curiously
enough, his writings have been even more successful in Italy than at home. He
showed me a copy of the Italian translation of *Self-Help*, which has passed
through many editions. The extent of the author's popularity and influence
with young Italy may be gathered from the fact that a prize was offered in 1867
by the Florence Society for the Education of the People, for a book of a like
character to his most famous production, founded upon Italian examples, and
that a circular was issued by the Italian Prime Minister, Count Menabrea, to
consuls in all parts of the world, citing Dr Smiles's *Self-Help*, and inviting them
to co-operate with him in the preparation of a similar book for Italian readers,
provided with examples drawn exclusively from the lives of Italian citizens. The
outcome was Lessona's 'Volere è Potere'.

When I asked Dr Smiles to tell me how he came to write *Self-Help*, he said he could not do better than give me a general outline of his career. Of course he turned out to be a Scotsman. In interviewing eminent people this is a surprise (pardon the parodox) that one is always prepared for.

'I have been engaged in business most of my life,' Dr Smiles began, 'and have been obliged to make my own way in the world. I was born in 1812, while Napoleon was crossing Russia with his beaten army over the snow. My birthplace is Haddington, where Mrs Carlyle was born. Her people lived practically next door to us, and Dr Welsh was our medical attendant.'

'Did you see much of Jane Welsh?' I interpolated.

'Of course I was quite a boy at the time. I used to see her walking about. Her mother was a much more beautiful woman than she was, Mrs Welsh had some of the gipsy blood in her.'

'Did you ever come in contact with Thomas Carlyle?'

'I knew him when he was in London. Mrs Carlyle called on me when I was at the South Eastern, and introduced herself. I saw her husband several times, but had no particular acquaintance with him. I met Mrs Carlyle oftener than Thomas. She was a very agreeable woman,' Dr Smiles went on, meditatively, wandering back into the days gone by – 'a little sarcastic, like Thomas. They were pretty well fitted for each other, I dare say.' That is certainly not the general impression; but Dr Smiles's suggestion may be right, after all.

Like so many others who have achieved greatness, Samuel Smiles was not an unusually promising scholar. He never took home any school prizes. With Douglas Jerrold he might have said, 'The only thing he took home from school was the measles.' Resuming the narrative, Dr Smiles said: 'In the early part of my life I practised as a country doctor in my native town. I was the oldest son at home, and my mother wished me to remain there, because we were a large family, and I might be of assistance in many ways. But there were already more than enough doctors in the town – eight to a population of three thousand – and my friends would not become sick even to oblige me. After I had gone on like this for years, keeping a horse and riding long distances, I decided to leave. I was not making anything, my mother kept me, and I wanted to do for myself, as I was now twenty-five or twenty-six. One day I met a Dr Mackintosh, whose classes I had attended in Edinburgh (where I was educated) for the practice of physic and midwifery. I rode out to meet him at Portobello, where I had a patient about whom I wished to consult him. "Well," said Dr Mackintosh, "how are you getting on at Haddington?" "Oh," I said, "I am not getting on at all; I am going off." "Going off! Why, the longer you live the better qualified you will be; you will become a well-known doctor in Haddington: you only want age." "But," I said, "I can't wait any longer, and I must go." "You know," said he, "there is an old proverb, 'A rolling stone gathers no moss.'" "Well," I replied, "I have been living there for about six years, and I have gathered no moss whatever, so I think I shall begin to roll." "Think of that proverb," said he in parting. But I did roll, and went first to Germany, where I remained to learn German and French.

'When I returned I was offered the editorship of a newspaper. Before I left England I had written an article for the paper, and was accustomed to write occasionally for the Edinburgh *Weekly Chronicle*. I had heard of the death of the editor of the *Leeds Times*, Robert Nicoll (who by the way was a poet: here is a volume of his verse), and had made an application through Tait of Edinburgh for the position. He asked me to write an article, which was published; but I heard no more of the matter before going to Germany. On my return to England, intending to settle at Doncaster, I called on a friend there and was surprised to find a letter offering me the editorship of the *Leeds Times*. The gentleman they had employed had not been a success; he sat in his house and wrote his articles without taking any interest in the politics of the place. They wanted to find another Scotsman, so fixed upon me. Eventually I took that position, and was there for many years, becoming a partner with the proprietor. But I didn't get much out of it, and as I had got married I decided to look out for something else.

'Railways were being started about that period, and I succeeded in obtaining the secretaryship of the Leeds and Thirsk Company. Of course the business was quite new to me, and I had to learn it. I retained this position until this and two other companies were amalgamated with the North Eastern, and as they of course wanted only one secretary, and had got him, I had to move off. It so happened that just at that time the South Eastern Railway in London were in want of a secretary, and I succeeded in obtaining the appointment.

'While the amalgamation of the Northern railways was in progress, I had to take books and documents of the Leeds and Thirsk Company to Newcastle, and remain there for six or eight months. I had previously thought of writing a biography of George Stephenson, the engineer; but although I had gone to Newcastle and made certain inquiries, I had never been able to push it through. But now I had more time at my disposal. When in London I had called on Robert Stephenson, the son of George, and when I mentioned the project he said, "It has often been proposed that my father's life should be written but I never found any one able to undertake it who cared enough about it. The fact is that when an engineer has done his work he is forgotten, though his work survives."

'It seemed to me, however, that the life of George Stephenson was a very interesting one, and I determined to get at the foundation of it, and the history of the man. So when Robert Stephenson came down to Newcastle, as he frequently did, we spent much time together, and he took me to all the places in the district with which his father had been associated – where he was born, where he worked, where he had been married, and I got to know the people whom he had known when he made the Darlington and Stockton railway – gathered, in short, the whole history of the man. Then when I came to London I used often to go and see Robert Stephenson himself, and got more information from him.

'The first edition of Stephenson's Life came out in 1857. It was very successful, and went through five editions in two years. I had before that written *Self-Help*, which was mostly in form of lectures I had delivered in connection with various societies, not for pay but for amusement and instruction of young people. A Leeds firm was willing to publish it and divide the profits, but I wanted it to come out in London. So I offered it to Routledge; but the Crimean War was then raging, and the book-trade was consequently at a very low ebb. I remember old Routledge saying, "Nobody will read books now-a-days; newspaper accounts of battles and fights are much more to the public taste. If you will call any day you will find the manuscript on the counter of my publishing house." So I went one day and saw my *Self-Help* lying amongst a lot of other documents; I picked it up and took it away with me, and put it on one side, thinking, "This won't do." But as soon as *Stephenson* was published, I thought, I will bring out that old manuscript of *Self-Help* and see if I can't make something of it. So I took it to Mr Murray and said, "Will you publish this?" "Yes – what is it?" "It is a book I have had beside me for some time: will you publish it on the same terms as *Stephenson?*" The arrangement was, I had two-thirds and he one-third of the profits. "I will be very glad to publish *Self-Help*," said Mr Murray, "but you must let me have half the profits." It was not quite finished, so I told him I would consider the matter. I eventually got him to publish the book at my own risk.

'*Self-Help* ran through a large number of editions; twenty thousand copies, I think, were sold the first year. It has been translated into all the languages of Europe without exception, and in some cases twice over–Italian, French, Spanish, German, Danish, Norwegian, Swedish, Russian; and also, curiously enough, into Japanese. The books went off, as a partner of Murray's used to say, like hot rolls. I afterwards proceeded to write the *Lives of the Engineers*, Stephenson's being one. That made a big book,' the author remarked, pointing to the five substantial volumes. Dr Smiles' other works are *Character*; *Thrift*; *Duty*; *Industrial Biography*; *Men of Invention*; *Life and Labour, or Characteristics of Men of Culture and Genius*; *Life of Thomas Edward*; *Life of Robert Dick*; *The Steam Hammer*; and *Jasmin: Barber, Poet, and Philanthropist*.

'And is *Self-Help* still selling?' I asked.

'Oh yes. The last edition consisted of five thousand copies. The type is getting so much worn that we are to have a new fount. It may possibly be brought out at a lower price.'

'Do you think that the virtues of thrift and perseverance are increasing or decreasing?'

'I think they are increasing. I receive a great many letters from all parts with respect to the influence these books of mine have had, and *Thrift* goes on steadily selling. I see there is still too much drinking going on. That appears to be because trade has been so good. Now if we have a depression of trade you will find the amount of spirits consumed decrease rapidly.'

'Don't you think there is a danger of over-doing what has been called "The Gospel of Getting On"? Isn't Help-One-Another a better working motto than Self-Help?'

'I have had some correspondence with people who brought to my notice a poem which appeared in the *Spectator* on that very subject. My own idea is that it is very important for a man to help himself and to push on and make the most of his skill and industry, but of course there is always mutual help going on at the same time. A man never can make progress merely by himself, he must have others to assist him; he thus helps them to some extent while helping himself. Of course I don't at all sympathise with a person whose only aim is to get on from a mere worldly point of view. A man should elevate himself in character and virtue and industry as well as in position. The greatest and best workers were originally poor men.'

'But don't you think selfishness is one of the most striking characteristics of the present age?'

'There is indeed a strong tendency towards selfishness. I think I have tried to rectify it. The selfish man becomes a curse to himself and to others. I see a great deal of it, but it is not Christian, it is not humane – anything but that. I have never advocated mere money-getting, or working solely for personal advantage.'

'What special advice would you offer to young men?'

'Industry, intelligence, application – these are the qualities that are required. George Stephenson used to say – I have heard him say it myself – "Now, my lads, be good, unselfish, and *persevere*" (with a strong north-country burr). What more can I say?' Dr Smiles asked. 'I think your publication is full of just the kind of advice young men need; I have been much interested in some of your excellent chapters. I would say to young men: Keep pegging away; if you fail, try again; with sobriety, integrity, and honesty, everything will come right in the end. Remember, I was forty-five years of age before I published a successful book. But I prided myself more upon my business qualities and habits, than upon my literary labours. I was for twenty-one years connected with railways (the public knows little of that part of my work), and I was prouder of being an active, punctual, business man than of being a writer of books. When I look back into the past, it all seems like a dream.'

●

ÉMILE ZOLA

Interviewed by V. R. Mooney
The Idler, June 1893

Émile Zola (1840–1902), the French novelist, was born in Paris, the son of an Italian engineer, who died when Émile was only seven. His upbringing thereafter, in Aix-en-Provence, was one of relative poverty. After failing his *baccalauréat* in 1859 he worked as a clerk in a publishing house before plunging into journalism and the writing of short stories. He was chief proponent of the naturalist technique of novel-writing and his first major work was *Thérèse Raquin* (1867). Between 1871 and 1893 he published a series of twenty novels, *Les Rougon-Macquart*, following the fortunes of a large family during the Second Empire and analysing the consequences of heredity and historical circumstances on their personalities. His novels were frequently criticized for their realistic depiction of human vices and social conditions. Like Balzac's great series of novels, they were impressive for the way in which Zola conveyed technical information about the various occupations and activities of his characters. *La Débâcle*, one of the Rougon-Macquart novels which is discussed in this interview, dealt with the politically sensitive subject of the Franco-Prussian War of 1870–71. Zola was an anti-clericalist and championed the cause of Dreyfus, the Jewish army officer who was wrongly accused of furnishing military secrets to a foreign government, court-martialled, and imprisoned on the penal colony of Devil's Island. Zola's article *J'accuse* (1898) attacked the government and military authorities for covering up this miscarriage of justice. He was prosecuted for libel and had to flee to England, although he returned a year later after an amnesty. Dreyfus was freed in 1906, but his champion had already died as a result of accidentally inhaling charcoal fumes.

'M. Zola?'

'No, monsieur, this is *not* No. 21 *bis* – this is No. 21.'

By way of justification for the asperity of the tones in which this reply is given forth the concierge of No. 21 proceeds to inform me that everyone makes the same mistake.

'It is a perpetual procession here,' she goes on. 'It is nothing but M Zola? M. Zola? M. Zola? without cease. I wish people would learn the right address.'

Now I at least ought to have known better, for I had visited M. Zola before, so, feeling rather small, I beat a hurried retreat, and betook myself to No. 21 *bis*.

Unlike most Parisians, Zola has a whole house to himself, and, as you perceive at a glance on entering, a very richly decorated house it is; tapestries, bronzes, bas-reliefs, sculptures in stone and marble, are studiously arranged about the hall and the handsome staircase, the general effect, in the subdued light of windows of stained glass, being most artistic.

On the first landing, lances and swords and armour of different kinds shine out from behind tropical plants. On this landing is Zola's studio, which is full of indications of his love for the antique – a love that is not carried to extremes, however, for the high-backed, uncomfortable chairs of our forefathers, in which so many of his fellow-collectors find it necessary to seat themselves (or their visitors), are here replaced by spacious modern armchairs.

I am not kept long waiting.

'Well, I am glad that this is a wet day, or else you would very likely have regretted losing the opportunity of going to the Bois.'

Such are the *maître's* first words after a hearty shake of the hand.

'So you want to know *all* about me. Now let me see what I can tell you without repeating myself.'

And Zola sinks down into a small but comfortable armchair, with a small Turkish inlaid coffee and cigarette stand covered with books on one side, and on the other an antique wrought iron fender placed in front of an immense fireplace, and commences placidly the following monologue, which I give as nearly as possible in his own words.

'My father's mother was a Corfiote, he himself a Venetian, and my mother was a Parisian. My father and mother met in Paris, during one of my father's numerous visits here in connection with an aqueduct which he wanted to construct at Aix in Provence. Within a very short time of their first meeting, they were married. It was a love match. I was born in Paris, in 1840, and to-day I am, therefore, fifty-three.

'In 1847 my father died, and left very little behind him, except lawsuits, which, through inexperience more than anything else, my mother and grandmother managed to lose.

'My education only then began, but until twelve, when I had finally to enter college, I had it pretty much my own way. That means I worked very little, and spent most of my time in the open air, running about in our glorious southern fields, and learning how to love and admire nature.

'At college I studied with varying success.

'What I liked best were mathematics and science. I hated Greek and Latin.

'It was during the last year of my college life that I made the acquaintance of two young fellows who may have been instrumental in making of me what I am now. As we had pretty much the same tastes it was our passion, whenever we could indulge in it, to run out in the fields, get on the banks of a stream, and for hours, under the shade of some tree, read the books of fiction which came to our possession. After each book had been gone through, we discussed its merits, chapter by chapter, studied the characters and the plot; all this more from a metaphysical than a literary point of view.

'I left college in 1848, and came to Paris to get work, in order to help my mother. I found a situation which I soon had to give up, and, till 1861, I went through all the hardships that a destitute young man can undergo in Paris.

'Often have I spent in my attic the best part of the day, lying in bed to keep warm.

'Although, as you see, I am better off now, I often look back upon that time regretting that it cannot return.

'*Voyez vous*, privations and suffering were my lot, but I had in me the fire of youth. I had health, hope, unbounded confidence in myself, and ambition.

'*Ah oui!* It was a glorious time. I remember how I used to write for hours and hours in my bed; how everything was then fresh to me, how my inexperience made me look hopefully forward. *Enfin*, life seemed bright, beautiful, and cheerful.

'After all, I really think hope is a higher satisfaction than possession.

'But I stray from the subject.

'Let me see, you left me in bed trying to get warm, and waiting for someone to provide the necessary number of coppers for a dinner.

'In 1861, I at last found a sufficiently remunerative situation at Hachette's, the publishers.

'I began at 200 francs a month. I did my work so thoroughly that I was soon raised. After a certain time I was placed in the advertising department, and there came in contact with the writers and newspaper men, who, in my first literary efforts, gave me a helping hand.

'During my stay in that office, I never ceased writing.

'You must know that I was all my life a very hard and conscientious worker.

'After my day's work at the office, I used to read and write for hours at home by candlelight. In fact, the habit of writing at night became so inveterate that, long afterwards, when I had time in the day, I pulled down the blinds in my room and lit the lamp in order to work.

'Towards this epoch I met my two college friends again. One had gained some notoriety as a painter, the other was a student at the *école polytechnique*. We resumed our rambles in the woods and our discussions. This, I am convinced, was of great use to me, as our different ways of looking at things enabled me to judge of characters, and to appreciate differing opinions.

'Before I left college, viz., when I was seventeen, I had written the '*Contes à Ninon*'. These I retouched a little, and determined to try my luck as a writer with them.

'As usual, with young and unknown writers, publishers received me and politely returned my manuscript. I tried my employer, but, although he encouraged me, and showed his sense of appreciation, by giving me a more responsible position, he refused to publish my story. Finally, I presented it to Mr Hetzel, and to my indescribable joy he accepted it.

'The book was very favourably reviewed, but sold very poorly.

'Soon afterwards, I began contributing to the *Vie Parisienne* and the *Petit Journal*, and thus got launched in journalism.

'As my evenings alone did not enable me to do all the work I had in hand, I resigned my situation in 1867, and devoted myself exclusively to literature.

'This did not improve my position, and I was obliged, for a certain time, to suffer new hardships and privations.

'It is needless to follow my career step by step. You know what I am now – you see I have succeeded.'

'Well, *mon cher maître*, not many men can boast of a success equal to yours. Indeed, there is evidence enough in this very room of that success.'

'That implies, of course, that you think I have an enormous account at the bank. You are mistaken. Every centime I get comes from the sale of my books, the rights of translation, etc. My royalty is 60 centimes per volume. This brings me about 300,000 francs a year, and I am not a man to economize. All this furniture, and the articles you see scattered about, I have slowly accumulated. I began to purchase with the first economies I ever made.

'This passion which obliged me frequently to change residences in order to find room for the ever increasing number of objects was acquired by me through reading Victor Hugo in my childhood. It is not so ardent now, I regret to say.'

As he got up to show me round, the light fell full on his face. I thought I noticed a look of melancholy, and made a remark to that effect.

With a sigh he replied, '*Mon cher monsieur*, I repeat I always think with pleasure of my garret. I had then no cares. I was, what I call, absolutely independent.'

'But in what way are you dependent now?'

'More than you think. I was then my own reader and my only critic. I lived in my writings, and thought them perfect. Since then I belong to the public, upon whose judgment my success depends, upon whose appreciation my reward lies. Do not imagine that I do not frequently suffer deeply, that I am not wounded, and that I do not feel mortified and become discouraged by the misinterpretation of my motives. These are passing clouds, but they are not pleasant, I can assure you.'

As he was unburdening his sorrows, we visited the apartment. It would be impossible to describe it in the short space of an article, as I must admit I seldom found such a mass, and at the same time such a variety, of objects collected.

Taste presides in everything; choice, disposal, grouping, and colouring. The southern nature of the host reveals itself in its love for bright colours; education and refinement in the subdued tones and harmonious *ensemble*.

He did not hesitate to show me everything; unfortunately, however, had I seen less, I would have remembered more.

As we walked back to the studio I returned to the previous subject, and asked him whether, as was generally supposed, he dashed through his books after a painstaking preliminary work.

He denied this.

'It is an error; I work very hard.'

'What way do you proceed then, *cher maître*?'

'Well, I never prepare a plot. I cannot do it. I have frequently meditated for hours, buried my head in my hands, closed my eyes, and got ill over it. But no use. I finally gave it up. What I do is to make three kinds of studies for each novel. The first I call a sketch, viz., I determine the dominant idea of the book, and the elements required to develop this idea. I also establish certain logical connections between one series of facts and another. The next *dossier* contains a study of the character of each actor in my work. For the principal ones I go even further. I enquire into the character of both father and mother, their life, the influence of their mutual relations on the temperament of the child. The way the latter was brought up, his schooldays, the surroundings and his associates up to the time I introduce him in my book. You see, therefore, I sail as close to nature as possible, and even take into account his personal appearance, health and heredity. My third preoccupation is to study the surroundings into which I intend to place my actors, the locality and the spot where certain parts may be acted. I enquire into the manners, habits, character, language, and even learn the jargon of the inhabitants of such localities.

'I frequently take pencil sketches and measurement of rooms, and know exactly how the furniture is placed. Finally, I know the appearance of such quarters by night and by day. After I have collected laboriously all this material, I sit down to my work regularly every morning, and do not write more than three pages of print a day.'

'How long does it take you to produce that?'

'Well, not very long. The subject is so vivid that the work proceeds slowly, but without interruption. In fact, I hardly ever make any erasures or alterations, and once my sheet is written and laid aside, I do not look at it again. The next morning I resume the thread, and the story proceeds to the end by logical progression.

'I work like a mathematician. Before I begin I know into how many chapters the novel shall be divided. The descriptive parts have an allotted space, and if they are too long for one chapter I terminate them in another. I try also to give some rest to the mind of the reader, or rather remove the tension caused by too long and stirring a passage, by interlarding something which diverts the attention for a time.

'Finally, I repeat, I have no preconceived plot. I do not know at the beginning of a chapter how it will end. Situations must logically follow one another, that is all.'

Of course, after this, the conversation rolled on some of his principal works, particularly *La Terre*.

In reply to the objection taken to that book, one of his arguments is that progress and science have made of man a being distinct from that of last century, and insisted that nowadays we must abandon the study of the metaphysical man of years gone by for an enquiry into the physiological creature of our days. That is my opinion, and it is in defence of this conviction that I worked for years.'

The next subject upon which I thought I might tackle him was the *Débâcle*.

'How did I prepare my *Débâcle*? Well, in the same way as all my other books. You know I went over most of the battle-fields described by me. Moreover, I received innumerable letters on the subject. The most interesting ones came from the professors of Paris schools, who, being left without employment, enlisted. These letters, coming from educated men, contain, without one exception, the same lamentations, and give similar accounts of privations and suffering. They all describe how for days they had to go without food, and ragged; and how fast their numbers were thinned. Each had in his memoirs accounts illustrating the blundering ignorance of the commanders! I was violently attacked when the *Débâcle* appeared. Everything was criticized as usual, and many details declared inaccurate. But I ask you whether it is always possible to be as absolutely accurate in small details in a novel as in a history?

'Some dates have been misplaced, and some details relating to the colour of the troopers' collars were not right; but criticism of such absurd details cannot affect the treatment and the development of the subject, and the conclusions arrived at. I am told that Marshal MacMahon is wild against me, and that he is preparing a reply to my book. It has always been my object to avoid personalities. I never once accused MacMahon, but the facts prove that he acted ignorantly. History will be severer, and when those who write it consult documents as I did, they will not treat him with the deference I used.

'General Gallifet is also my enemy. Do you know why? Because I have not mentioned him.'

'How does your *Débâcle* sell now, *cher maître?*'

'Not so well as at the beginning, and the cause of it is the Panama scandal. When the unscrupulousness of a certain class of men was made bare, the initiators of the enquiry were accused by a section of the nation with want of patriotism. Curiously enough, the same accusation was levelled against my book, therefore, instead of being thanked for the courage I had of disclosing the evils, I am punished for it. The same influences acted against me in the last Academy elections. Before the Panama affair, I was certain to have a chair.'

'Will you continue presenting yourself?'

'Certainly, until I get a seat. There is no reason why I should be excluded from that body, and if I abstain from presenting my candidature, it might be construed as an admission on my part that I considered justified the action of the academicians against me.'

'When is your novel about *Lourdes* going to appear?'

'Later than you think. I am working at present at *Dr Pascal*, which closes my series of the *Rougon-Macquart* novels.'

'Would it be indiscreet to ask you what subject you intend treating this time?'

'No. It will be a philosophical and scientific defence of the principal work of my life – the twenty volumes of the *Rougon-Macquart*. You see I attach the greatest importance to this, and therefore give special attention to my work, which is meant to be a justification of my theories and *hardiesses*. After this I'll take *Lourdes* in hand. *Lourdes* will be followed by *Rome*, and then by *Paris*. They will form a triptych.'

'Namely?'

'Well, in the first I shall try to prove that the great scientific development of our time has inspired hopes in the mind of all classes, hopes which it has not realized to the satisfaction of the most impressionable, therefore the most exacting and unreasonable minds. How such minds have returned with greater conviction to the belief in the existence of something more powerful than science, a something which can alleviate the evils from which they suffer, or imagine they do.

'Among these there may even be social philanthropists, who may think that divine intercession is more efficacious to cure the suffering of the people than anarchist theories. In my *Rome* I shall treat of the Neo-Catholicism, with its ambitions, its struggle, etc., as distinct from the pure religious sentiment of the pilgrims of *Lourdes*.

'Finally, in *Paris* I shall endeavour to lay bare the corruption and vice which devour that city; vice and corruption to which the whole civilized world brings its share. I need not say that these will be written in the shape of novels.

'For *Lourdes* I have collected all my material. As you know, I followed a pilgrimage, and was given the kindest assistance by the clergy, who allowed me to consult every document in their possession. As usual, I receive every day letters from laymen and priests, who spontaneously supply me with information.'

Zola thereupon got up, opened a drawer, and showed me piles of such letters. Among these I read one from a priest, who seemed convinced that before long Zola would be a convert. I asked him what he had seen at Lourdes.

'Nothing that I did not expect, considering that before going there I had had long conversations with eminent specialists in nervous diseases. I saw cures which would be called extraordinary by such as ignore the curative power of faith in hysteric complaints and its derivatives. But I did not see limbs straightened or replaced, nor has any monk or priest showed me or even alluded to such cures.

'But what struck me was that, contrary to what one is made to expect, I did not find among the clergy that aggressive and ostentatious proselytism. Everything is conducted in a dignified, quiet, unassuming manner.'

Continuing to look among the letters, I picked one from an English lady, expressing the sincere hope that the *Débâcle* would bear fruit, that the lesson it taught would be a warning to France, and save the nation from the errors it had fallen into during the Empire.

When I had done, Zola assured me that since the *Débâcle* he was happy to say that he receives numerous such letters from England. This shows him that the hostile feeling against him tends to disappear.

Before withdrawing, I asked him whether he had heard any more of the thief who, assuming the title of a journalist, had stolen some of his bronzes.

With a laugh, Zola replied in the negative, and explained that he had to thank *Lourdes* for the theft.

'Since it has become known that I prepare that book, the clerical papers send me their reporters. I receive them without exception. On this occasion, I was talking to a friend when a card was presented bearing the title of a small such paper. I requested the servant to show the bearer in the drawing-room.

'Five minutes later I was with the fellow, who asked a couple of questions. Instead, however, of waiting for complete information, which I volunteered to give, he very politely withdrew, and only the next day did I discover that he had removed valuables for about 700 francs.'

For how long I might have engaged the great and amiable novelist in conversation I don't know; but at this point, having listened to him for more than an hour and a half, I rose to leave.

And now that the heavy door has closed behind me, shall I attempt to compose a picture of Zola as I have seen him there in his room in his warm, many-pocketed Tyrolese jacket, braided with green, and buttoned up to the throat? Perhaps it is unnecessary, for his features must by this time be familiar to almost all.

Like all Southerners, Zola helps out his voice with frequent gestures; but he has none of the exuberant eloquence of his race. In society he is still, to a certain degree, and must always remain the victim of bashfulness; and his one attempt at public speaking was a complete failure. He has in him nothing of the boulevardier, and he is happy only when at work. Enforced idleness would mean misery to him.

●

HENRI ROCHEFORT

Interviewed by Marie A. Belloc
The Idler, April 1894

Victor Henri Rochefort, Marquis de Rochefort-Lucay (1832–1913), the French journalist and politician, started his newspaper *La Lanterne* in 1868. It was closed down by the authorities almost immediately. Rochefort left for Belgium, but returned the following year when he was elected to the Chamber of Deputies and launched another radical newspaper, the *Marseillaise*. One of his contributors, Victor Noir, was murdered by Prince Pierre Bonaparte, and Rochefort was put in jail. In 1871 he was elected to the National Assembly and launched yet another paper, *Le Mot d'ordre*, which championed the communard cause. He was sentenced to life imprisonment and transported to New Caledonia, from where he escaped in 1874. In 1880 there was an amnesty for political prisoners and exiles, and he returned to France. Again he produced a troublesome newspaper, appropriately entitled *L'Intransigeant*, and again he was elected to the National Assembly, though only from 1885 to 1886. In 1889 he left France for England, where he lived until 1895.

Marie Adelaide Belloc (1868–1947), the journalist and novelist, was the only sister of Hilaire Belloc. Their father was French and their mother English and well-connected in literary circles, being a friend of both George Eliot and Elizabeth Barrett Browning. Marie Belloc was introduced to W. T. Stead by Cardinal Manning, who was a friend of her mother, and Stead in turn introduced her to Edmund Garrett. She soon began writing for *The Pall Mall Gazette*, specializing in French literature. Because of her part-French background, she had no qualms about visiting men unchaperoned. She also spoke French, which assisted her greatly when interviewing men such as Henri Rochefort, Jules Verne and Alphonse Daudet. She formed many friendships in literary circles, in particular with Oscar Wilde, R. H. Sherard, George Meredith and Henry James. She later married F.S.A. Lowndes, a journalist on *The Times*, and, as Marie Belloc Lowndes, became a successful novelist.

Henri Rochefort, Marquis, journalist, dramatist, duellist, ex-convict, and exile, will probably remain as one of the most striking figures of the France of the Nineteenth Century, were it only through the rough, but often true, art of the caricaturist, for few politicians have been so often cartooned as the great journalist. His tall upright figure and keen eagle face, surmounted by a shock of snow-white hair, has made him a striking personality to the public imagination, whilst his paper, *L'Intransigeant*, brings him into close daily communion with hundreds and thousands of his fellow-countrymen of all ranks and conditions, for even those who do not in the least agree with the editor of that brilliant little sheet make it a point of seeing what Rochefort 'has to say' on the theme of the hour.

M. Rochefort has spent the last three years of his life as an exile, finding a hospitable shelter in England. Strange to say, he has made no attempt to learn the language of his hosts, for he fears that it might injure his style as a French pamphleteer; for in hourly communication with his Paris office, he boasts that he can keep his finger on the pulse of political France even more firmly than if he were on his beloved boulevards.

Every evening is sent off from the Regent's Park a short leader which may, the next morning, make or unmake the history of our lively neighbours. M. Rochefort's memory, as regards both friends and foes, is phenomenal; those who have skeletons abiding in their cupboards tremble when they see their name mentioned in *L'Intransigeant*.

Sitting in the large study of his London house, hung with splendid examples of Italian art, which makes it seem to the casual visitor an annex to the Louvre or National Gallery, M. Rochefort kindly consented to tell me something of his life and adventures.

'Yes, I have had a strange life,' he observed, thoughtfully. 'To begin with, I was brought up between a Conservative father and a Republican mother, and, as is generally the case with us, fell most strongly under her influence. I was twelve years old when I entered the College Saint Louis, and whilst there, instead of studying, I used to spend all my time in composing verses and reading novels. It was principally through the former habit that my political opinions first got me into trouble,' he continued, smiling grimly. 'The Archbishop of Paris, Monseigneur Sibours, announced that he was coming to pay a visit to the Lycée, and I was ordered to compose a poem in his honour. Now this worthy man had shortly before adopted the children of a certain Larr, who had been executed as having been a party to the political assassination of General Bréa. So, seeking about for what would most annoy my masters and please the Archbishop, I thought of this as a theme on which to compose my verses. Imagine the horror of everybody (for this was shortly after the insurrection of 1848) when I was heard declaiming, not the compliments which were expected, but a violent Republican tirade, congratulating the Archbishop on his humanity in having adopted the unfortunate children of a political murderer!'

'I suppose you began your journalistic career on leaving school?'

'Not so. My father, as you are doubtless aware, was himself a well-known dramatist and writer, but he died before I became of age, and, like many young men, I had to take what I could get. There had once been an idea of my becoming a doctor, but I was extremely nervous and impressionable, and dreaded even witnessing an operation, far less performing one. Therefore I was only too glad to get a small post as an *employé* in a government office, and it was whilst there, in order to add somewhat to my modest salary of £1 a week, that I wrote several short plays. I made my *début* as journalist,' added M. Rochefort, after a short pause, 'when I was twenty-seven, but I had already written many articles on theatrical criticism for the *Charivari*, and many other papers. Still, in those days critics were not paid what they are now, and I made but little way till two years later, when, to my infinite joy, for I had always had the keenest love and interest in everything that appertained to art, I was made Under-Inspector of the Fine Arts, with what then seemed a splendid salary of £120 a year. It was about this time that I began signing my articles 'Henri Rochefort', but none of our old family friends realized that it was Henri de Rochefort-Lucay who, on more than one occasion, got the papers for which he wrote suspended on account of the violence of his sentiments he expressed therein, for from the moment I was allowed my fling I began to write political articles.'

'I suppose it was about this time, Monsieur, that you became known as a formidable duellist?'

The editor of *L'Intransigeant* laughed gaily. 'I was trying the other day to count up the number of times I had fought, but I found that the number had escaped me. When I was a younger man, especially during the years between twenty and thirty, I used to accept challenges from all and sundry; I have become more wise with time, and know now that to do so very often simply means giving an enemy a chance of bringing his name before the public. For instance, I remember once a man sent me a challenge because I had written an article criticizing Marshal Ney. I think he was considerably surprised when I refused to go into the question, observing that to consider an historical judgment a cause for duelling would simply be to admit that anyone who has a fancy that way can lock the doors on the events of the past, and put the key in his pocket; and this, as a matter of principle, I would not allow to be done.'

'And which have been your most notable duels?'

'Four or five stand out in my memory,' he replied, meditatively. 'My first, which was with a Spanish officer, after I had written an article which he considered insulting to his sovereign; another with Prince Murat, in which I was wounded; one with Paul de Cassagnac, where the same fate befell me, and one, since the war, in Switzerland, with an individual who sent me a challenge on account of something I had written, though to this day I do not know what was his excuse, for I do not believe that I had given him cause for offence.'

The event which influenced the whole of Henri Rochefort's life was the publication, in the year 1868, of La Lanterne. The very words now invoke, in the mind of those who can remember what then occurred, the personality of the great journalist. Under the Empire the strictest censorship was exercised over the French press, but, notwithstanding this fact, on the first of January, 1868, a little red thirty-two page pamphlet made its appearance on the Boulevards, and had the widest success; every word of La Lanterne was written by Rochefort himself; and he put all his skill and wit in holding up once a week the Third Empire to public shame and ridicule. Even in the drawing-rooms of the aristocratic Faubourg Saint Germain the pamphlet was read with enthusiasm, and it became fashionable for ladies to have the tips of their fingers slightly tinged with the bright red which was known to rub off the back of M. Rochefort's organ.

The first step taken by the Government was to forbid the sale of La Lanterne on the Boulevards, but this only increased its vogue elsewhere. Finally, the eleventh number was seized, and the proprietor-editor was condemned, by default, to a year's imprisonment, and a fine of ten thousand francs (£400).

'But that did not trouble me,' exclaimed M. Rochefort, when talking over these glorious times, 'for from Belgium, where I had fled upon hearing of my coming doom, I continued editing my dear little paper, and we went on as far as seventy-four numbers. I often laugh when thinking of the way in which we eluded the police when sending thousands of copies of La Lanterne to Paris. You know it was made illegal to even carry a copy in your hand over the frontier; so we made use of every truc, including that of filling hollow busts of the Emperor with the seditious journal! Once in Paris it was only too easy to dispose of them, for everyone was anxious to read the pamphlet, and translations of La Lanterne were also published in Germany, Italy, Spain, and Russia.'

'What made you give up its publication?'

'I was extremely anxious to enter the French Parliament, and, feeling tired of living far away from all my interests and friends, I made up my mind to go back to Paris in disguise, and see what could be done. I was arrested very shortly after I crossed the frontier, but the Government, knowing I had opposed my candidature, and fearing, I imagine, that the news of my arrest would precipitate matters, gave me a safe conduct till the elections were over. My rival was, oddly enough, M. Sadi Carnot, who represented the Moderate Republicans of the Paris constituency for which I was standing. I won the seat by four thousand votes, and then entered for the first time the Corps Législatif.'

'It was shortly after this, Monsieur, that the sad affair of Victor Noir occurred?'

'Yes. Although I was compelled to give up the publication of *La Lanterne* on my return to Paris, I had started a new paper, the *Marseillaise*, and Noir was a member of my staff. The rights of this tragic affair will never be known. I have always held the theory that Pierre Bonaparte, when he fired at Victor Noir, believed that he was firing at me; for he had sent me a challenge a few days before, and had asked me to come and see him in his house at Auteuil. This I had not done. Now it so happened that Victor Noir was asked by another journalist to carry a letter for him to Bonaparte, and, before he had had time to explain his business, the latter had shot him dead! I need hardly tell you that the murderer was acquitted. On the other hand, I might, on account of a somewhat violent article which I wrote on the matter, have been judged and condemned to an ignominious punishment. However, the Government chose a more summary method of disposing of me. On the 2nd of February I was presiding over a public meeting, when suddenly a number of policemen burst into the hall, arrested me, and took me, without further ado, to the prison of Sainte Pelagie, and the next day the whole of my staff was also arrested. I was let out for a short time, in order to appear as a witness at the trial of Pierre Bonaparte, but, on the declaration of war with Prussia. I was once more put into prison, and there I languished, feeling, as you may imagine, terribly out of it, till the famous 4th of September, when the Republic was proclaimed, and my friends, accompanied by a large crowd, came and opened my prison gates.'

'How is it, then, Monsieur, that you were by this same Republican party afterwards exiled to New Caledonia?'

'Oh, that is a long story. My journalism was again responsible for that. I founded *Le Mot d'Ordre*, in which I started and carried on a violent campaign against Thiers and the Government of Versailles; but, on the other hand, I also attacked frequently the Communists, and told them what I thought of some of their actions. This put me wrong with both parties, and when I finally left Paris, I was arrested and taken to Versailles, where I was tried by a Council of War. Oddly enough, it happened that my judges meant to condemn me to death, but, all unknown to them – for soldiers are not lawyers – a new article had been added to the Code; and I could not help laughing in my sleeve when I saw how disappointed they looked when they discovered that the crime with which they had charged me, that of inciting the citizens to disregard the Government of the country, was punishable only by imprisonment and transportation. Still, though I was glad not to be taken out to the plain of

Sartory to be shot – for one does not recover from a correctly-aimed bullet – the idea of being sent away to the other side of the world did not please me, for it implied leaving my children, to whom I was most tenderly attached. For a long time I hoped that I should simply be confined in a French fortress, for Time seemed to have forgotten me. My little ones were being most kindly cared for by Madame Juliette Adam and her large-hearted husband, and I had news of them frequently. Imagine, then, my disgust when, on the 24th of May, 1873, I received an intimation that I was to be sent away to New Caledonia. My friend, Victor Hugo, did his best to obtain a commutation of sentence, but his letters received no reply; and on the 8th of August I started for the penal colony with a number of others, among whom was Louise Michel. We were looked upon by the people who had charge of us as wild beasts – that is the only explanation I can give for the fact that we were enclosed on deck in large iron cages.

'I did not entirely regret my sojourn in the convict settlement, for it taught me many things and won me many good friendships. That does not imply, however,' added M. Rochefort, laughing, 'that I was not exceedingly glad to get away on the 20th of March, 1874, when I and five others, among whom was the unfortunate Olivier Pain, persuaded a captain belonging to the British Merchant Service to help us make our escape. Everything went off without a hitch, and I shall never forget the kindly reception given us in Australia, for you must remember we had no money, and, I was going to add, no clothes: indeed, I had to borrow a small sum before I could send a telegram to Monsieur Adam, telling him where we were, and asking him to send me a thousand pounds. When this money arrived, we came straight to England, where I had once more the joy of clasping my children in my arms.'

'And during the last twenty years, Monsieur?'

'My history since then,' he replied, smiling, 'has been public property. The General Amnesty of July, 1880, enabled me to go back to Paris, and it was then that I started L'Intransigeant. I confess I am much attached to my halfpenny oriflamme; in it I try day by day to tell my readers something about those who are governing them,' and once more Monsieur Rochefort smiled grimly. 'I am never so happy as when I am writing. My methods of work? Well, I always use a stereoscopic pen, a most excellent little weapon, brought me from America by my son. As to my articles, I only make up my mind a few moments before sitting down to write what the subject is to be. You see I am in a peculiar position. People often bring me political documents of the greatest importance, and I make use of them as occasions arise. For instance, I possess a list of all the deputies and senators who accepted bribes over the Panama business.'

'And are you not afraid of assassination?'

'A man must take his chance of that sort of thing,' replied M. Rochefort, shrugging his shoulders. 'Of course I am aware that I have a good many enemies, and many of those in high places would not be sorry to see me disappear swiftly and quietly.'

'There have been rumours lately, Monsieur, of an amnesty.'

'Time will show us,' he replied, cautiously. 'I am quite content here. I have all my life taken a keen interest in art. Well, London is a vast storehouse of art treasures, and I am kept fully occupied, both with seeing those who come to confer with me on what is going on at home, and with visiting your splendid museums, galleries, and, may I add, picture auctions'; and with legitimate pride Monsieur Rochefort brought forward into the light a lovely sketch by Lawrence which he had lately picked up at a sale.

'One word more, Monsieur. How do you regard bomb-throwing Anarchism?'

A gloom came over Henri Rochefort's face. 'Such things do incalculable harm to the cause of Liberty, and, though you will probably not share my opinion, I may tell you that I am firmly convinced that many so-called Anarchist outrages are really planned and carried out by the police. The same may be said of political assassinations. It is so easy to use as a tool some poor half-crazy fool, who hopes in this way to win notoriety and fame.'

●

OSCAR WILDE

Interviewed by Oscar Wilde and Robert Ross
St James's Gazette, 18 January 1895

Oscar Fingall O'Flahertie Wills Wilde (1854–1900), the Irish playwright and poet, was born in Dublin, the son of Sir William and Lady Jane Francesca Wilde. He was educated at Trinity College, Dublin, and Magdalen College, Oxford, where he first developed the attitudes of an aesthete. His first book of poems was published in 1881 and the following year he embarked upon an ambitious and gruelling lecture tour of the United States during which he was frequently interviewed. He wrote several influential essays and articles; his only novel, *The Picture of Dorian Gray*, was published in 1890, and several theatrical successes came thereafter: *Lady Windermere's Fan* (1892), *A Woman of No Importance* (1893), *An Ideal Husband* (1895), and *The Importance of Being Earnest* (1895). This interview came close upon the opening of *An Ideal Husband*, after which the Scottish dramatic critic William Archer had suggested that the cult of 'Oscar' was threatening to get the better of Wilde the artist. *Salomé*, another play, was written in French and performed in Paris, though banned from the stage in Britain on grounds of indecency. 1895 was also the year of Wilde's downfall. The Marquess of Queensberry, father of Wilde's friend and lover Lord Alfred Douglas, accused Wilde of 'posing as a sodomite'. Wilde sued for libel and lost, and was then prosecuted and jailed for homosexual offences.

After his release he went to live in France, where he wrote a poem based on his experience of prison, *The Ballad of Reading Gaol* (1898).

Wilde was suspected as author of this interview, which was published anonymously under the heading of 'Mr Oscar Wilde on Mr Oscar Wilde; An Interview', but the editor of Wilde's letters, Rupert Hart-Davis, believes that it was a collaboration between Wilde and Robert Ross, his secretary. It is the earliest instance that I have found of the 'self-interview', a sub-genre of the interview which has occasionally appealed to writers with a flair for a witty and epigrammatic turn of phrase, whose public image is complex. The most famous modern examples are self-interviews by Truman Capote, Gore Vidal and Norman Mailer.

I found Mr Oscar Wilde (writes a Representative) making ready to depart on a short visit to Algiers, and reading, of course, nothing so obvious as a time-table, but a French newspaper which contained an account of the first night of *An Ideal Husband* and its author's appearance after the play.

'How well the French appreciate these brilliant wilful moments in an artist's life,' remarked Mr Wilde, handing me the article as if he considered the interview already at an end.

'Does it give you any pleasure,' I inquired, 'to appear before the curtain after the production of your plays?'

'None whatsoever. No artist finds any interest in seeing the public. The public is very much interested in seeing an artist. Personally, I prefer the French custom, according to which the name of the dramatist is announced to the public by the oldest actor in the piece.'

'Would you advocate,' I asked, 'this custom in England?'

'Certainly. The more the public is interested in artists, the less it is interested in art. The personality of the artist is not a thing the public should know anything about. It is too accidental.' Then, after a pause –

'It might be more interesting if the name of the author were announced by the *youngest* actor present.'

'It is only in deference, then, to the imperious mandate of the public that you have appeared before the curtain?'

'Yes; I have always been very good-natured about that. The public has always been so appreciative of my work I felt it would be a pity to spoil its evening.'

'I notice some people have found fault with the character of your speeches.'

'Yes, the old-fashioned idea was that the dramatist should appear and merely thank his kind friends for their patronage and presence. I am glad to say I have altered all that. The artist cannot be degraded into the servant of the public. While I have always recognized the cultured appreciation that actors and audience have shown for my work, I have equally recognized that humility is for the hypocrite, modesty for the incompetent. Assertion is at once the duty and privilege of the artist.'

'To what do you attribute, Mr Wilde, the fact that so few men of letters besides yourself have written plays for public presentation?'

'Primarily the existence of an irresponsible censorship. The fact that my *Salome* cannot be performed is sufficient to show the folly of such an institution. If painters were obliged to show their pictures to clerks at Somerset House, those who think in form and colour would adopt some other mode of expression. If every novel had to be submitted to a police magistrate, those whose passion is fiction would seek some new mode of realization. No art ever survived censorship; no art ever will.'

'And secondly?'

'Secondly to the rumour persistently spread abroad by journalists for the last thirty years, that the duty of the dramatist was to please the public. The aim of art is no more to give pleasure than to give pain. The aim of art is to be art. As I said once before, the work of art is to dominate the spectator — the spectator is not to dominate art.'

'You admit no exceptions?'

'Yes. Circuses, where it seems the wishes of the public might be reasonably carried out.'

'Do you think,' I inquired, 'that French dramatic criticism is superior to our own?'

'It would be unfair to confuse French dramatic criticism with English theatrical criticism. The French dramatic critic is always a man of culture and generally a man of letters. In France poets like Gautier have been dramatic critics. In England they are drawn from a less distinguished class. They have neither the same capacities nor the same opportunities. They have all the moral qualities, but none of the artistic qualifications. For the criticism of such a complex mode of art as the drama the highest culture is necessary. No one can criticize drama who is not capable of receiving impressions from the other arts also.'

'You admit they are sincere?'

'Yes; but their sincerity is little more than stereotyped stupidity. The critic of the drama should be as versatile as the actor. He should be able to change his mood at will and should catch the colour of the moment.'

'At least they are honest?'

'Absolutely. I don't believe there is a single dramatic critic in London who would deliberately set himself to misrepresent the work of any dramatist — unless, of course, he personally disliked the dramatist, or had some play of his own he wished to produce at the same theatre, or had an old friend among the actors, or some natural reasons of that kind. I am speaking, however, of London dramatic critics. In the provinces both audience and critics are cultured. In London it is only the audience who are cultured.'

'I fear you do not rate our dramatic critics very highly, Mr Wilde; but, at all events, they are incorruptible?'

'In a market where there are no bidders.'

'Still their memories stand them in good stead,' I pleaded.

'The old talk of having seen Macready: that must be a very painful memory. The middle-aged boast that they can recall *Diplomacy*: hardly a pleasant reminiscence.'

'You deny them, then, even a creditable past?'

'They have no past and no future, and are incapable of realizing the colour of the moment that finds them at the play.'

'What do you propose should be done?'

'They should be pensioned off, and only allowed to write on politics or theology or bimetallism, or some subject easier than art.'

'In fact,' I said, carried away by Mr Wilde's aphorisms, 'they should be seen and not heard.'

'The old should neither be seen nor heard,' said Mr Wilde, with some emphasis.

'You said the other day there were only two dramatic critics in London. May I ask –'

'They must have been greatly gratified by such an admission from me; but I am bound to say that since last week I have struck one of them from the list.'

'Whom have you left in?'

'I think I had better not mention his name. It might make him too conceited. Conceit is the privilege of the creative.'

'How would you define ideal dramatic criticism?'

'As far as my work is concerned, unqualified appreciation.'

'And whom have you omitted?'

'Mr William Archer, of the *World*.'

'What do you chiefly object to in his article?'

'I object to nothing in the article, but I grieve at everything in it. It is bad taste in him to write of me by my Christian name, and he need not have stolen his vulgarisms from the *National Observer* in its most impudent and impotent days.'

'Mr Archer asked whether it was agreeable to you to be hailed by your Christian name when the enthusiastic spectators called you before the curtain.'

'To be so addressed by enthusiastic spectators is as great a compliment as to be written of by one's Christian name is in a journalist bad manners. Bad manners make a journalist.'

'Do you think French actors, like French criticism, superior to our own?'

'The English actors act quite as well; but they act best between the lines. They lack the superb elocution of the French – so clear, so cadenced, and so musical. A long sustained speech seems to exhaust them. At the Théâtre Français we go to listen, to an English theatre we go to look. There are, of course, exceptions. Mr George Alexander, Mr Lewis Waller, Mr Forbes-

Robertson, and others I might mention, have superb voices and know how to use them. I wish I could say the same of the critics; but in the case of the literary drama in England there is too much of what is technically known as "business". Yet there is more than one of our English actors who is capable of producing a wonderful dramatic effect by aid of a monosyllable and two cigarettes.'

For a moment Mr Wilde was silent, and then added, 'Perhaps, after all, that is acting.'

'But are you satisfied with the interpreters of *An Ideal Husband*?'

'I am charmed with all of them. Perhaps they are a little too fascinating. The stage is the refuge of the too fascinating.'

'Have you heard it said that all the characters in your play talk as you do?'

'Rumours of that kind have reached me from time to time,' said Mr Wilde, lighting a cigarette, 'and I should fancy that some such criticism has been made. The fact is that it is only in the last few years that the dramatic critic has had the opportunity of seeing plays written by anyone who has a mastery of style. In the case of a dramatist also an artist it is impossible not to feel that the work of art, to be a work of art, must be dominated by the artist. Every play of Shakespeare is dominated by Shakespeare. Ibsen and Dumas dominate their works. My works are dominated by myself.'

'Have you ever been influenced by any of your predecessors?'

'It is enough for me to state definitely, and I hope once for all, that not a single dramatist in this century has ever in the smallest degree influenced me. Only two have interested me.'

'And they are?'

'Victor Hugo and Maeterlinck.'

'Other writers surely have influenced your other works?'

'Setting aside the prose and poetry of Greek and Latin authors, the only writers who have influenced me are Keats, Flaubert, and Walter Pater; and before I came across them I had already gone more than half-way to meet them. Style must be in one's soul before one can recognize it in others.'

'And do you consider *An Ideal Husband* the best of your plays?'

A charming smile crossed Mr Wilde's face.

'Have you forgotten my classical expression – that only mediocrities improve? My three plays are to each other, as a wonderful young poet has beautifully said,

> – as one white rose
> On one green stalk, to another one.

They form a perfect cycle, and in their delicate sphere complete both life and art.'

'Do you think that the critics will understand your new play, which Mr George Alexander has secured?'

'I hope not.'

'I dare not ask, I suppose, if it will please the public?'

'When a play that is a work of art is produced on the stage, what is being tested is not the play, but the stage; when a play that is *not* a work of art is produced on the stage what is being tested is not the play, but the public.'

'What sort of play are we to expect?'

'It is exquisitely trivial, a delicate bubble of fancy, and it has its philosophy.'

'Its philosophy?'

'That we should treat all the trivial things of life very seriously, and all the serious things of life with sincere and studied triviality.'

'You have no leanings towards realism?'

'None whatever. Realism is only a background; it cannot form an artistic motive for a play that is to be a work of art.'

'Still I have heard you congratulated on your pictures of London society.'

'If Robert Chiltern, the Ideal Husband, were a common clerk, the humanity of his tragedy would be none the less poignant. I have placed him in the higher ranks of life merely because that is the side of social life with which I am best acquainted. In a play dealing with actualities to write with ease one must write with knowledge.'

'Then you see nothing suggestive of treatment in the tragedies of every-day existence?'

'If a journalist is run over by a four-wheeler in the Strand, an incident I regret to say I have never witnessed, it suggests nothing to me from a dramatic point of view. Perhaps I am wrong; but the artist must have his limitations.'

'Well,' I said, rising to go, 'I have enjoyed myself immensely.'

'I was sure you would,' said Mr Wilde. 'But tell me how you manage your interviews.'

'Oh, Pitman,' I said carelessly.

'Is that your name? It's not a very *nice* name.'

Then I left.

●

PAUL KRUGER

Interviewed by Edmund Garrett
Cape Times, 22 July 1895

Paul (Stephanus Johannes Paulus) Kruger (1825–1904), the South African politician, was born in the Cape Colony. He took part in the trek to Natal, the Orange Free State, and the Transvaal, fighting against the British and being appointed as head of the provisional government of the Boer republic. He was elected president of the Transvaal in 1883 and returned to power on three subsequent occasions, the last being in 1898. His recalcitrant policy towards the British led naturally to the Boer War, during which he sought support from other European powers. Thereafter he lived in Utrecht, where he wrote *The Memoirs of Paul Kruger, Told by Himself* (1902).

Edmund Garrett (1865–1907), the son of a Derbyshire rector, was educated at Rossall and at Trinity College, Cambridge. He became President of the Cambridge Union, campaigned for the Liberal Party, and wrote verse. As an undergraduate aged twenty-two, he visited W. T. Stead, then sent him an account of their meeting entitled 'Interview with the Editor of *The Pall Mall Gazette*'. His first journalistic commission followed soon afterwards, and his career flourished, although it was constantly marred by illness and punctuated by visits to sanatoria. It was because his health had collapsed that Stead sent him out to South Africa as a special correspondent. The result was a series of reports that were subsequently turned into a book, *In Afrikanderland*, which Garrett's *Dictionary of National Biography* (1901–11) entry calls 'the best description of South Africa in that momentous phase of its development'.

Garrett's first interview with Kruger took place in January 1890 and much impressed E.T. Cook, Stead's successor as editor of *The Pall Mall Gazette*, who appointed Garrett as his assistant editor upon his return to England. Cook, who later wrote Garrett's life, said that the 1890 interview with 'Oom Paul' 'touches the high-water mark of skill in that sort . . . for such adventure Garrett was peculiarly well fitted; he was a capital talker, he had complete assurance, and a way with him which the grimmest and most consequential of men found it difficult to resent'.

This second interview took place at Pretoria a few weeks after Garrett had assumed the editorship of the *Cape Times*, a post which he held until his untimely death. Under the terms of his contract, Garrett was entitled to twelve months' notice of his dismissal, thus giving him a large degree of editorial independence and a licence for what he called 'a journalism that does things'. He was an ally of Alfred Milner, the British High Commissioner and another disciple of Stead's. Under Garrett's editorship, the paper's circulation rose. He was elected a member of the Cape Assembly.

It is six years, roughly, since I last picked my way across the streets of Pretoria – six o'clock of a sultry January morning it was, I remember – for the honour of a chat with President Kruger. In these six years much has happened in the President's republic; more in some ways if less in others than sanguine folk expected.

Materially, things have come true which I was able then, on due inquiry from those who knew, to promulgate as bold forecasts. The railways have come in with a rush, and the gold output gone up with steady strides. Long before the baptism of fireworks of the Delagoa Bay line, which the President then swore must come first, the Cape trunk line, let in by famine and tumult, has enabled the then bankrupt Rand to pay its way and that of the Republic; to rebuild Pretoria, and to change the lodgings of Oom Paul's Executive from Van Erkom's tobacco store to the great Raadzaal, which now dominates Church Square. And that extraordinary mortgage on the future known as 'Deep Levels' – the boring, at colossal cost, of a second set of holes beside the first along the miles of the great *banket* reef – this is one of many new signs that all this material development has come to stay, that the industrial *Uitlander*, outnumbering the pastoral Boer, is a feature of the situation absolutely permanent.

Yet politically it is 'as you were'. The Johannesburger is only a politician in lean times; and these are fat ones. The mob, despite two or three moments of crisis when a random shot would have fired South Africa, is still practically voiceless; the handful still rules; the impossible quietly continues; the Boer, rifle and *biltong* at saddle-bow, is still the man who counts across the Vaal. And Stephanus Johannes Paulus Kruger is still President, President for the third time; though there was talk of gerrymandering at the last election, and though some of Piet Joubert's men are said to have taken an oath, Boer-like, that they would not wash till they had shot Paul – and, as some say, kept it.

So at three o'clock of a crisp July afternoon, I once more sought the low-pitched bungalow-looking house opposite the little Dopper Church, for a talk with Paul Kruger. With me was the same interpreter as before, my good friend Johann Rissik. The six years have made him State Surveyor-General, and a rich man to boot, they tell me; but they have not touched Mr Rissik's simple readiness to take trouble for other people, nor his transparent straightforwardness, nor the President's complete trust of him, even as interpreter for a *courantschryver*.

A little more grizzled, a little more bent is Paul Kruger at seventy than he was at sixty-five; but he is still Paul Kruger, every inch of him.

In the stiff though homely parlour – just such a parlour as one knows in certain old countrified places in England, with just such rugs, just such antimacassars – the old man motioned us to a pair of chairs, and pulling up an armchair point-blank to them, sat down himself and faced us with the characteristic Boer air of masked vigilance. As he did so, he lit the inevitable long pipe and began puffing at it.

How stolid he looks! How ox-eyed! (And the comparison Homer meant as a compliment to a goddess may be permitted for the President of a pastoral Republic.) How mildly ruminative! But give him one little opening for the point he wants to make, and down he comes upon you, in under your guard, flashing and relentless as a rapier. 'Great men,' said Mr Chamberlain of another grand old man, 'are like great mountains': if so, the Paulberg is certainly a sleeping volcano.

'The next talk we have' (I had to open somehow) 'I hope, President, to be able to speak to you in the *taal*. Hitherto, I have had no opportunity to learn it.'

'Humph!'

A guttural and phlegmatic response showed me that my good intentions towards the cherished *patois* were discounted.

I reverted to our last meeting, and hastened to drag in the blessed word Swaziland – once a sure conventional 'open sesame'. 'I told you then, President, that you would get Swaziland as soon as people at home understood what you would do in return. Well, you have got it.'

The President fixed deep-set eyes on the interpreter while the words were translated; then suddenly, and with characteristic vehemence, he brought up that official phrase about Swaziland not being 'actually incorporated in the Republic'. Heaven knows what the phrase means.

'But, President, you know that is purely a question of words – diplomatic language meant to hoodwink a few people who want to be hoodwinked. You must understand that with our party-government a thing of this kind, that is in the teeth of certain prejudices, has to be done gingerly. There is a section of people in England – very good people – who become quite unreasonable on the least pretext where natives are concerned; a Government has to think of them.'

'But *I* have also my difficult people to think of. I have done my part, all the same; only the British Government have not done theirs. I risked my position here – yes, I risked it – carrying out what I promised, because I had promised.' . . .

' "Damping the trek," you mean?'

'Yes; it was a risk for me, but I did it; and then the British Government have got out of their promise.'

'But surely you have, or are on the point of having, everything that is of any use to you in Swaziland?'

'Swaziland? Swaziland is nothing . . . Swaziland is nothing at all . . . There is a little gold, perhaps; that is nothing to me; and some grazing; but Swaziland in itself is nothing at all!'

The sentences were given out with immense force and *intention*, the pipe being clutched in the right hand and withdrawn only momentarily for each sentence from the teeth, which closed upon each statement like a guillotine, then sent after it a great jet of smoke.

'But, sir, you did not say Swaziland was exactly *nothing* . . . six years ago . . .' I ventured.

'I always said it was nothing save as a way to the sea. I said that all along, and it was well understood. And now they no sooner give it to me than they take away altogether the only thing that made it worth having – the way to the sea.'

I knew of course that we must come to the Zambaan and Umbegiza business soon; but I could not have the Swaziland cession whistled down the wind so coolly; so I interjected the excellent Boer formula for all doubtful cases – *Wacht en beitje!*

'Wait a moment, President, I beg you. You used a phrase to me six years ago: 'Each hand must wash the other.' You could not expect to get everything for nothing. Swaziland, as I understood it, was for 'damping the trek'; expansion eastward for giving up claims to expand northward. The way to the sea surely was to be for a further *quid pro quo*: to wit, for joining the Customs Union.'

'See, it was like this!' the old man burst in so soon as he had grasped my statement of the case. 'There is the *trek* and there is the *haven*' – he actually laid down his pipe for a moment, and putting up two fingers of his right hand, no dapper one, ticked them off with the left.

'No! no!' I interjected, determined not to be mistaken, and copying his pantomime: 'here is the *trek*, and here is Swaziland only; then *here* (a third finger) is your haven against (fourth finger) our Customs Union.'

The President gave up the hand and fell back on still quainter symbols. Turning to the table, he seized a great leather tobacco-case which lay there close to the enormous family bible, and catching up in the other hand a matchbox, he set them up against each other like a man bartering.

'This' (the tobacco-pouch) 'is the way to the sea, including Swaziland (he hurried on), which is only useful as *part* of the way to the sea. *This* (the matchbox) is the piece of coast with means to make a port – *that* certainly is something more than the way to the sea. For *that* (matchbox again) *vryhandel*: (free trade, meaning customs union); but for *this* (tobacco-pouch) I have already given what I promised, and you have not yet given it me (brusquely withdrawing it, and throwing it on the table), you have made it now quite impossible.'

He recovered the pouch, refilled his pipe which had gone out, and puffed forth volumes of smoke, while his meaning was being made clear to me.

'This is to me quite a new conception of the case, President,' I rejoined. 'Granted, the way to the sea was always part of the bargain; but it was a distinct part, and belonged to the coast side, not the Swaziland side of the business.'

'I assure you it was as I say, it was clearly understood so in conversation after conversation with British statesmen.'

'But President' – a bright idea coming to my rescue – 'we gave you a chance of your way to the sea as well in the 1890 Convention; and your Raad rejected it. Then in the new Convention the chance was not repeated. But you had it, and lost it. How was that?'

The shot told. What the President would have liked to say was perhaps something about his recalcitrant Raad. What he did say was simply that the Raad did not consider the way to the sea which was then proposed acceptable in its method of arrangement. I asked what they really did want, and jumping up with the alacrity of excitement, the old man fetched from the next room a large school-map on a roller. We went to the table, where he spread it out, and talked rapidly over it, laying his hand now over Swaziland, now over the coast, now over that fateful little strip between the two which the recent annexation has turned into a 'No Road' notice-board. He depreciated the road to Kosi Bay proposed in the abortive Convention; it ran over ground not feasible: he depreciated Kosi Bay itself, talking of its shallowness and sandiness till I asked myself, 'Has the old man really grasped the utter futility of the dream of Kosi Harbour?' He wandered down the coast to Sordwana Bay, which is just opposite the point where the Republic most projects towards the coast, south of Swaziland and much more coastward – only forty miles off, in fact: but that bay surely is part of Zululand and a clear reversion of Natal's; Natal would always see to it that there should be an Imperial non-possumus there. He traced with one broad finger the northward course of the Pongo River, which connects this same south-east corner of the Republic, through the Tonga lowlands, with a southern coign of Delagoa Bay – as if it would really profit him to have a second string, besides the semi-Portuguese railway, to the wholly Portuguese port. But finally he made it clear that what he really yearns for is free leave to drive a wedge of Republican territory through the new annexation and the Tonga protectorate to anywhere that suits best on the coast between the Portuguese frontier and Zululand.

'But what is the use of talking – after this annexation?' He always came back to his point. 'They practically say to me, "You are shut in – shut into a *kraal* for ever!"'

He put his two hands together to make the kraal, just as he had done six years ago over the same expression. And as then, so now again, voice and gesture had a certain pathos, the note of an old man against Fate; and I noticed once more the sad gap on the rough left hand where the thumb should be – and recalled, with teeth on edge, the story of how the boy Paul amputated it himself long ago with his pocket-knife out on the lonely veldt. Truly that boy was father of this hard old man before me, who never forgets, never relents, always suspects.

'For ever is a long time, President. What if the British Government has only made its title clear to this strip of country so as to be able to bargain better – to have no questions next time which side the asset really belongs to?'

'I have been played with so often,' was the gloomy reply. 'Great Britain holds a thing out, and says: "We will consider the Republic's rights favourably, only you must just do something more"; then again it says: "*Now* you positively get it, only first there is one small thing we must have from you"; and so it goes on . . .'

What could I answer? The very expressions almost that I have written over and over again these dilatory years past. The President's sarcastic sketch of our diplomacy on the Swaziland question was an uncomfortably speaking likeness.

I turned the tobacco-pouch over in my hand rather stupidly, remembering in a vague way that the French *blague* means at once 'tobacco-pouch' and 'humbug'. To be sure, the dangling as of a bunch of carrots has not been all on one side in Transvaal *pourparlers*.

In my embarrassment I caught up the President's other symbol again, the match-box, and copying his own dumbshow of bartering the one against the other, I said:

'I think, President, you and we have been like two savages exchanging treasurers. Neither hand liked to give credit; neither would be the first to let go its prize before closing on the return value.'

The President was rolling up the map. We went back to our chairs, I assuring him earnestly that there was no real hostility to his sea ambitions in England, and quite a cordial feeling growing up in these latter days towards himself.

'You should visit England again, President, if you like being banqueted —'

'I have always found, when people banquet me, they want something out of me,' quoth the unmitigable old cynic without the ghost of a smile. And, after a smoky pause, he burst out again at the annexation grievance: 'It was the way it was done. I was never told – never consulted – never warned even.'

It must out. It was a thing I had come to say – the unpalatable truth that the oft-threatened annexation fell when it did fall simply as a sharp *riposte* to the German intriguing of Mr Kruger and his late inspirers.

'It was, after all, President, a kind of rude tit for tat.'

'Tit for tat! What had I done? What had I done, or failed to do, since the Swaziland Convention which this simply makes nothing of ?'

Of course there was but one possible answer to the challenge. Generalities would not serve here. That *gauche* speech of the President's at the *Kaiser-Kommers* playing off Germany against England was the easiest thing to name. I promptly named it.

Then did President Paul Kruger wax very wroth. He began with a volley against newspaper reports. Newspapers had to make something startling for their readers. He was utterly misrepresented. If I had been there I should have seen at once that his meaning was a perfectly harmless one.

Might I ask what it really was?

The explanation was tortuous. To my dull apprehension, it amounted to saying – well, pretty much what the papers always said he said. That did not surprise me. But the gloss was to the effect that, whatever he *said*, the President meant only a little joke, and his little joke was as much at the expense of Germany *versus* England as of England *versus* Germany. He would expect either to prevent his head being punched (were such a design conceivable) by the other. There was no mischievous bringing in of Germany – not more than of England. In fact (the President rounded off with this suggestion) the whole thing was after dinner.

'But on your own showing, President, I must join issue with your view of the German position here. We cannot allow that Germany has any right to be brought in here on a footing equal with England. What has Germany to do in this *galère* with any footing at all?'

'Do you deny my right to look to other Powers for moral support?'

'Certainly; it is treason to South African unity! . . .'

'Suppose England wanted to cut my throat! I do not for a moment say she ever would, but supposing! Should I not then have a right to moral support from Germany?'

'Giving you your independence does not look like cutting your throat; and as for moral support, what moral support got you that independence? Not German; not European at all; but just the moral support of your kinsmen, my friends down there in Cape Colony. You looked to them then, and surely it is them you should look to now, if support you want: not to France or Germany or *any* Power outside South Africa, President!'

'I know what they did! I do not forget their support! I do not wish to bring in European powers unnecessarily,' insisted the President with rising disquiet; and feeling I had the advantage of him, this time I pressed him for a pronouncement.

'Will you not say frankly, President, that you adopt the South African standpoint – the only one I hear taken in the Free State as well as the Colony: that every other European Power, beyond the maritime power of England which keeps the coasts, is an exotic, an intruder in the South African States and colonies. You are angry with England just now over this annexation; but you know that country is not lost to South Africa, as Madagascar is lost when France steps in, as Damara is lost when Germany steps in; it is only kept warm some day to be handed over as British Bechuanaland is being handed to Cape Colony, as Zululand will be handed to Natal –'

'It does not help me to have country taken from me and handed to Natal,' said the President hotly . . .

'And as Swaziland has been to the Republic,' I closed up my argument; 'as this very strip may yet be, for value received.'

'Swaziland was by right ours already! They were all ours! Natal itself was ours! It is like stealing my watch' – he pulled out a great clock, disengaging the chain and seals with trembling fingers, and thrust it into my embarrassed hands: 'You take my watch, then you say, "Look! we give you this. Here is a nice present for you; be grateful"! I will not say anything unfriendly to Germany!' Then, as if he had committed himself too far, he went on pettishly: 'I do not wish this conversation printed. It must not be published. I inform you that I was only giving you a friendly chat . . .'

Here was a pretty kettle of fish! It is ill to argue with the master of interviews, as of legions. I had won the argument, so I fondly told myself, and lost my paper the interview. I had angered Oom Paul; he knew his German speech was a blunder, and he was determined to punish me. Was he inexorable? Not at all, when the moment's testiness had been got over. There were explanations and apologies; the temperature resumed the normal; fairness and good temper reasserted themselves; the embargo on publication was removed; and my interview was saved by the skin of its teeth.

The old man, remembering his Boer hospitality, went out to order coffee, and on his return hastened to leave the dangerous topic for more attractive ground.

'President, will you bargain with me a moment for your seaport, as you did six years ago for Swaziland? I want another outspoken message to the English people. Imagine me plenipotentiary for them – all we journalists are that in a sense . . .'

'Well?'

'First, there is the railway question . . .'

The President frowned slightly.

'The Cape asks for too much. We cannot agree for so much. We have not yet a basis of agreement.'

'Granted. But after we have had all the lines working together, with no cutting down prices, so as to see where the trade will naturally run – say eighteen months or two years hence: suppose it were possible for a committee of railway experts to apportion the profits on the ascertained facts: would you consider the idea of a general pooling of the railway systems and of the customs at the same time – for customs are an asset in a railway fight, and *vice versa* – if the same conference which achieved this gave you out of hand and at once your port, your access, everything you want to get to the sea? No promises, mind; no more nonsense about "good will" on either side; but cash down – harbour for rail-and-customs union?'

Needless to say it took the President some time and a great deal of tobacco smoke to digest this portentous offer, which has all the sweeping largeness of the irresponsible diplomat.

'I cannot well say yes or no without knowing more of the Railway and Customs Union. All would depend on the terms,' he answered at last. 'Hitherto in all the unions proposed, this Republic has had all to give and nothing to gain.'

'But if it had the sea to gain, and union were the only condition? Put yourself for a moment in *Oma's* place,' I pleaded (*Oma*, Grandmother, is colloquial Boer for Her Britannic Majesty's Government).

'*Oma* has to think of her children. Natal and the Cape may say, "Why give the Transvaal a port which might be used to cut us out? The Transvaal is rich; we are poor; but we have our ports."'

'But I don't want a port to cut them out. I only want it to prevent them from joining together to bleed me.'

'Then surely you can have no objection to getting your port on terms which simply lay that down. Once come with a Customs and Railway Union, and any hostile action between the various ports is impossible. Surely you don't ask us for a port, and in the same breath refuse guarantees that the giver of the port shall not suffer by it?'

'I will give any guarantee of equal treatment at the port that England demands,' exclaimed the President. 'I will promise that it shall never be less favourably open to English or English Colonial trade than to any other in the world.'

'Not even by the expedient of differential railway rates?'

'No; that is also a point which can be settled beforehand, when we come to discuss the harbour.'

'Then, in effect, you are not opposed in principle to such a simultaneous settlement of all these open questions as I suggest?'

'I am in favour of a settlement. I have always been in favour of a settlement, so it be only fair and reasonable; then it is for the benefit of the republics as well as the colonies; it will help us all together.'

With this very proper sentiment the President evidently meant the interview to close. It had indeed lasted well over an hour, and I felt I must not abuse the old gentleman's courtesy longer. Yet there was one question yet in the bottom of the wallet that must out. I could not go away without a word about the franchise and the *Uitlander*. We had settled up South Africa; but the internal affairs of the Transvaal we had been ignoring.

'One thing more I must ask, President – and understand, please, that I speak now not in an English character. England claims no voice in your private affairs on the Rand or elsewhere.'

The President nodded slowly, and resigned himself to the unwelcome line of country.

'No doubt, you have there among the rest some of the scum of the earth,' I pursued, anxious to get out at once all my credentials of moderation. 'But you have also –'

Tramp, tramp, tramp! At this point in came half a dozen members of the Volksraad, evidently keeping an appointment with the President. They drowned my sentence unfinished. He rose to welcome them, and Mr Rissik to go. I surveyed the situation, and with a bold stroke brought the intruders into the conversation.

'Let us ask these gentlemen,' said I, turning to a bearded farmer in broadcloth: 'I appeal to your own burghers, President. Are there not, besides the scum of the earth in Johannesburg, thousands of honest folk who are building houses, and rearing children, and meaning to spend their lives here, and could be safely *inspanned* as citizens?'

The half-dozen must have all this translated, of course. There was handshaking and introductions; the talk became general. Platitudes were poured forth, and the President slyly dropped out of the conversation. At last I carried off Mr Rissik in triumph, and got back to his Honour.

'There are our own Afrikanders [*sic*] from Cape Colony, too, President. Surely *they* can be trusted with your independence. I know you suspect them as *Engelsche gesind* –'

'I have no hatred of the English,' was the wary answer. 'See this ring . . .' And he began working away at a big plain gold ring on his finger, wetting it and trying to push it off. I knew that old ring. It was a gift from an English sympathizer on one of the President's visits to us in the 'seventies or 'eighties. Bother the ring! I mentally ejaculated.

'Surely you could trust the Afrikanders [sic] with a vote,' I persisted, escaping from a vicious, if golden, circle.

'They can vote already,' said the President, impatiently enough. 'After only two years, they can vote for a Landdrost and a Commandant, and the Second Raad, which has to do with many important things, and will have more still given to it . . .'

'President, if I had cast my lot in with your Republic I should be willing to exchange British citizenship for yours; but I would not be put off with half-citizenship. I should not care a straw, if you will excuse me, about your Landdrost and your Second Raad; I should demand a voice in the real government of the country. As it is, you are less of a Republic here in reality than we in the Cape Colony.'

'What!' exclaimed the President; 'you can only vote for one Raad in the Colony . . .'

And he launched into a constitutional disquisition from which it appeared that he imagined that at the Cape the Assembly co-opts the Council.

I assured him the Council was elected by the very same voters as the popular chamber; whereon he fell back on comparing himself, directly elected by the people, with the Governor and the Prime Minister whom the Colony does not elect directly. I rejoined that we could at any rate make our Prime Minister responsible for his mistakes and turn him out. And so on and so forth. It was characteristic of much that, when at a loss for any other argument of Transvaal constitutional superiority, the President fell back on colour. 'You in the colony,' said he, 'are governed by black men. You let black men vote!'

At last we escaped from the constitution and returned to the point.

I asked him plainly what he would do if the Orange Free State proposed an assimilation of the oligarchical Transvaal franchise to their own liberal one as a condition precedent of the much-talked-of inter-Republican federation? He at once and firmly declined to discuss the question.

There was a pause; then Oom Paul said gravely, 'See, I will tell you what is the truth about this *stemregt*. I know neither English nor Dutch, Afrikander nor *Uitlander*; I only know good people and bad people. You yourself say, some of these people in the towns are the scum of the earth. Very well. We cannot let people in without proving them. We let them in once before the war, and therefore the war came; for it was people let in on this easy plan who misled the English Government into coming in and annexing us. Therefore we must first *prove* this population – we must *prove* them to see if they are good people or bad people. Then . . . we shall see.'

A most characteristic pronouncement! Derive from it, O reader, what sap thou may'st. Around, the faithful burghers sat drinking it in with heavy concentration; puffs of smoke were the commas, and the full-stops – well, you know how a Boer puts in the stops in a conversation . . . till you scarcely know where to tuck your feet.

We rose to go.

And so, with thanks on my side and mutual expressions of good will, ended my latest – not, I hope, my last – plain talk with the 'grand old man' of the Transvaal.

'Oom Paul is a bad enemy, as we have learned to our cost. He has proved to us of late that he can also be a leal friend. Slowly but surely, I believe, my countrymen are coming to realize that his friendship is worth having.' So I wrote six years ago, after a talk at Pretoria. My countrymen so far agreed with me that they gave Oom Paul Swaziland. If they now grumble that they have seen little friendship since, I answer that they got what they were promised, and that they dangled the gift too long for any further graciousness to cling to it. Do not suppose that now the strenuous old man is done with. In a sense, age is strength to him: I felt a touch of pathos, an impulse of hero-worship myself; how much more must his own burghers.

If there are two just men in South Africa who know what they want and hold by it in the teeth of fate, he is one of the two. For the *Uitlander* in the Transvaal, Oom Paul will do just so much as he is forced to, when he is forced: no sooner and no more. As well talk to the Paarl rock! But for a frank and bold policy of South African amity outside, may not the one strong man be as good to bargain with as ever the *Uitlander* in his thousands is likely to prove, when the *Uitlander* has come by his own? Be that as it may, I have the honour to offer President Kruger's words, through the *Cape Times*, to the consideration of England and South Africa.

●

'ARE INTERVIEWERS A BLESSING OR A CURSE?'

Barry Pain, *The Idler*, December 1895

Barry Pain was the pen-name of Eric Odell (1864–1928), who obtained a third-class degree in classics from Cambridge in 1886. He went on to become the most successful comic writer in England at the turn of the century, with his articles being published in a series of collections. He followed Jerome K. Jerome as the editor of *To-Day* in 1897.

I do not make this a personal question at all. I may once or twice have been interviewed, by mistake for somebody else, but I put any opinions and prejudices aside that I may have formed then. Looked at impartially, the question presents two important points – the point of right and the point of taste. They are both equally simple. With regard to the point of right, it will readily be acknowledged –

That the public has a right to wish to know something of its celebrities in their homes.

That the editors of periodicals have a right to tell the public what they wish to know.

That the celebrities have a right to refuse to tell the editors or the public anything whatever, and to refuse to have 'a cosy corner in the Library' photographed and reproduced.

At the same time, the celebrities should remember that, if they exercise their right, the periodicals will not contain interviews; that if they do not contain interviews the public will not buy them; that if the public does not buy them the periodicals will cease to appear; and, finally, that if there are no periodicals, the editors will all die of starvation and exposure; there will be no celebrities at all – for the press makes the celebrities, and without celebrities society will cease to exist. There would be other results – the coroners would be over-worked, and the housemaids would have nothing to light the fires with in the morning – but I need not go into these. The refusal of a fifth-rate burlesque actress to tell an interviewer that she loves her art, and that he will be surprised to hear that her favourite recreation is gardening, would therefore swell the ranks of the unemployed, and tend to disintegrate the social system. The celebrity has a right to refuse to be interviewed – otherwise, where is the liberty of the subject? But a merciful celebrity will not exercise the right.

We come to the point of taste. You, as a celebrity (I take it for granted that you are a celebrity – most people are), will consider that, since the public wishes to pry into your private concerns, the public taste is bad. You will also consider that, since it is the public which has made you a celebrity by its appreciation of your high-kicking, poetry, trained dogs, cycle record, or statesmanship, the public taste is, therefore, good. These two conclusions cancel one another, and may be allowed to go out. You pass to the consideration of your own taste. Good taste decides that you cannot possibly have the furniture of your house, the expression of your face, the geniality of your smile, and all the affairs of your private life exposed to the public gaze. Good taste demands a certain reticence. Therefore – this is very important – if you have good taste, you will be interviewed as often as possible, and you may even find it necessary, in the interests of your own privacy, to pay papers to interview you. Nothing conceals one's real self better than an interview, except more interviews. Vary the information which you give to the interviewers; never tell two of them the same thing, and never tell any one of them anything approaching the truth. Always see a proof; it is possible that the interviewer may have observed some little thing correctly, and it is necessary to strike it out. In this way, by the careful disposal of dummies supposed to be you, you will detract public attention from your real self and attain the privacy and reserve which your good taste demands.

●

HENRIK IBSEN

Interviewed by R.H. Sherard
The Humanitarian, January 1897

Henrik Ibsen (1828–1906), the Norwegian playwright, first became a celebrity in his native country in the 1860s with his plays *Brand* and *Peer Gynt*. However, it was not until 1880 that his plays began to be performed in England, in translations by the London dramatic critic William Archer. Another critic, George Bernard Shaw, was an enthusiast, but performances in England of *Ghosts*, *Hedda Gabler* and *The Master Builder* in the early 1890s had sparked controversy.

By the time of this interview, Ibsen was becoming accepted as a major playwright of international stature. Because of his interest in social and moral issues, it is not surprising to find this interview with him in *The Humanitarian*, which was the monthly magazine of the Humanitarian Society and which otherwise tended to interview churchmen, missionaries, philanthropists and social workers. This was one of a series of interviews that R.H. Sherard conducted for the magazine with writers whose work reflected humanitarian concerns, the others being Hall Caine and Alphonse Daudet. It was the result of several conversations.

It was noticed by many, during the recent festivities in Christiania in honour of Doctor Nansen, that Doctor Henrik Ibsen had abandoned the places where he is daily to be seen, and this appeared strange to those who have remarked his clockwork regularity and unvarying habits. Indeed, at the gala performance at the Christiania theatre, where a box had been reserved for his use, his non-appearance provoked much comment, although everybody knew, or ought to have known, that since the conservative and prudent manager of the municipal theatre refused to play *Ghosts* on his stage, Dr Ibsen has never set foot in a house which, with this exception, has been so hospitable to him. It had been expected, however, that on so special an occasion he would have made an exception, and all the more so, because the rival Björnson was to be present as his *vis-à-vis*. Ibsen, one thought, would come to share a triumph, which, as it was, was enjoyed by Björnson alone. However, he stayed away, just as he had stayed away from every one of the functions of that period of enthusiastic rejoicing, save and except the dinner at the Palace. It can be conjectured what was the nature of the comments passed in this connection, for malevolence is as rife in Christiania as in any other town. Now malevolence is invariably stupid, and here, none who so commented, saw the absurdity of attributing to Ibsen, the philosopher, jealousy of Nansen, the athlete. The real reason was, of course, that Dr Ibsen, an old man of methodical habits, was afraid to face the crush of the Karl Johann's Gade, down which he walks every day, and the crowd in the Grand Hotel, where twice a day he takes his favourite stimulants. There may also have been some reluctance on his part to witness scenes and manifestations, which, in their effect as in their cause, might seem to demolish the theory of human life and human character which he has so laboriously endeavoured to establish. For here was optimism radiant and roaring, here was faith vindicated, here was the exultation of the crowd at the triumph of those admirable qualities in man, which Ibsen would have us believe are lost to the world. Nansen, his crew, and their achievements, and the enthusiasm which these provoked in thousands and tens of thousands, seemed to deal a *coup de grâce* to the pessimism which Ibsen has preached so long and with such impressive earnestness. And then again, Ibsen is an unhappy man, and he may have felt that he would be out of place amongst people so exuberantly happy. If he went to the king's dinner, at the king's invitation, it was no doubt because the *mise-en-scène* appealed to the dramatist, just as King Oscar's excellent *cuisine* appealed to the finest epicure in Scandinavia. And it may be noted in this connection that the love of the table usually goes hand-in-hand with pessimism. One remembers Schopenhauer at his *table d'hôte* and the '*il n'y a que ça*' of Émile Zola. This love of the table appears to be the only consolation of those who have lost faith in all the many things which make for the joy of living. It certainly seems to be the only consolation that life affords to Henrik Ibsen, whose ingrained sadness impresses itself on all who approach him.

During six weeks, I saw him almost every day, for he pays two daily visits at fixed hours to the hotel at which I was staying, and on no single occasion did I ever see him in any company. He was always alone, whether sitting behind his glass in the little inner room at the Grand Hotel, reading the Norwegian papers, or perambulating the Karl Johann's Gade with his hands behind his back. And as he is out of doors, so he is also in his house in the Victoria Terrasse, a solitary man, manifesting a real dislike for family life. He never visits his one son, Dr Sigurd Ibsen, who is almost as great a recluse as his father. Indeed, when this son married one of the daughters of Björnstjerne Björnson, Dr Ibsen kept away from the wedding.

This sadness, this want of sociability on his part, struck me as so abnormal on the part of a Norwegian – for the Norwegians are in the main jovial and fond of society – that I could not help expressing my surprise on the subject to

Björnson, whose neighbour at table I was at a dinner given by Mr Thommessen, editor and part-proprietor of the *Verden's Gang*.

'But, Ibsen,' cried Björnson, 'is not a Norwegian at all. He comes of a Scotch family, and that explains his Calvinism, his despairing views on life and on men. It is indeed a grievance to the Norwegians that this export-trade of pessimism in Christiania should have been founded by a foreigner.'

However this may be, it is certain that Ibsen's pessimism is sincere, and the result to himself is that he is a very unhappy man. I had many conversations with him, but I only heard him laugh once, and that was one day when I asked him if he had seen in the Paris *Figaro* an article on 'The Influence of Ibsen on Modern Painting', which had recently appeared. He was much amused, and kept saying: 'What in the world have I to do with that? What do the journalists not invent?' For the rest he greatly prefers silence to conversation, and is particularly hostile to the interview in any form. On the day on which I first saw him, he had been much incensed by an article in the form of an interview which had appeared in a Berlin paper. He would not contradict it however, contenting himself by describing its writer as a *Schweinehund*, which conveyed also his comment on its accuracy. The same evening, however, he authorized me to contradict everything that had till then appeared in the papers on the subject of the new play which he was then finishing. Many particulars had appeared in the German papers, where it had also been announced that the title decided upon was *Leichengeruch* (*The Smell of Corpses*). 'I never speak of my new plays,' he said. 'No one knows anything about them – not even the slightest particular – until they have become public property.' His caution in this respect dates no doubt from the time when the agent of an enterprising publishing-house in America, obtained, by bribing a compositor in a Copenhagen printing-office, advance proofs of one of his plays, and by anticipated publication considerably spoiled its effect. In addition to this – not to mince matters – Dr Ibsen has but little inclination to oblige strangers. I should describe him as a typical misanthrope, by natural tendency and by the circumstances of his life. This has not been a happy one, and though great success has crowned him at last, it has come too late. Till he was nearly of middle age, he was held in his native land a man of no account, his work was derided and he had to suffer all the humiliations and stress of poverty. Not very long ago a Bergen publisher presented him with the copyright of one of his earlier works, which in the days before he left Norway to seek his fortunes abroad, he had sold to him outright for the sum of twelve pounds. His domestic life has not been a happy one and woman has woven but few celestial roses into his life. In his *Master-Builder* he expressed what were his ambitions as a young man, ambitions which he has scarcely been able to realize. He is, as Norwegian circumstances go, a rich man to-day – and is held to be worth between two and three hundred thousand kroners – but this money has come too late to compensate him for the real privations of his youth and middle age. So there is little joy in his life, except what may be derived from creature comforts and constant study. He is a great reader of the German philosophers, and told me of his particular delight in Kant. 'I read him first as a duty,' he said, 'and afterwards as a pleasure.' His only relaxation appears to be to spend an hour twice a day at the Grand Hotel, and to read the papers, with a glass of aqua vitae on his right hand and a glass of beer on his left, from which as he reads, he takes alternate sips. He spends one hour a day in perambulating the streets, clad in black, professional broadcloth, with his tall hat tilted back on his head. The rest of his day is spent in absolute seclusion in his house in Victoria Terrace, where visitors are rarely, if ever, admitted. He is never seen at the theatre, or in society, or at any place of entertainment. He is rarely seen in any man's company. It is a dismal and depressing life in a town which at its best is not a cheerful one. I shall not forget the astonishment with which he asked me one morning after I had been a month in Christiania: 'Still here? What can you find to do in this town?'

'It's all so new to me,' I said, seizing my opportunity, 'Christiania is a very interesting town for an observer.'

'Indeed I find it so,' said Dr Ibsen. 'It is the most immoral town in Europe, and there is no town in Europe where a student of social life can find better subjects. Marriage, for instance, is practically non-existent here, and that is due first to the abolition by the police of all government-controlled prostitution, such as used to flourish here until recently, an abolition which has driven our young men into the alcoves of their neighbours, as an alternative to disease of the worst kind, and secondly to the ease with which, thanks to recent legislation, divorces can be obtained in Norway.'

'Is that so easy a matter here?'

'Yes, a man or a woman can now get a divorce in a few weeks by a mere application to a magistrate, who decides the question administratively, that is to say without any civil process, and who never refuses to separate a couple who may have got tired of each other. So that, it being so easy for a man or a woman to get divorced, marriage is deprived of half its terrors in the eyes of our people, and there is little reason for the *union libre*, which flourishes in parts of Germany and France, where divorces are not so easily obtained.'

'Are you in favour of the free union?'

'I?' cried Dr Ibsen. 'I? I am in favour of nothing. I suggest no remedies. My plays are not doctrinary. They describe life as I see it —'

'Here in Norway?' I interrupted.

'Certainly. I am a Norwegian dramatist and my plays describe life as I see it in Norway. They do not profess to indicate how a better state of things could be introduced. I am not a teacher. I am a painter, a portrait-painter.'

'But a portrait, a picture can often be made to convey a lesson more effectively than any other means.'

Dr Ibsen slightly shrugged his shoulders, 'I am not a teacher,' he repeated.

It was some days before I could tackle him again, that is to say before I

found him once more in a talkative humour. I then reverted to the sociological
questions which I had been instructed to put to him.

'Do you think the woman question, *the* question of the future?'

He smiled. 'Why of the future?' he said. 'Has it not always been *the* question,
is it not *the* question now. There is no reason why it should ever cease to be *the*
question. If you mean, however, to ask; whether the immediate future will see
the emancipation of women, that is to say an equalization of their position with
that of men, I say, no. There are many years, centuries to pass before such
emancipation takes place. It will be the result of a natural *processus*, the gradual
increase of physical strength in women, combined with an increase of civil
power, of wealth, and so on – not at all the result of the isolated action of a few
foolish individuals.'

'Then you think women should be admitted to political power?'

'I never said so. *Gott bewahre!* I said they will gain an increase of civil power,
inevitably, whether you or I think they should have it or not. They will attain
equal powers with men. Have they not done so already in parts of America? But
there, no doubt, the women are endeavouring to anticipate. These things
cannot be yet. *Das muss sich so Alles entwickeln*. Little by little the restrictions as
to the holding of wealth, of property, by women will fall away, and simultaneously powers will be naturally conceded to the women to protect their property.
Whether all women will care to exercise political power, to vote and so on, is
another question.'

'Then you think their social condition will improve?'

'Most certainly, but as gradually as it has improved since, since say the days
of the Council of Trèves. It is certain; one can see its gradual development, that
the social condition of women is improving, that they are becoming less and
less mere drudges, mere breeders, and more the helpmates and comrades of
men.'

'Your preference, Doctor, seems to be for women, you seem to hold that sex
better –'

'I will not have you say that I hold such and such general opinions because I
have described such and such things. I do not generalize in my plays.'

'Do you think the economic condition of women will improve?'

'In proportion to the general improvement of economic conditions, if any
there is to be in Europe, which I doubt. From what I read in the papers there will
soon be terrible competition from the East. Women will be allowed to compete
freely with men in all branches of labour, but whilst the difference exists in their
physical powers they must always compete at a disadvantage. A woman cannot
get away from her sex and the impediments of it. During the periods of
menstruation, for instance, she is at a great disadvantage, and then there is
maternity. But I think legislation, when the fixation of a minimum wage comes to
be a fact, will concede to women for a similar amount of work, a similar wage. At
present in factories and mines and elsewhere women are expected to do a man's

work for half a man's pay. That injustice will be remedied by men themselves, that is to say, before the time when women will be able to remedy it themselves.'

'What is the position of women in Scandinavia?'

'In some ways advanced. You must have seen our "studentessen" walking about the streets in their academicals. Many of these girls come up from the country and live alone in lodgings, and, as you may have noticed, are very well able to take care of themselves. Again, where society is so thoroughly immoral as it is in the towns of Norway, and here in particular, woman enjoys more power than she does when the virtues are practised. Consider for instance, the position that woman holds in Paris, where the courtesan of the hour has more power than the corps of ministers. The position is not one that flatters the woman-idealist, but there it is none the less.'

'Is Christiania then so immoral a town? I am sure one sees little of it. The streets are singularly –'

'It is just because the streets are so singularly clean that the private houses, the family circles, are so singularly impure. The *ménage à trois* flourishes here as nowhere else, and, in illustration of the equalization of the sexes, the third party is as often as not a woman. People marry, divorce, re-marry, and after re-marriage return to a kind of *union libre* with their divorced spouses. It is very comic in Norway since the new divorce laws – far more droll than anything which any French *vaudevilliste* imagined.'

'I suppose that since the abolition of Government inspection of women, disease has spread very greatly here.'

'Yes, next to Stockholm there is perhaps more syphilis in Christiania in proportion to its population than in any other town in Europe.'

'Was not *Ghosts* –?' I began.

'Do not ask me,' said Ibsen. 'I don't want that old story raked up. The director of the theatre did what it was his right to do.'

'It was thought at the time that you intended *Ghosts* to be a protest against legislation likely to cause a spread of syphilis.'

Doctor Ibsen made no answer. 'What measures would you propose for the suppression of this terrible disease?'

'I? I? Why should I propose measures? I have nothing to do with that. And what use would there be in proposing measures? It has been suggested that syphilitic men should be forbidden to marry. How is one to tell a syphilitic man after the outward signs of his malady have disappeared. There is nothing to be done, except for the doctors to study how to remedy the disease, which at present they can not. By the way, it was a poor young fellow from this University who sacrificed himself in experimenting on the value of inoculation of attenuated syphilis as a preventive of the real disease, and died in consequence. Pasteur might have discovered some remedy, but, as I have been told, always refused to take up the question, having, as he said, no sympathy with the victims of this disease.'

'He might have had some with the innocent victims, the children of syphilitic parents, like the lad in *Ghosts*.'

'*Ghosts* hardly gives the meaning of "Gjengangere", which means *les revenants* – those who come again.'

'Which enables you to preach your doctrines of heredity?'

'Doctrines! I have no doctrines. How often am I to tell you that my plays are not doctrinary. I describe what I have seen. I have seen the immense importance of the question of heredity, and I have described its effect in certain instances.'

'Do you believe in hereditary transmission of mental and moral tendencies as well as in physical heredity?'

'Most absolutely. But the two things are the same, practically.'

'May not heredity be influenced by environment and education?'

'You know that as well as I do,' said Dr Ibsen, with some impatience. 'The conditions under which a child is trained, and the nature of its education, must have an immense influence on its moral tendencies, though less on its mental, and still less on its physical tendencies. All the training and education imaginable will not make the victim of hereditary syphilis less a victim, though they may save from the asylum a child predisposed to insanity or alcoholism.'

'Is there much drunkenness in Norway?'

'A great deal in all classes. But great efforts are being made to check the spread of alcoholism by legislation. There is a strong temperance party here. But I do not think they will effect much. Indeed, since recent laws were passed, one sees more drunkards in the street than formerly.'

'Do you regard drunkenness so much the cause of poverty as the result of it?'

'It's a vicious circle. A man drinks to console himself for the wretchedness of his position, the smallness of his wages, and he remains in a wretched position, and cannot improve his earnings because he drinks. On the whole, though, I should say it was cause rather than result.'

•

CECIL RHODES

Interviewed by Edmund Garrett
Cape Times, March 1898

Cecil John Rhodes (1853–1902), the South African politician, was born in England, the son of a vicar. Owing to ill health he was sent to Natal, where he made his fortune from the Kimberley diamond fields in the 1870s, and in 1888 he formed the De Beers Consolidated Mines Company. He returned to England and attended Oriel College, Oxford. He entered the parliament of the Cape Colony in 1881 and served as prime minister from 1890 to 1896. His commercial interests expanded rapidly. He persuaded the British to annex Bechuanaland in 1884, obtained the charter for the British South Africa Company in 1889 to administer the Matabeleland territory, and conspired to annex the Boer republic of the Transvaal by filibuster in 1895, an incident known as the Jameson Raid. This was part of his grand scheme to establish a British federal dominion in South Africa. He resigned after the Raid turned out to be a fiasco and devoted himself instead to the development of Rhodesia ('my North'), which territory had been named after him several months before the Raid. He dreamt of forming a quasi-masonic, secret society modelled on the Jesuits, which would aim to reunite the Anglo-Saxon peoples, including the citizens of the United States, in a single empire. During the Boer War he helped organize the defence of Kimberley and when he died shortly before his forty-ninth birthday his last words were: 'So little done, so much to do.' He never married and it was as a result of his generous bequest that the Rhodes scholarships at Oxford (for Americans and colonials) were created.

Sir Edward Cook, who described Stead and Garrett as 'the ablest interviewers I ever knew', held a high regard for this particular interview with Cecil Rhodes, referring to it as 'a masterpiece ... I do not think there is any statement of whatever compass which embodies so vividly so much of the manner, character and ideas of Rhodes as this presentation of the substance of several conversations'.

After further heart trouble in 1898, Garrett was obliged to abandon his editorship of the *Cape Times* and his role in South African politics. Back in Europe, he met and married a Quaker woman, Ellen Marriage, who had been a fellow-patient at a sanatorium in Suffolk. He had been given six months to live, but in fact managed three years of happy marriage.

A former colleague on the *Cape Times*, G.A.L. Green, later wrote that if Garrett had not been afflicted by ill-health 'his magnetic personality and gifts of oratory might well have been Rhodes's successor in South African politics'. Garrett's own epitaph was simple: 'In the brief opportunity given him he eagerly endeavoured to serve England and South Africa.'

'Speak? Of course I'm willing to speak if I'm wanted. I don't like speaking, as you know. I don't speak by choice. But if there's a definite purpose, if it's going to help in the election, and I'm asked to speak – why, what do you suppose I am waiting about here for? I am waiting over the election simply on the chance that one's influence may be of use to help the Progressive party. If I followed my own wishes, do you think I should be messing about down here?'

That set my eyes travelling from the broad white-pillared stoep of Groote Schuur away up past the trim Dutch garden, past the faint blue hydrangeas in the spinney, past the oaks and the pines, up the hill to the steep purple bluffs of the mountain, with the old Blockhouse at its edge – Mr Rhodes has just had a tree felled to open his view to the Blockhouse. I suggested that Groote Schuur grounds, even when shared with all Cape Town, as Mr Rhodes shares them, were not such a very bad place to be 'messing about' in.

'Yes, yes – it's a picture here, a picture one never tires of; but life isn't all looking at pictures, and I want to get back to my North, you see. They want one there, everything is moving; I ought not really to have left. Here one sits talking and talking and seeing people. Here it's all talking – in the North it's *doing*. Away on the veld I am always happy. Can't you see that if it was not for a purpose I should have been back there weeks ago?'

He threw himself on to one of the big sofas in the stoep with a bang.

'But, Mr Rhodes, you can hardly grudge, if you are going to take a leading place again in Cape politics –'

He bounced up again from the sofa even more impatiently than he had bounced into it.

'Don't talk as if it was *I* who want your Cape politics. You want *me*. You can't do without me. You discuss "Ought Rhodes to do this?" and "Will Rhodes keep in the background?" and so on – I am quite willing to keep out, but you have to take the feeling of the people, and the feeling of the people – you may think it egoism, but there are the facts – is that somebody is wanted to fight a certain thing for them, and there is nobody else able and willing to fight it. You say, "Oh, but that's your ambition; you want to get back into power –"'

'I never said –'

'Well, somebody else says it then. I reply, quite fairly, No humanly speaking, *qua* ambition at the Cape, one has had everything. There is no more to offer, only work and worry. *Qua* the North –'

He paused. This somewhat elliptical use of '*qua*' is very Rhodes-ian, by the by.

'*Qua* the North – well, there we are really *creating* a country. It's interesting to create, I can tell you; much more interesting than politics. We've had the war and rinderpest and rebellion and drought and so on, and now everything is pushing on; and there's the native question to solve and the new constitution to get under way; and that tariff arrangement I wanted to make – the treaties were in the way, but Laurier has got rid of them; and I have a big irrigation scheme on; and then the development to make way for a population – You will say, If it comes out all right; but I don't bother about that; I know the country too well, and with Heany crushing twenty penny-weights in May – I can wait. Then the railway and the telegraph – you know that telegraph of mine that the British public wouldn't look at. There is imagination in that. It is really an immense thing, only you people won't see it –'

Here a protest against the 'you' as quite incorrect passes unnoticed.

'You won't see it, though it was the dream of the ancients to pierce through this continent; and, if you look you will see Alexander got so far, and Cambyses so far – got to Memphis, didn't he, and then went mad? – and Napoleon so far – there's a tablet his soldiers stuck up at Philae, and we are pushing up from the other end right through. They used to say I was too soon, but the danger now is being too late in connecting, with the French cutting in. Really there are many other things to think of besides Cape Town parish pump.'

'Of course (I admitted) Cape Town is parish pump, if you take it as a localism apart from the broader unity; Bulawayo is even more parish pump, and Salisbury parish pump *in excelsis!*'

'Quite true. You have it exactly. Do you know our people up there are no more thinking about uniting than the people here, or at Johannesburg. They're hoeing their own patch for all they're worth; of course they are, and as for unity with the Cape, they look on the Cape as a sort of Bond-ridden place – Bond, varied by unctuous rectitude and all sorts of wobbling; and as to my ideas of working in with the Cape as to railway, and so on, I really believe they say "Oh, this is Rhodes's amiable lunacy – we must humour him because after all he does work for the country." You see, it's very amusing. Localism here and in Johannesburg, and in Natal and in Cape Colony; and that's where I think, to be frank, that one *is* perhaps able to be of a certain use, because one has a certain influence with a good many people in all these places, and you know my idea – Colonial Federation. One was trying the general federation before, with the Republics in; only Kruger and Leyds made it impossible, and then in the middle of the mess they had made one made a mistake, on the top, and so the whole plan is altered.'

'You say "made a mistake". The "unctuous rectitude" of some of us has consisted in wanting you just to say so much to your former Dutch supporters.'

'I said so much at Westminster; but I am not going on saying it, and crawling in the dust to please you or anybody, so I told some Dutch constituents of mine who made advances, after abusing one like a pickpocket at the time. "Oh," they said, "do say you repent! Only *tell* us you repent!" "That's *my* business," I answered. I know what my idea was – no race feeling at all – and what my motive was, and it all went wrong, and I and others made mistakes, and that's all about it.'

I now pass to Mr Rhodes's very frank and simple treatment of the supposed difficulty of his position in Cape internal politics.

We took the thorny points first, beginning with the Food Duties; but as about these the conversation took a rather argumentative turn, I prefer not to try to reproduce the *ipsissima verba*, but to leave Mr Rhodes's exact position to be stated by himself on Saturday. Broadly, however, his position is this. The meat duty he is prepared to abolish, recognizing that the duty is at present pinching the families of working men in the towns without being the slightest protection to the farmer, who has no stock left to protect; that it will take long to re-stock the country; and that a legislator's duty is to deal with the present. On food-stuffs apart from meat he is evidently prepared to make something of a new departure, though not nearly so large a one as his urban admirers would like. He frankly declines to give up his strong feeling that the community at large ought to be ready to sacrifice something to keep white men settled on the land, which he holds can only be secured in Cape Colony by giving *some* special consideration to the products of the soil; but he declares that the form and the amount of such consideration he has always treated purely as a question of degree and of fair adjustment between the claims of the various classes of the population. The times have changed. He once voted for an increase of duties; that is now utterly out of the question. He fully owns that any change in the present state of things must be in the other direction; and I think if the party strongly unites on the 50 per cent compromise adopted by the League – which itself contains many farmers – Mr Rhodes will see his way to pledge himself to that extent of reduction. Fortunately, Mr Rhodes's tendency to consider each local question, not only as between local producers and consumers, but with a view to the broader South African scheme, helps in this case on the right side. In 1895 he distinctly made use of the argument that increased duties would help to keep the Free State in the Customs Union. To-day his federal scheme looks rather towards Natal, and Natal still stands, though not so sharply as formerly, for low duties.

On all the other planks of the Progressive platform, Mr Rhodes claimed that, so far from having a past to bury, his record includes nearly all the real Progressive measures that have been actually carried in the Colony. The Rhodes Ministry passed the Scab Act, in the teeth of what Sir Gordon Sprigg called 'the demons of prejudice and ignorance', to improve the staple product of the colony. It also passed the Glen Grey Act, which took the first great step for the progress of the native in our social and economic scheme, by giving him an individual hold on the land.

'What about the Excise?'

'I voted against the Excise when it was levied in the wrong way, that is with a minimum of revenue and a maximum of irritation to the farmers with their small stills, but I have long had a plan for the Excise to be levied from the canteens and really paid by the consumer.'

'What about the Innes Liquor Bill for keeping drink from the aboriginal native?'

'Keeping drink from the native? Why, I might say that that has been my whole life. I have run De Beers on ginger beer. In Rhodesia the Native Liquor Law is the most stringent in South Africa. In the Transkei I found the traffic only checked by a fine, and substituted confiscation because the sellers could afford to pay the fine and go on. If anybody in South Africa has done more than I have to keep drink from the native, I should like to know his name.'

'And education?'

'Of course any one can see that education is the key to progress among us. As you know, I wanted to found a real South African University, and put the scheme aside only in deference to the susceptibilities of Stellenbosch, which you may call vested interests.'

'But what of the Progressive party's demand for compulsory education in centres?'

'I have a scheme for what I would call permissive compulsory education. That is to say, compulsory for the individual when adopted by the district and assisted by the consolidated fund on the £ for £ principle. The Colony might be divided into seven districts, of which five would adopt the permissive compulsory right away, and the others would have the strongest inducement to follow suit.'

Needless to say, Mr Rhodes is strong for redistribution. No need to enlarge on that.

'I do not pretend to be a town politician,' he says, summing up. 'Production interests me. My sympathy with the farmer is natural. Look at my own pursuits and tastes. I can conceive a time when the people in the towns who have stood by me so well in my time of failure, and for whose fair demands I hope to do something now, will say that I am too moderate for them in my politics. I say my Progressive record already is pretty good, considering that I was working with the Bond and for the Northern Extension, and you cannot do everything at once. Today what is the Bond – I mean the official Bond, the Bond which rejects Dutchmen like Faure and Bellingan because they are not narrow enough? It is not only against progress, it is against equality, against unity, and it is domineered by that continental gang from Pretoria. It is not a case of whether the Bond will forgive me. It is I who will have no compromise with them and their continental gang. You may find Mr Hofmeyr very moderate and very nice, but I take "Ons Land", which represents Mr Hofmeyr among his own people. Look at the line it takes. They talk of race hatred! Some of my greatest friends are Dutch; and in what I may call my own country, in Rhodesia, the only thing that is said sometimes is that the Dutch get actually favoured more than my own people. But these others with their eternal whine of Afrikanders [sic], Afrikanders, poor oppressed Afrikanders, and their abuse of England and Englishmen, and their support of everything rotten at Pretoria, they are simply spreading hatred as hard as they can spread it. Those are the people we are going to fight. We shall want all our discipline and all our organization and unity for that fight. But it will all come right later on. I may not live to see it, but you will all be putting up statues to me.'

The reader may be surprised, by the by, to find Mr Rhodes in his casual talk dipping into the remote past; hitching his telegraph wire on to Cambyses; and picturing himself, with Burns' lady,

> Gone, like Alexander,
> To spread his conquests further.

But this is quite characteristic. I remember once his going to Aristotle to explain experiences in the Matopos. At the historic *indaba*, for instance, he was not afraid because he thought he knew it was all right. That was one kind of courage, the courage of superior knowledge, as defined by Aristotle. In actual fighting, on the other hand, the noise of the elephant-rifle bullets fired close by always made him duck his head, and the sight of men hit and bleeding made him feel sick. In short, 'I was in a horrible funk. But I stayed at the front because of being far more afraid to be thought afraid' – which, he explained, corresponded to another Aristotelian classification of courage. Is it not a triumph for Oriel, for Oxford, and for Greats that Cambyses and Aristotle should thus mingle with the thread of the musings of a man of action in the whirl of Cape politics or in the wide spaces of life on the veldt? At any rate it is very quaint and interesting.

●

TWO MOON

Interviewed by Hamlin Garland
McClure's Magazine, September 1898

Two Moon, the Cheyenne chieftain, took part in the famous Battle of the Little Big Horn in Montana in 1876. Brevet Major-General George A. Custer, lieutenant-colonel in command of the Seventh Cavalry, led his troops as part of a military expedition to encircle and engage hostile Indians, who were under the leadership of the Sioux chieftain Sitting Bull. On 25 June, part of Custer's force, under the command of Major Reno, crossed the Little Big Horn River and attacked the Indian encampment in the valley, but was forced to retreat across the river. Custer, who had led his own column to attack the encampment by another route, was attacked and surrounded by superior numbers and every man was slaughtered as the column moved across open ground and up towards the brow of a hill in search of a defensive position.

There is some dispute as to how Custer met his end. He suffered a fatal body wound, but there was also a head wound caused by a firearm discharged at close range and some have suggested that he saved his last bullet for himself.

Hamlin Garland (1860–1940) was a Western 'realist' novelist, the son of an unsuccessful prairie homesteader in Iowa and Dakota Territory. Garland decided to become a teacher and to that end became an avid autodidact. He moved to Boston in 1884 and soon took a job as a lecturer at the Boston School of Oratory. He was influenced by such thinkers as Herbert Spencer, Hippolyte Taine, Walt Whitman and Henry George, and the doyen of the American 'realist' novel, William Dean Howells. He journeyed back to Iowa and Dakota before returning to Boston and writing a series of short stories, some of which appeared in *Harper's Weekly*. His most famous book, *Main-Travelled Roads* (1891), was a collection of these and other short stories that gave a bleak and anti-mythic portrait of rural life in the Midwest. Howells praised it for its realism, but Garland's subsequent attempts at fiction embodying political and economic themes revealed his limits where plot and characterization were concerned. He turned away from realism in the 1890s and during the next twenty years wrote a series of romances set in the mountain West, which were sympathetic to the native Indian. In 1917 he published to acclaim an autobiography, *A Son of the Middle Border*, which again portrayed human heroism in withstanding the travails of frontier life. He wrote three sequels to this book, and in 1929 moved to California with his daughter, where he wrote a further two books about spiritualism. He had already been elected to the American Academy of Arts and Letters and had received honorary degrees from the University of Wisconsin (his native state) and Northwestern University.

As we topped the low, pine-clad ridge and looked into the hot, dry valley, Wolf Voice, my Cheyenne interpreter, pointed at a little log cabin, toward the green line of alders wherein the Rosebud ran, and said:

'His house – Two Moon.'

As we drew near we came to a puzzling fork in the road. The left branch skirted a corner of a wire fence, the right turned into a field. We started to the left, but the waving of a blanket in the hands of a man at the cabin door directed us to the right. As we drew nearer we perceived Two Moon spreading blankets in the scant shade of his low cabin. Some young Cheyennes were grinding a sickle. A couple of children were playing about the little log stables. The barn-yard and buildings were like those of a white settler on the new and arid sod. It was all barren and unlovely – the home of poverty.

As we dismounted at the door Two Moon came out to meet us with hand outstretched. 'How?' he said, with the heartiest, long-drawn note of welcome. He motioned us to be seated on the blankets which he had spread for us upon seeing our approach. Nothing could exceed the dignity and sincerity of his greeting.

As we took seats he brought out tobacco and a pipe. He was a tall old man, of a fine, clear brown complexion, big-chested, erect, and martial of bearing. His smiling face was broadly benignant, and his manners were courteous and manly.

While he cut his tobacco Wolf Voice interpreted my wishes to him. I said, 'Two Moon, I have come to hear your story of the Custer battle, for they tell me you were a chief there. After you tell me the story, I want to take some photographs of you. I want you to signal with a blanket as the great chiefs used to do in fight.'

Wolf Voice made this known to him, delivering also a message from the agents, and at every pause Two Moon uttered deep-voiced notes of comprehension. 'Ai', 'A-ah', 'Hoh', – these sounds are commonly called 'grunts', but they were low, long-drawn expulsions of breath, very expressive.

Then a long silence intervened. The old man mused. It required time to go from the silence of the hot valley, the shadow of his little cabin, and the wire fence of his pasture, back to the days of his youth. When he began to speak, it was with great deliberation. His face became each moment graver and his eyes more introspective.

'Two Moon does not like to talk about the days of fighting; but since you are to make a book, and the agent says you are a friend to Grinnell, I will tell you about it – the truth. It is now a long time ago, and my words do not come quickly.

'That spring [1876] I was camped on Powder River with fifty lodges of my people – Cheyennes. The place is near what is now Fort McKenney. One morning soldiers charged my camp. They were in command of Three Fingers [Colonel McKenzie]. We were surprised and scattered, leaving our ponies. The soldiers ran all our horses off. That night the soldiers slept, leaving the horses one side; so we crept up and stole them back again, and then we went away.

'We traveled far, and one day we met a big camp of Sioux at Charcoal Butte. We camped with the Sioux, and had a good time, plenty grass, plenty game, good water. Crazy Horse was head chief of the camp. Sitting Bull was camped a little ways below, on the Little Missouri River.

'Crazy Horse said to me, "I'm glad you are come. We are going to fight the white man again."

'The camp was already full of wounded men, women, and children.

'I said to Crazy Horse, "All right. I am ready to fight. I have fought already. My people have been killed, my horses stolen; I am satisfied to fight."'

Here the old man paused a moment, and his face took on a lofty and somber expression.

'I believed at that time the Great Spirits had made Sioux, put them there,' – he drew a circle to the right – 'and white men and Cheyennes here,' – indicating two places to the left – 'expecting them to fight. The Great Spirits I thought liked to see the fight; it was to them all the same like playing. So I thought then about fighting.' As he said this, he made me feel for one moment the power of a sardonic god whose drama was the wars of men.

'About May, when the grass was tall and the horses strong, we broke camp and started across the country to the mouth of the Tongue River. Then Sitting Bull and Crazy Horse and all went up the Rosebud. There we had a big fight with General Crook, and whipped him. Many soldiers were killed – few Indians. It was a great fight, much smoke and dust.

'From there we all went over the divide, and camped in the valley of Little Horn. Everybody thought, "Now we are out of the white man's country. He can live there, we will live here." After a few days, one morning when I was in camp north of Sitting Bull, a Sioux messenger rode up and said, 'Let everybody paint up, cook, and get ready for a big dance.'

'Cheyennes then went to work to cook, cut up tobacco, and get ready. We all

thought to dance all day. We were very glad to think we were far away from
the white man.

'I went to water my horses at the creek, and washed them off with cool
water, then took a swim myself. I came back to the camp afoot. When I got
near my lodge, I looked up the Little Horn towards Sitting Bull's camp. I saw a
great dust rising. It looked like a whirlwind. Soon Sioux horseman came
rushing into camp shouting: "Soldiers come! Plenty white soldiers."

'I ran into my lodge, and said to my brother-in-law, "Get your horses; the
white man is coming. Everybody run for horses."

'Outside, far up the valley, I heard a battle cry, *Hay-ay, hay-ay!* I heard
shooting, too, this way [clapping his hands very fast]. I couldn't see any
Indians. Everybody was getting horses and saddles. After I had caught my
horse, a Sioux warrior came again and said, "Many soldiers are coming."

'Then he said to the women, "Get out of the way, we are going to have hard
fight."

'I said, "All right, I am ready."

'I got on my horse, and rode out into my camp. I called out to the people all
running about: "I am Two Moon, your chief. Don't run away. Stay here and
fight. You must stay and fight the white soldiers. I shall stay even if I am to be
killed."

'I rode swiftly toward Sitting Bull's camp. There I saw the white soldiers
fighting in a line [Reno's men]. Indians covered the flat. They began to drive
the soldiers all mixed up – Sioux, then soldiers, then more Sioux, and all
shooting. The air was full of smoke and dust. I saw the soldiers fall back and
drop into the river-bed like buffalo fleeing. They had no time to look for a
crossing. The Sioux chased them up the hill, where they met more soldiers in
wagons, and then messengers came saying more soldiers were going to kill the
women, and the Sioux turned back. Chief Gall was there fighting, Crazy Horse
also.

'I then rode toward my camp, and stopped squaws from carrying off lodges.
While I was sitting on my horse I saw flags come up over the hill to the east
like that [he raised his finger-tips]. Then the soldiers rose all at once, all on
horses, like this [he put his fingers behind each other to indicate that Custer
appeared marching in columns of fours]. They formed into three bunches
[squadrons] with a little ways between. Then a bugle sounded, and they all got
off horses, and some soldiers led the horses back over the hill.

'Then the Sioux rode up the ridge on all sides, riding very fast. The
Cheyennes went up the left way. Then the shooting was quick, quick. Pop-pop-
pop very fast. Some of the soldiers were down on their knees, some standing.
Officers all in front. The smoke was like a great cloud, and everywhere the
Sioux went the dust rose like smoke. We circled all round him – swirling like
water round a stone. We shoot, we ride fast, we shoot again. Soldiers drop, and
horses fall on them. Soldiers in line drop, but one man rides up and down the

line – all the time shouting. He rode a sorrel horse with white face and white fore-legs. I don't know who he was. He was a brave man.

'Indians keep swirling round and round, and the soldiers killed only a few. Many soldiers fell. At last all horses killed but five. Once in a while some man would break out and run toward the river, but he would fall. At last about a hundred men and five horsemen stood on the hill all bunched together. All along the bugler kept blowing his commands. He was very brave too. Then a chief was killed. I hear it was Long Hair [Custer], I don't know; and then the five horsemen and the bunch of men, may be so forty, started toward the river. The man on the sorrel horse led them, shouting all the time. He wore a buckskin shirt, and had long black hair and mustache. He fought hard with a big knife. His men were all covered with white dust. I couldn't tell whether they were officers or not. One man all alone ran far down toward the river, then round up over the hill. I thought he was going to escape, but a Sioux fired and hit him in the head. He was the last man. He wore braid on his arms [sergeant].

'All the soldiers were now killed, and the bodies were stripped. After that no one could tell which were officers. The bodies were left where they fell. We had no dance that night. We were sorrowful.

'Next day four Sioux chiefs and two Cheyennes and I, Two Moon, went upon the battlefield to count the dead. One man carried a little bundle of sticks. When we came to dead men, we took a little stick and gave it to another man, we counted the dead. There were 388. There were thirty-nine Sioux and seven Cheyennes killed, and about a hundred wounded.

'Some white soldiers were cut with knives, to make sure they were dead; and the war women had mangled some. Most of them were left just where they fell. We came to the man with big mustache; he lay down the hills towards the river. The Indians did not take his buckskin shirt. The Sioux said, 'That is a big chief. That is Long Hair.' I don't know. I had never seen him. The man on the white-faced horse was the bravest man.

'That day as the sun was getting low our young men came up the Little Horn riding hard. Many white soldiers were coming in a big boat, and when we looked we could see the smoke rising. I called my people together, and we hurried up the Little Horn, into Rotten Grass Valley. We camped there three days, and then rode swiftly back over our old trail to the east. Sitting Bull went back into the Rosebud and down the Yellow-stone, and away to the north. I did not see him again.'

The old man paused and filled his pipe. His story was done. His mind came back to his poor people on the barren land where the rain seldom falls.

'That was a long time ago. I am now old, and my mind has changed. I would rather see my people living in houses and singing and dancing. You have talked with me about fighting, and I have told you of the time long ago. All that is past. I think of these things now: First, that our reservation shall be fenced and the white settlers kept out and our young men kept in. Then there will be no trouble. Second, I want to see my people raising cattle and making butter. Last, I want to see my people going to school to learn the white man's way. That is all.'

There was something placid and powerful in the lines of the chief's broad brow, and his gestures were dramatic and noble in sweep. His extended arm, his musing eyes, his deep voice combined to express a meditative solemnity profoundly impressive. There was no anger in his voice, and no reminiscent ferocity. All that was strong and fine and distinctive in the Cheyenne character came out in the old man's talk. He seemed the leader and the thoughtful man he really is – patient under injustice, courteous even to his enemies.

•

LEO NIKOLAYEVICH TOLSTOY

Interviewed by Harold Williams
The Manchester Guardian, 9 February 1905

Count Leo Nikolayevich Tolstoy (1828–1910), the Russian novelist and religious and moral thinker, was born at his family estate on the Volga, Yasnaya Polyana, where this interview took place. Tolstoy read law and oriental languages at Kazan University, failed to graduate, led a decadent life and then joined an artillery regiment in the Caucasus. It was while serving in the army that he began to write, producing an autobiographical trilogy. He served as an officer in the Crimean War and wrote sketches of that conflict before travelling to St Petersburg and to Europe. In 1862 he married Sophie Andreyevna Behrs, by whom he had thirteen children. Thereafter he lived at Yasnaya Polyana and wrote his famous novels, *War and Peace* (1863–9) and *Anna Karenina* (1874–6). Apart from these he wrote many religious and moral tracts, though after he was excommunicated for his heretical theories in 1901 he attacked Christianity. He denounced his own novels, gave all his money to his wife and lived the frugal life of a serf on his own estate, to which pilgrims came in search of enlightenment. After rowing with his wife one evening, he left home and caught a chill, and died in the siding of a railway station.

Harold Williams was born in New Zealand, the son of a Methodist minister. By the age of eleven he knew Latin, Greek, Hebrew, French, German, Maori and Italian. In his thirties he had joined *The Times* and covered the Russian liberal exiles on their peripatetic tour of European capitals. In 1904, after just over a year with *The Times*, he was recruited by *The Manchester Guardian* as its correspondent in St Petersburg – the paper's first resident staff correspondent in a foreign capital – and during the next few years he witnessed the various liberal attempts to secure political reform. He was something of a Tolstoy disciple and was disappointed to find the novelist and thinker so disengaged from political events.

In the struggle and turmoil that agitate Russia today Tolstoy often seems to belong to a remote and silent past. One remembers that he is alive and at work; one notices the reverence with which his name is mentioned by all; everywhere one sees his portrait or his bust; in hundreds of families *War and Peace* is being read once more with a fresh and vivid interest. Tolstoy rests secure above all winds that shake the reputations of the hour, and this very security seems to raise him to a kind of Olympian detachment from the hopes and fears of those who are struggling for political liberty. Moreover, Russia has reached a stage when it will not listen to Tolstoy. There was a time when his teachings were popular here – the time when the repressive measures following upon the death of Alexander II had paralysed all political and social activity and forced high-hearted Russians to seek comfort in doctrines of abstinence and non-resistance. But now that the hope of liberty has aroused the political energies of every thinking man in the country Tolstoy has become a voice crying in the wilderness. The splendour of his artistic gifts is admitted, but no Liberal leader thinks of asking his advice on the conduct of a political agitation. Foreigners hold a different point of view. It is still of importance to us to learn what Tolstoy thinks of the great events of the hour, and when violence raises its head, as it did lately in St Petersburg, one naturally appeals to the greatest living Russian for his interpretation of the tragedy.

Travelling from Moscow and Tula, I reached Yasnaya Polyana on Thursday morning. A snowstorm had blown over, and the sun shone from a wind-swept sky on the rising ground upon which stands the plantation enclosing the well-known homestead. After the trepidations of St Petersburg and the gloomy forebodings of Moscow, Yasnaya Polyana seemed a very haven of peace. And about Tolstoy's own personality the atmosphere of peace seemed to be resting continually. He was very calm, with the calmness of one whose time of struggle is past, and though he talked freely about current events and was kind and courteous after the gracious manner of Russian noblemen of the old school, one felt that his real life was hidden in some remote world of quiet contemplation.

I need not describe again the familiar face. Age and illness have done their work; face and form are spare, and the hair is growing very thin, though not so white as one expected to see it. Tolstoy walks with a brisk step, but stoops slightly. He has not abandoned his habits of vigorous exercise, spends nearly every afternoon in riding or walking, and in spare moments indoors plays battle-dore and shuttlecock with his daughter or amuses himself with cup and ball. He is in excellent health, though a doctor living in the house assured me he was very liable to catch cold. He is as firmly convinced as ever of the value of a vegetarian diet, and referred with great approval to the works of Dr Haig and to the successes of vegetarian sportsmen in England. As to his literary work, it was rather disappointing to him that the novel of which so much has been heard lately is abandoned for the present, and may never be completed. During the autumn and the early part of the winter Tolstoy was engaged in the preparation of a breviary of thoughts of great men, a portion for every day in the year. His eyes sparkled as he described what pleasure the work had given him. He hopes to complete it by writing a series of short stories, one for the first day of every month, but the main portion of the work is already in the hands of a printer in Moscow. Of late, in response to repeated inquiries from England and other countries, he has been recording his views on the Russian Liberal movement, and on the morning of my arrival he completed an article on the subject which will shortly be published in the English press. He is now at work on a pamphlet in which he will expound afresh his views on the State and on political activity in general.

It was with the Constitutional movement that our conversation naturally began. Tolstoy's opinion of it was very summary. 'It is dangerous,' he declared, 'and useless, because it diverts men's activities from the true path. A Constitution cannot improve matters; it cannot bring freedom. All Governments are maintained by violence or the threat of violence and violence is opposed to freedom. A man is only free when no one can force him to do that which he believes to be wrong, and the right course of action for every man is to abstain from all participation in the acts of the Government, to refuse to serve in the army, to refuse to accept a position under the Government, and every day and always to do good. The agitation for a Constitution can only lead to false results.'

He was greatly interested in hearing of the recent events in St Petersburg, and was particularly anxious to learn more about Father Gapon. There was a link between him and the workmen's leader in the fact that Fainermann, one of Gapon's teachers in the ecclesiastical seminary, was a friend and disciple of Tolstoy's, and only a few days before. Tolstoy had received from Fainermann a letter describing his relations with Gapon. He deplored the massacre and was horrified to hear the details, but declared it was only what might be expected of the Government, which must maintain itself by violence.

'Do you think, then,' I said, 'that it was the agitation amongst the workmen that was responsible for this result?'

'No, no,' he exclaimed. 'I could not go so far as to say that. I only say that the whole movement for a Constitution is a movement in the wrong direction. The people does not want a Constitution, and those who are agitating for it do not know the people. With all their professions of love for the people, they have no real care for it; they simply despise it. The people only wants one thing – that is, land. Have you read Henry George's works?'

For Tolstoy, in spite of his abhorrence of political methods, is a great admirer of Henry George, and inquired eagerly as to the extent to which Henry George's theories had been put into practice in New Zealand. Now this was only one instance of the apparently irreconcilable inconsistency between the theoretical and practical sides of his nature. Returning to the question of the Constitutional agitation, he said: –

'I think the best thing would be a Zemsky Sobor (Assembly of Representatives of the zemstvos).'

'But how,' I asked, 'do you reconcile that with what you say of the wrongfulness of all political systems?'

'Oh,' he said, 'I simply mean that the Emperor is foolish, from the point of view of his own interests, not to convoke a Zemsky Sobor.' He added that his eldest son had written to the Emperor an appeal for a Zemsky Sobor, and that a friend of his from Nijni Novgorod had drawn up in the same sense a project of which he spoke with high approval.

He would not admit that the particular form of government prevailing in a country made any essential difference in the lives of its citizens.

'Don't you think,' I asked, 'that it is better to live, say, under the English political system than under the Russian? Look at the passport system here, for instance; the censorship, and the banishment of political offenders.'

'It is not a whit better in England,' he stoutly declared. 'Wherever there is violence people are deprived of their freedom. Why, my friend Tchertkoff, who lives outside the town of Christchurch, is compelled to pay a tax for the maintenance of a band which plays inside the town, and which he himself would much rather never hear at all. And as for banishment, that affects a man very slightly. I have been awaiting banishment for the last twenty years, and if it came I should not be disturbed. Banishment cannot prevent one from living the true life. And freedom of the press! Does the people need freedom of the press? These gentlemen may have freedom of the press, if they will, to air their own views, but that is a small matter.'

It should be added that Tolstoy himself suffers keenly from the effects of the censorship. Even such a distinguished writer as he is not spared the indignity of having many passages blacked out in the books and papers that are sent him from abroad. And the existence of the censorship prevents him from receiving copies of many works of his own that are published in England or Germany.

He spoke of strikes, and said the most effective would be a strike of those who provided the nation with bread. I mentioned a report I had heard in Moscow, to the effect that all the physicians in rural districts intended striking.

'All the better,' said Tolstoy, with a smile.

'But then,' I said, 'all the peasants will be without medical help.'

'So much the better,' he declared; 'forty or fifty years ago, when I was young, there were no doctors among the peasants, and the peasants got on very well without them. No, sickness is not an evil; death is not an evil. The one evil is that men do wrong.'

In the evening, after dinner, we forsook the thorny ground of politics, and Tolstoy began speaking of questions that affect him more nearly. Speaking of the choice of a profession, he said that a man's mode of life is the resultant of the action of two opposing forces – his own effort to reach the ideal, and the inertia of his past. 'There is a terrible saying of Kant's,' he said, 'a saying that for a long time I did not dare to accept, but which I now see to be true, to the effect that a man who does good merely from habit is not a good man. But it is a fact. When we have reached one stage of goodness we dare not rest there, but must strive to reach a higher. You reminded me,' he added, turning to the family physician, who sat close by, 'of a saying of Sutaieff's. It was not Sutaieff but another peasant who, when it was pointed out to him that divorce was un-Christian, said that to continue living with his wife must be, after all, the work pleasing to God, because it was so hard.'

'I am an old man now,' he said again, 'and must soon die, and for me, it is more important to think of the eternal life than of the forms of the world. And, moreover, as other men do not know how soon they may die, it seems to me important that they too should concern themselves with the life eternal. When I am asked about the future life, where I shall be after death, I can only refer again to my dear old Kant, who pointed out that the conceptions of space and time are merely formative principles of the human intellect. The question "where" involves a consideration of space, "shall I be" one of time. And in the eternal life there is neither space nor time. We are each one of us a part of the universal life that is above space and time.'

Tolstoy declares that he has no clearly elaborated metaphysical system of his own, but expresses great admiration for Kant, and wishes he were more frequently read than he is. 'There is no philosophy today worthy of the name,' he said. 'One can respect men like Kant and Hegel even when one doesn't agree with them. But as for Nietzsche, he is a mere feuilletonist.'

He was greatly interested, however, in learning that one of his own disciples, Dr Eugen Schmitt, had discovered excellent points in Nietzsche. He spoke slightingly of contemporary Russian philosophy, and was grieved that members of the new idealistic school sought to find a philosophical justification for the dogmas of the Orthodox Church. Of Vladimir Solovioff, the most distinguished of Russian philosophers, he said that he had formed a fatal intellectual habit of playing with great ideas.

Tolstoy's literary criticisms are always interesting. He has a poor opinion of Russian literature, and, in fact, of most other literatures of the present day. 'Formerly,' he says, 'art was like chamber-music, and appealed to the few; now it appeals to the taste of the great commercial and industrial classes. It will never come to its own until it appeals to the people as a whole.' He drew illustrations of his thesis from contemporary English literature.

'Look at Rider Haggard,' he said; 'he writes the most extraordinary fables'; and he proceeded with great gusto to relate to an artist who was of the company the contents of *She*. His estimate of Miss Marie Corelli and of Mr Hall Caine, particularly of the latter, was extremely unfavourable. For Dickens he has an unbounded admiration and has lately re-read with delight his *Child's History of England*. Ibsen is not to his taste, and he strongly criticized *When We Dead Awake*, which had recently been given in a Moscow theatre. Amongst German writers, he admires Von Polens, whose *Büttner-bauer* was translated into Russian at his instigation. Rosegger, the Austrian writer, whose descriptions of peasant life might have been expected to appeal to Tolstoy, is no favourite of his, but he spoke with enthusiasm of a short story by another Austrian, Anzengruber. Anatole France's *Crainquebille*, too, seems to have evoked his special admiration. He expressed his wonder at the perfection to which the technique of novel-writing had been brought. 'Why, the Russian ladies,' he said, 'nowadays write excellently – far better than Turgenieff or any of us; only, they have nothing to say.'

'Journalism,' he assured me, 'is a bad business. A newspaper is compelled to stand for a certain party, while the essence of thought is that it should be independent. And then journalism is bad because it forces a man to work hastily and makes him eager to forestall others. It has good points, it is true, and one is that it provides men with a means of communication.' 'The most Christian knowledge,' he added, 'is the knowledge of languages, because it draws men closer together.'

Much more he said during the day – much that I am unable to record here. And in the effort to report his words I have been unable to indicate the incessant play of his personality. The conversation was frequently interrupted; part of it was held over lunch, part in the study, part, again, at dinner and over the evening glass of tea. There were many interludes. Tolstoy's manner frequently changed from seriousness to playfulness, and he would pass in a moment from general questions to those of purely personal interest. He spoke simply and kindly, without the least pretence at dogmatism, and was always ready to listen to an opinion opposed to his own. And one never lost the impression of his inward calm, as of a man who had faced the deepest problems and had found in their solution peace.

I left him at midnight, and next morning was back in Moscow, hearing of agitation in the Nobles' Assembly, the radical resolutions of a meeting of lawyers, and excited discussions as to the probability of a conflict between the terror from above and the terror from beneath. Involuntarily I thought of Tolstoy's words – 'The Constitutional movement is a noisy movement, and this is not in its favour. God's work is wrought in stillness. To Elijah the prophet God spoke not in the earthquake, not in the wind, but in the still small voice.'

And yet it is in the stormy life of the cities that the battle of Russian freedom is now being fought out, and not, though one would like to believe it were, in the happy, peaceful haven of Yasnaya Polyana.

●

W.T. STEAD

Interviewed by Mrs Maud Churton Braby
The World of Dress, June 1905

Mrs Maud Churton Braby (1875–1932) was a journalist, a novelist and the author of *Modern Marriage, and How to Bear It* (1908). She certainly impressed Stead with this interview for a fashion magazine, which he felt had caught him to a tee, and he sent her a photograph bearing the inscription: 'To the best interviewer I have ever met!'

'I had rather dreaded interviewing Mr W.T. Stead. A chill remembrance of a *tête-à-tête* years ago with a prominent Salvation Army leader still lingered in my mind, and I feared the interview with Mr Stead might resemble it. My imagination depicted a stern, rugged, elderly individual who, metaphorically speaking, would breathe hell-fire upon me and rage against the wicked follies of the world in general, and of my unregenerate sex in particular. The prospect of broaching so frivolous a subject as Dress to him was terrifying in the extreme. Any topic of conversation more mundane than spirit draperies, say, at the very worst, would seem an insult to the strenuous atmosphere of Mowbray House.

Judge of my astonishment when – arriving several hours after the appointed time – I encountered, on the steps of that august building, a joyous gentleman whose white beard alone hinted at advancing years, whose cheerful, healthy countenance glowed with the joy of living, in whose bright blue eyes there shone a fire that would not have disgraced Endymion, and whose whole mien was one of over-flowing, irresponsible gaiety and innocent gladness.

'Is this what you call the morning?' he asked smilingly, as his portmanteau was hoisted into the waiting hansom. 'I'm just off to Stratford-on-Avon, to the Shakespeare festival. You shall come too – as far as the station. And on the way you shall tell me your views on *the* subject of which among all others I know least – Dress. That's the whole secret of successful interviewing – for the interviewer to talk all the time.'

Having delivered himself of this dictum, Mr Stead proceeded, to my great relief and delight, to talk steadily for the next twenty-five minutes.

'This Kodak,' he began, taking his seat in the hansom, and indicating an extremely battered leather object which he carried, 'this Kodak might be said to be typical of my views on Dress. I have had it so many years that they no longer make the films to fit it. I like old things – old books, old friends, old clothes. I wear my clothes until they are literally unwearable – until my wife forces new ones upon me, which I accept in groaning and lamentation of spirit

. . . Yes, my wife always buys my clothes; she sends for materials and drives me to the tailor's. When they are made, I try them on with reluctance. They're always cut on the same pattern, of course, and as it's a good many years since that pattern was taken, why, the tailor has to let them out accordingly!' And he beamed upon me like a young Apollo!

'Surely you wouldn't wish women to choose their costumes in the same way?' I interposed hurriedly, taking advantage of the temporary breathing space caused by the beaming process.

'Ah, women's clothes! That's a saddening thought. Meredith was right when he said that woman was the last animal to be civilized by man! How selfish you are, how deficient in the instinct of social altruism! Now, take women's hats. For the last six months I've been going to the theatre, you know.'

Mrs Braby knew – who did not?

Stead proceeded to hold forth on 'those dreadful matinée hats' and the discomfort they had given him.

'I think it terribly sad,' he continued, 'that woman, the loveliest object we have in the world – the most beautiful thing that God has created, should go about tricked out and disfigured by all the barbaric arts of the milliner.'

Here I anxiously scanned the narrow strip of mirror at the side of the hansom, and then noted with relief that the Endymion-like blue eyes were twinkling. The Mentor of Mowbray House evidently realizes the importance of the 'great task of happiness'.

'How would you wish women to dress, then?' I asked.

'Well, my two pet aversions are the wasp-waist and the trained walking-skirt. The Greek draperies might be too cold for this climate, but they would be no more inconvenient than those insane long skirts which offend my sense of cleanliness. The modern woman walking in a long skirt has either to act as a street sweeper or else practically amputate her left arm – for all the use it is to her.'

'And have you any opinion on the increasing extravagance of modern fashion?'

'Extravagance is purely relative. If you only have 12s 6d, and you pay 13s for a dress, it is extravagance, though the gown itself might be wholly vile. If you have £30,000 a year, and you spend a thousand of it on your clothes, you are not so extravagant as you would be in the other case. Now, my whole idea of the Dress Question in a nutshell is, firstly, that it should be healthy, warm, and comfortable; and, secondly, that it should be capable of being put on and off in the minimum of time. For instance, from the bath to the doorstep I can dress from top to toe in four minutes. What do you think of that?'

'Brilliant,' I murmured, 'how do you manage it?'

'Well, I strive to realize my ideal! To continue: thirdly, that it should last. It should last a very long time. Now, I have worn a pair of trousers at my country place for seven years.'

'Marvellous!' I commented.

'Wasn't it? I didn't wear them *all* the time, you understand, not quite all, but off and on very nearly the whole seven years.'

I was suitably impressed by this record of trousers-endurance.

'All trousers should be capable of being patched,' continued Mr Stead, solemnly, but still with that air of overflowing gaiety. 'They should have leather seats. Now, you know my whole views of Dress – warm and comfortable, easy to assume, capable of great endurance, and after that to be as nice-looking as you can afford – don't you think that an excellent ideal?'

'For you, perhaps –'

'Well, apropos of that point of view, a lot of men were once talking about me at a literary club, and some thought I was somebody, and some that I was nobody, and then a friend of mine settled my claims to distinction by saying: "Well, when all's said and done, Stead's the only man in London who dares dress as he does!" You see, I wear exactly what I choose, a privilege peculiar to beggars and to dukes.'

'I see. Morally, you're a duke?'

'No, I wouldn't say that, because dukes are often very immoral, but I'm a sartorial kind of duke!' Here Mr Stead positively roared with laughter.

'And as for women's clothes,' he continued, 'having fulfilled the above requirements in their attire, they should try in addition to look as charming as possible. Now, at this point, *I* ought to interview *you*, because I know nothing about being charming, whereas you, obviously . . .' Modesty here dictates the omission of Mr Stead's remarks. Then he suddenly asked: 'Am I not a flirtatious person?' – *so* astounding me by this unexpected ebullition of joyousness that I nearly fell out of the cab. 'It's one of my theories,' he continued, 'that nothing so adds to the innocent gaiety of the world as harmless flirtatiousness . . . Yes, and I always get on splendidly with women. Shall I tell you why? The whole secret of getting on well with women is to be absolutely faithful to one's wife. Yes, and to be so entirely innocent in your relations with women all your life that you can meet them on terms of absolute equality and friendship – just as one can another man.'

'Are you always as young as this, Mr Stead?'

'How old do you think I am? Seventy-five, I hope, for the reputation of my beard.'

'About twelve,' I answered.

'Twelve? Much too old, except by an almanac. A man once said of me, "Why, Stead's a mere child" – to which another friend replied, "Stead a child, why, he's an infant, he's not weaned yet!"'

And Stead enlarged a little on the value to him of his white beard – it had won him the deference he had never been able to get before.

'But despite my white beard and five-and-fifty years, I grow younger and younger every decade, although now I'm a grandfather. I've six children and two grandchildren; and, I say,' he went on eagerly, 'do you know the reason why new-born babies wear long clothes? Once I imagined it was to allow room for the baby's growth. I soon discovered, however, that by the time the length was right, the garment was too small at the top. Then at last I found out the true purpose of those long skirts. They were invented to enable the young father – or the younger grandfather – to swing the baby head downwards. Yes, I've done that to all my children, and consequently they learnt early to look at life from two points of view.'

'*Do* be serious, Mr Stead, what do you suppose Mrs Aria will say to all this? We're nearly at the station; now do say something about Dress for my interview.'

'Dress? But, good gracious, we've discussed the dress-topic threadbare; I've told you everything I think and know, and all I feel about Dress – what more can I do?'

I gave it up in despair, and wondered for the fiftieth time during the last twenty minutes why I had ever imagined Mr Stead to be a stern, pious person.

'But I am pious – very pious,' he assured me, when I had confided this thought to him. 'Why should piety be incompatible with flirtatiousness, which, as I've already explained to you, is the secret of true, innocent gaiety, and an inexhaustible spring of the joy of life?'

'I don't know why it should be but it certainly is as a rule.'

'Then that's not true piety. All nice people are pious. To be nice is to be a Christian on the surface . . . Here we are at the station; I *am* sorry. Don't go yet, my wife and daughter are here somewhere . . . Well, I'm delighted to have had this cheery talk, we must meet again. Come to lunch – I shall never forget you. Ah, there's Mother, how surprised she'll be to see you . . . Mother, here's a young lady I never saw in my life till half an hour ago, and she's been interviewing me about – er – Dress.'

●

CHRISTABEL PANKHURST

Interviewed by E.M. Evors, *Hearth and Home*, 10 November 1910

Christabel Harriette Pankhurst (1880–1958), the English suffragette, was the daughter of Emmeline Pankhurst, the founder of the Women's Franchise League, and Richard Marsden Pankhurst, a radical Manchester barrister who was responsible for drafting the first women's suffrage bill and the Married Women's Property legislation. In 1903 Christabel, with her mother, founded the Women's Social and Political Union, a more militant version of her mother's League. Christabel's sister Sylvia was also a prominent suffragette.

*

A finely balanced combination of brains, enthusiasm, and confidence characterizes the Votes-for-Women movement. Its organization is near to perfection, and
its vitality is as unquestionable as it is unquenchable.

When I went the other day to the headquarters of the Women's Social and
Political Union, at Clement's Inn, just off the Strand, to see Miss Christbabel
Pankhurst, it was with the idea not only of glancing, through her eyes, at the
present position of affairs, but of trying to inveigle her into divulging the
future 'surprises' awaiting Cabinet Ministers should they prove recalcitrant
during the coming session. Dreams of the siege of the Houses of Parliament, of
megaphone messages, of Suffragette airships, and all the rest of it, had assailed
me. But in this last particular Miss Christabel, like a good strategist, was wily
and reticent.

'Plans! Yes; lots of them. But I am not at liberty to unfold them before the
time. Week by week, you know, our doings and fixtures are chronicled in *Votes
for Women.*'

Miss Pankhurst looked singularly young as she sat there in her private room,
the signs and impedimenta of business all around her. She looked the picture of
health, too, with her frank, mobile face, clear pink and white complexion, blue-
grey eyes, and soft brown hair; and was gowned simply and artistically in green.
To a stranger it would have been a surprise to realize her self-possession and
dignity. And many a man would have envied the ease with which she could
switch herself off from the conversation in train to answer equally ably the
queries of all and sundry that came intermittently over the telephone by her
side. She is level-headed, confident, well-informed, and she is deadly in earnest.
You cannot draw her with chaff. She squashes the least note of levity with a
reproachful: 'This is a serious movement. We are strictly political.'

'Our business now is to get this Conciliation Bill passed,' she said; 'and a
very important event is the monster meeting to be held at the Albert Hall on
November 10th. All the speeches that night will be in support of the Bill, and
among the speakers will be Mr Israel Zangwill and Mr Gerald Arbuthnot, MP,
a member of the Conciliation committee. Mrs Pankhurst will be in the chair.'

'And after?'

'After that meeting the various resolutions asking for facilities towards the
passing of the Bill will be presented by a deputation of leading women to Mr
Asquith. If his answer is "No", a very much larger deputation of women will
go to Westminster on November 22nd.'

From the tone of Miss Pankhurst's voice something like a serious revolution
of women Suffragists may be anticipated if this Bill – which, it will be
remembered, was carried by a majority of 110 on its second reading – is not
allowed to go further.

'In the meantime,' Miss Pankhurst added, 'we are, of course, circularizing all
MPs to bring pressure to bear on Cabinet Ministers that they may give the Bill
fair play.'

'Importunity is one of your watchwords, is it not?'

'Yes. The concession of the vote is a just measure; we women want the vote, and we shall go on pestering Parliament till we get it. If MPs would fight for us we should not need to be such a nuisance to them. But they don't, even when pledged to our cause. They just knuckle under to Cabinet Ministers, instead of bringing the necessary pressure to bear upon them.'

'Men seem terribly frightened of doing anything so "revolutionary" as giving women the Parliamentary vote,' I said. 'They think it would mean a sex war. What is your view about that?'

'I don't see how that could be,' said Miss Pankhurst. 'It is a battle between women and the Government. A political war, not a sex war.'

'Still, some of them think it would lead to a sex war.'

'I don't think so. Men are already getting less antagonistic towards the movement. Indeed, some of our best friends are men,' added Miss Pankhurst. 'The fact is, men are afraid of change, although when the changes are made they accept them without any fuss. Look at the changes that have come to women in the last hundred years. And yet men like us still. They would not like us to be the fainting, weeping, weak-minded creatures we used once to be. They like us as we are now. If you come to think of it, changes made in defiance of men are always approved by them afterwards.'

New hope for women Suffragists lies in the changes in the Constitution involved in the movement towards 'All Round Home Rule' – Imperial federation beginning at home – which is creating so much attention just now, and being so eagerly discussed. These changes may come into the domain of practical politics sooner than we think. Commenting on this situation, Miss Pankhurst wrote the other day in a most interesting leader headed 'Will Women Get Home Rule?' as follows:

'If the Constitution is to be made over again, women will clamour for admission with more insistence than ever before. If there is to be self-government for England, for Ireland, for Scotland, for Wales, then there must be self-government for women too. If there are to be local Parliaments in the various parts of the United Kingdom women will claim a share in electing them. If, under a brand-new Constitution, the powers and functions of the Imperial Parliament are to be defined and settled anew, women will not consent to being left out of consultation. If all Britain's self-government dominions are to be given a voice in Imperial government, then the women of the Mother Country must have the vote, for they cannot any longer be held in political servitude while the women of Australia and New Zealand are free to share in the Imperial counsels.

'These considerations may or may not have presented themselves to the mind of our party politicians, but they cannot remain blind to them for very long. Women are able nowadays to express their point of view in a manner which cannot well be overlooked, and, moreover, there are men who are determined to see even justice done between the sexes.'

'When did you first become interested in Women's Suffrage?' I asked.
'I was brought up in the movement. My father, who was both a lawyer and a politician, drafted the first Women's Suffrage Bill, and also the Married Women's Property Act Bill. That association counts for a great deal, of course; yet I think one needs a kind of "personal conversion" as well, and that came to me when I was organizing women in trades' unions.'

'And how did you learn to become a public speaker?'

'By actually speaking. I made my maiden speech at college – Victoria University, Manchester – about ten years ago. I had no intention of speaking, but there was a debate and I felt strongly on the subject, so I just got up and spoke. That was the first plunge.'

Other claims on Miss Pankhurst's time brought our interview to a close. So regretfully I departed, thinking out a hundred unasked questions which the interview had suggested.

•

WOODROW WILSON

Interviewed by Isaac F. Marcosson

Munsey's Magazine, October 1911

Thomas Woodrow Wilson (1856–1924), the twenty-eighth president of the United States (1913–21), was educated in law at Princeton, the University of Virginia and Johns Hopkins University, where he took a PhD. In 1890 he was appointed Professor of Jurisprudence and Political Economy at Princeton, and in 1902 he was made president of the university. He stood as a reformist Democratic candidate for the governorship of New Jersey in 1910 and served as governor from 1911 to 1913. His administration was characterized by progressive reforms and he took this platform to the country in 1912 as a presidential contender, winning as a result of a split Republican vote. During his first presidential administration, he extended the powers of the federal government with the creation of the Federal Reserve System and the Federal Trade Commission, and the passing of anti-trust and child labour legislation. Wilson had pursued a policy of neutrality throughout most of the First World War, and was indeed re-elected to the presidency in 1916 on the platform of neutrality, but in 1917 he felt impelled to enter the conflict after persistent outrages against American shipping by German submarines. He was one of the key architects of the Treaty of Versailles and an enthusiast for the League of Nations. Although he won the Nobel Peace Prize in 1919, he failed to persuade the isolationist US Congress to ratify the Versailles Treaty and US membership of the League of Nations. After recovering from a stroke, Wilson made a final effort to steer his country towards an internationalist approach to foreign affairs. The Republican Warren Harding won the presidency the following autumn and Wilson's recovery from illness proved to be only temporary. He died the following year.

Isaac F. Marcosson (1876–1961) was born in Louisville, Kentucky. The son of a travelling salesman, his heart was set on a journalistic career by the age of fourteen and he started on the *Louisville Times* at eighteen. He quickly rose to become assistant city editor and books editor, and he began contributing to national magazines. In 1903 he went to New York City and joined the staff of Walter Hines Page's *World's Work*, a monthly magazine concerned mainly with business. He joined the staff of *The Saturday Evening Post* in 1907, writing a regular column called 'Your Savings', as well as interviews and other features. He served as an editor at *Munsey's* (1910–13) before returning to the *Post*, where he remained until 1936. Over the years he interviewed such figures as Lloyd George, the British First World War general Douglas Haig, and the Chinese nationalist leader Sun Yat-sen. Soon after he left the *Post*, his second wife died of cancer and he decided to study the disease. Independently wealthy by virtue of a substantial bequest from the wife of a friend, he became the public relations director of a New York hospital specializing in cancer treatment. He married for the third time and his wife helped him with his hospital work and with the corporate biographies that he wrote during the 1950s.

Because, figuratively speaking, he has worn a classic mantle for most of the years during which he has been conspicuously known to the public, you must not get the impression that Woodrow Wilson has the shy and sensitive soul of the student. A man who could step from a college office into a capitol where privilege, favor, and graft were so deeply rooted as to become part and parcel of the very structure, and could clean it out with a broom that fairly bristled with a scorching flame, is the personification of dramatic action.

Within six months from the time when he became Governor, he had prevented his party from sending a wealthy machine politician to the United States Senate; he had ordered the State chairman of his party, who had accused him of abuse of patronage, out of his office, never to return; he had forced through a Democratic Assembly and a Republican Senate a direct primary and election law which takes the organization of both parties in New Jersey out of the hands of the bosses; he had galvanized what had been a tottering attempt at executive power into an authoritative, discreet, and open-minded State-rule. In a word, he woke the whole commonwealth. He has proved that he bears to politics the same relation that a 'fighting parson' bears to a war for liberty. His ethics are sound, but his courage, vigor, and pugnacity are sounder.

Ask Governor Wilson how this seemingly miraculous transformation has been achieved, and he will tell you that he was born a political animal.

'From my boyhood,' he said to me, 'I have aimed at political life. The reason

I studied law was because, when I was a boy in the South, the law furnished the
shortest path to public life. I gave it up, later, because I found I could not be an
honest lawyer and a politician at the same time. At least, I did not know how to
then. I tried the next best thing, which was studying politics. I went back to
school, where I undertook to learn something of the facts of government. People
think I was born a scholar; as a matter of fact, I was born a man of affairs.'

There is an air of quiet and determined conviction about this spare, well-
formed, gray-eyed man in whom the thinker and the doer meet so admirably.
The face is long, the forehead high and smooth; the whole demeanor is that of
some high-bred, well-controlled, but emphatic organization. The face shifts
quickly from grave to gay, but there is always behind the bright, winning smile
some evidence of hidden strength, latent determination, steadfast purpose.
Governor Wilson's voice is clear, resonant, and distinct. Without effort he can
reach the remote ends of a large auditorium. Keep in mind, however, the fact
that he had been addressing audiences for twenty years before he began to
arouse the Jersey voter from his lethargy in a stirring campaign that set a new
mark for strenuosity.

When you go to see Governor Wilson at the State House in Trenton, two
things impress you very strongly. One is the striking and convincing personality
of the man; the other is the fact that the door of his office is wide open, so that
'all who would might enter, and no one was denied'. You can almost see him
from the moment you step into the long conference-room hung with portraits
of former Governors.

As you look across its stately stretch of space, you see a small chamber simply
furnished in oak. Here, with ranks of law books behind him, this militant
Governor sits at a real bar of the people. From the mantel on his left a bronze
Washington in a sort of Roman toga and a metal Lincoln in a nondescript attire
look down upon him. Through the windows in front of him he can see the tide
of Trenton traffic moving up and down State Street. He has only to turn in his
swivel chair to the left to see the shining Delaware fringed with green.

There is no 'gum-shoeing' about Governor Wilson's office; no whispered
and suspicious talk. Men who come there must speak their minds frankly and in
the open. This is why the sound of the old order of things has ceased in the
State House of New Jersey. Tuesday is 'Governor's Day', when the executive
office is a sort of forum for everybody. There is neither color line nor political
bar to free speech with the head of the State.

I walked with Governor Wilson down State Street to a modest hotel, where
we had luncheon. The humblest citizen of Trenton could not have been more
unassuming. When people recognized him, he acknowledged their greeting
with a dignified courtesy. At the restaurant he took a side table, and throughout
the meal any special attention almost embarrassed him. I cite this instance
merely to show one phase of the man, because a genuine sense of modesty
seems to be ingrained in him.

His attitude on this occasion made me think of another luncheon that I once had with a certain Governor of Kansas. He also took me down the main street of his capital city to a restaurant frequented by the general public. Instead of seeking a quiet table, as Governor Wilson did, he chose one near the street, where he kept up a running fire of conversation and greeting with passers-by. In short, he capitalized his democracy.

Later, I rode with Governor Wilson in his automobile from Trenton to Sea Girt, where the State troops were camped, and where the Governor's cottage – the New Jersey White House – is located. As we whirled through the country – and few parts of New Jersey are more beautiful than this – here and there a word of greeting was shouted at the Governor. In response there was always the same dignified courtesy – never anything of the 'hale and hearty' manner which is so often affected by the politician.

On this trip we talked of the great problems that press down upon the mind of the country, and thus, as we sped toward the sea, there developed the interview which now follows.

No issue in the next Presidential campaign will be more important than the tariff. I asked Governor Wilson to define his position, and he replied:

'I believe in a tariff for revenue only, but I recognize the fact that our existing economic system has been built on the opposite theory. Any change in our scale of duties ought to be brought about by prudent and well-considered steps, and with statesmanlike regard for every legitimate interest involved. We ought not to impair our industries or imperil the employment of our working people.

'Everybody will agree that if our tariff policy is indeed to be protective, and to seek the objects which it has always pretended to seek, it is perfectly legitimate that it should pay a very careful regard to the business interest of the country taken as a whole. But that is a very different matter from paying regard to the individual interests of particular undertakings and of particular groups of men. The long and short of the whole experience, as we now see it, is that our whole tariff legislation has degenerated from a policy of protection into a policy of patronage.

'The party which has stood most consistently for the so-called system of protection has derived not a little of its power from the support of the great business interests of the country. I do not mean the moral support merely. I mean that it has been supplied with immense sums of money for the conduct of its campaigns and the maintenance of its organization, and that, whether consciously or unconsciously, it has established a partnership with the manufacturing interests which has deprived it of its liberty of action in matters touching the tariff. It is bound by obligations, both tacit and explicit, to protect those interests which have been its most stalwart backers and supporters.

'It has again and again happened, therefore, to the scandal of the whole country, that items and clauses have been inserted into our tariff laws which were not even explained to the members of Congress, which were a matter of private arrangement between the representatives of certain great business interests and the members of the Ways and Means Committee of the House and the Finance Committee of the Senate. The Finance Committee of the Senate, in particular, during many years, was the stronghold of these special interests.

'I am not intimating direct corruption of any kind. I am speaking now only of that subtle corruption of the will to which I have already referred. The will dominant in the Finance Committee of the Senate has for many decades together been subservient to the dictates and to the interests of particular groups of men. Their interests have been served constantly, and often in defiance of the well-known opinions and purposes not only of the national administration, but of the members of the House as well, who struggled in vain against the dictates of the omnipotent leaders of the Senate. Here, displayed in its grossest form, was the intimate power of business over politics.'

'What do you think about Canadian reciprocity?' I asked.

'I welcome reciprocity with Canada,' replied Governor Wilson, 'as a breach in the tariff wall.'

So far, we had discussed politics. Now we turned for the moment to a problem which lies very close to the whole American people – a problem which really should have no politics, and yet which has been closely identified with the policies of both of the great parties. I refer, of course, to the Sherman Anti-Trust Act, around which a fierce strife has raged for years.

I asked Governor Wilson to tell me his opinion of the Sherman Act, and he replied:

'I believe in the policy of the Sherman Act. At the same time, I believe that some combinations in the field of business and industry make for efficiency and economy, and stimulate rather than destroy competition. So soon as the object and the operation of the combination come to be a restraint, it is illegitimate, because it is opposed to the common interest.'

'But what about the big corporations and their alliance with politics?' I asked the Governor.

'I am not hostile to corporations,' he answered, 'if corporations will prove that they are as much interested in the general welfare as we are. I am not opposed to anybody who is serving the public – who is giving them honest service, and at a reasonable rate, not with the primary idea of squeezing and exploiting them, but with the primary idea of serving them.

'America is willing to give abundant largess to anybody who will serve her, but she is very chary, if she can have her own way, of giving fortunes to anybody who imposes upon her.

'For example, there have been two kinds of railway promoters in this country. There have been those who, by special genius for organization, and by far-sighted vision of the things that were going to happen, have built up great transportation systems. You have never heard their names maligned. The names that you have heard traduced are the names of men who did not build up anything, but manipulated everything – the men who ran railroads from the stock-market, who manipulated prices, who made fortunes out of the changes in the quotations in stocks. Such men, by well-known processes, run up to a high price the securities of roads that they know are about to become insolvent, and sell out before the crash comes; or they buy in things they know to be valuable, which they have cheapened by misrepresentation. They have had more to do with embarrassing the development of this country than any other set of men. They are the panic-producers.

'In order to do these things they must have the protection of silence, of private understandings cemented by money, or in any other way that it is possible to cement such arrangements. They must be secure against inquiry, shielded against change. They must have a free hand to do what they please.

'The alliance of these men with politics is the most demoralizing thing that could possibly descend upon any country. And it has descended upon us.'

'Corporations do not do wrong,' continued the Governor. 'Individuals do wrong – the individuals who direct and use them for selfish and illegitimate purposes, to the injury of society and the serious curtailment of private rights. Guilt, as has been very truly said, is always personal. You cannot punish corporations. Fines fall upon the wrong persons, more heavily upon the innocent than upon the guilty, as much upon those who know nothing whatever of the transactions for which the fine is imposed as upon those who originated and carried them through – upon the stockholders and the customers rather than upon the men who direct the policy of the business.

'If you dissolve the offending corporations, you throw great undertakings out of gear. You merely drive what you are seeking to check into other forms, or temporarily disorganize some important business, to the infinite loss of thousands of entirely innocent persons and to the great inconvenience of society as a whole. Law can never accomplish its objects in that way. It can never bring peace or command respect by such futilities.

'I regard the corporation as indispensable to modern business enterprise. I am not jealous of its size or might, if you will abandon the fatuous, antiquated, and unnecessary fiction which treats it as a legal person, as a responsible individual. Such fictions were innocent and convenient enough so long as corporations were comparatively small; but it is another matter now. The modern corporation is an economic society, a little economic state – and not always little, even as compared with states. Many of our modern corporations yield revenues and command resources which no ancient state possessed, and which some present-day bodies politic do not approach.

'To sum it all up in one sentence, the big evil to be corrected is the control of politics and of our life by great combinations of wealth. Men sometimes talk as if it were wealth we were afraid of, as if we were jealous of the accumulation of great fortunes. Nothing of the kind is true. America has not the slightest jealousy of the legitimate accumulation of wealth. Everybody knows that there are hundreds and thousands of men of large means and large economic power who have come by it legitimately, and in a way that deserves the thanks and admiration of the communities they have served and developed. But everybody knows, also, that some of the men who control the wealth and have built up the industry of the country seek to control politics, and to dominate the life of common men, as no man should be permitted to do.'

'What is the remedy?' I asked.

'Simply this,' answered the Governor, with certainty and decision. 'The men who exert the wrong kind of control must change their point of view. They are trustees, not masters, of private property, not only because their power is derived from a multitude of men, but also because, in its investments, it affects a multitude of men. It determines the development or decay of communities. It is the means of lifting or depressing the life of the whole country. They must regard themselves as representatives of a public power.

'There can be no reasonable jealousy of public regulation in such matters, because the opportunities of all men are affected. Their property is everywhere touched, their savings are everywhere absorbed, their employment is everywhere determined, by these great agencies. What we need, therefore, is to come to a common view which will not bring antagonisms but accommodation.'

I asked Governor Wilson to define his Democracy, whereupon he answered:

'I am two kinds of a Democrat – first, a born Democrat; second, a convinced Democrat.

'I can best define what I mean by being a Democrat, perhaps, by first telling what a Republican is. As I see him, he believes in a government *for* and not *by* the people. The Republican party looks upon itself as a trustee, and it believes in the trustee principle. This is the very essence of the protective policy. It is not taking care of the people, but it is being taken care of.

'By a convinced Democrat I mean that I dissent from the Republican party's theory of government. The people as a whole should direct and control our affairs.'

'What is your formula for good government?' I asked the Governor.

'It is summed up in two single words – "common counsel",' he said.

'How does this express itself ?' I asked.

'In a free, frank legislation, expressive of the wishes of the people, as opposed to private understandings arrived at by hidden influences. As a matter of fact, the American people are waiting to have their politics simplified, because they realize that at the present time their politics are full of private arrangements, and they do not understand what it all means.

'This reminds me of an experience I had out in Oregon. That State is the center of real popular government, and the people have made discriminating choice of their officials. One of the reform leaders in Oregon is William S. U'Ren. It has been said that the State of Oregon has two capitals – one at Salem and the other under Mr U'Ren's hat. I made the remark, when I was out there, that I would rather have the government under the hat of one man whom I knew and could follow, than in the hands of a legislature guided and controlled by nobody knows whom.

'This was misconstrued as a statement on my part in favor of "one-man power". What I had in mind was simply this – if I had the choice, I would rather live under a legislature dominated by one man whom I could trust than a legislature dominated by secret influences.

'In the main, nobody knows where most legislative bills come from. When you can identify the real source of legislation, you will get a long way toward genuine popular government.

'The only way to defend yourself against improper legislation in America is to let Americans know that it is improper, and it will stop. The great antiseptic in America is public information and public opinion. You can clarify and purify the worst things in our life by simply letting the eyes of honest Americans have access to them.'

'What is the Democratic program as you see it?' was the next question.

'It is not difficult to answer that question,' was the ready response. 'The first item of that program is that the machinery of political control must be put into the hands of the people. That means, translated into concrete terms, direct primaries, a short ballot, and, wherever necessary, the initiative, the referendum, and the recall. These things are being desired and obtained, not by way of revolution, not even with a desire to effect such changes as will alter any fundamental thing in our governmental system, but for the purpose of recovering what seems to have been lost – the people's control of their own instruments, their right to exercise a free and constant choice in the management of their own affairs.

'Back of all reform lies the means of getting it. Back of the question what we want is the question how we are going to get it. The immediate thing we must do is to resume popular government.'

We had sped swiftly across the country. Already the tang of the sea was in the air; our journey was near its end.

'One more question. What of the so-called "new radicalism" of which you are the accredited leader?' I asked.

The Governor's face relaxed into a smile.

'All the people are radical,' he said. 'That is to say, the people are ready for any reasonable program that will get them the goods – the goods not being anybody's scalp, not anybody's ruin, not any damage to the honest business of the country, but the proper control of their own affairs. I will not permit without challenge the men who are holding back, the men who are afraid of the people, to appropriate to themselves the handsome word "conservative".

'I maintain that those of us who believe in the so-called radical program are intelligent conservatives. The distinction which I make is that time-old distinction between Liberals and Tories – between men who can move and men who are such Bourbons that they cannot forget anything and cannot learn anything.

'The so-called standpatter is a man who is fooling himself to the top of his bent. I suppose that a man on an ice-floe in the Arctic Ocean thinks he is standing still, but he is not. There is a great drift of the water under him. I suppose the so-called conservatives claim to be standing where their fathers stood. They are doing nothing of the kind, because the country is not where their fathers were. There is a great drift historically, a glacial movement, of which they are not aware.

'In a word, the so-called radicalism of our time is nothing else than the effort to release the powerful constructive energies of our time.'

•

GUGLIELMO MARCONI
Interviewed by Kate Carew
New York Tribune, 14 April 1912

Guglielmo Marconi (1874–1937), the Italian physicist and inventor of the wireless, was born in Bologna. He began experimenting with electromagnetic waves in his early twenties. In 1898 he transmitted signals across the English Channel and a few years later he was able to transmit across the Atlantic. He set up the Marconi Telegraph Co. in London in 1898. Marconi and his co-experimenter, the German physicist Karl Braun, received the Nobel prize for physics in 1909. He subsequently invented devices for transmitting and receiving short wave radio. Like Thomas Edison, he was made a Grand Officer of the Crown of Italy – hence OC.

Kate Carew was the pen-name of the caricaturist Mary Williams Reed, who wrote many interviews, initially for the New York *World* and later for the *New-York Tribune*, which were invariably illustrated by her own caricatures of her subjects. These included the novelist Jerome K. Jerome, the Broadway theatrical producer Charles Frohman, Mrs George Cornwallis-West (Winston Churchill's mother), G.K. Chesterton, Granville Barker, Sir Arthur Wing Pinero, Ben Tillett (the London dockers' union leader), Elie Metchnikoff (the microbiologist), Abdul Baha, and Father Vaughan.

If genius is only illimitable patience then I want to assure you, my dears, that Mr Guglielmo Marconi is not the only one who is entitled to write OC after his name and be spoken of in contemporary talk as a friend of kings.

For three days – three long; oh, such long, weary days – I sat in the Waiting

Garden of the Holland House, taking nourishment and sleep at stated intervals.

At the end of that time Mr Marconi's secretary appeared. He said:

'I think I can arrange the interview soon, but you must promise me not to stay longer than fifteen minutes.'

I promised, unhesitatingly.

In a little while he returned.

'I'm afraid I shall have to ask you to make it ten minutes.'

I promised, hesitatingly.

Later: 'I'm sorry, Miss Carew, but I can give you but five minutes with Mr Marconi. He's frightfully busy. Promise me you won't stay longer.'

'Oh, for a look at him,' I agonized, 'just a look.'

On the way the secretary told me of his amusement at the bluff American men threw about being so tremendously over-worked. 'My word, they do make a big noise about it, and they seem to have time for everything.'

Meantime I wondered, 'What can I say in five minutes?' Then I recalled hearing a Young Thing who had been introduced to Mr Caruso recently chirp:

'Oh, Mr Caruso, I do think you sing lovely.'

I thought I might say something like that as an initial transmitter.

'Oh, Mr Marconi, isn't your wireless telegraphy too interesting.'

He would bow a courtly assent, as Mr Caruso did; then I might add:

'It has made such a difference in our home lives.'

By that time the secretary would be making frantic dots and dashes in the atmosphere and I would know it was time for me to go.

What I did say was, in answer to a polite regret:

'It was a long time, but I imagine my profession is like yours, Mr Marconi, in one respect, that it requires a lot of patience.'

The famous inventor had no appearance of the hurry his bluff-hating secretary had intimated. He waited leisurely for me to install myself and my interviewing apparatus into a fixed station, and then said, with an indulgent, comrade-like smile:

'Yes, indeed. One of the first things a scientific man has to have is patience.'

We rigged our serial wires to the poles of question and answer and started right in to send and receive messages.

I asked: 'Do you believe, Mr Marconi, that power for commercial use, such as that of Niagara, for example, will ever be transmitted by wireless?'

He immediately began to make little zigzaggy lines, sort of Marcel – no, I mean Hertzian – waves along the table top as he spoke. It was an occupation he indulged in all through our tête-à-tête.

'It has already been transmitted experimentally. It may not be done absolutely in our' – an apologetic wave is drawn among the others – 'in my time, but it is sure to be. Mr Tesla is working on that problem now.'

'It is an appalling thing to think of, isn't it?' piped I.

'It is.'

We sat silent for a moment, our vibrations tuned to the pitch of wonder and enthusiasm. I came to first, and spent the interlude in taking notes of Mr Marconi's appearance.

There is still something of the schoolgirl left in your old Aunt Kate, and I had simply taken it for granted that a man so famous, engaged in such unusual doings, chaining the elemental forces to the use of man, giving airy nothings local habitation and name, would have an appearance to correspond – dark, lustrous eyes, flashing continuous sparks; hair prematurely white, witness of midnight vigils; body a mere human motor, charged with psychic force, ascetic, attenuated.

The man I faced is of medium height, with good breadth of shoulder, rather stockily built. In spite of the fact that he has Italian 'forbears' you would say, 'Oh, an Englishman,' if asked suddenly to classify him. He has the colouring of the Anglo-Saxon rather than of the Southron, blondish with hazel gray eyes, not large, but keen. His muscles have the taut look that indicate the out-of-door life. He has a determined chin, a good, generous mouth, set in lines of character, a broad, exposed forehead.

Wager he was a self-willed youngster, said I to myself.

There is nothing of the mystic in his appearance and nothing of the hard, aggressive business man with metallic tones. His face – if you think of emotion and mobility as one – is unemotional, but full of thought, directness, purpose. From his slicked hair, brushed smoothly back, to his shiny russet shoes he is perfectly unobtrusive in externals. He does not, apparently, take himself seriously overmuch, too intent on the big things to dwell on the little. His words, perfectly enunciated, have just a suspicion of a foreign influence, too vague to be definitely catalogued, not more evident than those of an English or American boy brought up in a Continental school.

To sum up, Mr Marconi suggested the Doer so much more emphatically than the Dreamer that I asked, not forgetful of the three days I had trailed him to his lair and waited in a state of siege:

'How many hours a day do you work?'

'I don't call the business that called me here, the lawsuit with the United States Wireless Telegraph Company, really work but when I am experimenting I spend sometimes seven, eight, ten, fourteen and even sixteen hours at a stretch.' He spoke the last figure with an enthusiasm that suggested he would like to get right back to the sixteen-hour labor law. 'When I was in Newfoundland, trying to get in touch with Poldhu, Cornwall, two thousand miles away, I worked many days with scarcely any rest.'

Mr Marconi's hands are not the least harmonious with the rest of his rugged appearance. They are beautiful artistic hands. As he tapped an occasional Morse S . . . and continued his Hertzian zigzags I watched them, fascinated. They are the only feature that makes you realize the magician, the supernatural being flinging his words across wild wastes of water, by dipping masts and spars, over storm-sprayed waves, through flocks of screeching sea birds, from sand

dunes to the centres of civilization. They suggested several questions. One was:
'Do you take any relaxation?'
'Yes, I am very fond of motoring and of music. I had a serious musical education. My piano playing, by developing my senses of delicate, harmonious sounds, has been of great use to me scientifically.'
'Your daily routine?'
'Eight – Rise.
'Eight-thirty – Breakfast.
'Nine – Work.'
That final monosyllable, embracing the major portion of his life, prompted me to ask, with a sigh, 'Do you never tire of the work?'
'I get physically fatigued, but I never have any sense of satiety in regard to my experiments.'
In this Mr Marconi resembles Mr Edison, who told me once he never tired of his work. Seems a bit strange to us women.
Just at this electric moment my sensory, auditory nerves detected from the secretarial retreat a sort of Br-r-r and sulphurous sparks as from an agitated mental battery. I installed myself more comfortably. The Marconi system is supposed to lend assistance to those at sea in a deep fog. It did. The inventor, casting a soothing look over his shoulder, gave me an inaudible signal to continue.
'What kind of boy were you?' I asked. 'Interested in science?'
'Oh, tremendously. I commenced experimenting when I was seven. I made my first wireless experiment when I was nineteen.'
I am a great believer in the attrition of domestic life. History shows but few lone children who arrive at eminence, so I inquired:
'Did an older brother act as inspiration?'
'I have an older brother' – the tone and boyish expression might be translated 'dear old chap!' 'I don't know that he was an inspiration, but he had a decided influence, although his tastes ran to agriculture and business. But he was most sympathetic always.'
'How about the family – tolerant?'
'Just that, in the beginning. They considered me fantastic, and the idea I had as a youngster of sending messages through the hills on our Italian place did not keep them awake nights with admiration, but they did not throw any obstacles in my way. I consider that a good deal, and as soon as my experimenting was taken seriously they were very proud and happy.'
I liked this reminiscent talk, so I sat still, for I was told that if you shift the reflector the slightest bit the messages will stop.
'Now, I know you'll think me a tremendous egotist, that I'm awfully self-assured, but I am going to confess to you that I always believed in myself, dreamed I was going to be somebody – make the world talk. I assume every boy believes that of himself, but I believe I believed it harder than most boys do.'

The zigzags were moving toward me in a confidential, quivery way.

'Don't you know it right now, from your mature standpoint, that a boy should feel that way?' I chirped.

'I believe it is the saving quality of the imaginative, dreamy temperament.'

'Were you inspired as a boy by the life of any particular scientist?'

Mr Marconi fell into an abyss of thought, from which he soon emerged.

'I don't recall that there was any special influence; but, unlike many scientists, I have always been tremendously interested in the experiments and discoveries of others.'

The secretary passed from door to door. He gave me a look in which I read that he considered me the original Bramley coherer. I didn't care. I didn't intend to discohere as long as Mr Marconi would talk. I pretended to be ignorant of that hurt expression of faith destroyed. Oh, these secretaries, who know me to be a false, perjured woman. If they should get together and form a trust my stock of Pon-My-Word-of-Honor wouldn't be worth the paper it was written on.

I inquired, perfectly callous to the suffering near me, 'Did you dream the wireless from the beginning?'

'No; I don't think I did. I had in mind always the idea of bringing countries closer in touch with each other, uniting remote spots and centres of life, but it was all so vague. As nearly as I can put that far-off ambition into words, it seemed to be that I wanted to engage in some form of scientific work that would keep me travelling.'

'So there IS romance?' I asked in a delighted told-you-so tone. We were back to the schoolgirl starting point again.

'Romance! I should say so.' Marconi's face lights up as with an inner fire. No lack of emotion now. The fingers trace agitated wavelets like those that might be made by a huge marine spider.

'When I leave here I travel for five days into the heart of the Canadian wilderness. It is stimulating to see New York, but after a little while I find myself longing to get back to the wireless.'

'To get back to the wireless.' Surely that is a good translation for the almost untranslatable term 'wanderlust'.

'You love tha' Great Beyond?' I almost whispered. I was so afraid that Marconi the poet would become Marconi the inventor again.

'Yes, indeed. Those vast expanses of sea and land; those vague sky lines. It is among them that one spends the wonderful moments of life. Your imagination faces the infinite, and you read infinite possibilities. As Tennyson said, "You see the vision of the worlds and all the wonders that may be."'

Under that quiet, that very quiet, exterior, I seemed to realize the force of his imagination and the will to put its dreams into deeds.

'The human side is interesting, too, I suppose?' asked I, slipping from the heights.

'Very. Queer lots. New types. Some clever, some not so clever. Many mere wasters of one's time.'

'Do the natives take you seriously?'

'They have to. In some of the remote stations, small footholds of earth, I have to depend on native help. I have to instruct the people, trust them when I go away, inspire them with confidence. It is not the least interesting part of my work, I assure you.'

I thought of all those little-heard-of places with which the name of Marconi is indissolubly linked. Salisbury Plains and Penarth, Alum and Glace bays, Wimereux and others. The walls of the sitting room seemed to fade away and I visioned him there – in a more suitable frame.

I had intended to ask something fluffy about the stage wireless, but the contrast of the Broadway stage with the other enormous one he had mentioned, where the dramas of Nature are played, where great primeval forces are used instead of petty theatric craft, made the interrogation impossible. I inquired, instead:

'Have the flying machines stolen your' – I hesitated between thunder and lightning, and, misunderstanding, Mr Marconi answered, quickly:

'I went up in one with some apparatus, but we were all so interested watching the aeroplane that we forgot the wireless.'

'When the air is filled with flying machines, as is predicted, will the presence of so much mechanical force interfere with the wireless vibrations?'

'Not in the least.'

'What nation has helped you most, financially, sympathetically?'

'Italy in both ways.'

'Do you believe in spiritualism?'

'Yes, but I haven't gone into the study of it very deeply.'

'Do you think the time is coming when we will dispense with the ordinary methods of communication, such as telephones, letters?'

Mr Marconi certainly has the penetrating power. I got it then all right.

'I certainly do! We'll be able to tune our minds. I am sure of it. We do it now in a measure, but some day when you go into a restaurant and the waiter asks you, "Alone?" you will say, "Oh, no; I expect somebody." You will send out a wave or two and soon the somebody will appear.'

He laughed at the perfectly rapturous expression on my face. Then I hedged on my delight:

'Suppose another somebody is asking me at the same time?'

'Oh, but you can't receive and send simultaneously, you know.' This still more gayly.

We got real jokey about that little luncheon.

Then I asked: 'Supposing I don't remember what you have said to me in this interview. If I send out a wave, will you get it and answer?'

'I won't promise.' The joker is the inventor now. 'We haven't gone that far yet. Telepathy is still a promise rather than a fulfilment?'

'Will the telephone wires be abolished finally?'

'The initial experiments have been successful. When you realize that before 1898 wireless had not been sent two miles, what can one not safely predict?'

'Did you take a personal interest in the first rescue at sea by the wireless?'

The Hertzian waves are very calm and collected now, the table top is allowed to rest. The serenity of my vis-à-vis is more marked than ever. There is no doubt that Mr Marconi is a real lion. There is also no doubt that he is not of the class that gnaws the bars of the cage.

'I am going to disappoint you, I had no thrill, no excitement, no ecstasy, no more than I have at present.' I don't think that very flattering. 'In my imagination it had happened a thousand times, so when the reality came it meant nothing except the gratification at the saving of life.'

'Are you working on any new inventions?'

'Several. I have my papers in the Patent Office now for a wireless compass which I believe will end all the perils of fog. It has been described at length in the newspapers.'

'When do you expect the wireless will get around the world?'

'I cannot answer that.'

'Does the curvature of the globe present any difficulties?'

'None at all at present.'

'What is the greatest distance wireless messages have been sent to the present time?'

'From Great Britain to the Argentine Republic.'

'Are they quicker than the cable?'

'From transmitter to the receiver I believe the wireless is a bit quicker, but the commercial difficulties of delivering the wireless messages makes the time of the two methods comparatively the same.'

'What is the comparative rate?'

'From New York to London messages cost a word 15 cents by wireless and 25 by cable.'

'And the exact time?'

'The fraction of a second.'

At that unfortunate word 'time' the secretary, like the genie of a lamp, suddenly appeared. It was quite easy to see that I was outside his friendly radius. He sent out danger signals into the ether, and Mr Marconi picked up an oscillating impulse which referred to the five minutes I had promised not to overstay.

My mind, perfectly tuned, caught the farewell pitch.

I rose hastily, and as we shook hands I had the impression that I had received in the beginning, firmly emphasized, that all the nice things his admirers say about Mr Marconi are true. He has the infinite patience, the acute observation, the practical skill and the active imagination attributed to him. He is the doer and the dreamer: the man of action and the poet.

And, as I caught the sly little twinkle in his eye, I added to this long but well deserved list the quality that makes the man, even the celebrated inventor, the O.C. and friend of kings, a good 'pal'.

●

G.K. CHESTERTON
Interviewed by Hugh Lunn
Hearth and Home, 17 October 1912

Gilbert Keith Chesterton (1874–1936), the English writer, was educated at St Paul's School in London and studied art at the Slade School. He wrote poetry, polemical essays and reviews, detective stories with a priest as sleuth (Father Brown), and biographies of Browning, Dickens and Robert Louis Stevenson. He was converted to Roman Catholicism in 1922 and thereafter wrote popular biographies of St Francis of Assisi and St Thomas Aquinas.

Hugh Kingsmill Lunn (1889–1949), too, was a biographer. He later published biographies of Matthew Arnold, Shakespeare, and Frank Harris, as well as essays, anthologies and travel books under the name Hugh Kingsmill. He was employed on *Hearth and Home* during the brief and controversial editorship of Frank Harris.

Everyone knows Mr Chesterton's appearance, 'a good portly man, i' faith, and a corpulence', like Falstaff. His writings, too, have become familiar, winning many disciples, especially among the young. At Oxford the Chestertonian and the Shavian are well-known types: the Shavian enthroned above human emotion is clever, but a prig; the Chestertonian, less brilliant, is more likeable. He doesn't care for advanced ideas, but he would like to combine wit and probity. So he welcomes a writer who defends old modes of thought with humour, and attacks modern thinkers on the ground that they are antiquated bores in disguise.

Yet underlying Mr Chesterton's geniality there is a real bitterness, at times the impatient intolerance of a man defending a difficult position. I was interested to see if this intolerance would be greater or less in speech. On the whole I found it far less.

Mr Chesterton began with characteristic words, 'I am always ready to be interviewed, for I hold the theory, nowadays completely forgotten – as forgotten as this matchbox was still this moment (fishing a box out of a bowl on the mantelpiece) – the theory that the Press is a public agora. I should not refuse an interview even to a paper owned by one of those capitalist millionaires, whom I hate. Nowadays the Press merely echoes the powerful; its real aim should be to give the public a chance to state its views.

'And now what do you want me to talk about? I am ready to give my opinion on any question, whether I know something about it or not. No, I'm not an Imperialist in the modern sense; the only theory of Imperialism that seems to me sound is Dante's. He defended the Roman Empire as the best human government, on the definite ground that the best human government would probably crucify God. Caesar had to be lawful; because Christ had to be killed by law.

'Neither do I believe in Cosmopolitanism: nowadays it's either run by financiers for their own profit, or it's the product of Atheistic Socialism, as in Germany. Christ didn't come to bring peace among the nations. When He said that a man should turn the other cheek, I fancy He meant that a man, when attacked, should humiliate his enemy by treating him with sudden and unexpected contempt.'

He paused with a smile to ask me what questions I really wanted to put. I wished to find out what he thought about writers dead and living, for I had noticed that he never spoke of literature for its own sake, but only with reference to what some would call broader issues. And now, though beginning to see that, whatever the subject, he would always be pulled back to express certain theories on life, I put a direct question to him:

'You are very hostile, aren't you, to the literary movement in the eighties and nineties?'

'Yes, I am. How can I make my feeling clear? It seems to me that at that time the two great ideals of life were dead. The French Revolution, so people thought, had destroyed Christianity, and the decadents didn't even believe in the French Revolution. They cared nothing either for the rights of man or the rights of God.'

'You don't like Housman's *Shropshire Lad*, then?'

'It's marvellous,' he answered, 'the singing beauty of it is extraordinary. But it was written by the devil. The suffering in Housman or in Hardy is evil – utterly unlike Milton's dignified sorrow. Peasants don't feel like that. Of course, we are all melancholy at times: you and I will quite probably be melancholy before we go to bed to-night. But really from the way they write, you'd think Hardy and Housman had been kicked through every village, and ducked in every horse-pond throughout the kingdom. In a healthy society you get the heroic peasant romances of France and Spain and Italy. But with a landed aristocracy like ours you get *A Shropshire Lad* and those Wessex stories.'

The words 'landed aristocracy' struck a danger-note, and I hurriedly asked him what he thought of Wells. 'He's inconclusive: his limitation is an unlimited mind. You know the sort of pocket-knife that boys love, and I love, too, furnished with every possible implement? Wells is like that knife, except that he hasn't got any nippers. He never really gets to grips with anything; doesn't know what a full-stop is. Those rows of dots that he puts at the end of his sentences represent him to me. He's like a hat floating on the sea of modern thought; you think that every wave will throw it on the shore, but there it is, still bobbing up and down. It hasn't got any tentacles; it can't grip. Of course Wells has a wonderful mind: *Tono-Bungay* is a great novel. People say his books are immoral, but that's all nonsense.

'Shaw is a greater fighter than Wells, but he loses terribly through fear of his emotions. The way he talks about love seems to me merely mad.'

'What do you think of Arnold Bennett?'

'He seems to me rather like Hardy and Housman; somebody must have broken his back.'

'But surely,' I remonstrated, 'he has real, genial humour?'

'Certainly: he is like that glorious hero of his, *The Card*, he has contributed to the greatest of causes, the "great cause of cheering us all up". Still I suspect he's against real joy. But it's difficult to talk about him. His books are finished works of art, and you can't discuss them simply because they are finished.'

'Do you agree with Frank Harris on Shakespeare?'

'Well, I think the book a blow to the Baconians, but he makes too much of Shakespeare's difference from the rest of us. We are all as poetical as Shakespeare; but we don't happen to be such great poets. Our temperaments are the same, but you and I haven't got the mind to write lines like "And all our yesterdays have lighted fools . . ."'

'You don't think the artist as near the centre of things as the ordinary man, do you?'

'No, I don't. Most people consider the joys and sorrows of the working-man chaotic and comic – only fit for a music-hall sketch. To me his emotions seem more permanent, less sophisticated than those of the artist. If Edward I came to life, he'd understand the workman, but Heaven only knows what he'd make of some of our modern artists.

'I put the artist and man of action on the same level. Byron worked through the medium of words; Napoleon through the medium of bayonets. I don't know that there's much to choose between them, though I own to a slight preference for Napoleon's medium.'

'Then, who do you think the highest type of man?'

'The saint: St Francis of Assissi could judge both Byron and Napoleon. By the way, a dialogue between the three would be amusing.'

'But, to take a greater artist than Byron, do you think Shakespeare could be judged by St Francis?'

'Yes; Shakespeare had got some of the literary man's vices. He talked too much about fame; the saint doesn't bother whether he'll outlive marble or the monuments of princes.'

The argument seemed to me unreal: St Francis too had his flaws. Self-torture is a vice as much as self-indulgence, though doubtless rare.

I went on: 'Don't you think the artist is underpraised nowadays in comparison with the practical man?'

'Yes. I don't think the balance is fairly held. Of course, one's sympathies aren't always on the same side. If a band of troubadour poets – manly, virile fellows – were bayonetted by a regiment of Prussian soldiers, I'd naturally sympathize with the poets. But if Nero – that eminent aesthete – collected a body of aesthetic young Romans round him, and proceeded to live for the moment's sake, I should be delighted to see a troop of Dacian legionaries disturbing the artistic harmony in their rude, artless fashion.'

The illustrations interested me; the second was so much more vivid and realistic than the first. It seemed that Mr Chesterton could not sympathize with the artist till he had pictured him as manly and virile, the characteristic qualities of the man of action.

However, I still pressed the point.

'Don't you think minor poets are unfairly sneered at nowadays?'

'Yes; and as a minor poet I feel it deeply. Journalists can't hit out at the powerful; they'd lose their jobs. So they hit the minor poet. It's like a man who has lost his nerve on the hunting field, but goes about boasting that he still hunts beetles.'

Mr Chesterton had missed my point. He thought minor poets should be spared, because they were beetles; clearly he didn't think capitalists the real beetles, and artists, however minor, the real powers.

The talk wandered over many subjects, lasting altogether two hours. A real kindness and sympathy, never quite hidden even when he was most intolerant, gave charm to everything he said. The flow of quaint imagery showed a quick receptive mind: the love of old fixed certainties a shrinking from the unknown future. The greatest souls search the darkness that lies in front, their backs turned to the pleasant landscapes of the past. The rustic inn where the countrymen gather stands back from the main road. One should not linger there; it charms as fatally as the arbour of the decadents.

•

'BARRIE AT BAY: WHICH WAS BROWN?'

Sir James Barrie
The New York Times, 1 October 1914

Sir James Barrie (1860–1937), the Scottish playwright, was the son of a weaver. He studied at Edinburgh University and worked as a journalist during the 1880s, before embarking on a successful career writing for the theatre in 1890. His plays include *The Admirable Crichton* (1902), *What Every Woman Knows* (1908) and *Peter Pan* (1904), a fairy-land adventure which became a staple of many a child's upbringing. His plays were mounted on Broadway by the producer Charles Frohman, and it was during a visit to New York that Barrie conceived this 'short story', satirizing the crass inquisitiveness and gullibility of a newspaper interviewer.

As our reporter entered Sir James Barrie's hotel room by one door, the next door softly closed. I was alone (writes our reporter). I sprang into the corridor and had just time to see him fling himself down the elevator. Then I understood what he had meant when he said on the telephone that he would be ready for me at 10.30.

I returned thoughtfully to the room, where I found myself no longer alone. Sir James Barrie's 'man' was there; a stolid Londoner, name of Brown, who told me he was visiting America for the first time.

'Sir James is very sorry, but has been called away,' he assured me without moving a muscle. Then he added: 'But this is the pipe,' and he placed a pipe of the largest size on the table.

'The pipe he smokes?' I asked.

Brown is evidently a very truthful man, for he hesitated. 'That is the interview pipe,' he explained. 'When we decided to come to America Sir James said he would have to be interviewed, and that it would be wise to bring something with us for the interviewers to take notice of. So he told me to buy the biggest pipe I could find, and he practised holding it in his mouth in his cabin on the way across. He is very pleased with the way the gentlemen of the press have taken notice of it.'

'So that is not the pipe he really smokes?' I said, perceiving I was on the verge of a grand discovery. 'I suppose he actually smokes an ordinary small pipe.'

Again Brown hesitated, but again truth prevailed.

'He does not smoke any pipe,' he said, 'nor cigars, nor cigarettes; he never smokes at all; he puts that one in his mouth to help the interviewers.'

'It has the appearance of having been smoked,' I pointed out.

'I blackened it for him,' the faithful fellow replied.

'But he has written a book in praise of My Lady Nicotine.'

'So I have heard,' Brown said guardedly. 'I think that was when he was hard up and had to write what people wanted; but he never could abide smoking himself. Years after he wrote the book he read it; he had quite forgotten it, and he was so attracted by what it said about the delights of tobacco that he tried a cigarette. But it was no good; the mere smell disgusted him.'

'Odd, that he should forget his own book,' I said.

'He forgets them all,' said Brown. 'There is this *Peter Pan* foolishness, for instance. I have heard people talking to him about that play and mentioning parts in it they liked, and he tried to edge them off the subject; they think it is his shyness, but I know it is because he has forgotten the bits they are speaking about. Before strangers call on him I have seen him reading one of his own books hurriedly, so as to be able to talk about it if that is their wish. But he gets mixed up, and thinks that the little minister was married to Wendy.'

'Almost looks as if he hadn't written his own works,' I said.

'Almost,' Brown admitted uncomfortably.

I asked a leading question. 'You don't suppose,' I said, 'that any one writes them for him? Such things have been. You don't write them for him by any chance, just as you blackened the pipe, you know?'

Brown assured me stolidly that he did not. Suddenly, whether to get away from a troublesome subject I cannot say, he vouchsafed me a startling piece of information. 'The German Kaiser was on our boat coming across,' he said.

'Sure?' I asked, wetting my pencil.

He told me he had Sir James's word for it. There was on board, it seems, a very small, shrunken gentleman with a pronounced waist and tiny, turned-up mustache, who strutted along the deck trying to look fierce and got in the other passengers' way to their annoyance until Sir James discovered that he was the Kaiser Reduced to Life Size. After that Sir James liked to sit with him and talk to him.

Sir James is a great admirer of the Kaiser, though he has not, like Mr Carnegie, had the pleasure of meeting him in society. When he read in the papers on arriving here that the Kaiser had wept over the destruction of Louvain, he told Brown a story. It was of a friend who had gone to an oculist to be cured of some disease in one eye. Years afterward he heard that the oculist's son had been killed in some Indian war, and he called on the oculist to commiserate with him.

'You cured my eye,' he said to him, 'and when I read of your loss I wept for you, sir; I wept for you with that eye.'

'Sir James,' Brown explained, 'is of a very sympathetic nature, and he wondered which eye it was that the Kaiser wept with.'

I asked Brown what his own views were about the war, and before replying he pulled a paper from his pocket and scanned it. 'We are strictly neutral,' he then replied.

'Is that what is written on the paper?' I asked. He admitted that Sir James had written out for him the correct replies to possible questions. 'Why was he neutral?' I asked, and he again found the reply on the piece of paper: 'Because it is the President's wish.'

So anxious, I discovered, is Sir James to follow the President's bidding that he has enjoined Brown to be neutral on all other subjects besides the war; to express no preference on matters of food, for instance, and always to eat oysters and clams alternately, so that there can be no ill-feeling. Also to walk in the middle of the streets lest he should seem to be favoring either sidewalk, and to be very cautious about admitting that one building in New York is higher than another. I assured him that the Woolworth Building was the highest, but he replied politely, 'that he was sure the President would prefer him to remain neutral.' I naturally asked if Sir James had given him any further instructions as to proper behavior in America, and it seems that he had done so. They amount, I gather, to this, that Americans have a sense of humor which they employ, when they can, to the visitor's undoing.

'When we reach New York,' Sir James seems to have told Brown in effect, 'we shall be met by reporters who will pretend that America is eager to be instructed by us as to the causes and progress of the war; then, if we are fools enough to think that America cannot make up its mind for itself, we shall fall into the trap and preach to them, and all the time they are taking down our observations they will be saying to themselves, "Pompous asses."

'It is a sort of game between us and the reporters. Our aim is to make them think we are bigger than we are, and theirs is to make us smaller than we are; and any chance we have of succeeding is to hold our tongues, while they will probably succeed if they make us jabber. Above all, oh, Brown, if you write to the papers giving your views of why we are at war – and if you don't you will be the only person who hasn't – don't be lured into slinging vulgar abuse at our opponents, lest America takes you for another university professor.'

There is, I learned, only one person in America about whom it is impossible, even in Sir James's opinion, to preserve a neutral attitude. This is the German Ambassador, whose splendid work for England day by day and in every paper and to all reporters cannot, Sir James thinks, be too cordially recognized. Brown has been told to look upon the German Ambassador as England's greatest asset in America just now, and to hope heartily that he will be long spared to carry on his admirable work.

Lastly, it was pleasant to find that Brown has not a spark of sympathy with those who say that, because Germany has destroyed art treasures in Belgium and France, the Allies should retaliate with similar rudeness if they reach Berlin. He holds that if for any reason best known to themselves (such as the wish for a sunnier location) the Hohenzollerns should by and by vacate their present residence, a nice villa should be provided for them, and that all the ancestral statues in the Sieges-Allee should be conveyed to it intact, and perhaps put up in the back garden. There the Junkers could drop in of an evening, on the way home from their offices, and chat pleasantly of old times. Brown thinks they should be allowed to retain all their iron crosses, and even given some more, with which, after smart use of their pocket combs, they would cut no end of a dash among the nursemaids.

As for the pipe, I was informed that it had now done its work, and I could take it away as a keepsake. I took it, but wondered afterward at Brown's thinking he had the right to give it me.

A disquieting feeling has since come over me that perhaps it was Sir James I had been interviewing all the time, and Brown who had escaped down the elevator.

●

FRANK HARRIS

Interviewed by Djuna Barnes

The New York Morning Telegraph Sunday Magazine, 4 February 1917

Frank Harris (1856–1931), the Irish journalist and writer, was born in Ireland and won a scholarship to Cambridge University. Instead of attending the university he used his £10 scholarship to travel to the United States, where he filled many jobs across the country. He studied law at a university in Kansas, then travelled to Europe to report on the Russo-Turkish War, then studied some more in German universities. Back in England, he embraced journalism once again, editing in succession the *Evening News*, *The Fortnightly Review*, and the *Saturday Review*, and befriending Oscar Wilde, H. G. Wells and George Bernard Shaw. He sold the *Saturday Review* in 1898 and his next editorship was that of *Vanity Fair*. This was followed by *Hearth and Home*, from which he was sacked for being too controversial, and *Modern Society*, for which he was obliged to serve a prison sentence for libel.

Harris was a maverick and a rogue. He returned to the United States from England and bought *Pearson's Magazine*; however, sympathy with the German cause caused trouble with the US Post Office and publication of *Pearson's* was eventually suspended. Later, Harris went to live with his second wife in the South of France, where he wrote his most notorious book, *My Lives and Loves* (1923–7), which some believe confirmed him in the role of a self-fantasist. Because of its explicit account of his promiscuous sexual liaisons, the book was banned from publication in the United States until 1964.

Djuna Barnes (1892–1982), the American poet, novelist, and caricaturist, was born in Cornwall-on-Hudson, New York. She was a reporter and illustrator for various newspapers and magazines, such as the *New York Press*, *The New York Telegraph Sunday Magazine*, the *New York Sun Magazine*, *Vanity Fair*, *Charm*, *McCalls*, *Theatre Guild Magazine*, *Physical Culture*, and *Unmuzzled Ox*. She also wrote 'vox pop' reportage as well as interviews with celebrities. Her subjects over the years included James Joyce, Jack Dempsey, D. W. Griffith, Raymond Hitchcock, David Belasco, Florenz Ziegfeld, Billy Sunday (the popular preacher), and Alfred and Lynn Lunt (the husband-and-wife theatrical team). In addition to her journalism, Barnes wrote one-act plays, short stories and a novel, *Nightwood* (1936).

I was dining at the house of a friend some eighteen months ago when the maid announced Mr Harris. 'Frank, you know,' my hostess said as she arose to greet him.

A short man came suddenly into the room, a man with thick, dark hair and a mustache like a mural painting, a decoration to the house of Harris. A man who seemed to be a favorite corridor where life had loved to stroll. When he spoke one became startled: the voice was the deep and rich voice of a large man; let me call it the echo of those who passed.

His eyes were keen at once and kind; not overoften, but once now and again one could see that this man had not flung the harpoon alone.

What more expressive thing can I say to describe him than that life had used him. I like this better than the phrase, he had used life.

This was the only time that I was to meet him and not know him, for he becomes a friend at once or he becomes nothing. He has also the terrible quality that goes with it: he can cease as abruptly and as decisively as he began.

It is a terrible thing that memories of great men die with their contemporaries. For only so short a space can one man say of another, 'I knew him well. He used to have a droll little trick –' So soon, too tragically soon, comes the remark instead, 'I knew a man once who knew a man –'

This is Harris. With him dies virtually all of the oldest and best in the last century of English letters. An eloquent potpourri of the petals fallen from the flowers of Europe, adding his own fine shower of leaves to the fragrant pile that too soon will pass into the unlimited where all limited things have couch and eternal sleep.

I remember walking up Fifth Avenue one night with him in the fall, and with what awe I watched this man's moods come and go. At one moment running and jumping a brook in the street, and the next denouncing America's insistent crying for 'a happy ending'. Some editor had got him to change one of his books and he was already beginning to regret it.

A fine strain of piracy runs through the veins of Harris. Like Benvenuto Cellini, he cannot help seeing the beauty of force. Ah, how his eyes shone when mentioning the diamond mines of Kimberley. 'There is a living for you,' he exclaimed again and again. And even Nellie, his wife, gets a great deal of amusement in watching him, swearing to do her part in holding up the train if he will; both of them amused, but something beyond amusement always in the hot, quick light in Harris's eyes.

I said, 'I'll see you swinging yet in Kimberley, see you swinging by the neck in Kimberley.'

It had a strange poetic rhythm to it, and Harris looked up and nodded. 'That's the way to die,' he said. 'Go out like a fine, brave fruit, not like a worm.'

For me, personally, the social side of Harris is the most charming. He is so human, often brilliant, so caustic, at times so bitter. Undying hate for his enemies and for those who have caused him trouble; such high wrath blazing always for pains brought to the artist's soul by the vulgar bourgeoise; such dynamic contempt for all who cramp and spoil – and yet always so much the gentleman.

This is how I love him, this is where my mind accepts as true the sinister in him.

But there is a business side as well, and to this I had to go also. For when he is being interviewed, he is another man again: not the writer, not the talker, not the host, he is the man who made the *Fortnightly Review* what it was in London and is making *Pearson's* what it is here. And I cannot but feel alienated by the knife that cuts the truth from top to base and lays it a quivering anatomical district before the eye.

Therefore I asked him if he thought he had already reached 'safe' with *Pearson's*.

'I believe so,' he said. 'The circulation manager tells me that the sales have quadrupled in New York in the last four months, and repeat orders are coming in from all parts of the country. Three days after the publication of the February number, we received repeat orders from Philadelphia and Chicago of twenty-five percent – and now another repeat order from Philadelphia for a further twenty percent.'

'Success comes running here, where she tiptoes in London?' I queried.

'I can only speak for myself,' he replied. 'For me, well, I find it more easily won here in America. Let me explain. In England a radical policy is disliked by the classes. Of course, if you get together five or six men of genius such as I had on the *Saturday Review*, an increase of circulation is almost assured. Shaw, Wells, Max Beerbohm, Cunningham-Grahame, and Arthur Symons give a weekly paper distinction and influence, but even in that case the advertiser does not follow the reader. Though I almost doubled the circulation of the *Saturday Review* in the first year, I lost more than half my advertisements. The moneyed classes in England dislike originality and hate all radical theories. The middle-class shopkeeper in England is the most obstinate foe to progress in the world. He is as much the snob as the aristocrat, and has besides an insane love of money and a corresponding hatred of those who hinder him from obtaining it.

'In America, on the other hand, you can reach success through a radical policy. That is, an editor can thus obtain circulation, and advertisements follow circulation. The coming success in American journalism will be a really radical daily paper in New York.

'That is the difference between Europe and America. In Europe you are radical till you get power; then you sell out to the privileged classes and get everything you want for yourself. Like Lloyd George and Briand, who both started as social reformers or Socialists and are now defenders of the privileged classes and money. Mr Wilson brought in an eight-hour bill while President – a radical reform, a thing unthinkable in Europe.

'America is radical at heart, and if you ever get a Moses, Americans will follow him into the promised land. In Europe Moses' only chance of getting the leadership is to become a lackey of the classes. He frightens everybody by telling them that the Red Sea is a sea of blood.

'My message at present is better than the paper it is printed on,' he added, smiling.

Then I asked him if he believed that Lloyd George would be unable to lead the English to success, and if he was not of the opinion that as a popular leader Lloyd George was already lost.

'Completely lost, I'm afraid,' he nodded. 'He is leaning not on the Liberals, but on the Tories; he is the last hope of the oligarchy. He thinks that energy, courage, and hard work will make the difference between success and failure in this war. Both the French and the English commanders encourage him in the belief that if sufficient munitions are provided, the Allies can break through on the West and drive the Germans back to their own frontier. He is practically pledged to achieve this by next August. In my opinion, he will fail; but even if he succeeds, he will get no better terms from the Germans than he could get now.

'By rejecting the peace proposal and by making exorbitant demands, he has made himself mainly responsible for at least another year of war; and the next year of war will cost more in blood and treasure than can possibly be gained by any or all of the combatants. He underrates his adversaries, or rather, he does not understand Germany at all or Germany's aims.'

'And the result will be?'

'A draw,' said Mr Harris, 'with the Germans winners on points.'

'Do you think President Wilson could end the war?'

'Yes, a year-and-a-half ago when England was dependent for her munition supply on America. The President could then have forced England to give reasonable terms, by threatening to put an embargo on the exportation of munitions; but now American munitions are not absolutely necessary to Great Britain. Accordingly, President Wilson could hardly enforce peace at the present time. By working for it steadily he may bring it about by next September or October, especially if the Allies fail to drive the Germans out of France or to break their lines. I believe that President Wilson will do all in his power to end it all, but I see no hope of peace until Lloyd George has had his trial and failed.'

'Then you think that if the Allies win and drive the Germans back to their own frontier, the war will go on?'

'Probably. The Germans will never accept terms the Allies have put forward till they are completely beaten, and that I regard as impossible.'

'What do you think will happen in the United States after peace is made?'

'The United States will either have to socialize her chief industries in order to meet the new competition of socialized Europe, or she will have to erect a high tariff wall and keep out competition, which will have the effect of increasing enormously the social inequality inside these United States. I was very glad to see that Secretary Daniels intends to socialize the manufacture of munitions. That is the best line to take. He seems to be doing much good work.

'I should like to see the telephones and the telegraphs taken over by the state, and the railways; but that will hardly happen the next year, and will never happen if the Frank Trumbulls are listened to.'

But I was thinking of Shaw and of Moore and of Wilde and those other brilliant minds that Frank had struck fire against. And so I asked him suddenly, breaking in on a reverie which he had fallen into, his hand set in between the first and second buttons of his coat as one sees them in old photographs.

'Tell me,' I said, 'something about those men who made up the genius of the *Saturday Review*.'

'You know,' he answered, 'Shaw and Bertrand Russell are about the only two men in England who have kept their heads in the general smashup. It is astonishing how infectious is the spirit of the herd in England. In America, too, you have persons talking of patriotism as the soul of the nation.'

'And Shaw,' I asked, 'what kind of letters does he write?'

'Shaw's letters are quite as funny as his plays. You had a specimen of that the other day when he replied to the invitation to come to America to speak. He said he was afraid to come, for he liked riding in railway cars with other men's wives – a home thrust for the way we treated Gorki.'

'And George Moore?'

'There is a man who writes letters as well as he writes books. Most men who come to the front are sincere – genius especially.'

'And what do you think of America in regard to literature and art?'

'There America has everything to do, and has hardly made a start as yet. In the long run, the composite character of America may be a great help. Every state should have a state art gallery, a state theatre and a state conservatory of music, and, of course, state endowment of scientific research.

'Every big city, too, should have its municipal theatre, municipal art gallery, municipal school of music, municipal schools of chemistry and physics. Art, literature, and science must be endowed and fostered, that is the most necessary thing in America today; that is the lesson Germany and France have taught the world. Statesmen should think of themselves as gardeners and not be satisfied till they can show specimens of every flower of genius in the gardens.'

'You believe that the endowment of art produces artists, and the endowment of literature, writers of genius?'

'The men of genius are always there,' replied Mr Harris, 'but if you do not help them, they will not be able to produce the great works. Shakespeare would never have done his best work, never have written *Hamlet* or *Othello* or *Antony and Cleopatra*, if Lord Southampton had not given him the one thousand pounds which made possible his high achievement. The popular taste of his day was worse than ours. His worst play, *Titus Andronicus*, was of the popular type, given hundreds of times in his life, whereas *Hamlet* was only given twelve times, and *Lear* once or twice.

'Only when New York has a municipal theatre and a state theatre shall we be equal to Paris, which has the Odéon and the Comédie Française, and we with a population half as large again. We endow common school education in America; but not the flower of education. We must endow genius in America, and every manifestation of it.'

He turned suddenly to the mantelpiece and dropping his lower lip, said, 'Ah,' as only he knows how to say it. The ejaculation of a man who will not weep when his heart is full, the desolate sound of a man who will not permit himself to be disillusioned; a half-sound between a truce and a challenge.

'It's dreadful, dreadful!' he said, clasping his hands behind him, walking to the window where he could see the park.

I asked him, 'What,' softly.

'The way they treat a man; the way they treat men of talent and of real worth in America. I don't see how you all stand it.'

I knew that he was referring to those of us who have been born with a little reverence for the things that are beautiful, and a little love for the things that are terrible; and I nodded my head.

•

EUGENE O'NEILL

Interviewed by Young Boswell
New York Tribune, 24 May 1923

Eugene Gladstone O'Neill (1888–1953), the American playwright, was born in New York. The son of an actor, his education was patchy and included only a year at Princeton; after doing some journalism he became a sailor, travelling to South Africa and Australia. He was struck down with tuberculosis and confined to a sanatorium where he decided to start writing plays. In 1915 he became a member of the Provincetown Players and wrote a play for them to perform, *Beyond the Horizon* (1920), which won a Pulitzer prize. He won several more Pulitzers: for *Anna Christie* (1922), *Strange Interlude* (1928), and *A Long Day's Journey into Night* (1957). His plays tend to be long, tragic in tone and boldly experimental in their presentation. He became the first American playwright to be awarded the Nobel prize for literature in 1936.

'Young Boswell' was the pseudonym adopted by Harold Stark for the purpose of conducting a series of short interviews. In 1923 Stark, then just out of Princebridge college, decided to interview Joseph Hergesheimer, the American novelist, as a speculative exercise. He wrote up the conversation and approached the editor of *The New York Tribune*, Julian Mason, with the idea of writing a daily interview column. Mason agreed and asked Stark how much he wanted to be paid. Stark's price was thirty-five cents, but Mason gave him 'a green note of a certain combination . . . the first money he had ever earned'. Among the various celebrities interviewed by Young Boswell for the *Tribune* were Hugh Walpole, Sergei Rachmaninov, Theodore Dreiser, William Allen White, H. L. Mencken, Hilaire Belloc, Ethel Barrymore, Leopold Stokowski, Isadora Duncan, Alla Nazimova, Dorothy Parker, Will Rogers, Chaliapin, and Joseph Conrad. These interviews were published the following year in book form as *People You Know*.

Eugene O'Neill leads the serious dramatists in America today. For two successive years his plays, *Beyond the Horizon*, and *Anna Christie*, were awarded the Pulitzer prize. His plays are being produced in England, France and Germany, and have been greeted with tremendous enthusiasm. *Emperor Jones* was a pioneer experiment in audience hypnosis. *The Hairy Ape* proved that tragedies may be popular successes.

O'Neill is the son of an actor. He has been, in rapid succession, a Princetonian, a gold miner, a sailor, an actor, a poet, a playwright, and is only thirty-three.

No man writing in this country at present has the poignant sense of tragedy that is manifest in the plays of Eugene O'Neill. Someone has said that he was over-sensitive and morbid as a child, and someone else, an academic critic, no doubt, that he wrote in the tragic vein, because he was young. Whoever may be wrong, Young Boswell was curious to know the source of that incisive, inevitable tragic quality, but found the young dramatist reticent, when the subject was mentioned.

EUGENE O'NEILL: I have an innate feeling of exultance about tragedy, which comes from a great reverence for the Greek feeling for tragedy. The tragedy of Man is perhaps the only significant thing about him.

He is a loosely built man, giving one the illusion of height. His face is long and narrow, young and sensitive. His eyes are serious and very dark, as though things might appear darkly through their medium. His brown hair has gone gray at the temples. He talked sincerely, though hesitantly, being impelled to speak of things private to him, and of theories which, he confessed, he hasn't formulated. He is not the self-conscious artist, but rather a virile man, who can't help writing. He is, however, not self-revelatory.

EUGENE O'NEILL: I want to write a play that is truly realistic. That term is used loosely on the stage, where most of the so-called realistic plays deal only with the appearance of things, while a truly realistic play deals with what might be called the soul of the characters. It deals with that thing which makes the character that person and no other. Strindberg's *Dance of Death* is an example of that real realism. In the last two plays, *The Fountain* and the one I am working on now, I feel that I'm getting back, as far as it is possible in modern times to get back, to the religious in the theater. The only way we can get religion back is through an exultance over the truth, through an exultant acceptance of life.

He hesitated as though he did not want to reveal any more and looked out of the window. Then he went on.

EUGENE O'NEILL: If there is anything significant about modernity, it is that we are facing life as it truly is. That fact differentiates this age from any other. We have no religion to evade life with. Like all the other evasions, religion is breaking down. We are looking life straight in the eye. And we see that our lives do not contain any of the qualities that we have always used to describe the good things of life. So, we must face life as it is, within ourselves, and do it with joy, and get enthusiasm from it. And it is a difficult thing to get exultance from modern life.

Again he fell into a silence. He stooped down to adjust a shoestring and Young Boswell was afraid he would not go on. And then he spoke of the theater.

What I am after, is to get an audience to leave the theater with an exultant feeling, from seeing somebody on the stage facing life, fighting against the eternal odds, not conquering, but perhaps inevitably being conquered. The individual life is made significant just by the struggle, and the acceptance and assertion of that individual, making him what he is not, as always in the past, making him something not himself. As far as there is any example of that in *The Hairy Ape*, it is his last gesture, when he kills himself. He becomes himself and no other person.

YOUNG BOSWELL: The full realization of the individual ego!

EUGENE O'NEILL: The struggle of Man to dominate life, to assert himself and insist that life has no meaning outside himself; where he comes in conflict with life, which he does at every turn; and his attempt to adapt life to his own needs, in which he doesn't succeed, is what I mean when I say that Man is the hero.

If one out of ten thousand can grasp what the author means, if that one can formulate within himself his identity with the person in the play, and at the same time get the emotional thrill of being that person in the play, then the theater will get back to the fundamental meaning of the drama, which contains something of the religious spirit which the Greek theater had. And something of the exultance which is completely lacking in modern life.

•

STANLEY BALDWIN
Interviewed by F.W. Wilson
The People, 18 and 25 May 1924

Stanley Baldwin (1867–1947), the English politician, was the son of an iron and steel manufacturer. He was educated at Harrow and Trinity College, Cambridge, and was first elected as a Conservative MP in 1906. He was a surprise choice as party leader and prime minister in 1923, but the party preferred him to the aristocrat Curzon. He served as prime minister three times: first from 1923 to 1924; then, after Ramsay MacDonald's short-lived Labour government, from 1924 to 1929; and finally from 1935 to 1937 as head of the national government. Baldwin was created the 1st Earl Baldwin of Bewdley upon his retirement in 1937. The period of his premierships had included the General Strike of 1926, when his government had outfaced the trade unions, and the Abdication of Edward VIII. His final premiership (1935–7) was criticized by Churchill for the failure to re-arm with sufficient dispatch in response to the continental aggression of Germany. He was a canny politician who prided himself on his reputation for honesty and considered it one of his prime duties to keep the dangerous and untrustworthy Lloyd George out of the political mainstream.

While in opposition, in 1924, Baldwin gave an interview to the political correspondent of *The People*, then a right-wing Sunday paper, in which he made some unguarded remarks about fellow Tory politicians Winston Churchill and Lord Birkenhead (the reference to his health was a veiled reference to his fondness for alcohol), as well as Lord Beaverbrook, the press baron. The interview caused a sensation. Within hours, Conservative Central Office issued a press statement saying that the interview contained inaccuracies. The next day a further statement was issued, this time specifying that the barbed remarks about certain public figures did not 'represent views that were ever expressed or held' by Mr Baldwin.

The press was extremely sceptical about the denial. 'The unfortunate thing from Mr Baldwin's point of view', commented the *Glasgow Weekly Herald*, 'is that the personal passages he repudiates are precisely those it would have been most difficult for the interviewer to imagine or invent.' Pressure was brought to bear on *The People*'s proprietor, a Canadian financier named Grant Mordern, to repudiate the interview and publish an apology. Instead, he published another article which contained further damaging revelations. The whole episode went against the grain of Baldwin's image as an honest politician. Former prime minister Lloyd George, who had long been accused of dishonesty by Baldwin, was able to be witheringly ironic in an address to the National Liberal Federation: 'Mr Baldwin is an honest man. He tells the truth, even in interviews.'

The interview had been arranged through the principal agent to the Conservative party, H.E. Blain. In the next edition of the paper, a week later, F.W. Wilson gave a fuller account of his interview with Baldwin.

A dramatic situation, with far-reaching consequences for a great political party and the country, has been unfolded to me by Mr Stanley Baldwin, the leader of the Conservative Party and ex-Prime Minister.

I asked Mr Baldwin what was the real significance of his new programme, expounded in his last three public speeches.

'I have attempted,' he said, 'to tell the country what I honestly believe. Every future Government must be socialistic, in the sense in which our grandfathers used the word. Personally, I don't know what Socialism means, but I do know that if the Tory Party is to exist we must have a vital, democratic creed, and must be prepared to tackle the evils, social and economic, of our over-populated, over-industrialized country.

'The cost of living must be reduced, the producer must get more reward for his article, and it ought to cost the consumer and buyer less.

'I believe the Tory Party is the only party that can tackle such problems satisfactorily. In the past we have been accused, and often rightly, of being too closely identified with vested interests. In the future we must put our house in order, and remove many of the abuses, whose existence is food for Socialistic argument. If we are to live as a party we must live for the people in the widest sense.

'Another reason why we should do this is because our party contains, and can command, the best brains and the best business experience in the country, which may be used to break rings and trusts. For trusts exist under Free Trade, just as much as they might do under Protection. We have people trained in national war service, who could help us, and it might be necessary to mobilize them, in a great campaign for cheaper food.

'We alone can tackle these social problems. The Socialists fall into class warfare difficulties and the Liberals are too idealistic.

'First and foremost, I attach tremendous importance to a speedy attack on food profiteering. Some facts which have come to my notice recently are very significant.

'An allotment-holder found it impossible to obtain more than a penny apiece for the cauliflowers she grew. These same cauliflowers she saw being sold at the local market next day for 6d each. A Worcestershire farmer told me that he sold pigmeat to Birmingham for 6d a pound; it was resold there for 1s 8d a pound. A Nottingham firm made a frock for 25s; it was sold at a Regent Street sale for £4 4s. These margins of profit and difference of price are, I am sure, too great.

'We want a strong Royal Commission to investigate all the facts before we formulate legislation. I am certain the index cost of living could be reduced, as a result of action in these matters, by 25 points.

'This is but a part of the programme I propose. It is part of the new spirit we have in industry. We must educate the workers in industrial matters. They should know all the details of management, all about the ratios of wages to sinking funds and depreciation, etc., and all about the competition with which their firm is faced. If trade unions had spent their money educating their members instead of fighting strikes, the workers would now be controlling industry everywhere.

'The Tory Party cannot go on on the old lines. I am certain that if we had not gone to the country and been defeated last year – though that, of course, is not why I went, I believed in something I wanted the country to adopt – we should have died of dry rot in two years, and Labour would have come in with a sweeping majority.

'We must recognize facts, and the new programme I have preached is an attempt to bring the Party up to date.

'But the lot of a leader in opposition is a difficult one. Read "C.B.'s" [Campbell-Bannerman's] life and see the kind of time he had. I know I am abused and jeered at, and intrigued against. But why?

'When I spoke at the Carlton Club meeting I never expected that we should win. I took my political life in my hands and I was prepared to retire from politics. I did not know that Bonar Law would lead us. In fact, the night before I spent two hours with him, and he had sealed a letter to the chairman of his Glasgow Association telling him that he would not stand for Parliament again. In that mood I left him.

'And then we won. I spoke because I was determined that never again should the sinister and cynical combination of the chief three of the coalition – Mr Lloyd George, Mr Churchill and Lord Birkenhead – come together again. But to-day you can see the signs of the times.

'But I didn't expect the exiled Conservative ex-Ministers would take things as badly as they did. Before the election last year I welcomed Mr Austen Chamberlain back, and I accepted his friends, though I could easily have stopped their return to our councils.

'With Austen came Lord Birkenhead, who had attached himself to the strings of Austen's apron the year before very cleverly. And Austen is one of those loyal men who could not see disloyalty or intrigue even if it was at his elbow. But I am under no illusions as to Lord Birkenhead. If his health does not give way he will be a liability to the Party. But can a leader of the opposition shut the door to an ex-Minister?

'And at the same time I am attacked by the Trust Press, by Lord Beaverbrook and Lord Rothermere. For myself I do not mind. I care not what they say or think. They are both men that I would not have in my house. I do not respect them. Who are they? I was attacked, I am told, in the *Evening Standard* over my arrangement for the Budget speakers. I did not read it. Why should I?

'This Trust Press is breaking up. The *Daily Mail* is dead; it has no soul. Northcliffe, with all his faults, was a great journalist, with a spark of genius. But this man! I get much correspondence about him. A post-card the other day said "If Lord Rothermere wants a halo in Heaven or a coronet on earth, why don't you get it for him?"

'The last time I spoke to Lord Beaverbrook was at Bonar's funeral. He had contracted a curious friendship with Bonar and had got his finger into the pie, where it had no business to be. He got hold of much information, which he used in ways in which it was not intended.

'When I came in, that stopped. I know I could get his support if I were to send for him and talk things over with him. But I prefer not. That sort of thing does not appeal to me.

'As I said, I do not mind attacks on myself. I often wonder if my silent contempt irritates them more than if I were to speak out. I suppose it is my lot to suffer disloyalty. But there are limits.

'Take the article in the recent number of *English Life*. That's a pretty dirty bit of work. It is written by "A Conservative ex-Minister", and I am pretty certain that if it is not written by the man I suspect, it was certainly inspired by him. It was a stab in the back. Now, it attacks my officials – the heads of the Central Office – and that I won't stand. If anybody had attacked a Treasury official when I was at the Treasury I would have come down to the House and made a very furious speech. And I intend to do so now.

'Besides, all this intrigue – this Churchill plotting – is bad for the party, for all the young men who are looking to Toryism for the salvation of the country. What do these intriguers want? Simply to go back to the old dirty kind of politics! Not while I'm leader of the party.'

And Mr Baldwin yawned with disgust and weariness at discussing for so long so unpleasant a subject.

●   ●   ●

Mr Baldwin, when I entered a large room on the first floor of Eaton Square, was at a desk in the far corner. He rose and greeted me, and my first words were, 'I'm afraid I am a very persistent man, Mr Baldwin. I have been trying to get you for weeks.' He replied, 'Not at all, Mr Wilson. I am seeing you because Mr Blain asked me to see you. Won't you sit down and smoke? I have been up at Wembley to-day and they gave me some Boer tobacco. The first time I smoked it was when I was given some by De Wet. I rather like it.'

'It's rather dry and difficult to keep in a pipe,' I said. 'I used to smoke it occasionally during the war, when it was given me by South African officers in the regiment. By the way,' I added, 'I know your son Oliver, as he was down at Bushey training with me during the war.'

Mr Baldwin, by this time, was sitting on a comfortable settee, armed with two cherrywood pipes. As he filled one, he said, 'Those were great days.'

I then asked him what he thought of Wembley, and he told me that he considered it the most wonderful show he had ever seen, that it ought to be made permanent or at least kept on for four years.

'The exhibition does not strike us, as educated men,' he said, 'the same as it would an ordinary member of the public. Take, for instance, those wonderful panoramas in the Australian exhibit. They give you the whole idea of sheep-farming. Of course, it is rather fatiguing. I found it so, as I was at top pitch the whole time. I got back and got into these,' he said, holding his tail coat, 'and went to a tea at the Duke of Devonshire's.'

'Now,' I said, 'Mr Baldwin, I must make quite clear to you what I want. After a sensible period of quietness, since the King's Speech, and your defeat at the last election, you have just made three speeches, which I think, contain your considered answer to Labour, and which offer the party a new policy on which they can reconstruct. It seems to me that you have formulated a new economic, with which to oppose the Socialist economic, and that you have at last given the country a lead which can be followed enthusiastically. I myself am particularly interested in your suggestions as to the necessity of tackling the profiteering question.'

Mr Baldwin interrupted me and proceeded to explain that he always attempted to tell the country in his speeches what he honestly believed.

'You see,' he said, 'every Government in the future, whatever party forms it, must be socialistic in the sense in which our grandfathers used the word.'

I was not surprised at this, as Harcourt once said 'we are all Socialists nowadays'.

He then continued expounding his new policy in the words which I faithfully reproduced last Sunday.

The only part I omitted was a passage in which he talked in a rather obscure way about the disparity between exports and imports to-day and exports and imports before the war. It struck me, as he spoke about this, that he felt himself in rather deep water and did not quite see his way through. It seemed more like thinking aloud rather than the expression of carefully worked-out judgment.

In fact, all the time that Mr Baldwin was talking I had the impression of a slow-thinking, very honest, earnest, likeable man, possessed of a strong sense of duty and obligation to his country, rather overwhelmed by a sense of his position, who was trying to tackle a very difficult subject with rather uncorrelated knowledge, and with few fundamental economic principles, but with a really true deep desire for the betterment of his more unfortunate countrymen.

All that I had previously thought about Mr Baldwin as being a typical honest Englishman, unsmirched by the rough-and-tumble, give-and-take of political life, became more and more confirmed. As he sat there, wreathed in smoke, filling one pipe after another, meditating in a low convincing attractive voice, I could understand why Bewdley loved him, and why his intimate friends speak of him with such real devotion.

There was none of the corruscating brilliance of Mr Lloyd George, none of that statesman's quickness and alacrity and subtleness, no attempt, which you so often felt with Mr Lloyd George, to attune himself with his audience. There was none of the canny, cautious, relentless logic of Mr Bonar Law, none of Asquith's carefully sorted-out pontifical thought, but just the simple political devotions of a simple man laid bare.

When we were talking about the new and the old Conservatism, I quoted to Mr Baldwin a remark from Lowes Dickinson's *A Modern Symposium*.

'Do you remember the opinion of the old Tory there? Mr Baldwin, "I like my gardener to take off his hat to me, and I like myself to stand bareheaded in the presence of the Queen."''

'Yes,' said Mr Baldwin, 'I remember. That book is the best Lowes Dickinson wrote.'

I congratulated him on his speech on the McKenna duties. 'It was not so much the matter, Mr Baldwin, I admired, as the tone of the speech. The Conservative cause is so often spoiled by exaggeration, and I was very pleased to read your speech with its calm tone and its admirable points.'

'I am glad you liked it,' he said. 'I made it like that purposely. I wanted Labour to listen to me. And they did, you know. They sat there with their tongues out. Labour listens to me, you know. I think it respects me. I was very disappointed with Mr Snowden's speech. It was unnecessary and a bad fall from his previous form, and you know the same night Mr MacDonald had a grave lapse at the Albert Hall.'

A little later.

'Whatever you can say about the Labour Party,' I said, 'you must recognize that the force behind Socialism is almost religious in its fervour and intensity.'

'Yes,' he said, 'but it is an extraordinary thing that when fanatics fall they so often fall on a dung heap.'

When Mr Baldwin had exhausted what he had to say on policy I said, 'Now, Mr Baldwin, you have apparently got a creed, which we can follow with enthusiasm and preach with conviction. But what is the use of trying to put it "over" when it is ignored by your hostile Press, laughed at, and when you are attacked and jeered at daily? Quite frankly, many members of your party go about whispering to one another that you are no use, and if one listened to many Tory MPs they would get the impression that you were a kind of effete moribund old man.'

Mr Baldwin smiled and replied, 'Of course, the life of a leader in opposition is always a difficult one. Every leader in opposition has intrigues. You remember how they treated "C.B." Read his life and see the kind of time he had. Even when he became Prime Minister it continued. I know I am abused and jeered at and intrigued against. I know it has been going on for a long time. But why?'

Mr Baldwin then told me the story of the Carlton Club meeting in the exact words which I used last Sunday. I must point out, however, that the published sentence, 'And Austen is one of those loyal men who could not see disloyalty or intrigue even if it was at his elbow,' is not as I actually reported it. Mr Baldwin was much more concrete. He used a word which could have been read as referring to a particular person, and in Mr Baldwin's interests my editor used a periphrasis.

Mr Baldwin also said that he knew that most of the intrigue proceeded from Lord Birkenhead, and he asked how he could refuse to have an ex-Minister in the councils of the party while he was in opposition.

'Do you recall,' he asked, 'any parallel in which a leader has taken such action?'

I could not recall one, but reminded him that Parnell was excluded from the executive of the Irish party after the divorce case. Mr Baldwin replied that the case was not parallel with his present difficulty.

He then proceeded to talk about the attacks made upon him by the newspapers. The connecting link was a reference to the last General Election, when I pointed out to him that Lord Birkenhead's speeches in Lancashire could hardly be said to be helpful.

'They were not,' he said. 'They did an unfortunate amount of harm. I think Birkenhead thought that we should come back with a small majority of between thirty and forty, and that he and his Coalition friends would hold the balance.'

'Yes,' I said, 'apparently that was the source of Lord Beaverbrook's estimate. He published the same figure.'

'Mind you,' said Mr Baldwin, 'if we had come back last year with a majority we should have had the full Chamberlain programme within four years. Naturally, these men were disappointed at the result. I was attacked all through the election, and I have been attacked since by the Trust Press.'

Mr Baldwin, at this point, rose and knocked his pipe out behind a firescreen, and his remark that he would not have either Lord Beaverbrook or Lord Rothermere in his house was made as he straightened himself in front of the fireplace.

When he spoke about that article in *English Life*, he said, 'I am perfectly certain that if it was not written by Lord Birkenhead it was certainly inspired by him.'

He also made some references to Commander Oliver Locker-Lampson, MP.

The interview, as written, did not contain everything that Mr Baldwin said about Mr Churchill.

'I do not think Churchill understands the post-war mind,' he said. 'I think if he got into the House he would only annoy Labour and there would be scenes. It is no use just denouncing Socialism as he does. You have got to have an alternative.

'Yes,' he mused, 'Churchill is a problem!'

When Mr Baldwin had finished, I thanked him for the frankness with which he had spoken, and the following conversation ensued.

'Do you think,' he said, 'that Lloyd George did himself any good when he attacked Northcliffe?'

I said, 'Yes. It made him really mad. Northcliffe was never the same after that terrible attack.'

'Well, then, Mr Wilson,' said Mr Baldwin, 'what do you advise me to do?'

'Besides this,' I replied (meaning the interview), 'I should, if I were you, make two or three speeches in the country pleading for purity in political life and denouncing this party intrigue. At the same time, I should take as many opportunities as possible of speaking on non-party subjects, in order to let people see your real personality.'

'I think I will,' said Mr Baldwin. 'When they attack my officials and when, as you have done, my attention is called to the effect on the party, they get me on one of my tenderest spots, and I think I will.'

By this time we were walking down his staircase.

'I hope, Mr Baldwin,' I said, 'you will allow me to come and see you again.'

'Whenever I have anything to say to you,' said Mr Baldwin, 'I hope you will come, or whenever you have anything to tell me.'

'It is, you know,' I said, 'most valuable for one writing about politics to get into touch with the main people in them. It is all very well studying the subject from books of anatomy, but it is very necessary to supplement that study with a little dissection.'

Mr Baldwin laughed, shook hands, thanked me for coming, and wished me good-night.

This ended the interview. I returned immediately to the office, and wrote an adequate and accurate summary of Mr Baldwin's statements. The verbal differences between my manuscript and the interview, as it appeared, were made by my Editor.

I wish to draw attention to the fact that I was, and am, perfectly convinced in my own mind that Mr Baldwin was aware of the terms on which the interview had been arranged between myself and Mr Blain, and that, while he was talking to me, he was talking perfectly honestly, with the full knowledge that I was on the staff of a newspaper, and going to report what he was saying.

●

WILLIAM HOWARD TAFT

Interviewed by Walter Tittle
The Century, September 1925

William Howard Taft (1857–1930), the American politician and jurist, was twenty-seventh president of the US (1909–13) and tenth Chief Justice of the Supreme Court (1921–30) – the only individual to hold both offices. He was the son of a politician who had served as President Grant's Secretary of War and Attorney-General. Taft himself was trained as a lawyer and served as US solicitor-general and first civil governor of the Philippines before being appointed President Roosevelt's Secretary of War (1904–8). He ran for the Republican Party as Roosevelt's successor, but in 1912 found himself running for re-election against his former patron, who stood as candidate for the Progressive Party, a Republican splinter that favoured a more aggressively reformist platform. The result was that the Republican vote was split and the Democratic candidate, Woodrow Wilson, was elected president instead. Taft subsequently became professor of law at Yale and his term in the Supreme Court was characterized by administrative efficiency.

Walter Tittle (1883–1966), the portrait painter and illustrator, was born in Ohio and contributed to magazines such as *Harper's*, *Scribner's*, *Life* and *The Century*. As well as sketching or painting public figures he occasionally wrote about them as well, a practice which gave rise to his 1948 book *Roosevelt as an Artist Saw Him*. In 1925 Tittle did a series of articles for *The Century* under the title 'Glimpses of Interesting Americans'. Each of these consisted of four interviews (with portrait drawings) of Americans who were prominent in different fields, such as literature or politics.

As I sat in a front parlor in the handsome residence of Chief-Justice Taft I was subconsciously aware of a droning of voices in a distant room. My mind was lazily inventorying the place: a Chinese cabinet filled with curios, a variety of furniture and objects suggesting gifts that may have come to the former President in his various official capacities, some interesting photographic portraits, a painting by Rubens. A half-formed thought running parallel to my observations was tinged with a bit of wonderment as to why it was that a very young man seemed to be doing most of the talking among the blurred voices that penetrated to me. Why was this youngster almost monopolizing the conversation in what must undoubtedly be distinguished company? The answer came in the only fragment of a sentence in which the words assumed a sudden distinctness. The young man remarked that such and such was the case, at least 'during my administration'. Thus, in considerable surprise, ended my involuntary eavesdropping.

The surprise was not abated when the 'young man' emerged. Nearly twelve years had elapsed since the end of his occupancy of the White House, but these years had been very kind to him. There was little apparent change in him to mark the passage of time. A bit thinner, though still of generous proportions, with clear and colorful skin, he seemed as young and vigorous as when he headed the affairs of the nation. His extraordinarily youthful voice at close range was filled with a jovial vitality that revealed not only a joyous and happy disposition, but a complete harmony of physical functioning as well. Before we settled to our task he answered a call on the telephone, and I remarked to him of the fitness and energy that his voice suggested.

'That's curious,' he said laughingly; 'a similar comment came just at this moment over the wire.'

With this jolly giant in a large chair beside a window, the process of delineation began. He told me of some of his previous experiences in sitting to artists, an anecdote of Zorn, whose able portrait hangs in the White House, being amusing.

'He was a curious person. I mentioned to him one day a portrait of his that I had seen and greatly admired. At my reference to this particular picture he displayed an utterly outraged spirit, nearly dropping his cigarette as he sputtered in complete disgust: 'That thing! Why, I had to do it from a photograph!' Sorolla painted me, too. He made me so fat that I looked like old King Gambrinus himself!' and the chief-justice laughed heartily at the recollection. He asked me my opinion of the Zorn portrait, and of that artist's work generally. I replied that I considered the portrait of him to be one of the artist's best. His chief value lay in his amazing technical facility that had dazzled me for a time, but gradually ceased to satisfy because, in a great majority of his performances, he was utterly content with a clever representation of surfaces viewed with the impersonal quality of the camera. Insight into character and psychology or sympathy with his subjects was almost wholly lacking. In these qualities Mr Sargent, with whom Zorn is naturally compared, excels to a great degree.

'Yes,' he said; 'Sargent has almost too much insight at times. It makes people afraid of him.'

There followed an account of his brother's notable collection of pictures in his house in Cincinnati. I had heard much of these canvases, and had made an effort to see them a few years before, but the family was away, and the beautiful old mansion was closed. It was designed by the architect who built the White House, about one hundred and twenty-five years ago, the chief-justice told me. Our discussion of pictures closed with an amusing remark from him about a group in a local museum.

'Some of them are of angels, and are so obviously painted from modern girls that there is a feeling of anachronism. One is likely to think of angels as looking more like the medieval representations of them. One sits with her knees crossed, and only a cigarette in her hand is needed to bring her entirely up to date.'

Justice Taft inquired in what part of the country I was born. I was proud to share with him his native Ohio, having first seen the light at no very great distance from his birthplace. I remarked upon the great productiveness of that State in contributing Presidents and other notable men in statesmanship as well as other important walks of life. He thought this was because of the great variety, as well as ability, of the early settlers, and of the fact that they intermarried freely, benefitting from the new infusions of blood. The melting-pot worked to better advantage in Ohio than in some other localities. The remarkable influence in national politics that has long been hers was due, to a considerable degree originally, he said, to the fact that she, with Indians, was an 'October State.' Down to about 1890 these two commonwealths held their congressional elections in October, providing in that way a sort of straw vote in Presidential years that was eagerly watched as indicative of the probable trend for the rest of the country. The rapidly growing population and wealth of this region caused it to maintain its reputation as a political pivot after the date of these elections was changed.

What the Ohio melting-pot did for the Taft family was confined to admixtures from various parts of England solely, with the possible exception of one ancestor on the *Mayflower* who is reputed to have married a Walloon. Otherwise, as far as he knows, the chief-justice is of pure English stock. There is a town in Massachusetts that has, in its public square, a monument to its founders. Of the thirty-odd names that are carved upon it, twenty-four are ancestors of his.

'We are of the Pilgrim stock that came in the *Mayflower*,' he said, 'but the real blue-bloods of New England are descended from the Puritans who came ten years later. They consider themselves vastly superior to the lowly Pilgrims. At a banquet in Boston some years ago I could not resist the temptation of a joking reference to this difference, remarking that we, as a family, had always adhered to the 'humbler walks of life'. Some of the Puritans were a bit teased by it, I think.'

A reference to the fullness and variety of his distinguished career achieved a reminiscent mood.

'My father was a judge, and I wanted to follow the same career. I remember well telling Mrs Taft that I would be quite content to be a common-pleas judge all of my life. I was fortunate in rising soon to more important posts than that, but it was a startling change for an average citizen to be taken from a judgeship and sent to preside over the welfare of islands in the antipodes whose name even I had hardly known. It was not easy to decide in favor of such a change. I recall Mr Root's argument that I accept this responsibility. He pointed out to me that I had had things pretty easy all my life, and here was a chance to be really useful. It would be much easier, naturally, to go on in the old way, but he hoped that I would accept the Philippines. Then to come to the White House from that world circle was another startling change. I didn't want to be President. It was the last ambition that would possibly have come to me. The whole thing was a curious sequence of unexpected occurrences.'

'I suppose you are more than content now,' I ventured, 'to be back on the bench, at the same time being at the top of your profession. It is a wonderful climax to your career, and undoubtedly involves much hard work.'

'The office of chief-justice has more hard work connected with it than the Presidency,' he replied, 'or, at any rate, more of sustained intellectual effort. I like it better. There is not the nervous drain in it that the President has to stand. Things proceed by systematic routine, and at the end of the day you have the satisfaction of knowing that something tangible has been accomplished. There is a feeling of futility connected with the position of President; at the end of most days one is exhausted and possessed of a feeling that nothing has really been done.' He paused to count up the time.

'It will be twelve years on the fourth of next March since I left the White House. It seems a dream to me that I was ever there as President. When I go there it never occurs to me that I once occupied the place, and I haven't the slightest desire to be back.'

'After the variety of titles that has been yours, I hardly know how to address you,' I declared, 'whether as Mr President, Mr Justice, or by one of the other prefixes that have been yours.'

'I claim that at last I am entitled to be called plain Mr Taft,' was the response. 'Just as the oldest daughter of a family is Miss Jones rather than Miss Helen Jones?'

'Precisely,' he replied.

'You have been extremely kind in giving so generously of your time and conversation to help me,' I said, 'and I am most grateful.'

'Justice Holmes spoke to me about you,' he replied. 'He is a wonderful man. He sits next to me on the bench, and is the keenest mind in the court. When he told me that he was sitting to you, I thought, "Far be it from me to deny you!"'

•

SIR EDWIN LUTYENS

Interviewed by Beverley Nichols
The Sketch, 5 May 1926

Sir Edwin Landseer Lutyens (1869–1944), the English architect, was born in London. Famous for his country houses, his civic architecture included the Cenotaph in Whitehall, the Liverpool Roman Catholic cathedral, the Viceroy's House in New Delhi, and the British Embassy in Washington.

(John) Beverley Nichols (1898–1983) was a writer and composer. The son of a solicitor, he was educated at Marlborough and Oxford, where he was president of the Union and editor of *Isis*. Thereafter he became a journalist, writing a diary for the *Sunday Chronicle* and interview-profiles for *The Sketch*, which were collected as *Are They the Same at Home?* (1927). He wrote prolifically in many spheres – plays and musical comedies, novels, children's stories, books about gardening, cats, cookery, and flower arrangement, detective novels, and four volumes of autobiography.

I was determined to stop him telling stories. Not that they were bad stories, but because they were good. They made me giggle, and took my mind off the things I really did want to talk to him about. And so, on this late afternoon in spring, as we together emerged through the gracious door of his office in Queen Anne's Gate, to take a walk, I fixed my eye upon him and said to myself: 'This time I am going to be a thoroughly bad listener.'

We began our walk. His pipe was now quite alight, and deep placid puffs were emerging from the figure on my right. I thought that the moment was ripe for broaching my deep-laid plans. 'Wouldn't it be rather marvellous to go for a long ride on top of a bus?'

He looked at me out of the corner of his eye. 'Talking of buses . . .' he said.

'Yes. I *was* talking of buses.'

'Talking of buses,' he repeated firmly, 'there was once a little boy who was travelling on the top of a bus, who said to his mother, "Ain't we ever going to get off this bloody bus?" Do you know what she replied?'

'No,' I said, with bitter resignation.

'She replied, "'Enery, 'ow often 'ave I told you not to say that word – ain't?"'

On the heels of this story another followed.

'Did I tell you about the Scotsman who was looking for a man in a mist?' he said.

Quickly I replied, 'Yes.' It was a shameless lie, because he had never told me the same story twice.

'No, I didn't,' said Lutyens, 'because I only heard it this morning.'

'Well, it must be a new Scotsman in a new mist,' I answered.

'Yes,' he said amiably. 'It must. There was once a Scotsman who met a man in a fog, and said, "Have you seen Macphierson?" "I'm not sure," replied the other. "I've seen one man, but he was either a very wee man wi' a beard, or a very tall man wi' a sporran."'

I refused to laugh (as a matter of fact, I had no great desire to laugh at that one), and with a sigh, he stopped telling stories, and became Sir Edwin Lutyens, chief architect of the Empire. For you see, we were at the foot of the Duke of York's steps, and, when you are at the foot of the Duke of York's steps, though you have probably never noticed it, a very curious phenomenon of the architect's craft is observable.

He stopped dead at the bottom of the steps and pointed upwards. 'Look!' he said. 'Do you see?'

I looked. I saw steps with the sunshine on them. I saw a pillar rising against a lemon-coloured sky. And – as I observed more closely I saw a sort of blob on the right. It looked like the head of John the Baptist, carelessly deposited there by one of the enviable residents of Carlton House Terrace.

'That blob?' I said. 'What is it?'

'Precisely,' replied Lutyens. 'What is it? It is the head of King Edward the Seventh. And it is in the wrong place.'

Then, with a sigh of relief, I noticed that his pipe had gone out, but that his eyes were alight with the artist's fire. And I knew he was going to talk as I wished him to talk.

'That ought to show you,' he said, 'something of the snares which we poor architects are always meeting. It's one of London's worst examples of foreshortening, or rather cross-shortening. It ought to have been placed on the steps, so that the feet of the horse were level with the top step. Still, it's too late now.'

With a disapproving frown at King Edward's desecrated head, of which the accompanying neck and body were now jerkily coming into view, he led the way up the steps.

'During the war,' he said, 'a certain great man asked me how much it would cost to take the Duke of York off the column and to put Kitchener in his place. I said it would cost five shillings.'

'Five shillings?' I was fascinated by the sight of King Edward's feet, which were just looming above us.

'Yes. Half a crown for each moustache.'

We paused on the top of the steps, feeling slightly awed by the monuments. 'How right Rosebery was,' said Lutyens, 'when he observed that the best possible monument to the last war would be to pull down all the monuments that were erected in the Boer War.'

It was then that he began to talk about his ideal city. I do not know how the subject was introduced. I have a faint suspicion that I badgered him into it by sheer persistence.

But I am not in the least ashamed of myself for doing so, for I wanted, as it were, to torture myself with the thought of the London that might have been. The London that is (and more especially the London that is yet to be) fills me with a pain that grows daily more acute. Sometimes I close my eyes and indulge in an orgy of mental spring cleaning. Imbued with the power that only comes to one in dreams, I dance down street after street, flicking portentous statesmen off their pedestals and watching them crash down in a cloud of dust. With a vast hammer I smash the horror that is Regent Street, throw the nauseous mess with a few giant handfuls into the Thames, and re-create, in a delicately coloured dream, the fairy fabric that was Nash's. I take a vast scraper and tear the vulgar signs from Piccadilly Circus, I destroy every single tile-faced abomination which houses the products of Messrs. Lyons and Company, I throw away the Marble Arch, kick up the Albert Memorial, and canter through Hyde Park, uprooting all those filthy little iron railings and sidewalks which do their daily worst to mar the gracious stretches of London's grass.

'My ideal city,' he said, 'could never exist. I should want endless women, sympathetic clients, and an inexhaustible supply of the right sort of stone.'

'I give you them all,' I said.

'That would be only demoralizing. One works far better with a certain amount of intelligent opposition. A building that is merely an abstract ideal is always a little inhuman.'

'Well, then, I give you the intelligent opposition.'

'In that case' – he paused a moment to allow a bus to snort itself past – 'in that case, my ideal city would be built, if it were in England, of Portland stone. Look at Wren's plan after the destruction of the Great Fire.'

'Or Washington,' I said perversely. 'At Washington the radiation from a central point is lovely, but it leads to a lot of nasty little grass plots, simply because of the geometry of the thing.'

'Well, you get over that by great open spaces. Look at Paris.' I looked at Paris.

'In Paris, everything radiates from the Arc de Triomphe. But there aren't any piffling little grass plots. The Champs Élysées is the ideal example in the whole world of the sort of vista which everybody like myself is always longing to achieve. When you look up the Champs Élysées it is like looking at the back-cloth of some marvellous scene painter. Everything is so graceful and so easy. The whole line is so melodious. One has no sense of difficulty. Yet there *were* colossal difficulties. They had to cut through a whole hill and lay the ground back in terraces. That's where Washington has failed.'

'How?'

'Because its vistas are blocked by objects bigger than they can hold. That great obelisk is far too big. Half the things there are far too big. There's no sense of a single rhythm.' He sighed, an almost melancholy sigh. We were passing a particularly hideous modern building (which I naturally may not name) and it seemed to weigh on his mind.

'Does London depress you, too, then?'

He did not answer my question. Instead he said: 'It would be so wonderful, if one were building one's ideal city. The arrangement of the vistas, I mean. I feel exactly like a scene painter. And that is the right feeling to have. To create something beautiful which always ended, at the finish of an interrupted avenue, with some form of spectacle. Everything else subdued to it. You know what Carlyle said when, for the first time, he noticed Chelsea Hospital?'

'No.'

'He said, "I have been passing this building for thirty years, and this is the first day that I have noticed it. I see that it is the work of a great gentleman." That's the fault of modern London, of any big city. We're all so damned anxious to be conspicuous that we achieve no sort of unity. And then, too, we have absurd ideas about what must be done and what mustn't.'

We were nearly in Trafalgar Square now, and I feared that Trafalgar Square might stop him talking. But no.

'When I was designing Delhi,' he said, 'they told me that, in order to show sympathy with India, I must employ a pointed arch. I had no intention of using a pointed arch. So I sent back the following reply: "*When God created India, He did not show His wide sympathy by pointing the rainbow.*"'

I wonder if the gentleman to whom that reply was addressed ever quite realized that it contained a whole philosophy of aesthetics?

We were now in Trafalgar Square, which has always seemed to me to be typical of the English race, because it is so full of glory and so full of muddle. Against a sky of red, white, and blue, the Nelson column rose like a warning finger. We stood by the parapet, hoping that the pigeons would behave themselves. And Lutyens turned to me and said:

'You see, it's really beyond criticism.'

'All this?'

'I mean, the thing for which it stands is so great that one can't say what one thinks about the execution of it.'

'Can't one?' I was certain that he could if he wanted. I remembered, with exquisite clarity, the design which a few years ago he had made for the clearing up of Trafalgar Square. If it had been adopted we should have had one of the finest open spaces in the world. But it was not adopted.

'Of course,' he said, as though he were saying something slightly naughty, 'it's all too big. Look over there.'

I looked. 'The scale of *that* is admirable. Now, if everything had been like that, and if the four lions . . .'

He paused. I looked to see what had caught his attention. His eyes seemed to be fixed on the distant sky. I followed their direction, and I saw flashing across a building on the other side of the Square a message in shimmering silver. It read: '*The price of the franc at noon in Paris to-day was* 135.75.'

This was terrible. If our examination of Trafalgar Square was to be interrupted in this rude manner by the enterprise of the *Daily Express*, we would never get anywhere.

'I wish I had francs to sell,' said Lutyens.

'It is only the influence of Trafalgar Square that makes you say things like that,' I said. 'You were saying something about lions.'

'Ah, yes, I should like them much better if they had been stuffed. Think what a subject for a really competent taxidermist! Think how they would be in keeping with the spirit of the age! . . . Think . . .'

His eye was fixed again on that damnable news message. It seemed to exercise a positively hypnotic effect on him. Feeling slightly dizzy, I traced out the message. It began: '*At the Crystal Palace this afternoon . . .*'

Lutyens turned away before the message was finished. I think it made him feel dizzy.

'Talking of the Crystal Palace,' he said, 'I was once informed by a celebrated peer of the realm that it might be bought for Imperial purposes. He asked me what was the most suitable purpose I could suggest for it.'

'And what did you suggest?'

'Well, I asked him how much money was available. And when I was informed that money was no object, I told him that the best thing to do with it would be to put it under a glass case.'

Again his eye wandered. But this time the snaky silver news was in the middle of a message:

'*Was found dead this afternoon with the bodies of her three children by her side.*'

'How disgusting civilization is!' he said, with a disapproving frown.

'Yes,' I remarked brightly. 'That's why I think it's so restful to look at those lions.'

He glanced at the lions for the last time.

'If I had my way,' he whispered, 'I would put a gramophone in the tummy of each of them, and make them purr.'

•

WILLA CATHER
Interviewed by the *Nebraska State Journal*
5 September 1926

Willa Sibert Cather (1876–1947), the American novelist and poet, was born in Virginia and brought up in Nebraska, attending the university there from 1891 to 1895. She wrote journalism for local newspapers and published books of poetry and short stories before going to New York in 1906 to edit *McClure's* magazine. Her first novel, *Alexander's Bridge*, was published in 1912, the year she left *McClure's*. Her next three novels formed a trilogy about immigrant life in the Midwest. She won the Pulitzer prize in 1922 for *One of Ours*. Her later novels, *The Professor's House* (1925) and *Death Comes for the Archbishop* (1927), were both set in New Mexico. Her work was characterized by subtly portrayed heroines of independent spirit struggling against conventionality in a frontier context.

Interviewed at the Grand Central station, where she was waiting for a train one hot July day, Willa Cather said:

'Yes, I'm getting out of town – it's rather evident. No, not west this time. I have just come back from three months in New Mexico. Now, I'm going up into New England.'

'What part of New England?'

'Oh, several places! Mr Knopf and Mr Reynolds will always have my address if you should wish to reach me about something important. Seriously, I'm going away to work and don't want to be bothered.'

'But this is vacation time.'

'I've just had a long vacation in New Mexico. I need a rest from resting.'

'Are you beginning a new novel?'

'No, I'm in the middle of one.'

'When will it be published?'

'The book? About a year from now. The serial publication will begin sometime this winter. I want to finish the manuscript by the middle of February and get abroad in the early spring.'

'I suppose, Miss Cather, it's no use to ask you for the title. You told me several years ago that you never announced the title of a new book until it was completed.'

'Did I tell you that? Well, this time I'll make an exception. I don't like to get into a rut about anything. I call this book *Death Comes for the Archbishop*.'

'And the scene?'

'Oh, that remains to be seen! My train is called.'

'One general question on the way down, please. What do you consider the greatest obstacle American writers have to overcome?'

'Well, what do other writers tell you?'

'Some say commercialism, and some say prohibition.'

'I don't exactly agree with either. I should say it was the lecture bug. In this country a writer has to hide and lie and almost steal in order to get time to work in – and peace of mind to work with. Besides, lecturing is very dangerous for writers. If we lecture, we get a little more owlish and self-satisfied all the time. We hate it at first, if we are decently modest, but in the end we fall in love with the sound of our own voice. There is something insidious about it, destructive to one's finer feelings. All human beings, apparently, like to speak in public. The timid man becomes bold, the man who has never had an opinion about anything becomes chock full of them the moment he faces an audience. A woman, alas becomes even fuller! Really, I've seen people's reality quite destroyed by the habit of putting on a rostrum front. It's especially destructive to writers, even so much worse than alcohol, takes their edge off.'

'But why, why?'

'Certainly, I can't tell you now. He's calling "all aboard". Try it out yourself; go lecture to a Sunday school or a class of helpless infants anywhere, and you'll see how puffed-up and important you begin to feel. You'll want to do it right over again. But don't! Goodbye.'

●

GEORGES CLEMENCEAU
Interviewed by George Sylvester Viereck
Liberty, 7 July 1928

Georges Clemenceau (1841–1929), the French politician known as the Tiger, came from La Vendée and started his adult life as a doctor in Paris. He lived in the United States from 1865 to 1869, then returned to pursue a political career, attending the French National Assembly in 1871. Five years later he won a seat in the Chamber of Deputies and assumed the leadership. He was also a journalist, in which capacity he founded *L'Aurore* and defended Dreyfus. He was premier of France from 1906 to 1909 and again from 1917 to 1920, as leader of a Coalition cabinet. He rallied the French people and spurred the French army on to victory. At the 1919 Paris Peace Conference, he was responsible for the tough terms applied to Germany under the Treaty of Versailles. Ironically, he lost the 1920 presidential election because he was thought to have been too lenient towards Germany.

George Sylvester Viereck (1884–1962) was an American of German-Jewish origin. His father was a scholar and had been a Socialist MP in the German Reichstag. The family emigrated to the United States in the 1890s. During the First World War, George Sylvester Viereck supported Germany until the United States was drawn into the conflict. He first came to public attention as a poet and one commentator sang his praises thus: 'From 1908 to 1914 he was the Puck of American letters – an impudent, irreverent, irrepressible boy, tickling the solemn donkey of puritanic ideals, shocking all good folks by teaching the Muse to sing shamelessly of things that proper people would not even whisper . . . For its liberation from ethical preoccupation, its enfranchisement in aesthetic freedom American poetry has George Sylvester Viereck to thank more than anyone else with the possible exception of Ezra Pound.'

He wrote a best-selling novel – *My First Two Thousand Years: The Autobiography of the Wandering Jew* – and described himself as a 'de luxe interviewer' for the Hearst papers, magazines such as *The Saturday Evening Post*, and *Liberty*, of which he was advisory editor for ten years. Some of his interviews with international celebrities were collected in a volume called *Glimpses of the Great*, which was published in New York, London, and Berlin in 1930. It contained interviews with thirty-two world figures, including George Bernard Shaw, Israel Zangwill, Frank Harris, Henry Ford, Ramsay MacDonald, Kaiser Wilhelm II, Sigmund Freud, Benito Mussolini and Albert Einstein, as well as the key figures of the First World War: General von Ludendorff, Clemenceau, and Marshals Joffre and Foch.

In the Introduction to *Glimpses of the Great*, Viereck offered this slightly rarefied assessment of his role: 'To me the men to whom I have talked and whose thoughts I record are flashes of the great World Brain. Some are incandescent in their intensity; in others the divine flame burns more dimly. Their colours are more varied than the spectrum. I am the spectroscope that reveals the stuff of which they are made, or, translating colour into sound, I am the trumpet through which they convey their message.'

'A parliament of peace changes nothing!' exclaimed Clemenceau with quiet fury. 'International leagues do not obliterate international rivalries.'

Upon his head the man who dictated the Peace Treaty of Versailles, overruling both Lloyd George and Woodrow Wilson, wore somewhat coquettishly the famous Greek cap, classically 'flapped', with which he is always depicted.

Clemenceau's stature was slight. In spite of the almost ferocious energy that one still suspected in his frame, he did not at first look like a tiger. In his lighter manner he seemed Puck at the age of a hundred; in his more serious moods, when the cap sat awry, there were touches and traits of King Lear.

'More than ten years ago,' I remarked, 'America entered the war. What is your view of the present state of the world in general and of France in particular?'

Imps seemed to leap from Clemenceau's eyes.

'Conditions will be satisfactory as long as the present balance of power on the continent of Europe remains. If that balance be upset by any revival of German imperialism, Europe will have another general war.'

'Will it be possible for diplomacy or philosophy to abolish war?'

'No.'

'What is the supreme lesson of the war for you, for France, for the world?'

'History repeats itself. Man should prevent history from repeating itself. Peace is made by the biggest battalions! Peace is the creation of the strongest power! Our "statesmen" have secured, with much expenditure of words, the admission of Germany into the so-called League of Nations. There her pledges will have the same value as those by which she guaranteed the neutrality of Belgium, only in the end to violate it openly without even seeking the ordinary resource of lying pretexts.'

'But,' I remarked, 'you disarmed Germany at Versailles. The German Republic is defenceless, an island surrounded by a sea of arms.'

'If my advice had been followed,' he snarled, 'there would be *permanent* peace.'

Precisely as it was said of Gladstone that he was the grand old man, it might be said of Clemenceau that he was the sardonic patriarch. The oddness and bluntness of his manner suggested that satirical Dean Swift who gave *Gulliver's Travels* to the nursery and to the university.

The beginning of our interview was not auspicious.

When I called on him in his simple house in Paris at 9.30, the appointed hour, his manservant conducted me into the library. The Tiger entered quietly, almost stealthily, with catlike tread.

'What is it? What's the matter?' were his first words. It was more a growl than a salutation.

I explained my mission.

'I am very happy to see you, but I will not be interviewed.'

'M. Clemenceau,' I interrupted, 'you yourself made the condition that I should obtain the consent of your publishers. "If they were willing"– such was the message I received from you –"you would talk to me at length on your philosophy of life." I procured the consent by cable. I am here at your invitation –'

'You must forgive me,' the Tiger replied somewhat petulantly, 'but I cannot depart from my principle.'

I subsequently learned that it was Clemenceau's favourite trick to embarrass his interviewers. He made startling statements, which he subsequently repudiated. The convenience with which the Tiger forgot an occasion was probably one of the reasons responsible for the nervous strain at Versailles and the breakdown of President Wilson.

'M. Clemenceau,' I replied, 'this interview has been arranged by a mutual friend.' I mentioned the name of the friend.

'Why isn't he here?' Clemenceau snapped back. 'The other day he brought me one of your countrymen, who afterwards misquoted every word I said.'

'To be misquoted,' I remarked, 'is the destiny of great men. They are always misquoted. That's no misfortune. Some of the best things attributed to great men were probably never said at all – at least, not by them. The world's imagination invents the appropriate word if the hero's own imagination fails him.'

The Tiger seemed unimpressed. But he considered it necessary to explain his aloofness from human contact.

'I hate no one. I love no one. I harbour no ill will toward the world. Maybe' – there was a dry chuckle in Clemenceau's voice as he pronounced these words – 'no good will, either.

'I have retired completely. At my age one is entitled to do only the things that amuse one. My stay in Paris is almost ended. I shall shortly return to the Vendée, where I am happy.'

'Will you write your memoirs?'

'No!' He shouted the word.

'Are you happy when you are not working?'

'Happiness! What is happiness? I take pleasure in simple things. It delights me to be in life and out of it at the same time.'

We were getting along famously.

I took out a questionnaire which I had prepared for my intellectual dalliance with the Tiger. He scanned my questions.

'I should love to answer them, not only for your sake, but for my own. It would be a pleasing intellectual exercise. But principle is principle. One must stand for something. There is nothing in life except principle. No, I cannot answer them.'

I made one more attempt to change his determination.

'I do not want an ordinary interview. I have no use for conventional journalism. I am not a journalist, I am a poet.'

Clemenceau rose.

'I congratulate you.'

He made a deep bow, with the grave dignity of a raven.

'As for myself,' he added, 'I am a positivist, not a poet.'

Once more the ice was broken.

'Will you,' I asked, 'inscribe your book for me?' The two huge paper-bound volumes of *Au Soir de la Pensée* (In the Evening of my Thought) were bulging out of my brief-case.

'With pleasure,' he said, somewhat mollified, and he began to write in a hand betraying no tremor of age. I think he used an ancient goose quill.

I looked around the room. It was evidently his workroom. There were reproductions of Greek scenes, a statue or two, and books in all languages. Clemenceau's English diction was perfect, but his inflection betrayed the Latin.

'I read a little in your book before I wrote to you,' I remarked, 'but it is a hard nut to crack.'

'At least,' Clemenceau answered, 'I don't use the endless words of the German philosophers.'

He continued to write.

'Are you German?' he asked.

'Aha!' I said to myself. 'Now the Tiger is about to spring.'

'I am an American of German descent. I was born in Munich. My mother is from San Francisco. My father was born in Berlin.'

Clemenceau looked up.

'The Germans are a great people,' he said. 'I admire thier achievements in art, in literature, in organization. Who wouldn't? Yes, they are great; but – I cannot forget Belgium.'

I took the bull by the horns, explaining the German attitude. Perhaps no one in recent years had dared to speak with such frankness to the Tiger.

'The Germans hold that Belgium had forfeited her neutrality before the war. They were convinced that France and England would march through Belgium first, if they didn't.'

'But why,' he insisted, 'did she make a treaty? Bethmann-Hollweg himself admitted that Germany committed a wrong.'

I urged military necessity. Clemenceau listened patiently.

'When a nation's existence hangs in the balance,' I added, 'safety is more important than treaties.'

'Ah,' Clemenceau replied, suddenly veering around, 'I too do not believe in treaties. But then, why have them?'

'The Kaiser,' I ventured to interrupt, 'told me that Bethmann-Hollweg's speech apologizing for the invasion of Belgium was made without his authorization. The Chancellor was misled by the desire to play up the liberal sentiment. Bethmann-Hollweg should have insisted that Belgium compelled the invasion by joining the iron ring forged by King Edward to smother the Germans.'

'The Kaiser?' Clemenceau asked. 'You know him?'

'Yes,' I replied. 'I have been his guest on several occasions.'

'I cannot forgive him,' Clemenceau remarked.

'You mean you consider him responsible for the war?'

'I was not referring to that. I mean I never forgave him for going away. He should not have gone away.'

'The Kaiser,' I said, 'explained to me with his own mouth his fateful decision of November 11, 1918. He said to himself: "If I stay, there will be a continuation of the war at the front, and civic strife at home. If I go, there will be an honourable peace, based on the Fourteen Points, and peace at home!" He determined to sacrifice himself to save his people.'

'That sounds plausible. Nevertheless, I do not believe it of William the Second. He is too pompous. He was hated by every one. He had no friends in Europe.'

'For that you must blame, in part, King Edward.'

'Why,' Clemenceau suddenly remarked, firing his question like a machine gun, 'did he survive his empire? Why does he live?'

'Napoleon did not commit suicide,' I replied. 'Suicide would have been regarded as a confession of guilt. He lives to combat the legend of Germany's guilt.'

'On the guilt question,' Clemenceau retorted with a snarl, 'don't you think our mind is made up? I know who started the war, if any one knows.'

He lapsed into silence.

'M. Clemenceau,' I remarked, 'did you say at the time when you made the Peace Treaty of Versailles: "There are twenty million Germans too many"?'

'I never said such a thing. I am old enough to tell the truth. It is one of the privileges of age. Nothing I say can harm me any more.'

'I am glad,' I remarked, 'thàt you did not make that statement. It seemed to me a cruel and callous thing to say at a time when German children were dying like flies as a result of the inhuman starvation blockade, continued for a year after the Armistice.'

Clemenceau smiled grimly. Once more he was the Tiger rather than Puck.

'Which is more dangerous, the vague idealism of men like Woodrow Wilson or the opportunism of men like Lloyd George?'

'All depends upon the man. A nebulous idealism fostered by a positive genius is better than a positive opportunism in the mood of Hamlet. We should study the circumstances in which each was placed before deciding anything. History is filled with characters who essayed to play a part for which their temperaments unfitted them. There is a time for all things. Hence there may be a time to be an idealist as well as a time to be an opportunist.'

'Is it true that you said you had a pretty tough job trying to make peace, sitting between one man who thought he was Napoleon Bonaparte and another who imagined he was the Messiah?'

'I did say it,' Clemenceau replied, grinning amusedly to himself.

'And did you say that Wilson was too much for you, because he issued fourteen commandments, whereas our Lord contented himself with ten?'

Again the pleased smile. Clemenceau loved his *bons mots*. Again the Tiger was submerged in Puck. Suddenly Clemenceau's mind reverted to Germany.

'I really did not make the remark about the Germans,' he reiterated. 'German literature was a great formative influence in my life.'

'Did you know,' I interjected, 'that Mussolini not only reads Nietzsche, but that he wrote an essay on Klopstock, a poet so dull that not one in a million Germans has the patience to wade through his works?'

'Klopstock?' Clemenceau repeated. 'I have not read "Klopstock". But I translated every line of Goethe's *Faust*.'

'In verse?' I questioned.

'Yes.'

'Did you publish your translation?'

'No. I' – he emphasized the personal pronoun grimly – 'make no claim to being a poet. I am a materialist.'

'When did you translate *Faust*?'

'As a young man, in America, with my teacher, an old lady who taught me German. I could not do it to-day. I have forgotten my German.'

'Did you forget it at Versailles?'

No answer. I did not pursue the subject.

'Do you consider,' I asked, 'Goethe's *Faust* the greatest of all poems?'

'It is one of the greatest.'

'Who is the greatest poet?'

'Shakespeare is the greatest of all poets. He overwhelms me. He is overtowering. But I certainly honour Johann Wolfgang.'

He stressed the last syllable of Wolfgang with the peculiar singsong of the French.

'Shakespeare,' Clemenceau continued, 'was not only a great poet, but a great personality. He embraced the world.'

'What a pity,' I remarked, 'that we know so little about his life.'

'What do you mean?'

'Everything seems to be veiled in mystery. We don't know the identity of the Dark Lady and the Fair Lad of the *Sonnets*. We know nothing of Shakespeare's love affairs.'

'Why should we?' Clemenceau replied, with a delightful Gallic smile. 'We are too busy with our own.' Then, more seriously, he added: 'It is the work that matters, not the man.'

The supreme human achievement, to Clemenceau at eighty-seven, was neither statesmanship nor literature, but philosophy. Clemenceau had given much thought to the problem of life and death.

'Can you,' I asked, 'summarize in a phrase what is the ultimate happiness?'

'The ultimate happiness,' and here Clemenceau chuckled, 'is not to be bothered.'

'And what,' I asked, 'is the supreme human achievement?'

'To be a philosopher.'

Clemenceau takes his place with philosophers. One of the masters of French politics, he also is one of the masters of French thought. Clemenceau is the incarnation of philosophy in its sceptical mood. He looked the part!

Take the bust of Socrates, imagine the beard swept away, substitute a cap for the flowing hair, and the result is Clemenceau. The illustration is apt; for the philosophy of Clemenceau, like that of Socrates, is a confession that he knows nothing, or rather that he knows that he knows nothing.

His hands habitually grip one another in his lap or on his desk as he leans forward. There is scrutiny and there is suspicion in that lined face. The neck is sinewy but firm. The ears are prominent but fine. The brows are shaggy but well arched. The lips are for ever describing angles – moving, unfolding, shutting, as if he means to make a sensation with a sentence, but thinks better of it. The nose is fit for such a grim countenance. I can see him now.

The chin is strong, well outlined, prone to an upward movement when he is delivering himself of an opinion in determined, even ringing tones. It is the same voice with which he upset ministries in the Chamber of Deputies, the voice in which he crushed all opposition with his epigrams.

He emphasizes a word now and then with a flourish of his hand – a long, thin, bony hand, opening and closing to reveal fine fluted fingers.

His movements are so quick, his ironical courtesy is so charming, his vivacity so overwhelming that I could not resist the question:

'How do you keep yourself so young? Are you interested in the attempts of Steinach and Voronoff to prolong human life?'

Clemenceau snarled something that may have been either approval or disapproval.

Perhaps my question was unfair, for it was rumoured that another operation performed many years ago, which unintentionally produced the Steinach effect, accounted for his astonishing vitality.

The Tiger knows the value of silence. In this case silence prevailed.

'Is not life too short to be worth living?' I asked.

'It depends upon how you define life,' Clemenceau growled.

'In the light of my own experience I have not found life too short to be worth living. It might easily be too long to be worth living. Life is no longer worth living when one has exhausted its possibilities.'

'Do you believe that modern science will be able to prolong life appreciably?'

'Yes.'

'To what do you ascribe your own extraordinary youthfulness?'

'I write, I read, I take exercise, I eat simply. That is the secret of youth,' he remarked. 'Moderation, exercise, work are my daily companions.'

'Do you believe with Bernard Shaw that man will live three hundred years eventually?'

'That,' Clemenceau replied, shaking his head impatiently, 'involves a prediction about the future of humanity; and all predictions about the future of humanity are liable to be falsified by the introduction of the element of the unforeseen. Granting that the element of the unforeseen does not upset the inference, it may be said that a time can be envisaged when the life of man will be prolonged very much beyond what we now think possible.'

'Do you think that life can teach us more in three hundred years than in eighty?'

'That depends upon the intelligence of the individual. Life might teach some individuals nothing in a thousand years.'

'Do you believe in the evolution of the superman, or do you believe that humanity will eventually be supplanted by another species: ants, sea animals, et cetera?'

'Man will never be supplanted by anything inferior to himself. And there is nothing earthly that is higher than the human being. Assuming that life on our planet in its highest manifestations will always be that of human beings, and since human beings seem progressive, it follows that our race must go on indefinitely unless a catastrophe of cosmic proportions should obliterate it.

'Man will get beyond his present stage of evolution. Compared with primitive man, is not the human being of to-day a superman?'

'As a psychologist and a philosopher,' I ventured, 'what is your attitude towards psychoanalysis?'

Clemenceau looked at me without comprehension.

'What do you think of Freud?'

He repeated the name, which, however, seemed to mean nothing to him.

'Who is he?' the Tiger roared. 'Has he written a book?'

I renewed my questioning along more familiar channels.

'Who is the greatest philosopher?'

'Plato.'

The reply was instantaneous.

'The greatest statesman?'

'Caesar.'

'The greatest soldier?'

'Napoleon.'

'Who is your favourite author?'

'My favourite author today may not be my favourite author tomorrow.'

Clemenceau likes to be amused. Authorship is one of his amusements.

By temperament a man of books, destiny made him a man of action. He longed for the solitude of his study at a time when he had to guide the destinies of a nation. His manner was that of a man who confronts his intellectual inferiors. He always had the courage of his opinions. He never hesitated or feared to throw them into the teeth of a disedified world.

He is one of the men, perhaps the very one, to whom Briand pointed when he proclaimed in that immortal speech of his: 'You have put out the lights of heaven!' For Clemenceau told the world that those lights do not shine.

'Is it possible to pierce the veil behind which the World Spirit hides itself?' I asked.

'However deaf, however mute it seems, the world,' Clemenceau replied, 'permits a piercing of its mysteries. This is what I try to explain in my book.'

I looked at the two volumes.

'It certainly is inspiring to think that it is possible to write such a book at eighty-seven. Will you,' I added, 'mark for me some passages which you yourself regard as the most illuminating?'

'Why don't you read the book yourself?'

Glaring at me ferociously, Clemenceau seized a paper knife and pointed to several passages in his book. They reveal how Clemenceau, denying both God and Devil, optimism and pessimism, reconciled himself to the universe.

I sat dumbfounded before this unsuspected Clemenceau, this new Clemenceau rising rosily and freshly out of the old Clemenceau.

The bell rang, announcing another guest.

I had spent an hour with Clemenceau.

Did he know that he had given me more than an interview? Had he deliberately bared his heart to me? Or had he been playing with me as a tiger-cat with a mouse?

•

GRETA GARBO

Interviewed by Mordaunt Hall
The New York Times, 24 March 1929

Greta Garbo (1905–90), the American film actress, was born Greta Lovisa Gustafsson in Stockholm, Sweden, where she grew up. She worked briefly as a shopgirl and won a bathing beauty competition before winning a scholarship to the Royal Theatre Dramatic School in Stockholm. She starred in just one Swedish film – whose director Mauritz Stiller came up with her professional name – before travelling to the United States in 1925. She gave this interview a year before her career took off with her first picture *Anna Christie*. There followed several classic Hollywood films during the 1930s – *Queen Christina*, *Anna Karenina*, *Camille*, and *Ninotchka* – but she retired from the movies in 1941, never to return. She lived as a recluse for the rest of her life, mainly in New York City, becoming a US citizen in 1951. Mordaunt Hall was being unwittingly prescient when he described her as a 'would-be hermit' and her most oft-quoted line – 'I vont to be alone' – echoes her remarks here about dining alone and looking at the skyscrapers.

That languid screen enchantress, Greta Garbo, was at the Hotel Marguery, Park Avenue, last Wednesday, having arrived the day before from Sweden. Her mere presence appeared to have its effect upon the room clerk, for most of the conversation was either uttered in a whisper or by signals. The Metro-Goldwyn-Mayer representatives could not have acted with greater deference had a visiting potentate been the object of their attentions, for Miss Garbo, like Charlie Chaplin or Sir James M. Barrie, is a shrinking violet when it comes to being interviewed.

The telephone bell broke the silence and the room clerk lifted a finger as a signal to the elevator operator that Miss Garbo would receive a representative of *The New York Times*. Soon the door of Miss Garbo's apartment was flung open and the sinuous figure of the alluring actress appeared as if from a ray of sunlight. In a low-toned voice that suited her bearing, she greeted the caller, whose eyes fell from her face to a bouquet of flowers on a table and then to the carpet.

'Won't you sit down?' she said.

The visitor's eyes once more challenged the chance of being caught: staring and forthwith became aware that Miss Garbo wore a black covering on her head, like a skull cap, with two tassels of hair bursting forth from each side. It was quite obvious after she had answered a few questions that Miss Garbo's magnetism was just as impressive off the screen as on. Like Pola Negri, whom she greatly admires, she is natural, being more amused than embarrassed by her none too extensive knowledge of English.

She wore a pink silk sweater with a short black velvet skirt, and coils of smoke rose to the ceiling from the cigarette she held in her long fingers.

When she first came here, three and a half years ago, Miss Garbo knew hardly any English, but now she succeeds fairly well in expressing herself and, in spite of occasional lapses, that are quite captivating, she declared that she was quite willing to try acting and dialogue in a talking picture.

What would she like to do as a pictorial story? She puffed her cigarette, threw back her head, lowered her eyelids and vouchsafed:

'Joan of Arc. But it probably wouldn't go so well. I would like to do something unusual, something that has not been done. I would like to get away from the usual. I don't see anything in silly lovemaking. I would like to do something all the other people are not doing. If I could get von Stroheim! Isn't he fine?'

Miss Garbo said that she liked the screen translation of Arlen's *Green Hat*, which was called *The Woman of Affairs*, better than any other of her films. Her first picture, one of the only two she made in her native Sweden, was the film version of *The Legend of Gosta Berling*, which was exhibited here in 1928. She was then seventeen years old and, according to her own description, 'twenty pounds bigger, or was it ten pounds?'

Crowds greeted her when she returned to Sweden this last time. She did not make much of the reception, but admitted that throngs had been at Guttenborg when she landed. She did not know, now that she was back in America, whether she was homesick or not. In Stockholm she said that she loved to wander along the streets looking in the smaller shop windows and then going off to dinner without returning to change her clothes. Her blue-gray eyes lighted up as she referred to this.

When she was asked whether many people recognize her in this city, she replied, as she has a habit of doing to other questions:

'I don't know.'

What did she do on her first evening in New York?

She had dinner alone.

'All alone?'

'Yes, quite alone, and I loved to look at the – what you call – shyscrapers – No, what it is?'

'Yes, skyscrapers. Let's not talk about me, let's talk about New York and the skyscrapers. They look so beautiful from this window. It is true I was invited to go to dine somewhere in the country at a house where Captain Lundborg was a guest. He, you know, is the man who flew over to Nobile and brought him back. But, as I said, I dined alone and looked always at the gorgeous, unreal skyscrapers – did I have it right, then?'

This would-be hermit admits that she knows very few people in Hollywood. She occasionally plays a little tennis and owns only one car, but drives in others belonging to friends.

The talk of necessity switched back to Sweden, when Miss Garbo was asked whether she had ever appeared on the stage. She said she had not but that a friend of hers asked her to act in *Resurrection* while she was in Stockholm. She, in evidently a rash moment, consented.

She went on so far as to memorize her lines and study the part. She was confident of herself, but the night before the dress rehearsal she began to be very nervous and she could not sleep a wink. She asked her friend to come and see her and she told him that she could not appear after all. She had not slept. No amount of pleading could change her mind. She simply could not appear before the footlights.

One would be almost inclined to believe that no matter where Miss Garbo goes she has a pretty dull time. But that seemed impossible. She takes about six weeks to make one of her pictures and so far has appeared in eight Hollywood productions.

She studies her stories before she appears before the camera.

'And when are you returning to Hollywood?'

'I don't know. Tomorrow, perhaps.'

Then the conversation turned to talking films, and Miss Garbo said:

'If they want me to talk I'll talk. I'd love to act in a talking picture when they are better, but the ones I have seen are awful. It's no fun to look at a shadow and somewhere out of the theatre a voice is coming.'

She was asked whether she knew Charlie Chaplin and answered that she knew him 'very little'.

There is no longer any Swedish coterie in Hollywood, for Victor Seastrom is no longer there. Lars Hanson is back in his native land, to which lesser lights have also flown.

Miss Garbo has a profound admiration for Pola Negri. She said that she loved the way in which Miss Negri kept to the Old-World atmosphere.

'There's hardly no one so good as Pola Negri,' said Miss Garbo., 'She is so amusing. It is always amusing to see her.'

Amusing as used by Miss Garbo means a combination of interesting and in-spiring.

She repeated 'Delighted to have met you,' and then turned her head in the direction of her beloved skyscrapers.

•

SIGMUND FREUD

Interviewed by George Sylvester Viereck
Glimpses of the Great, 1930

Sigmund Freud (1856–1939), the Austrian Jew who founded psychoanalysis, trained as a physician in Vienna. He also studied in Paris under Jean-Marie Charcot, who used hypnosis as a treatment for hysteria. Freud later developed his own therapeutic technique – conversational 'free association' – as well as the psychoanalytic theory of defence mechanism and repression, which argued that neurosis was the result of infantile sexuality (what he called 'seduction theory'). In 1990 he published *The Interpretation of Dreams* and in 1902 he was appointed extraordinary professor of neuropathology at the University of Vienna, thereafter concentrating on the study of psychological and psychopathological behaviour, and the role of sexuality in the unconscious. In 1938, when the Nazis annexed Austria (having already banned psychoanalysis in Germany), he emigrated to England with his daughter Anna, who later gained distinction as a child psychologist. He died from cancer of the jaw.

'Seventy years have taught me to accept life with cheerful humility.'

The speaker was Professor Sigmund Freud, the great Austrian explorer of the nether world of the soul. Like the tragic Greek hero, Oedipus, whose name is so intimately connected with the principal tenets of psychoanalysis, Freud boldly confronted the Sphinx.

Like Oedipus, he solved her riddle. At least no mortal has come nearer to explaining the secret of human conduct than Freud.

Freud is to psychology what Galileo was to astronomy. He is the Columbus of the subconscious. He opens new vistas, he sounds new depths. He changed the relationship of everything in life to every other thing, by deciphering the hidden meaning of the records inscribed on the tablets of the unconscious.

The scene where our conversation took place was Freud's summer home on the Semmering, a mountain in the Austrian Alps, where fashionable Vienna loves to forgather.

I had last seen the father of psychoanalysis in his unpretentious home in the Austrian capital. The few years intervening between my last visit and the present had multiplied the wrinkles of his forehead. They had intensified his scholastic pallor. His face was drawn, as in pain. His mind was alert, his spirit unbroken, his courtesy impeccable as of old, but a slight impediment in his speech alarmed me.

It seems that a malignant affection of the upper jaw had necessitated an operation. Since that time, Freud wears a mechanical contrivance to facilitate speech. In itself this is no worse than the wearing of glasses. The presence of the metal device embarrasses Freud more than his visitors. It is hardly noticeable after one speaks to him a while. On his good days, it cannot be detected at all. But to Freud himself it is cause of constant annoyance.

'I detest my mechanical jaw, because the struggle with the mechanism consumes so much precious strength. Yet I prefer a mechanical jaw to no jaw at all. I still prefer existence to extinction.

'Perhaps the gods are kind to us,' the father of psychoanalysis went on to say, 'by making life more disagreeable as we grow older. In the end, death seems less intolerable than the manifold burdens we carry.'

Freud refuses to admit that destiny bears him any special malice.

'Why,' he quietly said, 'should I expect any special favour? Age, with its manifest discomforts, comes to all. It strikes one man here, and one there. Its blow always lands in a vital spot. The final victory always belongs to the Conqueror Worm.

> Out – out are the lights – out all!
>   And over each quivering form
> The curtain, a funeral pall,
>   Comes down, with the rush of a storm,
> And the angels, all pallid and wan,
>   Uprising, unveiling, affirm
> That the play is the tragedy 'Man,'
>   And its hero the Conqueror Worm.

'I do not rebel against the universal order. After all,' the master prober of the human brain continued, 'I have lived over seventy years. I had enough to eat. I enjoyed many things – the comradeship of my wife, my children, the sunsets. I watched the plants grow in the springtime. Now and then the grasp of a friendly hand was mine. Once or twice I met a human being who almost understood me. What more can I ask?'

'You have had,' I said, 'fame. Your work affects the literature of every land. Man looks at life and himself with different eyes because of you. And recently on your seventieth birthday the world united to honour you – with the exception of your own university!'

'If the University of Vienna had recognized me, they would have only embarrassed me. There is no reason why they should embrace either me or my doctrine because I am seventy. I attach no unreasonable importance to decimals.

'Fame comes to us only after we are dead, and, frankly, what comes afterwards does not concern me. I have no aspiration to posthumous glory. My modesty is no virtue.'

'Does it not mean something to you that your name will live?'

'Nothing whatsoever, even if it should live, which is by no means certain. I am far more interested in the fate of my children. I hope that their life will not be so hard. I cannot make their life much easier. The war practically wiped out my modest fortune, the savings of a lifetime. However, fortunately, age is not too a heavy a burden. I can carry on! My work still gives me pleasure.'

We were walking up and down a little pathway in the steep garden of the house. Freud tenderly caressed a blossoming bush with his sensitive hands.

'I am far more interested in this blossom,' he said, 'than in anything that may happen to me after I am dead.'

'Then you are, after all, a profound pessimist?'

'I am not. I permit no philosophic reflection to spoil my enjoyment of the simple things of life.'

'Do you believe in the persistence of personality after death in any form whatsoever?'

'I give no thought to the matter. Everything that lives perishes. Why should I survive?'

'Would you like to come back in some form, to be reintegrated from the dust? Have you, in other words, no wish for immortality?'

'Frankly, no. If one recognizes the selfish motives which underlie all human conduct, one has not the slightest desire to return. Life, moving in a circle, would still be the same.

'Moreover, even if the eternal recurrence of things, to use Nietzsche's phrase, were to reinvest us with our fleshly habiliments, of what avail would this be without memory? There would be no link between past and future.

'So far as I am concerned, I am perfectly content to know that the eternal nuisance of living will be finally done with. Our life is necessarily a series of compromises, a never-ending struggle between the ego and his environment. The wish to prolong life unduly, strikes me as absurd.'

'Do you disapprove of the attempts of your colleague Steinach to lengthen the cycle of human existence?'

'Steinach makes no attempt to lengthen life. He merely combats old age. By tapping the reservoir of strength within our own bodies, he helps the tissue to resist disease. The Steinach operation sometimes arrests untoward biological accidents, like cancer, in their early stages. It makes life more liveable. It does not make it worth living.

'There is no reason why we should wish to live longer. But there is every reason why we should wish to live with the smallest amount of discomfort possible.

'I am tolerably happy, because I am grateful for the absence of pain, and for life's little pleasures, for my children and for my flowers!'

'Bernard Shaw claims that our years are too few. He thinks that man can lengthen the span of human life, if he so desires, by bringing his will power to play upon the forces of evolution. Mankind, he thinks, can recover the longevity of the patriarchs.'

'It is possible,' Freud replied, 'that death itself may not be a biological necessity. Perhaps we die because we want to die.

'Even as hate and love for the same person dwell in our bosom at the same time, so all life combines with the desire to maintain itself, an ambivalent desire for its own annihilation.

'Just as a stretched rubber band has the tendency to assume its original shape, so all living matter, consciously or unconsciously, craves to regain the complete and absolute inertia of inorganic existence. The death-wish and life-wish dwell side by side, within us.

'Death is the mate of Love. Together they rule the world. This is the message of my book, *Beyond the Pleasure Principle*.

'In the beginning, psychoanalysis assumed that Love was all important. Today we know that Death is equally important.

'Biologically, every living being, no matter how intensely life burns within him, longs for Nirvana, longs for the cessation of "the fever called living", longs for Abraham's bosom. The desire may be disguised by various circumlocutions. Nevertheless, the ultimate object of life is its own extinction!'

'This,' I exclaimed, 'is the philosophy of self-destruction. It justifies self-slaughter. It should lead logically to the world suicide envisaged by Eduard von Hartmann.'

'Mankind does not choose suicide, because the law of its being abhors the direct route to its goal. Life must complete its cycle of existence. In every normal being, the life-wish is strong enough to counterbalance the death-wish, albeit in the end the death-wish proves stronger.

'We may entertain the fanciful suggestion that death comes to us by our own volition. It is possible that we could vanquish Death, except for his ally in our bosom.

'In that sense,' Freud added with a smile, 'we may be justified in saying that all death is suicide in disguise.'

It grew chilly in the garden.

We continued our conversation in the study.

I saw a pile of manuscripts on the desk in Freud's own neat handwriting.

'What are you working on?' I asked.

'I am writing a defence of lay-analysis, psychoanalysis as practised by laymen. The doctors want to make analysis except by licensed physicians illegal. History, the old plagiarizer, repeats herself after every discovery. The doctors fight every new truth in the beginning. Afterwards they try to monopolize it.'

'Have you had much support from the laity?'

'Some of my best pupils are laymen.'

'Do you practise much yourself ?'

'Certainly. At this very moment, I am working on a difficult case, disentangling the psychic conflicts of an interesting new patient.

'My daughter, too, is a psychoanalyst, as you see . . .'

At this juncture, Miss Anna Freud appeared followed by her patient, a lad of eleven, unmistakably Anglo-Saxon in feature. The child seemed perfectly happy, completely oblivious of a conflict or tangle in his personality.

'Do you ever,' I asked Professor Freud, 'analyse yourself ?'

'Certainly. The psychoanalyst must constantly analyse himself. By analysing ourselves, we are better able to analyse others.

'The psychoanalyst is like the scapegoat of the Hebrews. Others load their sins upon him. He must exercise his art to the utmost to extricate himself from the burden cast upon him.'

'It always seems to me,' I remarked, 'that psychoanalysis necessarily induces in all those who practise it the spirit of Christian charity. There is nothing in human life that psychoanalysis cannot make us understand. "*Tout comprendre c'est tout pardonner*" – "To understand all, is to forgive all."'

'On the contrary,' thundered Freud, his features assuming the fierce severity of a Hebrew prophet. 'To understand all, is not to forgive all. Psychoanalysis teaches us not only what we may endure, it also teaches us what we must avoid. It tells us what must be exterminated. Tolerance of evil is by no means a corollary of knowledge.'

I suddenly understood why Freud had quarrelled so bitterly with those of his followers who had deserted him, why he cannot forgive their departure from the straight path of orthodox psychoanalysis. His sense of righteousness is the heritage of his ancestors. It is a heritage of which he is proud, as he is proud of his race.

'My language,' he explained to me, 'is German. My culture, my attainments are German. I considered myself a German intellectually, until I noticed the growth of anti-Semitic prejudice in Germany and in German Austria. Since that time I consider myself no longer a German. I prefer to call myself a Jew.'

I was somewhat disappointed by this remark.

It seemed to me that Freud's spirit should dwell on heights, beyond any prejudice of race, that he should be untouched by any personal rancour. Yet his very indignation, his honest wrath, made him more endearingly human.

Achilles would be intolerable, if it were not for his heel!

'I am glad,' I remarked, 'Herr Professor, that you, too, have your complexes, that you, too, betray your mortality.'

'Our complexes,' Freud replied, 'are the source of our weakness; they are also often the source of our strength.'

'I wonder,' I remarked, 'what my complexes are!'

'A serious analysis,' Freud replied, 'takes at least a year. It may even take two or three years. You are devoting many years of your life to lion-hunting. You have sought, year after year, the outstanding figures of your generation, invariably men older than yourself. There was Roosevelt, the Kaiser, Hindenburg, Briand, Foch, Joffre, George Brandes, Gerhart Hauptmann, and George Bernard Shaw . . .'

'It is part of my work.'

'But it is also your preference. The great man is a symbol. Your search is the search of your heart. You are seeking the great man to take the place of the father. It is part of your father complex.'

I vehemently denied Freud's assertion. Nevertheless, on reflection, it seems to me that there may be a truth, unsuspected by myself, in his casual suggestion. It may be the same impulse that took me to him.

'In your *Wandering Jew*,' he added, 'you extend this search into the past. You are always the Seeker of Men.'

'I wish,' I remarked after a while, 'I could stay here long enough to glimpse my own heart through your eyes. Perhaps, like the Medusa, I would die from fright if I saw my own image! However, I fear I am too well versed in psychoanalysis. I would constantly anticipate, or try to anticipate, your intentions.'

'Intelligence in a patient,' Freud replied, 'is no handicap. On the contrary, it sometimes facilitates one's task.'

In that respect the master of psychoanalysis differs from many of his adherents, who resent any self-assertion of the patient under their probe.

Most psychoanalysts employ Freud's method of 'free association'. They encourage the patient to say everything that comes into his mind, no matter how stupid, how obscene, how inopportune, or irrelevant it may seem. Following clues seemingly unimportant, they can trace the psychic dragons that haunt him to their lair. They dislike the desire of the patient for active cooperation; for they fear that once the direction of their inquiry becomes clear to him, his wishes and resistances unconsciously striving to preserve their secrets, may throw the psychic huntsman off the trail. Freud, too, recognizes this danger.

'I sometimes wonder,' I questioned, 'if we should not be happier if we knew less of the processes that shape our thoughts and emotions? Psychoanalysis robs life of its last enchantments, when it traces every feeling to its original cluster of complexes. We are not made more joyful by discovering that we all harbour in our hearts the savage, the criminal and the beast.'

'What is your objection to the beasts?' Freud replied. 'I prefer the society of animals infinitely to human society.'

'Why?'

'Because they are so much simpler. They do not suffer from a divided personality, from the disintegration of the ego, that arises from man's attempt to adapt himself to standards of civilization too high for his intellectual and psychic mechanism.

'The savage, like the beast, is cruel, but he lacks the meanness of the civilized man. Meanness is man's revenge upon society for the restraints it imposes. This vengefulness animates the professional reformer and the busybody. The savage may chop your head, he may eat you, he may torture you, but he will spare you the continuous little pinpricks which make life in a civilized community at times almost intolerable.

'Man's most disagreeable habits and idiosyncrasies, his deceit, his cowardice, his lack of reverence, are engendered by his incomplete adjustment to a complicated civilization. It is the result of the conflict between our instincts and our culture.

'How much more pleasant are the simple, straightforward, intense emotions of a dog, wagging his tail or barking his displeasure! The emotions of the dog,' Freud thoughtfully added, 'remind one of the heroes of antiquity. Perhaps that is the reason why we unconsciously bestow upon our canines the names of ancient heroes such as Achilles and Hector.'

'My own dog,' I interjected, 'is called "Ajax".'

Freud smiled.

'I am glad,' I added, 'that he cannot read. It would certainly make him a less desirable member of the household if he could yelp his opinion on psychic traumas and Oedipus complexes!

'Even you, Professor, find existence too complex. Yet, it seems to me that you yourself are partly responsible for the complexities of modern civilization. Before you invented psychoanalysis we did not know that our personality is dominated by a belligerent host of highly objectionable complexes. Psychoanalysis has made life a complicated puzzle.'

'By no means,' Freud replied. 'Psychoanalysis simplifies life. We achieve a new synthesis after analysis. Psychoanalysis reassorts the maze of stray impulses, and tries to wind them around the spool to which they belong. Or, to change the metaphor, it supplies the thread that leads a man out of the labyrinth of his own unconscious.'

'On the surface, it seems, nevertheless, as if human life was never more complex. And every day some new idea, put forward by you or by your disciples, makes the problem of human conduct more puzzling and more contradictory.'

'Psychoanalysis, at least, never shuts the door on a new truth.'

'Some of your pupils, more orthodox than you, cling to every pronouncement that has ever emanated from you.'

'Life changes. Psychoanalysis also changes,' Freud observed. 'We are only at the beginning of a new science.'

'It seems to me that the scientific structure you have erected is very elaborate. Its fixtures – the theory of "replacement", of "infantile sexuality", and of "dream symbols", etc. – seem to be fairly permanent.'

'Nevertheless, I repeat, we are only at the beginning. I am only a beginner. I was successful in digging up buried monuments from the substrata of the mind.

But where I have discovered a few temples, others may discover a continent.'

'You still place most emphasis on sex?'

'I reply with the words of the great poet, Walt Whitman: "Yet all were lacking, if sex were lacking." However, I have already explained to you that I place to-day almost equal emphasis upon that which lies "beyond" pleasure – death, the negation of life. This desire explains why some men love pain – as a step to annihilation! It explains why all men seek rest, why poets thank –

> Whatever gods there be,
> That no life lives for ever,
> That dead men rise up never,
> And even the weariest river
> Winds somewhere safe to sea.'

'Shaw, like you, does not wish to live for ever, but,' I remarked, 'unlike you, he regards sex as uninteresting.'

'Shaw,' Freud replied smiling, 'does not understand sex. He has not the remotest conception of love. There is no real love affair in any of his plays. He makes a jest of Caesar's love affair – perhaps the greatest passion in history. Deliberately, not to say maliciously, he divests Cleopatra of all grandeur, and degrades her into an insignificant flapper.

'The reason for Shaw's strange attitude toward love, and for his denial of the primal mover of all human affairs, which robs his plays of universal appeal in spite of his enormous intellectual equipment, is inherent in his psychology. In one of his prefaces, Shaw himself emphasizes the ascetic strain in his temperament.

'I may have made many mistakes, but I am quite sure that I made no mistake when I emphasized the predominance of the sex instinct. Because the sex instinct is so strong, it clashes most frequently with the conventions and safeguards of civilization. Mankind, in self-defence, seeks to deny its supreme importance.

'If you scratch the Russian, the proverb says, the Tartar appears underneath. Analyse any human emotion, no matter how far it may be removed from the sphere of sex, and you are sure to discover somewhere the primal impulse, to which life itself owes its perpetuation.'

'You certainly have succeeded in impressing this point of view upon all modern writers. Psychoanalysis has given new intensities to literature.'

'It also has received much from literature and philosophy. Nietzsche was one of the first psychoanalysts. It is amazing to what extent his intuition foreshadows our discoveries. No one has recognized more profoundly the dual motives of human conduct, and the insistence of the pleasure principle upon unending sway. His Zarathustra says:

Woe
Crieth: Go!
But Pleasure craves eternity,
Craves quenchless, deep eternity.

'Psychoanalysis may be less widely discussed in Austria and Germany than in the United States, but its influence in literature is nevertheless immense.

'Thomas Mann and Hugo von Hofmansthal owe, much to us. Schnitzler parallels, to a large extent, my own development. He expresses poetically much that I attempt to convey scientifically. But then, Dr Schnitzler is not only a poet, but also a scientist.'

'You,' I replied, 'are not only a scientist, but also a poet. American literature,' I went on to say, 'is steeped in psychoanalysis. Rupert Hughes, Harvey O'Higgins, and others make themselves your interpreters. It is hardly possible to open a new novel without finding some reference to psychoanalysis. Among dramatists Eugene O'Neill and Sydney Howard are profoundly indebted to you. *The Silver Cord*, for instance, is merely a dramatization of the Oedipus complex.'

'I know,' Freud replied. 'I appreciate the compliment, but I am afraid of my own popularity in the United States. American interest in psychoanalysis does not go very deep. Extensive popularization leads to superficial acceptance without serious research. People merely repeat the phrases they learn in the theatre, or in the press. They imagine they understand psychoanalysis, because they can parrot its patter! I prefer the more intense study of psychoanalysis in European centres.

'America was the first country to recognize me officially. Clark University conferred an honorary degree upon me when I was still ostracized in Europe. Nevertheless, America has made few original contributions to the study of psychoanalysis.

'Americans are clever generalizers, they are rarely creative thinkers. Moreover, the medical trust in the United States, as well as in Austria, attempts to pre-empt the field. To leave psychoanalysis solely in the hands of doctors would be fatal to its development. A medical education is as often a handicap as an advantage to the psychoanalyst. It is a handicap if certain accepted scientific conventions become too deeply encrusted in the mind of the student.'

Freud must tell the truth at all cost! He cannot force himself to flatter America, where he has most admirers. He cannot even at three score and ten bring himself to make a peace offering to the medical profession, which accepts him only grudgingly even now.

In spite of his uncompromising integrity, Freud is the soul of urbanity. He listens patiently to every suggestion, never attempting to overawe his interviewer. Rare is the guest who leaves his presence without some gift, some token of hospitality!

Darkness had fallen.

It was time for me to take the train back to the city that once housed the imperial splendour of the Hapsburgs.

Freud, accompanied by his wife and his daughter, climbed the steps leading from his mountain retreat to the street, to see me off. He looked grey and sad to me as he waved his farewell.

'Don't make me appear a pessimist,' he remarked, after the final handshake. 'I do not despise the world. To express contempt for the world is only another method of wooing it, to gain an audience and applause!

'No, I am not a pessimist, not while I have my children, my wife, and my flowers!

'Flowers,' he added smilingly, 'fortunately have neither character nor complexities. I love my flowers. And I am not unhappy – at least not more unhappy than others.'

The whistle of my train shrieked through the night. Swiftly the car bore me away to the station. Slowly the slightly bent figure and the grey head of Sigmund Freud disappeared in the distance.

Like Oedipus, Freud has looked too deep into the eyes of the Sphinx. The monster propounds her riddle to every wayfarer. The wanderer who does not know the answer she cruelly seizes and dashes against the rocks. Yet she may be kinder to those whom she destroys than to those who guess her secret.

●

GEORGE BERNARD SHAW

Interviewed by Hayden Church

Liberty, 7 February 1931

George Bernard Shaw (1856–1950), the Irish playwright, critic and polemicist, was born in Dublin of Irish Protestant parents. His mother, a singing-teacher, proved a powerful influence and he abandoned his job as a clerk in a firm of land-agents to follow his mother and sister to London. There, he started writing novels, before turning to music and dramatic criticism and the writing of plays in the 1890s. Between 1892 and the mid 1930s he wrote over twenty plays, both tragedies and comedies yet all concerned with social, moral or philosophical issues. Renowned for his wit, Shaw gave many interviews during his lifetime and enjoyed writing letters to the press as well as pamphlets on controversial issues. A socialist, he was one of the key figures in the Fabian Society and edited the influential volume *Fabian Essays* (1889).

Hayden Church served on the London staff of *The New York Times* during the 1930s and 1940s. He conducted many interviews with Shaw over the years.

*

'If you were Dictator of England,' I said to George Bernard Shaw, 'what would you do?'

'Probably go mad, like Nero,' he replied. 'Why ask silly questions?'

Mr Shaw rapped out this characteristic comeback in a recent interview, partly obtained during a strenuous walk with him on the Malvern Hills, that was perhaps as remarkable a one as even the world's greatest and wittiest dramatist ever has given.

In the course of it, replying to a question originally posed by Edison, he revealed how he would prefer to die, and denied that he, probably the wealthiest as well as the most renowned of living writers, has made a success of life.

Roving over a wide variety of topics, he expressed typically Shavian views on the recent triumphs of women over men, and while discussing the future of talking pictures gave his opinion, by inference, on the much debated question: Should Charlie Chaplin make talkies?

But it was with big subjects that Shaw was mainly concerned, at the outset, anyway. And one of my opening questions, while discussing world depression, was fortunate in drawing from him as forceful, as incisive, and incidentally as controversial a pronouncement as he has made in recent years.

'How do you view the economic future of England?' he was asked. 'Will things get steadily worse, or will the Old Country "muddle through", as usual?'

'It is rather late in the day,' he replied, 'to talk about England, or any other twopenny-halfpenny nationality, muddling through. The question today is, will Civilization muddle through? If the Big Ship goes down England will go down with it. And don't forget that these Big Ships always have gone down, so far. Mesopotamia was once more highly civilized than either old or new England; but it went under so completely that I was over sixty before I ever heard of Sumer. I see by your expression that you have not heard of it yet. And the Sumerian civilization was only one of half a dozen. We are adding to the list of extinct civilizations almost as fast as the astronomers are adding to the list of dark stars.

'Every serious student of the subject knows that the stability of a civilization depends finally on the wisdom with which it distributes its wealth and allots its burdens of labour, and on the veracity of the instruction it provides for its children.

'We do not distribute our wealth at all: we throw it into the streets to be scrambled for by the strongest and greediest who will stoop to such scrambling, after handing the lion's share to the professional robbers politely called owners. We cram our children with lies, and punish anyone who tries to enlighten them. Our remedies for the consequences of our folly are tariffs, inflation, wars, vivisections and inoculations – vengeances, violences, black magic. As to reform, we have not sense enough or energy enough to reform our spelling. Talk about something else!'

I obeyed by putting to him two questions that, with others, were propounded by Thomas A. Edison to candidates for the scholarship founded by the famous American inventor. When setting these questions, Edison probably little thought that any of them would draw replies from George Bernard Shaw, but I asked Mr Shaw to answer the most important ones, pointing out that his answers would be of immense interest. And so unquestionably they prove, particularly that to the first question.

This query of Edison's was, 'When you look back on your life from your death bed, by what facts will you determine whether you succeeded or failed?' In propounding it I remarked that any fool knows that Shaw has succeeded as few men do, but in his reply, as will be seen, he brushed this comment aside.

'I am not on my death bed,' he said, 'except in so far as we are all on our death beds. Personally I should prefer to die in a reasonably dry ditch under the stars. I have not succeeded: people have agreed to rank me as successful: that is all. Have I not written somewhere that life levels all men: death reveals the eminent. Well, I am not quite dead yet, only seven-eighths dead.'

The second of Edison's questions was: 'If you could prescribe and enforce a system of education for the world's whole population, on what essentials would you place the greatest emphasis?'

Mr Shaw dictated his reply to this, as follows:

'Reading (including music), writing, arithmetic, and manners, primarily and compulsorily; elementary law, economics, and physics (including astrophysics), as qualifications for employments other than the performance of manual operations under tutelage; and for the rest, what the learner is capable of.'

Mr Shaw is fully alive to the possibilities of talking pictures. He made a new talkie of himself not so long ago and also has agreed, for the first time, to two of his plays being turned into talkies.

'Is there any particular phase of the talkies that is interesting you at present?' I asked him. 'What do you consider is the best film yet made?'

'The best films I have seen are Russian ones,' he replied. 'We in England are doing our best to prevent them from being shown because they are too moral for us. I am not interested in any particular phase of the talkies: I am interested in the enormous fact that a method of projecting drama and acting has been discovered which reduces our cheap, shabby half-visible, half-audible old stage methods to absurdity. And our theater people are still blinking at it and saying it will not last because the public likes the real thing.

'As if Charlie Chaplin were not ten times more real to us than any stage actor in the world! If this is true of Charlie Silent what will Charlie Talking be? It is pitiable to hear our old theater managers prophesying nonsense on their way to oblivion through the bankruptcy court.'

As these replies of his make evident, Mr Shaw is as dynamic as ever, in spite of his seventy-four years. If he is 'seven-eighths' dead, as he asserts, he certainly contrives to make the fact imperceptible. His hair and his beard (which in the talkie he made recently he jestingly expressed his intention of dyeing) and his famous Mephistophelean eyebrows have, it is true, become snowy white, but he is as straight as a pine tree and brimful of 'pep'. A famous European scientist recently described him as 'the only old man living with a young man's brain'. More often than not, when in London, he walks across from his flat in Whitehall Court, on the Thames Embankment, to the Royal Automobile Club in Pall Mall and has a swim before breakfast!

My interview with him took place at Malvern, in Worcestershire, where, following the recent Festival of his plays there, he indulged in a holiday. Up to this point he talked while striding about his workroom in the suite that he and Mrs Shaw were occupying in a small but well run hotel. But then, declaring that he needed some physical exercise, he took me for what he called a 'walk' up the Worcestershire Beacon, the loftiest of the neighboring near-mountains that are known misleadingly as the Malvern Hills.

Several times, to the astonishment of Malvernites – most of whom prefer to ascend it on the backs of reluctant donkeys – GBS legged it right up to the summit of the Beacon, 1,440 feet above sea level. On this particular occasion, mercifully, he couldn't spare the time to repeat this performance, but contented himself with a lesser, but to his companion sufficiently strenuous, climb around the north side of the great 'hill' – scrambling up rocky declivities and striding around tricky bends in the winding and often nonexistent pathway, with fearsome depths yawning beneath, as jauntily as if he were still in the Malvern streets. By the end of an hour we were several hundred feet up, and had a glorious view of the other Malvern Hills, of the picturesque town, with its ancient Priory, and of the river Avon, winding its way towards Stratford.

During this man-size hike the talk ran from Emil Jannings' first talkie, which Shaw seemingly did not care for overmuch, to the play *Journey's End* (on which it appears the verdict of GBS was asked while it was going the rounds of theatrical managers), and on to prize fighting, in which, as everyone knows, the author of *Cashel Byron's Profession* maintains a lively and expert interest.

I asked him why he considered it is that England does not seem able to produce a heavyweight champion.

'There are dozens of men in every parish in England,' he replied, 'who could walk over all the champions in the ring as easily as Tunney walked over the apparently unconquerable Carpentier and his conqueror, Dempsey, if they gave their minds to it as he did. They prefer other careers, that is all.'

Inevitably the conversation turned to Shaw's plays and I mentioned that he had been quoted as saying, when asked if he had any personal favorite among them, that he rather liked *Heartbreak House*, a picture, in the words of the preface thereto, 'of leisured, cultured Europe' before and during the war.

'I may have said something like that,' GBS admitted. 'But plays like *Heartbreak House* are expensive.'

I looked at him inquiringly, imagining he meant that they call for expensive casts.

'Yes,' he added, 'it took half a century of international dry rot and a war on top of it to bring that one to birth.'

'There are always any number of subjects,' he remarked a moment later, 'crying for treatment on the stage, if only playwrights could see the possibilities in them. Housing conditions in the London slums had been a national scandal for a century before I dramatized them in *Widowers' Houses*.'

We talked of Macbeth apropos of Sybil Thorndike's production of that play, which Mr Shaw largely directed, and he remarked that he has always wished to see a performance of it given entirely in the Scotch dialect.

'I believe it would be tremendously impressive,' he declared.

Coming back to the subject of the pictures, I asked Shaw if seeing himself as others see him by means of his recent talkie and the one he made some months previous had resulted in his making any new discoveries about himself.

'Only that I am getting very old,' he replied and that my mouth is growing very crooked. But I made a small discovery about myself when first I saw myself on the screen in a picture I helped to make nearly twenty years ago. I had often noticed that my father bore a strong resemblance to Sir Horace Plunkett, the Irish agriculturist, and when I saw the first movie of myself I realized for the first time that I also looked like Plunkett.

'That film was an extraordinary affair that Barrie got up in pre-war days,' Shaw went on. 'It was intended to raise funds for some charity, I believe, and any number of celebrities of one kind and another took part in it. It began, I remember, with a dinner party at the Savoy, one of the diners being the then Mr Asquith.

'Afterwards Granville Barker and I and two or three other writers were taken out to Elstree and dressed up as cowboys. As such we did all sorts of insane things, such as chasing horses and riding motorcycles. At one time I had five people behind me on a motorcycle and I rode over several precipices. True, the precipices were only about seven feet high, but I don't greatly enjoy falling even seven feet at my age.

'The public, however, was denied the pleasure of witnessing these antics, as Barrie eventually decided to scrap the film. I believe he afterwards utilized part of it in a piece he wrote for Gaby Deslys.'

I wish I could reproduce the delicious Irish accent with which Shaw said all this. Listening to it is one of the joys of talking to him.

No interview with GBS, most ardent of feminists, would be complete without some commentary on women. So, as a final query, I asked:

'How comes it, do you consider, that women recently have been beating men in all directions? Amy Johnson, for instance, and the other Englishwomen who won the King's Cup air race and the King's Prize at the Bisley rifle championship meet.'

'What is there surprising about them?' demanded Shaw. 'Miss Johnson did not fly to Australia: a machine did; and she hung on to it and steered it. The

King's Prize was won by a rifle: is there any mortal reason why a woman's eyes should not align the sights of a rifle, and a woman's wits allow for the wind, and a woman's finger pull the trigger as well as a man's? If you look in the day's paper you will learn that several women had babies yesterday without any help from machines.

'Prove to me that a man has achieved that amazing and arduous feat, and I will sit up and discuss the significance of his triumph very seriously.'

•

WYNDHAM LEWIS
Interviewed by Louise Morgan
Everyman, 19 March 1931

(Percy) Wyndham Lewis (1882–1957), the English novelist, painter and critic, was born in Nova Scotia, Canada. Educated at Rugby and the Slade School of Art, he was fascinated by modernism, though not with the left-wing politics that usually accompanied it. With fellow maverick Ezra Pound, he founded the Vorticist movement and a magazine called *Blast*. During the First World War he fought as a soldier and then served as a war artist. He wrote three influential novels – *Tarr* (1918), *The Childermass* (1928), and *The Apes of God* (1930). He painted some highly regarded portraits, but otherwise he was an experimental painter. He emigrated to Canada for the duration of the Second World War, and went blind in 1951.

Louise Morgan interviewed several writers for *Everyman*, including W. B. Yeats, Sinclair Lewis, Sylvia Townsend Warner, Edgar Wallace, and Somerset Maugham. These were collected with other interviews in book form as *Writers at Work* (1931). Morgan later became a special correspondent for the *News Chronicle*.

Wyndham Lewis is, as he says himself, a Renaissance man. He has the Renaissance faculty, one that is all but lost today, for taking active part in things and at the same time observing them from the outside. He has also the Renaissance many-sidedness. He is a painter, with a profound understanding of the history and technique of painting; he is a critic in the broadest sense of the term, a novelist, a man of science, and a philosopher. He is also a brilliant pamphleteer. In this day of the specialist he has refused to be bound by the specialist code. In a world of civilization infinitely complicated and vast he has insisted on seeing the whole of things for himself.

Pretence is the one thing he cannot bear. He is ruthless in exposing the hundreds of pseudo-artists that are the peculiar plague of our generation. The genuine artist has never had an easy time, but his difficulties are more monstrous now than they have ever been, for art nowadays is not only commercialized but (worst fate of all) fashionable. Literary parties, lion-petting, log-rolling, and the back-to-nature, feministic movement of a devitalized post-War world are choking the life out of art. We have lost the things that were the common possession of artists in the Renaissance – the joyous experimenting and fighting spirit, the masculine capacity for work, the largeness of interest that finds no time for petty or namby-pamby amusements. But all these things Wyndham Lewis has. He stands alone in our timid, prettifying, back-scratching midst, and by his measure we suddenly see ourselves for what we are. No wonder some of us do not like him.

With all this vaguely in mind, I asked him if he ever ceases 'work'. It is obvious that any kind of life apart from active observation, thought, and shaping in paint and words has no interest for him.

'I work whenever convenient,' he said. 'That is, I work until I am interrupted. I'm often interrupted. I suppose apart from that you might say I worked the whole time. This morning I spent working on a portrait-drawing; this afternoon I was working upon a new critical essay until you came.'

'Is this where you do it all?'

'No. This is my office. Occasionally I work here, but not very often. I have a room in another house crammed full of books. I call that my library; there I do practically all my writing. Then I have a studio, an enormous shack of a place, in still another house, where I do my big paintings. That's not all! I have another room in a fourth house where I sleep. There's nothing but my bed in it. I live in a series of rooms in different houses.'

His 'office', in which we sat, in the neighbourhood of north Hyde Park, is the kind of room that would make a settled housekeeper shudder, and draw cries of ecstasy from the uninitiate in search of Bohemia. At first glance it appears a chaos. From the door one walks down a narrow lane made among small chests and piles of books and papers to the fireplace. Canvases large and small are tilted against the wall behind the door. There is an easel, more piles of books on the floor and shelves, and tables with pots of paint and brushes on them. Several old Eastern rugs cover the floor; the curtains are green baize with an orange band, the side of one tacked down its whole length with push-pins – evidently to avoid a draught; two Chinese rubbings hang on the walls. The chairs we sat in were very comfortable; mine was covered in sacking. By the fireplace next Mr Lewis's chair was a low writing table, with a still lower shelf beneath the top one, neatly equipped with blotting pad and writing paper. Plump in the middle of the room stood, flanked by the books and tables and cases, two breast-high, narrow, parchment-coloured barrels, the telephone directory sprawled open on top of one of them. I had not realized that barrels can look elegant. These two did. I could not resist enquiring about them.

'They're paint barrels,' he said. 'I believe all furniture should be very high or very low: though it is said that furniture gets *lower and lower* as the ethical standards of a civilization decline. I can't help that. Those old paint barrels have their uses. I put down my palette on them, or the book I'm reading. They're just the right height for the telephone.'

So the barrels, having arrived with paint in them, stayed because they were useful. The books which seemed dropped so casually about could be reached instantly. Mr Lewis put his hand on two or three which we referred to without a moment's hesitation. That room exists not for itself, not for show, but as the most convenient workshop possible for its owner.

'Your painting must help your writing,' I said.

'It must of course do that. The habit of thinking of things in plastic and pictorial terms must have its influence upon the writer's art, when you practise both as I do. First of all, I *see*! The first – and last – thing that I do is to use my eyes. The result is the art of the *visuel*, as Remy de Gourmont called it. Then the visual discipline began very young. I began – yes – with painting: as a small boy I was sent to a London art school. (I did not remain there long – I got a big prize at once: when I realized that I was about to become an infant-prodigy I hastily left and went to Paris, where I did nothing for some time – except attend the philosophy-courses of the Collège de France.) All serious writers should be encouraged to draw and paint – for myself, I suffer a great deal upon those occasions when I have time to read a few pages of a fellow-fictionist on account of the *bad drawing* and the confused sentimental and unreal colouring I find in his pages. The drawing in some novels is so bad I cannot read them.'

'You consider that a course of drawing would give a greater precision of observation to the fiction-writer?'

'Well, the art of draughtsmanship is in the fullest sense a scientific study – it *should* help the writer of fiction. Anything that trains the mind to close observation should do that. Great periods of painting have always followed close upon the heels of important scientific research. A. N. Whitehead says painting is the scientific mind at work. The Greek plastic artists came out of the researches of Greek surgeons and doctors. In the same way the Renaissance painters learned from their men of science. Michelangelo had corpses in his studio, which he peeled and probed – he learnt anatomy at first-hand. In writing, the only thing that interests me is *the shell*. It's the actions and the appearance of people that I am concerned with, not the "stream of consciousness" of any "mysterious" invisible Within. I think the normal human attitude is physical, not mental.'

'You think Joyce's method is not normal, then?'

'His method is romantic. The method preferred by me may be described as classical; it is objective, and rather scientific than sentimental. The classical is the form to which all romantic revolutions of style return. The romantic is a decadence, a constantly recurring decadence if you like, but a decadence.'

'The novel will not develop in the direction of Joyce, then?'

'I think not, because his *inside* method is too limited to be a universal method. I have used the inside method occasionally, but only under special circumstances. It can be very effective when dealing with the extremely aged, with young children, half-wits, or animals. But for the most part I use the *outside* method. I was glad to see what one of my critics said about the "Stendhalian detail" in *The Apes of God*. The same writer used the term *visuel* – that is as it should be, for *The Apes of God* is written mainly with the eye. No book ever written has paid so much attention to the *outside* of people, I think. To put that sort of technique in a nutshell, I prefer the ossature of an animal to its intestines. The trouble with the "thought-stream" method is that it robs work of all linear properties whatever, of all contour and definition: it breaks up or dissolves the shell. The romantic abdominal *within* method results in a jelly-fish structure, without articulation of any sort.'

He sat quietly in his chair, smoking one cigarette after the other, and speaking in an ordinary conversational tone. In only one way does he conform to the fads of the hour, and that is in not looking at all like an artist. I had expected something cadaverous and sinister – a touch of sulphur at least. Nothing could have been more different from my expectations than the tall, scholarly-looking, calm man with the really jolly smile who sat opposite me by the bright gas-fire.

This was the man who had hurled magnificent verbal thunder and lightning directed with deliberate intent to blast, at hundreds of his contemporaries. Was it possible that this thoughtful, sympathetic, almost bland man could hate? I wondered, and nerved myself to ask him.

'Hate?' he asked. 'Oh, not that at all. Everything I do is done in cold blood. *Kaltes Blut*, you know.' He smiled. 'The temperament of the duellist.'

'But you give the effect of tremendous emotional power. Hatred reverberates with the physical impact of a drum throughout a good deal of your writing.'

'That is good. So much the better, if I give the effect without feeling it!'

'Do you enjoy controversy?'

'No. I suffer it. I don't enjoy it. I am good, I am told, at controversy, but I would much prefer not to engage in it. It's a great waste of time, and I wish it weren't necessary. But I have to defend myself. London is divided into two or three big literary gangs. Each gang takes very good care of its members. I don't belong to any of these organizations. Whenever you get big groups like this it leaves a wide margin; there is a no-man's-land where an independent spirit can install himself and do quite well. There's a great deal of room in London for the solitary racketeer.'

'How far do you distinguish between your pamphleteering and your creative work?'

'There is, in fact, no connexion whatever between them. The pamphlets are written just as one talks, and nearly as fast as talking. To write they are often a great bore – they are usually quite carelessly written. With my non-polemical writing it is the reverse – that is written with the greatest attention, of course. Into such a book as *The Wild Body* (a book of ten pieces of fiction) I put twelve months' hard labour I dare say: *Paleface* (a squib about the Blacks and Redskins) a sixth of that time. I have a great deal to say about the technique of contemporary fiction.'

'Will you tell me something about your own technique? How do you go about creating a book?'

'The book, of course, is born in the head, not on the paper. But I get down upon the paper, in a rough draught, written at top speed, the action, or the structure of the argument, as the case may be. The detail comes afterwards. But a work of art is a sort of animal – it is not easy for me to tell you just how it is made. It grows all sorts of things on itself – for effect – as it goes along. The brain creates it by a fiat – having pondered upon an entire zoology, for some time. But then the mere craftsman takes it over. Or seen under the figure of its keeper, I often find it an exacting baby – when some years back I had in hand a *Lion* and a *Fox* at the same time, it cost me a summer and an autumn of reading. A book that makes you read for it is the hardest book. You have to read such terrible nonsense.'

'But you must read a great deal,' I said. '*The Lion and the Fox*, as you say, must have meant a great deal of research. *Time and Western Man* I should think even more.'

'No, not more. I have always read a good deal of philosophy. It is when one makes a raid into an unfamiliar field, as Shakespearean criticism was to me, that the reading is most painful. For that is, naturally, a happy hunting-ground of donnish persons; without the precision of mind required for a scientific study, they become parasites upon the Shakespearian corpus, and proceed dreamily to pick the Swan of Avon dry. That is a hard lot of books to read. Not that they all are stupid. But the time would be so much better spent in reading Shakespeare. It is not *reading* I object to.'

'Have you any particular principles of style?'

'I have a great variety of styles, adapted to my varied activities. In the matter of contemporary fiction what is, I should be inclined to say, the main fault is that *words in themselves* are not enough considered. A writer should look at a *word* as Frederick II looked at a tall fine-chested Pomeranian, to pick him for a grenadier, or as a trainer looks at an elegant horse. *Really* – that is a bad word: *indeed* or *in fact* are better than *really*: there are in English a whole class of weak words that it is a good habit to avoid; except in writing naturalist dialogue, or for comic purposes, then you have to use them.'

'Do you consider there are many great stylists writing in English to-day?'

'The style is the man, and as each generation produces (with infinite travail) about a half-dozen important men – so you can't get a lot of *stylists* – it would be unreasonable to look for that.'

'But are there any who can compare with the great stylists of the past?'

'The "past" was not packed with stylists either! The general level of style to-day is affected by that poisonous fungus called "Fiction". That must have the effect of degrading the art of writing. It is a great breeding-ground for the worst clichés. Naturally any "Fiction" that pretends to be art must answer the same tests as any other prose. It is the custom of the conscientious poet to remark that the best poetry should be as good as good prose. And the conscientious prose writer, in the same way, will say that good prose must be as good as the best poetry. Simply because a poor work happens to be narrative (and so to come under that dreadful classification "Fiction") that is no reason why it should be *let off easily*, as it were. If a book written in prose cannot be opened at any page whatever without our falling upon some passage that may certainly be "Fiction" but that is not art, then it is a bad book. A good book of narrative should be as easy to *cut* (at any page you choose) and to find something good in it, and of the nature of art, as, say, a volume of Donne or of Hopkins. Certainly those are high standards. But it is no use protesting that this is "breaking a butterfly upon a wheel" – that "Fiction" is just what it is, and not susceptible to these scrutinies: of course the highly remunerated "Fiction" critic likes "Fiction", and small blame to him: only he should not, so it seems in my humble opinion, treat his innumerable "butterflies", week by week, as though they were eagles! That I do think is only common sense. The cutting of the book – like a pack of cards – is an excellent device. It can be warmly recommended to the student of letters.'

He took his *Apes of God* down from the shelf, and 'cutting' it, read a page aloud. There was no mistaking the kind of stuff there; it was good cloth, of the soundest thread and the cleanest weaving. There was no filling in it, and it wasn't artificial silk either. We both agreed on its quality.

'With your endless capacity for work and your intensely active disposition,' I said, 'I suppose you never have such a thing as a barren interval?'

'I feel a slight diffidence about answering that question. I feel I ought to entertain a certain shame on the subject of my fertility, like a woman who has too many children. However, my reply is an uncompromising one – *No.*'

'What are you working on at present?'

'A long novel. The only thing I propose to write in the future is novels – with pamphlets swarming round them to defend them, like destroyers around a battleship or battle-cruiser. I am a double personality, in fact. Attached to the creative artist is the pamphleteer. Whenever I write a book I am obliged to write a pamphlet or two defending it. I couldn't wish for a more satisfactory co-worker, by the way. I have no complaint to make of the pamphleteer that is the right-hand man of the artist Wyndham Lewis.'

'Have you tried to analyse why you write?'

'Why I write? No. It's the most natural thing in the world for me to write. Why do I breathe? I might as well try to answer that question!'

•

AL CAPONE

Interviewed by Cornelius Vanderbilt Jr
Liberty, 17 October 1931

Al (Alphonse) Capone (1899–1947), the American gangster, was born in Brooklyn, New York. He was educated at New York's PS 7, in the same class and street gang as Salvatore Luciana (alias Lucky Luciano), and while at school he fell in with gang boss John Torrio. He worked for a while as a restaurant bouncer, married an Irish girl, and followed Torrio, when summoned, to Chicago. In 1924, when Torrio decided to retire after an assassination attempt, Capone took over his organization and ruthlessly set about eliminating the rival Irish, Polish, and Jewish gangs. He made a fortune as a bootlegger during Prohibition. He was always conscious of his image and used to entertain journalists, holding court in the Lexington Hotel (known as the Fort), where he kept his offices.

In 1929, following the murder of corrupt *Chicago Tribune* journalist Jake Lingle (with whom Capone had clashed), the Irish journalist Claud Cockburn obtained an assignment from *The Times* (London) to interview Capone. He found himself being lectured about the virtues of 'the American system'. Capone 'praised freedom, enterprise and the pioneers' and 'referred with contemptuous disgust to Socialism and Anarchism'. He insisted that his rackets were 'run on strictly American lines' and finished with a peroration: 'This American system of ours,' he shouted, 'call it Americanism, call it Capitalism, call it what you like, gives to each and every one of us an opportunity if we only seize it with both hands and make the most of it.' In the end, Cockburn decided not to write up the interview for his paper because 'I saw that most of what Capone had said was in essence identical with what was being said in the leading articles of *The Times* itself, and I doubted whether the paper would be best pleased to find itself seeing eye to eye with the most notorious gangster in Chicago.'

Capone was popular with many ordinary persons in Chicago because he had supplied the city's speakeasies with alcohol. He was also a charitable benefactor, paying for a soup kitchen for the unemployed and giving parties for the poor in Little Italy. The editor of *Liberty* introduced this interview as follows: 'When Al Capone gave this interview to Mr Vanderbilt, he was facing trial for evasion of the federal income tax law, with the prospect of several years in prison if he should be convicted. What was going on in the mind of this self-proclaimed dictator from the underworld? Was he sobered, deflated, as a man naturally would be in such circumstances? On the contrary, as Mr Vanderbilt shows, he was coolly holding forth on the affairs of the nation, telling the President of the

United States what to do and naming his possible successor, and – to crown the effrontery of it – denouncing grafters and swindlers. The interview is published as an astonishing and salutary object lesson in underworld mentality aggrandized by prohibition riches, sensational publicity, and the arrogance of a gangster, swollen with power.'

In October 1931 Capone was sentenced to eleven years' imprisonment – then the heaviest sentence ever for a tax evader. He languished in federal prisons, including the notorious Alcatraz, where he was humiliated and attacked by other prisoners, until 1940 when he was released, having been diagnosed as suffering from neurosyphilis. A pathetic figure, although still wealthy, he went to live with his wife and family in his Miami mansion, where he died at the age of forty-eight from the tertiary stage of the disease. In 1990 the American Bar Association held a mock re-trial of the Capone tax evasion case and concluded that Capone had been ill served by his lawyers and that the evidence against him would not have been allowed to go before a modern jury. Furthermore, Capone's defence team had been unaware that some of the federal witnesses against their client had been coerced.

Cornelius Vanderbilt Jr (1898–1974) was a scion of the wealthy New York financial dynasty, although his father had been cut off from the rest of the family, and from the bulk of his fortune, because he had married an older woman of whom his family had disapproved. His parents were still rich, however, as Vanderbilt Jr's maternal grandfather was also a wealthy business-man. Vanderbilt Jr was brought up in Newport, Connecticut, and frequently travelled to Europe as a child. He turned to journalism as soon as he was discharged from the army at the end of the First World War, despite his father's disapproval. He was a reporter for *The New York Herald*, for whom he interviewed the Irish poet Lord Dunsany, the Belgian playwright Maurice Maeterlinck, and Edward, Prince of Wales; he was Albany correspondent of *The New York Times*, then a Washington correspondent for United Press, the Universal Service, and as an independent. In 1923 he founded and became president of Vanderbilt Newspapers, which launched tabloid titles in Los Angeles, San Francisco and Miami. The papers closed after a few years and he got. his fingers burned. He was also associate editor of the *New York Mirror* from 1925 to 1929.

During the 1930s he became a special correspondent for *Liberty* magazine, specializing in interviews. His subjects included General Pershing, Pope Pius XI, Mussolini, General Pilsudski (the Polish leader), Stalin, Hitler, and President Hoover. He interviewed Hitler several times. On the first occasion, just after Hitler had been imprisoned for his role in the Munich beer-hall putsch, Vanderbilt Jr threw a brick through a window in order to get himself arrested, then bribed his way into the cell next to Hitler's – all for the sake of an interview. Years later, he turned down the offer of an interview with Hitler because he would not fulfil the condition of paying $5,000 into a fund for the families of

Nazis killed during Hitler's rise to power. He also interviewed Stalin (who 'appeared an ogre to some, to me a schoolmaster') several times. Stalin had been reading a book when Vanderbilt Jr had arrived to interview him the first time. He later learned that the book had been the Bible and that Stalin had read it in four languages. Also on this occasion, Stalin had 'talked to me more like an American businessman than like the leader of Red Russia'. The last time he interviewed Stalin, Vanderbilt correctly read into Stalin's remarks that Russia was about to form a non-aggression pact with Germany and he was able to tip off Roosevelt in advance.

During the 1930s Vanderbilt Jr worked tirelessly for the Roosevelt presidential campaigns. He turned down the offer of a job in the administration, but accepted the title of presidential agent, without salary or expenses, reporting directly to FDR on many matters. He was awarded the Distinguished Service Cross of the FBI in 1942 for his work in exposing a Japanese wireless operator on the Pacific coast. He wrote a number of travel books – *Reno* (1929), *Park Avenue* (1930), *Palm Beach* (1931) – and during the 1940s was a travel columnist for the *New York Post* and Affiliated News Features. He also wrote several books of memoirs: *Personal Experiences of a Cub Reporter* (1922), *Experiences of a Washington Correspondent* (1929), *Farewell to Fifth Avenue* (1935), and *Man of the World: My Life on Five Continents* (1959). Vanderbilt Jr was married no less than six times.

Before visiting Capone, Vanderbilt Jr left a note with his hotel manager with instructions that it should be opened after a certain time. Inside it revealed where he had gone. Meanwhile, the interview had been going so well that Capone and Vanderbilt Jr were considering an 'intimate dinner' the following week when the phone rang. Capone answered and passed the receiver to Vanderbilt Jr. 'Police Headquarters,' he explained. 'They say I kidnapped you.'

'Us fellas has gotta stick together.'

We were seated, Al Capone and I, in a large spacious office in the southeast corner of the fourth floor of the Lexington Hotel at Twenty-second and Michigan, Chicago. It was after 4 p.m. The day was Thursday, August 27. And this was the year.

Below us, on the sidewalks, cops and plain-clothes men bristled. Their light artillery was very much in evidence. Gangster hangouts had been brushed clean time after time during the past twenty-four hours. Hotels and apartments had been entered and raided. Pat Roche wanted the king, and wanted him badly. And Pat was the state's attorney.

Someone had been kidnapped. His name was Lynch. He published a race-track tip sheet. Rumor had it his captors demanded '250 grand' for his release. Believing that Al Capone might know something about it, the Chicago police had asked the king to help them find him. His Majesty had graciously acquiesced; and it was not long before Lynch was found. Nor had he been obliged to pay a nickel's worth of ransom.

Al Capone does not tolerate some kinds of rackets, and kidnapping is one of them.

He leaned a bit farther back in his comfortable office chair and lit, for the seventeenth time, his chewed Tampa cigar. We had been talking for more than an hour.

'This is going to be a terrible winter,' he went on. 'Us fellas has gotta open our pocketbooks, and keep on keeping them open, if we want any of us to survive. We can't wait for Congress or Mr Hoover or anyone else. We *must* help keep tummies filled and bodies warm.

'If we don't, it's all up with the way we've learned to live. Why, do you know, sir, America is on the verge of its greatest social upheaval? Bolshevism is knocking at our gates. We can't afford to let it in. We've got to organize ourselves against it, and put our shoulders together and hold fast. We need funds to fight famine.'

Could I be hearing correctly? Was I in my right senses? Here, in front of me, in the bay of a window, behind a long, large teak desk, sat the most feared of all our racketeers. Much taller than I had imagined, and much broader; a fellow with a winchlike handshake, a banker's bay window, and the winning smile of all the Latin races. And yet, instead of the usual line of talk that emanates from gentry of his kind, he had been giving me a discourse the like of which it had never been my fortune to hear.

He went on:

'We must keep America whole, and safe, and unspoiled. If machines are going to take jobs away from the worker, then he will need to find something else to do. Perhaps he'll get back to the soil. But we must care for him during the period of change. We must keep him away from red literature, red ruses; we must see that his mind remains healthy. For, regardless of where he was born, he is now an American.'

Boys were shouting extras in the streets below. Al 'Brown', as he likes to call himself, got up from his chair and walked over to the south side of the room. He drew from a cabinet a pair of field glasses, raised them to his eyes, and read slowly from an afternoon sheet's headlines: 'Pat Roche Confident He Will Soon Have Capone Under Arrest.'

He smiled broadly at me. 'Pat's a fine guy,' said he quietly, 'only he likes to see his name in print a bit too often.'

And, thought I, 'If Pat really was in earnest about arresting you he could do it in a jiffy.'

He practically answered the thought: 'I guess I'm like you, Mr Vanderbilt: I get more blame from the crowd for things I never do than praise for the good I do.

'The news gang are forever riding me. Seems as if I'm responsible for every crime that takes place in this country. You'd think I had unlimited power and a swell pocketbook. Well, I guess I got the power all right; but the bank book suffers from these hard times as much as anyone else's.

'My pay roll is about as big as it ever was, but the profits have done their share of dwindling. Say, you'd be surprised if you knew some of the fellas I've got to take care of.'

I could have answered that I wouldn't have been surprised at anything, but I held my peace. Al Capone is not the usual type of gangster who has risen to a high place. He is a capable organizer and politician.

At thirty-two he has about him the most perfectly oiled machine this country has ever seen. He is as powerful in Chicago as any Tammany boss ever was in New York. To do the many things he must do daily, he has a pay roll in excess of $200,000 a week.

At this writing the Capone machine has yet to meet a defeat. Just how can a man of his youth hold together the kind of organization he has built up? I asked him. His reply came without hesitation:

'People respect nothing nowadays. Once we put virtue, honor, truth, and the law on a pedestal. Our children were brought up to respect things. The war ended. We have had nearly twelve years to straighten ourselves out, and look what a mess we've made of life!

'War legislators passed the Eighteenth Amendment. Today more people drink alcohol from speakeasies than passed through all the doors of all the saloons in America in five years before 1917. That's their answer to law respect. Yet most of those people are not bad. You don't classify them as criminals, though technically they are.

'The mass feeling that prohibition is responsible for a lot of our ills is growing. But the number of law-breakers is increasing too. Sixteen years ago I came to Chicago with forty dollars in my pocket. Three years afterward I was married. My son is now twelve. I am still married and love my wife dearly. We had to make a living. I was younger then than I am now, and I thought I needed more. I didn't believe in prohibiting people from getting the things they wanted. I thought prohibition an unjust law and I still do.

'Somehow I just naturally drifted into the racket. And I guess I'm here to stay until the law is repealed.'

'Then you believe it will be repealed?'

'Certainly,' was his quick reply. 'And when it is I'd be out of luck if I hadn't arranged to do business elsewhere. You see, Mr Vanderbilt, prohibition forms less than thirty-five per cent of my income.'

His next statement fell like a thunderbolt.

'I believe Mr Hoover may make the text of his December message to Congress a suggestion that the nation's legislators raise the percentage of the alcoholic content of liquor. That will be his best card for renomination. Besides, you know he has always called the Volstead Act "a noble *experiment*".

'In time, though, people won't tolerate even that. They'll demand a return to normal drinking; and if they exercise enough pressure they'll beat the Anti-Saloon League and the industrialists who have waxed fat and wealthy at the expense of thirst.

'The law will be repealed. There will be no further need of secrecy. I will be spared an enormous pay roll. But as long as the act remains in effect and there are people left who will continue to break the law, then there must be positions for persons such as I, who find it devolves upon us to keep the channel open.

'People who respect nothing dread *fear*. It is upon fear therefore that I have built up my organization. Those who work *with* me are afraid of nothing. Those who work *for* me are kept faithful, not so much because of their pay as because they know what might be done with them if they broke faith.

'The United States Government shakes a very wabbly stick at the lawbreaker, and tells him he'll go to prison if he beats the law. Lawbreakers laugh and get good lawyers. A few of the less well-to-do take the rap. But the public generally isn't any more afraid of a government prison sentence than I am of Pat Roche. Things people know about amuse them. They like to laugh over them and make jokes. When a speakeasy is raided, there are a few hysterical people, but the general mass are light-hearted. On the other hand, do you know of any of your friends who'd go into fits of merriment if they feared being taken for a ride?'

Did I? That was one question I could answer, and quickly.

On the wall behind the king was a picture of Lincoln in a cheap frame. He seemed smiling benevolently down. A bronzed paperweight of the Lincoln Memorial statue of the Great Emancipator was on the royal desk. A copy of the Gettysburg Address adorned another portion of the wall. That Capone admired Lincoln more than any other American was easy to see.

I asked him how he felt about the 1932 elections.

'The Democrats will be swept in on a record vote,' he declared. 'The masses will think they'll get relief from the depression that way. I know very little about world finance; but I don't think the end of the depression is going to come like that. I think it will take longer. A series of circumstances will bring about a relief, if we don't let the Reds try to bring it about before.

'Owen Young has the best chance, in my own humble estimation. He's a swell guy, and they ought to let him get it. If not, then Roosevelt will; and I think Roosevelt has enough sense to make Young his Secretary of the Treasury. Roosevelt's a good fellow, but I'm afraid his health is pretty shaky, and a leader needs health.'

Capone's naïveté was charming. He did nothing for effect; and I am sure he wasn't trying to show off for my benefit.

Four days before I had been sitting in my Nevada ranch house. My Sicilian secretary, Peter Marisca, had brought me a telegram that had been mislaid earlier in the day. It read: 'Appointment arranged in Chicago Wednesday morning at 11. Call my office on arrival.' It was signed by a well known Mid-Western attorney. I had just had time to pack some bags and catch a late night train east.

Reaching Chicago Wednesday, I read of the kidnaping of Publisher Lynch, and of the Chicago police's bid to Capone for his help. Nevertheless, I called the attorney who had sent me the wire. Capone was in consultation with his counsel and could not see anyone.

Late that evening I purchased an early copy of a morning paper. Headlines told of Lynch's return home, and of Pat Roche's order for Capone's arrest. It was intimated that the king knew entirely too much about the cause of Lynch's sudden kidnapping.

All hopes of seeing Capone fled instantly. I had developed a bad cold in my head, and I went to bed.

Early Thursday morning there was a telephone message: 'Mr Al Capone's secretary says it will be entirely all right for Mr Vanderbilt to come to his office this afternoon at three.'

Peter Marisca didn't deliver it because he thought someone was playing a practical joke! Yet he told it to me as an aside that day at luncheon at the Drake; and I nearly burned my throat with the mock turtle.

And so here I had come through cordons of police and government agents. Down in the lobby of the Lexington we had entered an elevator, in which a colored boy as glum as glue had taken us up.

In the hallway a well upholstered young chap had been waiting. He was dressed in the lightest green suit I think I have ever seen. And he lost no time in asking me whom I wanted.

'I have an appointment with "Mr Brown",' I said.

'That guy with you?' He motioned to Pete. I replied that he was. We moved down the hall and into a private suite of rooms. Pete stayed outside to talk his native tongue with any number of other Sicilians.

During the interview I was brought back from my surmises by a question Capone put to me. 'In your talks with big men throughout the world,' he was saying, 'what have they to offer as a solution for the present depression?'

'Frankly,' said I, 'I've heard so many solutions, I feel as if none of them really knew anything. I think they're stumped.'

'Not stumped,' said Al. 'They can't all get together and stick to any one thought. They lack concentrated organization. Isn't it a peculiar thing that with one of the world's greatest organizers as our chief executive we lack organization more now than ever in our history?

'The world has been capitalized on paper. Every time a fellow had a new idea, they'd increase the capital stock – give themselves so much cash and their stockholders so much paper. The rich got richer; the stockholders speculated with the paper. Someone found out it paid to keep a rumour factory going. Someone else interested women in gambling on the big board. The world was wild.

'Amalgamations took place. The more clever a fellow was with turning paper recapitalizations into cash, the greater became his vice-presidential titles. Young men who ought, many of them, to be resting behind the bars of penitentiaries for stealing paper rose overnight in the world of prosperity. Our entire prospectus of living turned topsy-turvy.

'Crooked bankers who take people's hard-earned cash for stock they know is worthless would be far better clients at penal institutions than the poor little man who robs so that his wife and babies may live. Why, down in Florida, the year I lived there, a shady newspaper publisher's friend was running a bank. He had unloaded a lot of worthless securities upon unsuspecting people. One day his bank went flooey. I was just thanking the powers that be that he'd got what was coming to him when I learned of another business trick that would make safe-cracking look like miniature golf.

'The crooked publisher and the banker were urging bankrupt depositors who were being paid thirty cents on the dollar to put their money in another friend's bank. Many did so; and just about sixty days later that bank collapsed like a house of cards too.

'Do you think those bankers went to jail? No, sir. They're among Florida's most representative citizens. They're just as bad as the crooked politicians! I ought to know about them. I've been feeding and clothing them long enough. I never knew until I got into this racket how many crooks there were dressed in expensive clothes and talking with affected accents.

'Why, when I was held the other day for evasion of federal taxes I nearly got myself into a fine pickle. Certain officials wished to make a bargain with me. If I'd plead guilty and go to jail for two and a half years they'd dismiss the charges they had against me. A pretty penny had to be paid, but I thought that that was better than the strain of a long-winded trial. A day or so before the bargain was to be struck, though, I learned that someone was going to go to the Appellate Court and that there'd be a fly in the ointment and they'd have me in Leavenworth for ten and a half years. So I decided I could be just as foxy, and we entered a plea of not guilty, and when the case comes up we'll see what we will see.

'A little while ago in one of the Chicago newspapers it said that a local millionaire manufacturer had been found to be some fifty-five thousand dollars in arrears with his personal-property tax. A day later it was printed that this had been printed in error, and that the situation had been satisfactorily cleaned up.

'If Mr Hoover's government wants me to explain my federal taxes I shall be very glad to do so. I think I could enlighten him and several other officials a considerable bit, and any time they need any sensational matters to talk about I shall have them ready to give out.

'Graft,' he continued, 'is a byword in American life today. It is law where no other law is obeyed. It is undermining this country. The honest lawmakers of any city can be counted on your fingers. I could count Chicago's on one hand!

'Virtue, honor, truth, and the law have all vanished from our life. We are smart-Alecky. We like to be able to "get away with" things. And if we can't make a living at some honest profession, we're going to make one anyway.'

It was growing late. The setting sun's ruddy light enlivened the red-and-gold fancy plaster walls of his office. It intensified the dark-red window shades. The large moose's head on the wall; the stuffed fish and game; the short army rifle – all seemed resplendent in afternoon's final burst of glory. The big old-fashioned phonograph case should perhaps have opened of its own accord to play some triumphant march.

'The home is our most important ally,' Capone observed. 'After all this madness the world has been going through subsides, we'll realize that, as a nation, very strongly. The stronger we can keep our home lives, the stronger we can keep our nation.

'When enemies approach our shores we defend them. When enemies come into our homes we beat them off. Homebreakers should be undressed and tarred and feathered, as examples to the rest of their kind.

'There would be very little need for your home town, Reno, Mr Vanderbilt, if more men protected their homes. When the prohibition law is repealed there'll be less desire for birth control. Without birth control America can become as stalwart as Italy. With an American Mussolini she could conquer the world.'

The door opened quietly behind me. Peter and 'Mr Brown's' secretary were still in conversation. Al greeted Pete and they had a few words together in Sicilian.

'Remember, Mr Vanderbilt, us fellas has gotta stick together this winter,' he repeated. 'Last winter I fed three hundred and fifty thousand persons a day here in Chicago. This winter it's going to be worse. I think we both speak the same language; and I think we're both patriots. We don't want to see them tear down the foundations of this great land. We've got to battle to keep free. Good luck. I'm glad I met you.'

The iron study door swung to. My most amazing interview was at an end.

•

ADOLF HITLER

Interviewed by George Sylvester Viereck

Liberty, 9 July 1932

Adolf Hitler (1889–1945), the German dictator, was born in Austria, the son of a customs official who changed his surname to Hitler from Schicklgrüber. He had early ambitions to become an artist and an architect, but was thwarted because of his lack of academic success. He lived in Vienna for several years, working at various odd jobs and developing a distaste for Jews and trade unionists. He moved to Munich in 1913 to avoid military service, but the following year when war was declared he enlisted in the Bavarian army. Having risen to the rank of corporal, he was awarded the Iron Cross (first class) for his bravery as a runner, but by the end of the war he was an invalid, having been wounded and having suffered a temporary loss of sight as the result of a gas attack. Embittered by national defeat, which he blamed on the Jews and the Socialists, he spied for the army on minor political parties and joined one himself, which he quickly took over and renamed the National Socialist German Workers' Party. In 1923 he took part in the Munich 'beer-hall putsch', an attempted coup against the republican government in Bavaria. The police machine-gunned the marching Nazi stormtroopers and Hitler was imprisoned for nine months, during which he dictated *Mein Kampf* (*My Struggle*), his autobiographical political credo, to Rudolf Hess. After his release he began to attract mass support to the Nazi Party. Against the background of economic depression, Hitler used his intuitive understanding of crowd psychology, his manipulation of the anti-Semitic paranoia (which he shared), and his understanding of propaganda and the 'big lie', to enable him to build a coalition of disaffected workers, Ruhr industrialists, and financiers. He stood unsuccessfully in the presidential elections of 1932, but his opponent in that contest, Paul von Hindenburg, made him chancellor in January 1933. Within weeks he had brought about the burning of the Reichstag and blamed it on the Communists, and in the ensuing general election the Nazis intimidated other parties and secured a narrow majority. From that point, Hitler gradually assumed absolute power, using his bodyguard, the SS, to purge rival Nazis in 1934. He began to rearm Germany and to adopt an aggressive, expansionist foreign policy, taking back the Rhineland, annexing Austria, and invading Czechoslovakia. His attack on Poland led to the Second World War. He committed suicide with his mistress, Eva Braun (having married her at the last minute), in 1945, as the Russians were about to descend on his underground bunker.

As an interview subject, Hitler was far from ideal, being intensely self-absorbed. When H.R. Knickerbocker of the *Chicago Tribune* interviewed him, he had only to ask him a couple of questions before Hitler launched into a ninety-minute monologue as if he were addressing a mass audience. There is a similar element of monologue to this interview with George Sylvester Viereck. Viereck had first interviewed Hitler in 1923 'when he was still comparatively obscure . . . I wrote "This man, if he lives, will make history for better or for worse." He did both. I called him "the overcompensation of Germany's inferiority complex".'

Viereck was more accurate in his prediction than the American journalist Dorothy Thompson, who also interviewed Hitler in April 1932, for *Cosmopolitan*. Hitler kept Thompson waiting for an hour and failed to impress her: 'When I finally walked into Adolf Hitler's salon in the Kaiserhof Hotel, I was convinced that I was meeting the future dictator of Germany. In something less than fifty seconds I was quite sure that I was not. It took just about that much time to measure the startling insignificance of this man who had set the world agog. He was formless, almost faceless, a man whose countenance is a caricature, a man whose framework seems cartilaginous, without bones. He is inconsequent and voluble, ill-poised, insecure. He is the very prototype of the Little Man.' The interview was republished as a book called *I Saw Hitler*. Hitler was furious and blamed Putzi Hanfstaengl, his Harvard-educated liaison man with the foreign press, who said that Thompson had arrived for the interview drunk.

As for Viereck, he expressed doubts about the atrocity stories which emanated from Germany in the late 1930s and he tried to keep the United States out of the Second World War. He was subsequently imprisoned, suffering from war psychosis, and his interviewing career did not last into the post-war period.

'When I take charge of Germany, I shall end tribute abroad and Bolshevism at home.'

Adolf Hitler drained his cup as if it contained not tea, but the life blood of Bolshevism.

'Bolshevism,' the chief of the Brown Shirts, the Fascists of Germany, continued, gazing at me balefully, 'is our greatest menace. Kill Bolshevism in Germany and you restore seventy million people to power. France owes her strength not to her armies but to the forces of Bolshevism and dissension in our midst.

'The Treaty of Versailles and the Treaty of St Germain are kept alive by Bolshevism in Germany. The Peace Treaty and Bolshevism are two heads of one monster. We must decapitate both.'

When Adolf Hitler announced this programme, the advent of the Third Empire which he proclaims seemed still at the end of the rainbow. Then came election after election. Each time the power of Hitler grew. While unable to dislodge Hindenburg from the presidency, Hitler today heads the largest party in Germany. Unless Hindenburg assumes dictatorial measures, or some unexpected development completely upsets all present calculations, Hitler's party will organize the Reichstag and dominate the government. Hitler's fight was not against Hindenburg but against Chancellor Bruening. It is doubtful if Bruening's successor can sustain himself without the support of the National Socialists.

Many who voted for Hindenburg were at heart with Hitler, but some deep-rooted sense of loyalty impelled them nevertheless to cast their vote for the old field marshal. Unless overnight a new leader arises, there is no one in Germany, with the exception of Hindenburg, who could defeat Hitler – and Hindenburg is eighty-five! Time and the recalcitrance of the French fight for Hitler, unless some blunder on his own part, or dissension within the ranks of the party, deprives him of his opportunity to play the part of Germany's Mussolini.

The First German Empire came to an end when Napoleon forced the Austrian emperor to surrender his imperial crown. The Second Empire came to an end when William II, on the advice of Hindenburg, sought refuge in Holland. The Third Empire is emerging slowly but surely, although it may dispense with scepters and crowns.

I met Hitler not in his headquarters, the Brown House in Munich, but in a private home – the dwelling of a former admiral of the German Navy. We discussed the fate of Germany over the teacups.

'Why,' I asked Hitler, 'do you call yourself a National Socialist, since your party program is the very antithesis of that commonly accredited to Socialism?'

'Socialism,' he retorted, putting down his cup of tea, pugnaciously, 'is the science of dealing with the common weal. Communism is not Socialism. Marxism is not Socialism. The Marxians have stolen the term and confused its meaning. I shall take Socialism away from the Socialists.

'Socialism is an ancient Aryan, Germanic institution. Our German ancestors held certain lands in common. They cultivated the idea of the common weal. Marxism has no right to disguise itself as Socialism. Socialism, unlike Marxism, does not repudiate private property. Unlike Marxism, it involves no negation of personality, and unlike Marxism, it is patriotic.

'We might have called ourselves the Liberal Party. We chose to call ourselves the National Socialists. We are not internationalists. Our Socialism is national. We demand the fulfillment of the just claims of the productive classes by the State on the basis of race solidarity. To us State and race are one.'

Hitler himself is not a purely Germanic type. His dark hair betrays some Alpine ancestor. For years he refused to be photographed. That was part of his strategy – to be known only to his friends so that, in the hour of crisis, he could appear here, there, and everywhere without detection. Today he could no longer pass unrecognized through the obscurest hamlet in Germany. His appearance contrasts strangely with the aggressiveness of his opinions. No milder-mannered reformer ever scuttled ship of state or cut political throat.

'What,' I continued my cross-examination, 'are the fundamental planks of your platform?'

'We believe in a healthy mind in a healthy body. The body politic must be sound if the soul is to be healthy. Moral and physical health are synonymous.'

'Mussolini,' I interjected, 'said the same to me.'

Hitler beamed.

'The slums,' he added, 'are responsible for nine-tenths, alcohol for one-tenth, of all human depravity. No healthy man is a Marxian. Healthy men recognize the value of personality. We contend against the forces of disaster and degeneration. Bavaria is comparatively healthy because it is not completely industrialized. However, all Germany, including Bavaria, is condemned to intensive industrialism by the smallness of our territory. If we wish to save Germany we must see to it that our farmers remain faithful to the land. To do so, they must have room to breathe and room to work.'

'Where will you find the room to work?'

'We must retain our colonies and we must expand eastward. There was a time when we could have shared world dominion with England. Now we can stretch our cramped limbs only toward the east. The Baltic is necessarily a German lake.'

'Is it not,' I asked, 'possible for Germany to reconquer the world economically without extending her territory?'

Hitler shook his head earnestly.

'Economic imperialism, like military imperialism, depends upon power. There can be no world trade on a large scale without world power. Our people have not learned to think in terms of world power and world trade. However, Germany cannot extend commercially or territorially until she regains what she has lost and until she finds herself.

'We are in the position of a man whose house has been burned down. He must have a roof over his head before he can indulge in more ambitious plans. We had succeeded in creating an emergency shelter that keeps out the rain. We were not prepared for hailstones. However, misfortunes hailed down upon us. Germany has been living in a veritable blizzard of national, moral, and economic catastrophes.

'Our demoralized party system is a symptom of our disaster. Parliamentary majorities fluctuate with the mood of the moment. Parliamentary government unbars the gate to Bolshevism.'

'Unlike some German militarists, you do not favor an alliance with Soviet Russia?'

Hitler evaded a direct reply to this question. He evaded it again recently when *Liberty* asked him to reply to Trotsky's statement that his assumption of power in Germany would involve a life-and-death struggle between Europe, led by Germany, and Soviet Russia. 'It may not suit Hitler to attack Bolshevism in Russia. He may even look upon an alliance with Bolshevism as his last card, if he is in danger of losing the game. If, he intimated on one occasion, capitalism refuses to recognize that the National Socialists are the last bulwark of private property, if capital impedes their struggle, Germany may be compelled to throw herself into the enticing arms of the siren Soviet Russia. But he is determined not to permit Bolshevism to take root in Germany.'

He responded warily in the past to the advances of Chancellor Bruening and others who wished to form a united political front. It is unlikely that now, in view of the steady increase in the vote of the National Socialists, Hitler will be in the mood to compromise on any essential principle with other parties.

'The political combinations upon which a united front depend,' Hitler remarked to me, 'are too unstable. They render almost impossible a clearly defined policy. I see everywhere the zigzag course of compromise and concession. Our constructive forces are checked by the tyranny of numbers. We make the mistake of applying arithmetic and the mechanics of the economic world to the living state. We are threatened by ever increasing numbers and ever diminishing ideals. Mere numbers are unimportant.'

'But suppose France retaliates against you by once more invading your soil? She invaded the Ruhr once before. She may invade it again.'

'It does not matter,' Hitler, thoroughly aroused, retorted, 'how many square miles the enemy may occupy if the national spirit is aroused. *Ten million free Germans, ready to perish so that their country may live, are more potent than fifty million whose will power is paralyzed and whose race consciousness is infected by aliens.*

'We want a greater Germany uniting all German tribes. But *our salvation can start in the smallest corner. Even if we had only ten acres of land and were determined to defend them with our lives, the ten acres would become the focus of regeneration.* Our workers have two souls: one is German, the other is Marxian. We must arouse the German soul. We must uproot the canker of Marxism. Marxism and Germanism are antitheses.

'In my scheme of the German State, there will be no room for the alien, no use for the wastrel, for the usurer or speculator, or anyone incapable of productive work.'

The cords on Hitler's forehead stood out threateningly. His voice filled the room. There was a noise at the door. His followers, who always remain within call, like a bodyguard, reminded the leader of his duty to address a meeting.

Hitler gulped down his tea and rose.

•

TALLULAH BANKHEAD

Interviewed by Gladys Hall
Motion Picture, September 1932

Tallulah Bankhead (1903–68), the American actress, was born in Huntsville, Alabama, and educated in New York and Washington. She first appeared on the stage in 1918 and there followed a long career on Broadway and in Hollywood. She received Critic awards for her roles in *The Little Foxes* (1939) and *The Skin of our Teeth* (1942). Her most famous film role was in Alfred Hitchcock's 1944 film *Lifeboat*.

This interview caused an outrage. Bankhead's views about sexuality were more than her studio, Paramount Pictures, could bear. Paramount forced her to deny that she had made the controversial statements attributed to her. Thereafter, it became a rule that interviews with stars for fan magazines were conducted in the presence of a studio publicity representative.

Has Hollywood turned a cold shoulder on Tallulah Bankhead? Persons In The Know have it that Hollywood has given her a shoulder very cold and very rigid, indeed.

According to these women-about-town, Hollywood's most elite hostesses have run a blue pencil through the made up moniker of Bankhead.

These hostesses are pictured as confessing they are *afraid* of Tallulah. And the gossipers report that Marion Davies, Connie Bennett, and Bebe Daniels Lyon are among those who prefer not to be At Home to Tallulah.

It is said that, at formal dinner parties, where genteel elegance rests upon all, Tallulah is apt to give vent to words and expressions believed by our grandmothers to belong to truck drivers and longshoremen exclusively.

I am told that Tallul' is never decently hypocritical. She is never hypocritical at all. She conceals nothing. She reveals All – and more than all. She disguises nothing. She calls a spade nothing but a spade – in Hollywood, where dirt is dug with dinner forks. She gives to all the functions of living and loving, of body and soul their round Rabelaisian, biological *names*. Crimson faces and heaving bosoms and masculine guffaws slide off the bawdy Bankhead like oil off water. She is no respecter of persons and no respecter of personalities.

It is said that she speaks of her love affairs with equal frankness. She has a romantic interlude and, afterwards, discusses it with lurid details and complete unreserve. It matters not whether the recent recipient of her favors happens to be among those present or not. Whether he is or whether he isn't, she is said to dilate upon his ways and wiles, his abilities and disabilities, his prowess or his lack of prowess, with such consummate abandon that the unfortunate male, if present, can think of no recourse except immediate suicide.

No good hostess, I am informed, could dream of exposing her guests to such ribaldries. Tallulah's wit, I am told, is barbed. Her shafts and arrows fly wildly through the Hollywood atmosphere, striking willy-nilly, where least expected. She is like a gilded bomb invited to rest among lilies of the field. Thus I have been told.

But Tallulah denies all this. She denies it vehemently, amusedly, scornfully and – can it be? – a little sadly. She denies everything that has been said about her, rumored about her and printed about her.

She 'wears' an exterior as, for certain purposes, a mummer wears a mask. She wears this exterior for protection, to save her neck, her face, her feelings. She took it off for me.

She said, to begin with (and oh, the rapid, dynamite, restless things she said!): 'Hollywood has been divine to me. I don't know what you mean. If it *is* giving me the cold shoulder, I haven't felt the chill. It is news to me. It may be that *I* am suspected of giving *Hollywood* the cold shoulder because I accept so few invitations. Because I have never given parties. Because such hospitality as I have accepted I haven't returned. It has reached a point now where, if I gave a party at all, I would have to invite about five hundred people.

'But this is all absurd. Most of the things said about me and printed about me are absurd and untrue. Not that I mind what people say – it's all part of the game. They say, for instance, that Marlene Dietrich and I are furiously jealous, the one of the other. That we spend our spare time in brawling together like fish-wives all over the lot. I have just come, as it happens, from Marlene's dressing-room where we had a dish of champagne together . . .'

(On this I can confirm Tallulah. Marlene's dressing-room is next to Tallulah's. Just before Tallulah came in, I heard her call back, 'Thanks for the champagne, Marlene . . .')

'I am said to be lacking in seriousness, to have no serious side at all, to be unhurt by anything, to be incapable of hurt. Lies, of course. Here and now, for the first time, I deny that. I am serious. I am deadly serious. I am serious about my work. I am serious about love. I am serious about marriage and children and friendship and the whole stuff of life. *I pretend not to be.*

'I have an inferiority complex. It is my defense mechanism working. So that, if I take a fall, if I fail here or fail there, if the movies or a man chuck me out on my ear, people will laugh it off and say, "Oh, well, Tallulah doesn't care!" But I would care. I'd care all right, but not so much as if people knew that I cared. I can't bear pity. I can't endure sympathy. A kindly pat on my bowed shoulder would drive me nuts.

'I am deadly serious about my work. I'd have to be – anybody has to have any kind of lasting success. Nobody attains any kind of permanence unless he is serious. There are no such things as "the breaks". Not for long. I have had no "angels" in my life, nobody has ever helped me. I wouldn't be helped. What I have achieved, I have achieved by myself and I haven't done it by not caring.

'When I first started to make pictures, absurd stories began to circulate about me. I was said to be trying to "do a Garbo". A fatal thing to say about anyone. Words perfectly calculated to arouse the defensiveness and rage of thousands of Garbo fans. Do you think I didn't care about that? Don't be a fool. I was said to have ordered Adolph Zukor off the set, not knowing who he was. Do you think *I'm* a fool? I knew perfectly well who he was and what business he had there. I asked him to leave because I was working with a new medium, because I was frightfully nervous and edgy and because his presence, of all persons, made me more so.

'When I saw the preview of my first picture in the East, I managed to get out of the theatre, blind with tears as I was. I made my friends swear on my eyes (I'm superstitious about eyes, I'm something of an eye-worshiper) that they would never go to see that picture. I hadn't learned how to make up, how to be photographed. I was full of inhibitions and uncertainties.

'I am serious about money. I have my eye on a fixed sum. I may never reach it. I'm hideously extravagant. With all the money I made in London, I had to borrow a wad to get out of the place, skirts clean. I never leave a place owing bills. I'm serious about my credit, you know.

'I'm serious about my ambition. Know what it is? I'll give it to you – *to have no ambition*. To be without ambition of any sort is Heaven. Nirvana, the state of the blessed. I've been hag-ridden with ambition. It burns you up. It eats you alive. It drinks your blood and crumbles your bones. I want to be without it.

'I'm serious about love. I'm damned serious about it now, of all times. I haven't had an *affaire* for six months. Six months. Too long. I am not promiscuous, you know. Promiscuity implies that attraction is not necessary. I may lay my eyes on a man and have an *affaire* with him the next hour. But it is serious. The attraction is serious.

'I am serious about marriage – too serious to indulge in it. I know myself too well. I never fool myself. I do fool everyone else. I know that once I get a thing – or a man – I'll tire of it and of him. I am the type that fattens on unrequited love, on the unattainable, on the just-beyond-reach. The minute a man begins to languish over me, I stiffen and it is finis.

'I am serious about wishing I had children – beautiful children. I wouldn't care for the other variety. I love anything and everything that is beautiful. Perhaps beautiful is not the word – personality is more like it.

'Of course, I am an extremist. I'm in transports of mad delight with living one day and bored to a hellish desperation the next day. When I am in heaven, I'm liable to rip the stars out of the sky and gut the moon. When I'm bored – no hell is so dark-brown and odorous.

'I'm serious about the matter of good taste. Hollywood's cold shoulder or warm heart to the contrary. I would feel acutely if I thought I had hurt anyone. I am not religious, but I would make a wide detour and put myself to a lot of inconvenience before I would make a ribald remark about a minister, or priest or rabbi to one of the faithful. The things other people hold sacred I am careful of. I might offend morals, but never good taste – the more important of the two.

'My secretary says that I am mad, and tries to prevent me from saying it – and proving it – to the Press. At this moment she is making signs to me from the other room. Perhaps I am mad. How should I know? *I* think I am normal. I know that the things I do *seem* normal to me. And I repeat that I do not believe that mad people, or superficial people, or people who never take anything seriously get very far – or stay there.

'There is nothing more to say about this Hollywood cold-shouldering proposition. Other than that I've never heard of it, have not been aware of it. And certainly I feel no equivalent emotion in myself. I like Hollywood. I find the people interesting and, very often, especially delightful. I don't go around a great deal because it would bore me. I've done all the night-clubbing and partying I could swallow, in London and in Paris. It doesn't interest me any longer, that sort of thing. I've had some close and personal friends from London staying with me. I haven't needed outside entertainment. I play Bridge a little, very badly. I go to the movies, Garbo is a very great genius. I'm mad about her. *And I'm not, as a rule, very fond of women.* I'm crazy about Gary Cooper and Jackie Cooper, and Jack Oakie and Leslie Howard.

'If there's anything the matter with me now, it's certainly not Hollywood or Hollywood's state of mind about me, one way or the other. The matter with me is – I WANT A MAN! I told you I haven't had an *affaire* for six months. I'm bored to the point of suicide when I'm not in love. When I am in love, I want to die. I always want to die when I'm on the top. When I'm down again, I want to fight back. I wish to God I could fall in love now – find someone to fall in love with. Six months is a long, long while. *I want a man!*'

I felt, when I left Tallulah's dressing-room, that I had been closed in with a feverish, very tired, very mundane and effete tigress. She wore scarlet pajamas, tailored coat and trousers. Her nut-brown hair was long-bobbed and flying. She wore no make-up. Her eyes were strained and weary. She paced the floor, back and forth, to and fro.

She brought to mind the gallant, maniacal *Mad Hopes*, the obsessed *Royal Family of Broadway* – all of the fiercely desiring, fiercely living desperadoes, male and female, of theatre, of history, of life. She may be mad. But she is serious about it. She may be without a soul. She is not without a heart. She may make mock of lovers as dead to her as the dead yesterdays. She would never make mock of love. Nor of life. And if life or love make mock of her, she will answer back with an ironic laugh and a bawdy phrase – and tears in her heart.

●

BENITO MUSSOLINI

Interviewed by Emil Ludwig
Talks with Mussolini, 1933

Benito Mussolini (1883–1945), the Italian dictator, was born in Romagna province, the son of a blacksmith. He became a journalist, editing a socialist paper, *Avanti*, but after serving as a soldier in the First World War he founded a right-wing paper, *Popolo d'Italia*, and led the Fascisti, a group of extreme nationalists. In 1921 he was elected to parliament and founded the National Fascist Party, and the following year he led his blackshirt supporters in the March on Rome, which caused King Victor Emmanuel III to invite him to form a government. In 1928 'Il Duce', as he was now known, abolished the Italian parliament and in 1929 he signed the Lateran Treaty which acknowledged the Vatican as a separate state. His foreign policy was aggressive and expansionist. He formed an Axis with Hitler's Germany and supported Franco in Spain. His armies annexed Abyssinia and Albania to the Italian crown. In 1940 he entered the Second World War on the side of Germany and thereafter fortune deserted him. His armies were defeated in Greece and North Africa and his popularity began to ebb with these military failures. The King deposed him and had him imprisoned, but he was released by German parachutists and installed as a German puppet ruler in northern Italy. In 1945, when the Germans retreated, Italian partisans captured Mussolini and his staff by Lake Como. He was tried and shot and his body publicly shamed and reviled in Como and Milan.

Sir Charles Petrie, the British diplomat, gave an interesting assessment of Mussolini, which echoes Ludwig's perception: 'The impression which he used to make on me as I crossed the floor of that vast room in the Palazzo Venezia was not the dictator with forbidding manner and beetling brows, but the cultured man-of-the-world quite ready to indulge in the give-and-take of ordinary conversation. In particular, he had a winning smile which used to light up his face in a way reminiscent of that of de Valera and Neville Chamberlain. I never found that he made any attempt to "lay down the law", though whenever I spoke with him I was always conscious of his wide knowledge ... Perhaps Mussolini's most marked characteristic, just as his eyes were his most prominent physical one, was his extraordinary ability to dissociate in any question the important from the trivial. He went to the heart of a problem in a way that had the effect of clearing the brains of those with whom he was conversing, and of reducing apparently insuperable difficulties to their right proportions ... If one were asked what was Mussolini's most prominent attribute, the answer must be his encyclopedic knowledge – knowledge of affairs, of books and, until his last years, of his own fellow-countrymen. At the height of his power he is reputed to have said that the difference between the Führer and himself was that whereas he was the first-class head of a second-rate nation, Hitler was the second-rate head of a first-class nation. Had Mussolini kept this rather more prominently before him, many things might have been different.'

Emil Ludwig (1881–1948), the German biographer and journalist, was the son of Hermann Cohn, a professor of ophthalmology. He was given the surname Ludwig to avoid being automatically discriminated against as a Jew, although, while he embraced first Christianity then rationalism, he never repudiated his race. He received a law degree from Heidelberg University and spent his twenties writing plays and poems. After briefly working in London as a correspondent for a German paper, he returned to Germany after the outbreak of the First World War and became a correspondent for the next four years in those countries allied to the Central Powers. Although not a socialist, Ludwig was in favour of the Weimar Republic. His play on Bismarck was at first suppressed, but after Ludwig sued and won, it played a thousand performances in Berlin. He settled in Ancona, Switzerland, and became a Swiss citizen in 1932, after Hitler came to power in Germany.

The conversations in this book 'took place in the Palazzo di Venezia at Rome, being held almost daily for an hour at a time between March 23 and April 4, 1932, both dates inclusive'. The two men talked in Italian, Ludwig then wrote up each interview straight away in German, and Mussolini checked the German manuscript. 'No secretary was present to take notes,' explained Ludwig, 'no demand was made for the revision of a manuscript report; it was all a matter of personal confidence.' Ludwig was mistrustful of dictators, but chose to interview Mussolini for several reasons: because democracy was failing in parts of Europe, because dictators had apparently produced material prosperity in the Soviet Union and Italy, and because he surmised, wrongly as it turned out, that Mussolini was 'far from inclined to cherish plans of war'. Ludwig believed that 'in conversation a man discloses himself more freely than on paper with a pen . . .'; and he regarded his interviews with Mussolini as 'an attempt at indirect portraiture', an effort 'to characterize the man in action in general, and to show once again how closely akin are the poet and the statesman'. To this end he recorded each conversation 'as faithfully as possible and without additions. I compressed rather than expanded, and was careful to avoid any kind of staginess (to which fascism has been unduly prone).' Uppermost in Ludwig's mind was his determination to reveal Mussolini's 'feelings, self-knowledge, and motives'. He concluded that 'in conversation, Mussolini is the most natural man in the world'.

Interestingly, Mussolini had himself been an interviewer during his time as a journalist. He interviewed the French premier, Aristide Briand, at Cannes: 'Not so very long afterwards we met as prime ministers.' Mussolini confirmed to Ludwig that he studied the physiognomy of his subjects and prepared himself for the fray.

Someone had made me a present of the *édition de luxe* of Machiavelli, which the fascist State publishing organization has somewhat too fulsomely dedicated to the Duce. All the same, it is doubtless better that a dictatorial government should acknowledge its obligations to this instructor of dictators than that, while secretly acting on his theories, it should use 'Machiavellian' as a term of abuse. When Frederick the Great was yet only crown prince he wrote his moralizing *Anti-Machiavel*. In later days he became more straightforward, governing frankly in accordance with Machiavelli's principles.

'Did you make early acquaintance with Machiavelli's *The Prince?*' I asked Mussolini.

'My father used to read the book aloud in the evenings, when we were warming ourselves beside the smithy fire and were drinking the *vin ordinaire* produced from our own vineyard. It made a deep impression on me. When, at the age of forty, I read Machiavelli once again, the effect was reinforced.'

'It is strange,' I said, 'how such men as Machiavelli flourish for a time, pass into oblivion, and are then resuscitated. It seems as if there were seasonal variations.'

'What you say is certainly true of nations. They have a spring and a winter, more than one. At length they perish.'

'It is because there are recurring seasons in the national life that I have never been much alarmed that winter now prevails in Germany,' said I. 'A hundred years ago and more, when Germany had fallen on evil days, Goethe made fun of those who spoke of our "decay". Have you studied any of the notable figures of our political life?'

'Bismarck,' he promptly answered. 'From the outlook of political actualities, he was the greatest man of his century. I have never thought of him as merely the comic figure with three hairs on his bald head and a heavy footfall. Your book confirmed my impression how versatile and complex he was. In Germany, do people know much about Cavour?'

'Very little,' I answered. 'They know much more about Mazzini. Recently I read a very fine letter of Mazzini's to Charles Albert, written, I think, in 1831 or 1832; the invocation of a poet to a prince. Do you approve of Charles Albert's having issued orders for Mazzini's imprisonment should he cross the frontier?'

'The letter,' said Mussolini, 'is one of the most splendid documents ever written. Charles Albert's figure has not yet become very clear to us Italians. A little while ago his diary was published, and this throws considerable light upon his psychology. At first, of course, he inclined to the side of the liberals. When, in 1832 – no, in 1833 – the Sardinian government sentenced Mazzini to death *in contumaciam*, this happened in a peculiar political situation.'

The answer seemed to me so guarded that, in my persistent but unavowed determination to compare the present to the past, I considered it necessary to speak more clearly.

'Those were the days when *Young Italy* was being published illegally. Don't you think that such periodicals appear under all censorships? Would you have imprisoned Mazzini?'

'Certainly not,' he rejoined. 'If a man has ideas in his head, let him come to me, and we will talk things over. But when Mazzini wrote that letter, he was guided more by his feelings than by his reason. Piedmont in those days had only four million inhabitants, and could not possibly form front against powerful Austria with her thirty millions.'

'Well, Mazzini was jailed,' I resumed. 'Soon afterwards, Garibaldi was sentenced to death. Two generations later, you were put in prison. Should we not infer that a ruler ought to think twice before punishing his political opponents?'

'I suppose you mean that we don't think twice here in Italy?' he inquired with some heat.

'You have reintroduced capital punishment.'

'There is capital punishment in all civilized countries; in Germany, no less than in France and in England.'

'Yet it was in Italy,' I insisted, 'in the mind of Beccaria, that the idea of abolishing capital punishment originated. Why have you revived it?'

'Because I have read Beccaria,' replied Mussolini, simply and without irony. He went on, with the utmost gravity: 'What Beccaria writes is contrary to what most people believe. Besides, after capital punishment was abolished in Italy there was a terrible increase in serious crime. As compared with England, the tale in Italy was five to one. I am guided, in this matter, exclusively by social considerations. Was it not St Thomas who said that it would be better to cut off a gangrenous arm if thereby the whole body could be saved? Anyhow I proceed with the utmost caution and circumspection. Only in cases of acknowledged and exceptionally brutal murders is the death punishment inflicted. Not very long ago, two rascals violated a youth and then murdered him. Both the offenders were sentenced to death. I had followed the trial with close attention. At the last moment doubt became insistent. One of the two offenders was a habitual criminal who had avowed his crime; the other, a much younger man, had pleaded not guilty, and there were no previous charges against him. Six hours before the execution I reprieved the younger of the two.'

'You could put that in the chapter, "Advantages of Dictatorship,"' I said.

His repartee was swift, and couched in a tone of mockery:

'The alternative is a State machine which grinds on automatically without any one having the power to stop its working.'

'Would you like to leave this contentious topic, and talk about Napoleon?'

'Go ahead!'

'Despite our previous conversations, I am not clear whether you regard him as a model or as a warning.'

He sat back in his chair, looked rather gloomy, and said in a restrained tone:

'As a warning. I have never taken Napoleon as an examplar, for in no respect am I comparable to him. His activities were of a very different kind from mine. He put a term to a revolution, whereas I have begun one. The record of his life has made me aware of errors which are by no means easy to avoid.' Mussolini ticked them off on his fingers. 'Nepotism. A contest with the papacy. A lack of understanding of finance and economic life. He saw nothing more than that after his victories there was a rise in securities.'

'What laid him low? The professors declare that he was shipwrecked on the rock of England.'

'That is nonsense,' answered Mussolini. 'Napoleon fell, as you yourself have shown, because of the contradictions in his own character. At long last, that is what always leads to a man's downfall. He wanted to wear the imperial crown! He wanted to found a dynasty! As First Consul he was at the climax of his greatness. The decline began with the establishment of the empire. Beethoven was perfectly right when he withdrew the dedication of the *Eroica*. It was the wearing of the crown which continually entangled the Corsican in fresh wars. Compare him with Cromwell. The latter had a splendid idea: supreme power in the State, and no war!'

I had brought him to a point of outstanding importance.

'There can, then, be imperialism without an imperium?'

'There are half a dozen different kinds of imperialism. There is really no need for the blazons of empire. Indeed, they are dangerous. The more widely empire is diffused, the more does it forfeit its organic energy. All the same, the tendency towards imperialism is one of the elementary trends of human nature, an expression of the will to power. Nowadays we see the imperialism of the dollar; there is also a religious imperialism, and an artistic imperialism as well. In any case, these are tokens of the human vital energy. So long as a man lives, he is an imperialist. When he is dead, for him imperialism is over.'

At this moment Mussolini looked extraordinarily Napoleonic, reminding me of Lefèvre's engraving of 1815. But now the tension of his features relaxed, and in a quieter tone he continued:

'Naturally every imperium has its zenith. Since it is always the creation of exceptional men, it carries within it the seeds of its own decay. Like everything exceptional, it contains ephemeral elements. It may last one or two centuries, or no more than ten years. The will to power.'

'Is it to be kept going only by war?' I asked.

'Not only,' he answered. 'Of that there can be no question.' He became a little didactic. 'Thrones need wars for their maintenance, but dictatorships can sometimes get on without them. The power of a nation is the resultant of numerous elements, and these are not exclusively military. Still, I must admit that hitherto, as far as the general opinion is concerned, the position of a nation has greatly depended upon its military strength. Down to the present time, people have regarded the capacity for war as the synthesis of all the national energies.'

'Till yesterday,' I interpolated. 'But what about tomorrow?'

'Tomorrow?' he reiterated sceptically. 'It is true that capacity for war-making is no longer a dependable criterion of power. For tomorrow, therefore, there is need of some sort of international authority. At least the unification of a continent. Now that the unity of States has been achieved, an attempt will be made to achieve the unity of continents. But as far as Europe is concerned, that will be damnably difficult, since each nation has its own peculiar countenance, its own language, its own customs, its own types. For each nation, a certain percentage of these characteristics (*x* per cent, let us say) remains completely original, and this induces resistance to any sort of fusion. In America, no doubt, things are easier. There eight-and-forty States, in which the same language is spoken and whose history is so short, can maintain their union.'

'But surely,' I put in, 'each nation possesses *y* per cent of characteristics which are purely European?'

'This lies outside the power of each nation. Napoleon wanted to establish unity in Europe. The unification of Europe was his leading ambition. To-day such a unification has perhaps become possible, but even then only on the ideal plane, as Charlemagne or Charles V tried to bring it about, from the Atlantic Ocean to the Urals.'

'Or, maybe, only to the Vistula?'

'Yes, maybe, only to the Vistula.'

'Is it your idea that such a Europe would be under fascist leadership?'

'What is leadership?' he countered. 'Here in Italy our fascism is what it is. Perhaps it contains certain elements which other countries might adopt.'

'I always find you more moderate than most fascists,' said I. 'You would be amazed if you knew what a foreigner in Rome has to listen to. Perhaps it was the same thing under Napoleon at the climax of his career. Apropos, can you explain to me why the Emperor never became completely wedded to his capital, why he always remained le fiancé de Paris?'

Mussolini smiled, and began his reply in French:

'*Ses manières n'étaient pas très parisiennes.* Perhaps there was a brutal strain in him. Moreover he had many opponents. The Jacobins were against him because he had crushed the revolution; the legitimates, because he was a usurper; the religious-minded, because of his contest with the papacy. It was only the common folk who loved him. They had plenty to eat under his regime, and they are more impressed by fame than are the educated classes. You must remember that fame is a matter, not of logic, but of sentiment.'

'You speak sympathetically of Napoleon! It would seem that your respect for him has not diminished during your own tenure of power, in which you have become enabled to understand his situation from personal experience.'

'No, on the contrary, my respect for him has increased.'

'When he was still a youthful general, he said that an empty throne always tempted him to take his seat upon it. What do you think of that?'

Mussolini opened his eyes wide, as he does when in an ironical mood, but at the same time he smiled.

'Since the days when Napoleon was emperor,' he said, 'thrones have become much less alluring than they were.'

'True enough,' I replied. 'Nobody wants to be a king nowadays. When, a little while ago, I said to King Fuad of Egypt, "Kings must be loved, but dictators dreaded," he exclaimed, "How I should like to be a dictator!" Does history give any record of a usurper who was loved?'

Mussolini, whose changes of countenance always foreshadow his answers (unless he wants to conceal his thoughts), became earnest of mien once more. His expression of sustained energy relaxed, so that he looked younger than usual. After a pause, and even then hesitatingly, he rejoined:

'Julius Caesar, perhaps. The assassination of Caesar was a misfortune for mankind.' He added softly: 'I love Caesar. He was unique in that he combined the will of the warrior with the genius of the sage. At bottom he was a philosopher who saw everything *sub specie eternitatis*. It is true that he had a passion for fame, but his ambition did not cut him off from human kind.'

'After all, then, a dictator can be loved?'

'Yes,' answered Mussolini with renewed decisiveness. 'Provided that the masses fear him at the same time. The crowd loves strong men. The crowd is like a woman.'

'In my study of great careers,' I began, 'I have always made it my business to note in one particular respect the behaviour of men who have left the circle in which they grew up – how they have comported themselves as between their relationship to their old friends, on the one hand, and the loneliness which their new position has forced upon them, on the other. Herein there is disclosed the character, or part of it. What does the man do in such a conflict between human kindliness and authority? Does he not naturally tend to pass from the tropics to the North Pole? Tell me what happens when one of your sometime comrades enters this hall! How do you make shift without reopening one of the old discussions? You once wrote (and it is a fine saying): "We are strong because we have no friends."'

Mussolini made no movement, no gesture, as he sat opposite me; but there was something unusual, something almost childlike, in his expression which disclosed to me that the topic I had mooted had stirred him profoundly. When, at length, he answered, it was plain to me that his words were colder than his feelings, and that he was not disclosing all his sentiments or all his thoughts.

'I cannot have any friends. I have no friends. First of all, because of my temperament; secondly, because of my view of human beings. That is why I avoid both intimacy and discussion. If an old friend comes to see me, the interview is distressing to us both, and does not last long. Only from a distance do I follow the careers of my former comrades.'

'What happens when those who have been friends become foes, and when such a one calumniates you?' I asked, remembering my personal experiences. 'Which among your old friends have remained most faithful to you? Are there any former friends whose onslaughts are still a distress to you?'

He remained unmoved.

'If those who were once my friends have become my enemies, what concerns me to know is whether they are my enemies in public life; if so, I fight them. Otherwise they do not interest me. When some former collaborators attacked me in the press, declaring that I had embezzled money intended for Fiume, this certainly intensified my misanthropy. The most loyal of my friends are enshrined in my heart, but in general they keep their distance. Precisely because they are loyal! They are persons who do not seek profit or advancement, and only on rare occasions do they visit me here – just for a moment.'

'Would you trust your life to these, or to any one else?' I asked. 'You have made some of them life members of the Gran Consiglio.'

'Three, and only for three years,' he said drily.

'Such being now your position, I am led to ask when you felt yourself most lonely. Was it in youth, as in D'Annunzio's case; or when you were outwardly in close contact with your party comrades; or to-day?'

'To-day,' he answered without a moment's hesitation. 'But still,' he went on after a pause, 'even in earlier times no one exerted any influence upon me. Fundamentally I have always been alone. Besides, to-day, though not in prison, I am all the more a prisoner.'

'How can you say that?' I inquired with considerable heat. 'No one in the world has less ground for making the statement!'

'Why?' he asked, his attention riveted by my excitement.

'Because there is no one in the world who can act more freely than you!' I rejoined.

He made a conciliatory gesture and replied:

'Please don't think that I am inclined to quarrel with my fate. Still, to a degree I stand by what I said just now. Contact with ordinary human affairs, an impromptu life amid the crowd – to me, in my position, these things are forbidden.'

'You have only to go out for a walk!'

'I should have to wear a mask,' he answered. 'Once when – unmasked – I made my way along the Via Tritone, I was speedily surrounded by a mob of three hundred persons, so that I could not advance a step. Still, I do not find my solitude irksome.'

'If loneliness is agreeable to you,' said I, 'how do you find it possible to put up with the multitude of faces you have to look at here day after day?'

'In this way,' he replied, 'that I merely see in them what they say to me. I do not let them come into contact with my inmost being. I am no more moved by them than by this table and these papers that lie on it. Among them all, I preserve my loneliness untouched.'

'In that case,' said I, 'are you not afraid of losing your mental balance? Do you not recall how the reigning Caesar would, while enjoying a triumph in the Forum, have with him in his chariot a slave whose business it was to remind him continually of the nullity of all things?'

'Of course I remember. The young fellow had to keep the emperor in mind of the fact that he was a man and not a god. But nowadays that sort of thing is needless. For my part, at any rate, I have never had any inclination to fancy myself a god, but have always been keenly aware that I am a mortal man, with all the weaknesses and passions proper to mortality.'

He spoke with obvious emotion, and then went on in a calmer tone:

'You are perpetually hinting at the danger that may result from the lack of an opposition. This danger would be actual if we lived in quiet times. But to-day the opposition is embodied in the problems that have to be solved, in the moral and economic problems that perpetually press for solution. These suffice to prevent a ruler from going to sleep! Furthermore, I create an opposition within myself!'

'I seem to be listening to Lord Byron,' said I.

'I often read both Byron and Leopardi. Then, when I have had enough of human beings, I go for a voyage. If I could do whatever I liked, I should always be at sea. When that is impossible, I content myself with animals. Their mental life approximates to that of man, and yet they don't want to get anything out of him: horses, dogs, and my favourite the cat. Or else I watch wild animals. They embody the elemental forces of nature!'

This avowal seemed to me so misanthropical that I asked Mussolini whether he thought a ruler needed to be inspired rather with contempt for mankind than with kindly feelings.

'On the contrary,' he said with emphasis. 'One needs ninety-nine per cent of kindliness and only one per cent of contempt.'

The statement, from him, surprised me, and to make sure that I was not misunderstanding him I asked him once more: 'You really think, then, that your fellow human beings deserve sympathy rather than contempt?'

He regarded me with the inscrutable expression which is so common to him, and said softly:

'More sympathy, more compassion; much more compassion.'

This utterance reminded me that, when reading Mussolini's speeches, I had more than once been surprised by what seemed to me a parade of altruism. Why should he, the condottiere, refer with so much insistence to the interests of the community? I was led to ask him:

'Again and again, in exceedingly well-turned phrases, you have declared an increase of your own personality to be your aim in life, saying, "I want to make my existence a masterpiece," or, "I want to make my life dramatically effective." Sometimes you have quoted Nietzsche's motto, "Live dangerously!" How, then, can a man with so proud a nature write: "My chief aim is to promote the public interest"? Is there not a contradiction here?'

He was unmoved.

'I see no contradiction,' he replied. 'It is perfectly logical. The interest of the community is a dramatic affair. By serving it, therefore, I multiply my own life.'

I was taken aback and could find no effective repartee, but I quoted to him his own words: '"I have always had an altruistic outlook on life."'

'Unquestionably,' said he. 'No one can cut himself adrift from mankind. There you have something concrete – the humanity of the race from whose loins I sprang.'

'The Latin race,' I interrupted; 'that includes the French.'

'I have already declared, in the course of one of these conversations, that there is no such thing as a pure race! The belief that there is, is an illusion of the mind, a feeling. But does it exist any the less for that?'

'If so,' said I, 'a man could choose a race for himself.'

'Certainly.'

'Well, I have chosen the Mediterranean, and here I have a formidable ally in Nietzsche.'

The name aroused an association in his mind and, speaking in German, he quoted the proudest of Nietzsche's utterances: 'Do I seem to strive for happiness? I strive on behalf of my work!'

I pointed out that this idea really derived from Goethe, and I asked him whether he shared Goethe's notion that character is moulded by the blows of fate.

He nodded assent: 'It is to the crises I have had to pass through and to the difficulties I have had to surmount that I owe what I am. Because of that, one must always stake one's all.'

'Therewith you run the risk of destroying yourself and your work by taking needless risks.'

'Life has its price,' he answered confidently. 'You cannot live without risk. This very day I went into battle once more.'

'If you were consistent in that view, you would not seek to protect yourself,' I said.

'I don't,' he rejoined.

'What!' I exclaimed, 'Do you not recognize that again and again some one of your enemies risks his own life in the hope of depriving you of yours?'

'Oh, I understand what you are driving at. I know, too, the rumours that are current. It is said that I am watched over by a thousand policemen, and that every night I sleep in some new place. Yet in actual fact I sleep night after night

in the Villa Torlonia, and I drive or ride whenever and whithersoever fancy
seizes me. If I were to be continually thinking about my own safety, I should
feel humiliated.'

'Tell me,' I said in conclusion, 'what part does the desire for fame play in
your life? Is not that desire the strongest motive for a ruler? Is not fame the
only way of escaping death? Has not fame been your goal since you were a boy?
Has not all your work been animated by the desire for fame?'

Mussolini was imperturbable.

'Fame did not loom before me in boyhood,' he said; 'and I do not agree with
you that the desire for fame is the strongest of motives. In this respect you are
right, that it is some consolation to feel that one will not wholly die. Never has
my work been exclusively guided by the wish for fame. Immortality is the hall-
mark of fame.' He made a sweeping gesture towards a remote and uncontrollable
future, and added:

'But that comes – afterwards.'

•

JOSEPH STALIN

Interviewed by Emil Ludwig
Leaders of Europe, 1934

Joseph Vissarionovich Stalin (1879–1953), the leader of the USSR from 1924
until his death, was born in Georgia, the son of a cobbler named Dzhugashvili.
He was expelled from the Tiflis Theological Seminary because he had joined the
(Marxist) Social Democratic party. The authorities sent him to Siberia, but he
escaped and became a professional revolutionary, allying himself with Lenin. In
1912 he went to St Petersburg and was co-opted to the Bolshevik Central
Committee. Having taken the name Stalin (which means 'Man of Steel'), he was
arrested for the sixth time and again sent to Siberia, where he remained until
1917. With the 1917 Revolution, he joined the editorial board of the party
paper, *Pravda*, and when the Bolsheviks gained power later that year he was
appointed people's commissar of nationalities and a member of the politburo.
During the Russian Civil War (1918–20) he organized the Red 'terror' in
Tsaritsin (later to be named Stalingrad). In 1922 he was made general secretary
to the Central Committee and although Lenin, who died in 1924, had urged in
his testament that Stalin be dismissed because of his arbitrary conduct in
suppressing the short-lived independence of his native Georgia, Stalin succeeded
to the leadership. Thereafter, he outmanoeuvred his rivals Bukharin, Kamenev,
and Zonoviev, and drove Trotsky into exile (in 1928). At the same time
he introduced Five Year Plans of thrusting industrialization, and forcibly

collectivized Soviet agriculture, persecuting the *kulaks*, 10 million of whom
were either executed or allowed to starve to death. The 1930s were a period of
brutal repression in which Stalin's political rivals were forced to confess crimes
against the state, subjected to show trials and subsequently executed, while the
intelligentsia and the Red Army were purged. Stalin's foreign policy was based
on the need to contain Germany, but when he failed to secure alliances with the
Western powers he switched to making a non-aggression pact with Hitler
instead. Nonetheless, Germany invaded the Soviet Union in 1941 and some 20
million Soviet citizens died during the next four years. At the Teheran and
Yalta conferences, Stalin negotiated the concession from the Western powers of
a Soviet sphere of influence in Eastern Europe. Military conquest reinforced
this claim and an 'iron curtain' fell across Europe, leaving Stalin a modern
emperor.

When a visitor enters the inner courtyard of the Kremlin, which is like an
elevated fortress in the middle of the Bolshevic metropolis, he is greeted by
Napoleon. Thousands of cannons with their breaches turned towards the old
red battlements, together with the openings in the walls and the towers, are like
a thousand iron mouths that challenge the stranger. And each is marked with
the imperial N. The guard that stands at the old drawbridge simply asks the
visitor's name and the soldier by his side compares it with his book to see if it is
the same name as that which has been telephoned. A passport is not demanded.
It seemed to me that almost anybody who had laid a plan for the assassination
of the chief personalities in the Kremlin could very simply gain an entrance. At
the gate of the building where the Government of the Soviet Union has its
headquarters one is again asked the name. It is in this same building that Stalin
has his office as General Secretary of the Communist Party. Here we have
another instance of how these two powers are welded together even though the
Bolshevics so often deny this, just as the King of Prussia tried to distinguish
between himself in that capacity and as Emperor of Germany in the last tragic
moments of his rule. The truth is that in this office nine men of the Bolshevic
Party decide everything. Here the ministers make their speeches and from here
they take their orders.
    The three or four rooms and the corridors that we passed through were quite
simple but efficiently furnished as offices. A carpet with wide red borders leads
to Stalin's room. He received us there immediately. My companion was a young
journalist who speaks several languages excellently and translates very precisely.
Stalin and Mustapha Kemal are the only men with whom I have had to
converse through the medium of an interpreter. The room which we entered
was long and at the far end of it a medium-sized man in a light brown jacket
stood up from his chair. He was dressed with painful neatness, just as the room
was arranged with the hygienic accuracy of a doctor's consulting room. A large

table stood in the middle, as in an ordinary board-room, with plain water carafes and glasses and large ashtrays. Everything was in apple-pie order. The walls were coloured dark green. Pictures of Lenin and Marx and several other people unknown to me hung there, but they were all just enlarged photographs. Stalin's desk was also in perfect order and on it was a photograph of Lenin, beside four or five telephone apparatuses, such as one finds in all these government offices.

'Good evening,' I said, in stumbling Russian. He smiled and seemed somewhat embarrassed but he was extremely courteous and began by offering me a cigarette. He assured me that I was at full liberty to say what I liked and to ask whatever questions I liked and that he had an hour-and-a-half free. But when I drew out my watch at the end of the time he made a prohibitive gesture and kept us for another half-hour. A certain degree of embarrassment is as graceful in a man of power as it is in a beautiful woman. In the case of Stalin it did not surprise me at all because he scarcely ever sees people from the West. None of the present ambassadors or envoys, and scarcely any of the great experts, have ever seen him. The only foreigner who has free access to him is little old Cooper, the American hydraulic engineer, who is constructing the cofferdam on the Dnieper. Though my interpreter holds an important position in the Bolshevic Press organizations, he had never seen Stalin before. Since he had to speak constantly through the medium of the interpreter, Stalin was looking away from me practically all the time and for the whole two hours he kept on drawing figures on a piece of paper. With a red pencil he drew red circles and arabesques and wrote numbers. He never turned the pencil round though at the other end it was blue. During the course of our conversation he filled many sheets of paper with red drawings and from time to time folded them and tore them in pieces. The result was that I managed to get his glance straight into my face only for a few seconds and thus I beheld 'the great betrayer of mankind'. His look was dour and the expression veiled. But it was not the glance of a misanthropist. It was the glance rather of a man who has grown suspicious of his fellow-men from long experience and has lived a very lonely life. Though it may happen only seldom, I can imagine this man suddenly rising up and advancing slowly to his opponent and deliberately looking him straight in the eye. For, as a matter of fact, this plodding man is capable of sudden surprise. In 1919 or 1920 he unexpectedly got a divorce and married the sixteen-year-old daughter of a Georgian friend.

In the long pauses that were necessary for translation and re-translation I had a very good opportunity for observing his movements, especially as he speaks so slowly. Such pauses enable an interviewer to introduce a change of theme in the conversation and thus the better to search the mind of his interlocutor. Stalin's habit of sitting absolutely immobile and of scarcely ever emphasizing a word with a gesture made this all the easier. When I am conversing with anybody I have a habit of standing up and walking about. If I had done it here it might have been considered strange.

What completed the picture of Stalin, as I have already described it, was the heavy and muffled tone of his voice. It was the kind of voice that could never speak the word of destiny 'I Will' with fiery emotion. He could only let the syllables fall like heavy hammer blows. The chief impression that I got of him was that of a protector. Stalin is a man before whose name many men and women have quaked, but one could never imagine a child or an animal doing so. In a former age such a man would have been called the father of his country.

Since the stranger arriving in the Kremlin is always looked upon as an enemy, I decided to take that attitude in my questions. Stalin gave me an exhaustive answer each time and I shall not shorten it here. He spoke in short clear sentences, not as a man who is accustomed to simplify things before public audiences, but as a logical and constructive thinker whose mind works slowly and without the slightest emotion. This man who is now the exponent of the whole Moscow ideology struck me as a typical disciple of Hegel. In parenthesis, I may here call attention to the curious fact that so many foreign dictators have been educated by the Germans. Marx is the apostle in Russia, Nietzsche in Italy, and Hegel in both countries. Stalin takes the point of an argument immediately, lays it on the table, as it were, talks around it and then comes close to it and carefully brings historical data and statistical percentages to bear on it. When he spoke he seemed to me to be absolutely a contradiction of Prince Bülow. He scarcely ever gave me the merely official answer, the experience which I have had with most of the other Communists.

Although he could not have been prepared for most of my questions and although he has not had the experience of our European ministers of State who are asked the same questions week after week, and although he knew that I should publish his answers to the world, he did not correct himself once. He had all the historical data and names at his finger tips. He did not ask for any copy of what my interpreter wrote down and he did not ask for any corrections to be made. I had never before experienced the same kind of self-confidence. In all my conversations with other leaders, I have not taken down what they have said at the moment but have recorded it afterwards and submitted it to them for authorization. But here I took the stenographical text as it was taken down by another person and when I examined it I could not find the slightest omission and yet nothing had been bettered. Outside of one mere private question, he did not ask me to tone down anything or omit this or that. When I recall to mind the habits of our poor ministers, when they are preparing a parliamentary speech or having an interview corrected by the head of their press bureau, I am filled with respect for the shoe-maker's son from the Caucasus. He has never had anything like a systematic education and he is today the absolute ruler of such a large section of mankind.

'You have led a life of a conspirator for such a long time,' I said, 'and do you now think that, under your present rule, illegal agitation is no longer possible?'

'It is possible, at least to some extent.'

'Is the fear of this possibility the reason why you are still governing with so much severity, fifteen years after the revolution?'

'No. I will illustrate the chief reason for this by giving a few historical examples. When the Bolshevics came to power they were soft and easy with their enemies. At that time, for example, the Menshevics (moderate Socialists) had their lawful newspapers and also the Social Revolutionaries. Even the military cadets had their newspapers. When the white-haired General Krasnow marched upon Leningrad and was arrested by us, under the military law he should have been shot or at least imprisoned, but we set him free on his word of honour. Afterwards it became clear that with this policy we were undermining the very system that we were endeavouring to construct. We had begun by making a mistake. Leniency towards such a power was a crime against the working classes. That soon became apparent. The Social Revolutionaries of the right and the Menshevics, with Bogdanow and others, then organized the Junker revolt and fought against the Soviets for two years. Mamontow joined them. We soon saw that behind these agents stood the great Powers of the West and the Japanese. Then we realized that the only way to get ahead was by the policy of absolute severity and intransigence. The illegal campaigns which we ourselves had carried on in the old days were naturally valuable to us as an experience, but that was not the decisive factor.'

'This policy of cruelty,' I said, 'seems to have aroused a very widespread fear. In this country I have the impression that everybody is afraid and that your great experiment could succeed only among this long-suffering nation that has been trained to obedience.'

'You are mistaken,' said Stalin, 'but your mistake is general. Do you think it possible to hold power for fourteen years merely by intimidating the people? Impossible. The Czars knew best how to rule by intimidation. It is an old experiment in Europe; and the French Bourgeoisie supported the Czars in their policy of intimidation against the people. What came of it? Nothing.'

'But it maintained the Romanovs in power for three hundred years,' I replied.

'Yes, but how many times was that power not shaken by insurrections? To forget the older days, recall only the revolt of 1905. Fear is in the first instance a question of the mechanism of administration. You can arouse fear for one or two years and through it, or at least partly through it, you can rule for that time. But you cannot rule the peasants by fear. Secondly, the peasants and the working classes in the Soviet Union are by no means so timid and long-suffering as you think. You believe that our people are timid and lazy. That is an antiquated idea. It was believed in formerly, because the landed gentry used to go to Paris to spend their money there and do nothing. From this arose an impression of so-called Russian laziness. People thought that the peasants were easily frightened and made obedient. That was a mistake. And it was a three-fold mistake in regard to the workers. Never again will the workers endure the rule of one man. Men who have reached the highest pinnacles of fame were lost the moment they lost touch with the masses. Plechanow had great authority in his hands but when he became mixed up in politics he quickly forgot the masses. Trotsky was a man of great authority, but not of such high standing as Plechanow, and now he is forgotten. If he is casually remembered it is with a feeling of irritation.' (At that point he sketched something like a ship with his red pencil.)

I did not intend to mention Trotsky to Stalin, but since he himself had broached the subject, I asked: 'Is the feeling against Trotsky general?'

'If you take the active workers, nine-tenths speak bitterly of Trotsky.'

There was a short pause during which Stalin laughed quietly and then took up the thread of the question again: 'You cannot maintain that people may be ruled for a long time merely by intimidation. I understand your scepticism. There is a small section of the people which is really afraid. It is an unimportant part of the peasant body. That part is represented by the *kulaks*. They do not fear anything like the intimidation of the reign of terror but they fear the other section of the peasant population. This is a hang-over from the earlier class system. Among the middle-classes, for example, and especially the professional classes, there is something of the same kind of fear, because these latter had special privileges under the old régime. Moreover, there are traders and a certain section of the peasants that still retain the old liking for the middle-class.

'But if you take the progressive peasants and workers not more than fifteen per cent are sceptical of the Soviet power, or are silent from fear or are waiting for the moment when they can undermine the Bolshevic State. On the other hand, about eighty-five per cent of the more or less active people would urge us further than we want to go. We often have to put on the brakes. They would like to stamp out the last remnants of the intelligentsia. But we would not permit that. In the whole history of the world there never was a power that was supported by nine-tenths of the population, as the Soviet power is supported. That is the reason for our success in putting our ideas into practice. If we ruled only by fear not a man would have stood by us. And the working classes would have destroyed any power that attempted to continue to rule by fear. Workers who have made three revolutions have had some practice in overthrowing governments. They would not endure such a mockery of government as one merely based on fear.'

'When I hear repeatedly about the power of the masses,' I said, 'I am surprised at the hero worship that is more prevalent here than anywhere else, for this is the last place that one would logically expect to find it. Your materialistic conception of history, which is what separates me personally from you – for I hold that men make history – should prevent leaders and symbols from being shown in the form of statues and pictures on the street. You are the very people who, logically, ought not to revere the Unknown Soldier or any other individual. Now how can you explain that contradiction?'

'You are mistaken. Read that part of Marx where he speaks of the poverty of philosophy.'

Above Stalin's head hung a portrait of the white-haired Karl Marx. And every time that the conversation turned to the great Socialist, I had to look at the portrait.

'There,' continued Stalin, 'you will find that men make history. But not in the way that your fancy suggests. Men make history rather in their reactions to the definite circumstances in which they find themselves placed. Every generation has a new set of circumstances to face. In general it can be said that great men are of value only in so far as they are able to deal with the circumstances of their environment. Otherwise they are Don Quixotes. According to Marx himself, one should never contrast men and circumstances. As far as my opinion goes, it is history that makes men. We have been studying Marx for thirty years.'

'And our professors interpret him differently,' I suggested.

'That is because they try to popularize Marxism. He has himself never denied the importance of the rôle of the hero. It is in fact very great.'

'May I therefore conclude that here in Moscow also one man rules and not the council. I see sixteen chairs around the table.'

Stalin looked at the chairs: 'The individual does not decide. In every council there are people whose views must be taken into account but wrong views also exist. We have had experience of three revolutions and we know that out of one hundred decisions made by individuals ninety are one-sided. Our leading organ is the Central Committee of the Party and it has seventy members. Among these seventy members are some of our most capable industrialists and our co-operatives and our best tradesmen, also some of our ablest authorities on agriculture and co-operative as well as individual farming, finally some men who have a first-class knowledge of how to deal with the various nationalities that make up the Soviet Union. This is the Areopagus in which the wisdom of the party is centred. It gives the individual the possibility of correcting his partial prejudices. Each contributes his own experience for the general benefit of the Committee. Without this method very many mistakes would be made. Since each person takes his part in the deliberations our decisions are more or less correct.'

'So you refuse to be a dictator,' I said. 'I have found these same tactics are used by all dictators. In Europe you are painted as the bloodthirsty Czar or the aristocratic freebooter from Georgia.'

He laughed in a genial way and blinked at me as I continued: 'Since there are stories going around of bank robberies and other burglaries which you organized as a youth in order to help the party, or at least countenanced, I should like to know how much of all these we are to believe.'

The peasant instinct in Stalin now came to the fore. He went across to his writing-desk and brought me a pamphlet of about twenty pages which contained his biographical data in Russian but naturally nothing in answer to my question.

'There you will find everything,' he said, obviously pleased at this debonair way of giving a negative answer. I began to laugh and asked: 'Tell me if you do not feel yourself to be the follower of Stenka Rasin, the noble rapparee whose legendary deeds I have heard recounted on the Volga, where they were done.'

He returned to his constructive logical way of talking.

'We Bolshevics,' he said, 'apart entirely from our national origin, have always been interested in personalities like Bolotnikow, Stenka Rasin, Pugàtschew, because they emerged spontaneously from the first elementary uprising of the peasantry against the oppressor. It is interesting for us to study the first signs of that awakening. Historical allegories, however, are out of the question; and we have not idealized Stenka Rasin. Individual uprisings, even when organized with the rapacity that characterized these three leaders I have mentioned, lead to nothing. A peasant revolution can attain its ends only when it is united with the revolution of the workers and led by the latter. Only a revolution integrally organized and welded together in all its parts can lead to its goal. This you cannot have among the peasants because they alone form an independent class. Moreover, the three insurrectionary leaders that I have mentioned were all Czarists. They were against the landed gentry but *for our good Czar*. That was their battle cry.'

The hands of the watch that I had placed before me on the table showed that our time was growing short. I put another question in an innocent way, as if I did not know about America in Russia: 'Everywhere in this country,' I said, 'I find that America is respected. How is it possible that a State whose aim is to overthrow capitalism can pay its respects to a country in which capitalism has reached its highest grade of development?'

Without a moment's pause, Stalin gave a magnificent answer: 'You are overstating things. Here there is no general respect for everything that is American. There is only a respect for the American sense of practicality in everything, in industry, in literature and in business; but we never forget that it is a capitalist land. They are sound people, or at least there are many sound people there, sound in mind as well as in body, sound in their whole attitude towards work and towards everyday facts. The practical business side of American life and its simplicity has our admiration. In spite of its capitalistic character, the customs which are in vogue throughout the industrial and economic life of America are more democratic than in any European country, for in Europe the influence of the aristocracy is not yet obliterated.'

'You do not know how true that is,' I said in an undertone. But the interpreter heard me and translated it for Stalin.

'Yes, I know,' answered Stalin, 'in spite of the fact that the feudal form of government has been wiped out in many European lands, the feudal spirit still remains and is powerful. From the aristocratic environment, many technicians and specialists carry on the tradition of their origin. That cannot be said of America. It is a land of colonists without a landed gentry or an aristocracy, and hence the simple vigour of its customs. In industry and business they are simple, and our workmen who have become leaders of industry here notice that fact immediately when they go to America. There it is difficult to distinguish between the engineer and the simple workman while they are at their job.'

Here Stalin had formulated with simplicity and sureness of insight the parallel between those two utterly different nations, America and Russia. All at once and without any signs of making a transition and before I could put a question, he said:

'But if we feel friendly towards any one nation as a whole, or towards a majority in any nation, our friendship is for the Germans. There is no comparison between this friendship and our kindly feelings for America.'

'And why the Germans?'

'It is a fact.'

Stalin uttered these four words with such conclusive emphasis that he seemed to forestall any further questions on that point, but the spontaneous expression of his sympathy had so much behind it that I did not wish to lose the opportunity. Without mentioning the World Revolution, I said: 'I think you are deceiving yourself in your hopes of Germany. The Germans love order more than freedom. That is why we have had no revolutions, or at least, no revolutions that were successful.'

'As to the past you are right in what you say about the Germans,' he answered. 'When I was living in Berlin in 1907 I was often amused by the spirit of obedience shown by our German friends. I was told that once the leaders of the party had announced a demonstration to which the communists from the various parts of Berlin were to come at a given hour. About two hundred had come from one suburb. When they reached the railway gate where the tickets had to be handed over the ticket collector was not there. The Russians who were with them urged them to pass through the open gate as they all had their railway tickets. But they would not budge an inch and it looked as if they would have remained there for hours if the ticket collector had not come. When I was in Dresden and Chemnitz between 1905 and 1907 I found the law was respected there like frost or thunder or some other force of nature against which the will of man is of no avail. In Vienna, in 1912, when I went with my Russian friends into the park at Schoenbrunn, we noticed the sign *Verboten* everywhere, but we were not used to such things and we must have paid a fine of a crown apiece over twenty times for the pleasure of having broken the law. Our German friends laughed at us for the pleasure we had taken in that form of amusement. So it was in those days.

'But today? Where is the German sense of order today? Where is the respect for the law? The National Socialists break the law whenever they find it in their way. They shoot and bludgeon all round. In Germany today workers go out of the city and dig up other people's potatoes. Everything is changed since the old days.' He was silent. In that one reply he had shown himself a disciple of Hegel and I said to him:

'As far as I know you were only a few months in Europe, whereas Lenin was there for twenty years. Which do you think was the better preparation for a revolutionary leadership – at home or abroad?' He neither answered yes nor no but gave a general explanation.

'For Lenin,' he said, 'I would make an exception. Very few of those who remained here in Russia kept themselves so closely in touch with what was happening here as Lenin did while he was abroad. I visited him several times abroad, in 1907, 1908 and 1912, and I generally found that he daily received sheaves of letters from Russian politicians and that he knew more of what was happening in Russia than people who actually lived here. And yet he looked upon it as a great misfortune that he had always to remain abroad. As regards the others, who remained in Russia and whose number was of course much greater, they certainly helped the movement excellently. The number of those abroad who helped the movement was only as one to two hundred in comparison with those who carried on the work at home. And in the Central Committee today, out of seventy members, there are only three or four who have been abroad.'

'But did you not highly appreciate the knowledge of Europe that Lenin had?'

'What do you understand by the word *Europe*? You know many of those who have sojourned as immigrants in Europe. Anybody who desires to study Europe can certainly do so better in Europe than outside of Europe. In this sense those of us who have been there only for a little while have certainly missed something. But that lack is of no decisive importance when we come to the question of acquiring a knowledge of European economics, industrial technique, the education and training that takes place in the centres of leadership, the whole range of literature, belles-lettres and science. All things else being equal, it would of course be better to study these in Europe itself; but the minus quantity here is not of striking significance. I know several comrades of ours who spent twenty years in Europe, somewhere or other in Charlottenburg, but you might put a concrete question to them about Germany and they could not give an answer.'

Somewhat later I brought the conversation round to the surprising change of front that communism had made in abandoning the old theory of equality and introducing piece-work in its place, thus giving the energetic worker a chance to earn more than his companion. 'We were astonished,' I concluded, 'when you yourself characterized equalization as the remains of middle-class prejudice.' Stalin answered: 'A completely socialized State where all receive the same amount of bread and meat, the same kind of clothes, the same products and exactly the same amount of each product – such a Socialism was not recognized by Marx. Marx merely says that so long as the classes are not entirely wiped out and so long as work has not become the object of desire – for now most people look upon it as a burden – there are many people who would like to have other people do more work than they. So long, then, as the distinction of class is not entirely obliterated, people will be paid according to their productive efficiency, each according to his capacity. That is the Marxist formula for the first stage of Socialism. When Socialism has reached the complete stage everyone will do what he is capable of doing and for the work which he has done he will be paid according to his needs. It should be perfectly clear that different people have different needs, great and small. Socialism has never denied the difference in personal tastes and needs either in kind or in extent. Read Marx's criticism of Stirner and the Gotha programme. Marx there attacks the principle of equalization. That is a part of primitive peasant psychology, the idea of equalization. It is not Socialistic. In the West they look upon the thing in such a primitive way that they imagine we want to divide up everything evenly. That is the theory of Babeuf. He never knew anything about scientific Socialism. Even Cromwell wanted to level everything.'

Although I thought him wrong in regard to Cromwell it was not my business to enter into a historical argument with Stalin. I preferred to revert to the problem of stories and legend-mongering and, since he had just asked whether the cigarette he had given me did not please me – for I had stopped smoking – I said:

'You are supposed to be against the creation of legends. And yet surely nothing has made you so popular as the legend that you always smoke a pipe.'

He laughed. 'You see how little need I have of it. This morning I left it at home.'

'But are you really against legends?'

'Not when they are folk-legends.'

'It is late. Will you kindly autograph this pamphlet you have given me?'

He nodded. But he seemed bewildered because he was not used to this European custom. 'Yes, of course, but what shall I write?'

'Your own name, and that of Herr Ludwig,' said the translator. His shyness at that moment attracted me to him very much. He raised the red pencil with which he had been drawing and wrote on the pamphlet. I counted three sheets of paper which were completely filled with his pictures. I took none of them away because I felt that some disciple of Freud would have taken them from me later on and made them the subject of an essay on calligraphy. I stood up and asked:

'Would you be surprised at a question?'

'Nothing that happens in Russia could surprise me,' he said.

'That frame of mind is international. In Germany also, nothing that might happen could surprise us. Do you believe in Destiny?'

He became very serious. He turned to me and looked me straight in the face. Then, after a tense pause he said: 'No, I don't believe in Destiny. That is simply a prejudice. It is a nonsensical idea.' He laughed in his dark muffled way and said in German, '*Schicksal, Schicksal.*' Then he reverted to his native language and said: 'Just as with the Greeks. They had their gods and goddesses who directed everything from above.'

'You have been through a hundred dangers,' I said; 'when you were banned and exiled, in revolutions and in wars. Is it merely an accident that you were not killed and that someone else is not in your place today?'

He was somewhat annoyed, but only for a moment. Then he said, in a clear, ringing voice:

'No accident, Herr Ludwig, no accident. Probably there were inner and outer causes that prevented my death. But it could have happened by accident that someone else might be sitting here and not I.'

And as if he wished to break through this dense and annoying cloud and get back to his Hegelian clarity, he said: 'Destiny is contrary to law. It is something mystic. In this mystical thing I do not believe. Of course there were causes why I came through all these dangers. It could not have happened merely by accident.'

Schicksal (Destiny, Fate)! The echoes of that mighty German word were still in my ears as we took our seats in the waiting motor car.

In this citadel the Czars lived and ruled, sometimes wielding a power that had not been arrived at by natural means And here Death found them. Everything around us gleamed sinister in the dusk – sinister and embattled. And here, the son of the Georgian peasant had laughed defiantly when the word *Destiny* was mentioned. The circle of cannons in the forecourt reflected the evening light in a dull sheen. But on each muzzle glittered brightly the letter *N*, embossed in gold – the superscription which a little corporal from a barren island had dared to stamp on the mouth of Death.

'What have you to do with Destiny?' Napoleon asked Goethe. 'Politics are *Destiny*.'

•

ROYAL SCOTT GULDEN

Interviewed by John L. Spivak
New Masses, 9 October 1934

Royal Scott Gulden, a member of the wealthy Gulden mustard-producing family, was secretary of the Order of '76, an anti-Semitic organization. According to Spivak, 'its membership included federal, state and city government officials' and cooperated 'with paid Hitler agents in the distribution of anti-Semitic propaganda'.

New Masses was founded by a group of Greenwich Village socialists in 1911 as a monthly magazine called, simply, *Masses*. A pacifist as well as socialist publication, it was banned during the First World War and its editors were prosecuted unsuccessfully for conspiracy against the government. It was revived in 1926 as *New Masses* by Michael Gold and Joseph Freeman and became more and more associated with the Communist Party line. It went weekly in 1934 and continued publication on that basis until 1948 when, after a temporary break, it merged with another title and changed its name to *Masses and Mainstream*. During the 1950s it published interviews with persons involved on both sides of the McCarthyite debate. John L. Spivak was a regular contributor of interview features and other articles to *New Masses* during the 1930s. His favourite subjects were anti-Semites and anti-Communists.

There is an air of mystery on the seventh floor of 139 East 57th Street, New York City. Well-dressed men and women enter and leave Room 703. Sometimes they carry briefcases and look intent and serious. To the observer who wanders onto this floor, Room 703, the entrance to a suite, is just another office in an office building, possibly a private office because there is no firm's or individual's name on the glass door. Those running this office do not want any names on their doors, they do not want too many people to know that this is the head-quarters of the secret society for spying on 'Jews and Communists', the Order of '76.

There are a wooden bench and several desks in Room 703. To the right as you enter are two more rooms, each with desks at which serious looking men sit studying papers; and to the left, Room 704, is another office, the one where the files are kept and where Royal Scott Gulden, of the mustard king family, acts as secretary of the espionage society and as director of spreading the 'hate the Jew' creed. It is an exclusive organization, this one on the seventh floor of the building. It takes into its membership only men and women in the 'higher strata' of the military, business and political 'worlds of the country'. They want to 'save America from falling into the hands of the Jews and the Communists'.

Gulden himself is a neatly dressed, middle aged man with graying temples, thinning hair and washed-out gray eyes. He was at his desk, heaped high with letters and clippings when I walked in. The two men with whom he was talking turned around quickly while all of them looked at me with a startled air. Strangers do not wander into these offices by accident. Gulden raised his eyes interrogatively, a pleasant smile spreading over his pale face.

'My name is Spivak – John L. Spivak of the *New Masses* –'

The two men with Gulden closed in on me almost automatically.

'The *New Masses*!' Gulden exclaimed. 'The *New Masses*! He's from the *New Masses*!'

He was addressing no one in particular. It was just the exclamations of a startled man who automatically keeps on talking until he can gather his wits.

'We're running a series of articles on the growth of anti-Semitism in this country. I find that your organization has established an espionage system among Jews and Communists and carries on anti-Semitic propaganda –'

'Well?' said Gulden coldly.

'I should like to interview you.'

One of the men beside me started to laugh.

'You seem to know all about it,' returned Gulden suavely. 'You don't have to interview me.' He turned to his desk.

'But I'd like to very much,' I assured him sweetly.

He raised his head and looked at me steadily for a moment.

'All right,' he said curtly. 'What do you want?'

'These gentlemen?' I nodded to the two men still standing beside me.

'You want to know everything, don't you?'

'I know one of them. This man is Eugene Daniels who is supposed to have thrown the stink bomb in the stock exchange, isn't he?'

Daniels smiled embarrassedly. The head of the secret espionage order bowed gracefully.

'Pardon me. Mr Daniels – Mr Spivak. This gentleman is Mr Hemple – Jonas Hemple. Now let's get down to business. I'm very busy. What do you want?'

'I just want to know why you believe in anti-Semitism.'

'I don't believe in anti-Semitism,' Gulden smiled. 'I don't believe in measles either, but we have them. I don't believe in poison but you get it. It's the same with the Jews. We've got them. Our main work is patriotic, chiefly against Communism. And when we find that Communism and Judaism are one, then we fight Judaism.'

The other men nodded. Mr Daniels launched on a long dissertation to assure me that he did not mind the Jews. I finally had to explain that it was Mr Gulden's views I was interested in. Mr Daniels left.

'How did you discover that Communism and Judaism are one?' I asked.

'Oh, we got a barrel of clippings . . .'

He rose to get a folder out of a file. I noticed a slight bulge on his right hip. I got up and patted it gently.

'What's this – a gat?'

Gulden turned upon me with a startled air. The mysterious and heavy set Mr Hemple stepped quickly to my side. Gulden returned to his desk without the folder.

'Yes, a gun,' he smiled, his washed-out gray eyes boring into me.

'What calibre?'

'Thirty-two, Smith and Wesson –'

He drew the revolver from its holster and placed it on his desk.

'You needn't be afraid,' he smiled assuringly. 'We don't hurt people – unless they hurt us,' he added significantly.

'Maybe I'd better hold it then,' I laughed.

Gulden smiled grimly. 'I think maybe we'd better put it in my desk.' He opened a drawer and deposited the pistol.

'Got a permit?'

He turned upon me irritably.

'Who the hell –'

'Got a permit?' I repeated.

'What the hell –'

'Let's see your permit!'

Gulden looked startled. Without further word he fished a billfold from his coat pocket and handed me his pistol permit: C 23609.

I don't know why this head of the espionage society should have obeyed my sharp tone unless men with guilty consciences always try to avoid trouble. The man seemed bewildered after he handed me his permit and for a space eyed me narrowly as though trying to decide whether he should answer questions or throw me bodily out of his office. Hemple broke the silence.

'Before we go on with this interview,' he said quietly, 'I'd like to ask you some questions about the *New Masses*. Where does it get the money to carry on and pay you?'

I leaned over secretively. 'Are we talking confidentially now?'

Both of them nodded quickly.

'Moscow gold,' I whispered. 'There's a special consignment of one million dollars a month for the *New Masses* to pay its large staff. I get one hundred thousand dollars a week for my work –'

'Come on! Cut the comedy!' Gulden interrupted. 'I don't know why I should answer questions, but I said I would, so let's get it over with. I want you to get this straight. We're not opposed to the Jews as Jews, but every Jew is a potential Communist, and both are breaking down the laws of the land.'

'How do you know Jews are breaking the law any more than the Gentiles?'

'The Protocols of Zion prove it.'

'I thought they were discredited.'

'I don't care whether they're discredited or not. I don't care whether they're authentic or not. All I know is that they outline a program for the Jews to capture the world and that program is working out accurately and rapidly. If the protocols are forgeries, how did they guess what was going to happen today? I believe the protocols are genuine and events are proving their authority!'

'You think there's a conspiracy by the Jews to capture the world?'

'I absolutely do!'

'And that these Jews are financing the Communists?'

'Certainly. They are financing the Third International and the Soviets. And as evidence I give the statement of Mr Schiff –'

'What Mr Schiff ?'

'The financier,' said Gulden vaguely. 'This Mr Schiff loaned two or four million dollars to the Bolsheviks. I don't know the exact amount, but it was up in the millions. He bragged about it, I understand.'

'Didn't Germany, whose government hates the Jews and the Communists as enthusiastically as you, also loan millions to the Bolsheviks – in the form of trade credits?'

'Yes, but they did it as a war measure –'

'They have extended credits since Hitler got into power.'

Gulden turned irritably from me.

'I don't care what the Germans do! That's their business! I'm interested in America.'

'We'll get to that –' I started to assure him, when Mr Hemple interrupted:

'The Jews must be destroyed. Even the Old Testament says the Jews must be destroyed. Jeremiah: 34: "Behold, I will command, saith the Lord, and I will make the cities of Judah a desolation without an inhabitant."'

'That seems to settle it,' I agreed. 'But what do you do for a living?'

'I smoke cigarettes and hang around here,' he returned, with obvious distaste.

I turned again to Gulden.

'It's dawning on me that you don't like the Jews. However, there are millions of them. What does your organization think should be done with them?'

'They ought to be made to stop spreading their Semitism in our faces. It's just a question of how long our patience will hold out.' He hesitated, shrugged his shoulders and added, 'I suppose history will repeat itself.'

'What do you mean by that?'

'I mean the good old fashioned pogroms!'

'Your organization is in favor of pogroms against the Jews?'

'If I say that, I'll be liable to arrest, I assume,' he said slowly. 'But I will say this: we're trying to prevent pogroms by preventing the Jews from driving people to start pogroms against them. We must defend ourselves. If the Jews keep sweeping on, then we will defend ourselves. You can depend upon one thing: if pogroms are forced on us, we will not run away!'

'Forced on you!' I looked at him with amazement. 'Are the Jews making pogroms against you?'

'Yes,' he said heatedly. 'The Jews are making economic pogroms against us. They are taking our businesses, our professions away – and if that continues pogroms will start. And when they do you can bet the Order of '76 will be there!'

He paused and added, 'And I don't care if you do say that in your Communist *New Masses*.'

'I'll quote you exactly. But tell me, don't you realize that when this story comes out Jews will eat their hot dogs without Gulden's mustard?'

Gulden looked grave for a moment.

'In times like these,' he said very seriously, 'we must all make sacrifices.'

Whereupon the interview continued:

'Are you connected in any way with the Nazi distributed anti-Semitic propaganda in this country? The Nazis, as you know, would like to take it out on the American Jews for their boycotts and protests against the way the Jews are treated in Germany.'

'We have no connection with the Nazis or the Germans in any way!' he exclaimed. 'We are purely an American organization –'

At that moment, with the perfect timing of a dramatic stage entrance, a well dressed man of about thirty, with a Teutonic face, opened the entrance door, stepped to the doorway of the private office where we sat, threw his shoulders back, brought his feet together with a click and raised his hand in the Nazi salute!

Gulden and Hemple looked at me. Both of them smiled embarrassedly. I couldn't help letting out a loud laugh. My two hosts did not stir, so I raised my hand in an answering salute!

'Heil Hitler!' I said dryly.

'He's from the *New Masses*,' Gulden explained quickly.

A flush spread over the newcomer's face. Without a word he turned and walked out as though fleeing from some pestilence. I looked at Gulden and started to laugh again.

'Tell me,' I said, still chuckling, 'isn't Col. Edwin Emerson, the Nazi agent in this country who first organized anti-Semitism here on a national scale, a member of your secret order?'

Gulden hesitated a moment and then nodded.

'And you have a member by the name of Sidney Brooks, who is with the Republican Senatorial and Congressional Campaign Committee –'

'I've scarcely met him since he joined,' he interrupted quickly.

'And you know that as a member of this organization he made mysterious trips to 17 Battery Place, where the German Consul General has his offices?'

'I don't know anything about that!'

Mr Gulden was on the defensive, his face a little paler than its normal hue. Mr Hemple had lost his superior smile and leaned forward, studying me with a puzzled air.

'And you knew that this Brooks is really the son of Col Emerson, and this Brooks brought Pelley of the Silver Shirts to you to merge –'

'We never merged with the Silver Shirts!' Gulden exclaimed. 'I can prove it to you! I'm even willing to let you see our correspondence with them. There is no such letter or document –'

'The letter regarding that is not in your file,' I assured him. 'I have it.'

Gulden's washed-out eyes seemed to water. A haggard look appeared in them. Hemple sighed audibly.

'You don't know anything about organizing an espionage system, do you?'

'I was with the Department of Justice –'

'That's fine – but you don't really know anything about organizing an espionage system, do you? What I'm driving at is that you got someone to direct this spy system for you, didn't you?'

'I did not!'

'Didn't Emerson send a man named Fritz Duquesne to you?'

Gulden did not answer.

'Did you ever meet Duquesne, the German war time spy?'

'Yes, he came up here one day.'

'What for?'

'Oh, I don't know. He just wanted to look me over, I guess.'

'Why should he want to look you over?'

'I don't know!' he exclaimed irritably. 'Who the hell are you to ask me all these questions!'

'Just an American citizen interested in finding out how much money you are getting from a foreign government to carry on anti-Semitic propaganda in this country!'

'I never got a nickel from the Germans! I wish I had!' he exclaimed. Gulden rose and began to pace nervously about the room. It was quite evident that the secrecy in which the society had veiled its movements was not so secret.

'How long did you spend with Duquesne?'

'Oh, maybe ten or fifteen minutes.'

'Actually you were with him for two hours, weren't you!'

Gulden looked worried. He did not answer.

'Isn't it rather strange that this hundred percent "patriotic" organization is so close with German spies and secret service men in this country in the dissemination of anti-Semitic propaganda?'

'We will cooperate with anyone who will help to drive out the Jewish pest!' he said vigorously.

'Then you are cooperating with the Nazis?'

'I didn't say that!'

'You have been distributing anti-Semitic propaganda smuggled off German ships, haven't you?'

'No!'

'When did you see Duquesne last?'

'I haven't seen him since he was here. I haven't any knowledge of him at all!'

Gulden swallowed and scratched the gray hairs on his temple.

'You've been in touch with him at 51 West 46th Street recently –'

'Forty-one –' Gulden said automatically, and caught himself.

'That's right,' I laughed.

Gulden's pale face had turned a purplish hue. He was livid with fury.

'If you want to talk to me any more, you'll have to show me authority or take me into court!' he shouted. 'I've said all I intend to say. I've said enough!'

'Yes, you've said enough,' I agreed and rose.

●

JOSEPH STALIN

Interviewed by H.G. Wells

The New Statesman and Nation, 27 October 1934

This interview appeared under the heading 'A Conversation Between Stalin and Wells'. Wells had visited Stalin on his second journey to the Soviet Union. Wells later admitted that he had approached the exercise with the prejudice that Stalin was 'a very reserved and self-centred fanatic, a despot without vices, a jealous monopolizer of power'. Its publication provoked a controversy among left-wing intellectuals, with George Bernard Shaw and Ernest Toller penning comments for the subsequent issue of the magazine.

Shaw appreciated the comedy of the occasion: 'Stalin listens attentively and seriously to Wells, taking in his pleadings exactly, and always hitting the nail precisely on the head in his reply. Wells does not listen to Stalin: he only waits with suffering patience to begin again when Stalin stops. He has not come to be instructed by Stalin, but to instruct him.' Shaw went on to describe Stalin (whom he had met) as 'a first-rate listener' and Wells as 'the worst listener in the world'. Ernest Toller took the line that, compared to fascist countries, intellectual freedom in the USSR was growing.

In the next issue after that, J.M. Keynes wrote in defence of Wells: 'My picture of that interview is of a man struggling with a gramophone. The reproduction is excellent, the record is word-perfect. And there is poor Wells feeling that he has his one chance to coax the needle off the record and hear it – vain hope – speak in human tones. Shaw mocks Wells's little pretences which show him pathetically conscious that one must be polite to one's host even when it is a gramophone.' In hindsight it is perhaps easier to agree with Keynes than with Shaw.

The interview was reprinted, along with the various comments and letters that ensued (a comment by Wells on Shaw's first comment, another piece by Shaw, two more replies from Wells, yet another broadside from Shaw, and a letter from Dora Russell attacking Wells and Keynes) in December 1934 as *Stalin-Wells Talk.*

WELLS: I am very much obliged to you, Mr Stalin, for agreeing to see me. I was in the United States recently. I had a long conversation with President Roosevelt and tried to ascertain what his leading ideas were. Now I have come to you to ask you what you are doing to change the world.

STALIN: Not so very much.

WELLS: I wander around the world as a common man and, as a common man, observe what is going on around me.

STALIN: Important public men like yourself are not 'common men'. Of course, history alone can show how important this or that public man has been; at all events you do not look at the world as a 'common man'.

WELLS: I am not pretending humility. What I mean is that I try to see the world through the eyes of the common man and not as a party politician or a responsible administrator. My visit to the United States excited my mind. The old financial world there is collapsing; the economic life of the country is being reorganized on new lines. Lenin said: 'We must learn to do business,' learn this from the capitalists. To-day the capitalists have to learn from you, to grasp the spirit of Socialism. It seems to me that what is taking place in the United States is a profound reorganization, the creation of planned, that is, socialist economy. You and Roosevelt begin from two different starting points. But is there not a relation in ideas, a kinship of ideas and needs, between Washington and Moscow? In Washington I was struck by the same thing that I see going on here; they are building offices, they are creating a number of new State regulation bodies, they are organizing a long-needed civil service. Their need, like yours, is directive ability.

STALIN: The United States is pursuing a different aim from that which we are pursuing in the USSR. The aim which the Americans are pursuing arose out of the economic troubles, out of the economic crisis. The Americans want to rid themselves of the crisis on the basis of private capitalist activity without changing the economic basis. They are trying to reduce to a minimum the ruin, the losses caused by the existing economic system. Here, however, as you know, in place of the old destroyed economic basis, an entirely different, a new economic basis has been created. Even if the Americans you mention partly achieve their aim, i.e., reduce these losses to a minimum, they will not destroy the roots of the anarchy which is inherent in the existing capitalist system. They are preserving the economic system which must inevitably lead, and cannot but lead, to anarchy in production. Thus, at best, it will be a matter, not of the reorganization of society, not of abolishing the old social system which gives rise to anarchy and crises, but of restricting certain of its bad features, restricting certain of its excesses. Subjectively, perhaps, these Americans think they are reorganizing society; objectively, however, they are preserving the present basis of society. That is why, objectively, there will be no reorganization of society.

Nor will there be planned economy. What is planned economy; what are some of its attributes? Planned economy tries to abolish unemployment. Let us suppose it is possible, while preserving the capitalist system, to reduce unemployment to a certain minimum. But surely, no capitalists would ever agree to the complete abolition of unemployment, to the abolition of the reserve army of unemployed, the purpose of which is to bring pressure on the labour market, to ensure a supply of cheap labour. Here you have one of the rents in the 'planned economy' of bourgeois society. Futhermore, planned economy pre-supposes increased output in those branches of industry which produce goods that the masses of the people need particularly. But you know that the expansion of production under capitalism takes place for entirely different motives, that capital flows into those branches of economy in which the rate of profit is highest. You will never compel a capitalist to incur loss to himself and agree to a lower rate of profit for the sake of satisfying the needs of the people. Without getting rid of the capitalists, without abolishing the principle of private property in the means of production, it is impossible to create planned economy.

WELLS: I agree with much of what you have said. But I would like to stress the point that if a country as a whole adopts the principle of planned economy, if the Government, gradually, step by step, begins consistently to apply this principle, the financial oligarchy will at last be abolished, and Socialism, in the Anglo-Saxon meaning of the word, will be brought about. The effect of the ideas of Roosevelt's 'new deal' is most powerful, and in my opinion they are socialist ideas. It seems to me that instead of stressing the antagonism between the two worlds, we should, in the present circumstances, strive to establish a common tongue for all the constructive forces.

STALIN: In speaking of the impossibility of realizing the principles of planned economy while preserving the economic basis of capitalism, I do not in the least desire to belittle the outstanding personal qualities of Roosevelt, his initiative, courage and determination. Undoubtedly Roosevelt stands out as one of the strongest figures among all the captains of the contemporary capitalist world. That is why I would like once again to emphasize the point that my conviction that planned economy is impossible under the conditions of capitalism does not mean that I have any doubts about the personal abilities, talent and courage of President Roosevelt. But if the circumstances are unfavourable, the most talented captain cannot reach the goal you refer to. Theoretically of course, the possibility of marching gradually, step by step, under the conditions of capitalism, towards the goal which you call Socialism in the Anglo-Saxon meaning of the word, is not precluded. But what will this 'Socialism' be? At best, bridling to some extent the most unbridled of individual representatives of capitalist profit, some increase in the application of the principle of regulation in national economy. That is all very well. But as soon as Roosevelt, or any other captain in the contemporary bourgeois world, proceeds to undertake something serious against the foundation of capitalism, he will inevitably suffer utter defeat. The banks, the industries, the large enterprises, the large farms are not in Roosevelt's hands. All these are private property. The railroads, the mercantile fleet, all these belong to private owners. And, finally, the army of skilled workers, the engineers, the technicians, these too are not at Roosevelt's command, they are at the command of the private owners; they all work for the private owners. We must not forget the functions of the State in the bourgeois world. The State is an institution that organizes the defence of the country, organizes the maintenance of 'order'; it is an apparatus for collecting taxes. The capitalist State does not deal much with economy in the strict sense of the word; the latter is not in the hands of the State. On the contrary, the State is in the hands of capitalist economy. That is why I fear that, in spite of all his energy and abilities, Roosevelt will not achieve the goal you mention, if indeed that is his goal. Perhaps, in the course of several generations it will be possible to approach this goal somewhat; but I personally think that even this is not very probable.

WELLS: Perhaps I believe more strongly in the economic interpretation of politics than you do. Huge forces striving for better organization, for the better functioning of the community, that is, for Socialism, have been brought into action by invention and modern science. Organization, and the regulation of individual action, have become mechanical necessities, irrespective of social theories. If we begin with the State control of the banks and then follow with the control of the heavy industries, of industry in general, of commerce, etc., such an all-embracing control will be equivalent to the State ownership of all branches of national economy. This will be the process of socialization. Socialism and individualism are not opposites like black and white. There are many intermediate stages between them. There is individualism that borders on brigandage, and there is discipline and organization that are the equivalent of Socialism. The introduction of planned economy depends, to a large degree, upon the organizers of economy, upon the skilled technical intelligentsia who, step by step, can be converted to the socialist principles of organization. And this is the most important thing. Because organization comes before Socialism. It is the more important fact. Without organization the socialist idea is a mere idea.

STALIN: There is not, nor should there be, an irreconcilable contrast between the individual and the collective, between the interests of the individual person and the interests of the collective. There should be no such contrast, because collectivism, Socialism, does not deny, but combines individual interests with the interests of the collective. Socialism cannot abstract itself from individual interests. Socialist society alone can most fully satisfy these personal interests. More than that; socialist society alone can firmly safeguard the interests of the individual. In this sense there is no irreconcilable contrast between 'individualism' and Socialism. But can we deny the contrast between classes, between the propertied class, the capitalist class, and the toiling class, the proletarian class? On the one hand we have the propertied class which owns the banks, the factories, the mines, transport, the plantations in colonies. These people see nothing but their own interests, their striving after profits. They do not submit to the will of the collective; they strive to subordinate every collective to their will. On the other hand, we have the class of the poor, the exploited class, which owns neither factories nor works, nor banks, which is compelled to live by selling its labour power to the capitalists and which lacks the opportunity to satisfy its most elementary requirements. How can such opposite interests and strivings be reconciled? As far as I know, Roosevelt has not succeeded in finding the path of conciliation between these interests. And it is impossible, as experience has shown. Incidentally, you know the situation in the United States better than I do, as I have never been there and I watch American affairs mainly from literature. But I have some experience in fighting for Socialism, and this experience tells me that if Roosevelt makes a real attempt to satisfy the interests of the proletarian class at the expense of the capitalist class, the latter will put another President in his place. The capitalists will say: Presidents come and Presidents go, but we go on for ever; if this or that President does not protect our interests, we shall find another. What can the President oppose to the will of the capitalist class?

WELLS: I object to this simplified classification of mankind into poor and rich. Of course, there is a category of people which strives only for profit. But are not these people regarded as nuisances in the West just as much as here? Are there not plenty of people in the West, for whom profit is not an end, who own a certain amount of wealth, who want to invest and obtain an income from this investment, but who do not regard this as their main object? They regard investment as an inconvenient necessity. Are there not plenty of capable and devoted engineers, organizers of economy, whose activities are stimulated by something other than profit? In my opinion there is a numerous class of capable people who admit that the present system is unsatisfactory and who are destined to play a great role in future capitalist society. During the past few years I have been much engaged in, and have thought of the need for conducting, propaganda in favour of Socialism and cosmopolitanism among wide circles of engineers, airmen, military-technical people, etc. It is useless approaching these circles with two-track class-war propaganda. These people understand the condition of the world. They understand that it is a bloody muddle, but they regard your simple class-war antagonism as nonsense.

STALIN: You object to the simplified classification of mankind into poor and rich. Of course there is a middle stratum; there is the technical intelligentsia that you have mentioned and among which there are very good and very honest people. Among them there are also dishonest and wicked people, there are all sorts of people among them. But first of all mankind is divided into rich and poor, into property owners and exploited; and to abstract oneself from this fundamental division and from the antagonism between poor and rich means abstracting oneself from the fundamental fact. I do not deny the existence of intermediate, middle, strata which either take the side of one or other of these two conflicting classes, or else take up a neutral or semi-neutral position in this struggle. But, I repeat, to abstract oneself from this fundamental division in society and from the fundamental struggle between the two main classes means ignoring facts. This struggle is going on and will continue. The outcome of the struggle will be determined by the proletarian class, the working class.

WELLS: But are there not many people who are not poor, but who work and work productively?

STALIN: Of course, there are small landowners, artisans, small traders; but it is not these people who decide the fate of a country, but the toiling masses, who produce all the things society requires.

WELLS: But there are very different kinds of capitalists. There are capitalists who only think about profits, about getting rich; but there are also those who are prepared to make sacrifices. Take old Morgan, for example. He only thought about profit; he was a parasite on society, simply; he merely accumulated wealth. But take Rockefeller. He is a brilliant organizer; he has set an example of how to organize the delivery of oil that is worthy of emulation. Or take Ford. Of course Ford is selfish. But is he not a passionate organizer of rationalized production from whom you take lessons? I would like to emphasize the fact that recently an important change in opinion towards the USSR has taken place in English-speaking countries. The reason for this, first of all, is the position of Japan, and the events in Germany. But there are other reasons besides those arising from international politics. There is a more profound reason, namely, the recognition by many people of the fact that the system based on private profit is breaking down. In these circumstances, it seems to me, we must not bring to the forefront the antagonism between the two worlds, but should strive to combine all the constructive movements, all the constructive forces in one line as much as possible. It seems to me that I am more to the Left than you, Mr Stalin; I think the old system is nearer to its end than you think.

STALIN: In speaking of the capitalists who strive only for profit, only to get rich, I do not want to say that these are the most worthless people capable of nothing else. Many of them undoubtedly possess great organizing talent, which I do not dream of denying. We Soviet people learn a great deal from the capitalists. And Morgan, whom you characterize so unfavourably, was undoubtedly a good, capable organizer. But if you mean people who are prepared to reconstruct the world, of course you will not be able to find them in the ranks of those who faithfully serve the cause of profit. We and they stand at opposite poles. You mentioned Ford. Of course, he is a capable organizer of production. But don't you know his attitude towards the working class? Don't you know how many workers he throws on the street? The capitalist is riveted to profit, and no power on earth can tear him away from it. Capitalism will be abolished not by 'organizers' of production, not by the technical intelligentsia, but by the working class, because the aforementioned strata do not play an independent role. The engineer, the organizer of production, does not work as he would like to, but as he is ordered, in such a way as to serve the interests of his employers. There are exceptions of course; there are people in this stratum who have awakened from the intoxication of capitalism. The technical intelligentsia can, under certain conditions, perform miracles and greatly benefit mankind. But it can also cause great harm. We Soviet people have not a little experience of the technical intelligentsia. After the October Revolution, a certain section of the technical intelligentsia refused to take part in the work of constructing the new society; they opposed this work of construction and sabotaged it. We did all we possibly could to bring the technical intelligentsia into this work of construction; we tried this way and that. Not a little time passed before our trained intelligentsia agreed actively to assist the new system. To-day the best section of this technical intelligentsia are in the front ranks of the builders of socialist society. Having this experience, we are far from under-estimating the good and the bad sides of the technical intelligentsia, and we know that on the one hand it can do harm, and on the other hand it can perform 'miracles'. Of course, things would be different if it were possible, at one stroke, spiritually to tear the technical intelligentsia away from the capitalist world. But that is Utopia. Are there many of the technical intelligentsia who would dare break away from the bourgeois world and set to work to reconstruct society? Do you think there are many people of this kind, say, in England or in France? No, there are few who would be willing to break away from their employers and begin reconstructing the world.

Besides, can we lose sight of the fact that in order to transform the world it is necessary to have *political power*? It seems to me, Mr Wells, that you greatly under-estimate the question of political power, that it entirely drops out of your conception. What can those, even with the best intentions in the world, do if they are unable to raise the question of seizing power, and do not possess power? At best they can help the class which takes power, but they cannot change the world themselves. This can only be done by a great class which will take the place of the capitalist class and become the sovereign master as the latter was before. This class is the working class. Of course, the assistance of the technical intelligentsia must be accepted; and the latter, in turn, must be assisted. But it must not be thought that the technical intelligentsia can play an independent historical role. The transformation of the world is a great, complicated and painful process. For this great task a great class is required. Big ships go on long voyages.

WELLS: Yes, but for long voyages a captain and a navigator are required.

STALIN: That is true, but what is first required for a long voyage is a big ship. What is a navigator without a ship? An idle man.

WELLS: The big ship is humanity, not a class.

STALIN: You, Mr Wells, evidently start out with the assumption that all men are good. I, however, do not forget that there are many wicked men. I do not believe in the goodness of the bourgeoisie.

WELLS: I remember the situation with regard to the technical intelligentsia several decades ago. At that time the technical intelligentsia was numerically small, but there was much to do and every engineer, technical and intellectual, found his opportunity. That is why the technical intelligentsia was the least revolutionary class. Now, however, there is a superabundance of technical intellectuals, and their mentality has changed very sharply. The skilled man, who would formerly never listen to revolutionary talk, is now greatly interested in it. Recently I was dining with the Royal Society, our great English scientific society. The President's speech was a speech for social planning and scientific control. To-day, the man at the head of the Royal Society holds revolutionary views, and insists on the scientific reorganization of human society. Your class-war propaganda has not kept pace with these facts. Mentality changes.

STALIN: Yes, I know this, and it is to be explained by the fact that capitalist society is now in a *cul de sac*. The capitalists are seeking, but cannot find, a way out of this *cul de sac* that would be compatible with the dignity of this class, compatible with the interests of this class. They could, to some extent, crawl out of the crisis on their hands and knees, but they cannot find an exit that would enable them to walk out of it with head raised high, a way out that would not fundamentally disturb the interests of capitalism. This, of course, is realized by wide circles of the technical intelligentsia. A large section of it is beginning to realize the community of its interests with those of the class which is capable of pointing the way out of the *cul de sac*.

WELLS: You of all people know something about revolutions, Mr Stalin, from the practical side. Do the masses ever rise? Is it not an established truth that all revolutions are made by a minority?

STALIN: To bring about a revolution a leading revolutionary minority is required; but the most talented, devoted and energetic minority would be helpless if it did not rely upon the at least passive support of millions.

WELLS: At least passive? Perhaps subconscious?

STALIN: Partly also the semi-instinctive and semi-conscious, but without the support of millions, the best minority is impotent.

WELLS: I watch Communist propaganda in the West and it seems to me that in modern conditions this propaganda sounds very old-fashioned, because it is insurrectionary propaganda. Propaganda in favour of the violent overthrow of the social system was all very well when it was directed against tyranny. But under modern conditions, when the system is collapsing anyhow, stress should be laid on efficiency, on competence, on productiveness, and not on insurrection. It seems to me that the insurrectionary note is obsolete. The Communist propaganda in the West is a nuisance to constructive-minded people.

STALIN: Of course the old system is breaking down, decaying. That is true. But it is also true that new efforts are being made by other methods, by every means, to protect, to save this dying system. You draw a wrong conclusion from a correct postulate. You rightly state that the old world is breaking down. But you are wrong in thinking that it is breaking down of its own accord. No, the substitution of one social system for another is a complicated and long revolutionary process. It is not simply a spontaneous process, but a struggle; it is a process connected with the clash of classes. Capitalism is decaying, but it must not be compared simply with a tree which has decayed to such an extent that it must fall to the ground of its own accord. No; revolution, the substitution of one social system for another, has always been a struggle, a painful and a cruel struggle, a life and death struggle. And every time the people of the new world came into power they had to defend themselves against the attempts of the old world to restore the old order by force; these people of the new world always had to be on the alert, always had to be ready to repel the attacks of the old world upon the new system.

Yes, you are right when you say that the old social system is breaking down; but it is not breaking down of its own accord. Take Fascism for example. Fascism is a reactionary force which is trying to preserve the old world by means of violence. What will you do with the Fascists? Argue with them? Try to convince them? But this will have no effect upon them at all. Communists do not in the least idealize methods of violence. But they, the Communists, do not want to be taken by surprise, they cannot count on the old world voluntarily departing from the stage, they see that the old system is violently defending itself, and that is why the Communists say to the working class: Answer violence with violence; do all you can to prevent the old dying order from crushing you, do not permit it to put manacles on your hands, on the hands with which you will overthrow the old system. As you see, the Communists regard the substitution of one social system for another, not simply as a spontaneous and peaceful process, but as a complicated, long and violent process. Communists cannot ignore facts.

WELLS: But look at what is now going on in the capitalist world. The collapse is not a simple one, it is an outbreak of reactionary violence which is degenerating into gangsterism. And it seems to me that when it comes to a conflict with reactionary and unintelligent violence, Socialists can appeal to the law, and instead of regarding the police as the enemy they should support them in the fight against the reactionaries. I think that it is useless operating with the methods of the old rigid insurrectionary Socialism.

STALIN: The Communists base themselves on rich historical experience which teaches that obsolete classes do not voluntarily abandon the stage of history. Recall the history of England in the seventeenth century. Did not many say that the old social system had decayed? But did it not, nevertheless, require a Cromwell to crush it by force?

WELLS: Cromwell operated on the basis of the constitution and in the name of constitutional order.

STALIN: In the name of the constitution he resorted to violence, beheaded the king, dispersed Parliament, arrested some and beheaded others!

Or take an example from our history. Was it not clear for a long time that the Tsarist system was decaying, was breaking down? But how much blood had to be shed in order to overthrow it?

And what about the October Revolution? Were there not plenty of people who knew that we alone, the Bolsheviks, were indicating the only correct way out? Was it not clear that Russian capitalism had decayed? But you know how great was the resistance, how much blood had to be shed in order to defend the October Revolution from all its enemies, internal and external.

Or take France at the end of the eighteenth century. Long before 1789 it was clear to many how rotten the royal power, the feudal system, was. But a popular insurrection, a clash of classes was not, could not be, avoided. Why? Because the classes which must abandon the stage of history are the last to become convinced that their role is ended. It is impossible to convince them of this. They think that the fissures in the decaying edifice of the old order can be mended, that the tottering edifice of the old order can be repaired and saved. That is why dying classes take to arms and resort to every means to save their existence as a ruling class.

WELLS: But were there not a few lawyers at the head of the great French Revolution?

STALIN: I do not deny the role of the intelligentsia in revolutionary movements. Was the great French Revolution a lawyers' revolution and not a popular revolution, which achieved victory by rousing vast masses of the people against feudalism and championed the interests of the Third Estate? And did the lawyers among the leaders of the great French Revolution act in accordance with the laws of the old order? Did they not introduce new, bourgeois-revolutionary law?

The rich experience of history teaches that up to now not a single class has voluntarily made way for another class. There is no such precedent in world history. The Communists have learned this lesson of history. Communists would welcome the voluntary departure of the bourgeoisie. But such a turn of affairs is improbable, that is what experience teaches. That is why the Communists want to be prepared for the worst and call upon the working class to be vigilant, to be prepared for battle. Who wants a captain who lulls the vigilance of his army, a captain who does not understand that the enemy will not surrender, that he must be crushed? To be such a captain means deceiving, betraying the working class. That is why I think that what seems to you to be old-fashioned is in fact a measure of revolutionary expediency for the working class.

WELLS: I do not deny that force has to be used, but I think the forms of the struggle should fit as closely as possible to the opportunities presented by the existing laws, which must be defended against reactionary attacks. There is no need to disorganize the old system, because it is disorganizing itself enough as it is. That is why it seems to me insurrection against the old order, against the law, is obsolete, old-fashioned. Incidentally, I deliberately exaggerate in order to bring the truth out more clearly. I can formulate my point of view in the following way: first, I am for order; second, I attack the present system in so far as it cannot assure order; third, I think that class war propaganda may detach from Socialism just those educated people whom Socialism needs.

STALIN: In order to achieve a great object, an important social object, there must be a main force, a bulwark, a revolutionary class. Next it is necessary to organize the assistance of an auxiliary force for this main force; in this case this auxiliary force is the party, to which the best forces of the intelligentsia belong. Just now you spoke about 'educated people'. But what educated people did you have in mind? Were there not plenty of educated people on the side of the old order in England in the seventeenth century, in France at the end of the eighteenth century, and in Russia in the epoch of the October Revolution? The old order had in its service many highly educated people who defended the old order, who opposed the new order. Education is a weapon the effect of which is determined by the hands which wield it, by who is to be struck down. Of course, the proletariat, Socialism, needs highly educated people. Clearly, simpletons cannot help the proletariat to fight for Socialism, to build a new society. I do not under-estimate the role of the intelligentsia; on the contrary, I emphasize it. The question is, however, which intelligentsia are we discussing? Because there are different kinds of intelligentsia.

WELLS: There can be no revolution without a radical change in the educational system. It is sufficient to quote two examples – the example of the German Republic, which did not touch the old educational system, and therefore never became a republic; and the example of the British Labour Party, which lacks the determination to insist on a radical change in the educational system.

STALIN: That is a correct observation.

Permit me now to reply to your three points. First, the main thing for the revolution is the existence of a social bulwark. This bulwark of the revolution is the working class.

Second, an auxiliary force is required, that which the Communists call a party. To a party belong the intelligent workers and those elements of the technical intelligentsia which are closely connected with the working class. The intelligentsia can be strong only if it combines with the working class. If it opposes the working class it becomes a cipher.

Third, political power is required as a lever for change. The new political power creates the new laws, the new order, which is revolutionary order.

I do not stand for any kind of order. I stand for order that corresponds to the interests of the working class. If, however, any of the laws of the old order can be utilized in the interests of the struggle for the new order, the old laws should be utilized. I cannot object to your postulate that the present system should be attacked in so far as it does not ensure the necessary order for the people.

And finally, you are wrong if you think that the Communists are enamoured of violence. They would be very pleased to drop violent methods if the ruling class agreed to give way to the working class. But the experience of history speaks against such an assumption.

WELLS: There was a case in the history of England, however, of a class voluntarily handing over power to another class. In the period between 1830 and 1870, the aristocracy, whose influence was still very considerable at the end of the eighteenth century, voluntarily, without a severe struggle, surrendered power to the bourgeoisie, which served as a sentimental support of the monarchy. Subsequently, this transference of power led to the establishment of the rule of the financial oligarchy.

STALIN: But you have imperceptibly passed from questions of revolution to questions of reform. This is not the same thing. Don't you think that the Chartist movement played a great role in the reforms in England in the nineteenth century?

WELLS: The Chartists did little and disappeared without leaving a trace.

STALIN: I do not agree with you. The Chartists, and the strike movement which they organized, played a great role; they compelled the ruling classes to make a number of concessions in regard to the franchise, in regard to abolishing the so-called 'rotten boroughs', and in regard to some of the points of the 'Charter'. Chartism played a not unimportant historical role and compelled a section of the ruling classes to make certain concessions, reforms, in order to avert great shocks. Generally speaking, it must be said that of all the ruling classes, the ruling classes of England, both the aristocracy and the bourgeoisie, proved to be the cleverest, most flexible from the point of view of their class interests, from the point of view of maintaining their power. Take an example, say, from modern history – the general strike in England in 1926. The first thing any other bourgeoisie would have done in the face of such an event, when the General Council of Trade Unions called for a strike, would have been to arrest the Trade Union leaders. The British bourgeoisie did not do that, and it acted cleverly from the point of view of its own interests. I cannot conceive of such a flexible strategy being employed by the bourgeoisie of the United States, Germany or France. In order to maintain their rule, the ruling classes of Great Britain have never foresworn small concessions, reforms. But it would be a mistake to think that these reforms were revolutionary.

WELLS: You have a higher opinion of the ruling classes of my country than I have. But is there a great difference between a small revolution and a great reform? Is not a reform a small revolution?

STALIN: Owing to pressure from below, the pressure of the masses, the bourgeoisie may sometimes concede certain partial reforms while remaining on the basis of the existing social-economic system. Acting in this way, it calculates that these concessions are necessary in order to preserve its class rule. This is the essence of reform. Revolution, however, means the transference of power from one class to another. That is why it is impossible to describe any reform as revolution. That is why we cannot count on the change of social systems taking place as an imperceptible transition from one system to another by means of reforms, by the ruling class making concessions.

WELLS: I am very grateful to you for this talk, which has meant a great deal to me. In explaining things to me you probably called to mind how you had to explain the fundamentals of Socialism in the illegal circles before the revolution. At the present time there are in the world only two persons to whose opinion, to whose every word, millions are listening – you and Roosevelt. Others may preach as much as they like; what they say will never be printed or heeded. I cannot yet appreciate what has been done in your country; I only arrived yesterday. But I have already seen the happy faces of healthy men and women and I know that something very considerable is being done here. The contrast with 1920 is astounding.

STALIN: Much more could have been done had we Bolsheviks been cleverer.

WELLS: No, if human beings were cleverer. It would be a good thing to invent a Five Year Plan for the reconstruction of the human brain, which obviously lacks many things needed for a perfect social order. (*Laughter.*)

STALIN: Don't you intend 'to stay for the Congress of the Soviet Writers' Union?

WELLS: Unfortunately I have various engagements to fulfil, and I can stay in the USSR only for a week. I came to see you, and I am very satisfied by our talk. But I intend to discuss with such Soviet writers as I can meet the possibility of their affiliating to the PEN Club. This is an international organization of writers founded by Galsworthy; after his death I became president. The organization is still weak, but it has branches in many countries, and what is more important, the speeches of its members are widely reported in the press. It insists upon this, free expression of opinion – even of opposition opinion. I hope to discuss this point with Gorki. I do not know if you are prepared yet for that much freedom . . .

STALIN: We Bolsheviks call it 'self-criticism'. It is widely used in the USSR . . .

•

HUEY P. LONG

Interviewed by Sender Garlin
New Masses, 26 March 1935

Huey Pierce Long (1893–1935), the American politician, was the Governor of Louisiana from 1928–31. Known as the 'Kingfish', he was a demagogue who used methods associated with the European dictators of the period to drive through a programme of social and economic reform. In 1930 he was elected to the US Senate, though he continued to control his home state through a nominee governor. He aspired to be president and devised a 'Share the Wealth' platform, but he was assassinated in Baton Rouge, Louisiana, before he could run. His career was the inspiration for Robert Penn Warren's novel, *All the*

King's Men. His son, Russell Billiu Long, served as US Senator for Louisiana from 1948 to 1987.

Sender Garlin also wrote a short book about the 'Kingfish': *The Real Huey P. Long* (1935).

'Special Session Called' was the headline in the *Shreveport Journal,* an afternoon paper. It reported that the session was due to convene that night at 10 o'clock. Shreveport is a six-hour train ride from the capitol at Baton Rouge, and if you were a senator or representative from Caddo Parish (county) where all the cotton and oil comes from, you'd have just time enough to pack your bag and kiss your wife goodbye if you wanted to get to the opening session of the Louisiana legislature in time to be counted for a day's pay by the state auditor. Nor is the ten-cent-a-mile transportation expense money which the state generously allots to be despised by *any* Lousiana statesman.

At 5:30 a.m. the next morning, just as dawn was breaking, I arrived at the Heidelberg Hotel in Baton Rouge. Slumping into one of those soft, brown leather chairs they have in those swell hotels in which Communist reporters do not generally register, I took up my position of watchful waiting for the Kingfish. I approached the hotel clerk for information about the habits of the Kingfish. What time did he usually rise? Would he answer the telephone if I called up? How watchful were his famed bodyguards?

At eight o'clock I called United States Senator Huey P. Long and the voice which answered, I later learned, was that of Joe Messina, Huey's chief bodyguard. 'Naw, you can't see him,' he snarled derisively. 'Huey's busy today.'

Undaunted, I walked to the Capitol and entered the legislature hall. It was empty except for the presence of a tall, red-haired young man in a black derby seated at the press table. 'Reporter?' I inquired. 'No, representative,' he answered proudly.

'Well, maybe you can help me get hold of Huey.' I had learned that if you say 'Senator Long' no one will know whom you're talking about.

'Maybe I *can* get you to him,' answered the representative doubtfully. 'But I took another newspaperman from New York to see Huey and I sure caught hell for it. It was this fellow Westbrook Pegler. He later wrote some snotty stuff about Huey.'

'You won't catch hell if you take *me* to him,' I assured the young man. 'I don't belong to *his* crowd.'

The young man led me to the room on the tenth floor where the Ways and Means Committee was 'considering' bills for the legislature.

I recognized my man at once. He was sitting at the head of a long walnut table 'explaining' various bills to the committee members, most of whom showed not the slightest interest in them. In one hour the Kingfish had succeeded in explaining and having voted favorably nearly twenty bills. When time hung heavily on the hands of the bored legislature, Huey waxed witty.

'Talking about this here business about the state insane asylums,' remarked the Kingfish, 'I may as well tell you that a relative of mine has taken over the business of running it, and we've got quite a surplus. Fact is, the insanity rate is getting mighty low these days what with the decline in the anti-Long movement.'

The legislators guffawed appreciatively.

At another point when the Kingfish was at a loss to 'explain' one of his bills to Jack Williamson, of St Charles Parish, youthful opposition leader on the Ways and Means Committee, Huey declared:

'This is a fine bill, a fine bill. George, here [Wallace, assistant Attorney General] tells me it removes some of the clockwork and gives the hands a chance to move.'

By such profound analysis Long prepared his bills for speedy passage in the Legislature.

Along about noon the solons decided on a luncheon recess. Seeing my chance, I approached the Kingfish and remarked, 'I've been wanting to meet you for a long time, Senator. How are you?' I didn't bother to go into details about credentials at the moment.

'Could I talk to you for a few minutes now, Senator? I'm making a study of conditions in Louisiana and I'd like to ask you a few questions, if you don't mind.'

'I'm very busy right now,' Long countered, turning his back on me politely and addressing himself to the Hon. George Wallace, assistant Attorney General of Louisiana and reputed to be Huey's 'braintruster.' I stood hesitating for a second, then approached the Kingfish once more.

'You don't mind if I accompany you down the elevator, do you, Senator?'

'Hell, no!' Long continued talking with his Attorney General.

'Quite a building, this capitol, eh, Senator?'

'Sure is,' replied the Senator, glancing around with evident satisfaction.

'Expect the session to last very long?'

'Few days.'

We passed through the doorway of the committee room into the wide spacious hall-way of the capitol. Huey and I were being followed by the watchful Attorney General, several members of the Ways and Means Committee and at least two members of Huey's omnipresent bodyguards.

We finally landed in the elevator. Ten floors, even in a modern $5,000,000 capitol, are good for a few questions.

'Is the Standard Oil Company the only corporation you're hostile to, Senator, or do you fight big business all over the state?'

'I'm not hostile to anything. All we're doing is reducing rates and getting taxes out of them.'

That very evening Huey's subservient legislature – at his bidding – was to revoke the tax on the Standard Oil Company!

'How do you feel about Roosevelt's program, Senator?'

'I don't know what his program is. I wish someone would explain it to me.' (Sixth floor).

'Just who is behind this Square Deal outfit?'

'Oh, hell,' Long grimaced, 'they got nobody.' (Third floor).

'Is it true that the Standard Oil Company is paying their expenses?'

'They ain't doing enough work for anybody to make them worth a cent.'

Thus with a wave of the hand the Kingfish brushed away the latest manifestation of opposition to his policies.

The elevator landed on the main floor. Huey made for the governor's office and I tagged along.

Once inside, Huey threw himself into a luxurious leather chair. I sat down at the table, while the Kingfish's retinue, including a number of legislators and the Attorney General, waited patiently on the sidelines.

'You're considered quite a friend of labor in this state, aren't you, Senator?'

'Aw, hell, yes. Ever since I was Railroad Commissioner way back in 1918, and all along the line I've always been 100 percent for labor and labor's always been 100 percent for me.'

'Senator, some of the union people in New Orleans tell me that men got as low as ten cents an hour on state construction work under your administration. No truth in that, is there?'

'I guess that's so. But, hell, that didn't have anything to do with me. That was a question of bidding. Whoever turned in the lowest bid got the contract.'

'But, as a friend of labor, you could have stipulated union scales for all state construction work, could you not, Senator?'

'There's no such thing as unions on state highways around here,' the Kingfish replied. Our eyes met.

'Senator, from what you hear in Washington, do you think there is any danger of war breaking out?'

'They'd go in for it if they could. It's been the method of all condemned and rebuked administrations since the beginning of time.'

'Don't you think, Senator, that the government should use the money appropriated for war preparations, that is, battleships, etc., to feed the unemployed and their families?'

'Absolutely. I ain't in favor of this government battleship business a-tall. Of course, I wouldn't scrap all of 'em, but I *would* have a better unified airplane study made.' Huey is apparently in favor of a more efficient war machine.

'Your opponents say that Negroes will now vote in Louisiana as a result of your abolition of the poll tax. Is that really so?'

'Not a-tall, sir!' Huey barked. 'The poll tax don't change the status of the nigger one damn bit! All it does is to eliminate the one-dollar poll tax. Of course the niggers are registering in droves, but the Registrar of Voters *still* has charge of setting the qualifications for all voters.'

Several months previously Huey had got out a leaflet to this effect in order to reassure his lily-white supporters that he had no intention of helping to enfranchise the hundreds of thousands of Negro workers and share-croppers in Louisiana.

Over Huey P. Long's signature, the leaflet declared:

An underhanded and secret lie is being spread about that this amendment for free poll taxes will let the Negro vote in our elections. That is not true and everybody telling it either does not know the truth or doesn't want to know the truth. The free poll tax will not affect the status of the Negro at all. Negroes can pay and do pay their poll taxes now, but that doesn't give them any better chance to vote. It is the registration law and the white primary that keeps the Negro out of our elections.

Shifting the subject, I asked Long if it were true that Harvey Couch, power man and railroad president, was one of his main supporters.

'Those fellows (the opposition) would have it that I shouldn't speak to Couch, but I speak to them all, and tax 'em.' Long was evidently conscious of the box-office value of the slogan, 'tax the rich'.

'What do you think of Upton Sinclair's "Epic" program, Senator? John Klorer, the editor of your paper, tells me that Sinclair was one of the first to subscribe to it and has said some nice things about your ideas.'

'I don't know much about what he's aiming for, but I believe it calls for confiscation. I'm not for that, my program is for limiting fortunes above a certain amount.'

'What amount, Senator?'

'Oh, if a man has a million dollars, we let him he'p himself to it, but if he has a few millions, why then we put a tax on it.'

'Senator, I recall that you once debated Norman Thomas in New York. Just what do you think of the socialist program? It has something in common with your "Share-the-Wealth" plan, hasn't it?'

'No, we're about as far apart as the poles. They believe in government ownership. I'm against that; the government's messing around in business too much as it is.'

'Well, how do you feel about the Communist program for fighting the depression, Senator?'

'Oh, I don't know much about them.'

Our eyes met for the second time.

'I do know, though, that they are a-seeking for the government to own everything. We call for the government to keep out of business. Our plan is nothing but limiting property.'

'I'm not entirely clear, Senator. Didn't I understand you to say that it was the socialists who want the government to own everything?'

'Well, sir, I don't just catch the difference myself. Some say there is a difference between 'em, but I'll be damned if I know what it is.'

Huey's eyes fell on a newspaper clipping on the table. He chuckled. I caught a glimpse of a cartoon portraying him as a crowned dictator.

'I understand that practically all the important newspapers of the state are against you, Senator. Is that true?'

'Yes, it's true, all right, and it's a damn good thing. We thrive on opposition. Senator Noe, here, will tell you a thing or two about it. Why, up in Monroe and Shreveport our boys had told us that the papers were a-layin' low and that we'd carry the election only three to one. Hell, I said, that will never do. It ain't fair for them papers to lay quiet against them bills of ours. Sometimes those sons-of-bitches make like they're on our side, and we have to get out our handbills to convince them to the contrary. Now, as I was saying, we got out the handbills up in Monroe and Shreveport and after a while the papers started printing front-page attacks against me and m'bills, and the finish was that we carried the election there eight to one instead of three to one.'

'Senator, I've just visited the cotton country up North. The farmers, especially the poor ones, don't seem to be getting on very well. What do you think about it?'

'This damn AAA or whatever you call it hasn't he'ped anybody anywhere, in any way.'

'How would you handle the farmers, Senator?'

'If you'd read my speeches like you said you did, you'd know that my idea is to store up the crops and hold it for a year until we got a good price for it. In the meantime we'd put the farm fellows to work on highway building and such.'

'Well, isn't that fundamentally the same thing that Roosevelt is doing; you both seem to be in agreement about the necessity for crop curtailment?' The Kingfish grunted.

'Your program is considered quite radical by the people of Louisiana, isn't it, Senator?'

'Hell, I don't give a damn what folks call it or me – radical, conservative or reactionary. All I'm advocating is right out of the Bible. It comes straight out of the Scriptures.'

'A little while back, Senator, you stated that you were in favor of organized labor. How, then, do you account for the fact that labor organization is so weak in the state of Louisiana? You have considerable influence in this state; couldn't you help unionization along a bit?'

'No, sir, I couldn't do that. I'm for labor, have always been, and labor's for me. But I couldn't get messed up in that.'

'Senator, I understand that your legislature defeated the Child Labor Amendment. How did *that* happen?'

'The rural vote wouldn't support it, I voted for it in Congress, though,' he hastened to add.

'But couldn't you swing the rural vote around if you took the stump and spoke for the amendment throughout the state?'

'Well, now, I caint make the rural people do it without I ruin myself to do it, do you understand?'

I walked out of the governor's office, out of the capitol and into the Louisiana sunshine. At the head of the steps I recognized Joe Messina, Long's six-foot bodyguard. A few days earlier he had beaten and nearly murdered a diminutive newspaper photographer who had tried to snap a picture of the senator and the utility man Harvey Couch, in the latter's private railroad car.

•

GERTRUDE STEIN

Interviewed by John Hyde Preston
The Atlantic Monthly, August 1935

Gertrude Stein (1874–1946), the American writer, was born in Pennsylvania. She was brought up in Vienna, Paris and San Francisco, studied psychology and medicine at American universities, but settled in Paris, where she mingled with writers and artists and developed her own modernist ideas about literary form. She lived with her friend and companion from San Francisco, Alice B. Toklas, who became the subject of Stein's *The Autobiography of Alice B. Toklas* (1933). Her works of fiction included *Three Lives* (1909), *The Making of Americans* (1925), and *Brewsie and Willie* (1946), about the American liberation of Germany, which she witnessed because she had been living in a German village during the Second World War. Her attempt to apply the techniques of abstract painting to literary composition were not successful, and she wrote more comprehensibly than popular myth has suggested.

John Hyde Preston was born in 1906. He published a biography of the American Revolutionary soldier Anthony Wayne, *A Gentleman Rebel: The Exploits of Anthony Wayne* (1928), a popular history of the American Revolution, *Revolution, 1776* (1933), and a couple of novels during the 1930s.

I

This morning I went to see her at her hotel. All the arrangements had been made by her friend and secretary who was there at the door and seemed shy that I shook hands with her first, as if for fear I had mistaken her for the woman I had come to see. The other woman was standing in the middle of the small sitting room, and I saw her through a door, very alert and ready to smile without smiling. She is a short person, strong and round, close to the earth, with an earth face and marvelous eyes. When she looks at you they are straight, but when she looks to one side the right eye seems a little out of focus, seems to go a little further away from you than the other. Her hair is close-cropped, gray, brushed forward or not brushed at all but growing forward in curls, like the hair of the Roman emperors. She looks sun-beaten, but not Indian like her secretary, for the wrinkles around her eyes are sharp, quick, and not wide like Indian wrinkles and she never quite closes her eyes, which are deep brown, but holds them closely with her lids.

If I had seen her a year ago I should have expected a legend, but I had learned to expect a woman, and I came to find something more – more, I mean, than one who had been a fountainhead not so much for herself as for others and certainly for all the young Americans who were writing in Paris after the war. She is more than that because she has grown beyond and most of them have gone only as far as she took them; they repudiated her when they thought they were adult and they went into costume and have never come out. That is the terrible thing which happens to many Americans because they feel that they have a new literature to create, as if it were a duty; so they go into costume, and when the literature is created, if at all, they do not know it or do not know when to stop, and so they go on creating a literature that is already born out of them and has a life of its own; they go on giving birth every day to a thing already alive and on two legs, all because they are in costume and can't get out. For all I know she may be in costume too, but not in mind and not personally.

She talks freely and volubly and sometimes obscurely, as if she had something there that she was very sure of and yet could not touch it. She has that air of having seen in flashes something which she does not know the shape of, and can talk about, not out of the flashes but out of the spaces between when she has waited.

I do not mean that there is in her conversation any trace of that curious obscurity which dims so much of her prose, for me at least – and I was frank (without wanting to be) in telling her that I could only guess sometimes at the written words. She seems peacefully resigned to the attacks that have been made upon her all her life and she has that air, so rare in writers, of living outside of both fame and criticism.

II

We talked with great freedom from the outset. We started naturally and there was no feeling on my part that I had to tell her why I had come. She seemed to know why I had come and she knew it better than I did, and she started right off to talk about the problem of the young writer in America and she talked about it better than anyone I have ever known because she did not reduce it to elements and harp on any one element that she knew and understood, and there was not the feeling that writers get from writers, – 'Yes, I've gone through that myself, and I'll tell you what it is and what I did about it,' – but the true feeling of one before your eyes who was growing into a scene, your scene, without your really telling her about it, and then bringing you into a feeling with the world, not by taking you as an individual, but by taking a world and a spirit of creation and taking them so fully and so happily that you were drawn in suddenly to know that you were there, not by transition, but by recognition. I think that in some of her prose pieces you get that – you do not have to follow; you suddenly know. (Of course you have followed, but it has not been by following that you have it.)

I had been so miserable, despairing, self-doubtful about my work and for so long a time that I was able to give her the picture clearly, and she got it more clearly than I had given it, and her lids really seemed to take hold on her eyes, not in a squinted, contracted way, but firmly and evenly and restfully.

'You will write,' she said, 'if you will write without thinking of the result in terms of a result, but think of the writing in terms of discovery, which is to say that creation must take place between the pen and the paper, not before in a thought or afterwards in a recasting. Yes, before in a thought, but not in careful thinking. It will come if it is there and if you will let it come, and if you have anything you will get a sudden creative recognition. You won't know how it was, even what it is, but it will be creation if it came out of the pen and out of you and not out of an architectural drawing of the thing you are doing. Technique is not so much a thing of form or style as the way that form or style came and how it can come again. Freeze your fountain and you will always have the frozen water shooting into the air and falling and it will be there to see – oh, no doubt about that – but there will be no more coming. I can tell how important it is to have that creative recognition. You cannot go into the womb to form the child: it is there and makes itself and comes forth whole – and there it is and you have made it and have felt it, but it has come itself – and that is creative recognition. Of course you have a little more control over your writing than that; you have to know what you want to get; but when you know that, let it take you and if it seems to take you off the track don't hold back, because that is perhaps where instinctively you want to be and if you hold back and try to be always where you have been before, you will go dry.

'You think you have used up all the air where you are, Preston; you said that you had used it up where you live, but that is not true, for if it were it would mean that you had given up all hope of change. I think writers *should* change their scenes; but the very fact that you do not know where you would go if you could means that you would take nothing truly to the place where you went and so there would be nothing there until you had found it, and when you did find it, it would be something you had brought and thought you had left behind. And that would be creative recognition, too, because it would have all to do with you and nothing really to do with the place.'

But what if, when you tried to write, you felt stopped, suffocated, and no words came and if they came at all they were wooden and without meaning? What if you had the feeling you could never write another word?

'Preston, the way to resume is to resume,' she said laughing. 'It is the only way. To resume. If you feel this book deeply it will come as deep as your feeling is when it is running truest and the book will never be truer or deeper than your feeling. But you do not yet know anything about your feeling because, though you may think it is all there, all crystallized, you have not let it run. So how can you know what it will be? What will be best in it is what you really do not know now. If you knew it all it would not be creation but dictation. No book is a book until it is done, and you cannot say that you are writing a book while you are just writing on sheets of paper and all that is in you has not yet come out. And a book – let it go on endlessly – is not the whole man. There is no such thing as a one-book author. I remember a young man in Paris just after the war – you have never heard of this young man – and we all liked his first book very much and he liked it too, and one day he said to me, "This book will make literary history," and I told him: "It will make some part of literary history, perhaps, but only if you go on making a new part every day and grow with the history you are making until you become a part of it yourself." But this young man never wrote another book and now he sits in Paris and searches sadly for the mention of his name in indexes.'

III

Her secretary came in and out of the room, putting things away in a trunk that stood open at the end of the couch (they sail to-morrow noon), exchanging a few words in a voice that was new for its softness; and suddenly out of something that we were saying about America came the discovery that both she and I were from Seattle and that she had known my father when he was a young man and before he went into the Klondike. And then as her secretary spoke a strange deep kinship of land seemed to take possession of the other woman – who had been born in Pennsylvania and raised in Oakland, California, and had been in far-off Paris for thirty years without sight of her native earth – for she began to speak with deep-felt fervor of her American experience in the past six months.

'Preston,' she said, 'you were saying that you had torn up roots ten years ago and tried to plant them again in New England where there was none of your blood, and that now you have a feeling of being without roots. Something like that happened to *me*, too. I think I must have had a feeling that it had happened or I should not have come back. I went to California. I saw it and felt it and had a tenderness and a horror too. Roots are so small and dry when you have them and they are exposed to you. You have seen them on a plant and sometimes they seem to deny the plant if it is vigorous.' She paused when I lit a cigarette; I could not make out whether she had been alarmed at my smoking so much or whether she was instinctively silent in the face of any physical activity on the part of her listener. 'Well,' she went on, 'we're not like that really. Our roots can be anywhere and we can survive, because if you think about it, we take our roots with us. I always knew that a little and now I know it wholly. I know because you can go back to where they are and they can be less real to you than they were three thousand, six thousand miles away. Don't worry about your roots so long as you worry about them. The essential thing is to have the feeling that they exist, that they are somewhere. They will take care of themselves, and they will take care of you too, though you may never know how it has happened. To think only of going back for them is to confess that the plant is dying.'

'Yes,' I said, 'but there is something more. There is the hunger for the land, for the speech.'

'I know,' she said almost sadly. 'America is wonderful!' Then without any warning she declared: 'I feel now that it is my business here. After all, it *is* my business, this America!' And she laughed with a marvelous heartiness, a real lust. When I asked her if she would come back she looked up slyly and was smiling still and she opened and shut her eyes with the same zestful expression with which a man smacks his lips.

'Well,' I said, 'you have had a long time to look. What is it that happens to American writers?'

'What is it you notice?'

'It is obvious. They look gigantic at first. Then they get to be thirty-five or forty and the juices dry up and there they are. Something goes out of them and they begin to repeat according to formula. Or else they grow silent altogether.'

'The trouble is a simple one,' she said. 'They become writers. They cease being creative men and soon they find that they are novelists or critics or poets or biographers, and they are encouraged to be one of those things because they have been very good in one performance or two or three, but that is silly. When a man says, "I am a novelist," he is simply a literary shoemaker. If Mr Robert Frost is at all good as a poet, it is because he is a farmer – really in his mind a farmer, I mean. And there is another whom you young men are doing your best – and very really your worst – to forget, and he is the editor of a small-town newspaper and his name is Sherwood Anderson. Now Sherwood' – he was the only man she called by his first name, and then affectionately – 'Sherwood is really and truly great because he truly does not care what he is and has not thought what he is except a man, a man who can go away and be small in the world's eyes and yet perhaps be one of the very few Americans who have achieved that perfect freshness of creation and passion, as simple as rain falling on a page, and rain that fell from him and was there miraculously and was all his. You see, he had that *creative recognition*, that wonderful ability to have it all on paper before he saw it and then to be strengthened by what he saw so that he could always go deep for more and not know that he was going. Scott Fitzgerald, you know, had it for a little while, but – not any more. He is an American Novelist.'

'What about Hemingway?' I could not resist asking her that question. Her name and the name of Ernest Hemingway are almost inseparable when one thinks of the Paris after the war, of the expatriates who gathered around her there as a sibyl. 'He was good until after *A Farewell to Arms*.'

'No,' she said, 'he was not really good after 1925. In his early short stories he had what I have been trying to describe to you. Then – Hemingway did not lose it; he threw it away. I told him then: "Hemingway, you have a small income; you will not starve; you can work without worry and you can grow and keep this thing and it will grow with you." But he did not wish to grow that way; he wished to grow violently. Now, Preston, here is a curious thing. Hemingway is not an American Novelist. He has not sold himself and he has not settled into any literary mould. Maybe his own mould, but that's not only literary. When I first met Hemingway he had a truly sensitive capacity for emotion and that was the stuff of the first stories; but he was shy of himself and he began to develop, as a shield, a big Kansas City-boy brutality about it, and so he was "tough" because he was really sensitive and ashamed that he was. Then it happened. I saw it happening and tried to save what was fine there, but it was too late. He went the way so many other Americans have gone before, the way they are still going. He became obsessed by sex and violent death.'

She held up a stubby forefinger. 'Now you will mistake me. Sex and death are the springs of the most valid of human emotions. But they are not all; they are not even all emotion. But for Hemingway everything became multiplied by and subtracted from sex and death. But I knew at the start and I know better now that it wasn't just to find out what these things were; it was the disguise for the thing that was really gentle and fine in him, and then his agonizing shyness escaped into brutality. No, now wait – not real brutality, because the truly brutal man wants something more than bullfighting and deep-sea fishing and elephant killing or whatever it is now, and perhaps if Hemingway were truly brutal he could make a real literature out of those things; but he is not, and I doubt if he will ever again write truly about anything. He is skillful, yes, but that is the writer; the other half is the man.'

I asked her: 'Do you really think American writers are obsessed by sex? And if they are, isn't it legitimate?'

'It is legitimate, of course. Literature – creative literature – unconcerned with sex is inconceivable. But not literary sex, because sex is a part of something of which the other parts are not sex at all. No, Preston, it is really a matter of tone. You can tell, if you can tell anything, by the way a man talks about sex whether he is impotent or not, and if he talks about nothing else you can be quite sure that he is impotent – physically and as an artist too.

'One thing which I have tried to tell Americans,' she went on, 'is that there can be no truly great creation without passion, but I'm not sure that I have been able to tell them at all. If they have not understood it is because they have had to think of sex first, and they can think of sex as passion more easily than they can think of passion as the whole force of man. Always they try to label it, and that is a mistake. What do I mean? I will tell you. I think of Byron. Now Byron had passion. It had nothing to do with his women. It was a quality of Byron's mind and everything he wrote came out of it, and perhaps that is why his work is so uneven, because a man's passion is uneven if it is real; and sometimes, if he can write it, it is only passion and has no meaning outside of itself. Swinburne wrote all his life about passion, but you can read all of him and you will not know what passions he had. I am not sure that it is necessary to know or that Swinburne would have been better if he had known. A man's passion can be wonderful when it has an object which may be a woman or an idea or wrath at an injustice, but after it happens, as it usually does, that the object is lost or won after a time, the passion does not survive it. It survives only if it was there before, only if the woman or the idea or the wrath was an incident in the passion and not the cause of it – and that is what makes the writer.

'Often the men who really have it are not able to recognize it in themselves because they do not know what it is to feel differently or not to feel at all. And it won't answer to its name. Probably Goethe thought that *Young Werther* was a more passionate book than *Wilhelm Meister*, but in *Werther* he was only describing passion and in *Wilhelm Meister* he was transferring it. And I don't think he knew what he had done. He did not have to. Emerson might have been surprised if he had been told that he was passionate. But Emerson really had passion; he wrote it; but he could not have written *about* it because he did not know about it. Now Hemingway knows all about it and can sometimes write very surely about it, but he hasn't any at all. Not really any. He merely has passions. And Faulkner and Caldwell and all that I have read in America and before I came. They are good craftsmen and they are honest men, but they do not have it.'

IV

I have never heard talk come more naturally and casually. It had none of the tautness or deadly care that is in the speech of most American intellectuals when they talk from the mind out. If sometime you will listen to workingmen talking when they are concentrated upon the physical job at hand, and one of them will go on without cease while he is sawing and measuring and nailing, not always audible, but keeping on in an easy rhythm and almost without awareness of words – then you will get some idea of her conversation.

'Well, I think Thomas Wolfe has it,' I said. 'I think he really has it – more than any man I know in America.' I had just read *Of Time and the River* and had been deeply moved.

'I read his first book,' she said, misnaming it. 'And I looked for it, but I did not find it. Wolfe is a deluge and you are flooded by him, but if you want to read carefully, Preston, you must learn to know how you are flooded. In a review I read on the train Wolfe was many things and among them he was Niagara. Now that is not so silly as it sounds. Niagara has power and it has form and it is beautiful for thirty seconds, but the water at the bottom that has been Niagara is no better and no different from the water at the top that will be Niagara. Something wonderful and terrible has happened to it, but it is the same water and nothing at all would have happened if it had not been for an aberration in one of nature's forms. The river is the water's true form and it is a very satisfactory form for the water and Niagara is altogether wrong. Wolfe's books are the water at the bottom and they foam magnificently because they have come the wrong way, but they are no better than when they started. Niagara exists because the true form ran out and the water could find no other way. But the creative artist should be more adroit.'

'You mean that you think the novel form has run out?'

'Truly – yes. And when a form is dead it always happens that everything that is written in it is really formless. And you know it is dead when it has crystallized and everything that goes into it must be made a certain way. What is bad in Wolfe is made that way and what is good is made very differently – and so if you take what is good, he really has not written a novel at all.'

'Yes – but what difference does it make?' I asked her. 'It was something that was very true for me, and perhaps I didn't care whether it was a novel or not.'

'Preston,' she said, 'you must try to understand me. I was not impatient because it was not a novel but because Wolfe did not see what it might have been – and if he really and truly had the passion you say he has, he would have seen because he would have really and truly felt it, and it would have taken its own form, and with his wonderful energy it would not have defeated him.'

'What has passion got to do with choosing an art form?'

'Everything. There is nothing else that determines form. What Wolfe is writing is his autobiography, but he has chosen to tell it as a story and an autobiography is never a story because life does not take place in events. What he has really done is to release himself, and so he has only told the truth of his release and not the truth of discovery. And that is why he means so much to you young men, because it is your release too. And perhaps because it is so long and unselective it is better for you, for it it stays with you, you will give it your own form and, if you have any passion, that too, and then perhaps you will be able to make the discovery he did not make. But you will not read it again because you will not need it again. And if a book has been a very true book for you, you will always need it again.'

Her secretary came into the room, looked at her watch, and said: 'You have twenty-five minutes for your walk. You must be back at ten minutes to one.' I arose, suddenly conscious that, having asked for fifteen minutes out of her last day in America, I had stayed over an hour utterly unaware of time. I made to go.

'No,' she said abruptly, 'there is still more to say. Walk with me because I want to say it.' We went out of the hotel. 'Walk on my left,' she said, 'because my right ear is broken.' She walked very sturdily, almost rapidly, and shouted above the traffic.

'There are two particular things I want to tell you because I have thought about them in America. I have thought about them for many years, but particularly in America I have seen them in a new light. So much has happened since I left. Americans are really beginning to use their heads – more now than at any time since the Civil War. They used them then because they had to and thinking was in the air, and they have to use them now or be destroyed. When you write the Civil War you must think of it in terms of then and now and not the time between. Well, Americans have not gone far yet, perhaps, but they have started thinking again and there *are* heads here and something is ahead. It has no real shape, but I feel it and I do not feel it so much abroad and that is why my business is here. You see, there is something for writers that there was not before. You are too close to it and you only vaguely sense it. That is why you let your economic problem bother you. If you see and feel you will know what your work is, and if you do it well the economic problem takes care of itself. Don't think so much about your wife and child being dependent upon your work. Try to think of your work being dependent upon your wife and child, for it will be if it really comes from you, and if it doesn't come from you – the *you* that has the wife and child and this Fifth Avenue and these people – then it is no use anyway and your economic problem will have nothing to do with writing because you will not be a writer at all. I find you young writers worrying about losing your integrity and it is well that you should, but a man who really loses his integrity does not know that it is gone, and nobody can wrest it from you if you really have it. An ideal is good only if it moves you forward and can make you produce, Preston, but it is no good if you prefer to produce nothing rather than write sometimes for money alone, because the ideal defeats itself when the economic problem you have been talking about defeats *you.*'

We were crossing streets and the crowds were looking curiously at this bronze-faced woman whose picture had been so often in the papers, but she was unaware of them, it seemed to me, but extraordinarily aware of the movement around her and especially of taxicabs. After all, I reflected, she had lived in Paris.

'The thing for the serious writer to remember,' she said, 'is that he is writing seriously and is not a salesman. If the writer and the salesman are born in the same man it is lucky for both of them, but if they are not, one is sure to kill the other when you force them together. And there is one thing more.'

We turned off Madison Avenue and headed back to the hotel.

'A very important thing – and I know it because I have seen it kill so many writers – is not to make up your mind that you are any one thing. Look at your own case. You have written, first a biography, then a history of the American Revolution, and third a modern novel. But how absurd it would be if you should make up your mind that you are a Biographer, a Historian, or a Novelist!' She pronounced the words in tremendous capitals. 'The truth is probably that all those forms are dead because they have become forms, and you must have felt that or you would not have moved on from one to another. Well, you will go on and you will work in them, and sometime, if your work has any meaning and I am not sure that anything but a lifework has meaning, then you may discover a new form. Somebody has said that I myself am striving for a fourth dimension in literature. I am striving for nothing of the sort and I am not striving at all but only gradually growing and becoming steadily more aware of the ways things can be felt and known in words, and perhaps if I feel them and know them myself in the new ways it is enough, and if I know fully enough there will be a note of sureness and confidence that will make others know too.

'And when one has discovered and evolved a new form, it is not the form but the fact that *you are the form* that is important. That is why Boswell is the greatest biographer that ever lived, because he was no slavish Eckermann with the perfect faithfulness of notes – which are not faithful at all – but because he put into Johnson's mouth words that Johnson probably never uttered, and yet you know when you read it that that is what Johnson would have said under such and such a circumstance – and you know all that because Boswell discovered Johnson's real form which Johnson never knew. The great thing is not ever to think about form but let it come. Does that sound strange from me? They have accused me of thinking of nothing else. Do you see the real joke? It is the critics who have really thought about form always and I have thought about – writing!'

Gertrude Stein laughed enormously and went into the hotel with the crowd.

•

F. SCOTT FITZGERALD
Interviewed by Michel Mok
New York Post, 25 September 1936

Francis Scott Key Fitzgerald (1896–1940), the American novelist, was born in Minnesota and educated at Newman School, New Jersey, and Princeton. He volunteered as a soldier in the First World War, but never saw active service in Europe. In his novels and short stories, he was the memorialist of the 1920s 'Jazz Age'. The hedonistic life of Princeton undergraduates was portrayed in *This Side of Paradise* (1920), while *The Beautiful and Damned* portrayed hedonism in an adult context. His most famous novel, *The Great Gatsby* (1922), dealt with the moral decay that came with wealth and success. Another novel, *Tender is the Night* (1934), related Fitzgerald's dissatisfaction with the moneyed, rootless life that he led on the French Riviera, his wife Zelda's mental illness, and his own alcoholism and melancholia.

Michel Mok (1888–1961) was born in Amsterdam, in the Netherlands. He was on the staff of European and Canadian newspapers before joining the *Philadelphia Record*. From 1933 to 1940 he worked for the *New York Post*, covering the trial and execution of Bruno Hauptmann for the murder of the Lindbergh baby, and writing features and theatre reviews. He later became a stage publicist, working for various Broadway showmen and, in particular, for Rodgers and Hammerstein. He also helped translate the essays, short stories and diary of Anne Frank. His son Michael Mok became a legendary reporter and an inspiration to young journalists like Tom Wolfe.

Long ago, when he was young, cock-sure, drunk with sudden success, F. Scott Fitzgerald told a newspaper man that no one should live beyond thirty.

That was in 1921, shortly after his first novel, *This Side of Paradise*, had burst into the literary heavens like a flowering Roman candle.

The poet-prophet of the post-war neurotics observed his fortieth birthday yesterday in his bedroom of the Grove Park Inn here. He spent the day as he spends all his days – trying to come back from the other side of Paradise, the hell of despondency in which he has writhed for the last couple of years.

He had no company except his soft spoken, Southern, maternal and indulgent nurse and this reporter. With the girl he bantered in conventional nurse-and-patient fashion. With his visitor he chatted bravely, as an actor, consumed with fear that his name will never be in lights again, discusses his next starring role.

He kidded no one. There obviously was as little hope in his heart as there

was sunshine in the dripping skies, covered with clouds that veiled the view of
Sunset Mountain.

Physically he was suffering the aftermath of an accident eight weeks ago,
when he broke his right shoulder in a dive from a fifteen-foot springboard.

But whatever pain the fracture might still cause him, it did not account for
his jittery jumping off and onto his bed, his restless pacing, his trembling
hands, his twitching face with its pitiful expression of a cruelly beaten child.

Nor could it be held responsible for his frequent trips to a highboy, in a
drawer of which lay a bottle. Each time he poured a drink into the measuring
glass on his bedside table, he would look appealingly at the nurse and ask, 'Just
one ounce?'

Each time the nurse cast down her eyes without replying.

Fitzgerald, for that matter, did not attempt to make his injury an excuse for
his thirst.

'A series of things happened to papa,' he said, with mock brightness. 'So
papa got depressed and started drinking a little.'

What the 'things' were he refused to explain.

'One blow after another,' he said, 'and finally something snapped.'

Before coming to North Carolina, however, his visitor had learned something
of Fitzgerald's recent history from friends in Baltimore, where he lived until last
July.

The author's wife, Zelda, had been ill for some years. There was talk, said his
friends, of an attempt at suicide on her part one evening when the couple were
taking a walk in the country outside Baltimore. Mrs Fitzgerald, so the story
went, threw herself on the tracks before an oncoming express train. Fitzgerald,
himself in poor health, rushed after her and narrowly saved her life.

There were other difficulties. Mrs Fitzgerald finally was taken to a sanitarium
near this city, and her husband soon followed her, taking a room in the rock-
built Park Grove Inn, one of the largest and most famous resort hotels in
America.

But the causes of Fitzgerald's breakdown are of less importance than its
effects on the writer. In a piece entitled 'Pasting It Together,' one of three
autobiographical articles published in *Esquire*, which appeared in the March
issue of that magazine, Fitzgerald described himself as 'a cracked plate'.

'Sometimes, though,' he wrote, 'the cracked plate has to be retained in the
pantry, has to be kept in service as a household necessity.

'It can never again be warmed on the stove nor shuffled with the other plates
in the dishpan; it will not be brought out for company, but it will do to hold
crackers late at night or to go into the ice box under the left-overs.

'Now the standard cure for one who is sunk is to consider those in actual
destitution or physical suffering – this is an all-weather beatitude for gloom in
general and fairly salutory daytime advice for every one. But at 3 o'clock in the
morning . . . the cure doesn't work – and in a real dark night of the soul it is

always 3 o'clock in the morning, day after day. At that hour the tendency is to refuse to face things as long as possible by retiring into an infantile dream – but one is continually startled out of this by various contacts with the world.

'One meets these occasions as quickly and carelessly as possible and retires once more back into the dream, hoping that things will adjust themselves by some great material or spiritual bonanza. But as the withdrawal persists there is less and less chance of the bonanza – one is not waiting for the fadeout of a single sorrow, but rather being an unwilling witness of an execution, the disintegration of one's own personality . . .'

Yesterday, toward the end of a long, rambling, disjointed talk, he put it in different words, not nearly as poetic but no less moving for that reason:

'A writer like me,' he said, 'must have an utter confidence, an utter faith in his star. It's an almost mystical feeling, a feeling of nothing-can-happen-to-me, nothing-can-harm-me, nothing-can-touch-me.

'Thomas Wolfe has it. Ernest Hemingway has it. I once had it. But through a series of blows, many of them my own fault, something happened to that sense of immunity and I lost my grip.'

In illustration, he told a story about his father.

'As a boy, my father lived in Montgomery County, Maryland. Our family has been mixed up quite a bit in American history. My great-grandfather's brother was Francis Scott Key who wrote 'The Star-Spangled Banner'; I was named for him. My father's aunt was Mrs Suratt, who was hanged after the assassination of Lincoln because Booth had planned the deed in her house – you remember that three men and a woman were executed.

'As a youngster of nine, my father rowed spies across the river. When he was twelve he felt that life was finished for him. As soon as he could, he went West, as far away from the scenes of the Civil War as possible. He started a wicker-furniture factory in St Paul. A financial panic in the nineties struck him and he failed.

'We came back East and my father got a job as a soap salesman in Buffalo. He worked at this for some years. One afternoon – I was ten or eleven – the phone rang and my mother answered it. I didn't understand what she said but I felt that disaster had come to us. My mother, a little while before, had given me a quarter to go swimming. I gave the money back to her. I knew something terrible had happened and I thought she could not spare the money now.

'Then I began to pray. "Dear God," I prayed, "please don't let us go to the poorhouse; please don't let us go to the poorhouse." A little while later my father came home. I had been right. He had lost his job.

'That morning he had gone out a comparatively young man, a man full of strength, full of confidence. He came home that evening, an old man, a completely broken man. He had lost his essential drive, his immaculateness of purpose. He was a failure the rest of his days.'

Fitzgerald rubbed his eyes, his mouth, quickly walked up and down the room.

'Oh,' he said, 'I remember something else. I remember that when my father came home my mother said to me, "Scott, say something to your father."

'I didn't know what to say. I went up to him and asked, "Father, who do you think will be the next President?" He looked out of the window. He didn't move a muscle. Then he said: "I think Taft will."

'My father lost his grip and I lost my grip. But now I'm trying to get back. I started by writing those pieces for *Esquire*. Perhaps they were a mistake. Too much de profundis. My best friend, a great American writer – he's the man I call my artistic conscience in one of the *Esquire* articles – wrote me a furious letter. He said I was stupid to write that gloomy personal stuff.'

'What are your plans at the moment, Mr Fitzgerald? What are you working on now?'

'Oh, all sorts of things. But let's not talk about plans. When you talk about plans, you take something away from them.'

Fitzgerald left the room.

'Despair, despair, despair,' said the nurse. 'Despair day and night. Try not to talk about his work or his future. He does work, but only very little – maybe three, four hours a week.'

Soon he returned. 'We must celebrate the author's birthday,' he said gayly. 'We must kill the fatted calf or, at any rate, cut the candled cake.'

He took another drink. 'Much against your better judgment, my dear,' he smiled at the girl.

Heeding the nurse's advice, the visitor, turned the talk to the writer's early days and Fitzgerald told how *This Side of Paradise* came to be written.

'I wrote it when I was in the army,' he said. 'I was nineteen. I rewrote the whole book a year later. The title was changed, too. Originally, it was called, "The Romantic Egotist".

'Isn't *This Side of Paradise* a beautiful title? I'm good at titles, you know. I've published four novels and four volumes of short stories. All my novels have good titles – *The Great Gatsby*, *The Beautiful and Damned* and *Tender Is the Night*. That's my latest book. I worked on it four years.

'Yes, I wrote *This Side of Paradise* in the army. I didn't go overseas – my army experience consisted mostly of falling in love with a girl in each city I happened to be in.

'I almost went across. They actually marched us onto a transport and then marched us right off again. Influenza epidemic or something. That was about a week before the armistice.

'We were quartered at Camp Mills, in Long Island. I sneaked out of bounds into New York – there was a girl concerned, no doubt – and I missed the train back to Camp Sheridan, Ala., where we had been trained.

'So this is what I did. Went to the Pennsylvania station and commandeered an engine and a cab to take me to Washington to join the troops. I told the railroad people I had confidential war papers for President Wilson. Couldn't wait a minute. Couldn't be intrusted to the mails. They fell for my bluff, I'm sure it's the only time in the history of the United States Army that a lieutenant has commandeered a locomotive. I caught up with the regiment in Washington. No, I wasn't punished.'

'But how about *This Side of Paradise?*'

'That's right, I'm wandering. After we were mustered out I went to New York. Scribners turned my book down. Then I tried to get a job on a newspaper. I went to every newspaper office with the scores and lyrics of the Triangle shows of the two or three previous years under my arm. I had been one of the big boys in the Triangle Club at Princeton and I thought that would help. The office boys were not impressed.'

One day, Fitzgerald ran into an advertising man who told him to stay away from the newspaper business. He helped him to get a job with the Barron Collier agency, and for some months Fitzgerald wrote slogans for street car cards.

'I remember,' he said, 'the hit I made with a slogan I wrote for the Muscatine Steam laundry in Muscatine, Iowa – "We keep you clean in Muscatine." I got a raise for that. "It's perhaps a bit imaginative," said the boss, "but still it's plain that there's a future for you in this business. Pretty soon this office won't be big enough to hold you."'

And so it turned out. It didn't take Fitzgerald long to get bored to the point of pain and he quit. He went to St Paul, where his parents again were living and proposed that his mother give him the third floor of her home for a while and keep him in cigarettes.

'She did, and there in three months I completely rewrote my book. Scribner's took the revised manuscript in 1919, and they brought it out in the spring of 1920.'

In *This Side of Paradise*, Fitzgerald had one of his principal characters take a crack at the popular authors of the period – some of whom are popular still – in these words:

'Fifty thousand dollars a year! My God look at them, look at them – Edna Ferber, Gouverneur Morris, Fannie Hurst, Mary Roberts Rinehart – not producing among 'em one story or novel that will last ten years. This man Cobb – I don't think he's either clever or amusing – and what's more, I don't think many people do, except the editors. He's just groggy with advertising. And – oh, Harold Bell Wright and Zane Grey, Ernest Poole and Dorothy Canfield try, but they are hindered by their absolute lack of any sense of humor.'

And the lad wound up by saying, it was no wonder that such English writers as Wells, Conrad, Galsworthy, Shaw and Bennett depended on America for over half their sales.

What does Fitzgerald think of the literary situation in this country today?

'It has improved a lot,' he said. 'The whole thing broke with *Main Street*. Ernest Hemingway, I think, is the greatest living writer of English. He took that place when Kipling died. Next comes Thomas Wolfe and then Faulkner and Dos Passos.

'Erskine Caldwell and a few others have come up just a bit after our generation, and they haven't done quite so well. We were products of prosperity. The best art is produced in times of riches. The men who came some years after us didn't have the chance we had.'

Has he changed his mind on questions of economics? Amory Blaine, the hero of *This Side of Paradise*, predicted the success of the Bolshevik experiment in Russia, foresaw eventual government ownership of all industries in this country.

'Oh, but I made an awful boner,' said Fitzgerald. 'Do you remember I said publicity would destroy Lenin? That was a fine prophecy. He became a saint.

'My views? Well, in a pinch they'd still be pretty much towards the left.'

Then the reporter asked him how he felt now about the jazz-mad, gin-mad generation whose feverish doings he chronicled in *This Side of Paradise*. How had they done. How did they stand up in the world?

'Why should I bother myself about them?' he asked. 'Haven't I enough worries of my own? You know as well as I do what has happened to them.

'Some became brokers and threw themselves out of windows. Others became bankers and shot themselves. Still others became newspaper reporters. And a few became successful authors.'

His face twitched.

'Successful authors!' he cried. 'Oh, my God, successful authors!'

He stumbled over to the highboy and poured himself another drink.

●

DAVID LLOYD GEORGE

Interviewed by Harry Boardman
The Manchester Guardian, 12 April 1940

David Lloyd Geogre (1863–1945), the Welsh Liberal politician, was born in Manchester and after his father's death was brought up near Criccieth, in Wales, at the home of his uncle. He became a solicitor in 1890 and the Liberal MP for Carnarvon Boroughs, with Welsh nationalist tendencies, a couple of years later. As president of the board of trade from 1905 to 1908 and as chancellor of the exchequer from 1908 to 1915 he presided over a programme of social reforming legislation, introducing the basis of the welfare state with old age pensions and national insurance. A little Englander during the Boer War, he nonetheless supported the war against Germany in 1914. He served first as munitions minister then as war minister before replacing Asquith as prime minister of the coalition government. After negotiating the peace at Versailles and Irish partition, his coalition fell. The Liberal Party was routed in the 1922 general election and thereafter split and declined. Lloyd George, however, retained his seat until 1945, when he was created 1st Earl Lloyd-George of Dwyfor just before he died. He published his *War Memoirs* from 1933 to 1936 and *The Truth about the Peace Treaties* in 1938. During the early years of the Second World War he was a critic of Churchill's war cabinet (which he regarded as chock-full of sycophantic mediocrities, whereas his own war cabinet from 1916 to 1918 had been a cabinet of all the talents). He also favoured a negotiated peace with Hitler, and both Chamberlain and Churchill suspected that he had dreams of emerging as a British Pétain.

Harry Boardman (1886–1958) was born in Macclesfield, Lancashire, the son of a hand-loom silk weaver. He worked as a journalist on local newspapers in the West Midlands before the First World War, served in the army during the war, and joined *The Manchester Guardian* in 1919, having been talent-spotted some years earlier by its editor, C.P. Scott. He was immediately sent out to Ireland to cover the 'troubles'. There then followed a spell as a political correspondent outside London. From 1929 to 1945 he was Westminster political correspondent, and from 1945 till his death he was parliamentary correspondent. His parliamentary sketches were published in a collection, *The Glory of Parliament*, in 1960.

Mr Lloyd George kindly granted me an interview at Churt two days before he completes his fifty years' membership of the House of Commons. He was in lively trim. He was also impatient for news, and he would still have been unsatisfied had the BBC been broadcasting its news every half-hour. That will convey some idea of his concern at what has happened and is happening. But he would not discuss the situation – at least not for publication here – because he wants to know much more before pronouncing a public judgement. He does feel, however, that we have reached a fateful phase of the war that may decide its whole course within the next fortnight.

His views of the present Government we all know, but they seemed perfectly epitomized when at the end of the one o'clock news bulletin the announcer gave us his last piece of information: 'The War Cabinet met this morning.' Slapping his knee Mr Lloyd George exclaimed with mock relief, 'Ah! Now everything's all right. Let us go out and look at the garden.' He took this theme of the War Cabinet farther. Its present organization he unreservedly condemns.

'Take the present position,' he said. 'There is Winston Churchill; he has been put in command of the co-ordination of defence. In the first place he himself represents one of the Services, and you know there is great jealousy between the Services. Neither the Army nor the Air Force will feel that he is giving a fair judgement if it happens to be against them. Again, co-ordination is a thing to take the whole time of a man. Churchill should not be embarrassed by all the demands that the detailed work of the Admiralty makes on a First Lord – plans for convoys, for dealing with submarines, magnetic mines, attacks from the air on ships. How can he do that and at the same time deal with general policy and the big defence issues? If he were not sixty-five, if he were even thirty-five, I should still say he could not do all this.

'Much the same is true of Sir John Simon. How can he apply himself to the general conduct of the war? He has a tremendous task at the Treasury, a much bigger task than the Chancellor of the Exchequer had in the last war. No, you must have men in your War Cabinet, in your small War Cabinet, who are free from departmental ties. There is not a single department of State to-day that is not a whole-time job, and it takes a man all his time to master the work of one department. How are other departmental Ministers going to judge what ought to be done in that particular department? Oh, no, it is a fatal error to have your War Cabinet composed of Ministers with departments.

'It was not so in my War Cabinet. I had men without departmental responsibilities who could be turned on to anything at a minute's notice. There was Milner. If I found difficulties arising in a particular department I asked him to investigate them and report to me. It was the same with Smuts and Curzon. I also had Henderson and Barnes to deal with Labour problems. None of these men had anything to do but to take up special problems. What is more, being without departments themselves, their decisions were invariably accepted by the departments because they were seen to have no departmental bias of their own. My War Cabinet sat every morning and afternoon and sometimes in the evening to receive the reports of the free-lance Ministers on the particular problems referred to them.'

Mr Lloyd George could rejoice over the setting up of unity of command from the beginning, and recalled his own hard fight to get it. 'I started my fight for it in 1917, but the military caste did everything they could to prevent its coming, and if it had not been for the terrific catastrophe of 1918 we should probably not have carried it at all.'

When it came to looking back over the years, Mr Lloyd George talked much of Ireland. He recalls very clearly the debates on Gladstone's second Home Rule Bill. A particularly lively memory is a speech of Salisbury's in the House of Lords just before the bill was rejected. 'I was a young member then, and Salisbury impressed me tremendously. His speech was a massive piece of oratory.' I suggested that at that moment he little dreamed of the part he himself was to play in Irish history, and he agreed, which brought him at once to the London conference of 1920. He cherishes a fond remembrance of Michael Collins. 'He was what you might call a broth of a boy,' said Mr Lloyd George. 'You felt he would be a great fellow in a guerrilla raid. Daring was stamped all over him. And yet he was extraordinarily nice and genial.

'But,' Mr Lloyd George continued, 'Arthur Griffith was the ablest man of them all. He was a silent man. He said little but it was always very much to the point. He was a much abler man, in my judgement, than De Valera. I think it was a disaster to Ireland that he did not live. He was a man of intellect and balanced judgement, of composure and foresight.'

Mr Lloyd George ran over some of the earlier Irish leaders. John Redmond, 'there was a nobility about him'. Dillon, 'more Castilian than Irish, and, like the Castilian, incapable of compromise'.

Joseph Chamberlain always had a great admirer in Mr Lloyd George. It seems odd in the man who was nearly killed by the Birmingham mob for opposing Chamberlain and the Boer War, but Mr Lloyd George sees that Jingo episode as a lapse in a consistently Radical career informed with a passion for social reform much like his own.

He told me this hitherto unpublished story to prove his point. After the Tory disaster of 1906 the party, sick of Balfour's tight-rope walking on Protection, sent a deputation to Chamberlain begging him to accept the Tory leadership (Balfour having just been defeated in East Manchester). The deputation was led by Sir John Lawrence, who told Mr Lloyd George of Chamberlain's reply, which was this: 'There is one objection to my leading a party that is predominantly Conservative and it is a fatal one. I am a Radical.'

From the beginning of the Boer War until 1906 Mr Lloyd George did not speak to Chamberlain, but immediately after he became President of the Board of Trade Mr Lloyd George introduced a bill providing for a census of industry, and one night he heard, as he says, a sibilant voice saying over his shoulder: 'I cannot tell you, Mr Lloyd George, how much I approve your Census of Industry Bill.' It was Chamberlain. 'I meant to do this thing myself, but the difficulties were too great.' Chamberlain pursued. 'They told me they were not going to have a screw manufacturer probing into their business.' 'Yes,' said Mr Lloyd George, 'Chamberlain was a Radical, not a Liberal but a Radical.'

Towards the end of our talk a mutual friend joined us. He asked Mr Lloyd George if he would like to live his wonderful career over again. The reply was at once heroic and moving. And for an instant, too, one felt the touch of the seer who takes command of Mr Lloyd George at times. This is no journalistic hyperbole. The phenomenon will be attested by anyone who has known him.

'No,' said Mr Lloyd George brooding a little. 'No,' he repeated, this time emphatically. 'I should not like to go over it again. What is behind me I know. Before me all is new. I want to go forward.'

●

STEFAN ZWEIG

Interviewed by Robert Van Gelder
The New York Times Book Review, 28 July 1940

Stefan Zweig (1881–1942), the Austrian biographer and novelist, was born in Vienna of Jewish parentage. He wrote popular biographies of Balzac, Dickens, Mary Stuart and Marie Antoinette, as well as popular novels such as *Letter to an Unknown Woman* (1922) and *Beware of Pity* (1939). Two years after this interview, Zweig committed suicide in Brazil. His autobiography *The World of Yesterday*, which was published in 1943 after his death, proved to be one of his most successful books.

Robert Van Gelder (1904–52) graduated from the Columbia University School of Journalism in 1928 and worked on various newspapers in New Haven, Connecticut, before joining *The New York Times* as a reporter in 1928. He was editor of *The New York Times Book Review* from 1943 to 1946 and a collection of his interviews with authors during the early 1940s was published as *Writers and Writing* (1946).

'The artist has been wounded,' said Stefan Zweig, 'in his concentration.' He rapped his breast with the knuckles of his left hand. 'How can the old themes hold our attention now? A man and woman meet, they fall in love, they have an affair – that was once a story. Sometime again it will be a story. But how can we lovingly live in such a trifle now?

'The last months have been fatal for the European literary production. The basic law of all creative work remains invariably concentration, and never has this been so difficult for the artists in Europe. How should complete concentration be possible in the midst of a moral earthquake? Most of the writers in Europe are doing war work of one kind or another, others had to flee from their country and live in exile, wandering about, and even the happy few who are able to continue working at their desks cannot escape the turmoil of our time.

'Reclusion is no more possible while our world stands in flames; the "Ivory Tower" of aesthetics is no more bomb-proof, as Irwin Edman has said. From hour to hour one waits for news, one cannot avoid reading the papers, listening to the wireless, and at the same time one is oppressed by the worries about the fate of near relatives and friends. Here flees one without home in the occupied area, others are interned and ask for freedom, others wander about begging from one consulate to another to find a hospitable country which will accept them. From all sides every one of us who has found a haven is daily assailed by letters and telegrams for help and intervention; every one of us lives more the lives of a hundred others than his own.'

He spoke of external hindrances occasioned by blackouts, by lack of freedom of movement, by inability to obtain access to research materials.

'For instance, I was just about to lay the last hand to my favorite book on which I had been working for twenty years, a large and really the first comprehensive biography of the great genius Balzac. Reluctantly I had to abandon this nearly finished volume because the library of Chantilly which contains all of Balzac's manuscripts had been closed for the duration of the war and brought away to an unknown and inaccessible place; on the other hand, I could not take with me the hundreds and thousands of notes because of the censorship. Just as in my case, for thousands of artists and scientists work of many years has been stopped, perhaps for a long time, by purely technical difficulties.

'And the internal difficulty – what means psychology, what artistic perfection at such an hour, where for centuries the fate of our real and spiritual world is at stake? I, myself, had soon after completing my last novel, *Beware of Pity*, prepared the sketch for another novel. Then war started and suddenly it seemed frivolous to represent the private fate of imaginary persons. I had no more the courage to deal with private psychological facts and every "story" appeared to me today irrelevant in contrast to history.'

He said that most of the other writers he knew had experienced this same distraction in their own work. Paul Valéry, Roger Martin du Gard, Duhamel and Romains all had confessed to him that they could no longer concentrate on their work. 'I would be suspicious against any European author who would now be capable to concentrate on his own, his private work. What was allowed to Archimedes, the mathematician, to continue his experiments undisturbed by the siege of his town, seems to me quasi inhuman for the poet, the artist, who does not deal with abstractions but whose mission it is to feel with the greatest intensity the fate and sufferings of his fellow beings.'

Yet out of this war will come vast realms of experience in which the artist may work, and Mr Zweig paced the floor excitedly as he talked of this:

'On each ship, in each travel bureau, in each consulate, one may hear from quite unimportant, anonymous people the stories of adventures and pilgrimages which are no less dangerous and thrilling than those of Odysseus. If any one would print, without altering a single word, the documents of the refugees which are now kept in the offices of charity organizations, by the Society of Friends, in the Home Office in London, it would make a hundred volumes of stories more thrilling and improbable than those of Jack London or Maupassant.

'Not even the First World War drove so many lives to such crises as this one year, never has human existence known such tensions and apprehensions as today – too much tension to be dissolved immediately into artistic form. That is why, in my opinion, the literature of the next years will be more of a documentary character than purely fictional and imaginative.

'We assist at the most decisive battle for freedom that has ever been fought, we will be witnesses of one of the greatest social transformations the world has ever gone through, and we writers before all have the duty to give evidence of what happened in our time. If we reproduce faithfully but our own life, our own experiences – and I intend to do so in an autobiography – we have perhaps done more than by an invented novel.

'No genius can nowadays invent anything which surpasses the dramatic events of the present time, and also the best poet has again to become student and servant of the greatest master of us all; of history.'

Mr Zweig says that the one thing he can work on now is his autobiography, which will carry the title *Three Lives*.

'My grandfather lived a life, my father lived a life. I have lived at least three. I have seen two great wars, revolution, the devaluation of money, exile, famine. The period of the French Revolution and the Napoleonic wars, the period of the Reformation – they were times not unlike this. No other times can equal the change we who are of middle age now have seen.'

He commented that he was once 'the most translated author in the world'.

'My books were published in Italian, Japanese, in practically all the countries on earth. They had – how do you say – universal coverage. When Hitler came in, my books were banned in Germany, now they are banned in Italy, perhaps next week in France. There were large Finnish editions and Polish – no more. Every fortnight I lose a country.

'Oh, that is not important. So long as they can be published in one language, that is enough. And I believe that over here you will resist the death of freedom for a long time. It is inconceivable that liberty could be destroyed here. It will be regained in France; here it will not be lost.'

Mr Zweig is here only on a visitor's visa. He intended to leave shortly for South America, where he will lecture. Then he will return to England. 'I cannot miss what is happening there.'

He said that he is writing his autobiography as he writes everything else – 'four times too long'.

'I write the first time to please myself. I put in everything that I think of. I am a contented writer who can write all day and be happy. So the early drafts of my books are very, very long.

'On the other hand, I am a nervous reader. I become very impatient when any author – including myself – strays from his point. So when I read what I have written I cut it in great chunks. I chop and chop until there is not a spare word, a sentence that can be done without.'

•

PABLO PICASSO

Interviewed by Jerome Seckler
New Masses, 13 March 1945

Pablo Picasso (1881–1973), the Spanish painter, entered the academy at Barcelona at the age of fourteen and later studied in Madrid. In 1901 he went to Paris, taking a studio in Montmartre, where he was influenced by neo-Impressionist painters such as Toulouse-Lautrec and Degas. His own output went through many transformations over his remarkably productive career. In the first decade of the century alone he went through a blue, a pink and a brown period before embarking on Cubism, the movement which he founded with the French painter Georges Braque and which rejected traditional forms of representation based on perspective. Picasso and Braque parted company in 1914, however.

In the 1920s Picasso designed costumes for Diaghilev's Ballets Russes while continuing to paint in the Cubist style. One of his most famous paintings, *Guernica* (1937), expressed his horror at the bombing of the Basque town of Guernica during the Spanish Civil War. He was director of the Prado Gallery in Madrid from 1936 to 1939 under the Republic, though an absentee throughout. He spent much of the Second World War in Paris and joined the Communist Party after the liberation of the city, thus prompting the interest of *New Masses*. His later career was spent experimenting with different forms, such as lithography, sculpture and ceramics, as well as producing numerous canvases.

For the past ten years my friends and I had discussed, analysed and rehashed Picasso to the point of exasperation. I say exasperation because very simply it was just that. The only conclusion we could ever arrive at was that Picasso, in his various so-called 'periods', quite accurately reflected the very hectic contradictions of the times, but only reflected them, never painting anything to increase one's understanding of these times. Various artists and critics who make their living by putting labels on people identified him with a wide variety of schools – surrealist, classicist, abstractionist, exhibitionist and even contortionist. But beyond this lot of fancy nonsense, these people never did explain Picasso. He remained an enigma.

Then came the bombshell. In the midst of the last agonized hours of Loyalist Spain Picasso painted his Guernica mural, and with this mural emerged as a powerful and penetrating painter of social protest. But there was only the Guernica. Up to the time France entered the war there were no echoes in Picasso's painting of the furious protest that had produced the Guernica. Then came France's military disaster and her humiliating occupation by the Germans. Nasty stories circulated about Picasso. That he was living well in Paris under the Germans; that he played ball with the Gestapo, which in return permitted him to paint unmolested. That he was selling the Nazis fakes – works he signed, but which were actually painted by his students. Still another that he was dead. From 1940 until the liberation of Paris, Picasso remained a figure completely surrounded by mystery and obscurity.

Then in October following the liberation came the electrifying news that Picasso had joined the Communist Party.

In that same month liberated Paris held a gigantic exhibition of contemporary French art, one room of which was especially devoted to Picasso – seventy-four paintings and five sculptures, most of them executed during the occupation. The exhibition startled me. It was the Picasso of the Guernica, painting powerfully, painting beautifully, painting of life and hope.

I was so excited by Picasso's work I determined to see him. Through a young French artist who knew him I managed to get his address. At his studio I was told, after a whispered conversation in another room, that Picasso was 'not at home'. His secretary explained, 'Picasso has not painted for two months what with all that was happening, and now he wants to settle down and do some work.' But finally my young artist friend arranged a meeting for me, and at 11.30 of a Saturday morning I arrived at his studio, was ushered in and told to wait.

Picasso occupies the top two floors of a definitely unpretentious place, a four-story building close to the Seine. To get up to his studio one enters one of the holes in the wall that pass for doorways and climbs three flights up a narrow winding stairway with bare walls and worn wooden steps. This has been his home and his studio for the past eight years. You enter directly into one of the studios, a room with several easels, paintings, books – without order. As I waited I noticed one of his recent paintings on an easel, of a metal pitcher on a table. Tacked above the painting was a small pencil sketch of the composition, which the painting duplicated down to the last line and detail. Though it was only a quick sketch, he had followed it so closely that when he crossed lines at the corner of a table he also crossed them in the painting.

I asked his secretary if Picasso had had trouble with the Germans. 'Like everyone,' he said, 'we had hard times.' Picasso was not permitted to exhibit. Once the Gestapo came and accused Picasso of being in reality a man called Leipzig. Picasso simply insisted, 'No, I am Picasso, that's all.' The Germans did not bother him after that, but they kept a close watch on him at all times. Nevertheless, Picasso maintained a close contact with the underground resistance movement.

After about ten minutes, Picasso came down from the upstairs studio, and approached me directly. He gave me a quick glance, looked me squarely in the eyes. He was dressed in a light grey business suit, a blue cotton shirt and tie, a bright yellow handkerchief in his breast pocket – small hands but solid. I introduced myself and Picasso offered me his hand immediately. He had a warm, sincere smile, and spoke without restraint, which put me at once at ease.

I explained that I had always been interested in his work, but that he has always puzzled me, and how I felt suddenly at his recent exhibition that I understood what he was trying to say. I wanted to know him personally, and to ask him if my analyses of his paintings were correct, and if they were, to write about them for America. Then I described for Picasso my interpretation of his painting, *The Sailor*, which I had seen at the Liberation Salon. I said I thought it to be a self-portrait – the sailor's suit, the net, the red butterfly showing Picasso as a person seeking a solution of the times, trying to find a better world – the sailor's garb being an indication of an active participation in this effort. He listened intently and finally said, 'Yes, it's me, but I did not mean it to have any political significance at all.'

I asked why he painted himself as a sailor. 'Because,' he answered, 'I always wear a sailor shirt. See?' He opened up his shirt and pulled at his underwear – it was white with blue stripes!

'But what of the red butterfly?' I asked. 'Didn't you deliberately make it red because of its political significance?'

'Not particularly,' he replied. 'If it has any, it was in my subconscious!'

'But,' I insisted, 'it must have a definite meaning for you whether you say so or not. What's in your subconscious is a result of your conscious thinking. There is no escape from reality.'

He looked at me for a second and said, 'Yes, it's possible and normal.'

Picasso then asked if I were a writer. I told him the truth – I was not a writer, had never written before. That by vocation I worked in lumber. I was a painter too, but only by avocation, because I had to make a living. Picasso laughed and said, 'Yes, I understand.' Then I asked if I had his consent to write an article about him.

'Yes,' he said, and then added, 'For which paper?'

I told him the *New Masses*. He smiled and answered, 'Yes, I know it.'

He looked at the open door. There were several people waiting for him. 'Let's go upstairs to the studio for a moment,' he said. So we climbed the stairs to the large studio where he actually does his painting. The room was neat and clean. It didn't have the dusty, helterskelter appearance of the room downstairs.

I told Picasso that many people were saying that now, with his new political affiliations, he had become a leader in culture and politics for the people, that his influence for progress could be tremendous. Picasso nodded seriously and said, 'Yes, I realize it.' I mentioned how we had often discussed him back in New York, especially the Guernica mural (now on loan to the Museum of Modern Art in New York). I talked about the significance of the bull, the horse, the hands with the lifelines, etc., and the origin of the symbols in Spanish mythology. Picasso kept nodding his head as I spoke. 'Yes,' he said, 'the bull there represents brutality, the horse the people. Yes, there I used symbolism, but not in the others.'

I explained my interpretation of two of his paintings at the exhibition, one of a bull, a lamp, palette and book. The bull, I said, must represent fascism, the lamp, by its powerful glow, the palette and book all represented culture and freedom – the things we're fighting for – the painting showing the fierce struggle going on between the two.

'No,' said Picasso, 'the bull is not fascism, but it is brutality and darkness.'

I mentioned that now we look forward to a perhaps changed and more simple and clearly understood symbolism within his very personal idiom.

'My work is not symbolic,' he answered. 'Only the Guernica mural is symbolic. But in the case of the mural, that is allegoric. That's the reason I've used the horse, the bull and so on. The mural is for the definite expression and solution of a problem and that is why I used symbolism.'

'Some people,' he continued, 'call my work for a period "surrealism". I am not a surrealist. I have never been out of reality. I have always been in the essence of reality [literally the "real of reality"]. If someone wished to express war it might be more elegant and literary to make a bow and arrow because that is more aesthetic, but for me, if I want to express war, I'll use a machine-gun! Now is the time in this period of changes and revolution to use a revolutionary manner of painting and not to paint like before.' He then stared straight into my eyes and asked, '*Vous me croirez?*' (Do you believe me?)

I told him I understood many of his paintings at the exhibition, but that quite a few I could not figure out for myself at all. I turned to a painting of a nude and a musician that had been in the October Salon, set up against the wall to my left. It was a large distorted canvas, about five by seven feet. 'For instance this,' I said, 'I can't understand at all.'

'It's simply a nude and a musician,' he replied. 'I painted it for myself. When you look at a nude made by someone else, he uses the traditional manner to express the form, and for the people that represents a nude. But for me, I use a revolutionary expression. In this painting there is no abstract significance. It's simply a nude and a musician.'

I asked, 'Why do you paint in such a way that your expression is so difficult for people to understand?'

'I paint this way,' he replied, 'because it's a result of my thought. I have worked for years to obtain this result and if I make a step backwards, [as he spoke he actually took a step back] it will be an offense to people [the French was just that, *offense*] because that is a result of my thought. I can't use an ordinary manner just to have the satisfaction of being understood. I don't want to go down to a lower level.

'You're a painter,' he continued; 'you understand it's quite impossible to explain why you do this or that. I express myself through painting and I can't explain through words. I can't explain why I did it that way. For me, if I sketch a little table,' he grabbed a little table just alongside to illustrate, 'I see every detail. I see the size, the thickness, and I translate it in my own way.' He waved a hand at a big painting of a chair at the other end of the room (it had also been in the Liberation Salon), and explained, 'You see how I do it.'

'It's funny,' he went on, 'because people see in painting things you didn't put in – they make embroidery on the subject. But it doesn't matter, because if they saw that, it's stimulating – and the essence of what they saw is really in the painting.'

I asked Picasso when I could see him again, and he said he would be glad to see me any time I wished. We shook hands and I left.

I found it difficult to visit Picasso again as promptly as I wished, but on a Saturday morning some weeks later I paid him a second call. Picasso received me in his bedroom where, when I entered, I could hear him discussing political problems to be solved within the unity of the Allies with several friends. As soon as he saw me he came over, smilingly shook hands and greeted me, '*Bon jour! Ca va bien?*' Again he was so simple and sincere that I felt as though I had known him for years. He apologized for receiving me in his bedroom. 'I've had to organize myself in this little room,' he said, 'with my dog, my papers, my drawings, my bed, because I was freezing downstairs.' His hands as usual were expressively accompanying his words, like those of an orchestra conductor's. For a small room, it certainly was crammed full. The unmade bed, several bureaus, a slanting drawing table and a large gentle-eyed dog all revolved about a little coal stove, capped by a pot of water. Scattered on the bed and table were seven or eight large etchings in color which he had just finished – with bright reds, blues and yellows laid down in mass. On the bed also were five or six newspapers, including *L'Humanité*. Resting on a bureau on the wall was an etched zinc plate with two prints from it, of a lemon and a stemmed wine glass, done in the same beautiful bright colors. Over another bureau was an old photo-gravure of a Rubens – a man and woman bursting with love, very richly and sensitively done. On another wall was a small Corot landscape.

I brought out my report of our first interview and we went over it together. The article being in English, I had to translate into French. Everything was agreeable to him, but in translating what he had said about the bull, palette and lamp painting, I must have slipped in my French and he misunderstood me, thinking I was quoting him as saying the bull represented fascism.

'No,' he protested, 'it doesn't represent fascism.'

I explained what he had said was that it did not represent fascism but that it did represent darkness and brutality. 'But that's just the point,' I said. 'You make a distinction between the two. But what distinction can there be? You know and the

the people of the world know the two are the same, that wherever fascism has gone there is darkness and brutality, death and destruction. There is no distinction.'

Picasso shook his head as I spoke. 'Yes,' he said, 'you are right, but I did not try consciously to show that in my painting. If you interpret it that way then you are correct, but still it wasn't my idea to present it that way.'

'But,' I insisted, 'you do think about and feel deeply these things that are affecting the world. You recognize that what is in your subconscious is a result of your contact with life, and your thoughts and reactions to it. It couldn't be merely accidental that you used precisely these particular objects and presented them in a particular way. The political significance of these things is there whether you consciously thought of it or not.'

'Yes,' he answered, 'what you say is very true, but I don't know why I used those particular objects. They don't represent anything in particular. The bull is a bull, the palette a palette and the lamp is a lamp. That's all. But there is definitely no political connection there for me. Darkness and brutality, yes, but not fascism.'

He motioned to the color etching of the glass and lemon. 'There,' he said, 'is a glass and a lemon, its shapes and colors – reds, blues, yellows. Can you see any political significance in that?'

'Simply as objects,' I said, 'no.'

'Well,' he continued, 'it's the same with the bull, the palette and lamp.' He looked earnestly at me and went on, 'If I were a chemist, Communist or fascist – if I obtain in my mixture a red liquid it doesn't mean that I am expressing Communist propaganda, does it? If I paint a hammer and sickle people may think it's a representation of Communism, but for me it's only a hammer and sickle. I just want to reproduce the objects for what they are and not for what they mean. If you give a meaning to certain things in my paintings it may be very true, but it was not my idea to give this meaning. What ideas and conclusions you have got I obtained too, but instinctively, unconsciously. I make a painting for the painting. I paint the objects for what they are. It's in my subconscious. When people look at it each person gets perhaps a different meaning from it, from what each sees in it. I don't think of trying to get any particular meaning across. There is no deliberate sense of propaganda in my painting.'

'Except in the Guernica,' I suggested.

'Yes,' he replied, 'except in the Guernica. In that there is a deliberate appeal to people, a deliberate sense of propaganda.'

I pulled out my cigarettes and we lit up, Picasso smoking his in the ever-present cigarette holder. He took a few puffs meditatively as though waiting for me to say something, then said quietly and simply, 'I am a Communist and my painting is Communist painting.' He paused for a moment, then went on. 'But if I were a shoemaker, Royalist or Communist or anything else, I would not necessarily hammer my shoes in a special way to show my politics.'

'And yet,' I said, 'what a man is and thinks can be deduced from his paintings. But it is not necessary for a socially conscious painter, for instance, to show a scene of Nazi horror or destruction, of a person with blood dripping from the mouth, or a soldier shooting, a rifle.' I pointed to the small coal stove with the open pot of water on it, and continued, 'You can paint that, you can paint a mother and son, or a child, as you did, or a family eating dinner around a table – you can paint the glass and lemon. By its very objects, colors, forms it becomes a beautiful thing, the kind of beauty we want to surround our lives with, the kind of life we are fighting this war for. Being social beings we think politically whether we intend to or not.'

Picasso rested his hand on my shoulder and kept nodding his head vigorously as I spoke, saying, 'Yes, yes, that's right, that's so very true.'

I told him of the stir his joining the Communist Party had caused in the art world – how the critics, still labelling him 'surrealist', hopefully wanted him to continue painting as he had some years before – how they quoted him as saying there was no connection between art and politics.

Picasso laughed and said, 'But we know there is a connection, yes?' and added smilingly, 'but I don't try myself, that's all.'

I asked Picasso if my article, and I meant to include what he had just been telling me, had his approval. 'Yes,' he said, 'go ahead with it.'

At this point some of his friends drifted over and we discussed some of the trends in American and French painting. Picasso seemed unacquainted with our leading American painters. I mentioned some, including Thomas Benton, but Picasso did not know them or their work.

'That shows the distance between our two countries,' said one of Picasso's friends.

'In the United States,' I said, 'we don't have as many artists as France, but on the whole our artists are more vigorous, more vital, more concerned with people than the French painters. France has had the same big names in art for the past forty or more years. From what I observed in the exhibition at the Salon d'Automne, the younger artists were mostly introspective, concerned mainly with technique and hardly at all with living reality. French art is still concerned with the same techniques and still lifes.'

'Yes,' Picasso said, 'but the Americans are in the stage of the general sense. In France, that is past for us and we are now at the stage of individuality.'

By then someone decided it was time for lunch. I thanked Picasso and he told me again to drop around whenever I wanted, and with a warm handshake we said *au revoir*.

•

MAHATMA GANDHI
Interviewed by H.N. Brailsford
Harijan, 14 April 1946

Mahatma (Mohandas Karamchand) Gandhi (1869-1948), the Indian moral and
political leader, was born in Gujarat, Western India. He practised as a barrister
in London and went to South Africa where he first became politically active,
championing the cause of civil rights for Indians who had settled there. His
favoured method of protest was non-violent civil disobedience. He again used
this method (known as *satyagraha* in India) as leader of the Indian National
Congress. His first campaign back in his homeland, the Non-Co-operation-cum-
Khilafat, ran from 1920 to 1922. Later, he and his followers embarked upon the
Civil Disobedience Movement (1930-34). He was opposed to rural poverty, the
cartelization of the British imperial textiles industry which discriminated against
India, and the caste system. In 1942 Gandhi had launched another non-violent
movement, called Quit India, and was thereupon arrested along with other
Congress leaders. At the end of the Second World War he renewed his call for
independence. The rise of Muslim nationalism forced the British to partition
India and in 1948 Gandhi was assassinated by a Hindu zealot who believed that
he had not done enough to resist partition.

    Henry Noel Brailsford (1873–1958), the son of a clergyman, was educated at
Glasgow University and was briefly assistant professor of logic there before
joining the Greek Foreign Legion for the war with Turkey in 1897. His
influential book *The War of Steel and Gold* gave an international socialist analysis
of the imperialist rivalry that led to the First World War. Brailsford worked as a
leader-writer on a succession of newspapers – *The Manchester Guardian, Tribune,*
the *Daily News,* and *The Nation.* From 1922 to 1926 he edited *The New Leader.*
He had already interviewed Gandhi for *Young India* back in October 1931, and
he wrote several books on political subjects, including *Rebel India* (1932) and
Subject India (1942).

When last I was in Poona, Gandhi was a prisoner, and I was not allowed to
meet him. Then the town, gloomy and angry, was involved in a general strike.
Today it is celebrating the spring carnival in a mood of gaiety.

    Gandhi in his turn was happy when I met him, for Mr Attlee's speech in the
Indian debate had just opened the road to independence. He looked well and
very much less than his age . . . His manner was never solemn and often he
relaxed in a humorous chuckle. In a way, hard to define, one felt that this man
was speaking for India . . . He warned me, nonetheless, that he would be

speaking only for himself and not for the Congress. Our talk took its start from the Prime Minister's recognition of India's right to choose independence. This, Gandhi welcomed, and not only this, but the whole tone of the speech. He went on:

'But I can't forget that the story of Britain's connection with India is a tragedy of unfulfilled promises and disappointed hopes. We must keep an open mind. A seeker of truth will never begin by discounting his opponent's statement as unworthy of trust. So I am hopeful, and, indeed, no responsible Indian feels otherwise. This time I believe that the British mean business. But the offer has come suddenly. Will India be jerked into independence? I feel today like a passenger who has been hoisted in a basket-chair on to a ship's deck in a stormy sea and has not yet found his feet. There should have been some psychological preparation, but even now it is not too late. The tide of bitterness had risen high and that is not good for the soul. The last two months should have been filled with generous gestures. This is a milestone not only in India's history and Britain's, but in the history of the whole world.'

Gandhi's meaning was clear. The British Government had done the right thing, but in its manner of doing it, he missed the big touch. When I asked him for concrete illustrations, he chose two. The release of the political prisoners had been gradual and was still incomplete. He added: 'There was no danger to fear. If independence is coming, would these men have opposed it? A complete amnesty would have captured the people's imagination. When you are about to transfer power, you should do it boldly.'

He went on to speak of the Salt Tax. 'Its abolition would be a gesture the poorest peasant could understand. It would mean even more to him than independence itself. Salt in this climate is a necessity of life, like air and water. He needs it for himself, his cattle and his land. This monopoly will go, the instant we get independence. Then why not abolish it today? By such acts the Government could have created a feeling among the masses that the new era has already dawned . . .'

I . . . reminded Gandhi that many Englishmen find it hard to understand why Indians prefer independence to Dominion Status. His answer was startling. 'There was a time when I used to swear by Dominion Status, and actually preferred it to independence. That was my attitude during the First World War. I even used, in writing to Lord Chelmsford, the Viceroy of those days, an expression that has often been quoted against me. I wanted to evoke in the Indian breast the same loyalty to the British Crown that there is in the breast of an Englishman. It was an English footballer who converted me to independence.'

With a laugh, Gandhi explained that he was referring to C.F. Andrews, who had been a notable athlete at Cambridge, as well as a don. Gandhi added: 'Andrews made me understand the significance of the King-Emperor's title. The British king is king also in the Dominions, but he is the Emperor of India.

India alone makes the Empire. The Dominions are peopled by your cousins. But we Indians, with our different culture and traditions, can never belong to the British family. We may belong to a world-wide family of nations, but first we must cease to be under-dogs. So I set myself to win independence. You may object that by so doing I am throwing away the protection of the British army and navy. India would not need them, if she were truly non-violent. If, in the glow of freedom, she could live up to that creed, no power on earth would ever cast an evil eye upon her. That would be India's crowning glory and her contribution to the world's progress.

'If only Englishmen could follow this argument of mine, they would make their offer of independence in a different tone altogether. Today they insist that Dominion Status is the best gift they can possibly bestow: still, if Indians do choose independence, they shall have it. No, that is the wrong attitude. I should like to hear Englishmen saying: "For the world's sake and for ours as well as your own, you shall have independence today, even as we have it . . ."'

I asked Gandhi to face the anxieties of his English listeners and tell them whether Indian independence would make for Britain's security and the world's. He answered that the British need never fear an independent India. If they leave India as willing friends, she in her turn will always remain friendly. But Britain, I told him, might hope for some assurance of friendship. Would an independent India be willing to enter into an alliance with Britain? Gandhi's answer came promptly:

'Supposing India said "No", would you make the recognition of India's independence contingent upon her entering into an alliance with Britain? If you did that, it would immediately lower the value of your offer and rob it of all grace. The proper attitude is to meet India's claims as a matter of right, even if she wanted to be unfriendly and pay you back in your own coin. No calculations entered into the British mind, when they settled with the Boers at the end of a bloody war, and the Boers have stayed friends ever since.'

I replied that Britain has made up her mind to end the coercive connection with India. But living as she does in a perilous world it is inevitable that she should ask the question whether as an ally in a defensive war she would be entitled to use India's strategic bases and ports against the aggressor. If that question were asked in no bargaining spirit, could India give a reassuring reply? Gandhiji answered;

'Englishmen must learn to be Brahmins, not Banias. The Bania, I should explain, is the trader, or as Napoleon put it, the shopkeeper. The Brahmin is the man who is intelligent enough to rank the moral above the material values of life.

'A Gujarati novelist has said that Englishmen are soldiers and Brahmins, but not Banias. That was a generous verdict, but it was mistaken. Englishmen have still to evolve the Brahminical spirit. Even the British soldier still calculates and bargains like a Bania, and fails to reach the highest type of courage. I still cherish the hope that the British will respond to the non-violent spirit of India. As the author of that movement, I know what it has meant for the world. The non-violent spirit is the greatest thing in life. I feel it is my responsibility to help my brothers not to degrade themselves by bargaining. If you and we can rise to this moral height, no danger can alarm us. It is probable that many members of the Congress will not take this view and may be willing to discuss an alliance today. But independence would come free as air; don't let us bargain over it.'

In reply to a further question, whether a defensive alliance might be discussed when independence is ratified by treaty, Gandhi replied: 'If India feels the glow of independence, she probably would enter into such a treaty of her own free will. The spontaneous friendship between India and Britain would then be extended to other powers and, among them, they would hold the balance, since they alone would possess moral force. To see that vision realized, I want to live for 125 years . . .'

He said that he hoped for a mutually helpful commercial treaty between a friendly Britain and an independent India. For goods that India needed to import, he was even ready to give Britain a preference.

While we talked of Pakistan, Gandhi said that if no other method of solution succeeded, he was prepared to submit the whole issue to international arbitration. Nor should we forget that expedient, if any insoluble question arose between Britain and India, for example, over debts. But he saw no blank wall of difficulty ahead. His last words were that difficulties make the man . . .

I came away with the sense that I had been talking to a brave man who has the courage to believe that human society can be built only on moral principles. Amid our preoccupations over military perils, he stands aloof and repeats with unshaken faith his creed that safety is attainable, only when men learn to treat each other as brothers and equals. No lesser means will avail.

●

'THE GENTLE ART OF BEING INTERVIEWED'
Evelyn Waugh
Vogue, July 1948

According to Evelyn Waugh's diary for 19 August 1947, he was interviewed by a 'dull young woman, fat'. The interview appeared under the heading of 'Huxley's Ape makes hobby of graveyards' in the Stockholm paper *Dagens Nyheter*. Apart from being published in the US edition of *Vogue*, Waugh's piece was also printed in the British magazine *Nash's* (Winter 1948–9).

*

Was it a peculiarity of my own, or do you, Gentle Reader, as I once did, keep a black list of public characters? Mine grew longer every year. It comprised men and women, quite unknown to me except through the newspapers, for whom, nevertheless, I had a sharp personal dislike.

In a few cases, no doubt, the trouble was visual – a smirk in the photographer's flashlamp, a jaunty step in the news-reel, a hat; sometimes it was aural – adenoids at the microphone; but the vast majority of the people, at any rate on *my* list, were there for intellectual offences. It was something they were reported to have said to the press.

I refer, of course, to those utterances which seem to gush out spontaneously, washing away the patient camouflage of years in a great cataract of self-revelation. These people are kind in the home, good at their jobs, but when there are reporters about something comes over them, and it is then that they make their atrocious, unforgettable utterances – or so I used to think, when I watched them chatting to the men with the notebooks, posing for the men with the cameras.

The classic ground for the sport is a liner arriving in New York. New Yorkers still retain a friendly curiosity about their foreign visitors – indeed, believe it or not, a bulletin is printed and daily pushed under your door in the chief hotels, telling you just what celebrities are in town, where they are staying, and nominating a Celebrity of the Day, an introduction to whom is often included among the prizes in radio competitions.

To satisfy this human appetite, the reporters come on board with the first officials and have ample time before the ship finally berths to prosecute their quest. They are not got-up to please. Indeed, their appearance is rather like Poe's Red Death – a stark reminder of real life after five days during which one has seen no one who was not either elegantly dressed or neatly uniformed. American papers have at their command most prepossessing creatures of both sexes, but they choose only those who look like murderers to greet visitors. They are elderly and, one supposes, embittered men. They have not advanced far in their profession and their business is exclusively with the successful. Their revenge is a ruthless professionalism. They look the passengers over and make their choice, like fish-brokers at market. One of their number, the grimmest, stalks into the lounge, breaks into a distinguished group, taps an ambassador on the arm and says: 'The boys want a word with you outside.'

I have often watched the process and decided that the fox, on the whole, rather enjoyed it. Eminent people get the feeling of moving everywhere among flashlamps and questions, and miss them if they are not there, as dog-lovers like to be greeted by a hairy, dribbling, barking herd whenever they enter their own house. I suppose it is like being an officer in the army. One's first day in uniform one was embarrassed at being saluted; after a short time one expected it. Anyway, I used to think, as I saw the distinguished goats segregated from the sheep and hustled away so brusquely, that they would greatly have resented being left out, and I read the results with stony heart. How they gave themselves away, I thought.

But I have become altogether a softer man in this matter since last year when, for one ghastly afternoon, I found myself one of the victims – not, I need hardly say, in the open competition of the first-class deck of a Cunarder, but in far more modest but equally disturbing circumstances.

It was shortly before it became a criminal offence to travel abroad. I made a last-minute rush to a country which I will call 'Happiland'; a small, friendly country never much visited by the English, and last summer quite deserted by them, so that my arrival was, to that extent, remarkable.

I came by air. We landed at what should have been lunch-time, at what indeed *was* lunch-time for the various officials whose consent was necessary for our entry. This is no season in which to expect a sympathetic hearing of vexations of travel. We will all go through hell cheerfully nowadays to get abroad. I did not repine, but I was weary when at length some hours later I reached my hotel. It was a stuffy afternoon; Happilandic trams rattled below the window. I shut out their sound, and with it every breath of fresh air. I lay down on the bed, lit a cigar, and before I had smoked half an inch was asleep. It was still in my fingers when I awoke at dusk; there was ash all over me, a hole in the top sheet and a smell of tobacco and burned linen. There was a strange figure in my room. It turned on the light and revealed itself as a young woman dressed as though for sport – not 'le sport' of Mr Michael Arlen; athletics, putting the weight, most likely.

'Good night, Mr Wog,' said this apparition. 'Excuse please, I must make a reportage of you.'

I sat up and began slowly to remember where I was; much more slowly than in detective stories the heroine comes round from chloroform.

'I am of . . .' said my visitor, uttering some deep Happilandic gutturals, 'our great liberal newspaper.'

'Do sit down.' I waved to the armchair; then noticed that it was full of my clothes. 'I am sorry to receive you like this.'

'How you are sorry to receive me? I represent all anti-Fascist intellectual activities.'

'Ah, well; do you smoke?'

'Not too much.'

She sat on my clothes and looked at me for some time without noticeable interest.

'Well,' I said at length, 'I suppose this is really worse for you than for me.'

'Excuse please?'

'I simply said this was worse for you than for me.'

'In what directions, please?'

'Well, perhaps it isn't really.'

'I am not understanding what is worse, Mr Wog.'

'No, it meant nothing.'

'So.'

There was another pause in which I began slowly to regain my self-possession. It was a game of snakes and ladders. The next throw set me back six squares.

'Mr Wog, you are a great satyr.'

'I assure you not.'

'My editor says you have satirized the English nobility. It is for this he has sent me to make a reportage. You are the famous Wog, are you not?'

'Well, I'd hardly say that. Some of my books have been fairly popular . . . a very ordinary Wog, you know.'

'I know, like the great Priestley.'

'No, much more ordinary. Quite different.'

'How different, Mr Wog? You have said "Fairly", "Popular", "Ordinary". I have those words written down. I understand well. You believe in social justice, you write for the people, yes? You represent the ordinary man? That is why you satirize the nobility. They abuse you?'

'Yes, come to think of it, some of them do.'

'Of course. In Happiland we are having many such proletarian writers. But since we have no nobility, they must satirize the secretaries of the trades unions. Do you also satirize the secretaries?'

'No, I can't say I do. You see, I've never met one.'

'They are high people?'

'Yes, very high.'

'So. I find you are a timid man, Mr Wog, to be afraid of the secretaries. In Happiland are many jokes about them.'

She seemed cast down by her memories of Happilandic humour and sat silent for some time. When she next spoke it was in the *plume de ma tante* tradition.

'Mr Wog, how are your pens?'

I did not try. I simply said, 'Very well, thank you.'

'Here are many pens. I am not a pen. My editor has been an international pen in Swissland. Were you an international pen, Mr Wog?'

Light broke. 'The Pen Club? I'm afraid I am not a member, myself.'

'How can that be? In Happiland all the great authors are pens. There is much jealousy to belong. Some say the elections are by intrigue, but it is not so. It is all by merit. Is it not so in England?'

'Yes, I am sure it is.'

'How then, please, are you not a pen? Do the great English writers scorn you?'

'That's exactly it.'

'Because you are a proletarian?'

'I expect so.'

'Oh, Mr Wog, how I will satirize them in my reportage! It will enrage my editor. He will protest to the International Committee of Pens.'

'Jolly decent of him,' I said, perhaps rather weakly.

She wrote busily, in longhand, covering several leaves of her notebook. Then she said: 'Mr Wog, you have come here to satirize Happiland?'

'Certainly not.'

'Why then have you come?'

'Oh, just for the change.'

'That is interesting me very much. You think Happiland is greatly changed?'

'I mean for myself.'

'In what directions, please, do you wish to change?'

'In all directions.'

'So. And you come to Happiland for these changes? Because of the new Age-Spirit?'

That was a long snake, leading me back half-way down the board. 'Yes,' I said, contemptibly.

'And your school? That will change too?'

'Oh, I expect so. All the schools are changing every day, I'm told . . . I know what you're going to ask; in what directions? Well, not so much classics, you know, modern languages, more stinks.'

This seemed a ladder.

'I am not understanding stinks, Mr Wog.'

'That's what we used to call science at my school.'

'Yes, yes, now I understand you. It is an American idiom. Science stinks, yes? You suffer the cosmic despair because of the atom bomb. You antagonize the sciences. In Happiland we are having many such desperate intellectuals. And to express this world-sorrow you are leading your school of proletarian satyrs to new language-forms away from the classics. Mr Wog, this will be a fine reportage. I must go with it to my editor.'

She was gone, and as I lay back among the singed bedclothes I felt deep gratitude that none of my friends read Happilandic and deep compunction for the injustice which for years I had been doing a number of suffering fellow humans.

Think of this more or less true story, Gentle Reader, when you next feel moved to intolerance. It may be your turn next.

●

DYLAN THOMAS

Interviewed by Harvey Breit
The New York Times Book Review, 17 February 1952

Dylan Marlais Thomas (1914–53), the Welsh poet, was born in Swansea. The son of an English teacher, he worked as a journalist until the publication of his *Eighteen Poems* (1934) brought him fame. His *Collected Poems 1934–1952* was published in 1952 and was, in poetry terms, a bestseller. His poetic voice, his interest in sound sensations, and his humour came together in *Under Milk Wood* (1954), his radio play about life in a Welsh village. He also wrote short stories and broadcasts for the radio. He died young, as a result of his alcoholism, while on a lecture tour of the United States.

Harvey Breit (1913–68) was educated at New York University and was a columnist and assistant editor of *The New York Times Book Review* from 1948 to 1957. He helped adapt Budd Schulberg's novel *The Disenchanted* for the stage and co-edited *The Selected Letters of Malcolm Lowry* (1964). He also contributed to *Atlantic, Paris Review, Poetry* (Chicago) and *New Directions*. He also wrote articles on boxing and baseball. Many of his talks with authors, which appeared regularly in *The New York Times Book Review* while he was on its staff, were published as a collection, *The Writer Observed* (1956).

In 1950 the brilliant, aseptic Welsh poet Dylan Thomas (Dylan rhymes with penicillin) visited us for the first time. He is back a second time now – to read his own and other poets' verses at the Ninety-second Street YMHA, the Modern Museum and scores of colleges and universities – as much by popular demand as by his own wish. In celebration of this event, *New Directions* is bringing out his new poems, *In Contrary Sleep*, and in celebration of a more personal sort this writer engaged Mr Thomas in a repeat performance talk. Though Mr Thomas – it was an absolutely reliable bet – wouldn't repeat himself, couldn't repeat himself. And so, inexorably, it turned out.

In the course of the first talk (14 May 1950), Mr Thomas described himself as 'thirty-five years older, small, slim, dark, intelligent, and darting-doting-dotting-eyed'. He then added, 'Say I am balding and toothlessing. I am also well-dressed.' Mr Thomas wasn't slim then, and still isn't; he is still fair, with plenty of unruly hair, enough teeth, and his eyes are round and sleepy-looking. His tweeds are definitely unpressed. Mr Thomas, as a matter of fact, could easily have stood in for Heywood Broun on the occasion when he was described as resembling an unmade bed. Mr Thomas, it is nice to be able to report, continues all in all to remain intelligent, imaginative and unreconstructed.

The talk at first was on poetry in general and Thomas Hardy in particular, who turned out to be Mr Thomas's favorite poet of the century. But Mr Thomas was also a prose writer of talent, and one wondered how he thought about the two mediums. Did he, for example, care less and less about prose? 'No,' Mr Thomas said, 'as you grow older they are more and more separate in what you feel. When you are young you are liable to write this bastard thing, a prose-poetry. When you get a bit older you find they get separated, and prose becomes more clean and spare.'

One felt that about Eliot's prose. Mr Thomas nodded. 'Eliot does keep them separate. He writes beautiful prose – only because it's nothing to do with the verse. A poet can't write extravagant prose: it would be a slopover. A prose writer can write extravagant poetry. Joyce is the direct reverse. He wrote simple, clean poetry and marvelously imaginative prose. With most people it's the opposite. Writers should keep their opinions for their prose.'

Supposing, the interviewer said, you were not you and I were not I –
'I'd believe it,' Mr Thomas said succinctly.

And then not-I asked not-you, why shouldn't poets have opinions in their poetry?

'Opinions,' Mr Thomas proceeded, 'are the result of self-argument and as most people can't argue with anybody and especially with themselves, opinions are bloody awful. There are opinions, of course. In dramatic poetry for one, but most of us are lyric poets. It was Eliot in this century who showed that one could talk about any subject in verse, except one's self.'

Then wasn't there some sort of discrepancy in what Mr Thomas was saying? 'I suppose,' Mr Thomas said, 'the thing about opinion should be qualified.' That was precisely what Mr Thomas had been doing, hadn't he? 'The slant,' Mr Thomas went on, 'the tilt of the mind informs the poetry.'

Mr Thomas kept his Between-the-Acts little cigar in the corner of his mouth, his head tilted at an angle away from the smoke. 'I like to put down the word "blood". It's a curious kind of word; it means insanity, among other meanings. It's part of the tilt of my mind that I put it down often.'

Mr Thomas and his guest drank. 'What is interesting,' he pursued, after a while, 'is the way in which certain words either lost their meaning or their goodness. The word "honor", for instance. A world fit for heroes. A world fit for Neros is more like it.'

Why did words lose their meaning or goodness? 'The wrong people crowed about them,' Mr Thomas said, looking like an owl.

How long was he going to be here? 'About three months,' Mr Thomas said. 'It will be my last visit for some time. I will have had the universities and they will have had me.'

The writer wasn't taking that statement seriously at all.

'Well,' Mr Thomas said, '*I* am.'

Would he sum up?

'Poetry,' Mr Thomas summed up, avoiding what might have sounded theatrical, 'poetry. I like to think of it as statements made on the way to the grave.'

●

SAMUEL BECKETT

Interviewed by Israel Shenker
The New York Times, 6 May 1956

Samuel Beckett (1906–89), the French novelist and playwright, was born and educated in Ireland. He wrote his early poems and first two novels in English, but after his decision to settle in France in 1932, his later trilogy of novels,

Molloy (1951), *Malone Meurt* (1951), and *Innommable* (1953), and his bleak yet comic plays, *Waiting for Godot* (1956) and *End Game* (1957), for which he is best known, were written in French. These plays were described as belonging to the theatre of the absurd. He was awarded the Nobel Prize for literature in 1969.

Israel Shenker (b. 1925) was a correspondent in Europe for *Time Magazine* from 1949 to 1968. He then joined *The New York Times* as a reporter.

Samuel Beckett is a gaunt, imposing figure who looks like a fiery apostle sent to scourge the sinners of the world.

His Paris apartment is on the eighth floor of a middle-class apartment house – not shabbier than the Paris average.

He speaks precisely like his characters – with pained hesitation, afraid to commit himself to words, aware that talk is just another way to stir dust.

'I came to Paris for the first time as a student at Trinity in 1926, and I graduated from Trinity in 1927 with a degree in French and Italian. Then I came back here in 1928 as an exchange lecturer at the École Normale Supérieure . . .

'I left the École Normale in 1930. I was appointed the assistant to the Professor of French in Dublin for a period of three years . . . I resigned after four terms . . . I didn't like teaching. I couldn't settle down to the work . . . then I left Ireland.

'I was in Germany, in London, I was back in Dublin. I was battering around the place. That's a very confused period in my own mind. I wrote *More Pricks than Kicks* and *Echo's Bones*. I wrote my first novel – *Murphy*. In London. The poems all over the place, here and there.

'I had an elder brother, a quantity surveyor – like my father. A quantity surveyor is an intermediate between architect and builder. My brother had taken over my father's business when my father died.

'I didn't like living in Ireland. You know the kind of thing – theocracy, censorship of books, that kind of thing. I preferred to live abroad. In 1936 I came back to Paris and lived in a hotel for a time and then decided to settle down and make my life here. That was in 1933.

'While my mother was alive I went to her for a month every year, during the summer. My mother died in 1950.

'I was doing a fair amount of translation, teaching (tutoring in English), some work for UNESCO. But that's getting ahead of the story.

'When I was at École Normale in 1928, 1929, that was when I did a tentative translation into French of the Anna Livia passage in *Finnegans Wake* with a friend of mine. That was the first translation. It appeared later, worked over by others – a group including Joyce. The original draft was by me and Alfred Peron, now dead also, massacred by the Germans.

'I was never Joyce's secretary, but like all his friends I helped him. He was greatly handicapped because of his eyes. I did odd jobs for him, marking passages for him or reading to him. But I never wrote any of his letters.

'I was in Ireland when the war broke out in 1939 and I immediately returned to France. I preferred France in war to Ireland in peace. I just made it in time. I was here up to 1942, and then I had to leave, so I went to the Vaucluse – because of the Germans. Because I didn't keep quiet. I did – how shall I put it? – I don't like talking about the Resistance – it was a French group with my friend Peron. The function was to collect information of all descriptions and to get it over to London. I did all kinds of odd jobs – to receive the bits of information as they came in and classify them and type them up.

'During the war I wrote my last book in English – which was *Watt*. After the war I went back to Ireland in 1945 and came back with the Irish Red Cross as interpreter and storekeeper. The Irish Red Cross had offered St Lo a hospital entirely stocked with food and medical equipment and I went to St Lo. But I didn't stay long with the Irish Red Cross.

'In spite of having to clear out in 1942 I was able to keep my flat. I returned to it, and began writing again – in French. Just felt like it. It was a different experience from writing in English. It was more exciting for me – writing in French.

'I wrote all my work very fast – between 1946 and 1950. The French work brought me to the point where I felt I was saying the same thing over and over again. For some authors writing gets easier the more they write. For me it gets more and more difficult. For me the area of possibilities gets smaller and smaller.'

Beckett has been compared to Kafka, but he sees differences rather than a similarity. 'It seems to me – I've only read Kafka in German – serious reading – except for a few things in French and English – only *The Castle* in German. I must say it was difficult to get to the end. The Kafkaen hero has a coherence of purpose. He's lost but he's not spiritually precarious, he's not falling to bits. My people seem to be falling to bits. Another difference. You notice how Kafka's form is classic, it goes on like a steamroller – almost serene. It *seems* to be threatened the whole time – but the consternation is in the form. In my work there is consternation behind the form, not in the form.

'At the end of my work there's nothing but dust – the unnameable. In *l'Innommable* there's complete disintegration. No "I", no "have", no "being". No nominative, no accusative, no verb. There's no way to go on ... *Textes pour rien* – was an attempt to get out of the attitude of disintegration, but it failed.

'With Joyce the difference is that Joyce was a superb manipulator of material – perhaps the greatest. He was making words do the absolute maximum of work. There isn't a syllable that's superfluous. The kind of work I do is one in which I'm not master of my material.

'The more Joyce knew the more he could. He's tending toward omniscience and omnipotence as an artist. I'm working with impotence, ignorance. I don't think impotence has been exploited in the past. There seems to be a kind of aesthetic axiom that expression is an achievement – must be an achievement. My little exploration is that whole zone of being that has always been set aside by artists as something unusable – as something by definition incompatible with art.

'I think anyone nowadays, anybody who pays the slightest attention to his own experience, finds it the experience of a non-knower, a non-can-er. The other type of artist – the Apollonian – is absolutely foreign to me.

'The calm, abstract, Valéryan statement seems to me completely spurious – unless there are people whose inner experience is like that. I can't conceive of that.

'I'm not interested in any system. I can't see any trace of any system anywhere.'

Why did he choose to write a play after writing novels?

'I didn't *choose* to write a play. It just happened like that.'

Critics have said that the structure and message of *Waiting for Godot* left the author free to lay down his pen at any moment. Beckett disagreed: 'One act would have been too little and three acts would have been too much.'

What to do, then, when there is nothing more to say? Just what others do – go right on trying?

Beckett replied: 'There are others, like Nicolas de Staël, who threw themselves out of a window – after years of struggling.'

●

BRENDAN BEHAN

Interviewed by Robert Robinson
Sunday Graphic, 15 July 1956

Brendan Behan (1923–64), the Irish playwright, was born in Dublin, the son of a house-painter. He was sent to Borstal in 1939 for trying to blow up a British battleship in the Cammel Laird dockyards in Birkenhead on behalf of the IRA, and in 1942 was sentenced to fourteen years' imprisonment for the attempted murder of a policeman (he served five years). Thereafter he painted houses and wrote stories for a Dublin magazine, while assuaging his thirst for alcohol – almost a full-time occupation by anyone else's standards. Behan quickly gained a reputation as an opinionated roustabout who shocked the British public by appearing drunk and incoherent on BBC Television. He wrote a prison drama, *The Quare Fellow* (1956) and a farce, *The Hostage* (1958). His autobiography, *Borstal Boy*, was published in the same year. Behan was a natural joker with a zest for living and a favourite exclamation was 'Fuck the begrudgers!', though he was compassionate and always interested in ordinary people. Fame encouraged his duel with Fate, but it did not spoil his character. He had started drinking alcohol at the age of six and he eventually died from drink at forty-one.

Robert Robinson (b. 1927) was educated at grammar school and at Oxford, where he edited *Isis*. His first job in journalism was as TV columnist for the *Sunday Chronicle*. By the time of this interview he was film and theatre critic of the *Sunday Graphic*, an Irish paper, and radio critic of *The Sunday Times*. He later devoted his energies to broadcasting, mainly for the BBC.

The bright spot in my week was a small celebration I had with that great Dubliner, playwright and star of British TV, Mr Brendan Behan.

Mr Behan, you recollect, appeared with Malcolm Muggeridge in an interview, and permitted his Dublin accent and a quantity of beer to get between him and coherent utterance.

'It is a great sadness to me,' said Mr Behan, as we stood at the door of a public bar and watched two men-about-town in bowler hats, 'that Englishmen dress as though they were undertakers, and that the pubs close about four times a day.'

He broke into song as we entered the pub, and cheered up slightly.

He shook hands all round, placed himself in a strategic position behind a battery of bitters and clinked glasses as we drank to the West End contract he had just signed for his play *The Quare Fellow*, to be staged at the Comedy.

'Please,' he said, 'you must understand I only write plays when I'm short of a couple of bob. I don't give a damn for art. I'm just in it for the dough.'

(At this stage, I must indicate that my report does Mr Behan the injustice of removing the expletives. Mr Behan is unable to make conversational progress without a series of expletives exploding behind him like squibs.)

'I like England,' said this stout Irishman who has seen the inside of Her Majesty's jails.

'I like the bitter, I like the cockles and the Billingsgate boys. But I find the Covent Garden porters too refined.'

I asked him – as he broke once more into song – what he will do with the money he makes from his West End contract.

'Why,' he said simply, 'I shall eat it and drink it, like anyone else.'

And he broke off to inquire of Mr Stanley Devon . . . [the photographer] why he was not drinking. Mr Devon explained he was a teetotaller.

'Then,' said Mr Behan with missionary fervour, 'you deserve to be hung.'

'I shake hands,' he said somewhat irrelevantly, 'with no member of the upper class except the Guinness family. They've done a lot for me.'

'Ah,' said I, 'but look what you've done for Guinness . . .'

'Yes,' he continued, even more irrelevantly, 'me uncle wrote the Irish national anthem, and with a bit of luck I'd have been gauleiter of London this day.'

He started speaking French, and a Frenchman who had been following the conversation with his mouth hanging open asked him where he learnt to speak it so well.

He told him, solemnly and untruthfully, that he had lived in France since he was six years old, went stone deaf at the age of five, and picked it up lip-reading.

The Frenchman walked out with his mouth wider than ever.

We left by taxi, and in the middle of crowded Piccadilly Mr Behan roared the driver to a halt.

He climbed out, walked up to a beggar in the street, gave him half a crown, and climbed back in again.

Slàinte to Brendan Behan, say I.

•

NIKITA KHRUSHCHEV

Interviewed by Tom Driberg
Reynold's News, 9 and 16 September 1956

Nikita Sergeyevich Khrushchev (1894–1971), the Soviet politician and leader, was born in Kalinovka. He was a shepherd boy, a locksmith and a pipe-fitter in a Donbass coal mine before joining the Communist Party in 1918. He fought in the Civil War, then became a party official. Elected chief of the Moscow Communist Party in 1935, he was elected a full member of the Politburo in 1939 – the first of those who had joined the party after the Revolution to attain this status. During the Second World War he organized the guerrilla resistance in the Ukraine, but after the defeat of the Nazis he purged the anti-Stalinist opposition in the region. In 1949 he applied his organizational skills to the overhauling of Soviet agriculture. After the death of Stalin in 1953 Khrushchev was the only man to hold a position in the party secretariat (he was its head) and the Politburo, thus securing his succession.

In 1956, at the 20th Congress of the Communist Party, he boldly attacked Stalin's policies and personality cult (though the text of his speech was not published until 1989). He led the Soviet Union from 1956 to 1964, relaxing the worst excesses of the police state, pursuing policies of decentralization and economic reform, and making diplomatic efforts to achieve 'peaceful coexistence' with the West. In 1964, while on holiday at his villa on the Black Sea, he was deposed by a combination of Leonid Brezhnev and Alexei Kosygin. He died in obscurity and was not accorded the honour of a state funeral or interment in the Kremlin wall. A machine-made politician, he was destroyed by the machine.

According to Harrison Salisbury, who was the Moscow correspondent of *The New York Times* during the 1950s, Khrushchev 'was a newspaperman's delight because he was always open to interviews. He talked incessantly, and his talk was interesting. He was a mugger, he liked to be in the spotlight; he liked to talk about himself and his experiences.'

Thomas Edward Neill Driberg (1905–76) was a British journalist, schooled at Lord Beaverbrook's *Daily Express*, who had been elected to Parliament as an Independent in 1942 and had later joined the Labour Party. He was created a peer as Lord Bradwell in the year that he died. A notorious homosexual, his memoirs, *Ruling Passions*, were published posthumously.

In 1956, through his old friend Guy Burgess, who had defected to the Soviet Union before being unmasked as a Soviet spy, Driberg was able to interview Khrushchev. The interview, which took place soon after the famous 20th Congress of the Communist Party at which Khrushchev had attacked 'the errors of Stalinism', lasted for four and a half hours and was published on two succesive Sundays. This is the second part.

My interview with Mr Khrushchev, First Secretary of the Central Committee of the Communist Party of the Soviet Union, lasted two hours twenty minutes.

After our argument about the British Labour Party I turned to the subject on which I was really more anxious to question him – the present situation in the Soviet Union.

I mentioned two words that have been much in the air since the historic 20th Congress of the CPSU – the words 'decentralization' and 'legality'. As part of the general current process of decentralization, the All-Union Ministry of Justice has been dissolved, and its powers transferred to ministries in the various Republics of the USSR.

I had heard it said that this would prevent a repetition of those breaches of legality which have now been condemned, and I asked Mr Khrushchev if he thought this was so.

KHRUSHCHEV: 'We think that this decision will help to prevent violations in future, and improves the work of justice in the Soviet Union, because the Soviet Union is composed of sovereign republics, with their own economies and cultures.

'Justice concerns the people, and the people live in the Republics, the Soviet Union itself is an abstract concept: there is no territory of the Soviet Union as such. Therefore legislation should be legislation by and for the Republics. The Soviet Union itself can simply provide co-ordination, to guard against contradictory legislation. For this purpose, the supervision of the procurator is enough, with an All-Union special commission.'

DRIBERG: 'To what extent is there uniformity of punishment in the various republics? Could there be capital punishment for murder in one Republic, and not in another?'

KHRUSHCHEV: 'It is quite possible. Every national Republic has its own criminal code. Even now, there are some differences. But there is some co-ordination.'

I mentioned one minor respect in which decentralization did not seem to be occurring adequately as yet. The Soviet authorities set great store by visual education through large satirical posters. A few days earlier I had seen a number of these – satirizing drunkenness, nepotism, and other anti-social vices – at a crowded country fair in Uzbekistan. I took a photograph of one of the posters, and a youth standing by pointed to it and spoke to me.

My interpreter explained that he was asking what the poster meant like most of the people there, he was an Uzbek; Uzbek is the official language of Uzbekistan; yet the explanatory captions on all these posters were in Russian, which most of the people at the fair could not read.

'That shows,' said Mr Khrushchev, 'inadequate organization by our propaganda services.' He added that he was 'amazed by the silliness' of such a mistake.

I next raised the question of the Supreme Soviet, as compared with the British House of Commons, as a forum for the criticism and questioning of ministers.

KHRUSHCHEV: 'The character and procedure of the two assemblies are different. The Supreme Soviet is not in session all the year round, but only for definite, and comparatively brief, times. There would hardly be time for an hour of questions each day, as in the House of Commons.

'We were present at your question-time when we were in London. I like it. It is a democratic feature of your Parliament. To some extent I think it raises the blood-pressure of the ministers. It is democratic and interesting.

'Probably we ought to find some way of introducing a similar procedure in the Supreme Soviet. I cannot now say exactly what it would be like, but something of the kind is not excluded.

'Nevertheless, your question-time is a bit theatrical, because of your two-party system: it is chiefly the Opposition that asks questions, while Government MPs mostly support their leaders.'

DRIBERG: 'To some extent that is so but it is not entirely true. At question-time the House of Commons is less rigidly divided in two than at other times; it is much more the House as a whole *vis-à-vis* the Executive. If there is some case of injustice to an individual, it will be taken up at question-time by that person's MP whether he is Labour or Conservative

I added that I had been told that the most effective forum of democratic criticism in the Soviet Union was the ordinary Party meeting. I had wished to attend one of these, but was told that it might be difficult to do so as non-members were (naturally) not usually admitted. Could Mr Khrushchev help?

KHRUSHCHEV: 'I promise to speak for you.'

He went on to say that great importance was attached to party meetings, trade union meetings, 'and general meetings of the workers at which every question can be raised'. At one time they used to have evenings of questions and answers.

Workers had the right to question their factory managers or trade union officials: no question was barred, and if the answer wasn't known it had to be given at the next meeting.

I asked if these valuable meetings were no longer held. Not so often as before, said Mr Khruschchev, but they were 'not rejected'. Formerly they had been compulsory; now they were voluntary.

DRIBERG: 'If they are voluntary, isn't there a tendency on the part of managers and officials to avoid organizing them? If question-time in the House of Commons was voluntary, very few ministers in the British Government would insist on having it.'

He agreed that bureaucratic human nature was the same the world over – 'but we have a great medicine against bureaucracy in the mass correction of our Party, and it is compulsory on leaders and officials to answer every question.'

This sometimes wastes a lot of time, he said, because there are some people who are never content with an answer and go on fussing and nagging at everyone.

He told me of two of his own personal experiences during a recent visit to the Ukraine.

An old woman had complained to him ('she was a nervous and garrulous type') that she couldn't get a satisfactory answer to her problem, though she had been round to every official in turn.

There is a law that, if a collective farmer stops working on the collective, he loses his private plot of land (which varies in size in different districts). This woman had two sons, both of whom had formerly worked on the collective: now they had gone to work in a factory, and had accordingly been deprived of their plots of land. But they, and their mother, could still go on living at the collective; and they still had the much smaller portions of land that non-members were allowed.

The mother, however, was not satisfied with this. She wanted her sons' former plots of land back as well.

KHRUSHCHEV: 'After I'd looked into it, I had to tell her that I thought she'd been given the correct answer first time. So now she's not satisfied with me, either!'

DRIBERG: 'At least you can be sure that she won't vote against you.'

KHRUSHCHEV: 'Yes – besides she's not in my constituency!'

Next he told me of the complaint of another woman, the wife of a mining engineer. Her husband had been sent to jail for three years because a worker in a pit that he was in charge of had fallen and died. The woman said it was the worker's own fault, because he hadn't bothered to wear a safety-belt. But her husband had been convicted for negligent supervision.

KHRUSHCHEV: 'In this case I could not take sides. I asked the higher judicial authorities to investigate it.'

DRIBERG: 'Had the man the right of appeal to a higher court?'

KHRUSHCHEV: 'Certainly, I'm afraid I do not know if he had exercised it – I think perhaps I came on the scene before he had had time to.'

I then turned to the subject of the Soviet press. I said that I had gathered that the newspapers were full of criticism of individuals and institutions.

KHRUSHCHEV: 'Yes and this must make our enemies abroad think that we are in a terrible state, and are about to collapse, when they read our papers full of nothing but criticisms. Still, year after year goes by, and we survive!'

DRIBERG: 'And if there were no criticism in your papers, people abroad would say you had not a free Press. Besides the criticism at Party meetings and elsewhere, the Press is also a valuable medium for raising questions and grievances?'

KHRUSHCHEV: 'It is most important. In the public interest, because it affects not only the person criticized but the readers, who can learn the proper lessons from it.'

DRIBERG: 'I am not quite sure how high criticism can go. I hope you won't mind my asking this, but has a newspaper the right to criticize you?'

KHRUSHCHEV: 'Yes.'

DRIBERG: 'They didn't criticize Stalin. At present, I know, they are particularly pleased with you and the other Soviet leaders for doing what Stalin failed to do – going round and visiting the various Republics.'

KHRUSHCHEV: 'You are quite right, we are getting a great response on these tours of ours.'

DRIBERG: 'But if at some future time, for some reason, an editor thought that you deserved criticism, would he print it?'

KHRUSHCHEV: 'So far as criticism of my work as First Secretary of the Central Committee is concerned, the Party organ will not criticize me because – like my own work – it is guided by the directives of the Central Committee. If my work is not according to the policy of the Party, then the Central Committee and the Party press will criticize me openly.

'If any member of the Central Committee is not doing his job properly, the Central Committee can expel him, and if this person insists on his mistakes, he will be criticized in the press; and if he still insists, he would be expelled from the Party. This is essential Party discipline.'

DRIBERG: 'If in the past, editors had been more in the habit of criticizing the leaders, isn't it possible that the errors of Stalinism would have been avoided, or might have been corrected sooner?'

KHRUSHCHEV: 'Certainly – but such situations develop over a long period of time. They are like the Ukrainian funeral mounds: it was a tradition that, when a leading man had been buried, every passer-by should throw a handful of earth on the grave – and so, gradually, a great hill grew . . .

'It was the same with Stalin's authority. His freedom from criticism grew out of his positive work for the Party and the people. Then, in the conditions of the time, his peculiar temperament transformed what had been positive and good into a negative force. Things have been put right again by the 20th Congress.'

DRIBERG: 'Are you satisfied that collective leadership is now so well established that there cannot be a repetition of the errors of Stalin?'

KHRUSHCHEV: 'I think so. But this is a matter of relations between people as well as the creation of a democratic framework. Our aim is to prevent any repetition of the cult of the individual and to return to the Leninist position and methods. Lenin was very strict in this respect.'

At this point, rather abruptly but amicably, the interview ended, because Mr Khrushchev had to go to a luncheon that Mr Bulganin was giving in honour of the President of Indonesia. It was after 12.45. The discussion had lasted for two hours, twenty minutes.

The interpreter and I came out into the anteroom, where the Foreign Ministry official was awaiting us. He told me later that the private secretary's various telephones had been ringing constantly, but that all who rang had been told that Mr Khrushchev could not be disturbed. Freedom from interruption on such an occasion is as rare as it is welcome.

●

ALFRED HITCHCOCK
Interviewed by Pete Martin
The Saturday Evening Post, 27 July 1957

Sir Alfred Joseph Hitchcock (1899–1980), the English film director, was born in East London. He started as a technician in 1920 and directed his first film in 1925. He developed a reputation for suspenseful storytelling and was fascinated by themes of mistaken identity, transference of guilt and voyeurism. His career as a director lasted for just over fifty years and included such classics as *The Thirty-Nine Steps* (1935) and *The Lady Vanishes* (1938) in Britain, and *Rebecca* (1940), *Rear Window* (1955) and *Psycho* (1960) for Hollywood studios.

After a brief career as a bit player in Hollywood movies, Thornton Martin (b. 1901), better known as Pete Martin, turned to writing. His fiction was not a great success, but his non-fiction reporting for *The Saturday Evening Post* was. His first Hollywood assignment was in 1944. In 1953 he did his first major interview assignment, 'Call Me Lucky' – a four-part series of autobiographical articles about Bing Crosby, as told to Pete Martin. This and a similar series he did about Bob Hope set new circulation records for the *Post*. Thereafter he did an excellent series of celebrity interviews for the *Post* during the 1950s and 60s. Always headed 'I Call on . . .', they often ran to several thousand words. His subjects were usually film stars, singers or, that new breed of celebrity, the television personality, and they included Groucho Marx, Kirk Douglas, Jackie Gleason, Julie London, Phil Silvers, Clark Gable, Dinah Shore, Mike Wallace (himself a television interviewer), Ed Sullivan, Dean Martin, Lucille Ball and Desi Arnaz, Lawrence Welk, Maurice Chevalier, and Zsa Zsa Gabor. Apart from these interviews, which were collected in book form as *Pete Martin Calls on . . .* (1962), his co-written autobiographies of Crosby and Hope were published as books, and he co-wrote similar autobiographies of Ethel Merman and a couple of Second World War heroes, Sgt Charles 'Commando' Kelly and Lieutenant Commander John Morrill. He also wrote books about Marilyn Monroe and Walt Disney.

Alfred Hitchcock's office was on the first floor of the Paramount Studio. As I walked in, it all came back to me. I had been in that office before, to talk to Frank Capra or to Willie Wyler. I couldn't remember which. It had been a long time ago and both Capra and Wyler had been gone from Paramount for years. For all I knew, they might be on their way back. Things happen that way in Hollywood.

The small round man who occupied that office now had a long pink nose and a slow voice that wheezed as he talked. He was neither Capra nor Wyler. Instead, he was his own highly individual self, but a number of intelligent people believe that in his own bailiwick Alfred Hitchcock has no remote rival as a directorial genius.

I'd been trying to see him for a week, but he'd been very ill. Then he was reported convalescent. At last I got the word if I'd be at Paramount at three o'clock the following afternoon, he'd be happy to talk to me. When I saw him he looked amazingly well. I was surprised. I'd met him once before while covering the Hollywood beat and he looked better now than he had then.

'I hear you had more than one operation,' I said. 'Coming one on top of the other, they must have been quite a shock . . .'

'A New York doctor once told me that I'm an adrenal type,' he said. 'That apparently means that I'm all body and only vestigial legs. But since I'm neither a mile runner nor a dancer and my present interest in my body is almost altogether from the waist up, that didn't bother me much.'

'Who drew that cartoon of you I see on my TV screen?' I said. 'The one composed of two or three lines that gradually turns into you.'

'I drew it myself,' he said. 'I began to draw it years ago, when I was a movie art director. With one exception, there's been little change in it since then. At one time I had more hair. All three of them were wavy.'

'TV viewers are funny,' I said. 'I've noticed that one of the things about you which seems to appeal to them is the fact that when they stare at you on a TV screen, you stare right back at them contemptuously. But what seems to fascinate your viewing audience even more than your superciliousness is your lack of reverence for your sponsor.'

'Remember the old saying, "A knock is as good as a boost,"' he said. 'My guess is that my sponsor enjoys my lack of obsequiousness, but in the beginning they had difficulty in getting used to my approach and they took umbrage at my less worshipful remarks. However, the moment they became aware of the commercial effects of my belittling – they took a look at their sales chart – they stopped questioning the propriety of my cracks. But there's no getting around it, I did take getting used to. The tradition is that the sponsor must be coddled. In such an atmosphere I was a novelty.

'The type of humor I wanted to use on TV was the type I employed in my film, *The Trouble With Harry*. In that film, Harry was a dead body who was a botheration to those who were alive. The awkward question, "What'll we do with Harry?" was always popping up. There were those who found the notion gruesomely amusing, so I told myself that if no reverence for a dead body is amusing, no reverence for a live sponsor might be amusing too.

'In selecting the stories for my television shows, I try to make them as meaty as the sponsor and the network will stand for. I hope to offset any tendency toward the macabre with humor. As I see it, that is a typically English form of humor; even a typically London type of humor. It's of a piece with such jokes as the one about the man who was being led to the gallows to be hanged. He looked at the trap door in the gallows, which was flimsily constructed, and he asked in some alarm, "I say, is that thing safe?"

'A story about the comedian Charles Coborn is cut from the same bolt of cloth,' Hitchcook said. 'I mean the original Charles Coborn, not the Hollywood one, whose name is spelled slightly different. The first Charles Coborn, who was famed for singing "The Man That Broke the Bank at Monte Carlo", attended the wartime funeral of another comedian named Harry Tate, who'd been hit by some anti-aircraft-shell fragments. A large assembly of comedians was gathering at the graveside. Old Charles was so ancient that he was retired, and as the coffin was being lowered into the grave, one curious young sprout leaned over and whispered, "How old are you, Charlie?"

"Eighty-nine," Coborn said.

'"Hardly seems worth while you going home," the young 'un said.

'That's an example of the kind of humor I'm talking about,' Hitchcock said. 'But in case you've already heard that one, here's another story about two charwomen having a day off at a fair. They were in a sideshow watching a man whose quaint notion of entertaining the public was to bite the heads from live rats and chickens. In carnival lingo, parties who purvey such entertainment are called "gooks". The two chars stared at the gook, horrified, but one of them couldn't help trying to make a bit of a joke. "Wouldn't you like a piece of bread with it?" she called out.'

Hitchcock looked at me with a pleased expression, as if he'd just unburdened himself of a fragile and delicious witticism, but I was glad that I'd already had my lunch. However, his mention of hens triggered my next remark.

'I hear your father was a poulterer,' I said.

'He was,' Hitchcock told me. 'And there's a theory that I've never liked eggs because of my father's occupation. It's true that I do regard eggs as loathsome, and to me, the most repulsive smell in the world is that which reeks up from a hard-boiled egg, but my father's occupation has nothing to do with my reaction. I hate the whole idea of eggs so much that when I can, I drop one of them negatively, shall we say, into my pictures to cover them with the obloquy they so richly deserve. For example, in *To Catch a Thief* I had a woman stub out her cigarette in an egg yolk.'

'I do remember that,' I said, 'but it's the only one of your egg scenes I do remember.'

'In a picture made years ago, *Shadow of a Doubt*,' he said, 'there was a moment in which I wanted a man to be shocked by something someone had said. His knife was headed straight for a fried egg, and the instant the remark was made, the knife punctured the yolk and immediately yellow goo spread all over his plate. To me, it was much more effective than oozing blood.

'People constantly ask me, "Why are you so interested in crime?"' Hitchcock went on. 'The truth is I'm not. I'm only interested in it as it affects my profession. Actually I'm quite terrified of policemen; so much so that in 1939, when I first came to America, I refused to drive a car, for fear a policeman would stop me and give me a ticket. The thought that if I drove I would face that possibility day after day frightened me horribly, for I can't bear suspense.'

My face must have registered amazement, for he hastily explained, 'I mean I hate it when I'm on the receiving end. People told me, "Maybe if you will open a door in your subconscious, behind which you are concealing a psychosis acquired in your childhood, you'll lose your fear of policemen."

'I grubbed back into my memory and opened the following door: when I was a small lad my father sent me to the local chief constable with a note. The constable read the note, laughed and locked me into a cell for a minute or two while he said, "That's what we do to naughty boys." It was my father's idea of teaching me an object lesson. When they hear that, everyone says, "Of course! That's why you're afraid of police." Unhappily, however, the fact that I have exposed that incident to the light has not allayed my fears. Cops still give me goose pimples.'

I told him that one of my favorite Hitchcock touches was the sequence in the film *The Lady Vanishes*, in which the two Englishmen discuss news of the latest cricket scores.

'You mean Basil Radford and Naunton Wayne,' he said. 'When I discovered

Wayne, he was a compère at a cabaret in the Dorchester Hotel in London. A compère is a man who is not really in the show at all. He can be the anonymous flunky who hands the illusionist the silk hat stuffed with rabbits. In Wayne's case, his compèring meant that he announced each act and said a few words between turns. Radford was the leading man in the original company of *Night Must Fall* – he is also known for his portrayal of the commander of the Home Guard in the film *Tight Little Island* – but I'm proud of the fact that, having found those two, I put them together. They formed a combination that complemented each other as happily as arf and arf or fish and chips.'

'To me,' I said, 'one of the all-time classic motion picture scenes was that pair, sitting in a small station in a European city with all hell breaking loose in the world around them while their only concern was to find out what the cricket scores were back in England. As an American,' I went on, 'it was the quintessence of Britishness. Did the British think it thoroughly British too?'

'No,' Hitchcock said. 'They knew that it was merely a humorous exaggeration. Such things have been called the Hitchcock touch, but they're really examples of English humor based on carrying understatement to an absurd extreme.

'I suppose you might call it the oblique approach to melodrama. Melodrama is the most highly colored form of storytelling. Its villains, heroes and heroines are usually played heavy-handedly and bumblefootedly. I approach it somewhat differently. I've never gone in for the creaking-door type of suspense. To me, murder by a babbling brook drenched in sunshine is more interesting than murder in a dark and noisome alley littered with dead cats and offal.

'My hero is always the average man to whom bizarre things happen, rather than vice versa. By the same token, I always make my villains charming and polite. It's a mistake to think that if you put a villain on the screen, he must sneer nastily, stroke his black mustache or kick a dog in the stomach. Some of the most famous murderers in criminology – men for whom arsenic was so disgustingly gentle that they did women in with blunt instruments – had to be charmers to get acquainted with the females they murdered. The really frightening thing about villains is their surface likableness.

'Not long ago I did a piece for *The New York Times Sunday Magazine* describing the appeal of the true murder tale as opposed to the fictional variety. Once more I made the point that part of the fascination of the true murder lies in the fact that most real-life murderers are very ordinary, very polite, even engaging. I've heard the complaint that a true murder lacks mystery. I don't agree that that's a weakness. To me, suspense is immeasurably more potent than mystery, and having to read a fiction murder story through in order to find out what happened bores me.

'I've never used the whodunit technique, since it is concerned altogether with mystification, which diffuses and unfocuses suspense. It is possible to build up almost unbearable tension in a play or film in which the audience knows who the murderer is all the time, and from the very start they want to scream out to all the other characters in the plot, "Watch out for So-and-So! He's a killer!" There you have real tenseness and an irresistible desire to know what happens, instead of a group of characters deployed in a human chess problem. For that reason I believe in giving the audience all the facts as early as possible.'

I could hardly wait for him to finish, to tell him that I couldn't agree with him more; that one of my hobbies – in fact, my principal hobby – is the collecting, reading and rereading of accounts of true crimes, with a special leaning for those which took place against a British background. 'Someday,' I said, 'I hope to find an editor interested in persuading me to compile an anthology of such diverting writings. I would have cheerfully paid my own way over to England to cover the trial of Doctor Adams, the Eastbourne physician with the strange appeal for elderly and generous English gentlewomen.' Reluctantly I stopped riding my hobby and returned to a discussion of the Hitchcockian technique.

I asked, 'How would you handle a potential bomb explosion in one of your stories?'

'The point is to let the audience know where the bomb is, but not let the characters in my story know,' he said. 'For example, you and I are sitting here chatting. We needn't talk about death or anything of serious consequence, but if the audience knows that there's a bomb under my desk, set to go off, the suspense will be harrowing to them. But if we don't tell our audience about the bomb ticking away under my desk, and it goes off and blows us to smithereens, the only thing the audience will get is a shock, and a one-second shock at that, as opposed to sixty to ninety minutes of breath-holding waiting.'

'The thing you do that really wrings me out,' I said, 'is that sometimes you have a device like a basket or a box slowly opening while I'm sitting on the edge of my seat, waiting to see what nameless horror will emerge from it. Then something as dangerous as a small black kitten wanders out. You've prepared me for something catastrophic, but what happens is something harmless.'

'By judicious hinting it is possible to persuade an audience to put a shattering interpretation on the most innocuous things,' he explained. 'But you must be careful not to disappoint them completely. They'll react with a gratifying crawling of the flesh to things that turn out not to be so bad as they thought, but only if you ultimately come through with a real marrow chiller. Otherwise they'll feel let down and they'll leave your show resenting you as a cheat.'

'I've noticed that you let the public supply its own conclusion for some of your TV half-hour shows,' I said. 'That's a new technique to me. At least I've never seen it done before.'

'It's quite a trick to find thirty-nine shows a year, each with a twist at the end,' he told me. 'So we sometimes let you supply your own twist after you switch your set off, based, of course, on what you've just seen and heard.'

'They tell me you'll be doing something different on TV this fall,' I said. 'But I'm not quite sure just what it is.'

'In addition to our weekly half-hour show, I'll do ten one-hour shows,' he said. 'I'll have more time to develop character in them. For that matter, some stories deserve a longer telling than others. One of the first stories I'll do is the Cornell Woolrich story, *Three O'Clock*. It's about a man who makes a homemade bomb because he suspects his wife of having a lover and he's determined to blow them both up, even if it means blowing up his own home. However, immediately after he's started his bomb's timing device going, two burglars break into his house, truss him up and put him in the cellar while they rob the house. Then they leave. There he is, helpless, facing his own ticking bomb and not finding the situation all that it might be. In fact, he feels that it's extremely doubtful if there's any future in it.'

I waited; then asked, 'Well?'

Hitchcock blinked large, oyster-shaped eyes at me and said, 'If you think I'm going to tell you what happens, you're quite wrong. I suggest that you tune in this fall and find out.

'I've never thought of the motion pictures I've made as being primarily commercial,' he said thoughtfully. 'Nevertheless, I've usually encountered a firm insistence from the front offices of the studios for which I've worked that I attach a satisfactory ending. In this community, to have what is known as an unhappy ending is to commit the unforgivable Hollywood sin called "being downbeat". And while you'll find heated denial in film circles that the average movie audience is only of teen-age intelligence, and whereas a number of people in motion pictures take it for granted that TV is only for morons, the truth is that we who make TV films are allowed to end our stories on a downbeat note as often as not. So, in spite of bleats from some TV writers, we have more freedom on TV than we do in motion pictures. Perhaps all that this proves is that people will accept more mature entertainment if they don't have to pay for it. It may be that when they pay to go to a movie they feel they have bought the right to come out with a satisfied feeling.

'It has been said of me that if I made *Cinderella*, the audience would start looking for a body in the pumpkin coach,' Hitchcock went on. 'That's true. Although my product hasn't been wholly melodramatic – I once tried an ill-starred comedy with Carole Lombard – there's no point in denying that I'm thoroughly typed. If an audience sees one of my productions with no spine-tingling, they're disappointed.'

'Do you remember Robert Vogeler?' I asked. 'He was the American business-man who was mysteriously snatched on a journey between Budapest and Vienna, disappeared as if a crack in the earth had swallowed him, although he finally showed up in an Iron Curtain prison and eventually was released. As I read about him I thought, *How can Alfred Hitchcock make any more motion pictures, now that things are happening in real life which once only happened in his films?*'

'That question has presented a problem,' he said. 'After all, I couldn't dream up a more bizarre episode than Rudolf Hess's flight to Scotland during World War Two. The fact is, if I had put that into a movie before it happened, nobody would have believed it. Not only that, things have reached a point where those who live a life of wild and improbable adventure are copying devices from my movies.'

'Such as?' I asked.

'Such as my picture *Foreign Correspondent*,' he replied. 'In it, a man was assassinated by a pistol concealed in a camera. In my film a photographer said, 'Just a moment', to a diplomat on the steps of a large building; then pointed his camera at him and shot him dead. It gave me a turn when, a year later, the same thing occurred in real life in Teheran.'

'I can see how it might rock you,' I said.

'At first I thought I had suggested a *modus operandi* to the real-life assassins,' he admitted, 'but eventually I comforted myself with the thought that the whole thing was a coincidence. But I have to be careful that the pressure of real-life competition doesn't make me go too far with the bizarreness of my film situations, for the key to effective suspense is believability. The simpler and more homely the peril, the more real that peril.'

'You've edited a book called *Stories They Won't Let Me Do On TV*,' I said. 'I've noticed it in the bookstores. Why were those stories turned down?'

'Too macabre,' he said. 'I won't try to outline the plot of the short story called 'Two Bottles of Relish', by Lord Dunsany, for you, because I'm sure your editor would be stuffy about it and find it distasteful, but there's another one in that book of mine that he may not find unpalatable. In it, a man murders his wife, then transforms her into chicken feed. Afterwards he serves a pair of his chickens to the local police inspector when he has him in for dinner.'

I gulped and fished a piece of paper from my wallet. From it I read aloud this statement written about him by Ernest Havemann for *Theater Arts*:

Almost any director can come up with a good, rousing historical epic or he can translate a first-rate Broadway play to the screen, but it's something else to take a simple little idea for a melodrama and use it in such a way that it keeps the audience half swooning with fear and half falling out of their seats with laughter.

'It *is* something else,' Hitchcock said. 'The secret is the way in which the story is pieced together. With me, all the little bits of business and the situations must be planted and established before a camera rolls. Sometimes I plan as many as six hundred camera setups before I begin to shoot. If I ever tried to improvise a plot structure on the set, I couldn't get the effects or the reactions I want to get.'

'There must be very little wastage when you're done,' I said.

'There's practically no spare footage,' he told me. 'It's been said of my stories that they are so tightly knit that everything depends on everything else, and that if I ever made a change before the camera I might as well unravel the whole sweater. That's true too. Take a ready-made stage play like *Dial M For Murder*. As the director of that play in its filmed form, there was almost no work for me to do. The various bits and pieces had already been put together on the stage. I've often wondered why so many successful stage plays fail as movies. I think the reason is this: someone has decided to 'open up' the stage play with added exteriors and turn it into a movie and, as a result, the tightness and tautness of the stage play is lost.'

One of the questions I wanted to ask him was: 'In one of your stories is one of your problems the job of offering an explanation for all the hush-hush stuff; the mayhem and the villains still pursuing? In other words, don't the baddies have to be after something?'

'That is what I call the McGuffin,' he told me. 'It's the gimmick; it's what the excitement is all about. In a spy story the McGuffin is what the spies are after. In *The 39 Steps* the spies were after an airplane-engine formula, but the odd part of it is that the McGuffin never matters very much. In a film called *Notorious* I had Ingrid Bergman go to South America and get mixed up with some German spies. The question arose, What were the spies after? In other words, what was the McGuffin?

'Although it was a full year before Hiroshima, I said, "Let's make it uranium samples." I had a hunch that somewhere some spies from some country or other must be after an atom bomb or the knowledge of how to make one. So with Ben Hecht, the writer of my film story, I went to see Doctor Millikan of Cal Tech, to ask him what was to us a natural and not startling question: "How big is an atom bomb?"

'Doctor Millikan almost dropped his teeth. "Do you want to be arrested?" he blurted. "Do you want me to be arrested too?" But after those anguished questions, he pulled himself together and spent an hour telling us how impossible it was to make an atom bomb. We didn't know it, but the Manhattan Project had already been launched, and Doctor Millikan was one of the big wheels in it. It must have given him quite an odd feeling when we walked in with our question, but, as I say, he did his best to keep his knowledge top secret by telling us how ridiculous our notion was. However, when we left, I said to Hecht, "I'm going ahead with the uranium McGuffin anyhow." We made the picture and it grossed seven millions. Today, it would gross two or three times that much.'

I asked him to explain the origin of the term 'McGuffin'.

'Using the McGuffin to mean the papers, jewelry, whatever the spies are after, is my own adaptation of the word,' he said. 'It comes from an old English music-hall joke about two men on a train. One of the men says to the other, "What's that package on the rack above your head?" and the other man says,

"Oh, that's a McGuffin." The first man asks, "What's a McGuffin?" and the second man replies, "A McGuffin is an apparatus for trapping lions in the Adirondacks."

' "But there are no lions in the Adirondacks," the first man says. "Then that's no McGuffin," the second man says.'

I said I had heard that he had a reputation as an outstanding practical joker. 'I have pretty much outgrown that now,' he said. 'And I'm afraid that if I tried to describe them to you, they'd seem pretty flat and contrived, but I still have a little fun in elevators. Sometimes in a crowded elevator I turn to someone with me and say, "Of course, I didn't know the gun was loaded, but when it went off it blasted a great hole in his neck. A flap of his flesh fell down, and I could see the white ligaments uncovered. Presently I felt wetness around my feet. I was standing in a pool of blood." Everyone in the elevator stiffens; then I get out and leave them standing there. Once when I described that imaginary shooting one woman begged the operator, "Let me out of here, please." and she got out at the next floor.'

I asked him where he got such Hitchcock touches as people losing themselves in funeral processions or ducking into amusement parks or into halls where political speeches were being made to hide from their pursuers.

'I simply look around and ask myself what background I can use next,' he explained. 'Someday I'll have a character dash into a hospital, pretend to be a patient, lie down on one of those litters on which they wheel you into the operating room, and before it's over, I'll have him operated on.'

I had heard that he'd once told one nervous young actor who was jittering around in front of a camera, 'I can't understand why you are all of a twitter. There's nothing depending upon your performance except your whole career.'

I wanted to ask him what had happened to that young man. Had his career taken him on to become an Academy nominee? But I didn't get a chance to ask.

He stood up and said, 'I know you'll forgive me, but I'm fifteen minutes late to look at screenings of various actresses I am considering for my next film. It turns out that the girl I had selected for the part has made a previous engagement with a bird who has a nose even longer than mine – a stork.'

There are some things that even a great director, who anticipates every move before he turns a camera, can do nothing about.

●

FRANK LLOYD WRIGHT

Interviewed by Henry Brandon
The Sunday Times, 3 November 1957

Frank Lloyd Wright (1867–1959), the American architect, was born in Wisconsin. He trained as a civil engineer but turned to architecture when part of the State Capitol building fell down. He practised in Chicago and produced innovative designs in the fields of both domestic and civic architecture, designs renowned for their use of technology and open-space interiors.

Henry Oscar Brandon was born in Czechoslovakia in 1916 and educated at the Universities of Prague and Lausanne. He joined the staff of *The Sunday Times* (London) in 1939 and served as a war correspondent in North Africa and Western Europe from 1943 to 1945. After spells as Paris correspondent and roving diplomatic correspondent, he was sent to Washington in 1950 where he remained until his retirement. He received the Foreign Correspondent award from the University of California at Los Angeles in the year of this interview and the Hannen Swaffer award in 1964.

In 1956 Brandon suggested to the editor of *The Sunday Times* in London that his paper should publish a series of tape-recorded conversations with prominent Americans, pointing out to him that 'it was becoming increasingly important for newspapers to prove that they are capable of doing certain things which up to then enjoyed something of a monopoly on television and radio . . . and that this was a way of enlisting important personalities, whom otherwise it would be difficult to persuade to write articles for newspapers . . .'

His guinea-pig for this exercise was the American architect Frank Lloyd Wright, whom Brandon correctly anticipated would give a bravura performance for the microphone. 'He was an ideal person for an interview,' wrote Brandon. 'He was belligerently creative, and hence he invited controversy. And because he loved controversy, he not only enjoyed pouring oil on it but also to set it aflame himself. He could afford it. He not only had pride of accomplishment, but he was also so articulate, he had such a gift of phrase, such a command of language that he felt certain of winning every argument. If necessary he would shut you up by an authoritative statement that one could not possibly dare to contradict. Then he was intimidating. But Wright could equally well shrug you off with a mellow, humorous remark. That was the time he exuded greatness to me.'

Brandon's 'Conversation Pieces' for *The Sunday Times* included interviews with John F. Kennedy, Sir Isaiah Berlin, Dr Margaret Mead, Arthur Rubinstein, Edmund Wilson, Marilyn Monroe and Arthur Miller, Peter Brook, Peter

Ustinov, and James Thurber. They were later collected and published in book form as *Conversations with Henry Brandon* (1966).

Frank Lloyd Wright is one of the most controversial and authentically American Americans alive. At the age of eighty-eight he is now working on a mile-high office building for Chicago, a synagogue for Philadelphia, the Arizona State Capitol, the Guggenheim Museum in New York, a factory in San Francisco, a chain of motels across the country, a memorial in Venice, a commercial building in Venezuela and forty houses in twenty States of the United States.

I have just been to see him, and the tape-recorder enables me to give his precise words. I began by suggesting that what we usually call 'modern' architecture has run its course.

BRANDON: Before you answer, perhaps you would like to define 'modern' architecture.

WRIGHT: Well, modern architecture is anything built today. It's an ambiguous term, but 'modern architecture' does not necessarily mean new architecture. The *new* architecture is organic architecture.

BRANDON: Your organic architecture is really –

WRIGHT: A natural influence.

BRANDON: Isn't it an Oriental influence?

WRIGHT: No – except that the philosophy is perhaps Oriental. It was Tao who declared that the reality of the buildings did not consist in the walls and the roof, but in the space within to be lived in. The interior space was the reality of the building. Now that means that you build from within outward rather than from the outside in, as the West has always been building. In so far as that's Taoism, I suppose the philosophy is Eastern. But somehow only the West has ever built according to that philosophy. And our 'organic' architecture happens to be the original expression of that idea. The space concept in architecture is organic, and 'organic', as we use the term, means 'natural', it means 'essential'. It means *of* the thing instead of *on* it.

BRANDON: I quite agree there should be a close link between architecture and nature. That's what entranced me about the setting of the Japanese house. But how can you adapt this philosophy or organic architecture to the cities of today? They lack space.

WRIGHT: You can't. The city of today will have to run its course. It's being finished now by excess. Excess is ruining it. When we need a new city we're going to have it on our own organic terms and it will be more an agronomy, it will be part of the ground and it will be pretty nearly everywhere. The concentrations that are now cities are feudal survivals. We've got to go forward and make better use of the ground.

BRANDON: But aren't we going to lose whatever privacy and serenity there is left of our landscapes, of our countryside?

WRIGHT: On the contrary. If we have the right sort of architecture we won't do violence to the landscape as we do now. I would dread to see the kind of architecture that we have in cities go out into the country. But in organic architecture the nature of the thing prompts the fashioning of the thing, and the buildings that would be built would make that country more beautiful rather than less so. Of course, that's a long journey along the line of a culture that we don't have yet.

BRANDON: You've recently been to London. You probably saw that much was destroyed, that much has also been rebuilt. What sort of advice would you have for a city like London?

WRIGHT: London has a dormitory town, London has *sub*urbia, and I think for London *ex*urbia is important – getting out into the country as far as possible – maintaining the old city, the old buildings, and the old conditions as a memorial. I'm sorry to see the skyscraper about to invade London. I saw it in an illustrated magazine, a high hotel building like an office building, making of the hostelry a rat trap, right in the heart of London. I hope they never build it.

BRANDON: Why are you against skyscrapers? They are one of the outstanding American contributions to architecture.

WRIGHT: The skyscraper is responsible for the congestion, and is making the city of today impossible to use. The skyscraper piles the crowd up high, dumps it on the street, stuffs it in again, and the streets are not nearly wide enough.

Paris is so beautiful today because it has that sense of space without the skyscraper. London has something of that, and if it's invaded by the skyscraper, it will lose what it has. I think they should not build up those bombed areas either. They should plant them to greenery. The greenery of London is one of its beauties. Why not extend that and let the people push out into the countryside in becoming buildings in a way that does not damage the country but benefits the invader?

BRANDON: What impression did London make on you?

WRIGHT: I think most buildings in London are worth preserving: they're interesting examples of the old order. But, as compared with what we can build now, they are extremely inutile and will eventually be relics and unbecoming. London is rather far behind in what we call modern architecture and has very few, or no, examples of organic architecture.

See, the architecture we call organic is a natural architecture and it does not use steel like lumber. The steel framing in the nineteenth century was just like lumber framing. They made steel into lumber and used it as beams, as posts and all that. But that's not organic. We use steel suspended in strands for its tensile strength, buried in concrete for its compression strength. The system was invented by the French and we called it ferro-concrete.

BRANDON: Certainly what you have been building is daring and revolutionary. But looking at some of your structures I often wonder what holds them up?

WRIGHT: They hold themselves up. Take my 'Mile-High' building. It has a spine with ribs growing out from it. In the Guggenheim Museum the spine is coiled and the ribs or, if you want, the floors, grow only inward. The outer wall is the spine or support and the floor is cantilevered from it.

BRANDON: But is it safe without support on the inner edges?

WRIGHT: My thumb is not supported at the end! Its only support comes from where it joins my hand. This is the twentieth-century way of using steel. But all that is practised now in our big cities is nineteenth-century architecture – extensive steel frames that are rusting at the joints. Most of the architects we have called 'modern' are really wallpaper hangers, papering façades. Posters for whisky, posters for soap. They're not really architecture. They're all right for cities and they're all the cities are entitled to now, but don't call them architecture.

BRANDON: Personally, I prefer the façades of the old buildings on Park or Fifth Avenue. The avenues' majesty, dignity, and sense of proportion will be lost when those old buildings are replaced by these new austere structures of glass and steel, looking all alike.

WRIGHT: This is a matter of taste, and taste is always a matter of ignorance. You taste because you don't know. And if you like the taste of the old, you like the old. If you like the taste of the new, you like the new. But none of it is really architecture. Architecture is a deeper thing. It is the frame of human existence. We must dedicate this existence more to beauty. For if poetic principle has deserted us, how long are we going to last? How long can civilization without a soul last? Science cannot save us; it has brought us to the brink. Art and religion, which are the soul of civilization, have to save us.

Architecture is the only record you can read now of those civilizations that have passed into distance. Water closets, washbowls, and radiators, that's what they would find of our present-day civilization centuries hence. Architecture means *of* the nature of the thing whatever it may be and *for* the nature of the thing whatever that may be.

Most of this educated taste today is an acquired taste. It has nothing whatever to do with certain senses or the beneficial character of the thing tasted; it's only whether you like it or not. And who are you? You are only an artificial thing whose taste may be atrocious. So when we have a taste-built culture, we have a haphazard jamboree of all kinds of things. But if we go back to nature, and make things according to nature, we have a sense of propriety. Not propriety, but proper character in everything.

BRANDON: And you firmly believe that modern architecture will develop in that direction?

WRIGHT: Yes, it will be organic architecture. It was the basis of the present so-called modern. But organic architecture made first a negation and that negation was extremely narrow and affected a great many architects. And they followed the negation rather than going along into the affirmation of which it was capable and which we are now practising.

BRANDON: Modern architecture was born at a time of scarcity, a utilitarian period. Now we live in an age of greater plenty than, say, twenty years ago. Will this be reflected in architecture, will it make greater use of artful decoration? WRIGHT: Inevitably it will, but not in decoration as we know it. It will be more like the things we see in nature, in the garden, in the trees, everywhere about. If there is ornament it will be natural to the environment. And if there is a building it will be natural to its purpose in certain senses. It will all have the truth of nature.

Of course, that's all a large order. It's going to take time to reach it. But that's where we're headed for, and architecture is gradually getting a little deeper into nature, which is the mother of architecture, and without which there is no culture.

We Americans have a vast civilization and no culture because we have no architecture of our own. Washington, our capital, does not represent architecture of our own. The Capitol, for instance, represents American history. I do not judge its architecture but respect it for what it is. We have for a long time been flat on our faces, copying nineteenth-century Europe. But now Americans are waking up to the importance of having their own architecture, the importance of organic architecture. Yesterday I gave a lecture on the subject for the International Institute of Contemporary Art, and some fifteen hundred people came to listen. That's encouraging. There is a rebirth of architecture in America, and we're getting our own: organic architecture.

•

ERNEST HEMINGWAY
Interviewed by Milt Machlin
Argosy , September 1958

Ernest Hemingway (1889–1961), the American writer, started out as a journalist during the First World War. He stayed in Europe after the war and his first novel, *The Sun Also Rises* (1926), dealt with the desolation of American expatriates living in Paris. His second novel, *A Farewell to Arms* (1929), was a love story set during the First World War on the Austrian-Italian front, a theatre where Hemingway had been present, and a later novel, *For Whom the Bell Tolls* (1948), was set against the backdrop of the Spanish Civil War, in which Hemingway was again a correspondent. These novels all had rootless American heroes who were drawn into the moral and political conflicts of twentieth-century Europe and exhibited 'grace under pressure'. They were written in a direct style which dispensed with conventional punctuation and eschewed fine writing. In 1945 he went to live in Cuba, where he wrote the novella *The Old Man and the Sea*. He was awarded the 1954 Nobel Prize for literature. His final years were spent in Idaho, USA, where he continued to lead an outdoors life, falling prey to depressive illness which drove him to suicide.

Robert Milton Machlin was born in New York City in 1924 and after serving in the US army during the Second World War he obtained degrees from Brown University and the Paris-Sorbonne. He started out in journalism as a reporter and columnist with the *Morning Leader* in Clifton, NJ, and worked for Magazine House from 1953 to 1955. This was followed by a couple of years as an editor for *People* magazine. From 1960 to the present day he has been managing editor of *Argosy* magazine and was its executive editor from 1960 to 1975. He has contributed articles to *New York* magazine, *The New York Times*, *Coronet*, *This Week* and *Pageant*. He co-wrote *Ninth Life* (1961), about the long-drawn-out Chessman case and execution, and wrote *The Search for Michael Rockefeller* (1972), which was made into a TV movie. He also wrote *The Private Hell of Hemingway* (1962), a couple of books about UFOs, and various non-fiction and fiction books, winning the Mystery Writers special award in 1976.

The last time I saw Papa he nearly flattened me. Of course, it was all a misunderstanding. But still, I figured The Boss overestimated my influence with Ernest Hemingway, the Great White Father of American literature, and the greatest adventure writer that ever was.

'You claim to be such a buddy of Hemingway's,' The Boss told me. 'Why don't you go down to Cuba and ask him what's new?'

Before you could say 'Farewell to Arms', I was hustled onto a plane, and the next thing I knew I was wrestling with a giant Daiquiri in Havana's Floridita bar. This particular Daiquiri was called a Papa's Special because it was invented by Hemingway. It contained a squirt of lime, a squirt of grapefruit juice, some ice, and four ounces of rum. It usually takes me about a pint of rum just to get up the nerve to call Papa at his fortress, Finca Vigia, in San Francisco de Paula, about twenty miles from Havana.

The situation was this. One: Hemingway is the world's greatest writer and authority on hunting, fishing, drinking and other manly occupations. Two: This is Hemingway's year, being the year in which no less than three new Hemingway films are on view to the public. Three: The most recent Hemingway opus is the guttiest, fishiest, *masculinest* fish story ever to reach the silver screen – *The Old Man and the Sea*.

That was the situation from The Boss's point of view. From Hemingway's point of view it was a little different.

One: Papa hates interviews and doesn't give them except when his arm is twisted, and who'd want to do that?

Two: Papa wouldn't give two baits in a bucket for all the movies ever filmed, including the Hemingway masterpiece.

Three: Papa is now writing the most comprehensive work of his life, rumored to be a series of anywhere from three to six novels dealing largely with World War II and thereafter, and is in no mood to be interrupted. When Papa is working he doesn't answer phones. When he is not working he answers them sometimes, if he feels like it, and if the caller can explain in Spanish to René, the houseboy who answers the phone, what is on his mind. When Papa is not working, he prefers fishing, on the *Pilar*, his forty-two-foot 'fishing machine', for white marlin, if they are running, or for anything else big and exciting enough, if they aren't.

Papa is a very kind man. Everybody says so and it is true. But Papa is a man to whom privacy is a precious thing. The first time I saw Papa I sloped up to his verandah uninvited while Papa was reading his mail and having his evening medication of MacNish. This was before the great African plane accident in which he jammed his spine, ruptured his right kidney, collapsed his intestine and suffered a concussion. This was when Papa was in magnificent condition. Having heard tales of journalists being forcibly bounced from the premises by the master himself, I had fortified myself in the village with a local anaesthetic – barreled rum.

I rapped on the door frame with authority. There was a pained roar from inside the comfortable Spanish-style house.

'What the hell do you want?'

I explained my pilgrimage.

'What in hell do you think I moved out here for?' Papa asked, and answered his own question: 'To get away from bastards like you!'

This was where the rum-priming I'd done in village paid off. I was fearless.

'Look, Mr Hemingway,' I said with simple dignity. 'I was brushed off this afternoon by your houseboy, then by your maid. I've made up my mind that I'm either going to be brushed off by the boss himself or – or something.'

I guess it was my fearless reply that reached him, because he asked me to come in, sit down, have a drink, have a chat, and don't print anything. This was a big fat help, but I figured, what the hell. No point in going home thirsty.

I don't know about Papa, but I had a high old time that afternoon, drinking and talking. Papa likes to drink and he likes to talk. A fifth and a half of scotch later we had touched on the subjects of: women (Spanish, French, Italian, Japanese and Greek); fish (trout, marlin, and *sierra en escabeche*; a type of pickled *cero* mackerel); sports-writers (he likes Jimmy Cannon); fighters (Joe Louis); ball-players (DiMaggio, who else?); wine (*valpolicella, orvieto, manzanilla*); beer (he once wrote an endorsement for an American brand), and football, among other things.

I might say that Papa is an expert in all these things and more. But, surprisingly, he listens more than he talks, and if you don't watch out you're *giving* him an interview instead of *getting* one.

When we got to football, I started to explain how the outside tackle pulled out to run interference at my alma mater, dear old Brown. Papa was demonstrating how centers immobilized tackles when he played for Oak Park High, in

Illinois. Somehow we both ended flat on our duffs, a condition Miss Mary, Hemingway's blonde wife, found us in when she came to announce that it was time for Papa to go to dinner and for me to go home. I guess she was right. I went home, and before I went Papa promised me that *next* time he'd give me a *real, real* interview.

Six months ago I popped in on Papa again. The revolution was in full swing down in Cuba. I showed up in the middle of the night in a set of GI fatigues, dark glasses and sneakers. When the excitement died down (this was the time I nearly got flattened), it was explained that there were things you didn't do around Finca Vigia. You didn't come unannounced, especially in the middle of the night during a revolution. You didn't do this, especially if you were wearing noiseless sneakers. You didn't wear fatigues or Army clothes anywhere in Cuba unless you were ready to shoot it out with one side or the other. And you didn't come without an invitation more recent than five years old. Still, Papa was gracious.

We did some drinking and we talked about Paris (Dome, Coupole, and the changes since the war); fighters (he still liked Louis but admired Ray Robinson, too), magazines (he got some of his first rejection slips from *Argosy*), and why I couldn't have the story I wanted. I, at that time, was interested in Hemingway's gun collection.

'In the first place, I don't collect guns. I have some guns I like to shoot with. I like my Springfield 30–06. But it isn't a good idea to keep guns around the house in times like these.'

It wasn't even a good idea to talk about them much, I gathered.

Papa didn't look so good. He'd put on some weight and was drinking only a little light wine. He had something of a gut. Papa generally goes to bed about ten at night since the accident. Part of his kindness is that he doesn't seem to have the nerve to put out a guest once a pleasant drinking-talking relationship has been established. But Miss Mary serves well as watchdog and conscience. At nine-thirty she cleared her throat, and at nine-thirty-five I was shaking hands, headed for the door, with a promise that *next* time, 'true', I'd get a real story.

On my third go-round with Papa I discovered certain things. Papa will never break a promise to a friend, or even an acquaintance, but Papa is not going to louse up his work schedule for anyone. From just after daylight to at least one-thirty in the afternoon, Hemingway writes in a white tower (really) which surmounts the Finca Vigia and is probably responsible for its name (it means 'Lookout Ranch' and commands a startling view of Havana and the surrounding countryside).

After three days of trying, I reached Papa on the phone. He said he'd be glad to see me sometime but was not free at the moment to talk. He'd call me when he was ready.

After another day or so I had lost $150 playing a nervous game of blackjack in the casino of the Hotel Riviera, where I was staying, waiting impatiently for the phone to ring.

Time passed. I cast about for the bait that would hook Papa before I ran out of expense money and was left to work my way back on a banana boat. I looked up all of Papa's old friends. I went to Cojimar, the fishing village where he docks his boat, and talked to the fishermen who knew him. I talked to his boatman, Gregorio Fuentes, a Canary Islander, who is celebrating his twentieth year of skippering the *Pilar*. I talked to Elicio Arguelles, millionaire Cuban sportsman who is Papa's principal fishing buddy, along with Arguelles' cousin, Mayito Menocal, another millionaire Cuban sportsman. I found out that Papa's friends are almost all Cubans, and none, as far as I could determine, are writers or in any other way connected with the arts. Aside from being a writer and a great reader, Papa is one of the most unartistic bastards you'd ever meet, to the external eye.

Finally, almost by accident, I hit it. I was reading Papa a tidbit, on the phone, about *The Old Man and the Sea*, from a Warner Brothers handout I happened to have with me. The item referred to Arguelles in an ambiguous way, which I called to Papa's attention. I indicated that I had other releases put out by the movie people and – who knows? – maybe they were confusing too, if not downright inaccurate. Papa hit the bait like a myopic marlin.

'Be out here at six-thirty and bring those Warner things with you!' he growled.

At six-twenty-five, Cuban photographer Tony Ortega and I rolled up to Papa's white-painted gate. There was a big sign: NO VISITORS EXCEPT BY APPOINTMENT. For the first time I had one.

I noticed a new adornment on Papa's front gate since my last visit. About five rows of sharp barbed wire topped the fence around Hemingway's fifteen-acre property and entrance gate. I asked the old man who watched Papa's gate for him what was the pitch. Rebels?

'*Ladrones de mangos*.' He grinned through his toothless gums.

Mango thieves? That's all I could get out of the old man. It was already dark. We drove up the unlighted road serenaded by the cackle of chickens, barking of dogs, grunting of pigs, and crying of children, which welled up from the houses joining Papa's property on our right. Over this came the throb of a *danson* from the overloud juke box of the town bar a quarter of a mile away.

Papa greeted us at the door. He was friendly, but restrained. For one thing, the photographer made him nervous. I promised we wouldn't take any photos, but Tony begged for one shot for his own use.

Papa said, 'I'd rather take a punch in the nose,' but he posed.

I've never seen a man so scared by a camera. He froze.

'You guys are always trying to make a guy look foolish. What are you trying to do?' he asked Tony. 'Get me with my mouth open? This is Sunday. I'm trying to take it easy. I'm no movie star. Put away the camera.'

He was terrified. I'd discovered the one thing Papa was afraid of! I told Tony to pack away his Rollei.

'Look,' said Papa, 'it's Sunday. I don't get much time to relax. If you want to talk and take it easy, okay. Otherwise . . . ' He dismissed the subject. 'Want a drink?'

I accepted a scotch. He handed me the bottle to pour for myself, and eyed me critically as I poured.

'Lost some weight, didn't you?'

I had noticed before that he had a phenomenal memory, even recalling most of the details of that first meeting five years earlier. He stood up. He was wearing a sleeveless Cuban *guayaberra* – a sort of pleated sports shirt which hangs outside the trousers, and English-style shorts which he wears habitually around the house and the boat. The pants were about six inches too big around the waist. He unbuckled his belt and patted the flat place where his gut was the last time I had seen him.

'I lost, too. I'm down to two hundred and seven. That's a good weight for me.'

He looked at me again. Even minus thirty pounds, I'm no lightweight.

'Get any exercise?' he asked.

I acknowledged that I ran for the subway with some regularity, but that was all.

'No good. You should get exercise regularly. You got to start to watch out for heart attacks and things.' He patted his stomach again. 'I do the eight-eighty down in the pool every day.'

Sitting down, he leafed through the Warner releases I had brought, reading intensely and quickly as I looked around the forty-foot living room.

On the walls were an assortment of trophies, including a huge cape buffalo and many graceful deer and antelope. There were also bullfight posters and, on one wall, a jai-alai cesta. On the floor was a wall-to-wall Tahitian grass mat. The room was furnished comfortably with old-fashioned stuffed armchairs and some Cuban wicker and mahogany chairs. Between two armchairs stood the bar, with an assortment of spirits and some wine.

Hemingway snorted over a release claiming he had presented a cup to Batista.

'That's a lot of crap. I never saw the man!' Otherwise, he seemed satisfied. He wasn't inclined to talk about *The Old Man and the Sea*, though.

'Kid, I don't want to talk about the picture until I talk with Hayward (Leland Hayward, the producer). It's like a magician who's trying to saw a woman in half. He doesn't tell the audience how it's done before he does it, does he?'

I saw there was something that bothered him about the picture, but he wasn't inclined to tell me what it was. He did say that he pretty much liked it and that it was true to the book. According to published reports, he got $250,000 for the rights to the Nobel-prize-winning novelette, plus a one-third share of the profits, splitting equally with Hayward and the picture's star, Spencer Tracy. This is the most he ever got for film rights, and this is the only picture in which he has accepted participation.

Somehow Hemingway has always got the dirty end of the stick on movie deals. For *To Have and Have Not*, now being made, against his protest, for the third time, he got a measly $10,000. For *The Sun Also Rises*, he got nothing, having granted the rights to his first wife, who sold them for $10,000. *The Killers*, the picture he has despised least of those made from his works, earned him $37,500 and contained less than five minutes of his own dialogue.

The Old Man and the Sea retains the Hemingway dialogue almost intact, in the form of a running comment behind the action of the world's most classic fish story. It's a tale of the three-day battle between Santiago, an old Cuban drift-fisherman, and the biggest marlin ever seen, and how, after capturing the fish, the old man must fight futilely to the last ounce of his strength against the sharks which eventually claim his catch.

The setting is the little fishing village of Cojimar, a few miles from Hemingway's home. Papa knows almost every fisherman in this town personally and by name. He prides himself on his acquaintanceships with professionals, who are the only ones he really enjoys swapping fish talk with.

When *The Old Man and the Sea* came out, there was a rash of guesses as to who the 'real' old man was. Some said it was an old fisherman named Anselmo who lived in Cojimar. Another old waterfront habitué told journalists that *he* was the old man.

Hemingway fumed. He dragged the old pretender into the Teraza, Cojimar's famous sea-food restaurant, and had him face a kangaroo court of his fellow townspeople. The pretender confessed not only that he wasn't the old man, but that he wasn't even a fisherman.

'Then why did you say you were the old man?' Hemingway asked.

'Because they gave me five dollars.'

Papa says all this speculation as to the identity of the old man is bushwah.

'The story is fiction – the conflict between a man and a fish. The old man is nobody in particular. That's stupid. A lot of people have been claiming that this person is the old man and somebody else is the kid. That's a lot of bull. I wrote that story from thirty years of fishing around here, and before that, too. Most of these fishermen in Cojimar have had experiences like that. One was out two days with a fish, and when they found him he was out of his mind. That's even worse than what my old man experienced.

'If the old man is anybody, it's Chago's father, who died four years ago. I fished with him many times.'

'Chago' is Santiago Puig, the elder, a fisherman Hemingway met in his early days in Cuba. His son, who has the same name and also became a friend of Hemingway's, follows the same occupation and acted as a stand-in and oc-casional double for Spencer Tracy. We met him later and he told us this story of the meeting between Hemingway and his father, the man who, Papa said, is 'as much the real old man as anybody.'

*

'We were fishing in my father's boat, the small boat you see in the movie which they bought from me for fourteen hundred dollars, and took to Hollywood. We had caught a big marlin and we were having trouble boating it. I was still a young boy then (he's in his late forties now). Hemingway came along in his boat and helped us. Afterward, he asked if we wanted a drink. My father said he would like a drink of water, but Papa gave him a beer. Papa asked if he could have the head and sword of the marlin for the honor of it, and my father was proud to give it to him. Then he tried to give my father five dollars for it, but my father said he would throw the money in the sea if Papa did not take it back. So Papa took it back but said they would be friends, and they fished together many times after that.'

The villain of the picture is the shark, naturally. In real life, Hemingway has been an implacable enemy of the shark. 'I think it is the one thing he really hates,' a friend said of him.

The first big fish Papa ever hooked, a tuna he battled for hours off Key West, was finally gotten by a shark. That night Papa turned up with a submachine gun which he persuaded millionaire Bill Leeds to give or sell him. Since then, he's gone after shark with tommyguns, rifles, shotguns and a .22.

'With the .22, it's a brain shot,' says Hemingway. 'You have to know the spot and hit them just right when they surface.' He hits them, too.

Papa has an invention all his own for sharks. It's a wooden lance about twelve feet long, with a blade honed from a Ford spring leaf, and tempered. He always has two or three of these aboard the *Pilar*.

It's part of sport-fishing history, of course, that he brought in the first tuna in the Bahamas undamaged by shark.

'Hell,' he says, 'I brought in the first *two*. You got to boat them fast to keep the sharks off. If you let them get tired or sluggish, that's when the sharks move in.'

His pal Arguelles says Papa boated that first tuna in two hours.

'He was fishing barefoot, and by the time he was finished, the bottoms of his feet were cut and bloody from holding against the fighting chair.' It was largely by dint of sheer physical strength that Papa was able to pull those fish in – with a stiff, unyielding rod, at that.

Underneath Papa's hatred, though, is a deep respect for some sharks. The mako – *dentuso* in Spanish – is the first shark to strike the old man's marlin in Hemingway's story.

'He's not a carrion eater,' says Papa. 'He chases and overtakes the fastest game fish in the sea. He'll fight as good as any sport fish, too, when you hook him.' Talking, Papa almost verged into admiration for this champion of sharks. This was something he liked to talk about.

'Hammerheads and tigers will attack if they're hungry or if the water is roily. Some of them are dangerous because they're dumb. A tiger will even swallow an oil can if it's hungry. Thinks it's a tortoise. Mako is a good fish – hell of a lot of action. It'll jump higher than a marlin. It's a big sport fish down in New Zealand. If you go out with the boys from Cojimar, watch out when they boat him. He smashes up a lot of good equipment. A lot of times, after they club him and harpoon him, he'll come back to life in the bottom of the boat and take a big piece out of someone's leg.'

Hemingway's opinions on sharks and other fish are highly expert and respected even by museum ichthyologists. One of them once named a rosefish after him.

'There's only two sharks that are really bad. The *dentuso*, and the big white shark. Some of these guys get near a nurse shark and when they don't get any action they say that sharks aren't dangerous. In all these movies, it's nurse sharks you see them wrestling. They wouldn't dare try that with a mako. That's why they had so much trouble trying to get shark footage for *The Old Man*. I told them to go to Bimini during the tuna run. That's when the mako are running, too. But they horsed around until it was too late, and then they went to Nassau, where there aren't any.'

I could see a piece of Papa's profits bitten off like a chunk of red tuna meat. He began to think about another thing. One of the most expensive boondoggles in the making of the movie – which came in at more than double its original expected cost of $2,000,000 – was the $100,000 trip Hayward sent him on to Cabo Blanco, Peru, for the big marlin.

'First we had some great footage shot in the beginning when they started making the film, but it had to be junked because it was in Cinemascope and they decided not to make the film in Cinemascope.

'Then we had this stuff shot by Fred Glasell. It was terrific, and it was of the biggest marlin ever caught – a world's record. I told Hayward we wouldn't be able to get anything better than that, but he told us to try, anyway. The biggest marlin ever caught was fourteen and a half feet and about fifteen hundred pounds, but Hollywood wanted one eighteen feet.'

Hemingway went down to Peru with Gregorio, his boat and Arguelles. Miss Mary went along, too.

'We fished for twenty-three days without getting a bite. The fun was out of it anyway, because we had to use such heavy lines to simulate the hand line in the picture, that even if we caught one it wouldn't be anything. Arguelles boated a nine-hundred-pounder in two hours on the heavy line. We finally got three or four big ones and sent them back to Havana, but they weren't big enough, and they didn't jump – not once. There were three boats on the job and it was costing a fortune. I offered to stay down with one boat and one camera, but by that time they had decided to give up making the picture for a while. They finally wound up using the Glasell footage anyway.'

Gregorio was humiliated. He was sure that he could come up with a record breaker if they gave him enough time.

I poured myself another scotch and held out the bottle to Papa. He waved it away.

'I'll be drinking this one long after you're gone.' He clutched the scotch and lime he was nursing. 'I only get two a night and I have to make them last.'

I told him that I'd been drinking 'Papa's Specials' with a friend of his the previous night. We'd been matching capacities.

Papa looked interested and a little wistful for the old days.

'Did you break my record?'

'What was that?'

'Fifteen.'

'*Fifteen!*' I'd gotten pretty crocked on four. 'What was your time?'

'Well, from about ten-thirty in the morning, until seven o'clock at night. Guillermo (a famous jai-alai player) came into the Floridita. He was down. He'd just lost a *partido* (jai-alai game) thirty to sixteen. I said, "Cheer up, kid, let's have a drink." We started drinking easy, that way. It wasn't a contest, but we were still there by seven, and I went home and worked.'

'I know I drank fifteen because I signed for it on the tab.'

'You *worked*?'

'Wait a minute. No, I didn't work. I read.' He started to figure. How much booze was that? Let's see . . . there's four ounces in a special . . .'

I had already figured it. 'Sixty ounces – more than two fifths!'

'Of course, we drank standing up. You can drink more that way. I guess we had some *saladitos* (hors-d'oeuvres), too, and something else to eat. You have to eat something.'

'What about Vasco Da Gama, down there, does that bother you?' I was referring to the bronze bust of Hemingway they have in Papa's corner of the Floridita.

'It's getting so I hardly like to go in any more. These bastards won't let you drink in peace. I don't have any privacy any more. A lot of people think the statue is of Constante (the owner). Mrs Constante had it done down the road here.'

He sipped his lime and scotch sparingly. In the old days he used to navigate his boat by the bottle. Two Fundadors north by one Bacardi east.

I asked him how he'd like to go to Russia as a correspondent for *Argosy*.

'They already asked me to go about three times – as an exchange writer, whatever that is. The State Department asked me, too. What the hell would I do? Pose for pictures, sign autographs and make a lot of speeches? I don't know the language. You can't find out a damned thing if you don't know the language. I'm okay any place they speak French, Italian, Spanish or Swahili. That's all.'

Miss Mary came into the room, wearing neat white shorts with a small printed pattern, emphasizing her well-tanned legs.

'I saw you in the movies,' I told her, referring to the flash of a moment she appears at the end of *The Old Man and the Sea*.

'Oh that was a silly business,' she said, distracted. She turned to Papa. 'Miss Puss is missing. I haven't seen her in hours.'

Hemingway seemed to tense up, but he reassured Miss Mary. 'Don't worry, she'll turn up.'

Miss Mary retreated to the back of the house again, but after she was gone Papa seemed nervous. He stood up and listened for noises in the night. All you could hear was the insistent throbbing of drums.

I thought to myself, 'The natives are restless,' but realized it was only the distant boom of the juke box in San Francisco de Paula.

I asked about the recent addition of the barbed wire to the fence, and Papa looked at me sharply.

'Mango thieves?' I asked innocently.

He nodded distractedly, still listening into the night. 'Maybe.'

There was a sound in the darkness like a baby crying. Papa smiled and untensed.

'She's back. Miss Puss is back,' he said. I realized it had been a missing cat that had upset him. There are cats all over the place at Finca Vigia. 'Just Cuban alley cats, but we love 'em,' says Miss Mary.

Miss Mary came back into the room and looked at me significantly. I got the signal.

'Let me know if you want to do a story on the broadbill and sharks. That's a good story and it hasn't been done,' Papa said.

I said I would, and drifted out into the drum-throbbing darkness.

•

MONTGOMERY CLIFT

Interviewed by Roderick Mann
The Sunday Express, 16 August 1959

Montgomery Clift (1920–66), the American actor, was born in Omaha, Nebraska (as was his near-contemporary Marlon Brando). He was in amateur theatricals and made his Broadway début as a teenager in 1935. His first released film was Fred Zinneman's *The Search* (1948), which was followed by the Howard Hawks Western *Red River*. There followed films like *A Place in the Sun* (1951), *I Confess* (1952), and *From Here to Eternity* (1953). In 1957 he suffered a car crash, with the result that one side of his face was paralysed. He made several more films, including *The Young Lions*, *Judgement at Nuremberg*, *The Misfits, and Wild River*.

Roderick Mann was born in 1922. He was educated at Glasgow High School, King Edward's Grammar School, Brimingham, and in Paris. He joined *The

Sunday Express in 1956 where he wrote a weekly column for the paper until 1988. In 1978 *The Los Angeles Times* invited him to move Los Angeles and he wrote three columns a week for the paper, also until 1988. He wrote several segments of the American TV series *Hart to Hart*, has published three novels and has a new novel coming out in Britain in 1994. He wrote many interviews with show-business celebrities over the years, but he recalls that 'the one I did with Monty Clift has always stuck in my memory because it was so bizarre'.

It was an extraordinary encounter. A brief, penetrating glimpse into the unhappy mind of one of Hollywood's youngest and – you may think – greatest virtuosos: Montgomery Clift.

Ninety restless minutes during which time he alternately wept, mimicked me, lay on the floor, swore and pretended to be deaf.

His new film, *Suddenly, Last Summer* – in which he co-stars with Elizabeth Taylor and Katharine Hepburn – had just been completed.

It is a raw, emotional, Tennessee Williams shocker and even as he paced the floor of his hotel suite – while the long-player in the next room echoed Sinatra – Clift was still tense.

'I play the doctor,' he said. 'It's a long part, but a lousy part. There's no spark. The others, Liz and Katie, they spark off me.' I asked if he had discussed the part with Tennessee Williams – recalling how he had made a special journey to see author James Jones about his role in *From Here to Eternity*.

He looked at me bleakly.

'No. Tennessee doesn't give a damn – as long as he gets his film rights. I never even met him. James Jones *cared*. So I went to see him.'

'You must be one of the few actors ever to bother seeking out an author?' I said. He looked hard at me.

'Yes? Hey, what a bore I must be. What a damn dreary bore.'

'Not if it helps you turn in a good performance,' I said.

'What did you think of me in *The Young Lions*?' he asked.

'It was a fine performance,' I said.

Tears coursed down his cheeks. He wept silently, and without embarrassment. And the words, no longer hesitant, tumbled over themselves.

'I was proud of that. That was one of the few films I was really proud of. But you know the only impact it had on some people? It was my first film after I'd had my car crash in Hollywood – and when people saw my face on the screen they shrieked:' "Oh, God – poor Monty. What's happened to his face?"'

'I'd lost 12lb to play the part you see and had my ears glued forward. I wanted to look like a rodent that's why. Lean and slim like a rodent. Or let's say a rat passing for a mouse. But they didn't see that. Oh, no. All they saw was that my face looked different and they shrieked.'

'Are you ever moved by your own performances on the screen?' I asked.

'What's that?' he said sharply. 'What's that?' He came over to me and I repeated the question. 'Hey,' he said. 'You've got nice teeth. I wish I had teeth like those. I hate mine. How did you get teeth like those?'

Then he was back to the original question.

'Of course I'm moved if I've got the part right. I cried when I saw myself in *The Young Lions*. There was that scene with the girl in Brooklyn you know. It was so good I didn't even realize it was *me*. I was so pleased and proud.'

'Are you proud of many of your pictures?'

He laughed wildly and buried his head in his hands.

'That's a pretty silly question.'

'Is it?'

'Of course it is. How can any actor be proud of many of his pictures? There was only one other picture that really meant anything to me and that was *Lonelyhearts*.'

'One of the worst things you've ever done.' I said.

'I'm proud of *Lonelyhearts*,' he said. 'That and *The Young Lions*. Nothing else.'

He fumbled for a cigarette, and lit the cork-tipped end.

I asked: 'Did your car crash change you at all?. It was a pretty bad bash wasn't it?.'

'Oh, yes,' he mimicked. 'It was a bad bash all right. A terribly bad bash. No, of course it didn't change me. I'm exactly the same person I was before. And this is the same face. My nose was broken in two places, and my cheek got gouged and my teeth had to be straightened. But now it's just as it was before. I ought to know. It's my face.'

His eyes grew wet again. Suddenly he flung himself on the floor and lay stretched out, his suit rumpled, his face buried in the carpet.

'Since you first went to Hollywood you've worked very hard to keep your private life to yourself.' I said. 'Do the trappings of stardom really appal you so much?'

He looked up from the carpet. 'Some actors get their satisfaction from giving performances. Others get theirs from giving autographs. You have to pay a high price to be a public figure, and I find it offensive. And you have to be polite all the time. That's difficult. I can be polite in the morning and in the afternoon, but by the time five o'clock comes . . .' he shrugged his shoulders despairingly.

I left the talented tortured Monty Clift standing shoeless by the door, his suit crumpled, his tie awry.

'It hasn't been much good has it?' he said. 'I kept trying to think of things to say but I couldn't . . .'

●

JOHN F. KENNEDY
Interviewed by Henry Brandon
The Sunday Times, 3 July 1960

John Fitzgerald Kennedy (1917–63), the thirty-fifth president of the United States, was born in Brookline, Massachusetts. He was the son of multi-millionaire Joseph Kennedy, who after making his fortune during Prohibition emerged as a supporter of Roosevelt, and was later appointed by him as ambassador to Britain (1938–40). John Kennedy was educated at Harvard and in London. During the Second World War he served as a torpedo boat commander in the Pacific and was decorated with a Purple Heart for his bravery in saving members of his crew. He was elected as a Democrat representative in 1947 and as Senator for Massachusetts in 1952. In 1960 he became the youngest person ever to be elected president and the first Catholic to hold that office, though the victory was a narrow one. He was a champion of civil rights reform and overrode state governors and legislatures in the Deep South in enforcing desegregation in schools and universities, and he showed himself to be a tough negotiator over foreign policy matters, particularly during the Cuban missile crisis. He was assassinated in Dallas, Texas, on 22 November 1963, and it is a cliché that everyone can remember what they were doing when they heard the news.

Brandon interviewed Kennedy over breakfast, shortly before he became president, 'between orange juice and poached eggs, in Kennedy's charming old house in Georgetown'. The interview started at 8.45 a.m. 'After a sip of juice,' Brandon later recalled, 'Kennedy indicated that he did not want to lose any time, that I should proceed. There were no last-minute questions, no reservations, no fuss, no nervousness. It seemed all part of normal business. This was a politician who knew what his duties were and he accepted them not without relish. His answers never betrayed emotion or excitement or irritation. Nor did his face twitch or his eyes blink when I thought I might have touched a sensitive nerve. No question, however personal or wide-ranging, seemed to present a problem. This was an orderly mind speaking. It had sifted every problem in sight and the answers came forth crisp and concise and without hesitation. In spite of the bland, monotonous voice he sounded deeply involved in the great issues of our time. In spite of his casual, dispassionate manner, what he said carried conviction in a sober, reasonable way, yet it was difficult to judge how deeply these convictions were moored in his conscience . . . He was so self-contained, so detached that it was not easy to discern what moved him inside, what inner forces sustained him . . . The interview ended as abruptly and as casually as it had started. There was an urgent meeting on the Hill and he dashed out and into his convertible and drove off. As I closed up my tape recorder and got ready to go, I noticed that while I had gobbled up everything on the breakfast tray, he had hardly touched the eggs or the bacon or the toast . . .'

BRANDON: When did it first occur to you to try for the Presidency?

KENNEDY: I suppose after the Vice-Presidential race for the nomination at the 1956 Democratic Convention. I began to play a more active part in the 1956 campaign more as a national figure than just merely a Massachusetts figure. And then after Governor Stevenson was defeated in 1956, in early 1957 I began to consider the prospect very strongly.

BRANDON: Was it because you felt there was an open field, or was it because of some compulsion?

KENNEDY: Well, I think there were two reasons. First, in a sense, there was an open field and, therefore, there was the opportunity – there were indications that my name was being considered along with other candidates. The most important part, of course, is that it's quite obvious that the Presidency has become the key office. I've been in Congress now for fourteen years, and while the Constitution makes us an equal and coordinate branch of the government, the pressure of events and the change in circumstance give the President a predominant influence. This is essential – particularly for the successful conduct of foreign affairs. Therefore, I really run for the Presidency for the same reason that I ran for the House fourteen years ago and for the Senate eight years ago: I'm strongly interested in the direction in which the United States goes and the role it plays and the responsibilities it meets, and the Presidency is the centre of action.

BRANDON: What do you think are the basic qualities a President must have and that you feel you have?

KENNEDY: Well, I think a President certainly must have, we would hope, character, judgment, vigour, intellectual curiosity, a sense of history, and a strong sense of the future. Many other qualities would be advantageous but I would say these qualities were essential for any successful President.

BRANDON: It has been said that your youth and your Catholic religion are against you.

KENNEDY: Yes. Both of those factors were regarded strong on the debit side; but they were not wholly debit. Youth – I've come on to the political scene at a time when the leadership is old. The President is old, his health has been affected, his leadership is not wholly successful and therefore I think there is a desire to turn a new page and start with a newer leadership, fresher, and we hope more vigorous. I am not sure that youth has not been a real asset, even though it has its debit side too.

My religion is a matter of great political concern and has made me a controversial figure. In that sense I was evidently born into controversy. But I don't know whether it wasn't advantageous – looking at the situation as it was in '57, '58 and '59 – to be controversial in one way or another.

BRANDON: It makes the whole country aware of you –

KENNEDY: Well, I think you have to look at the way it turned out. I think the prospects of my being nominated are good – and my religion and my youth are with me – so I can't say that they were wholly obstacles to be overcome, in the political sense.

BRANDON: Do you think now, after your victory in West Virginia which has only five per cent Catholics, that religion is still a key issue in American politics?

KENNEDY: Yes, it is, but I think it's far less. For a while it looked like it was the only issue and that was, of course, most unfortunate. Now it is an issue among many issues – but it is an issue. The whole fight for religious freedom, the whole struggle of the Reformation, the whole character of the United States, all these things make the prospect of a Catholic President a matter of serious concern to a good many Americans. The majority of these Americans want certain questions answered, and when they're answered in a responsible way I think they are then prepared to move on to the other serious problems facing the United States. Some will never accept any answer –

BRANDON: One's always heard about the opposition among protestant voters, but do you think there is an opposition to you among the Catholic hierarchy?

KENNEDY: Some – but I would hope that those that are Republican would support a Republican candidate. The corollary of the desire not to be voted against merely because of my religion is also the hope that those who are co-religionists will not vote for me because of my religion. So if there is opposition among the hierarchy, I would hope that it's confined to those members of the hierarchy who are Republican.

BRANDON: There have been signs . . . for instance, in the statement on birth control and some of the editorials in *Osservatore Romano* that, in one way or another, were critical comments on your candidacy.

KENNEDY: I don't hold that view. I don't think my candidacy was in their minds. That may be a good or a bad fact, but I think they have a longer view than the 1960 election. They, therefore, were not really thinking of the implications of their statements on my candidacy, and I think that's probably just as well. If the hierarchy ever began to bend its statements to suit my candidacy, then the charge would be proved that there is an improper, or unwise, connection between Catholic politicians and the Catholic Church. My point is that there is not, and the very fact that these statements have been made, which have had in some ways a potentially harmful effect on my candidacy, indicates that they're not engaged in a Popish plot.

BRANDON: I've heard it said that one of the reasons why the Catholic Church would not like to see a Catholic President in this country is that the United States is one of the few – perhaps the last country – where the Church can still gather new members, where there is still a fairly wide field for the missionaries, and the figures prove the Catholics have made great gains in this country in the last few years and that more gains can still be made, but that with a Catholic President perhaps this would not be quite so easy.

KENNEDY: Well, I don't know who holds that particular view, but I don't hold it at all and I don't feel that it would be wise for Catholics to withhold themselves from the office of the Presidency in order to affect the policy of the Church in the United States. I can't believe that view is held seriously by many members of the hierarchy and if it is, I disagree with it. I can't believe that the religion of the President is going to affect the decision by many Americans as to which church they're going to embrace. If it does, then their conversion is not very soundly based. I don't know what President Eisenhower's religion is – what is he, a Presbyterian?

BRANDON: Yes.

KENNEDY: I'm not sure he has many converts, has he? Or prevented many from moving into the Presbyterian church?

BRANDON: Well, I think they're not in the same – conversion 'business' are they? (*Laughter*)

KENNEDY: They all follow the desire to spread their message. I hope they do.

BRANDON: Well, if, as a President, you've got to contradict the dogma, don't you think that would create difficulties for the Church?

KENNEDY: What dogma?

BRANDON: The idea, for instance, that as the *Osservatore Romano*, the Vatican mouthpiece put it, although members of the Church enjoy a 'wide autonomy', they should allow no split between 'the believer and the citizen'.

KENNEDY: It seems to me that the position of the Catholic Church in the United States is quite clear in support of the Constitution – in support of the separation of church and state; I strongly support it. If one held the view suggested in the question, it seems to me really I shouldn't be a United States Senator because I take the same oath the President takes in regard to defending the Constitution.

BRANDON: Well, take the issue of birth control –

KENNEDY: What about it?

BRANDON: I mean, if the Church says, 'This is our position,' and you contradict it, you don't think that would create problems for them?

KENNEDY: The office holder is bound by his oath of office which he takes to defend the Constitution, which he swears to in an oath or affirmation, an oath he swears to God. It would be an extremely serious offence to violate that oath. The separation of church and state provides for the President to exercise his best judgment as to what is the way the Constitution can best be defended and the United States can be defended.

In my opinion there is no conflict. If there were, then, of course, you would say that no man of my religion could take that oath. Catholic judges grant divorces every day, even though they, themselves, do not believe in divorce. You have to make a distinction between your private obligation and then your public duty as a public official. I find it not difficult at all to make this distinction.

It seems to me the point is belaboured. If you accepted the view that a President was unable to fulfil his Constitutional oath of office because of his religion, then you'd really have to say that a senator or a congressman of that religion was unable to fulfil his oath of office. The principle is the same. We've worked all this out quite successfully in this country. Two chief justices of the Supreme Court have been Catholics, for instance. I don't think we've found it difficult to make a distinction on the whole between what is Caesar's and what is God's.

BRANDON: Politicians who have a sense of responsibility are confronted with the dilemma between fierce public pursuits of their partisan ideas and the ethics of political fair play. What are the rules that guide you in the art of politics?

KENNEDY: Well, I think a breach of the canons of fair play usually ends in defeat. I think there are self-regulators in politics as there are in other areas of life. I think the most successful politicians rarely transgress.

BRANDON: It is often said about the father-son relationship that sons either rebel against their father or, on the contrary, they are a chip off the old block. How do you see your relationship to your father?

KENNEDY: I would say that the great majority of cases of father-son relationships really don't fall into either category that you describe. There are many disagreements. In my particular case there are many disagreements on policy and have been for a great many years. He has a wholly different view of what the role of the United States ought to be in the world than I have had in the fourteen years I've been in Congress. And on many domestic matters he has substantial differences of opinion. But it's not a matter really of discussion. We do disagree and therefore I'm not going to attempt to convert him, and he does not attempt to convert me, so it's outside of our personal relationship which is very satisfactory.

BRANDON: Is perhaps his pride in a son who might become President greater than his desire to see him agree with his own ideas?

KENNEDY: No, I don't think it's that at all. I think it's merely that he feels he has a large family, that they should determine their own lives and make their own decisions. His responsibility is not to impose his political views on his children. It makes a much more successful and lasting relationship, I think, when a parent does not.

BRANDON: If it isn't the father, then, who, or what, influenced you in your political thinking?

KENNEDY: Experience and my own observation, pragmatic judgment – all these. In addition, I think the world around us influenced me and my judgment. Now he may see the world from a different perspective. But I can't believe that all sons fall into either echoing their father's view or being rebels, I would hope that for the great majority the relationship would be comparable to mine. Living in a different generation, facing entirely different problems, they make their own decisions – but their personal relationship remains harmonious.

BRANDON: Arthur Miller said to me the other day that if an international crisis sufficiently intense gripped the United States, McCarthyism would recur, because it was the conservatives that defeated him, not the liberals or the left, not the people who knew what he was about. Do you agree with this?

KENNEDY: Well, I'm not sure that any historical period repeats itself in the exact same form. I do think the words 'appease' and 'soft on Communism' and all the rest have been thrown around with some vigour in the last month or so since the U-2 crisis. Senator Scott of Pennsylvania stated that it was necessary for Governor Stevenson and myself to come and relieve ourselves of the suspicion of being 'appeasers' because we didn't happen to agree with the way the administration handled the U-2 flight. Now, it does indicate that there are those in the United States who would be glad to take the axe off the wall if political pressures sufficiently disturb them and go back to the old techniques.

BRANDON: Would you take a much stronger position in future than you once took on McCarthyism?

KENNEDY: I don't agree with the technique, if that's your question, nor did I ever.

BRANDON: It used to be Churchill's definition that Britain's foreign policy is based on three circles with Britain in the middle: one, the Anglo-American Alliance; the other, Europe; and the third, the Commonwealth. I think this basis has become somewhat obsolescent. I am wondering how you see the role of Britain in the world today.

KENNEDY: I would say the three circles are still there. The Anglo-American Alliance is certainly a basic element in the foreign policy of both countries. The Commonwealth tie is pre-eminent. The area of recent concern, of course, has been the third circle, the relationship between Great Britain and Europe. As the power of the United States, the Commonwealth, and Europe have developed, of course, it has affected the relative position of Great Britain, but she still remains a connecting link between the three circles.

BRANDON: Do you think Britain should actually join the Common Market?

KENNEDY: That's a decision that Britain ought to make. It's not for an outsider to recommend any trade policy towards a country with all the complex problems that Great Britain faces. Her people are better judges whether she should do that or not. Perhaps the British could have taken a more affirmative policy in the last three years towards that whole development, but I'm not sure it would be wise for us to attempt to advise her at this point.

BRANDON: Would you like to see a supra-national authority in Europe? I mean, a development in that direction?

KENNEDY: Yes, I would. I think we can go ahead in trade and we can go ahead in other areas. But I think there is a quite obvious limit beyond which, at least in the near future, it won't proceed.

BRANDON: Sooner or later the United States will have enough ICBMs not to need bases in Europe. Do you think this would lead to a policy much more independent of Europe?

KENNEDY: No, I think that the ties are very basic between the United States and Europe, and the need for co-operation will persist, perhaps even more strongly. There are many areas that we can approach on a common basis. I don't think that our need for bases abroad explains our interest in the development of the resurgence of Europe in the last fifteen years at all. I think a vigorous, free Europe, with expanding economics, playing a proportionate role in assisting the underdeveloped world, playing its proper role in the defence of the West – these are great common objectives which transcend the location of military bases.

BRANDON: You mean that NATO would survive this development?

KENNEDY: Well, NATO in the sense of military guarantees of Western Europe against attack – in the sense that there's a pooling of military effort – that would certainly survive, and I hope would survive in a more vigorous form in other areas so that the energies of Western Europe and the United States can be more effectively pooled in the newer areas of responsibility. The military situation may change, but I think the basic tie will remain which can be expressed through NATO.

BRANDON: When you say 'military', you mean the question of American troops in Europe?

KENNEDY: No, I mean bases. It certainly would be wise to continue American troops in Europe even when we may no longer need the air bases. Those troops are there not merely to defend the air bases, but also as a guarantee of our determination to meet our commitments under NATO and to West Germany and to Berlin. As long as Berlin is in a state of inflammation, I would think the troops would remain regardless of whether the bases would be needed or not.

BRANDON: In view of the fact that Germany will remain divided for ten years – maybe more – will it be possible to maintain the present situation in Berlin that long?

KENNEDY: I don't think anybody can say what's going to happen in the next ten years. I would say that the United States could not afford, nor could Europe, nor could West Germany, nor Berlin, afford to see West Berlin's freedom lessened. I would think that would continue to be our objective. I don't know what the situation in Germany is going to be or what the situation is going to be in Berlin; I don't know what the policy of the Soviet Union is going to be for the next decade but, at least, that basic premise must remain in our hearts.

BRANDON: Do you think we could maintain a free Berlin with the help of the United Nations?

KENNEDY: Though the main burden for the freedom of West Berlin will continue to rest on the United States, Britain, France, and the Germans themselves, nevertheless, the participation of the United Nations in their guarantees would be advantageous.

BRANDON: If you look in a broad sweep at American-Russian relations, say, for the next ten years, what do you foresee?

KENNEDY: I envisage it as a continuing competitive struggle with periods of relative warmth and periods of bitter cold. I don't imagine there will be a sharp enough change within the Soviet Union itself, or within China, in the next decade to cause a complete reversal of the present policies. The tempo may change; the goals will not. I say this with some degree of hesitation because the world has changed in so many ways the last ten years, certainly in the last fifteen years. But I would judge – based on the information we have at present – that the competitive struggle will continue and will be affected in its vigour by the actions that we take.

BRANDON: De Gaulle seems to think that sooner or later we may be able to bring Russia on to the side of the West in defence against the Chinese. Do you think it would be impossible to –

KENNEDY: There isn't any doubt that there seems to be some difference in outlook and in philosophy between the Soviet Union and China. But I would think it would be some years away before you could expect there would be a greater community of interest between the Soviet Union and the West than there is between the Soviet Union and the Chinese Communists.

BRANDON: Do you think it will be possible to keep the Chinese as much excluded from the world community, from the United Nations, as at present?

KENNEDY: I would think if their policies would change, if there would be some indication they wish to live in harmony with us and with the countries to the south, that they desire to work out the problems of the areas on which there is disagreement then I would think the relationship would become more harmonious. But I think anyone's naïve to believe that under present conditions, by bringing the Chinese Communists into the United Nations they would relax their vigour, their outward drive or inward drive.

BRANDON: Do you think the US could afford to give up Formosa?

KENNEDY: In exchange for what? Or for what reason, or under what conditions? It might be possible that Formosa would be recognized as an independent country, and so on, but it would depend a good deal on what the relationship was between the United States and Communist China – how vigorous they were in carrying out their present Stalinist policies – how hard they were pushing against India and Burma. I think that the United States should attempt to encourage the Chinese Communists to come into the present negotiations at Geneva on disarmament and nuclear testing. If they are successful, we can possibly get other areas of negotiation on problems which may divide us: the admission of newspaper men, travel, and so on, and begin to lay a foundation for a more satisfactory relationship. But, under present conditions,

I'm not optimistic that the Chinese Communists are at all desirous of paying a price they would have to pay – at least in relaxing their aggressive intentions – by entering into harmonious relations with us or by meeting the conditions which are set for admission to the United Nations. I think they're far more determined, far more ruthless, and that they in some ways rather like the present condition which permits them to pursue their objective with little restraint.

BRANDON: And how do you feel about the offshore islands?

KENNEDY: I think it was unwise for us to draw the line at Quemoy and Matsu. They're not essential to the defence of Formosa and they are rather difficult to defend. I objected at the time of the Formosa Resolution to their inclusion five years ago, and I said on several occasions that this was not the place to draw the line. Formosa we should defend, however.

BRANDON: What kind of lessons do you draw from the summit fiasco?

KENNEDY: Well, I think we should realize how tentative are the signs of *improvement* in the relations between the United States and the Soviet Union. They can always turn cold again and we should maintain our strength in every area of national life so that if the negotiations are successful, we gain; if they're unsuccessful, we have the means of protecting our security and our commitment. That's the first.

Secondly, I thought it was unwise to have the U-2 flights so close to the summit. I thought the lack of executive co-ordination and the lack of preparation for this engine failure contributed to the disastrous summit meeting.

BRANDON: Would you want to resume the U-2 flights again?

KENNEDY: No, I think they're gone as a method of gaining intelligence – it would be far too provocative and dangerous to continue them.

BRANDON: And how do you feel about going to another summit meeting?

KENNEDY: Not unless there had been some reasonably successful action at the secondary level, either at the foreign minister level or the ambassadorial level or at the United Nations so that we had some reason to believe the summit would be successful, that the Russians were genuinely interested in it.

BRANDON: You've done so much in promoting aid to India, have you thought about an approach to the African problem?

KENNEDY: Well, it's somewhat different because, in the first place, there are many countries and few of them are in the advanced state of development which permits the kind of effective assistance which I think we could provide for India. You have therefore a lower level of economic development in the free African nations which requires a different kind of effort by the United States than India does. Teachers, economic assistance, grants, educational funds, medical exchanges – all these we can do usefully. And, I think, we need to have a more sympathetic attitude towards their aspirations.

BRANDON: In your Algerian speech in July 1957 you used a phrase: 'The Western house must be swept clean of its own lingering imperialism.'

KENNEDY: Well, I think an impressive job has been done on that. There are still areas where the Western house isn't clean, and there are people who are compelled to maintain their ties to Western Europe unwillingly. But I would say that great progress has been made in the last fifteen years in freeing Africa from the remnants of Western imperialism.

I don't think there's any doubt at all that Africa is going to be free in another decade. The big problem now is going to be what will happen in those free countries, whether they will be able to maintain a free society. Are they going to be able to solve the staggering problems that they face? As people hope more and more that life will be more generous to them, the great problem is making the benefits of life shared more generously. That's going to be a great problem for the African leaders and for us who have a stake in free Africa.

BRANDON: You know, the British have been trying to meet the African problem, or the African people, more than half-way, and I think they've come to the conclusion that there is no more half-way.

KENNEDY: Well, democracy is a very sensitive plant. The desire for political independence is, so to speak, the tide that is sweeping Africa. Building something on it, particularly building democracy on it, I think is going to be extremely difficult.

The Africans are determined to take the road to freedom, and it's proper they should take it. The most challenging days for Africa are still ahead. And one of the problems is that there is a great area of ignorance here and lack of interest about Africa. African policy is a matter of great debate among the British parties and there's a good deal of discussion in all the political periodicals of Great Britain. There's comparatively little information about Africa here in the United States. It's not a political issue. There's no strong feeling. It is still the Dark Continent from the point of view of information.

BRANDON: A lot has been written about the waste of American wealth for the production of unnecessary goods. How should the United States use its affluence wisely to live up to its global commitments and to enable her to lead Western society?

KENNEDY: I do think that if we're going to play our role as a great defender of freedom – to meet all of our commitments, to prepare ourselves for a population which is going to be double what we have today – we have to continue to maintain our 'capital structure'. We have to develop our natural resources, build schools and hospitals, homes and recreational facilities and all the rest. And that requires a public effort, not merely a private satisfaction of our needs. That requires the local, state, and national governments to meet their responsibilities. And that's always a struggle because it requires draining off from private consumption, which is immediate, funds for public consumption, which is less obvious to the individual.

BRANDON: But how are you going to persuade people to produce, say, fewer television sets?

KENNEDY: I'm not suggesting really that they produce fewer television sets –
BRANDON: Well, washing machines –
KENNEDY: Well, washing machines – I don't think that is particularly affluence. I think that the washing machines and television sets contribute to our life. Washing machines relieve heavy burdens and television does open up a window to a lot of people. I would say that we must persuade people that there are certain expenditures in the public sectors that must be made – that this is a commitment which must be met. With what remains – with everything the government is not required to appropriate through the taxing powers – the people themselves shall determine how they shall spend it. They can do a better job on that perhaps than we can. But I do think that the needs of the public services must be met.

BRANDON: You are really talking about regulation by taxation rather than by rationing.

KENNEDY: The purpose is not regulation. The purpose is to secure sufficient tax funds so that we can fulfil these public commitments that must be met so that we have a harmonious life for our people. We're not attempting to direct tastes. I don't think we've come to that yet and I don't think we're particularly equipped to do it in the government.

●

MARILYN MONROE

Interviewed by Georges Belmont
Marie-Claire, October 1960

Marilyn Monroe (1926–62), the American film actress, was born Norma Jean Baker. She studied at Lee Strasberg's Actors' Studio and achieved fame as one of Hollywood's most enduring sex symbols. She starred in films such as *Bus Stop, Some Like It Hot, Gentlemen Prefer Blondes*, and *The Misfits*. She was married first to the baseball player Joe DiMaggio, then to the playwright Arthur Miller, from whom she was divorced in 1961. She had affairs with both John F. Kennedy and Bobby Kennedy shortly before she descended into a severe depression which culminated in her suicide by means of an overdose of barbiturates.

She rarely gave interviews. This – her last – was given to the French journalist Georges Belmont, and is more or less a monologue. It shows that she was an intelligent and thoughtful person behind her screen image of sexy, dumb blonde. This was the Marilyn who so captivated Truman Capote and W.J. Weatherby that they each published records of their conversations with her some years after her death.

Georges Belmont was born in 1909 and received a diploma in English at the École Normale Supérieure. From 1932 to 1940 he combined journalism for *Paris-Midi* and *Paris-Soir* with poetry and criticism for various magazines. He was director and co-founder (with Raymond Queneau, Henry Miller, Le Corbusier and Frédéric Joliot-Curie) of the magazine *Volontés* (1938–40). During the Second World War he served as chief of the bureau of information (1941–2) and secretary-general of the general secretariat of youth (1942–3). From 1945 to 1953 he was literary director of the publishers Robert Laffont. Thereafter he returned to journalism for *Paris Match*. He was subsequently editor-in-chief of *Jours de France, Marie-Claire and l'Action Automobile*. From 1964 to 1979 he held his former post at Robert Laffont, and from 1980 to 1985 he was literary director of another publishers, Acropole. He is one of France's most distinguished translators of novels in English and has translated works by Graham Greene, Evelyn Waugh, Anthony Burgess, Henry James and Erica Jong. He has published three novels and a book of interviews with his friend Henry Miller, called *Face to Face with Henry Miller: Conversations with Georges Belmont* (1971).

MARILYN MONROE: I'd much rather answer questions. I simply can't tell the whole story, that's terrible . . . Where to begin? How? There are so many twists and turns.

GEORGES BELMONT: *Still, it began somewhere. What are your earliest childhood memories?*

It's the memory of a struggle for survival. I was still very small – a baby in a little bed, yes, and I was struggling for life. But I'd rather not talk about it, if it's all the same to you. It's a cruel story, and it's no one's business but my own, as I said.

It's true that I was illegitimate. My mother's first husband was named Baker. Her second was Mortenson. But she'd been divorced from both of them by the time I was born. When I was very young, I was always told that my father was killed in a car crash in New York before I was born. Strangely enough, on my birth certificate under father's profession there's the word 'baker', which was the name of my mother's first husband. When I was born, my mother had to give me a name. She was just trying to think quickly, I guess, and said 'Baker'. Pure coincidence . . . At least, I think that's the way it was.

Anyway, my name was Norma Jean Baker. It was in all my school records. Everything else that's been said is crazy.

During the war I worked in a factory. The work was very boring and life was pretty awful there. The other girls would talk about what they'd done the night before and what they were going to do the next weekend. I worked near where the paint sprayers were – nothing but men. They used to stop their work to write me notes.

And then one day the Air Force wanted to take pictures of our factory. I worked as a model here and there for several days, holding things in my hand, pushing things around, pulling them . . .

The pictures were developed at Eastman Kodak and the people there asked who the model was and one of the photographers – David Conover – came back and said to me, 'You should become a model. You'd easily earn five dollars an hour.' Five dollars an hour! I was earning 20 dollars a week for 10 hours a day and I had to stand all day on a concrete floor. Reason enough to give it a try. And I was able to pursue one of my dreams. From time to time I took drama lessons, when I had enough money. They were expensive; I paid 10 dollars an hour.

I got to know a lot of people, both good and bad. Sometimes when I was waiting for a bus a car would stop and the man at the wheel would roll down the window and say, 'What are you doing here? You should be in pictures.' Then he'd ask me to drive home with him. I'd always say, 'No, thank you. I'd rather take the bus.' But all the same, the idea of the movies kept going through my mind.

Of course, a lot of people said, 'Why don't you go and get a job in a dimestore?' But I don't know. Once I tried to get a job at Thrifty's and because I didn't have a high school education they wouldn't hire me. And it was different, really – being a model, trying to become an actress, and I should go into a dimestore?

There are a lot of stories told about those calendar pictures. When the story came out, I'd already done *Asphalt Jungle* and was rehired at Fox with a seven-year contract. I still remember the publicity department calling me on the set and asking, 'Did you pose for a calendar?' And I said, 'Yes, anything wrong?' Well, they were real anxious and they said, 'Don't say you did, say you didn't.' I said, 'But I did, and I signed the release, so I feel I should say so.' They were very unhappy about that. And then the cameraman on the film got hold of one of the calendars and asked me if I'd sign it, and so I said yes, I would. And I said, 'This isn't my best angle, you know.' And the studio got even madder.

Anyone who knows me knows that I can't lie. Sometimes I leave things out or I don't elaborate, to protect myself or other people – who probably don't even want to be protected – but I can never tell a lie.

People are funny. They ask you a question and when you're honest, they're shocked. Someone once asked me, 'What do you wear in bed? Pyjama tops? Bottoms? Or a nightgown?' So I said, 'Chanel Number Five.' Because it's the truth. You know, I don't want to say 'nude', but it's the truth.

There came the time when I began to, let's say, be known, and nobody could imagine what I did when I wasn't shooting, because they didn't see me at previews or premières or parties. It's simple. I was going to school. I'd never finished high school, so I started going to UCLA at night, because during the day I had small parts in pictures. I took courses in the history of literature and the history of this country, and I started to read a lot, stories by wonderful writers.

It was hard to get to the classes on time because I worked in the studio till six-thirty. And since I had to get up early to be ready for shooting at nine o'clock, I was tired and sometimes I would fall asleep in the classroom. But I forced myself to sit up and listen.

The professor, Mrs Seay, didn't know who I was and found it odd that the boys from other classes often looked through the window during our class and whispered to one another. One day she asked about me and they said 'She's a movie actress.' And she said, 'Well, I'm very surprised. I thought she was a young girl just out of a convent.' That was one of the nicest compliments I ever got.

But the people I just talked about, they liked to see me as a starlet: sexy, frivolous and dumb.

I have a reputation for always being late. Well, I don't think I'm late all the time. People just remember the times I come too late. Besides, I really don't think I can go as fast as other people. They get in their cars, they run into each other, they never stop. I don't think mankind was intended to be like machines. Besides, it's a great waste of time – you get more done doing it more sensibly, more leisurely. If I have to get to the studio to rush through the hairdo and the make-up and the clothes, I'm all worn out by the time I have to do a scene. When we did *Let's Make Love*, George Cukor thought it would be better to let me come in an hour late, so I'd be fresher at the end of the day. I think actors in movies work too long hours anyway.

I think that we're rushing too much nowadays. That's why people are nervous and unhappy – with their lives and with themselves. How can you do anything perfect under such conditions? Perfection takes time.

I'd like very much to be a fine actress, a true actress. And I'd like to be happy, but who's happy? I think trying to be happy is almost as difficult as trying to be a good actress. You have to work at both of them.

If I can realize certain things in my work, I come the closest to being happy. But it only happens in moments. I'm not just generally happy. If I'm generally anything, I guess I'm generally miserable. I don't separate my personal life from my professional one. I find that the more personally I work, the better I am professionally.

My problem is that I drive myself, but I do want to be wonderful, you know? I know some people may laugh about that, but it's true.

Once in New York my lawyer was telling me about my tax deductions and stuff and having the patience of an angel with me. I said to him, 'I don't want to know about all this. I only want to be wonderful.' But if you say that sort of thing to a lawyer, he thinks you're crazy.

There's a book by Rainer Maria Rilke that's helped me a lot, *Letters to a Young Poet*. Without it I'd probably think I *was* crazy sometimes. I think that when an artist – forgive me, but I do think I'm becoming an artist, even though some people will laugh; that's why I apologize – when an artist tries to be true, you sometimes feel you're on the verge of some kind of craziness. But it isn't really craziness. You're just trying to get the truest part of yourself out, and it's very hard, you know. There are times when you think, 'All I have to be is true.' But sometimes it doesn't come so easily.

I always have this secret feeling that I'm really a fake or something, a phoney. Everyone feels that way now and then, I guess. My teacher, Lee Strasberg at the Actors' Studio, often asks me, 'Why do you feel that way about yourself? You're a human being.' I answer, 'Yes, I am, but I feel like I have to be more.' 'No,' he says, 'you have to start with yourself. What are you doing?' I said, 'Well, I have to get into the part.' He says, 'No, you're a human being so you start with yourself.' 'With *me*?' I shouted the first time he said that. 'Yes, with you!'

I think Lee probably changed my life more than any other human being. That's why I love to go to the Actors' Studio whenever I'm in New York. My one desire is to do my best, the best that I can from the moment the camera starts until it stops. That moment I want to be perfect, as perfect as I can make it.

When I worked in a factory during the war, I used to go to the movies on Saturday nights. That was the only time I could really enjoy myself, really relax, laugh, be myself. If the movie was bad, what a disappointment! The whole week I waited to go to the movies and I worked hard for the money it cost. If I thought that the people in the movie didn't do their best or were sloppy, I was really angry when I left because I didn't have much money to go on for the next week. So I always feel that I work for those people who work hard, who go to the box office and put down their money and want to be entertained. I always feel I do it for them. I don't care so much about what the director thinks. I used to try to explain this to Mr Zanuck at Fox.

Love and work are the only things that really happen to us. Everything else doesn't really matter. I think that one without the other isn't so good – you need both. In the factory, I used to take pride in doing my work really perfectly, as perfectly as I could. And when I dreamed of love, then that was also something that had to be as perfect as possible.

When I married Joe DiMaggio in 1954, he had already retired from baseball, but he was a wonderful athlete and had a very sensitive nature in many respects. His family were immigrants and he'd had a very difficult time when he was young. So he understood something about me, and I understood something about him, and we based our marriage on this. But just 'something' isn't enough. Our marriage wasn't very happy, and it ended in nine months.

My feelings are as important to me as my work. Probably that's why I'm so impetuous and exclusive. I like people, but when it comes to friends, I only like a few. And when I love, I'm so exclusive that I really have only one idea in my mind.

Above all, I want to be treated as a human being.

When I met Arthur Miller the first time it was on a set, and I was crying. I was playing in a picture called *As Young As You Feel*, and he and Elia Kazan came over to me. I was crying because a friend of mine had died. I was introduced to Arthur.

That was in 1951. Everything was pretty bleary for me at that time. Then I didn't see Arthur for about four years. We would correspond, and he sent me a list of books to read. I used to think that maybe he might see me in a movie. So I wanted to do my best.

I don't know how to say it, but I was in love with him from the first moment.

I'll never forget that one day he said I should act on the stage and how the people standing around laughed. But he said, 'No, I'm very serious.' And the way he said that, I could see he was a sensitive human being and treated me as a sensitive person, too. It's difficult to describe, but it's the most important thing.

Since we've been married we lead, when I'm not in Hollywood, a quiet and happy life in New York, and even more so on the weekends in our country house in Connecticut. My husband likes to start work very early in the morning. Usually he gets up at six o'clock. Then he stops and takes a nap later on in the day. Our apartment isn't very large, so I had his study sound-proofed. He has to have complete quiet when he works.

I get up about eight-thirty or so, and sometimes when I'm waiting for our breakfast to be ready – we have an excellent cook – I take my dog, Hugo, for a walk. But when the cook is out, I get up early and fix Arthur's breakfast because I think a man should never have to fix his own meals. I'm very old-fashioned that way. I also don't think a man should carry a woman's belongings, like her high-heeled shoes or her purse or whatever. I might hide something in his pocket, like a comb, but I don't think anything should be visible.

After breakfast, I'll take a bath, to make my days off different from my working days, when I get up at five or six in the morning and take a cold shower to wake me up. In New York I like to soak in the tub, read the *New York Times*, and listen to music. Then I'll get dressed in a skirt and a shirt and flat shoes and a polo coat and go to the Actors' Studio – on Tuesdays and Fridays at 11 o'clock. On other days I go to Lee Strasberg's private classes.

Sometimes I come home for lunch, and I'm always free just before and during dinner for my husband. There's always music during dinner. We both like classical music. Or jazz, if it's good, but mostly we put it on when we have a party in the evening, and we dance.

Arthur often goes back to work after his nap, and I always find things to do. He has two children from his first marriage, and I try to be a good stepmother. And there's a lot to do in the apartment. I like to cook – not in the city, where it's too busy, but in the country. I can make bread and noodles – you know, roll them up and dry them, and prepare a sauce. Those are my specialities. Sometimes I invent recipes. I love lots of seasonings. I love garlic, but sometimes it's too much for other people.

Now and then the actors from the studio will come over and I'll give them breakfast or tea, and we'll study while we eat. So my days are pretty full. But the evenings are always free for my husband.

After dinner we often go to the theatre or to a movie, or we have friends in, or we visit friends. Often we just stay home, listen to music, talk, read. Or we go for a walk after dinner in Central Park, sometimes; we love to walk. We don't have a set way of doing things. There are times when I would like to be more organized than I am, to do certain things at certain times. But my husband says at least it never gets dull. So it's all right. I'm not bored by things; I'm just bored by people who are bored.

I like people, but sometimes I wonder how sociable I am. I can easily be alone and it doesn't bother me. I don't mind it, it's like a rest, it kind of refreshes my self. I think there are two things about human beings – at least, I think there are about me: they want to be alone and they also want to be together. I have a gay side to me and also a sad side. That's a real problem. I'm very sensitive to that. That's why I love my work. When I'm happy with it, I feel more sociable. If not, I like to be alone. And in my private life, it's the same way.

If I asked you what does it feel like being Marilyn Monroe, at this stage in your life, what would you answer?

Well, how does it feel being yourself?

Sometimes I'm content with myself, at other times I'm dissatisfied.

That's exactly how I feel. And are you happy?

I think so.

Well, I am too, and since I'm only thirty-four and have a few years to go yet, I hope to have time to become better and happier, professionally and in my personal life. That's my one ambition. Maybe I'll need a long time, because I'm slow. I don't want to say that it's the best method, but it's the only one I know and it gives me the feeling that, in spite of everything, life is not without hope.

•

NORMAN MAILER
Interviewed by Eve Auchincloss and Nancy Lynch
Mademoiselle, February 1961

Norman Mailer, the American novelist and journalist, was born in New Jersey in 1923. The son of an accountant, he was brought up in Brooklyn and attended Harvard University at the age of sixteen, where he majored in engineering, intending to become an aeronautical engineer. His first story was published when he was eighteen and won *Story* magazine's college writing prize. During the Second World War he served with the 112th Cavalry from Texas in the Philippines, an experience which formed the basis for his first novel *The Naked and the Dead* (1948), which became an international bestseller. His subsequent books have included *Barbary Shore* (1951), *The Deer Park* (1957) and *Advertisements for Myself* (1959). In 1955 he co-founded the New York magazine *Village Voice* and from 1952 to 1963 he edited another magazine, *Dissent*. In the 1960s he became active in the anti-Vietnam war movement, publishing *An American Dream* (1965), *Why Are We in Vietnam?* (1967), and *Armies of the Night* (1967). The latter described the 1967 protest march on the Pentagon for which Mailer and others were sent to prison, and it earned him both the Pulitzer prize and the National Book Award. His subsequent books have included *The Executioner's Song* (1979), a 'New Journalism' novel about the life and ultimate execution of killer Gary Gilmore, and two historical novels, *Ancient Evenings* (1983), about Ancient Egypt, and *Harlot's Ghost* (1991), about the CIA since the Second World War. Married four times, Mailer has always been conscious of the need to maintain his image carefully and has been a keen subject of interviews. Like Gore Vidal and Truman Capote, he once wrote a memorable self-interview.

Eve Auchincloss and Nancy Lynch were staff writers for *Mademoiselle*. Their other *Mademoiselle* interview subjects included James Baldwin and Gore Vidal.

Norman Mailer wrote the great book of World War II twelve years ago. Since then he has written much and though none of this work has had unequivocal success some of his peers have gone on looking to him not only as a major American novelist in the making but as a spokesman of an embattled generation – however antipathetic they may have found his later doctrines. We interviewed him in mid-November. A few days later he is alleged to have stabbed his wife and was committed to a hospital for mental observation. He has since been adjudged sane; his wife is recovered; his future as a writer remains the challenging question it has long been. The following is excerpted from what turned out to be a long, somewhat 'existential' discussion.

MAILER: Are we going to chat or are we going to have formal questions?

INTERVIEWERS: Formal questions, sort of, which might lead to anything.

MAILER: How long do you think it will be? Half an hour? An hour?

INTERVIEWERS: Well, it might be more if we get talking.

MAILER: You mean, just talking and talking? I'd rather not do that. I've noticed that if you know you're going to do a half-hour you do better. It's a bit like the difference of intensity between a canned television program and one where you're on live. If you know a million people are hearing you at this moment it makes you more stuffy or nervous or disagreeable or hysterical or misplaced in one way or another, but you really do feel that every bit of you is going every moment. And you have an existential situation. What I'm against in all this just talking is that I'm a terribly slack man. If I'm given too many allowances, I'll do exactly the sort of charming, thin thing that's good at the moment but doesn't transcribe. At the same time, I'm not capable of formal remarks. I don't have that kind of mind any longer. If we're going to chat I want to chat on a reasonably high level.

INTERVIEWERS: All right. In an article about the Democratic Convention you recently suggested that Kennedy is a hipster. Why do you think so?

MAILER: If I say why he is a hipster just head-on, it's going to be false. It's going to sound very dogmatic. What compounds the difficulty astronomically is that there is no agreement on the meaning of the word hipster. You see, to some people a hipster is an adventurer and to other people a hipster is a rather hideous sort of evil beatnik. So if I were to say directly that I think Kennedy is a hipster, to some people this would mean that an evil beatnik is President of the United States. The possibility this offers of deadening America's view of its own reality is so bad that I'd rather ignore the question.

INTERVIEWERS: One of the things we wanted to talk about was this idea that you've written about – that you look forward to a moral and sexual revolution in this country.

MAILER: Where have I said that?

INTERVIEWERS: You said it in *Advertisements for Myself*.

MAILER: Never did I say it that way. Never. I said in *Advertisements for Myself* something about hoping to create a revolution in the consciousness of my time. By implication I obviously meant a moral revolution and a sexual revolution, but I don't think I ever said it directly because then, you see, it would mean that I'm programmatic about things that are absolutely alien to program. The difficulty and the beauty of moral and sexual revolutions is that they are unpredictable.

INTERVIEWERS: What triggers them?

MAILER: What triggers them is the notion that if people became more authentic the world would be better. And this does have a rather tender optimism to it. It's like an old joke: 'People are no damn good.' If you assume that people are no damn good, then you need police, you need authorities, you need restraints. But if you believe that people in their natural state are more beautiful than in their conditioned state, you are optimistic, and you do believe in moral and sexual revolutions. But you don't believe that they are necessarily arrived at by me making statements and looking for planks. It means that you believe in the notion of a hero – a man who will dare the gods . . . and the mass media . . . Do you have any questions about existentialism?

INTERVIEWERS: Well, what about Sartre? You put him on the side of the squares in your list of square and hip.

MAILER: Yes, square, because I think he's programmatic – he tells us exactly what to do. He talks about the authentic but he never gives you any clue to the quality of an authentic moment.

INTERVIEWERS: What do you think the quality of the authentic is?

MAILER: I think it's the moment where our aesthetic and theological and ecclesiastical sense of meaning and the beatnik sense of kick, the hipster sense of cool, all come together. It's that moment, the Spanish moment of truth, where one feels that it's no use arguing about anything, because this is the way it is really and this is what we must do. The moment of faith.

INTERVIEWERS: Does your moment of faith ever come out of a negative reaction against things as they are? Like morals and sex as they now are? Or marriage?

MAILER: You want me to say something programmatic about marriage?

INTERVIEWERS: No, no, talk about it in your own way.

MAILER: You know, I was once on a television show, Mike Wallace. He was trying to get me to say something about marriage and sex and morality. And finally I said with small despair at my dullness – because, you know, when you're on television for half an hour, the things you say have to be said very quickly and with great wit and they must always go to the center, just like an ice pick. And I have a rather dull, slow mind and I talk in private, languorous terms that interest no one but myself. And so what happens is that I very often become strident when I'm in a situation where I have to do things in a hurry. So I became strident. I said, in effect, that I believed in promiscuity. And he said: 'What do you mean by that?' (They always say that.) I said I believed in *serious* promiscuity and I thought that no voice could ever indicate the wonderful meaning of 'serious' – and I did sound terribly dogged and dogmatic – so I added: 'I mean joyful promiscuity.' Well, what happened is that my wife saw the taped show on television later – we were sitting around watching it. And when that came on she said: 'You son of a bitch.' And she walked out of the room. And I was caught between all the delights of watching myself, because I was in reasonably good form, and having to go out and make up with her. I have this terrible feeling that to talk about marriage can just, you see, be beyond my means.

INTERVIEWERS: Well, you didn't really have much to say about marriage. Does that mean that you don't want to talk about it?

MAILER: Well, can I say that America is about as totalitarian and vicious and – I'm going to coin a word – liquidational about the uses of marriage as the Soviet Union is about the uses of the proletariat. It's been the great scandal of our national life.

INTERVIEWERS: Do you think we've made marriage too important a goal? One talks to a lot of college students who say that their primary goal in life is to have a happy marriage.

MAILER: Yes, well, I don't know how to talk to students like that and they wouldn't talk to me. We've nothing to say to one another. If there were a war, we'd be on opposite sides.

INTERVIEWERS: You and younger people?

MAILER: No, no. Some of the young. I don't think all students are serious about marriage responsibilities. There aren't too many responsibilities left. I think Eisenhower used them up.

INTERVIEWERS: What's taking their place? Or is that programmatic again?

MAILER: Yes, you're right. I was programmatic for the first time. It's not fair to old Eisenhower. Now that he's gone I'm not going to be the first to say he wasn't bad because I think he was terrible. But I think he was really terrible because he never allowed anyone in America to see his charm except the people who were close to him. And this is much too royal for a man who has nothing but democratic notions in his head. Eisenhower was not authentic and this is the tragedy of the man.

INTERVIEWERS: Didn't we impose the personality on him?

MAILER: We helped him out to a great extent, but a man of character is able to resist a favorable tide too. He was not a hero finally. He was the Republican Hemingway.

INTERVIEWERS: What does make a hero?

MAILER: Courageous moments. It's *not* living in certain courageous moments that gives one cancer. Of course, if it were simple, any time something really big is happening you'd just decide to be brave in order to avoid cancer. Then everyone would be brave. The tragedy of it all is that if you choose to be brave at a certain moment and you fail, that's even more likely to give you cancer than not doing anything at all. And since everyone has lost faith and a sense of certain values nobody acts any more. And more and more courageous moments are being lost all over the world, particularly in this country. And for that reason cancer is spreading. One of the causes of cancer must be the absence of action.

INTERVIEWERS: How can one be a real hero? What sort of brave moments *can* we live? It's easy to think of bravery in terms of the bull ring or war, but here in a city it's different.

MAILER: Bravery is doing something that engages grave risk without the certainty that you're going to win.

INTERVIEWERS: Without any moral references at all?

MAILER: Look at what I'm saying: Courage is something that engages grave risk without the certainty that you're going to win. If you do this in a vacuum, without moral references, then you are what society calls a psychopath.

INTERVIEWERS: You mean a hipster?

MAILER: Well, you would say that hipsters do this in a vacuum. I don't. It's just that a hipster's notion of morality is so complex. A great many people hate hip because it poses a threat to them. They feel that if they admit that I'm right about the hipster, then they have got to go out and become a hipster themselves, which is something I'd *never* ask of anyone. I just ask that the hipster be considered at least as interesting and serious a person as a young congressman.

INTERVIEWERS: It's hard to accept the idea of a person who seems to be withdrawn from history, withdrawn from the future, withdrawn from any kind of action.

MAILER: This is the corporation notion of the hipster. I'm a hipster, for example – a middle-aged hipster. I've turned terribly philosophical and mellow but still that's what I am.

INTERVIEWERS: Are you naturally a hipster or do you have to work at it?

MAILER: I think you're charming. (*Laughter*)

INTERVIEWERS: Will you say just what, at this stage, you feel a hipster is?

MAILER: It's not so important what the background of a hipster is, or their attainments, their education, their station in life. Originally they existed among the Negroes and a few whites. By now I think it's spread out so far, there's been such a promiscuity – let's coin another terrible word – a promiscuization of personality that you find him almost anywhere. A hipster is someone who, no matter how complex or how simple he might be, no matter how good or evil in the old sense of the words (and they never did have any meaning), is still someone who pays more attention to his body than to his mind. He's an existentialist.

INTERVIEWERS: Is a hipster competitive in any way?

MAILER: All the time. With everyone, with himself, with every moment, with every nuance of existence.

INTERVIEWERS: What is he competing for?

MAILER: For more existence. He's underprivileged. He's a true proletarian, a psychic proletarian. Marx's proletariat has disappeared – they went when the refrigerator arrived – but there's a new proletariat of people who consider themselves good people, who have a vision of themselves, of people they know, of the world, of existence, of eternity. And they feel that their vision is exquisite and extraordinary and they want others to know about it. They want to rule the world, every last one of them.

INTERVIEWERS: May not this will to rule be a dead end?

MAILER: Will without tenderness is one of the more dangerous things. Will without the ability to recognize anything but its own will is something that has to be assassinated.

INTERVIEWERS: Does the hipster try to kill his will?

MAILER: He tries to keep his will. But he remains tender.

INTERVIEWERS: You mean he feels tender as he grinds the heel of his boot into the face of the dying man!

MAILER: May I say this? If we are going to be extreme let's put it on record that you were extreme first! People always think I start these things but I don't. If you're going to grind your heel into the face of a dying man I still insist on the authority of my existential logic: let the act finally be authentic. If you're going to do it, do *it*.

INTERVIEWERS: You mean enjoy it?

MAILER: The poor soul is going out of existence. You might as well enjoy yourself! If you're going to grind your boot in his face, don't do it with the feeling, 'I'm horrible, I'm psychotic, I should be in a bughouse.' Do it. There are very few people who grind their feet into the face of anyone else, because when you get down to it people are much tougher, much more capable of defending themselves than anyone ever believes. And this is the old dim liberal notion of existence. I hate to end up as a liberal but I do think that people are a little bit more resistant than is generally given them credit . . . Are you really interested in the problem?

INTERVIEWERS: Yes.

MAILER: I mean, you've asked me to look into the abyss haven't you?

INTERVIEWERS: Don't we have to? Don't you want us to? Don't you think an awful lot of us want to look into the abyss?

MAILER: No, I don't. I think it's very hard. I think people are petrified of it. But if it's gotten so bad that one of America's better writers is talking about somebody grinding his heel into someone else's face, then let us consider this moment. Let's use our imaginations. It means that one human being has determined to extinguish the life of another human being. It means that two people are engaging in a dialogue with eternity. Now if the brute does it and at the last moment likes the man he is extinguishing then perhaps the victim did not die in vain. If there is an eternity with souls in that eternity, if one is able to be born again, the victim may get his reward. At least it seems possible that the quality of one being passes into the other, and this altogether hate-filled human, grinding his boot into the face of someone, destroying that most private part of a person (remember, in the twentieth century one's sexual privates are no longer so private as one's face), in the act of killing, in this terribly private moment, the brute feels a moment of tenderness, for the first time perhaps in all of his existence. What has happened is that the killer is becoming a little more possible, a little bit more ready to love someone. (*Pause*)

INTERVIEWERS: To refer to the abyss again, if we don't want to look into it, why do so many people go to analysts, why are so many interested in Zen?

MAILER: Because they *don't* want to look into the abyss. Beg your pardon, but psychoanalysis and Zen, in my private psychic geometry, are equal to nicotine. They are anti-existential. Nicotine quarantines one out of existence.

INTERVIEWERS: What do you mean?

MAILER: Whenever one feels an emotion which is a little bit new one lights a cigarette. The emotion is converted into textual material.

INTERVIEWERS: What about marijuana?

MAILER: I'd rather not talk about that.

INTERVIEWERS: What about your self-analysis?

MAILER: All right. I capitulate. My self-analysis started with marijuana for better or for worse. Whether marijuana is an invention of God or the devil, I really have no idea by now. My self-analysis started with marijuana because I found that, smoking marijuana, I became real to myself for the first time. About five, six years ago.

INTERVIEWERS: In what way did you become real?

MAILER: I found that a lot of things I did that I thought were silly turned out to have a reason. If I was crossing the room and I was telling a story in a rather nice way and I suddenly clumsily ran into something and banged my knee, it wasn't because I was neurotic but because I had a profound shame at the way I was betraying something that was true in me in order to tell a good story to people who didn't like me that much anyway. And so marijuana gave me a certain sense of my own importance.

INTERVIEWERS: Does it bring out things that are there below the surface already?

MAILER: It's a subtle drug. Most people get almost nothing from it the first time. I smoked it for six months and nothing happened to me.

INTERVIEWERS: Why did you go on?

MAILER: I don't know why. I suppose because some tiny part of the drug reached into me and said: There is something here if you want to use it. But you have to be desperate. I was very sick at the time, in Mexico. I really thought I'd had it. I really thought I was going to go, because I had a very bad liver and I was following my doctor's instructions, not drinking, eating exactly what I was told to eat and living a very orderly life. And absolutely nothing was happening. I was just getting sicker every day. And then finally I took it a few more times and it gave me a sense of something that was new. I had a few new emotions.

INTERVIEWERS: How were they new? What were they?

MAILER: They were larger than any I had had.

INTERVIEWERS: Larger anger?

MAILER: Oh, yes. But also a larger sensuality.

INTERVIEWERS: More love too?

MAILER: For a while, yes.

INTERVIEWERS: Why does one feel that love is a dirty word nowadays?

MAILER: It's because love, mother and family now belong to the flag and the FBI. There's a war of words going on in America and the difficulty for a writer, precisely for a writer like me, is that I am now forced to use the words my enemies have captured to say anything at all. I have to tie myself in knots not to use the word *love* when I want to talk about love. But I can't use the word because the moment I say *love* or *God* I'd lose three-quarters of the people who might read me. I don't think we can talk about it. I think thirty years may have to go by before one can use the word *love* again without the feeling that one is betraying one's friends.

INTERVIEWERS: So what happened when all these big emotions came?

MAILER: Well, what happened is something that one really cannot talk about. That's one thing marijuana did to me – it destroyed my memory in a most odd and disturbing way. I meet someone, I'm talking to them, I like them, I heard their name a half-hour ago – and I can't remember it.

INTERVIEWERS: Well, everyone has that problem. But when you talk about your memory being gone, is it just in respect to things like people's names? Or your childhood and the sort of things one might want to recall in great detail?

MAILER: Well, marijuana's terribly personal and it's entirely possible that certain people who wish to recall their childhood will recall it in great detail. I've never had any large feeling about my childhood. I never write about it. But to get back to marijuana, I don't know whether I trust it or not. It did a lot for me, but I may have to pay for it yet. And I don't know that I can recommend it. I think it's far better if these things happen to people without it. But I got to the point where nothing could happen to me without it and so I took it and I got a great deal from it and I lost quite a bit, I think.

INTERVIEWERS: Do you still take it? Does it do for you what it did in the beginning?

MAILER: On occasion I give in to it and it does a great deal, but it costs more. It gives me a great day but I lose three or four days – my mind is feverish, disconnected for three or four days afterward and then there's a terrible apathy and depression because I've used up too much for too little.

INTERVIEWERS: Which you might have been able to achieve in some other way?

MAILER: Yes, instead of trying to do your best at a time when it counts you just do your best no matter how, because there's so much in you at the moment that you have to give it out.

INTERVIEWERS: It's a sprint?

MAILER: Yes, it's a sprint.

INTERVIEWERS: Do you think that our society exacts sprints from people? Is that part of the trouble? That people are asked to give too much at a particular moment?

MAILER: Oh, that's an excellent image. People who are ambitious and proud and wish to succeed have to become sprinters. But you don't even win by winning the sprint any more. It's gotten so desperate that you can be the most charming person at the party and the next day people go around saying, 'That poor desperate man or woman had to be so extraordinary and why? Because they have no center to their lives.' So the ones who aren't charming begin to have an interest in destroying the sprinters and at the same time they are continually electing the sprinters. And so if one's going to keep one's sense that life conceivably has a bit of beauty to it, some way or other one has to enter the underground.

INTERVIEWERS: Yes, what about the underground? Somewhere you described it as a concentration of ecstasy and violence that is the nation's dream life. Is it a state of mind or does it exist somewhere?

MAILER: Well, assume that New York had an underground. Would I be likely, as apostle-leader of this underground, to announce where it existed? (*Laughing*) Oh you're marvelous, kids. I'll tell you this about you: I'd hate to go ten rounds with you. If you were a man and I was a good club fighter, I'd hate to go ten rounds with you. Because I'd win, you know, and I'd get a unanimous decision, but you'd wreck me for my next fight.

INTERVIEWERS: We were thinking that it seems from his writing that Mailer has an absolute problem about fatigue!

MAILER: He does. He is tired prematurely. You see, I'm an infantryman. I started as one. And I don't say this with any pride, because it's nothing to be proud about. It's something that's done to you rather than something you do. And I wasn't in a good war. I was in a dull war, in the Philippines. So we just walked off ten years of what was to have been our private lives and when we came out, you know, that fatigue has entered into one. There's a way of walking as an infantryman which is not describable and it never got into any war movie I ever saw. Nobody walks like this in the movies, which is why war movies are so very bad. If they'd just get that for one minute you'd know what war was about.

INTERVIEWERS: How do infantrymen walk?

MAILER: Without any sense of gesture or pride or individuality. But actors don't have any sense of this because actors are people who don't walk. They are usually carried in the laps of ladies – they are the children of kangaroos. They're carried in pouches until they become men and then they stand up and say a few words and then collapse back into the pouch again.

INTERVIEWERS: That fixes actors! What about writers? Let's talk about what you read now, if anything. Or who you think the writers are.

MAILER: All right, the only thing I read is that which is thrust under my nose by people whose quality attracts my fast-dimming attention. So I'll read anything. I think it's impossible to say who's going to be the writer of the ones we know – who's going to come along with something very good. I do think that the one thing that was not absolutely disastrous in the last ten years of our literary history was that we all had enough of a small sense of one another to be able to read one another just enough so that we all did learn from one another a bit. Naturally I learned from my contemporaries and I learned very grudgingly. I mean, I hated their talents. I despised and loathed everything about them that was the least bit good. It killed me every time they did something that I couldn't quite do. I went that way for years. Then I realized that it oughtn't to be that way if I was ever going to grow at all.

INTERVIEWERS: How important is style to you?

MAILER: Style? Style's an embrace. If I were to choose a style, I think a man who writes better than I do is William Burroughs. I think he's going to last a long time after me because he's more intense. He's got a quality I don't have. I mean, I write sentences that embrace people. But he writes sentences that stab people and you never forget the man who stabs you. You can forget an embrace.

INTERVIEWERS: What do you consider the brave things you've done?

MAILER: The bravest thing I've done? It was the worst piece I ever wrote –

'The Homosexual Villain'. It was the bravest thing I ever did because it was done out of a dim, dull sense of duty.

INTERVIEWERS: What about the piece you did on Kennedy in *Esquire*? Wasn't that done out of a sense of duty?

MAILER: Oh, well, by the time I wrote that I felt, for better or worse, that I was finally a mature artist in command of his powers, doing something wilfully. I wanted to accomplish a few things: I wanted to affect the election; I wanted to advance my career; I wanted to advance Kennedy's career; and I wanted to do something reasonably well written. What bothered me was that I felt I could have written something really extraordinary, but I had to rush it. I had only seventeen days. It was excellence of a sort, but I don't think it's going to last as long as *The White Negro*. You see, it's too attractive. I'm not enamored of the piece as much as some people are, because it's the first piece I wrote in my life which was written with deliberate political intention; I wanted to get a man elected and I wanted to warn the Democrats about something that I thought was terribly important. I thought there was a great danger that Kennedy'd lose at the last minute. I think that if the piece had any important effect, you know, on Democrats of some power and influence, it was that they didn't stop working in the last three days. I think they were worried all the way down and it was good that they were worried. I think that if they had eased up a little bit, Nixon might have won.

INTERVIEWERS: How are you different from other men?

MAILER: I'm less strong, more fidgety, more determined, more inept, more successful. I don't like myself well enough to follow my instincts as I should. I think I've not had the courage to be authentic ... but that's enough, ladies.

INTERVIEWERS: You have a wonderful way of dissipating ...

MAILER: Enthusiasm. Yes. Well, if I give something to people, why can't I take it back again? You see, you never gave me a chance to say that *The White Negro* is no longer true.

INTERVIEWERS: Isn't it?

MAILER: No. Because what I said then was true as I saw it for the time, but it wasn't true enough. There weren't enough White Negroes around and so the organized world took on my notion of the White Negro and killed the few of us a little further. And I betrayed my own by writing that piece. It's even remotely conceivable I would have done better to have kept silent. I advanced my career at the expense of my armies. As a general, you see, I gained strength and lost troops.

INTERVIEWERS: What things in *The White Negro* don't you believe any more?

MAILER: I don't know that I want to lose any more troops. I've said enough. The mood has been marvelous, but it's all over, dear ladies.

●

ALF LANDON
Interviewed by Thomas B. Morgan
Esquire, October 1962

Alfred Mossman Landon (1887–1987), the American businessman and politician, was born in Pennsylvania but made his fortune as an oil man in Kansas. He was Governor of Kansas when he stood as Republican presidential candidate in 1936 against the Democrat incumbent, Franklin D. Roosevelt. Although Landon had balanced his state's budget and was critical of extravagant public expenditure, he nonetheless endorsed many of the welfare initiatives of Roosevelt's New Deal. Called the Kansas Lincoln, Landon was a gentleman who described his opponent as 'a fine and charming gentleman'. Landon did not think he could win, but he was not much helped by the antics of a vocal Republican, Mrs Preston Davie, who counted down the days from Landon's nomination until election day – 'One hundred-and-sixty . . . days to save the American way of life' . . . and so on. America disagreed with her analysis and Roosevelt won a landslide victory, gaining every state other than Maine and Vermont. Landon and Roosevelt were the first presidential candidates to meet during a campaign since Wilson and Taft in 1912. Landon's daughter later served as a US senator for Kansas. He died in Topeka, Kansas, from where he had launched his campaign fifty years earlier.

Thomas B. Morgan was born in 1926 in Springfield, Illinois, and between 1954 and 1964 he wrote many articles – usually profiles – for *Esquire, Harper's, Cosmopolitan, Good Housekeeping, Holiday, Look, Redbook* and *TV Guide*, though he never made as much money from his journalism as equivalent profilists do today. His profile subjects include Brigitte Bardot, Gary Cooper, John Wayne, Nelson Rockefeller, and Sammy Davis Jr. 'I have learned that I am unable to hate in public. I may be amazed, offended, disgusted, antagonized, or saddened, but getting to know a subject always rules out hate . . . I am sentimental. I prefer to write about evil in terms of its victims.'

From 1969 to 1973 he served as press secretary to Mayor John V. Lindsay, and in 1975–6 he edited *The Village Voice*. His five books include two novels; the latest, *Snyder's Walk*, was published by Doubleday in 1987. He is currently president of the WNYC Communications Group, New York City's radio and TV public broadcasting service, to which he was appointed by Mayor David Dinkins in 1990.

This interview, 'The Late Spring of Alf Landon', was a comparatively short assignment for Morgan, taking him only a week to research and write. Often he would spend several weeks on a profile, priding himself on his 'involvement' with his subjects. He has what he has called 'a disarming Corn Belt dialect' which tends to put people at ease. Landon (like several other profile subjects) agreed to be interviewed on the condition that he could check what Morgan wrote, although Morgan reserved the right to ignore his observations. Landon took exception to the closing paragraph of this article. 'I had quoted a long, funny story he had told his son and me about the fiery mistress of an Oklahoma politician.' Landon wanted the quote to be excised on grounds of taste. 'In the short time I had spent with Landon . . . he had captivated me. I cherished our relationship. But I wanted to use the quotation. At *Esquire*, Harold Hayes said the decision was up to me. So, the article ran as I had written it. Landon wasn't pleased, but he wasn't as angry as I had expected, either. Today [1967], we still correspond.'

Most of Morgan's profiles, which were invariably of high quality (several were published as a collection called *Self-Creations: Thirteen Impersonalities*), do not qualify as interviews since they contain little in the way of reported speech from the subject. This is an exception.

Early in 1960 at Madison Square Garden along with such ubiquitous liberals as Eleanor Roosevelt, Norman Thomas, Walter Reuther, and Harry Belafonte, a mass meeting of the National Committee for a Sane Nuclear Policy was addressed by, of all people, Alfred Mossman Landon from Topeka, Kansas. In the demonology of American politics, circa 1936, Landon is 'the Kansas Coolidge'; the thin-smiling, respectable businessman-politician peering out from the pistil of a cartoonist's sunflower; the desperate and finally fuddled leader of the Republicans' terrible 'Life, Liberty, and Landon' campaign against the New Deal. He is America's only ex-candidate for the presidency ever to carry Maine and Vermont and that's all. Yet, said he to the multitude of SANE bomb-banners: 'Now – more than ever – world opinion must be aroused to demand that the attempt to ban atomic tests continue in energetic good faith . . .' (Alf Landon?)

Then, last December and again in May of this year, Landon turned up in Washington to plug another unlikely cause: the establishment of a partnership between the United States and the Common Market nations of Europe. Had he been four-square for the conservation of American independence and sovereignty, he would have seemed more in keeping with his alleged character. He is, after all, dimly remembered for his attacks on Roosevelt's reciprocal trade program. Nevertheless, Landon told his Washington audience: 'The time is past for any nation to travel alone . . . The United States must take the leadership . . . to unify the military, economic, and political resources of the free peoples.' He even said he might consider leaving the Republican Party if President Kennedy's new trade program, first step on the road to partnership, ever became a clear-cut issue between the two parties. 'Landon astonished everyone,' Washington columnist Mary McGrory wrote after his December speech. 'His high-level defense of the Common Market would have done credit to McGeorge Bundy or Paul-Henri Spaak.' *Alf Landon?*

With this question in mind, I wrote Landon last spring and was invited to pay him a visit. I flew to Kansas City and rode sixty-odd miles on the Santa Fe Railroad west along the Kaw River, through the wheat, to Topeka, arriving at nightfall. I checked in at the Jayhawk Hotel and then stopped at a bookstore on Kansas Avenue. I was waited on by a young salesgirl who could find no books, old or new, about the Big Loser, neither Frederick Palmer's *This Man Landon* nor *What It's All About* by William Allen White, late editor of the Emporia *Gazette*.

'You know Mr Landon?' I asked.

'Who's he?' she asked.

So, I bought a copy of Arthur Schlesinger, Jr's *The Politics of Upheaval*, which covers the 1936 elections, and read parts of it at dinner. Schlesinger says that Landon was essentially a moderate Republican. 'He simply did not see the New Deal, as Hoover did, as a conspiracy to subvert American institutions. He was, after all, a man who had offered to enlist with Roosevelt in 1933, who supported the administration's agricultural and conservation programs, endorsed the principle of social security, had never criticized the securities or banking or holding company or labor legislation, and seemed to hold against the New Deal chiefly its administrative inefficiency and its fiscal deficits.' As the campaign wore on, however, Landon was impelled to express the true sentiments of his party, 'the hysterical certitude that the republic was on the verge of collapse'. In the final weeks, Schlesinger says, 'The man of modesty and moderation and charm had turned into a tired, groping, stumbling figure, moving somnambulistically from railroad train to limousine to auditorium, reading strident speeches in a flat, earnest voice before crowds which came to cheer him and, after ten minutes, sank into fretful apathy.' While FDR went on to his rendezvous with history, Landon failed himself and passed into our folklore.

After dinner, I found Alf M. Landon listed in the telephone directory just that way (as I learned later, only his wife and the *New York Times* call him 'Alfred') and he answered the phone when I called. He said I'd picked a good, average week to come to town. He would be running WREN, his Topeka radio station, and keeping tabs on his two other Kansas stations; visiting his oil leases down by Madison, Kansas; and enjoying his hobby, which was politics. He told me to hop a taxi and come on out.

On the way, the hackie circled around the state capitol, a green-domed granite pile lit by spotlights. 'Best governor we ever had in there,' he volunteered, 'was old Alf Landon – um, um, 1932 to 19 and 36.'

'You know Governor Landon?'

'And like him, the old buzzard.'

We passed the Menninger Foundation, the Topeka zoo, and the city line.

Quarter of a mile off the highway on Westchester Road, we turned sharply and drove up to Landon's white house. In the glare of the headlights, we could see that it was only a little smaller than Monticello. Old Alf Landon had been making the best of it.

Upheld by stately columns, the roof extended high over the long, wide porch. When I rang the doorbell, I half-expected Big Daddy or Tennessee Williams himself to appear, but there was Alf himself, wearing a checked shirt, baggy gray suit and unlaced brogans. At age seventy-four soon to be seventy-five, he appeared hale. He was sunburned and weathered, almost bald, with hair like white mist, and his eyes were pursed behind rimless glasses. Around the mouth, he was Will Rogers. He had square jowls and a square frame. He said he was glad to see me and gave me a solid handshake.

Walking heavily, Landon led me from the foyer through a vast living room containing six or seven groupings of splendid furniture and into the study. This room was less grand, just about the size of a four-wall handball court. At one end it had a fireplace and at the other the massive desk he had used as governor. According to a brass marker on it, the desk had been built by the Student Cabinet-Making Department of the Kansas School for the Deaf. It had been given to Landon by his 'Democrat successor', Walter Huxman. Two walls of the study were lined with books and the floor space easily accommodated two couches and several easy chairs. Landon sat in his favorite chair under a reading lamp, holding the *Christian Science Monitor* in his lap. He lit a cigarette and turned on the radio so that it would be warmed up, he exclaimed, when the St Louis Cardinals' night game with the Houston Colts came on WREN. He was in good spirits. He asked me about my trip and about the weather back in New York. He said spring had been very late in Kansas this year. Farmers were complaining. Then he seemed amused by some inner joke, slapped himself on the knee with the newspaper, and said, 'I'm enjoying the role in life that I play. After the campaign of 1936, Mrs Landon and I came back here with the three children and we built this house because I wasn't going to run for office again. We would never have built a house this big if I had decided the other way – I could have been elected to the Senate in 1938 if I'd wanted it. We would have kept the old homestead in Independence, Kansas. It had just a yard and not thirty acres like we have here. It would have been small and crowded, but we would have lived there until we went to Washington. Fellers running for office shouldn't have big homes. Nixon made that mistake. First thing he did when he went back to California was to build himself a two hundred thousand dollar house. Only Kennedys and Rockefellers can get away with something like that. Well . . . I've been playing my role in business and in politics. I think about the issues as they come up and I say something about them when I want to. Don't like to say too much, but I speak up when I've got something to say. I've had a rule for ten years now that I won't make a speech if it keeps me away from home at bedtime. I've made two or three exceptions that you know about, but mostly I don't even go drill an oil well if it keeps me away from this house overnight. A while ago, we brought one in and I stayed up thirty-six hours in the field south of here, but when I slept, I came back and slept in my own bed.'

Mrs Landon joined us. Back in 1936, she had tried to help her husband by emphasizing the differences between herself and the peripatetic Mrs Roosevelt. She had promised the American people that she would not be seen outside of the White House. As it had turned out, of course, even this prospect had failed to cut any ice with the voters. She was a pretty, matronly woman now, with gray hair tinted blue and an expression of great firmness.

'Just look at Alfred's desk!' she said. It was piled high with newspapers, books, reports, letters and other clutter. 'It's always a mess, but if you cleaned it up, he'd never find anything.'

'Nobody wants to hear about that, Theo,' he said.

Landon turned up the radio and listened for a moment. Mel Tormé was singing. 'Game's not started yet,' he said to himself, turning it down again. He saw that I had the Schlesinger book with me. He advised me to give the section on the 1936 campaign a careful reading. Schlesinger, he said, had spent a week with him in Topeka while gathering research for the section. He had lunched every day at Landon's and had studied his campaign correspondence on file at the local historical society. 'What he's got in there is the most balanced thing that anybody's written on what happened in '36,' Landon said. He was openly fond of Schlesinger and pleased that once in a while the younger man called him on the phone from the White House. 'The President made a speech a while ago saying that Hoover *and Landon* had been against Roosevelt on social security,' Landon said, 'and Arthur Schlesinger told me he was going to inform the Kennedy camp that I had not been against social security.' Landon laughed as he said this to show that it did not make any difference to *him* whether or not people still thought of him as a reactionary, but it was not really an easy laugh.

Landon was interrupted by a phone call from Dale Gates, manager of his oil leases – thirty-six active wells producing about 110 barrels of three dollar oil per day. Landon was trained as a lawyer, but he had become wealthy in the Twenties on the profits from his oil interests, although not tycoon-wealthy. Now he was getting only enough output to meet his overhead and show a relatively small profit. He listened to Gates' nightly report, gave a few terse instructions and hung up. Then he tried the radio again. The Cardinals were at bat. As soon as the announcer reported the score, he seemed satisfied and turned down the volume once more. He said he'd had a very good reaction to his Common Market speech. The coverage in Eastern papers had been extensive and lots of Kansans had heard about what he had said in Washington. 'That's because news travels east to west in the United States. You have something to say to the American people, you go east to say it and then nature takes its course. You say it here and they might not get wind of it in Wichita. But you say it in New York or Washington and everybody in the country hears it. By the time I got home from Washington last December, I was scheduled right away to make a speech before the Chamber of Commerce. I gave them the Common Market and they gave me a standing ovation.'

Landon stared at me for a moment and said I looked like I could use a drink before going back to my hotel. He went to the kitchen, brought out ice and glasses, and suggested I pour the Scotch. '. . . Now a little branch water,' he said, filling our glasses at the tap.

Back in the study, he sipped his drink and sighed. He said he could not understand why everyone was so surprised to hear him support lower tariffs and freer trade. He recalled that his father had been a Bull Moose progressive in 1912 and that he himself had been a Bull Moose precinct worker in 1914. He talked as though it had been only yesterday and nothing had happened in between. 'I didn't have to change. I've always been a progressive. Didn't I get up on the platform in 1924 and speak out against the Ku Klux Klan? And who was it, in 1934, that agreed to introduce Norman Thomas when he was making a speech here? Nobody else would do it, so I did it. I quoted Voltaire – about dying for his right to speak though I disagreed with what he was speakin' about.' Landon piled up further proofs of his changelessness. In 1929, when one lone Kansan in Congress voted against the infamous Smoot-Hawley tariff bill, Landon as Republican state chairman sent him a wire of congratulations. In 1944, he was chairman of the Republican platform sub-committee on tariff reform and got through a plank that somehow satisfied GOP protectionists and still gave the Presidential candidate, Thomas E. Dewey, something he could interpret the other way. 'Well, sure, I know I took a weasel-worded position on reciprocal trade in 1936,' Landon said, 'but I was a candidate. If you're a candidate, you've got to stand on the record of your party. Mr Stevenson learned that, didn't he? Funny thing about him, Stevenson – I never could understand what he was saying.'

After we had finished our nightcap, Landon said he would drive me to the Jayhawk Hotel. He backed the Cadillac out of the garage, turned around in the drive, and we headed for town. On the car radio, he picked out a news station which was just then summing up developments in the fight between President Kennedy and US Steel. 'There's one group in this country that don't know anything about politics,' Landon said, disgustedly, 'and that's the businessmen. They know nothing at all about it. Oh, you find a few country bankers who have a feel for it, but they're few and far between. Businessmen – that's what's wrong with the Republican Party. They ought to quit fightin' labor and start fightin' Democrats.' Landon drove in silence for a while. Then, as we approached the hotel, he apparently decided that not only the Republican Party but also the US economy was in a peck of trouble because of poor judgment among business leaders. He said there was a conflict of interest going on right now in every big corporation that gave stock options to its management. 'Ever since the war, these business fellers have been payin' dividends instead of putting money into new plants and equipment. And now, they're crying to the government for tax relief so they can get enough money to modernize their plants. They're so far behind! I ask you – why did management in steel, oil, and railroads choose dividends and stock splits over modernization? I'll tell you – it was because those fellers have more interest in their own pocketbooks than they have in running a prudent operation. Stock options are supposed to be an incentive, but they've brought us to the point where now big business has to have more profits and more tax breaks and more depreciation allowances just to compete with old Europe. It's funny, isn't it?'

Next morning about ten, I returned to Landon's house. As usual, Alf Landon had awakened with the sun. Before breakfast, he had thoroughly read the Topeka and Kansas City morning newspapers, some research materials pertaining to the Common Market, and *Newsweek*, a magazine that he preferred to *Time* because 'those *Time* fellers are too willing to sacrifice accuracy for a wisecrack'. He had dressed in breeches, boots, and a lumberjack shirt with a gaping hole in each elbow. About nine a.m. he had eaten a light breakfast, going easy, as he would say, on the hydrocarbates. Soon after I had arrived, he saddled up two of his horses (he had three, including a twenty-eight-year-old mare). We rode across the turnpike that sets the rear limit of his property, through the backyards of several neighbors, and up to the cliff edge looking over the Kaw River. Landon quietly sized up the river's depth and current and said spring sure was late this year. Back at the house, he changed into his city clothes: a white shirt badly frayed around the collar, a bright blue tie, a shiny gray-green suit, brown shoes with the well-worn heels, and a brown fedora so old that it was turning black. Then, as he waited outside for Mrs Landon to drive him into Topeka, he was approached by an elderly Negro driving a polished, well-kept 1937 Ford coupe. The man wanted a job as caretaker and Landon told him he would think it over. 'You should have seen his Ford car, Theo,' Landon said to his wife moments later. 'It was twenty-five years old if it was a day and it looked like new. Any man who's that conservative about property might be a good man for us to hire.'

Mrs Landon dropped us on Kansas Street at the Chocolate Shop, a modest café one flight below street level. It was patronized by politicians, officeholders, and office seekers and Alf had been eating lunch there for years. He was, of course, different than the other customers: *they* wore white-on-white shirts and, once in his life, *he* had played for all the marbles. The difference was pointed up during the meal as fellers paused at Landon's table to whisper in his ear or talk aloud in an abstruse lingo that only a State House denizen could really understand. Ultimately, the difference was that Landon alone wanted nothing for himself from anybody.

'Did the candidate call you, Alf?' a certain judge asked.

'What candidate?' asked Landon.

'You know who.'

'Oh, *him*.'

'Did he call?'

'When?'

'You know what I mean, Alf.'

'Well, Judge, he did and he didn't.'

'Primary's coming – you'll have to make a statement for the voters.'

'I don't have to.'

'You've got to.'

'No – I don't have to go out on the limb anymore.'

'But *he* may be the candidate, Alf.'

'Well, maybe I'll have to say something.'

'You ought to, Alf.'

'I might – and then again, Judge, I might not.'

'That's good enough for me, Alf. Funny weather we're having, ain't it?'

'Spring is really late this year.'

'Sure is. I never saw the like to beat it.'

'Me neither.'

By two p.m., the Chocolate Shop was all but deserted. The politicians had gone back to work. A busboy was mopping the floor. Landon, however, dawdled over his coffee. He said he was just now, this late in life, having the best time he had ever had in politics. 'I was the first Republican to come out and support President Kennedy's trade program. Then the newspaper boys asked me if I was speaking as a Republican or a Democrat. I said I was speaking as neither but as an American. But then I thought I'd just jar 'em a little so I said, near as I can remember, I said I might become a Democrat depending on what happened to this Common Market legislation. But I went on to say that I thought both parties would be split over it . . . Anyway, I won't make that statement anymore. No, I won't say I'll become a Democrat.' Landon finished his coffee and lit a cigarette. As he sat there, at that very moment, many of the leaders of his party were in Abilene, Kansas, not more than two hours' drive from Topeka. They had assembled there for the dedication of former President Eisenhower's library. Landon said he had not gone because I had come to visit him. When I replied that we could have driven over to Abilene together, he said, 'Well, I'm just being pragmatic. Not that I know what it means . . . Everyone is using the word pragmatic these days. I looked it up several times, but I don't see how they can use it the way they do if it means what the dictionary says it means. People use that word almost as much as "image". I'll tell you, you won't find many speeches except mine that don't have *image, dedication*, or *challenge* in them. I hate those words.' And we were off the subject of Eisenhower.

By phone, Landon ordered a car from station WREN. Then we went up to the street to wait for it. The sun was bright and Alf's eyes seemed tight shut behind his glasses. 'Yes sir,' he said, 'once I called publicly for Dulles' resignation – of course, before anyone knew he had cancer. He made the "liberation" speech and got all those people on the other side all steamed up. We've got to take our share of the blame for the Hungarian Revolution on account of that. And for what happened in East Germany, too. You see, the difference between Eisenhower and me is this: his policies were to the left of what mine would have been, but his appointments were way to the right. Now, that's all I'm going to say about it. I'm still in the Republican Party . . . I was head of the Kansas delegation to the Republican convention in 1940. We went for Willkie on the fifth ballot and then I returned to my hotel pale and white fearing for my party and my country for the way we voted . . . In 1944, I was head of the delegation again. We were for Dewey on the first ballot and that's when he got it. I like Tom Dewey, but I wasn't for him in 1948. I'd already seen what kind of a campaign he would run, so I was for Taft. You know, Bob Taft might have got it. You remember the Ohio primary of 1948, he had some difficulties with Harold Stassen? Being the way he was, Taft did nothing to repair the damage and asked me to see what I could do. I called up Fred Seaton and Fred Seaton talked to Stassen and Stassen flew in to Topeka – let's see, it was May 30, 1948 – to see me. I told Stassen he didn't have a chance to get the nomination himself but if he acted quickly, he could nominate Bob Taft or Dewey and have a hand in working out the ticket. Now it seemed as though Stassen would agree to that. Meanwhile Taft called and said he'd been thinking of Alf Landon for Secretary of Defense. I replied that I found it difficult to make people believe that neither Mrs Landon nor I was interested in living in Washington. As it turned out, Stassen seemed to think that Taft did not want him and besides, he began thinking he really did have a chance for the nomination. So, the upshot was Stassen finally wound up trying to deadlock the convention and Taft didn't get the nomination . . . That reminds me. I was telling you last night what was the trouble with the Republican Party. Well, there was a good example in 1948. We were all at the convention in Philadelphia and there was a party given by the president of the Pennsylvania Railroad. Wouldn't you know that the leading candidates *went to it*! Sure enough, next morning in the papers, here's this railroad president weighing two hundred and twenty pounds with his arms around you know who – *Dewey and Taft*. That is what's wrong with the Republican Party!'

Landon suddenly realized that the driver of his bright-red radio car (with WREN painted on both sides and the trunk) had been waiting at the curb for some minutes. Alf said he had some appointments to keep and would again go riding with me in the morning. Then he climbed in beside the driver and, lacking only the blare of far-off trumpets, drove off in the brilliant afternoon light.

*

The following morning, I overslept. I skipped breakfast and read the Topeka paper in the taxi going out to Landon's house. I read all about the dedication of Eisenhower's library and looked over the special picture page. Of all the pictures, the one that was most arresting showed a little girl down on all fours watching the ceremonies between the boots of a soldier standing at parade rest. By the time I arrived at Landon's house, he was waiting for me on the porch and, with Mrs Landon at the wheel, we headed right back to town. Mrs Landon drove carefully and never took her eyes from the road – not even when Alf chatted with her at a stoplight.

'Well, I had a call from M——,' he said, 'and he asked me if I'd been to Abilene for the dedication. I told him no, because I had this feller from New York here to see me.'

'You wouldn't have gone anyway, Alfred,' Mrs Landon said.

'Well, I didn't want to say anything like that. It was Ike's day and he'd earned it.'

'If you'd have gone, you probably would have had your picture taken.'

'Theo, I've had my picture took.'

'You'd have been in the paper like that little girl they showed watching the parade on all fours.'

'They'd probably've given me a seat like hers,' Alf said, happily.

This seemed an opportune moment to remind Landon that he had not said anything to me about the Republican conventions of 1952, 1956 and 1960. 'I didn't go to any of those conventions,' he said, 'I was for Taft in 1952 and knew he wasn't going to be nominated, so what was the use of me going? The convention in 1956 was way out in San Francisco and there wasn't any reason for me to go to that either. The 1960 convention was up in Chicago, but I still didn't see any reason to go . . . About 1964, it's futile to ask. Who've we got? Nixon, Rockefeller, Romney maybe, and Goldwater. Besides them, I think Fred Seaton is a possibility if he gets himself elected governor of Nebraska. He was a good Secretary of the Interior . . . Nixon's already said he thought Kennedy would win in 1964. Rockefeller's divorce makes him a dubious prospect. Romney's not tested yet. Now, I must say I've been amazed at the reception Goldwater's been getting. There are more crusaders for Goldwater than any other candidate. He drew twenty-five hundred people to an auditorium in a little town in Wyoming when there weren't but two thousand people in the town. I don't know that he's got much to say, but you can't rule him out. He campaigned against labor in Arizona – he was *for* right-to-work laws as much as I was *against* them – and the Republicans can't carry the big cities by kicking labor in the pants. Yet, I think the 1964 convention might nominate Goldwater. Never can tell.'

It turned out that our destination was the WREN studio and offices on Fillmore Street. The station had been founded in 1926 and acquired by the Landon family in 1952. Of the four AM stations in Topeka, it was the only one with a union and an employee profit-sharing program. Moreover, it had given the employees something to share since Landon had managed to double the station's annual net profit in less than a decade. Architecturally, the station was unique; it combined an old Mid-western gothic house with a modern, glass-front extension – but otherwise, it was just another station devoted to music, news and sports. At the door, Landon was met by his station manager.

'How's things?' Landon asked.

'Okay,' the manager said, smiling.

'Anything new?'

'Nothing.'

'Any new business?'

'Nope.'

'So, what are you smiling about?'

'Well, sir, we didn't lose any.'

Landon's offices were in the gothic section of the building. Over the mantel in what had once been someone's parlor, he had hung a large painting of sunflowers. On the walls were old cartoons by Berryman, Ding Darling and McCutcheon, photos of Teddy Roosevelt, Abe Lincoln, Landon's father, Tom Dewey, and the first stone hauled to build the Kansas State Capitol, but no pictures of Eisenhower or Nixon. The furniture was old and most of it was uncomfortable. Apparently, Landon did not feel the need to impress anyone with his business surroundings. Instead, he seemed to be running a tight, economical ship. This morning, he read his mail, signed some checks, and talked on the phone. Then two Negroes arrived for a conversation. Landon talked with them for over an hour. When they had left, he told me that they had proposed a partnership with him in a business deal that might be worth a lot of money. He said he had pretty well made up his mind to go into it with them. 'I've never had the money that the newspapers have attributed to me,' he said. 'I'm an oil man who never made his million. A lawyer who never had a case. And a politician who only carried Maine and Vermont. I never was worth a million dollars or even half that much. But I like a good proposition as much as the next man and this seems to be one.'

With his son, Jack, an advertising man in Manhattan, Kansas, and his son's friend who was the accountant for Landon enterprises, Alf had spent much of the following day in Greenwood County near Madison looking over his oil leases. There was nothing romantic about the 'Landon Pool', just small pumps scattered over the countryside sucking up small quantities of oil and pushing the stuff through pipes into small storage tanks. After a late lunch at Dale Gates', Landon had said it was time to head back to Topeka. In the front seat while his son drove, Alf had been smoking quietly, looking out at the placid, bluestem grass country. Now and then, he had commented on the terrain or on the price of Texas cattle sent north to Kansas for the rich grass.

'Late spring,' he had also said.

'Sure is,' said his son.

'Latest I ever saw,' said the accountant.

An hour had gone by on the highway and there was another hour to go, when the car shot past a farmer pounding metal fence posts into the ground. Instead of a sledgehammer, the farmer was using a more efficient device, a metal hood that he held in both hands and brought down over the posts with a short, hard, driving motion. The scene set off a chain of spoken thoughts about work done with sledgehammers, post-driving and steel-driving and stake-pounding for circus tents. Then Alf touched his son's arm and said:

'Down in Oklahoma, there was Jake Hamon, an ambitious feller with big ideas who was a little short of cash. He had the idea that what Oklahoma needed was another railroad, so he sat down and tried to figure out where he could get the kind of money you need for that sort of thing. He thought a while and then he remembered the days when he'd been a sledgehammer man driving stakes to put up the tents of the Ringling Brothers circus. It just came to him that Mr Ringling might have some spare cash to spend on a railroad. It didn't bother Jake that Ringling was in New York at the time. This being nearly fifty years ago, people thought no more about spending days getting where they wanted to go than we think about spending hours. Jake just scraped together ticket money and rode the day coach all the way to New York. When he got there, he unwrapped the package he was carrying with his clean shirt and socks, spiffed up in the washroom, and went over to the Waldorf-Astoria Hotel where, as everybody knew, Mr Ringling came in for a cocktail every afternoon. Jake got there a little ahead of time and, with his last five-dollar bill, he tipped the bartender to point out Mr Ringling when he came in.

'So, Ringling came in and the bartender pointed him out to Jake and Jake waited until Mr Ringling had his cocktail in his hand and was just about to drink it. Then Jake sidled up to him at the bar and bumped his arm, on purpose. The drink spilled on Mr Ringling and made him a little peevish, but then Jake started talking about how he'd driven stakes for Ringling's circus tents in Oklahoma. And one thing led to another until pretty soon they'd formed a partnership to build Jake's railroad – the Oklahoma, New Mexico & Pacific Railroad Co. They bought up the necessary land and got the railroad about half-finished when, all of a sudden, they struck oil all along the right-of-way. Of course, Jake Hamon and the Ringlings cleaned up – made millions, in fact.

'Well, after that, Jake went on and became an important feller in Oklahoma politics and in 1920, he headed the Oklahoma delegation to the Republican nominating convention. From the first, Jake decided he was going to vote for Warren G. Harding and keep on voting for him until Harding won it. Days later, when Harding finally got the nomination, Jake was right next to him and stayed with him, helping him get elected.

'Now, President Harding was a grateful man and he decided to show his gratitude by making Jake Hamon Secretary of the Interior in his first Cabinet. He told Jake about it and Jake said he'd like it fine. But Harding said there was just one thing keeping him from making the announcement. Everybody knew that Jake had a girl friend back in Tulsa and Harding said he'd have to get quit of her before he came to Washington. All right, Jake said, and got on a train and went back to Oklahoma to tell the girl friend, who, as it turned out, shot him dead.

'Well, if Jake'd been Secretary of the Interior, it might have been him all mixed up in the Teapot Dome scandal, so perhaps it's just as well that Albert Fall got the job instead.'

Alf's son, Jack, laughed. 'Is that a true story, Dad?' he asked.

'True story? Well, sure it's a true story. The oil's still being produced, son. If it wasn't for that, in this day and age, how do you think the Ringling Brothers could keep their circus going?'

●

HAROLD MACMILLAN
Interviewed by Jocelyn Stevens
Queen, May 1963

Sir Harold Macmillan, 1st Earl Stockton (1894–1986), the English politician, was educated at Eton and Oxford and wounded in action during the First World War. He married Lady Dorothy, daughter of the Duke of Devonshire, Governor-General of Canada, to whom Macmillan served as *aide de camp*. Macmillan worked in his family publishing firm and entered politics in 1924 as Conservative MP for Stockton-on-Tees. He lost the seat in 1929, won it back in 1931 and held it until 1945. During the Second World War he served first as a junior minister, then in Churchill's cabinet as a special minister resident at Allied Headquarters, dealing masterfully with the many disputes that arose between the British, Americans and Free French. He won a by-election in Bromley in 1945 and served as minister of housing from 1951 to 1954, presiding over a building programme of 300,000 houses a year. After holding the ministries of Defence and Foreign Affairs as well as the chancellorship of the Exchequer, he emerged as prime minister following Anthony Eden's resignation over Suez in 1957. He won a general election in 1959 on the strength of Britain's economic resurgence and ushered in the decolonization of Africa. Macmillan's later years as prime minister were marked by internal party pressures and political scandals, and he resigned for health reasons in October 1963.

Jocelyn Edward Greville Stevens was born in 1932, educated at Eton and Cambridge and served in the army before joining Hulton Press as a journalist in the mid 1950s. With his own money he set up and edited *Queen*, one of the most influential new magazines of the 1960s. He sold out his interest in the magazine in 1968 and joined Beaverbrook Newspapers as a senior executive. He stayed with the company throughout the 1970s, gaining a reputation for a tough management style. It was apparently this that ensured his appointment in 1984 as Rector and Vice-President of the Royal College of Art, widely regarded as an appointment in the spirit of the Thatcherite age. He became chairman of English Heritage in 1992.

The Macmillan interview was a great success for Stevens. The *Daily Mirror* bought second British rights and ran it on the front page and centre spread, *Life* magazine made a six-page feature out of it, and Macmillan wrote Stevens a friendly note. Other notables interviewed by Stevens for *Queen* included the press baron Cecil King (his board of directors asked him to repudiate certain remarks in the interview as inaccurate, but he refused -- thereafter the board resolved to get rid of him); another press baron, Lord Beaverbrook, who returned a galley proof with various corrections and the comment 'You are a hard man'; and Harold Wilson, then leader of the Opposition -- when Stevens's tape recorder went haywire he asked if Marcia Falkender could take shorthand notes of the interview and a 'beautifully typed' transcript arrived the next day. *Queen* also published a memorable interview with John F. Kennedy by Robin Douglas-Home.

'He won't like this much,' said Harold Evans, the Prime Minister's Press Secretary, when he looked through the list of questions I had sent to the Right Honourable Harold Macmillan, MP.

Three days later I was ushered into the Cabinet Room at Admiralty House. Mr Macmillan was seated half-way along the huge square-ended oval Cabinet table. Behind him, over the fireplace, a portrait of Robert Walpole. Before him on a large sheet of yellow blotting-paper, the inevitable telephone, its green handle betraying its importance, the ultimate weapon of diplomacy. His handshake was unimportant. He pulled out a chair next to him.

His is a marvellous face. An Identi-kit designed by Vicky for a Conservative prime minister (Edwardian model). Now its familiarity gave me that false confidence that leads people to greet television faces as old friends. 'Come and sit down,' he said. For a moment we sat beside each other looking across the wide table. I pushed my chair back. 'I particularly asked if I could see you, Prime Minister, because to me and so many of my generation you are a remote figure, growing more remote.' His eyebrows depressed. I began:

'Why did you go into politics?' The Prime Minister picked up his pipe and a box of matches from the blotter in front of him and walked away from me towards two long windows overlooking Horse Guards Parade. For an awful moment I thought he was leaving. Then, at last, he turned like a bowler at the beginning of his run.

'It seemed at the time the only possible thing I could do. On the one hand I could see all the misery and suffering of the slump and on the other, the apparent incapacity of our economic society to do anything about it.'

In 1923 Mr Macmillan was defeated by 73 votes in his first election. His constituency, Stockton-on-Tees. In 1924 he was elected.

'My father was a Christian Socialist, which was regarded in those days as being almost subversive. I was brought up in a strong radical tradition. England was governed at that time by an upper middle-class intelligentsia. My family were scholars. I was a scholar. My family moved in a literary circle with such men as Morley and Asquith.' He elaborated at length about his early literary days.

'I was twenty when the First World War broke out. In those days they used to sell newspapers all through the night. I was on my way back from a party in London and I remember the newsboys shouting "Archduke Murdered". It didn't seem important at the time. Three weeks later we were at war. I had been at Oxford for two years.'

Mr Macmillan was a scholar at Eton. (Nineteen of Britain's forty-four prime ministers have been Etonians, but only Macmillan and Walpole were scholars.) He won an 'exhibition' to Balliol.

'I always ran second to my brother Daniel. You see, he got a scholarship to Balliol.

'It would be hard for you to understand that there was a great divide between the intelligentsia and, for example, the Services. The war dissolved all that. A whole generation was submerged.'

The Prime Minister was once again in his chair, his pipe unlighted on the blotter in front of him. He turned away and looked out of the window. A long pause. 'I managed to fix myself up in the Grenadier Guards and got to know men I would never otherwise have met. I shall never forget the suffering. 70,000 men killed in one day on the Somme.' He told a story of one of his corporals. 'One of the finest men I ever knew.' Another long pause as he stared out of the window. 'I was lucky to survive.'

Mr Macmillan was wounded three times – the third time seriously.

A story is told of this incident that he rolled into the bottom of a shell crater where he feigned death as the Germans counter-attacked over him. Twelve hours later his sergeant-major found him, half-conscious, reading a copy of Aeschylus he had had in his pocket. He was in hospital for two years.

'I worried as I lay in hospital. I felt that I must get something done. Soldiering had been quite new to me. Why not politics? Oliver Stanley, Duff Cooper, Anthony Eden and a few other friends got together. They called us the YMCA.'

The Prime Minister stopped. 'It's rather cold in here.' He got up, turned on an electric switch by the fireplace and sat down again. Harold Evans came round the table, put the plug in and returned noiselessly to his place across the table.

'Where was I? Oh yes. Well, things went along. One tried but there was very little one could do in those years.'

In fact, Mr Macmillan ceaselessly harried the complacent Tories with a passion and an impetuosity sharpened by Balliol and tempered by the suffering which he had seen in the war and the misery of the poverty at Stockton. In an early speech in the Commons, he called the Front Bench of his own party 'a few disused slag-heaps which might well be tidied up'. Although a rebel he was swept out of his constituency by the Socialist landslide in 1929 only to be re-elected in 1931, still a vehement critic of his own party.

'Then along came Munich. It was inevitable the way things were going.'

At the time Mr Macmillan described Chamberlain's agreement at Munich as hypocrisy and when the House of Commons cheered the Prime Minister he was one of the few MPs who protested.

'When the Second World War started, Winston sent for me. I can remember him saying There's one thing you can say for Hitler. He's made me a Prime Minister and you an Under-Secretary of State!"

'There are two kinds of politics – policy and things. At the Ministry of Supply I was dealing with things. When I was sent to North Africa as Minister Resident I had to deal with policy. Two people turned the job down before me. I wasn't too sure about it myself. Winston wanted me to go in uniform but I didn't feel that a Grenadier Captain on the Reserve would carry much weight in General Eisenhower's headquarters. I explained this to Winston who replied "I quite understand. You mean that there's no place between the Baton and the Bowler." I enjoyed that job tremendously. One met everybody.'

In 1945 his constituents rejected Mr Macmillan again and he lost his seat by 8,644 votes. However, in a by-election at Bromley the same year he was once again returned to the House of Commons.

'Winston asked me if I could build 300,000 houses in a year and if so, would I be a Minister of Housing. I agreed on condition I could run it my way. We ran it, in fact, like a war department. You see, I'd learnt a thing or two at the Ministry of Supply working with the tycoons. Then I was made Foreign Secretary but Anthony didn't want me there so I became Chancellor of the Exchequer. I was rather sad about that because I enjoyed the Foreign Office.

'I never had any feeling about becoming Prime Minister. I took things as they came and I still do.

'Power? It's like a dead sea fruit. When you achieve it there's nothing there. The art of government is mixing the thinkers and the doers. When we're having a Cabinet Meeting, Lord Home sitting over there,' he pointed across the table (suddenly he was Peter Cook), 'will say "What about –?" We discuss it. "Will So-and-So fall?" (pause). "Will they move in?" (pause). "What will he do?" (pause). We think about it.

'Then someone else,' another wave of the hand, 'will say "What about the railways?" Now Dr Beeching is a doer.'

Then as suddenly as he had come 'on the air,' he was off – reflecting on the historical role of the Prime Minister.

'Pitt had to deal with the Closet first and then Parliament. Then it became Parliament first and then Closet. Then Parliament and People. Now it's People and Parliament.

'I've been accused of caring too much for the material well-being of the people. I don't think that you can care too much about the well-being of the people. You would agree with me if you had seen what I saw in the First World War and the 1920s. People who criticize me on that score are the first to leap to their feet when we have 2 per cent unemployment.

'Yes, I am sensitive to criticism. One has to be. There are moments when I loathe everybody and then I retire and read Gibbon for a few hours. Don't I, Harold?'

Meaningful assent from across the table.

The strain of being Prime Minister?

'I'm a Highlander. That's why I'm so pale. People often think I'm ill. They're wrong. It's true, I get a bit tired but soon pop up again. Isn't that right, Harold?'

Nodded assent from Harold Evans across the table. In six and a half years as Prime Minister Mr Macmillan has not missed a day's work.

'My clothes Edwardian? I thought that cardigans were rather smart at the moment. My grandchildren gave me this one.' He plucked at his black cardigan. 'Suits? I always wear the same suit. When it wears out I tell my tailor to send another one round. I've got three shooting suits. I rather like them.

'What do I dislike? Questions in the House of Commons. I can't bear them. What else? Things that have no purpose – formalities – like the function I'm going to this evening. Now I enjoyed Princess Alexandra's wedding. That was very pretty.

'What do I like? Most of all being with Dorothy and my family. They are my chief interest. As I get older, I find that I am more tolerant. I like people more. My father was very shy. I learnt books before people. But what I really like to do is to go off with Dorothy in the car, alone, to Scotland. I love Scotland. Where the hedges cease there is real freedom.'

A Private Secretary came in, reminded the Prime Minister that he was due to look in on an exhibition in a few minutes.

'What do I have to do? Just walk round. Oh, that's all right.'

The Prime Minister pulled out a pair of what appeared to be very old horn-rimmed spectacles, and peered owlishly at the list of his day's engagements which was propped up in front of him like a menu.

The Private Secretary withdrew.

'Let's have a little whisky. It's a bit early but never mind.'

He pressed a bell. A messenger brought three glasses of whisky on a silvery tray. No ice.

'My work centres round the box. I'm rather good at doing the box. In fact, I'm very good at doing the box. Aren't I, Harold?'

Ready assent.

The 'box' is the Prime Minister's Despatch Box. Every evening the mass of papers he has to read are placed in it.

'I only require six hours' sleep a night and I normally do the box when I get home in the evening, whatever time it is. In fact, I have two boxes. Into one I place everything that I can decide upon at the time and into the other all matters that require further consideration. If I don't do the box in the evening, then I do it as soon as I wake in the morning. Anyway it's always done. The only difficulty arises at times like Easter or Whitsun when all the other Government Departments, in a rush to clear their boxes, fill my box with all sorts of problems that they have been meaning to deal with for ages. But we're putting an end to that. Aren't we, Harold?' Heavy assent.

'No, I don't get enough exercise, although yesterday I had a four-hour walk through the woods. I went to see my game-keeper. He wasn't too hopeful about next season's prospects.'

The Prime Minister is a hard and fast worker and when his work is done he appears to be able to relax and forget it. Every day he reads for at least two hours. His conversation is laced with quotations and literary references. He sleeps easily. 'It's the quality of sleep that counts, not the quantity.' He likes forestry, shooting and being out-of-doors. He goes to church every Sunday and reads the lesson, enjoys theatre and ballet, is not particularly interested in food or drink. When trapped into a choice, he is said to ask for cold meat and salad. He appears to have the constitution of an ox. 'I was weak as a child but have grown stronger and stronger.' 'Do I find my position lonely? No, if you mean the number of people I meet. Yes, if you mean whom can one ask for advice. That's quite a different story.'

The Private Secretary reappeared. The same dialogue was repeated.

The Prime Minister rose and walked to the door. Seventy minutes had passed in five. Outside the Cabinet Room we shook hands again, 'I hope I've been some help to you,' he said, and disappeared into a black Humber, leaving me with the distinct impression that Britain and Macmillan would go into the Seventies together.

●

EVELYN WAUGH
Interviewed by Julian Jebb
The Paris Review, Summer/Fall 1963

Evelyn Arthur St John Waugh (1903–66), the English novelist, was born in London. The son of a publisher, he was educated at Lancing and at Hertford College, Oxford, where he obtained a third-class degree in history. He became a schoolmaster for a couple of years, during which time he attempted suicide. His first publication, in 1926, was an essay on the Pre-Raphaelites, followed in 1928 by a biography of Dante Gabriel Rossetti and his first novel, *Decline and Fall*. That same year he married, although he and his wife were divorced two years later and he converted to Roman Catholicism. During the 1930s his reputation grew as he published several satirical novels that are renowned for their literary style, including *Vile Bodies* (1930), *Black Mischief* (1932), *A Handful of Dust* (1934), and *Scoop* (1938). He also wrote journalism, book reviews, and travel reportage. In 1937 he married Laura Herbert and settled down to life as a country gentleman. During the Second World War he served as a junior officer in the British Army, and in 1945 he published his most famous novel, *Brideshead Revisited*, about the decline of a Catholic aristocratic family. There followed a trilogy of war novels and the eccentric, semi-autobiographical novel, *The Ordeal of Gilbert Pinfold* (1957). His *Diaries* and *Letters*, published posthumously, were much praised for their fascinating gossip about contemporaries and their vicious wit.

Julian Jebb (1934–84) was educated at Downside and Cambridge. He was a fiction reviewer for *The Sunday Times*, the *Observer* and the *Spectator*, as well as an occasional film critic for *Sight & Sound* in its heyday. In the 1970s he moved to television and subsequently made documentaries about Virginia Woolf, Nancy Mitford and Dame Edna Everage. He also made documentaries with Sir John Betjeman, Poet Laureate.

The interview which follows is the result of two meetings on successive days at the Hyde Park Hotel, London, during April 1962.

I had written to Mr Waugh earlier asking permission to interview him and in this letter I had promised that I should not bring a tape recorder with me. I imagined, from what he had written in the early part of *The Ordeal of Gilbert Pinfold*, that he was particularly averse to them.

We met in the hall of the hotel at three in the afternoon. Mr Waugh was dressed in a dark-blue suit with a heavy overcoat and a black Homburg hat. Apart from a neatly tied small brown paper parcel, he was unencumbered. After we had shaken hands and he had explained that the interview would take place in his own room, the first thing he said was, 'Where is your machine?'

I explained that I hadn't brought one.

'Have you sold it?' he continued as we got into the lift. I was somewhat nonplussed. In fact I had at one time owned a tape recorder and I had indeed sold it three years earlier, before going to live abroad. None of this seemed very relevant. As we ascended slowly, Mr Waugh continued his cross-questioning about the machine. How much had I bought it for? How much had I sold it for? Whom did I sell it to?

'Do you have shorthand, then?' he asked as we left the lift.

I explained that I did not.

'Then it was very foolhardy of you to sell your machine, wasn't it?'

He showed me into a comfortable, soberly furnished room, with a fine view over the trees across Hyde Park. As he moved about the room he repeated twice under his breath, 'The horrors of London life! The horrors of London life!'

'I hope you won't mind if I go to bed,' he said, going through into the bathroom. From there he gave me a number of comments and directions:

'Go and look out of the window. This is the only hotel with a civilized view left in London . . . Do you see a brown paper parcel? Open it, please.'

I did so.

'What do you find?'

'A box of cigars.'

'Do you smoke?'

'Yes. I am smoking a cigarette now.'

'I think cigarettes are rather squalid in the bedroom. Wouldn't you rather smoke a cigar?'

He re-entered, wearing a pair of white pajamas and metal-rimmed spectacles. He took a cigar, lit it, and got into bed.

I sat down in an armchair at the foot of the bed, juggling note-book, pen, and enormous cigar between hands and knees.

'I shan't be able to hear you there. Bring up that chair.' He indicated one by the window, so I rearranged my paraphernalia as we talked of mutual friends. Quite soon he said, 'When is the inquisition to begin?'

I had prepared a number of lengthy questions – the reader will no doubt detect the shadows of them in what follows – but I soon discovered that they did not, as I had hoped, elicit long or ruminative replies. Perhaps what was most striking about Mr Waugh's conversation was his command of language: his spoken sentences were as graceful, precise, and rounded as his written sentences. He never faltered, nor once gave the impression of searching for a word. The answers he gave to my questions came without hesitation or qualification, and any attempt I made to induce him to expand a reply generally resulted in a rephrasing of what he had said before.

I am well aware that the result on the following pages is unlike the majority of *Paris Review* interviews; first it is very much shorter and secondly it is not 'an interview in depth'. Personally, I believe that Mr Waugh did not lend himself, either as a writer or as a man, to the form of delicate psychological probing and self-analysis which are characteristic of many of the other interviews. He would consider impertinent an attempt publicly to relate his life and his art, as was demonstrated conclusively when he appeared on an English television program, *Face to Face*, some time ago and parried all such probing with brief, flat, and, wherever possible, monosyllabic replies.

However, I should like to do something to dismiss the mythical image of Evelyn Waugh as an ogre of arrogance and reaction. Although he carefully avoided taking part in the market place of literary life, of conferences, prize-giving, and reputation-building, he was, nonetheless, both well informed and decided in his opinions about his contemporaries and juniors. Throughout the three hours I spent with him he was consistently helpful, attentive, and courteous, allowing himself only minor flights of ironic exasperation if he considered my questions irrelevant or ill-phrased.

INTERVIEWER: Were there attempts at other novels before *Decline and Fall*?

WAUGH: I wrote my first piece of fiction at seven. *The Curse of the Horse Race*. It was vivid and full of action. Then, let's see, there was *The World to Come*, written in the meter of 'Hiawatha'. When I was at school I wrote a five-thousand-word novel about modern school life. It was intolerably bad.

INTERVIEWER: Did you write a novel at Oxford?

WAUGH: No. I did sketches and that sort of thing for the *Cherwell*, and for a paper Harold Acton edited – *Broom* it was called. The *Isis* was the official undergraduate magazine: it was boring and hearty, written for beer drinkers and rugger players. The *Cherwell* was a little more frivolous.

INTERVIEWER: Did you write your life of Rossetti at that time?

WAUGH: No. I came down from Oxford without a degree, wanting to be a painter. My father settled my debts and I tried to become a painter. I failed as I had neither the talent nor the application – I didn't have the moral qualities.

INTERVIEWER: Then what?

WAUGH: I became a prep-school master. It was very jolly and I enjoyed it very much. I taught at two private schools for a period of nearly two years and during this I started an Oxford novel which was of no interest. After I had been expelled from the second school for drunkenness I returned penniless to my father. I went to see my friend Anthony Powell, who was working with Duckworths, the publishers, at the time, and said, 'I'm starving.' (This wasn't true: my father fed me.) The director of the firm agreed to pay me fifty pounds for a brief life of Rossetti. I was delighted, as fifty pounds was quite a lot then. I dashed off and dashed it off. The result was hurried and bad. I haven't let them reprint it again. Then I wrote *Decline and Fall*. It was in a sense based on my experiences as a schoolmaster, yet I had a much nicer time than the hero.

INTERVIEWER: Did *Vile Bodies* follow on immediately?

WAUGH: I went through a form of marriage and traveled about Europe for some months with this consort. I wrote accounts of these travels which were bundled together into books and paid for the journeys, but left nothing over. I was in the middle of *Vile Bodies* when she left me. It was a bad book, I think, not so carefully constructed as the first. Separate scenes tended to go on for too long – the conversation in the train between those two women, the film shows of the dotty father.

INTERVIEWER: I think most of your readers would group these two novels closely together. I don't think that most of us would recognize that the second was the more weakly constructed.

WAUGH [*briskly*]: It was. It was secondhand too. I cribbed much of the scene at the customs from Firbank. I popularized a fashionable language, like the beatnik writers today, and the book caught on.

INTERVIEWER: Have you found that the inspiration or starting point of each of your novels has been different? Do you sometimes start with a character, sometimes with an event or circumstance? Did you, for example, think of the ramifications of an aristocratic divorce as the center of *A Handful of Dust*, or was it the character of Tony and his ultimate fate which you started from?

WAUGH: I wrote a story called *The Man Who Liked Dickens*, which is identical to the final part of the book. About two years after I had written it, I became interested in the circumstances which might have produced this character; in his delirium there were hints of what he might have been like in his former life, so I followed them up.

INTERVIEWER: Did you return again and again to the story in the intervening two years?

WAUGH: I wasn't haunted by it, if that's what you mean. Just curious. You can find the original story in a collection got together by Alfred Hitchcock.

INTERVIEWER: Did you write these early novels with ease or –

WAUGH: Six weeks' work.

INTERVIEWER: Including revisions?

WAUGH: Yes.

INTERVIEWER: Do you write with the same speed and ease today?

WAUGH: I've got slower as I grow older. *Men at Arms* took a year. One's memory gets so much worse. I used to be able to hold the whole of a book in my head. Now if I take a walk whilst I am writing, I have to hurry back and make a correction, before I forget it.

INTERVIEWER: Do you mean you worked a bit every day over a year, or that you worked in concentrated periods?

WAUGH: Concentrated periods. Two thousand words is a good day's work.

INTERVIEWER: E.M. Forster has spoken of 'flat characters and round characters'; if you recognize this distinction, would you agree that you created no 'round' characters until *A Handful of Dust*?

WAUGH: All fictional characters are flat. A writer can give an illusion of depth by giving an apparently stereoscopic view of a character – seeing him from two vantage points; all a writer can do is give more or less information about a character, not information of a different order.

INTERVIEWER: Then do you make no radical distinction between characters as differently conceived as Mr Prendegast and Sebastian Flyte?

WAUGH: Yes, I do. There are the protagonists and there are characters who are furniture. One gives only one aspect of the furniture. Sebastian Flyte was a protagonist.

INTERVIEWER: Would you say, then, that Charles Ryder was the character about whom you gave most information?

WAUGH: No, Guy Crouchback. [*A little restlessly*] But look, I think that your questions are dealing too much with the creation of character and not enough with the technique of writing. I regard writing not as investigation of character, but as an exercise in the use of language, and with this I am obsessed. I have no technical psychological interest. It is drama, speech, and events that interest me.

INTERVIEWER: Does this mean that you continually refine and experiment?

WAUGH: Experiment? God forbid! Look at the results of experiment in the case of a writer like Joyce. He started off writing very well, then you can watch him going mad with vanity. He ends up a lunatic.

INTERVIEWER: I gather from what you said earlier that you don't find the act of writing difficult.

WAUGH: I don't find it easy. You see, there are always words going round in my head; some people think in pictures, some in ideas. I think entirely in words. By the time I come to stick my pen in my inkpot these words have reached a stage of order which is fairly presentable.

INTERVIEWER: Perhaps that explains why Gilbert Pinfold was haunted by voices – by disembodied words.

WAUGH: Yes, that's true – the word made manifest.

INTERVIEWER: Can you say something about the direct influences on your style? Were any of the nineteenth-century writers an influence on you? Samuel Butler, for example?

WAUGH: They were the basis of my education, and as such of course I was affected by reading them. P.G. Wodehouse affected my style directly. Then there was a little book by E.M. Forster called *Pharos and Pharillon* – sketches of the history of Alexandria. I think that Hemingway made real discoveries about the use of language in his first novel, *The Sun Also Rises*. I admired the way he made drunk people talk.

INTERVIEWER: What about Ronald Firbank?

WAUGH: I enjoyed him very much when I was young. I can't read him now.

INTERVIEWER: Why?

WAUGH: I think there would be something wrong with an elderly man who could enjoy Firbank.

INTERVIEWER: Whom do you read for pleasure?

WAUGH: Anthony Powell. Ronald Knox, both for pleasure and moral edification. Erle Stanley Gardner.

INTERVIEWER: And Raymond Chandler!

WAUGH: No. I'm bored by all those slugs of whisky. I don't care for all the violence either.

INTERVIEWER: But isn't there a lot of violence in Gardner?

WAUGH: Not of the extraneous lubricious sort you find in other American crime writers.

INTERVIEWER: What do you think of other American writers, of Scott Fitzgerald or William Faulkner, for example?

WAUGH: I enjoyed the first part of *Tender Is the Night*. I find Faulkner intolerably bad.

INTERVIEWER: It is evident that you reverence the authority of established institutions – the Catholic Church and the army. Would you agree that on one level both *Brideshead Revisited* and the army trilogy were celebrations of this reverence?

WAUGH: No, certainly not. I reverence the Catholic Church because it is true, not because it is established or an institution. *Men at Arms* was a kind of uncelebration, a history of Guy Crouchback's disillusion with the army. Guy has old-fashioned ideas of honor and illusions of chivalry; we see these being used up and destroyed by his encounters with the realities of army life.

INTERVIEWER: Would you say that there was any direct moral to the army trilogy?

WAUGH: Yes, I imply that there is a moral purpose, a chance of salvation, in every human life. Do you know the old Protestant hymn which goes: 'Once to every man and nation/Comes the moment to decide'? Guy is offered this chance by making himself responsible for the upbringing of Trimmer's child, to see that he is not brought up by his dissolute mother. He is essentially an unselfish character.

INTERVIEWER: Can you say something about the conception of the trilogy? Did you carry out a plan which you had made at the start?

WAUGH: It changed a lot in the writing. Originally I had intended the second volume, *Officers and Gentlemen*, to be two volumes. Then I decided to lump them together and finish it off. There's a very bad transitional passage on board the troop ship. The third volume really arose from the fact that Ludovic needed explaining. As it turned out, each volume had a common form because there was an irrelevant ludicrous figure in each to make the running.

INTERVIEWER: Even if, as you say, the whole conception of the trilogy was not clearly worked out before you started to write, were there not some things which you saw from the beginning?

WAUGH: Yes, both the sword in the Italian church and the sword of Stalingrad were, as you put it, there from the beginning.

INTERVIEWER: Can you say something about the germination of *Brideshead Revisited*?

WAUGH: It is very much a child of its time. Had it not been written when it was, at a very bad time in the war when there was nothing to eat, it would have been a different book. The fact that it is rich in evocative description – in gluttonous writing – is a direct result of the privations and austerity of the times.

INTERVIEWER: Have you found any professional criticism of your work illuminating or helpful? Edmund Wilson, for example?

WAUGH: Is he an American?

INTERVIEWER: Yes.

WAUGH: I don't think what they have to say is of much interest, do you? I think the general state of reviewing in England is contemptible – both slovenly and ostentatious. I used to have a rule when I reviewed books as a young man never to give an unfavorable notice to a book I hadn't read. I find even this simple rule is flagrantly broken now. Naturally I abhor the Cambridge movement of criticism, with its horror of elegance and its members mutually encouraging uncouth writing. Otherwise, I am pleased if my friends like my books.

INTERVIEWER: Do you think it just to describe you as a reactionary?

WAUGH: An artist must be a reactionary. He has to stand out against the tenor of the age and not go flopping along; he must offer some little opposition. Even the great Victorian artists were all anti-Victorian, despite the pressures to conform.

INTERVIEWER: But what about Dickens? Although he preached social reform he also sought a public image.

WAUGH: Oh, that's quite different. He liked adulation and he liked showing off. But he was still deeply antagonistic to Victorianism.

INTERVIEWER: Is there any particular historical period, other than this one, in which you would like to have lived?

WAUGH: The seventeenth century. I think it was the time of the greatest drama and romance. I think I might have been happy in the thirteenth century, too.

INTERVIEWER: Despite the great variety of the characters you have created in your novels, it is very noticeable that you have never given a sympathetic or even a full-scale portrait of a working-class character. Is there any reason for this?

WAUGH: I don't know them, and I'm not interested in them. No writer before the middle of the nineteenth century wrote about the working classes other than as grotesques or as pastoral decorations. Then when they were given the vote certain writers started to suck up to them.

INTERVIEWER: What about Pistol . . . or much later, Moll Flanders and –

WAUGH: Ah, the criminal classes. That's rather different. They have always had a certain fascination.

INTERVIEWER: May I ask you what you are writing at the moment?
WAUGH: An autobiography.
INTERVIEWER: Will it be conventional in form?
WAUGH: Extremely.
INTERVIEWER: Are there any books which you would like to have written and have found impossible?
WAUGH: I have done all I could. I have done my best.

●

SAMMY DAVIS JR

Interviewed by Oriana Fallaci
1964 - published in *The Egotists: Sixteen Amazing Interviews*, 1968

Sammy Davis Jr (1925–90), the American singer and entertainer, was the son of vaudevillians. He made his first stage appearance at the age of two and appeared in an Ethel Waters film aged six. The following year he joined his father and uncle in the family song and dance act and was tutored in dance by Bill 'Bojangles' Robinson, quickly becoming the star attraction. After the Second World War he rejoined the act, which became a headliner in variety shows, but lost his eye in an automobile accident and decided to concentrate on a solo singing career. He was signed to a recording contract by Decca and had hits with a couple of standards and versions of songs from films and shows. In 1956 he made his Broadway début as the lead in *Mr Wonderful*. There followed a series of cameo film roles, in *Porgy and Bess* and *Sweet Charity* and in a couple of Frank Sinatra 'ratpack' films. He left Decca and signed a new recording contract with Sinatra's Reprise label. His first million seller came in 1962 with the Bricusse–Newley ballad *What Kind of Fool Am I?* Like Sinatra, Davis had performed in Las Vegas since the early days and it was there that he collapsed on stage in 1970, exhausted from overwork. In 1971 he had his first American Number One with *Candy Man*, another Bricusse–Newley song. He died from throat cancer. Asked what his golf handicap was, Davis once famously remarked that he thought being a one-eyed black Jew was enough.

Oriana Fallaci was born in Tuscany, Italy, in 1930. Her father was involved in socialist politics and was military chief of the Anarchist Party for Tuscany. He was arrested by the Italian SS, tortured and imprisoned, and Oriana carried messages and hand-grenades for the Resistance as a teenager. Her mother was a committed anti-Fascist and it was she who encouraged Oriana not to marry but to go to work instead. Since then she has been a journalist and writer and has had interviews published in the Italian press, as well as in *Life*, *The Washington Post* and *The New York Times*.

Her early interviews were mainly with show-business celebrities such as Sean Connery, Alfred Hitchcock, and El Cordobés. Later she turned her attention to political leaders and her subjects included Henry Kissinger, Yasser Arafat, Lech Walesa, Indira Gandhi, Golda Meir, Muamar Qadaffi, the Shah of Persia, Teng Hsiao-p'ing and the Ayatollah Khomeini. She has described her interviews, which always follow the Q and A format, as 'pieces of theater with a story inside' and she has insisted that she publishes virtually every word uttered on these occasions and does not edit the interviews for publication. She can be very provocative in her questioning. 'I make scenes,' she once told *Time*. 'I yell and scream.' One commentator has described her as 'perhaps the most famous – and feared – interviewer in the world'. She dedicated her collection of political interviews, *Interview With History*, to 'all those who do not like power' and has said that she sees power 'as an inhuman and hateful phenomenon'. She has strong emotional reactions to her subjects. When Khomeini needled her during their conversation, she tore off her *chador* (Muslim veil) causing him to storm out (he eventually returned). She conceived what she later called 'a physical hate' for Qadaffi, but thought Teng Hsiao-p'ing 'very nice, very cute'. Lech Walesa, in her interview with him, predicted that if the communist regime failed Solidarity would go into government and that he would be president. Perhaps her most famous interview was the one with Kissinger, which was published by *The New Republic* in 1972. He told her that he saw himself as a 'lone cowboy entering a village... alone on his horse'. This was widely regarded as evidence of Kissinger's outsize ego and he later described the hour he spent with Fallaci as 'the most disastrous conversation I ever had with any member of the press'. Fallaci, for her part, 'thought it was a very bad interview. *My worst interview!* I almost did not publish it. In fact, everybody was surprised at the indulgence and tolerance I demonstrated towards him during the interview.'

Apart from books of her interviews, Fallaci has published novels including *A Man* (based on her Greek poet-lover who was tortured for resisting the regime of the colonels) and *Inshallah* (1992), about Beirut in the 1980s.

The most talked about couple in America lived in a house in New York City, on Ninety-third Street East, halfway between the luxury of Park Avenue and the desolation of Harlem. A mile or so north and you find only whites, a mile or so south and you find only blacks: they lived in that limbo because she was white as white and he was black as black. They married, not caring that she was white and he black, and brought into the world a daughter who was neither white nor black and adopted a son. They went on loving each other, living together, cost what it might. It might have cost him his death at the hands of a criminal or a madman; it had already cost her the contempt of a lot of people. She was Mai Britt; he was Sammy Davis Jr. The house was elegant; before it stood their Rolls Royce; inside it there triumphed a happiness to us incomprehensible. Mai said, 'It's four years now since I made a film, and I have no intention of returning to making films. Being an actress didn't matter to me, I became one by accident. It was all through Mario Soldati, who saw me in Stockholm. But it was only when I met Sammy that I realized that my real vocation was this, being a wife and mother. And what more can I want? When you see my husband, you'll understand that I can't want more: he's such a beautiful man, in every sense. He has a beautiful heart, beautiful courage, a beautiful intelligence. For me everything about him is beautiful, his smile, his expression, his face. Oh, you should see him with his short haircut, he looks like a boy! But he's no boy, he's a real man, a man who lives his life in reality, not waiting for kingdom come, and that's another reason why I like him, I love him, I'll always like him, I'll always love him.' Together they were beautiful, what a pity they have parted.

Waiting for me, that November, in the big living room was Mai, with Tracey, their coffee-colored daughter, and Mark, their adopted son, also Negro. 'We love children. Whether the world approves or not, we intend to have lots of children, our own and adopted.' After a while Sammy arrived, the ugliest man I'd ever seen. Perhaps being next to Mai, who is so beautiful, made him look even uglier, so small and skinny and twisted, with his huge nose flattened by punches, his mouth that opens wide like a pink oven, like the mouth of an ogre, his glass eye (he lost the sight of it in a motor accident many years ago) that always looks in the same direction while the other looks all around. But a very strange thing happened. As the minutes, the hours, passed, he grew steadily less ugly, until he almost wasn't ugly, and then he wasn't ugly at all, and then he was almost beautiful, and then beautiful: the paradox of Mai. He was beautiful in his ingenuousness, his honesty, his optimism, the youthful joy with which he showed me his rich man's house, his hundred suits, his two hundred pairs of shoes, his three hundred shirts, his dozens of cameras, gold cuff links, gold watches, gold rings, gold cigarette holders, gold tie tacks, the absurd and useless luxury that compensates for his hard life, his youth spent washing dishes, cleaning out toilets, the humiliations, the disappointed hopes. But his greatest compensation was the woman he had managed to marry, as in a fairy tale, the tale of the princess and the toad. The princess falls in love with the toad, and the toad turns into a gorgeous young man, a miracle for which he pays dearly every day, for which he will go on paying as long as he lives. So it's plain that he talked of nothing else, that he was able to talk of nothing else, it was an obsession. Actor, dancer, singer, convert to the Jewish faith, friend of the Kennedys, star of movies, plays, and a musical, *Golden Boy*, which was reaping success on Broadway, author of a book entitled *Yes, I Can*, he could have talked about a great many things. And instead he talked only about one thing; he was obsessed by it. About his compensation. About his fairy tale. About his love for the blonde white woman who was in love with him. And it is the quality of that love that makes this interview remain so fresh, so worthy of our continued attention.

ORIANA FALLACI: *On my way to your house, Mr Davis, I had a very disturbing thought. You have absolutely everything to make you hated by the multitudes of mean-minded and stupid people: you're a Negro, a Jew, married to a beautiful blond ... Truly there's no other internationally famous person who contrives to combine so many 'sins' into one. And I concluded: goodness, this man must positively enjoy doing battle with the world, irritating people, provoking them, defying them ... But do you really enjoy it, Mr Davis, or does it make you unhappy?*

SAMMY DAVIS JR: I don't enjoy it in the least. I've no taste for quarreling. I'm not much of a quarreler, and a lot of years have passed since the day when, as a boy, I realized that you can't spend your life coming to blows with your neighbor. In any case, brawls don't get you anything except a broken nose and an ugly face. I don't want to fight anybody intentionally, on principle. I only want to lead my life according to those standards I believe to be right, and the 'sins' that are combined in me aren't aimed at irritating, provoking, defying anyone. They arise out of reality, logic, out of being consistent. I'm a Negro, and that's a reality. I'm a convert to Judaism because in Judaism I found the religious faith I was looking for, the solution to a spiritual crisis that was troubling me, and so that was an act of logic. I married a beautiful blond because I loved her and she loved me, so that was simply being consistent. Nothing else. I never thought, 'I'll be a convert to Judaism in order to annoy the Catholics, the Methodists, the Presbyterians, and the rest.' I never said, 'I want to marry a blond, beautiful white woman.' All I ever said was, 'I'll marry the woman I fall in love with, and she will bear my children.' That's all. Chance or destiny willed it that the woman should be blond, beautiful, and white. Period.

Not period, seeing you don't enjoy it, you said so. Not period, seeing it precipitates and redoubles and trebles all the prejudices, the outrage, and the hostility. Not period, seeing ...

... seeing it makes me unhappy. And it certainly does make me unhappy. I get hurt easily, and who wouldn't get hurt in my position? Wouldn't you? You can't even have the faintest idea; you can go wherever you want, you can, with your white skin. You can enter any place, you can, with your white skin. Nobody throws you out of a hotel because you're white. Nobody stops you from entering a restaurant because you're fair. Nobody! And it isn't very nice, believe me, to go into the El Morocco with your own wife and see people making faces, turning their backs on you. It isn't even logical. It's absurd! Why should they make faces, turn their backs on you? Because you married a white woman, Sammy, obviously. And why shouldn't I have married a white woman? Because it's against the rules, obviously. What rules? The rules, Sammy. Rules? I've never gone by rules set by other people; I've always felt that they don't count for anything, rules, if your own conscience doesn't want to accept them.

So don't tell me I can't play this piano because it's against the rules; don't tell me I can't have that Rolls Royce because it's against the rules; don't tell me I can't marry a white woman because it's against the rules. If I love her, the white woman, if she loves me, if I can be a good husband to her and give her what she desires, why can't I marry her? Because it's never been done before, Sammy, obviously. Ah, yes? It's never been done? Then I'll do it. If the law of it's never-been-done were a valid logical, consistent law, the world wouldn't exist. Progress wouldn't exist. Houses, ships, the printed word, radio, cars, rockets wouldn't exist, Fellini's movies wouldn't exist, Ingmar Bergman's movies wouldn't exist, the window wouldn't exist, nothing would exist. Who made the first window? Assuredly someone who was told you can't because it's never-been-done. To which he replied: then I'll do it. And he did it. Not because he enjoyed doing battle with people, irritating, provoking them. Not to give offense. But because he was within his rights to try. Just as I was within my rights to leave Catholicism for Judaism, to marry Mai . . .

Sacred rights, Mr Davis, but I have a question to ask you – an unpleasant question, maybe, and a very serious one. When you married, you and Mai, didn't you think about the responsibility of bringing into the world children who would be neither black nor white? Weren't you at all scared at the thought of imposing too hard a life on your offspring? The world is what it is, Mr Davis, society is as you know it. It isn't comfortable to be neither black nor white: rejected by the whites because you aren't white, by the Negroes because you aren't black. It presents terrible problems, not belonging to any particular race, finding oneself in the middle . . .

Problems? No offspring of woman's womb is without problems. You, white and fair as you are, are you without problems? You think maybe you have fewer problems or substantially different problems from a Negro with crinkly hair? Let's have a look at them, these problems. Physical problems? The answer to that one is my daughter Tracey: a beautiful child, exquisitely made, wonderful. Mental problems? It's common knowledge that to mingle races does good, it's common knowledge that pure races always end up producing idiots. Aristocratic families, royal dynasties, have died out because as a result of being pure they bred idiots. This is a genetic law, not a personal point of view; it's true of plants, animals, human beings. And this leaves aside the fact that there's no such thing as a completely pure race; each of us has a drop of blood from some other race, a little drop of Jewish or Arab or Negro or Chinese blood, or whatever. Human, social problems? The world is improving. Believe Sammy, it's improving. Prejudices are growing fewer. What once even the imagination balked at is now beginning to be accepted in reality. Life for Tracey will be much easier than it has been for me, for my wife, for you, for today's adults. I am convinced that Tracey will have fewer problems being half white and half black than you, all white, and myself, all black, have had.

It's comforting and good too that you should be so optimistic, Mr Davis. But are you sure you're not living in a world of hopes and dreams rather than of cruel realities?

Ah! I live in the most tangible reality, believe me. I know very well that I could be killed for the choice I've made, that anyone might take a shot at me: that's a reality too. But I'm an optimist, and I also know that those who'd like to shoot at me constitute a mad minority; the majority is composed of good folk, decent folk. If this weren't so, we'd still be living in caves and eating each other like fish, snakes. I'm optimistic, yes, and I have my own reasons for being so. I'm optimistic because when I met this woman, I said to myself no, she can't love me, there's no future in it, Sammy, don't even think about it, you're ugly, you're black, you've only got one eye, you've got a broken nose, and she looks like a fairy. Come on, Sammy, come on! And then I discovered that she loved me, that there was a future in it even though I was black and ugly and had only one eye and a broken nose. I'm optimistic because everyone said, 'All right, but even so you can't marry.' But we did. I'm optimistic because they said, 'All right, you've done it, but it can't last.' But it is lasting, and it'll go on lasting. This doesn't mean I'm saying, 'Go ahead, baby, marry a Negro yourself, bring a baby into the world who's neither white nor black.' No, I'm only saying that I've done it and it worked for me. It showed I was right, and that makes me optimistic.

But you're in a privileged position, Mr Davis. You're famous, you're popular, you're rich, surrounded by admirers. Like Duke Ellington, Louis Armstrong, Harry Belafonte, Sidney Poitier, you can do things other people can't. People will always more easily accept rebellion, affirmations of principle, audacities from someone who is someone. When all is said and done, yours isn't a typical case. In the El Morocco they might make faces, turn their backs on you, but the doors of the El Morocco are open to you.

I never open a door, I never let anyone open a door to me, unless I'm sure, confident, that the door will stay open for whoever follows me. I never enter a club that won't admit other Negroes. I never enter a restaurant that won't admit other Negroes. I never work in a theater or a movie that doesn't give work to other Negroes, because I can't forget that if I'm admitted, it's because others entered before me, because they opened those doors, one by one, little by little, so that I can open them a little wider. And so I must see to it that after me another will open them a little wider still, until they are flung wide open. In short, the fact that many doors are open to Sammy Davis, Jr, means that the same doors are open to others. James Baldwin would never have started writing books if Richard Wright hadn't written them before him. I would never have succeeded if other Negro actors and singers hadn't succeeded before me. A Negro, you see, whatever he's doing, a Negro never does it just for himself. He always does it both for himself and for the others of his race, even though he might not be aware of it. And I know, my wife knows, that by getting married we have contributed something. I know, she knows, that we have contributed something by bringing Tracey into the world, and we are proud of it. You see, look, take my musical comedy on Broadway, *Golden Boy*. I'm proud to be on Broadway, I feel ten feet tall. When I think of it, my goodness, I can feel both my eyes. Las Vegas, Hollywood, London, for me nothing was worth Broadway. But I know that being on Broadway doesn't help only me. It helps twenty Negro boys who are in the show along with the same number of white boys. It helps to stir the stagnant waters of a theater of which people ask only gay musicals that raise no problems. When on Broadway has there ever been seen such real integration? When on Broadway has there ever been shown the love story of a Negro and a white girl? *Golden Boy* wasn't that originally, either; it was the story of a Jew who from being a violinist becomes a boxer. Well, now it's the story of a Negro who from being a violinist becomes a boxer and loves a very fair white girl. And people come to see it, every night the theater is full, people are accepting it!

No, Mr Davis, people come to see, but they don't accept it. People fill the theater for your sake, not for the love story of the Negro and the white girl. For weeks now there have been articles about the 'inopportunity' of showing a love story between a Negro and a white girl. People leave the theater making faces, saying, 'How about that, what a thing.' I quarreled with a friend of mine over it, Mr Davis, and . . .

Yes, I know. They're the same people who make faces and turn their backs when Mai and I go into the El Morocco: decent, democratic, maybe even cultured Americans. Americans who maintain they're totally in favor of the Civil Rights laws, ready to defend the theory but not to accept the reality, not to recognize that a Negro and a white girl can love each other, marry, bring children into the world. Americans who go lightheartedly to see Tennessee Williams plays, which in the name of art show the most degrading sides of our society, without batting an eyelid. It doesn't mean a thing. I'm sorry for them, sincerely, but it doesn't mean a thing; they're a minority. And even this minority must feel something when I cry to the woman I love: 'What color, what color are my hands? No color! No color!' At the bottom of their hearts they themselves must also feel that love has no color, love is simply love. I added those lines myself; *Golden Boy* is me in a way. I know exactly what it means to be involved in a love story of that kind, to feel yourself stared at when you walk down the street, to feel humiliated, knowing that, however things go, you're going to get very hurt. And in any case the central problem of *Golden Boy* isn't that either; it's the problem of a man who, halfway between the worlds of the whites and the Negroes, feels at ease with neither the whites nor the Negroes and rejected by both whites and Negroes.

But that's the problem I meant when I spoke of the responsibility of bringing into the world children who are neither white nor Negro, Mr Davis. It's the problem . . .

It's not my daughter Tracey's problem.

Isn't it your problem, either, Mr Davis?

No. No. No. I know a lot of Negroes who can't manage to communicate either with Harlem people or with Park Avenue people, and they're rejected both by Harlem and Park Avenue. But I'm not one of them. They are misfits, and I am not a misfit. They don't get on with either whites or Negroes, while I get on with both whites and Negroes.

There's one thing I've heard said, Mr Davis: that you prefer being with whites to being with Negroes. Your greatest friends and supporters – Frank Sinatra, Peter Lawford, Danny Kaye, Jack Benny – are white, after all, are they not?

And Sidney Poitier, Harry Belafonte, Duke Ellington are Negroes, are they not? And my great friends? Harry and Sidney belong to my generation, we grew up together, we read books together, together we chose the road we did. No, there's no truth in the idea that more of my friends are whites than Negroes. The fact is that many of my friends are actors, and there are more white actors than Negro actors, in the proportion of a hundred to one, I'd say. Obviously I'm seen more with white people than with Negroes. Obviously I am going to be talked about, publicized, supported by a greater number of whites. So what? I love the Negroes. God knows I love them!

But do the Negroes love you, Mr Davis? Especially since your marriage to Mai, are you sure the Negroes love you? There's a racism that's never spoken of, Mr Davis, the racism that Negroes display toward whites or toward Negroes who marry whites. Shall we talk about that, Mr Davis? Because I haven't quarreled only with . . .

During the electoral campaign I was alongside Bob Kennedy. I was fighting for him because I believed, I do believe, in him, because I was, I am, convinced that he will be a good senator and as good for America as his brother was. Well then, Bobby's last big rally was held in Harlem, the evening before the elections. And I was there, together with Mai, to ask the Negroes to vote for Bobby. Thousands and thousands of Negroes. And . . . well . . . it's ridiculous, it's incredible even, but they applauded me more than Bobby. Yes, the Negroes love me, and since my marriage to Mai they've loved me even more. Their racism . . . but who denies it? Does a white skin maybe give exclusive rights to hatred, contempt, error? Don't you understand that we Negroes have just as many idiot racists sick with fascism as you whites have? As many full of the same fears, the same arrogance as the whites, the same lack of dignity and generosity? Ah, those who belong to the Ku Klux Klan are neither better nor worse than those who belong to the racist Negro Black Muslim movement. They are both extremists, both disgusting, and I reject the one as strongly as I do the other because I believe that the answer to the race issue does not lie in reciprocal hatred, reciprocal contempt. I do not believe the Negro race to be an inferior race, but nor do I believe it to be a superior race, a model race. Quite simply, it's a race like any other: with its geniuses and its imbeciles. God! These things have to be said! We're in 1964, we're no longer in 1925, when an actress would walk around with a leopard on a leash! It has to be said that not only love has no color, hatred and violence have no color either!

Neither more nor less, Mr Davis. In fact, as I was going to say, I haven't quarreled only with a white friend over Golden Boy, *I've also quarreled with a Negro girl friend of mine. She also twisted her mouth into grimaces, and I asked her why. Wouldn't you marry a white man? And she replied: 'No! No! No!'*

I know girls like that, too. One of them is in my company. A lovely Negro girl who's very intelligent and talented, she can't stand white men, white people, and she'd never marry a white man, she'd never even talk to a white woman. My wife is the only white woman who gets a word or a smile out of her. What should I say to her? She makes me angry and sad, but I console myself with the thought that Negroes of this kind are in the minority. Months ago when there were the Harlem riots, only two thousand Negroes joined in. And there are three million Negroes in Harlem. One mustn't judge the Negroes and the whites by the worst of them. It would be the same as judging Italians by the gangsters with Italian names. When I think about Italians, I don't think of the Al Capones, the Anastasias, the Johnny Dios, the Frank Castellos. I think of the good folk, the vast majority, who come to America in the hope of finding something – a good life, happiness – work hard to get it, and decently and honestly build their families and their fortunes. Or else . . . yes, or else it would be the same as judging the Jews by the grasping moneylenders who have Jewish names. When I think about Jews, I never think of the characters who lend money. I think of the millions of martyred victims of the pogroms, the millions killed in concentration camps, I think of the unhappy people whose religion I have embraced. Or else . . . yes, or else it would be the same as judging racism solely in an American context. When I think about the people who make faces and turn their backs on me, I don't think only of New York and the El Morocco; I think of London, Rome, Paris, Stockholm. Bigotry and prejudice aren't limited only to my country, to my people. My marriage to Mai had a bad reception elsewhere too: in Europe, in Italy . .

I don't think so, Mr Davis, it's not so. In Italy you have been treated very decently. We Italians have many defects, but they do not include making faces at a Negro because he's a Negro. We're not racist.

Ah, no? I read more mean articles in the Italian press, after my marriage to Mai, than I don't know where. I even took proceedings against the weeklies. It isn't at all true to say that there's no racism in Italy. Try asking an Italian: 'Would you marry a Negro? Would you let your daughter marry a Negro? Would you bring children into the world with a Negro? In short, would you do what Sammy Davis and Mai Britt have done?' Try it, and then tell me what they answer. Even the nicest, most cultured, most democratic people, even the people who cried out against Goldwater, would in the majority of cases react like your white friend and the Negro girl you know. They'd answer, 'No! No! No!' In Italy, in Europe, you can go into any hotel you want, any restaurant you want, certainly, but the feelings that follow you when you walk down the street with your wife who is white are the same. At most, they respect you because you're a success. But this doesn't mean a thing when you deserve it. And I deserve it. Success didn't come to me by chance, I worked thirty-five years of my life to get it. I've washed dishes in kitchens, I've cleaned out toilets, I've emptied trash cans, and I started acting when I was four. When I was four years old, I used to act and sing with my parents. When I was six years old, I was engaged by some other people and left my parents' company, I never even went to school, because of it. I studied by correspondence course, or by reading books, and I sweated plenty, I still sweat plenty today, just as I used to, more than I used to, every night is my first night, every song is my first song, I deserve what I have, I deserve it down to the last drop, so why should people even want to deny this much to me?

Mr Davis, one question. Do you count yourself a happy man? A lucky man and a happy man?

Of course I'm a happy man! The happiest you'll ever meet. Of course I'm a lucky man! The luckiest man you'll ever meet! What more can I ask than what I have? God has given me everything, everything: money, popularity, family. And he gave me this extraordinary wife, so good, so beautiful. And he not only granted that I should love her but also that she should love me, ugly as I am, with only one eye, and a broken nose, and small too, and black. How can I complain? I can't complain about anything, anything!

Not even about your broken nose, your one eye, your ugliness?

I know I'm dreadfully ugly, one of the ugliest men you could meet, but ugliness, like beauty, is something you must learn how to use. All my life I've resisted the temptation to be a little less ugly, to have my nose fixed, for example. My bone structure is good, my jaw line is good, my cheek bones are good, my body is well proportioned. Maybe, if I'd had my nose fixed, I'd have become almost passable. But what does being passable make you? It makes you mediocre: neither ugly nor handsome. Complete ugliness, utter ugliness, like mine, though, is almost attractive. Yes, yes, I'm convinced that a really ugly man, in the end, seems attractive. A man who is so-so you don't even stop and look at, much less follow. A man like me you see, you stop and look at him, you follow him to go on looking at him, to assure yourself that he really is the ugliest thing you ever saw, and from looking at him so much you know what happens? What happens is that you find something attractive about him, and you like him. Isn't this what happened to Mai? As for my eye, ah, the optician did such an extremely fine job on it that you can't tell the false one from the real. I look more as if I have a squint than as if I'm blind in one eye. Look, my eyelid doesn't even droop, it stands up nice and straight, a masterpiece, and . . . you want to know something? I see much more now that I have only one eye than I used to see before, when I had both. With my one eye I've discovered a lot of things: Judaism, for example. With my one eye I found my wife and married her. With my one eye I have made her the mother of our children: me so black, her so white, me so ugly, her so beautiful. God, isn't she extraordinary, my beautiful wife? Look what a woman! Look! With one eye I got her, with one eye! And it doesn't matter to her at all that I only have one eye, not to her it doesn't.

●

MARGARET BOURKE-WHITE

Interviewed by Roy Newquist

Counterpoint, 1964

Margaret Bourke-White (*née* Margaret White) (1906–71), the American photo-journalist, was born in New York City. The daughter of a print designer, she studied photography at Columbia University. In 1927 she started working for *Fortune* magazine, and joined *Life* magazine when it was founded in 1936, as a staff photographer. She was married to the American writer Erskine Caldwell from 1939 to 1942 and took the photographs for his book about poverty in the Deep South, *You Have Seen Their Faces*. As a war correspondent for *Life*, she was the first ever woman photographer to be granted official status by US armed forces when she covered the siege of Moscow in 1941. She was there to record the ghastly scenes when the concentration camps were liberated at the end of the Second World War, and thereafter reported from India, Pakistan, South Africa and Korea. Her autobiography, *Portrait of Myself*, was published in 1963.

Roy Newquist was born in 1925 in Wisconsin. He was educated at Marquette University and the University of Wisconsin. From 1951 to 1963 he worked as a copy supervisor for advertising agencies in Minneapolis and Chicago. In 1963 he became literary editor of *Chicago's American* and his book reviews were syndicated. In addition, he was a critic for the *New York Post* and host of a radio programme called *Counterpoint* on New York's station WQXR. Newquist also wrote interviews as a freelance for *Show* magazine. His first book of interviews, *Counterpoint* (1964), consisted of interviews with sixty-three authors out of 252 he interviewed on tape in New York, London, Paris and elsewhere. Portions of some interviews were broadcast on his radio programme of the same name. For print purposes, however, he would record roughly an 'hour's worth of tape' and then turn 'the raw transcript into a piece that had some measure of continuity, deleting stuff that wasn't pertinent, catching the inconsistencies in tense, person, etc. Once this was done the transcript was submitted to the interviewee for any corrections, additions or deletions the interviewee wished to make.' Newquist explained that his subjects proved 'so cooperative, so congenial, that I finished up the series ten pounds heavier and a bit alcoholic'. Newquist's other books of interviews were *Showcase* (1966), *Conversations* (1967), *A Special Kind of Magic* (1967), and *Conversations with Joan Crawford* (1982).

Note: At fourteen a youngster, no matter how sophisticated, is apt to dream of being Tarzan or President. I was fourteen when *Life* made its début, forever establishing photography as a medium, not merely an adjunct.

I gave up Tarzana and the Presidency. For though I couldn't even handle a Brownie I wanted to be Margaret Bourke-White.

The greatness of Miss Bourke-White's work is apparent to even the casual reader who has watched the photo-essay develop as an art form during her years with *Fortune* and *Life*. Technically, of course, she performs miracles. But angles and lighting and composition are forgotten when we observe the miracle Miss Bourke-White repeats again and again in capturing the essence of a mood, an emotion, the soul itself. We feel the weariness of a GI, the quiet strength of Gandhi, the terror of death, the cruel grip of poverty, the exhilaration of victory.

But over the years, as though the immortality won with camera were not enough, Miss Bourke-White began writing. All her books – particularly her moving autobiography, *Portrait of Myself* – have borne the impressive Bourke-White signature in words and pictures. As most readers know, Miss Bourke-White has fought a long and noble and victorious fight against Parkinsonism.

When this interview was recorded, in July of 1963, she had recovered enough muscular control to show me about her stunning homesite near Darien, Connecticut, and enough control of speech to make this tape. Talking to this beautiful and determined woman, before, during, and after the interview, remains my most moving memory of time, place, and person involved in these interviews.

N.: In talking to Miss Bourke-White I would like to use her autobiography, *Portrait of Myself*, as a springboard. In it, as I recall, you seem to dismiss your childhood far quicker than most writers do when they recap their lives. Was there a reason?

B.-W.: Yes, it was a happy childhood on the whole, not at all dull or uneventful, and it probably provided a stable foundation for all that has followed. I was greatly influenced by my father who had a great love for all forms of natural life, and a great respect for anything that walked or crawled or slithered or flew or simply 'was'. He probably taught me to respect the whole of life, and to observe. Yet other than this it was not a dramatic childhood, and I'd have bored the reader if I'd carried it beyond a few chapters.

N.: Oddly enough, despite this love of nature, you first made your reputation in industrial photography, didn't you?

B.-W.: Yes. I worked in Cleveland and Pittsburgh. Actually I first started touring factories with my father, and they never seemed dull to me. They seemed very beautiful. Then I made a series of steel-mill pictures that came to the attention of Henry Luce, at a time when he was about to launch *Fortune*. So I went to work with him eight months before the first issue came out.

N.: You had the first cover, didn't you?

B.-W.: No, that was on *Life*. But the photo essays we did for *Fortune* were very exciting, especially for that time. We even did the stockyards. In those days making a pig look artistic wasn't dreamed of.

N.: The idea of a young woman climbing ladders in steel mills wasn't dreamed of either, was it?

B.-W.: No. But all that was a part of the challenge – we were determined to do new and different and better things.

N.: Then you helped launch *Life*. Yours was the first cover and the first photo-essay.

B.-W.: Yes. This was when I really started working with people, with faces. I'd never done that before. The faces showed so much – in the Dust Bowl assignment, for example – that I couldn't ignore them any longer.

N.: This came to characterize your work, didn't it? I mean, it's the faces you shot – the range of expression – that we recall so well from your World War II assignments, for example, and your work with Gandhi. Did this become a conscious objective?

B.-W.: I know that with Gandhi this is a thing I wanted to do very badly – to probe as deeply as I could. He had such an extraordinary personality. He used to have a nickname for me. When I'd come with the cameras he'd say, 'There's the torturer again.' It was said in fun, of course. But he hated flashbulbs, and I'm a great flashbulb user. It was very funny with Gandhi, but before I had a chance to take his picture his secretary insisted that I learn to spin. I'd never used a spinning wheel, and it seemed like very peculiar preparation for taking a photograph. But later I saw why – the spinning wheel was a symbol with Gandhi. The homespun cloth that he and his followers wore expressed their fight for freedom. They were imposing a boycott against British textiles, and it was Gandhi's idea that if he could get all Indians to wear their own homespun cloth it would help their cause.

N.: During World War II, when you established some sort of record for experiences that women simply shouldn't encounter, you were torpedoed off the African coast. It's one of the dramatic highlights of the book.

B.-W.: It was a dividing time in my life. It wasn't only dramatic, it went much deeper than that. I had the feeling that this was bringing out the best in people. There was such extraordinary courage. I remember standing there in the moonlight, waiting to get into our lifeboat, which was flooded by the splash of the torpedo, and I thought to myself that this was one time in my life when I had no idea of what was going to happen to me, I may live or die. Then I noticed several nurses standing nearby, and the way they were trembling, and I thought, 'This must be fear,' and I had to admire their discipline because aside from the trembling they controlled themselves so well. I think it was then I realized that every normal person has great courage that's just waiting to be called on.

N.: What theaters of war did you travel into?

B.-W.: I was in Africa and England with the Air Force, and then I wanted to see ground warfare where I worked with the Fifth Army under General Clark. When we were beginning to move into Germany, *Life* pulled me out of that theater and sent me through the greater part of the German campaign. When the war ended I stayed on in Germany.

N.: Miss Bourke-White, the courage you mentioned in regard to the nurses on the torpedoed ship was something you caught on the faces of even grievously wounded GIs in Italy.

B.-W.: Yes. They went through so much. It was a dreadful part of the war – the Cassino Valley, especially. It seemed we moved just an inch a day. I remember how ironical it was to see the boys slogging their way through the mud and slush, and we'd see signs that would say, '10 Miles to Cassino', and there they were, moving just a slow step at a time.

N.: In Germany, as I recall, you added another career: you became a looter.

B.-W.: I was fascinated by looting, and finally succumbed to the fever. It may not be a very pretty side of war, but it's definitely there. You're in the land of the enemy and you're curious about how they live, and as far as the things in their houses are concerned, you feel they've stolen it from others. You have no morals about that. There is a curious moral code, however. It was all right to loot an empty house, but you never looted a house that had people in it. Or if a house was smashed flat it was all right to loot, as long as the owner wasn't there. We also had another unwritten rule, which was that only the persons who had actually been under gunfire had the right to loot. It seemed so strange to have a code of morals for an immoral act, but there it was. We used to joke about it a lot, and wonder, if we visited each other in peacetime, if we'd have to nail down all the valuables in the house.

I had one great haul – I got to Nuremberg and Munich with the Rainbow Division and they took over Hitler's private apartment as headquarters. Before I got there everything had been looted except a couple of statues of dancing girls that were too heavy for normal looters, but I wanted them. So some of the boys helped me wrap them in blankets and I sent them out by carrier plane. This supposed to be inviolate, but somewhere between Munich and Paris the statues disappeared. I felt badly because these looters wouldn't know they came from Hitler's apartment – to them they'd just be heavy junk.

N.: Before we were in World War II you spent a long stretch of time in Moscow, photographing the Nazi bombing of that city. I'd never realized the Germans had attacked Moscow so heavily.

B.-W.: Yes, the first bombers came over on July 22, 1941, and the Germans were apparently determined to destroy Red Square and the Kremlin. Despite the number of pictures I took, the Russians just didn't want to admit there were so many planes over Moscow. No stories were allowed to go out concerning the bombing of the Kremlin. Actually, I know of one direct hit they made, right across the street from the little hotel where I was living. There was one very bad night when bombs and fire-bombs were falling especially heavily, and there was one direct hit that blew me and my cameras off the windowsill where I was working. I rushed back to the window when I could get to my feet, and a whole building seemed to be frozen in the air with stones and sticks and bricks falling out of it. It just seemed to hang there, and then it came down with a great crash. I learned later it was the palace that housed the Kremlin guard. Ninety-three men were housed there, and I don't know how many were killed, but the Russians would never let the story be released.

N.: Now I'd like to back up to a question that can be called basic and theoretical, but I would like to know how you feel about the obligations of a news and feature photographer, particularly a photographer like you who works in depth, to the public.

B.-W.: I feel that utter truth is essential, and to get at that truth may take a lot of searching and long hours and the difficulty of analyzing two sides of a question, but I feel that that's our great responsibility. I had this feeling particularly strong in Germany, when we moved into Buchenwald, and the sights were so terrible I couldn't think about them. Still, I felt driven to report them because I felt I must record whatever concerns the course of history. There were at least eight hundred corpses in Buchenwald when we got there, a great pile of naked bodies and we could even see the pieces of skin to be made into lampshades. Many men still alive in the camp, even though we arrived to feed them, died before morning. It seemed to me that this was a sacred mission, that we photographers must get pictures of this because it was the ultimate in race hatred, and I knew, if the truth were shown, that humanity would not forget quite so soon.

N.: If you were to give advice to the aspiring journalist, what would that advice be?

B.-W.: Learn to look on both sides of the question. And most questions have *more* than two sides. This should become a firmly fixed habit of the journalist. He should never stop at the obvious. He should investigate just a little further than his job requires to get that plus-quality that characterizes the finest journalists.

N.: In looking at culture today, what aspect do you find most encouraging as far as the utilization of talent is concerned?

B.-W.: I admire people who are trying to use television constructively. I admire those who have used this new medium to good creative effect – Leonard Bernstein, for instance. And there are many others who are working through difficulties to put something fine on the air.

N.: Miss Bourke-White, in the last part of your book you discuss your battle with Parkinson's Disease, its onslaught, the operation, and the therapy I believe you're still undergoing. How did you first notice the disease coming on?

B.-W.: Just by dragging a foot. If I sat down, say for lunch, and I didn't get up for an hour or two I'd find that the first three steps were terrible staggers. Then I'd be all right again. I was completely mystified about what was wrong, and so were most of my doctors.

N.: It was some time, wasn't it, before the disease actually slowed you down?

B.-W.: Yes. It was about eight years, and I feel so very fortunate that the new type of brain surgery had been discovered before I became a total victim. If it had been developed just five years later it would have been too late to help me. Yet, surgery, as wonderful as it is, is only 50 per cent of the battle. The rest of it we have to do ourselves. In my case it's been my very intensive and faithful physical therapy. One of the things I've always been grateful for is the fact that if this had to come to me, I'm so glad it's something I could work with – and I'm still working with it.

I've relearned walking, running, and I was so proud when I found out I could skip. I was practicing jumping rope, without much success because it took more co-ordination than I had. One morning I woke up early and grabbed my jumping rope and actually jumped. It all came back like a childhood dream. In fact, childhood games have helped me greatly. I can even play jacks – not all the fancy games children nowadays play, but I can play a straight game of jacks pretty well.

N.: You've been working with speech therapy, too, haven't you?

B.-W.: Yes. I've been doing everything from singing with Mitch Miller to performing facial exercises.

N.: I never realized, before, that the onslaught of Parkinson's Disease is so total.

B.-W.: It's a funny thing to discover that you direct your body to make a movement, and that you haven't made that movement at all – you've just been standing there. To bring the body back to obedience takes long, long practice. In my case I feel there are certain things I must do as health insurance. I always walk at least one mile a day and sometimes three or four.

N.: You've got a rocky surface out here, too. I don't imagine that's been the easiest to navigate.

B.-W.: It's been hard. For instance, I took you out to that little cliff this morning, and there was a time when I couldn't have made that short walk because the ground is so uneven. Now I make it easily, and I'm both glad and proud of it because it's a beautiful spot.

N.: To turn back once more to your book – I'd like to touch on two episodes you handled so wonderfully well – namely, your marriages. First, what we might call the student union, and second, your marriage to Erskine Caldwell.

B.-W.: I've always been glad that, even though my marriages broke up, I was married to wonderful men for whom I had great respect. I feel that each time was a notch in my growing process.

N.: The first time you were the victim of a rapacious mother-in-law?

B.-W.: Yes. She's dead, now, but she was a terror. She was very beautiful – she had masses of white hair, like a duchess, and if she'd given me half a chance I'd have loved her very much. But she was opposed to the fact that I was going on to school after marriage. She felt Margaret was indulging herself because she wouldn't quit college. It seemed the set of values I'd grown up with was completely foreign to her. Later I was glad because if I'd stayed married and had children, it would have changed my life completely. Not that having children isn't a worthwhile objective, but if it had happened to me I wouldn't have been able to see the world as a photo-journalist. I wouldn't want to change any of my life, even if I had the chance, because it's been the life I wanted.

N.: Your marriage to Erskine Caldwell came after one of the most colorful courtships I've ever read.

B.-W.: It was both funny and touching, the way he'd send cables to 'Honey-Chile' all over the North Pole area. Actually, Erskine and I worked together in his Tobacco Road country, doing a book that was very important to both of us. It came at a time when I hadn't worked much with people, and wanted so badly to do more. He showed me that he hadn't exaggerated conditions at all, and he was such a patient and sensitive man that he taught me a great deal. He has a strong, instinctive feeling for the sufferings of others, and I respected this deeply and began trying to probe as deeply.

N.: Then the inevitable problems of careers in conflict –

B.-W.: It's a complex problem, of course – it always is. I thought everyone knew, as I did, that my devotion to the camera came first. Perhaps it's true, as someone said, that I have a lens for a heart.

You know, when a person digs into his life thoroughly enough to write an autobiography, it's possible to call so many things tragic and to rationalize errors. I think I've been particularly fortunate; even my two broken marriages and this illness have been important to my own growth and development. Probably that's the essence of the tragedies and triumphs in any person's life. Whatever happens signifies growth, if we're wise enough or fortunate enough to see it that way.

•

MAO TSE-TUNG

Interviewed by Edgar Snow
The New Republic, 27 February 1965

Mao Tse-tung (1893–1976), the founding chairman of the People's Republic of China, was born in Hunan province. The son of a peasant farmer, he was educated at the University of Peking, where he discovered Marx. He was one of the first members of the Chinese Communist Party. He adapted Marxism to peasant conditions, creating a rural soviet at Jiangxi in south-east China in the early 1930s, and in order to escape persecution by Chiang Kai-shek's Nationalist forces he led his followers on the Long March (1934–6) to Yan'an in north-west China, during which he was elected chairman of the Communist Party. From 1937 to 1945 Mao's guerrilla warriors kept the Japanese at bay, and in 1949 the Red Army ousted Chaing Kai-shek from the largest part of mainland China. The Great Leap Forward, Mao's economic programme from 1958 to 1960, was a failure and he resigned as chairman of the Republic, although he retained control of the Communist Party's politburo until his death. In the late 1960s he reasserted his power with the Cultural Revolution, a vicious campaign of ideological purification in which he purged his enemies. During the 1970s his life was overshadowed by ill-health and the increasing influence of the Gang of Four, led by his (third) wife Jiang Qing. In 1972 he reversed his previous policy of hostility to the West when he met with the US president Richard Nixon and agreed to adopt diplomatic relations. Nonetheless, Maoism has remained influential as a revolutionary creed, particularly in the Third World.

Edgar Parks Snow (1905–71) was born in Kansas City, Missouri. He was educated at the University of Missouri and joined the *Kansas City Star* as a reporter. In 1928 he went to China for the first time, aged twenty-two, and became assistant editor of the *China Weekly Review*. He learnt the language, studied the country and its customs, and lectured at Yenching University. He subsequently reported on the Far East for the *Chicago Tribune*, the *New York Sun*, the *New York Herald-Tribune*, and the *Daily Herald*. He first interviewed Mao in the mid 1930s for the *China Weekly Leader*. During the Second World War he was an associate editor and war correspondent for *The Saturday Evening Post*, specializing in China, India, and the USSR. He also wrote several books about China. This interview has been slightly abridged.

In a rare interview which lasted about four hours, Mao Tse-tung conversed with me on topics ranging over what he himself called *shan nan hai pei*, or 'from south of the mountains to north of the seas'. With China's bountiful 200-million-ton 1964 grain harvest taxing winter storage capacities, with shops everywhere offering inexpensive foods and consumer goods necessities, and with technological and scientific advances climaxed by an atomic bang that saluted Khrushchev's political demise, Chairman Mao might well have claimed a few creative achievements. I found him reflecting on man's rendezvous with death and ready to leave the assessment of his political legacy to future generations.

The seventy-two-year-old warrior greeted me in one of the spacious Peking-decor rooms of the Great Hall of the People, across the wide square facing Tien An Men, the Heavenly Peace Gate of the former Forbidden City.

At the start of our conversation Chairman Mao agreed to be photographed informally in a film I believe to be the first ever made of him for foreign television. From this film political clinicians may make their own diagnosis of his condition, lately rumored to be much deteriorated. On 9 January, coming at the end of strenuous weeks of daily and nightly conferences with many regional leaders drawn to the capital for the annual National People's Congress, his talk with me might have been more speedily terminated by a sick man. He seemed wholly relaxed throughout our conversation, which began before six, continued during dinner and went on for about two hours after.

One of the chairman's doctors informed me that Mao has no organic troubles and suffers from nothing beyond the normal fatigue of his age. He ate moderately of a peppery Hunanese meal shared with me and drank a glass or two of wine, rather perfunctorily.

It was reported abroad that other 'government officials' were present during my interview. These officials were two friends from pre-revolutionary days in China: Mme Kung Peng, now an assistant to the Chinese Foreign Minister, and her husband, Chiao Kuan-hua, an assistant minister in the same department. I submitted no written questions and took no notes during the interview. Fortunately I was able to refresh my memory by reviewing the conversation with one of those present who had kept a written record. It was agreed that I might publish, without direct quotation, such of the chairman's comment as is given below.

'Some American commentators in Saigon have compared the strength of the Viet Cong there with the 1947 period in China, when the People's Liberation Army began to engage in large-scale annihilations of Nationalist forces. Are the conditions comparable?'

The chairman thought not. By 1947 the People's Liberation Army already had more than a million men, against several million troops on Chiang Kai-shek's side. The PLA had then used divisional and group army strength, whereas the Vietnamese liberation forces were now operating at battalion or at most regimental strength. American forces in Vietnam were still relatively small. Of course, if they increased they could help speed up the arming of the people against them. But if he should tell that to United States leaders they would not listen. Had they listened to Diem? Both Ho Chi Minh and he (Mao Tse-tung) thought that Ngo Dinh Diem was not so bad. They had expected the Americans to maintain him for several more years. But impatient American generals became disgusted with Diem and got rid of him. After all, following his assassination, was everything between heaven and earth more peaceful?

'Can Viet Cong forces now win victory by their own efforts alone?' Yes, he thought that they could. Their position was relatively better than that of the Communists during the first civil war (1927–37) in China. At that time there was no direct foreign intervention, but now already the Viet Cong had the

American intervention to help arm and educate the rank and file and the army officers. Those opposed to the United States were no longer confined to the liberation army. Diem had not wanted to take orders. Now this independence had spread to the generals. The American teachers were succeeding. Asked whether some of these generals would soon join the liberation army, Mao said yes, some would follow the example of Kuomintang generals who had turned to the Communists.

'United States intervention in Vietnam, the Congo and other former colonial battlefields, suggests a question of some theoretical interest as seen within Marxist concepts. The question is whether the contradiction between neo-colonialism and the revolutionary forces in what the French like to call the "third world" – the so-called underdeveloped or ex-colonial or still colonial nations of Asia, Africa and Latin America – is today the principal political contradiction in the world? Or do you consider that the basic contradiction is still one between the capitalist countries themselves?'

Mao Tse-tung said that he had not reached an opinion about that but he recalled something that President Kennedy had said. Had Kennedy not declared that as far as the United States, Canada and Western Europe were concerned, there was not much real and basic difference? The President had said that the problem was in the Southern Hemisphere. In advocating 'special forces warfare' training for 'local [countersubversive?] warfare' the late President may have had my question in mind.

On the other hand, contradictions between imperialists were what had caused two world wars in the past, and their struggles against colonial revolutions had not changed their character. If one looked at France one saw two reasons for de Gaulle's policies. The first was to assert independence from American domina-tion. The second was to attempt to adjust French policies to changes occurring in the Asian-African countries and Latin America. The result was intensified contradiction between the capitalist nations; but was France part of its so-called 'third world'? Recently he had asked some French visitors about that and they had told him no, that France was a developed country and could not be a member of the 'third world' of undeveloped countries. The matter was not so simple.

'Perhaps it could be said that France is in the third world but not of it?'

Perhaps. This question which had engaged the interest of President Kennedy had led Kennedy, Mao had read, to study Mao's own essays on military operations. Mao had also learned from Algerian friends during their struggle against France that the French were reading his works and using his information against them. But he had told the Algerian Prime Minister, Abbas, at that time, that his own books were based on Chinese experience and would not work in reverse. They could be adapted only to the waging of people's wars of liberation and were rather useless in an anti-people's war. They did not save the

French from defeat in Algeria. Chiang Kai-shek had also studied the Communists' materials but he had not been saved either.

Mao remarked that the Chinese also study American books. For instance, he had read *The Uncertain Trumpet* by General Taylor, the United States Ambassador in Saigon. General Taylor's view was that nuclear weapons probably would not be used, therefore non-nuclear arms would decide. Taylor wanted priority given to the Army. Now he had his chance to test out his theories of special warfare. In Vietnam he was gaining some valuable experience.

The chairman had also read some articles issued by US authorities to their troops on how to handle guerrillas. These instructions dealt with the shortcomings and military weaknesses of the guerrillas and held out hopes for American victory. They ignored the decisive political fact that whether it was Diem or somebody else, governments cut off from the masses could not win against wars of liberation.

Since the Americans would not listen to Chairman Mao, his advice would do nobody any harm.

'In Southeast Asia as well as in India and certain countries of Africa and even Latin America, there exist some social conditions comparable to those that brought on the Chinese revolution. Each country has its own problems, and solutions will vary widely, yet I wonder if you agree that social revolutions will occur which may borrow much from the Chinese?'

Anti-feudal and anti-capitalist sentiments combined with opposition to imperialism and neo-colonialism, he replied, grew out of oppression and wrongs of the past. Wherever the latter existed there would be revolutions, but in most of the countries I was talking about, the people were merely seeking national independence, not socialism – quite another matter. European countries had also had anti-feudal revolutions. Though the United States had had no real feudal period, still it had fought a progressive war of independence from British colonialism, and then a civil war to establish a free labor market. Washington and Lincoln had been great men of the time.

'Do you still believe that the bomb is a paper tiger?'

That had just been a way of talking, he said, a kind of figure of speech. Of course the bomb could kill people. But in the end the people would destroy the bomb. Then it would truly become a paper tiger.

'You have been quoted as saying that China had less fear of the bomb than other nations because of her vast population. Other peoples might be totally wiped out, but China would still have a few hundred millions left to begin anew. Was there ever any factual basis to such reports?'

He answered that he had no recollection of saying anything like that but he might have said it. He did recall a conversation he had had with Jawaharlal Nehru, when the latter visited China (in 1954). As he remembered it, he had said China did not want a war. They didn't have atom bombs, but if other countries wanted to fight there would be a catastrophe in the whole world, meaning that many people would die. As for how many, nobody could know. He was not speaking only of China. He did not believe one atom bomb would destroy all mankind, so that you would not be able to find a government to negotiate peace. He mentioned this to Nehru during their conversation. Nehru said that he was chairman of the Atomic Energy Commission of India and he knew about the destructiveness of atomic power. He was sure that no one could survive. Mao replied that it would probably not be as Nehru said. Existing governments might disappear but others would arise to replace them.

Not so long ago, Khrushchev said that he had a deadly weapon capable of killing all living things. But then he immediately retracted his statement – not only once but many times. Mao would not deny anything he had said, nor did he wish me to deny for him this so-called rumor (about China's millions' power of survival in a nuclear war).

Americans also had said very much about the destructiveness of the atom bomb and Khrushchev had made a big noise about that. They had all surpassed him in this respect, so that he was more backward than they, was not that so? Yet recently he had read reports of an investigation by Americans who visited the Bikini Islands six years after nuclear tests had been conducted there. From 1959 onward research workers had been in Bikini. When they first entered the island they had had to cut open paths through the undergrowth. They found mice scampering about and fish swimming in the streams as usual. The wellwater was potable, plantation foliage was flourishing, and birds were twittering in the trees. Probably there had been two bad years after the tests, but nature had gone on. In the eyes of nature and the birds, the mice and the trees, the atom bomb was a paper tiger. Possibly man has less stamina than they?

'Nevertheless, you would not exactly consider nuclear war to be a good thing?'

Certainly not, he replied. If one must fight one should confine oneself to conventional weapons.

He was interested to hear that I had attended a conference where professors had debated whether he had or had not made any original contributions to Marxism. I told him that I had asked one professor, at the close of such a conference, whether it would make any difference in their controversy if it could be shown that Mao himself had never claimed to have made any creative contribution. The professor said, 'No.'

Mao was amused. More than 2,000 years ago, he remarked, Chuang Chou wrote his immortal essay on Lao Tzu (called the *Chuang Tzu*). A hundred schools of thought then arose to dispute the meaning.

In 1960, when I had last seen Mao Tse-tung, I asked him whether he had ever written or had any intention of writing an 'autobiography'. He had replied in the negative. Nevertheless, learned professors had discovered 'auto-biographies' written by Mao. The fact that they were fraudulent did not in the least affect their documentary terminology.

A question currently exercising the professors was whether Mao had in fact written his celebrated philosophical essays *On Contradictions* and *On Practice* in the summer of 1937, as asserted in his collected works, or whether they had really been composed later.

He replied that he had indeed written them in the summer of 1937. During the weeks preceding and immediately following the Liukouchiao incident, there had been a lull in his life in Yenan. The army had left for the front and Mao had found time in which to collect materials for some lectures on basic philosophy for use in the anti-Japanese academy. Some simple and yet fundamental text was needed for the young students being prepared, in brief, three-month courses, for political guidance during the years immediately ahead. At the insistence of the party Mao prepared *On Contradictions* and *On Practice* to sum up the experiences of the Chinese revolution, by combining the essentials of Marxism with concrete and everyday Chinese examples. Mao wrote most of the night and slept during the day. What he had written over a period of weeks he delivered in lecture form in a matter of two hours. Mao added that he himself considered *On Practice* a more important essay than *On Contradictions*. As for a treatise entitled *On Dialectical Materialism*, which has been attributed to Mao's authorship by foreign Sinologists, he said that he had no recollection of having written any such work and he thought he would not have forgotten it had he done so.

'Youths who heard you lecture at Yenan later learned about revolution in practice but what could be the substitute for youths in China today?'

Mao said that of course those in China now under the age of twenty had never fought a war and never seen an imperialist or known capitalism in power. They knew nothing about the old society at first hand. Parents could tell them, but to hear about history and to read books was not the same thing as living it.

'Western commentators, and especially the Italian Communists, severely criticized the Soviet leaders for the conspiratorial and undemocratic way in which Khrushchev was thrown aside. What is your view?'

He replied that Mr K had not been very popular in China even before his fall. Few portraits of him were to be seen. But K's books were for sale in the book-stores before the fall and they were still for sale here but not in Russia. The world needed Khrushchev: his ghost would linger on. There were bound to be people who liked him. China would miss him as a negative example.

'On the basis of your own 70/30 standard – that is, a man's work may be judged satisfactory if it is 70 per cent correct and only 30 per cent in error – how would you grade the present leadership of the Soviet party? How far is it still below passing?' I asked.

Mao said he would not choose to discuss the present leaders in those terms. As for any improvement in Sino-Soviet relations, there was possibly some but not much. The disappearance of Khrushchev had perhaps only removed a target for polemical articles.

'In the Soviet Union,' I said, 'China has been criticized for fostering a "cult of personality".'

Mao thought that perhaps there was some. It was said that Stalin had been the center of a cult of personality, and that Khrushchev had none at all. The Chinese people, critics say, have some (feelings or practices of this kind). There might be some reasons for saying that. Was it possible, he asked, that Mr K fell because he had no cult of personality at all?

'Naturally I personally regret that forces of history have divided and separated the American and Chinese peoples from virtually all communication during the past fifteen years. Today the gulf seems broader than ever. However, I myself do not believe it will end in war and one of history's major tragedies.'

Mao said that forces of history were also bound, eventually, to bring the two peoples together again; that day would surely come. Possibly I was right that meanwhile there would be no war. That could occur only if American troops came to China. They would not really get much out of it. That simply would not be allowed. Probably the American leaders knew that and consequently they would not invade China. Then there would be no war, because the Chinese certainly would never send troops to attack the United States.

'What of the possibilities of war arising over Vietnam? I have read many newspaper stories indicating that the United States has considered expanding the war into North Vietnam.'

No, Mao said, he thought otherwise. Mr Rusk had now made it clear that the US would not do that. Mr Rusk may have earlier said something like that, but now he had corrected himself and said that he had never made such a statement. Therefore, there need not be any war in North Vietnam.

'I do not believe that the makers and administrators of United States policy understand you,' I said.

Why not? China's armies would not go beyond her borders to fight. That was clear enough. Only if the United States attacked China would the Chinese fight. Wasn't that clear? The Chinese were very busy with their internal affairs. Fighting beyond one's own borders was criminal. Why should the Chinese do that? The Vietnamese could cope with their situation.

'American officials repeatedly say that if United States forces were withdrawn from Vietnam, then all Southeast Asia would be overrun.'

The question was, said Mao, 'overrun' by whom? Overrun by Chinese or overrun by the inhabitants? China was 'overrun', but only by Chinese.

In reply to a specific question, the chairman affirmed that there were no Chinese forces in Northern Vietnam or anywhere else in Southeast Asia. China had no troops outside her own frontiers.

(In another context; it was said that unless Indian troops again crossed China's frontiers, there would be no conflict there.)

'Dean Rusk has often stated that if China would give up her aggressive policies then the United States would withdraw from Vietnam. What does he mean?'

Mao replied that China had no policies of aggression to abandon. China had committed no acts of aggression. China gave support to revolutionary movements but not by sending troops. Of course, whenever a liberation struggle existed China would publish statements and call demonstrations to support it. It was precisely that which vexed the imperialists.

Mao went on to say that on some occasions China deliberately makes a loud noise, as for example around Quemoy and Matsu. A flurry of shots there could attract a lot of attention, perhaps because the Americans were uneasy so far away from home. Consider what could be accomplished by firing some blank shells within those Chinese territorial waters. Not so long ago the United States 7th Fleet in the Taiwan Strait was deemed insufficient to reply to the shells. The US also dispatched part of its 6th Fleet in this direction and brought over part of the Navy from San Francisco. Arrived here, they had found nothing to do, so it seemed that China could order the American forces to march here, to march there. It had been the same with Chiang Kai-shek's army. They had been able to order Chiang to scurry this way and then to hurry off in another direction. Of course when Navy men are warm and have full bellies they must be given something to do. But how was it that shooting off empty guns at home could be called aggression, while those who actually intervened with arms and bombed and burned people of other lands were not aggressors?

He continued: some Americans had said that the Chinese revolution was led by Russian aggressors, but in truth the Chinese revolution was armed by Americans. In the same way the Vietnamese revolution was also being armed by Americans, not by China. The liberation forces had not only greatly improved their supplies of American weapons during recent months but also expanded their forces by recruiting American-trained troops and officers from the puppet armies of South Vietnam. China's liberation forces had grown in numbers and strength by recruiting to their side the troops trained and armed by the Americans for Chiang Kai-shek. The movement was called 'changing of hats'. When Nationalist soldiers changed hats in large numbers because they knew the peasants would kill them for wearing the wrong hat, then the end was near. 'Changing hats' was becoming more popular now among the Vietnamese puppets.

Mao said that the conditions of revolutionary victory in China had been first, that the ruling group was weak and incompetent, led by a man who was always losing battles. Second, the People's Liberation Army was strong and able and people believed in its cause. In places where such conditions did not prevail the Americans could intervene. Otherwise, they would stay away or soon leave.

'Do you mean that the circumstances of victory for the liberation front now exist in South Vietnam?'

Mao thought that the American forces were not yet ready to leave. Fighting would go on perhaps for one to two years. After that the United States troops would find it boring and might go home or somewhere else.

'Is it your policy now to insist upon the withdrawal of United States forces before participating in a Geneva conference to discuss the international position of a unified Vietnam?'

The chairman said that several possibilities should be mentioned. First, a conference might be held and United States withdrawal would follow. Second, the conference might be deferred until after the withdrawal. Third, a conference might be held but United States troops might stay around Saigon, as in the case of South Korea. Finally, the South Vietnamese front might drive out the Americans without any conference or international agreements. The 1954 Geneva conference had provided for the withdrawal of French troops from all Indochina and forbade any intervention by any other foreign troops. The United States had nevertheless violated the convention and that could happen again.

'Under existing circumstances,' I asked, 'do you really see any hope of an improvement in Sino-American relations?'

Yes, he thought there was hope. It would take time. Maybe there would be no improvement in his generation. He was soon going to see God. According to the laws of dialectics all contradictions must finally be resolved, including the struggle of the individual.

'Judging from this evening you seem to be in good condition,' I said.

Mao Tse-tung smiled wryly and replied that there was perhaps some doubt about that. He said again that he was getting ready to see God very soon.

'I wonder if you mean you are going to find out whether there is a God. Do you believe that?'

No, he did not. But some people who claimed to be well-informed said that there was a God. There seemed to be many gods and sometimes the same god could take all sides. In the wars of Europe the Christian God had been on the side of the British, the French, the Germans, and so on; even when they were fighting each other. At the time of the Suez Canal crisis God was united behind the British and French, but then there was Allah to back up the other side.

At dinner Mao had mentioned that both his brothers had been killed. His wife had also been executed during the revolution and their son had been killed during the Korean War. Now, he said that it was odd that death had so far passed him by. He had been prepared for it many times but death just did not seem to want him. What could he do? On several occasions it had seemed that he would die. His personal bodyguard was killed while standing right beside him. Once he was splashed all over with the blood of another soldier, but the bomb had not touched him. There had been other narrow escapes.

After a moment of silence Mao said that he had, as I knew, begun life as a primary school teacher. He had then had no thought of fighting wars. Neither had he thought of becoming a Communist. He was more or less a democratic personage such as myself. Later on, he sometimes wondered by what chance combination of reasons he had become interested in founding the Chinese Communist Party. Anyway, events did not move in accordance with the individual human will. What mattered was that China had been oppressed by imperialism, feudalism and bureaucratic capitalism.

'Man makes his own history, but he makes it in accordance with his environment,' I quoted. 'You have fundamentally changed the environment in China. Many wonder what the younger generation bred under easier conditions will do. What do you think about it?'

He also could not know, he said. He doubted that anyone could be sure. There were two possibilities. There could be continued development of the revolution toward Communism, the other possibility was that youth could negate the revolution, and give a poor performance: make peace with imperialism, bring the remnants of the Chiang Kai-shek clique back to the mainland, and take a stand beside the small percentage of counter-revolutionaries still in the country. Of course he did not hope for counter-revolution. But future events would be decided by future generations, and in accordance with conditions we could not foresee. From the long-range view, future generations ought to be more knowledgeable than we are, just as men of the bourgeois-democratic era were more knowledgeable than those of the feudal ages. Their judgement would prevail, not ours. The youth of today and those to come after them would assess the work of the revolution in accordance with values of their own. Mao's voice dropped away, and he half closed his eyes. Man's condition on this earth was changing with ever increasing rapidity. A thousand years from now all of them, he said, even Marx, Engels and Lenin, would possibly appear rather ridiculous.

Mao Tse-tung walked me through the doorway and, despite my protests, saw me to my car, where he stood alone for a moment, coatless in the sub-zero Peking night, to wave me farewell in the traditional manner of that ancient cultured city. I saw no security guards around the entrance, nor can I now recall having seen even one armed bodyguard in our vicinity all evening. As the car drove away I looked back and watched Mao brace his shoulders and slowly retrace his steps, leaning heavily on the arm of an aide, into the Great Hall of the People.

●

ANTHONY WEDGWOOD-BENN

Interviewed by Susan Barnes
The Sun, April 1965 (first published in
The Spectator, October 1987)

Anthony Wedgwood-Benn (b. 1925), the English Labour politician, was the son of a Labour politician, Viscount Stansgate, who had been granted an hereditary peerage by Churchill at the end of the Second World War. Wedgwood-Benn was elected as a Labour MP in 1950, but was obliged to stand down when he succeeded to his father's peerage in 1960. He fought and won a couple of by-elections on the issue of whether he should be entitled to renounce his title and as a result the Conservative government introduced legislation enabling him to do so. He served in Harold Wilson's cabinets as postmaster general (1964–6) and minister of technology (1966–70). From 1970 to 1974 he held the opposition portfolio of trade and industry, and when Labour was returned to power he was secretary of state, first for industry and later for energy. He was progressively radicalized by the frustrations of office and gained the conviction that even the Labour Party was essentially anti-democratic in structure. Hence he campaigned for internal reforms such as the right of constituency parties to de-select MPs and for extreme policies of wholesale public ownership and workers' control. He failed in his bid for the party's deputy leadership in 1981, and in 1983 he lost his Bristol seat at the general election. He won a by-election in Chesterfield the following year and challenged Neil Kinnock unsuccessfully for the party leadership in 1981.

Susan Crosland, née Barnes, was born in Baltimore, Maryland, USA. She came to England and married the writer Patrick Skene-Catling. Her first journalism was done for *The Sunday Express* (1960–64) and consisted largely of interviews with showbusiness and political personalities. She married the Labour politician Anthony Crosland in 1964 and thereafter wrote as a freelance, mainly doing interview-profiles for *The Sunday Times.* These have been collected in two books, *Behind the Image* (1974) and *Looking Out, Looking In* (1987). She has also written a biography of her deceased husband, *Tony Crosland* (1982), and a couple of blockbuster novels, *Ruling Passions* (1989) and *Dangerous Games* (1991).

This is an interesting example of how an interview can upset a public figure. Anthony Wedgwood-Benn knew Susan Barnes socially through her husband, Anthony Crosland, who was also a member of the Labour cabinet. His reaction when he read the finished article can be gauged from an entry in his published diaries for 3 April 1965: 'This evening Susan Crosland brought her unspeakable article for me to vet. It was the bitchiest, most horrible thing I've ever read and I decided to be bold and ring her up and asked her not to publish it. She was much taken aback, no doubt hurt, but she assented immediately. I should never have accepted in the first place.'

The article was commissioned by *The Sun*, which was then a Labour paper. Although it may seem somewhat tame by today's standards, it brings out Benn's eccentricity with evidently uncomfortable accuracy.

'Mr Benn is a pest!' said a weary telephone manager to me shortly after Anthony Wedgwood-Benn became Postmaster General. This was because I had asked the manager to show me a gadgety telephone like one the PMG straps on his head in order to be able to free his hands for writing and whatnot. (Mr Benn is a zealot for using time efficiently.)

The same telephone manager now concedes that it is the 'pest' aspect of Mr Benn – his intense tenacity for going after something – that is, in fact, already getting results in the GPO. It was this same tenacity which sharply advanced the lumbering modernization of Britain – for it was of course Mr Benn alone who against enormous odds forced through the Lords Reform Bill in 1963.

'People who wanted to be cynical said, "Oh, the chap is ambitious" and that may be true,' said Mr Benn when we met in his office. 'But equally I used to be humiliated by the idea of being a peer.

'People *will* think that because my father was made a peer and I went to Westminster, that I'm an aristocratic progressive. I'm not. I come from four generations of fierce radicalism . . . My origins are East End origins. My great-grandfather was a lay preacher in Stepney Green.'

It should be said that as well as being radical, Mr Benn's grandfather and father were highly successful in public life, the one being made the first baronet, Sir J. Williams Benn, the other being made the first Viscount Stansgate.

'It's partly the non-conformist and radical inheritance that accounts for my being a teetotaller,' Mr Benn went on, drawing on the pipe which is a good companion for his intensity. In his dark grey flannel suit and white shirt and black tie and short haircut, he looks not unlike a successful young advertising executive on Madison Avenue. 'Drink *was* a great problem in the East End of London. My grandfather was a great campaigner against it. My great-aunt never saw the joke when she used to sing, "The good ship Temperance is heading for the port".

'I don't campaign. I just don't drink. There are teetotallers and teetotallers.'

Indeed there are. A number of Mr Benn's friends who drink protest that they inevitably come reeling out of his house because he pours alcohol for others as if it were water. He and his glamorous American wife excel at hospitality. Some of it, it is true, is laid on a little early for everyone's taste. Currently they have people to breakfast at 7.30 in the morning.

'Not *every* day,' Mr Benn assured me. 'This week in fact I had somebody come as late as eight. You see, I'm at my brightest and best in the morning.'

Did not some people, I asked, take a dim view of conversing at that hour? 'Nobody's ever refused,' said Mr Benn cheerfully. Perhaps because they couldn't easily plead a previous engagement?

He maintains that his alleged interest in gadgetry is not for the sake of gadgetry but for efficiency. 'The organization of my day is an interesting thing to me. The thing about the Post Office is that it's the only department that is really *administrative*. I like getting things done. I like my dentist, because all he's interested in is teeth. He talks to me continuously about teeth. I like people who want to do their jobs well.'

A sinister buzzing noise, alarmingly like a dentist's drill, suddenly began to issue from one of the instruments on Mr Benn's desk. Sternly he fixed his large brown eyes upon one of the machines. 'That's very strange,' he said, in his reassuring baritone voice. 'It's a telephone. It isn't making a normal noise. Don't worry.'

So I stopped worrying, and in time the buzzing dentist's drill stopped, and Mr Benn returned his eyes to the distant corner of the room and puffed some more on his pipe.

Sometimes he is teased for his regular platform performance of loosening his tie and eventually removing his jacket, but he refuses to accept this as a consciously developed mannerism. 'I take off my coat because I get very hot,' he said. 'I like fiery meetings in the old style. And I like informality. It creates an entirely different atmosphere from *addressing* a meeting. I like being on the same level.'

Last September the Benns entered the eldest of their four children in the comprehensive school just across from their home in Holland Park Avenue. 'The idea that there was a conflict between our preference and principle just isn't true,' said Mr Benn, propping his feet against the top of his desk and tucking his knees under his chin. 'When our first child was born in 1951, there were not any comprehensive schools in existence.' So they put him down for Westminster.

'I have always admired the naturalness of US high schools. American education is underrated by people in this country: in order to keep ourselves comforted, we always compare our best with the American average. When history comes to be written, the comprehensive schools will be seen to be the famous mark of educational advancement in the twentieth century. My eldest boy will die about 2040. You've got to look ahead.'

Not able to look ahead that far, I asked Mr Benn about a remark he was reported to have made early in his career: 'I want to get rid of the stigma of being an intellectual' – a remark which led his close friend Anthony Crosland to reply, 'You'd better get the stigma first before you worry about losing it!'

'Actually, I never said that,' said Mr Benn, 'because I know I'm not an intellectual. This is not said out of false modesty. I'm just *not*. I'm a very unfabian Fabian. I'm a short-haired Socialist rather than a long-haired one.' (Mr

Benn's new crew cut electrified Parliament when he appeared on the Government front bench.)
   'For many years my father kept a chart on how to eliminate the waste of
time. If your hair is short, you don't have to brush it. I calculate that at the end
of the year you've saved a day over people with long hair,' he added, clearly
delighted at the thought.
   In fact, the only time Mr Benn was in the least querulous was on the subject
of the Post Office. 'You haven't asked me anything about it,' he said in some
aggrievement. 'I'm longing to tell you about it. It's *such* an interesting subject.
But I won't impose my views on you.'
   He doesn't need to. He's imposing them where it counts.

●

VLADIMIR NABOKOV

Interviewed by Penelope Gilliatt
Vogue, December 1966

Vladimir Nabokov (1899–1977), the American novelist, was born in St
Petersburg in Russia. He came from an aristocratic family which left Russia
after the Bolshevik Revolution in 1919, and studied Russian and French
literature at Cambridge. Thereafter he lived in Berlin until the late 1930s,
moved to Paris for a couple of years, and emigrated to the United States, taking
out US citizenship in 1945. He published novels, written in Russian, in both
Berlin and Paris. In the USA he became a university teacher and started writing
novels in English, including *Bend Sinister* (1962) and *Lolita* (1959), the latter of
which provoked an uproar because of its explicitly paedophiliac content. It also
brought sufficient fame to enable Nabokov to devote himself to writing on a
full-time basis. After 1959 he lived in Montreux, Switzerland.
   Penelope Ann Douglass Gilliatt (1932–93) was educated at Queen's College,
London, and Bennington College, Vermont. She was a staff writer for *Vogue,*
then for *Queen,* as well as film critic of *The Observer,* and from 1967 to 1979 she
shared the film critic's job on *The New Yorker* with Pauline Kael. She also
contributed short stories to *The New Yorker* and interview-profiles of such
people as Woody Allen, Jacques Tati, Jean-Luc Godard, Diane Keaton and
Graham Greene. She received an Oscar nomination for her screenplay of
Sunday, Bloody Sunday in 1971. She was married twice, to Professor Roger
Gilliatt, a neurologist, and to the playwright John Osborne, by whom she had a
daughter. Both marriages were dissolved.

*

'Is the Queen pregnant?' said Vladimir Nabokov.

'I don't believe so,' I said.

'When I saw her on television at the World Cup watching football she kept making this gesture.' He did a mime of smoothing a dress.

'She always does that.'

'Oh, I see. A queenly movement. Permanently with child. With heir.' He chuckled and looked interested.

We met in a distant part of Switzerland. I had said to him on the hotel telephone, sounding to myself ludicrously like a character in *Sherlock Holmes* but assuming that he wouldn't know it, that he could identify me downstairs in the lobby because I had red hair.

'I shall be carrying a copy of *Speak, Memory*,' he had said back. (*Speak, Memory* is his autobiography.)

His ear for the idiom was instant and exact. It turned out that his father had known Sherlock Holmes's creator, Sir Arthur Conan Doyle. ('Though Conan Doyle was much more proud of his intolerably boring books on South Africa.') Nabokov has a writer's passion for the physical details and likes Holmes's habit of passing half-a-crown through a chink in the cab to the cabdriver. He also has an intentness on the nuances of speech – Holmes's, mine, anyone's who uses English – that is made much more urgent by his exile from his own language.

Twenty-nine years ago he abandoned his 'untrammelled, rich, and infinitely docile Russian tongue', which he had already used to write novels unpublishable in the Soviet Union and so not published at all, for an English that he learned first from his governesses. Perhaps his command of it now is partly due to the obstacle, as a man will often think more swiftly who speaks with an impediment. Nabokov now writes a dulcet and raffish English that has found more of the secret springs of our language than most writers born to it can ever get under their fingers. For instance, he knows precisely the mechanism of an Anglo-Saxon use of bathos and rudeness, which will plant an anti-climactic word or vernacular insult in a suave context where it goes off with a peculiar mixture of self-mockery and shabby bombast. For all that, his distress about losing Russian is obviously gnawing and will never be appeased. In the preface to *Lolita* he writes briefly about it as if he were an illusionist robbed of his luggage, performing on a stage where his plundered trickery has to be practiced without any of the apparatus of association.

It occurs to me that perhaps this is exactly what makes him write better about love than any other novelist in modern English. The afflictions of exile carry a taste of theft that is the pang of intimacy itself. The tricked focus in the experience of loving, the one that hideously connects rapture with mortality and causes lovers to hoard the present as though it were already gone, bestows a psychic foretaste of loss that is close to the one that gave the privileged Russian children of Nabokov's age a genius for recollection. They lived their Russian youth with the intensity of the grown-up in love, mysteriously already knowing too much about losing it. The ache that clings to good fortune or great accord is one of time's ugly gags, like the grasping housewife already secreted in the rapturous frame of little Lolita.

Humbert Humbert is in love with a booby trap. His whole situation hoaxes him. *Lolita* is an account of the passionate involvement of a man constantly ambushed by *dépaysement* and consigned to the plastic exile of motels. *Dépaysé*: de-countried: we need a word for it now in English far more than we need 'deflowered'. It isn't at all fully expressed by 'alienation', or 'rootlessness', for like the comic agony of love in *Lolita*, it is a concept of loss that includes the knowledge of what it can be to possess. Before I met Nabokov I had wondered sometimes how it was possible for a writer to live permanently in hotels, as he has done since 1960, mostly in Switzerland; but it was a stupid speculation about a great novelist of *dépaysement* who carries his country in his skull. His landscape isn't Russia, but Russian literature.

His permanent address now is a hotel in Montreux that he described as 'a lovely Edwardian heap'. We met in the Engadine, where he and his wife had come for the butterflies, in another Edwardian heap with spa baths in the basement. He is a tall, loping man whose gait and way of peering reminded me faintly of Jacques Tati's.

'I am six foot,' he said. 'I have very thin bones. The rest is flesh.' He picked at his arm as if it were a jacket.

In his autobiography he describes himself as having the Korff nose, passed on from his paternal grandmother's side: 'A handsome Germanic organ with a boldly boned bridge and a slightly tilted, distinctly grooved, fleshy end.' He wears spectacles, but switches to pince-nez after six to alter the ache in his nose. His accent is neither Russian nor American: I think it originates in the upper-class English undergraduate speech of immediately after the First World War, when he went to Cambridge. ('Cambridge, Cambridge, not Cambridge, Mass.,' he said.) His French is delicate and pure. He hears it as dated: 'The slang goes back to Maupassant.' His Russian is the authentic sound of pre-Revolutionary St Petersburg. He did a mischievously expressive example of the boneless accent of standard Pravda speech now. I don't suppose that either he or his wife can detect that their birth in itself is a distinct and commanding fact about them both; but then the upper-class people of Europe never do. It is only the rest who can see the difference, and the well-born truly believe themselves to be indistinguishable.

The Nabokovs think of going back to America to live, perhaps in California. They are looking for what? A climate; and far more than that, a language. 'We were in Italy, but we don't want to live there. I don't speak Italian. And the *scioperi* (strikes) . . . Véra found a château in France, but it would have cost a lot of money to convert it. It had drawbridges. It had its drawbridges and drawbacks.' He has a habit of going back over what he has said and correcting it that is rather like the way he immediately uses an eraser on his notes. 'I don't much care for De Gaulle. I fear things will happen there when he dies. I would go to Spain but I hate bullfights. Switzerland: lakes, charming people, stability. All my publishers pass through from one festival to another.'

He had been up since six, as usual, and had a bath in the curative basement. 'I discovered the secret of levitation,' he said. 'One puts the feet flat braced against the end of the bath and rises covered with bubbles like a fur. I felt like a bear. A memory of a former state.'

We had a drink rather early in the morning. The whiskies looked small as he asked for soda. 'Make the glass grow,' he said, and then muttered: 'The grass glow.'

His books are written on index cards so that it is possible to start in the middle and insert scenes as he wants. He writes in 3B pencils that he says he sharpens compulsively. They have India rubbers on the ends which he uses to exorcise mistakes instead of simply crossing them out. My own error in writing with a pen struck him as technically cardinal. His pocket notebooks are made of paper squared like an arithmetic book. The formal pattern that might distract most people obviously stimulates him. I could understand this: it must be a little like seeing figments in the black-and-white tiles in public lavatories.

'Some of my best poems and chess problems have been composed in bathrooms looking at the floor,' he said.

At some stage we started to play anagrams. I gave him 'cart horse' (the solution is 'orchestra'). He took the problem away on what was meant to be a nap, and came bounding into the bar two hours later with an expression that was a very Russian mixture of buoyancy and sheepishness. The tartanned paper of his little note pad was covered with methodically wrong steps. 'Her actors,' he said, in try-on triumph, eyeing me, and knowing perfectly well that the answer had to be one word. Then he started to laugh at his picture of the creature whose property the actors would be. Bossy women strike him as irresistibly comic: they trudge through his books, absurd, cruel, creatures of inane placidity who see everything in the world as a mirror of their womanliness and who will speak sharply about something like Bolshevism as though it were an obvious minor nuisance, like mosquitos, or the common cold. I believe his woman producer also amused him because he finds the theatre inherently funny when it is earnest: something to do with its thickness, I think, compared with the fine mesh of novels he likes.

When he taught in America he lectured on *Anna Karenina*, Tolstoy's *The Death of Ivan Ilyitch*, *Ulysses*, Kafka's *The Metamorphosis*, and Jane Austen's *Mansfield Park*, which was suggested by Edmund Wilson. The precise butterfly-pinner discovered that Tolstoy made the two families in *Anna Karenina* age on a different time scale, so that more years have passed for one than for the other. He also says that Joyce left out any reference to Bloom's coming back from the cemetery.

'I know Dublin exactly. I could draw a map of it. I know the Liffey like the

Moskva. I have never been to Dublin but I know it as well as Moscow. Also, I have never been to Moscow.'

He and his wife both lived in St Petersburg, but they first met in Berlin in exile. They could have met many times when they were children; at dancing class, perhaps; it bothers them and they go over it.

'Véra's coming down in a moment,' he said. 'She's lost something. A jacket, I think. When she loses things, it is always something very big.' He started to shake again. His sense of humor is very Russian, and the sight of its taking him over is hugely pleasurable. There is a lot of the buffoon in it. He is one of the few people I have seen who literally does sometimes nearly fall off his chair while laughing.

'Véra has been doing "cart horse" as well,' he said. 'Eventually she suggested "horse-cart". She hadn't much hope.'

In the lounge there was an Edwardian mural of naked lovers, except they were not naked and seemed to have nothing much to do with loving. The woman was vulgarly draped and the man wore, as well as a tulle scarf across his groin, a vaporish example of early Maidenform around his chest. After days of looking at the picture Nabokov still found it mildly interesting. It happened to be a rather obvious demonstration of the intimacy in art between silliness and prudery. The high-flying Philistinism of protected art tastes strikes him often as richly foolish. Long ago the Empress of Russia gave him pleasure by being an eager admirer of Ella Wheeler Wilcox. *Invitation to a Beheading*, one of his early Russian-language novels, has a sulphurous passage about an imaginary book considered to be 'the acme of modern thought' in which world history is seen from the point of view of an elderly and apparently sagacious oak tree. Nabokov detests literature that has sweeping social pretentions. He also loathes prurience. The bad art of the past that has lost its power to bamboozle will often reveal that a large share of its badness consists in failing to go too far, which is the only course that is ever far enough in aesthetics. The streak of blue nerve in Nabokov's work is part of its quality. It has an effect that is close to the exhilaration of flair and courage in real conduct.

In the actual world, the vice for which Nabokov seems to have most loathing is brutality. He finds it in tank-shaped political bullies, 'swine-toned radio music', the enjoyment of trained animals, the truisms of Freudianism, the abhorrence of Germany between the wars. (There is a German in one of his books who believes 'electrocution' is the root of 'cute'.) In the world of art his equivalent loathing is for mediocrity, which is perhaps only the aesthetic form of the same brutality. There are celebrated writers in whom he detects a naïveté that he obviously finds almost thuggish. He detests Zola, Stendhal, Balzac, Thomas Mann.

Nabokov spoke eagerly about the descriptions of the fish in Hemingway's *The Old Man and the Sea* and about the jungle passages and close physical descriptions in Graham Greene's *A Burnt-Out Case*. 'The avant-garde French novels that I've read don't stir my artistic appetite. Only here and there. Even Shaw can do that.' I asked him about Genet: 'An interesting fairyland with good measurements.' Ostrovsky, the Russian playwright, he described as having 'a streak of poetry that he unfortunately put down because he was so intent on writing about the merchant class'. Tin-eared translators torment him. '*Vive le pedant*,' he writes defiantly in one of his prefaces, 'and down with the simpletons who think that all is well if the spirit is rendered (while the words go away by themselves on a naïve and vulgar spree – in the suburbs of Moscow for instance – and Shakespeare is again reduced to play the king's ghost).'

The English translations of his Russian novels have been done by Nabokov himself, generally with his son, Dmitri, who is a racing driver and a singer. Nabokov has just finished doing a Russian translation of *Lolita*, typeset in New York. 'To be smuggled in, dropped by parachute, floating down on the blurb.' His attachment to words is urgent and moving. A copy of the unabridged Webster's dictionary is carried about in the back of Nabokov's Lancia; in his hotel room on holiday it was open among the M's, halfway through, which is the way he leaves it so as to save the spine. In his autobiography he speaks of turning even now to the last page of any new grammar to find 'that promised land where, at last, words are meant to mean what they mean'.

'In Massachusetts once I was ill with food poisoning,' he said. 'I was being wheeled along a corridor. They left the trolley by a bookcase and I drew out a big medical dictionary and in the ward I drew the curtains around myself and read. It wasn't allowed because it looked as if I were dying. They took the book away. In hospitals there is still something of the eighteenth-century madhouse.'

'Pasternak?' I asked.

At once he talked very fast. '*Doctor Zhivago* is false, melodramatic, badly written. It is false to history and false to art. The people are dummies. That awful girl is absurd. It reminds me very much of novels written by Russians of, I am ashamed to say, the gentler sex. Pasternak is not a bad poet. But in *Zhivago* he is vulgar. Simple. If you take his beautiful metaphors there is nothing behind them. Even in his poems: what is that line, Véra? "To be a woman is a big step." It is ridiculous.' He laughed and looked stricken.

'This kind of thing recurs. Very typical of poems written in the Soviet era. A person of Zhivago's class and his set, he wouldn't stand in the snow and read about Bolshevist regime and feel a tremendous glow. There was the *liberal* revolution at that time. Kerensky. If Kerensky had had more luck – but he was a liberal, you see, and he couldn't just clap the Bolsheviks into jail. It was not done. He was a very average man, I should say. The kind of person you might find in the Cabinet of any democratic country. He spoke very well, with his hand in his bosom like Napoleon because it had almost been broken by handshakes.

'Yet people like Edmund Wilson and Isaiah Berlin, they have to love *Zhivago* to prove that good writing can come out of Soviet Russia. They ignore that it is really a *bad book*. There are some absolutely ridiculous scenes. Scenes of eavesdropping, for instance. You know about eavesdropping. If it is not brought in as parody it is almost Philistine. It is the mark of the amateur in literature. And that marvellous scene where he had to get rid of the little girl to let the characters make love, and he sends her out skating. In *Siberia*. To keep warm they give her her mother's *scarf*. And then she sleeps deeply in a hut while there is all this going on. Obviously Pasternak just didn't know what to do with her. He's like Galsworthy. Galsworthy in one of his novels gave a character a cane and a dog and simply didn't know how to get rid of them.

'And the metaphors. Unattached comparisons. Suppose I were to say "as passionately adored and insulted as a barometer in a mountain hotel",' he said, looking out at the rain. 'It would be a beautiful metaphor. But who is it about? The image is top-heavy. There is nothing to attach it to. And there is a pseudo-religious strain in the book which almost shocks me. *Zhivago* is so feminine that I sometimes wonder if it might have been written by Pasternak's mistress.

'As a translator of Shakespeare he is very poor. He is considered great only by people who don't know Russian. An example.' His wife helped him to remember a line of Pasternak translation. 'What he has turned it into in Russian is this: "all covered with grease and keeps wiping the pig iron". You see. It is ridiculous. What would be the original?'

'Greasy Joan doth keel the pot?'

'Yes. "Keeps wiping the pig iron!"' He expostulated and looked genuinely angry. 'Pasternak himself has been very much *helped* by translation. Sometimes when you translate a cliché – you know, a cloud has a silver lining – it can sound like Milton because it is in another language.'

'Isn't that what happened to Pushkin?' said Véra.

'He had translated the French writers of his day. The small coin of drawing-room poets and the slightly larger coin of Racine. In Russian it became breathtaking.' I remarked that someone had once said to me that the first man who compared a woman to a flower was a genius and the second, a fool. 'And the third, a knave,' said Nabokov.

We went for a drive in the new Lancia through the mountains. Mrs Nabokov drove, rather fast, mostly in third gear on a tricky road, in the face of jibes from her husband about sheer drops that she had chosen on other days as suitable places to turn.

'Sometimes my son wishes I wouldn't joke so much,' he said with melancholy.

I sat on the back seat, which was still insulated in cellophane, and took off my shoes to keep the cover intact. A hat for butterfly-hunting and walks was on the back shelf.

'You could cover your toes with my hat,' said Mrs Nabokov.

He looked for good meadows for butterfly-hunting and memorized promising paths off the road. His feeling about nature is communicable even to people who don't share it. He is the only man I have ever heard who responds to mention of Los Angeles not with abuse of the city but with glory in the vegetation. He wrote once that when he hunted butterflies it was the highest experience of timelessness, a way 'to picket nature' and 'to rebel against the void fore and aft'. I think it is also an expression of the great writer's passion to define.

We had lemon tea and cream cakes in another hotel looking out across the mountains. He was charming to a waitress who had seemed to have heard the order and said peacefully after a long wait: 'I can tell by the nape of her neck that the cakes are coming.' He has a comic affection for girls' bodies that is rather like his tenderness for gaffes, as though the naked toes or napes of girls absorbed by other things fall unknowingly into a category of farcical and touching blunders.

I asked him whether Lolita would have turned into a boy if his own real child had been a girl.

'Oh, yes,' he said at once. 'If I had had a daughter Humbert Humbert would have been a pederast.'

I thought perhaps that he might cherish a little hatred for *Lolita* now, as writers often do for books that have had more attention than anything else they have written, but his feelings seem not to have swerved. The book remains his favorite, though he says that *Pale Fire* was more difficult to write.

'I had written a short story with the same idea as *Lolita*. The man's name there is Arthur. They travel through France. I never published it. The little girl wasn't alive. She hardly spoke. Little by little I managed to give her some semblance of reality. I was on my way to the incinerator one day with half the manuscript to burn it, and Véra said wait a minute. And I came back meekly.'

'I don't remember that. Did I?' said Mrs Nabokov.

'What was most difficult was putting myself . . . I am a normal man, you see. I travelled in school buses to listen to the talk of schoolgirls. I went to school on the pretext of placing our daughter. We have no daughter. For Lolita, I took one arm of a little girl who used to come to see Dmitri, one kneecap of another.'

He says in his preface that the book originated in a story in *Paris-Soir* of an ape that had been taught to draw: its first drawing was of the bars of its cage. The brawl around *Lolita* and the fierce humor that stylizes all of his work often seems to obscure the extreme tenderness that impels it. His sensitivity to suffering and the exploited makes the attention paid to the plot facts of *Lolita* seem even more brutishly literal-minded than usual. When he was in Hollywood to do the script, the producers asked him to make Lolita and Humbert Humbert get married: apparently this would have pulled some knot of embarrassment for them. The idea of the book being classified as obscene – as it still is in Burma, for instance – is much more gross than anything in most pornography, for it is a book that extends exceptional gentleness to the yearning and the out of step. Elsewhere, in his *Laughter in the Dark*, a murderer thinks 'impossible to kill while she was taking off her shoe': it is a modern equivalent of the moment in *Hamlet* when a man cannot be murdered at prayer. In Nabokov's work sexuality stands for tenderness, and tenderness is the remaining sanctity.

In the car again I asked him about something he had once written about the author of *Alice in Wonderland*.

'I always call him Lewis Carroll Carroll,' he said, 'because he was the first Humbert Humbert. Have you seen those photographs of him with little girls? He would make arrangements with aunts and mothers to take the children out. He was never caught, except by one girl who wrote about him when she was much older.'

He started to answer something I was saying, and turned it into an imitation of Edmund Wilson saying, 'Yes, yes.' Nabokov and Edmund Wilson are old friends, but they have recently conducted a waspish public fight about Mr Wilson's knowledge of Russian, involving claims that seem fairly foolish in the face of a Russian-speaker. Nabokov's private feelings seem affectionately caustic. The imitated 'Yes' involved a head-movement like a man trying to get down a pill when he is gagging on it. 'Apparently consent with him is so difficult he must make a convulsive effort,' said Nabokov warmly enough, and came back to *Lolita*.

'It was a great pleasure to write, but it was also very painful. I had to read so many case histories. Most of it was written in a car to have complete quiet.' He says in *Speak, Memory* that 'in a first-rate work of fiction the real clash is not between the author and the characters but between the author and the world'. This is the force of *Lolita*. The most unsparing love-novel of our literature of glib and easy sex is about an obsession that is locally criminal, written by an alien attacking the numbness of a culture from the inside of the machine that best represents its numbness.

●

JOE ORTON

Interviewed by Giles Gordon
The Transatlantic Review, Spring 1967

John Kingsley (1933–67), the English playwright better known as Joe Orton, was born in Leicester. He left school at the age of sixteen and trained as an actor before becoming a successful writer of dark, witty farces with themes of sexual perversion and death such as *Entertaining Mr Sloane* (1964), *Loot* (1966) and *What the Butler Saw* (1969). A homosexual, he was beaten to death with a hammer by his lover Kenneth Halliwell, who then killed himself. This was his last interview, and was published shortly after his death.

Giles Alexander Esmé Gordon (b. 1940) was educated at the Edinburgh Academy and (briefly) at the Edinburgh College of Art. He went into publishing in 1959 and has worked as both an advertising manager and an editor. He was plays editor of Penguin Books at the time of this interview and was editorial director of Victor Gollancz from 1968 to 1973. That year he decided to become a literary agent and has been with Sheil Land Associates (formerly Anthony Sheil Associates) ever since. He has also written many book and theatre reviews and edited several collections of short stories. Among other interviews he did for *The Transatlantic Review* were those with Tom Stoppard, David Mercer, Edward Bond, and Arnold Wesker.

In his memoirs, *Aren't We Due a Royalty Statement?* (1993), Giles Gordon has recalled the occasion of this interview: 'Joe Orton relished being interviewed by a *literary* periodical of which he had not heard, and insisted upon donning a tie in front of the interviewer before the tape recorder was switched on: he wanted to *sound* properly dressed.'

Joe Orton has had two plays successfully put on in London. Both have been critical and box office hits. First *Entertaining Mr Sloane* and currently *Loot*, though when the latter was given a pre-London run in a much truncated form a few years back it got no nearer to London than Golders Green. Which in theatrical terms might as well be Aberdeen. His first play, *The Ruffian on the Stair*, a one acter, recently received a Sunday night production without décor at the Royal Court Theatre.

Mr Orton's plays are funny – he is surely the nearest to a writer of farce working in the serious theatre in English at present – and he has style; he is not afraid of artificiality in dialogue, nor is he at all pretentious or 'committed'.

He lives in Islington in London, in what is probably termed a flatlet, though he has his own front door. His room has yellow walls and a red and grey ceiling. The walls are covered with innumerable colour pictures extracted from magazines: he has created a Christian cross by cutting out reproductions of icons, plus a gorilla. There is a poster for *Loot*, and one for *Seid Nett Zu Mr Sloane*! The room has two single beds, scores of records, a huge television set, some books, a pair of shoes under the bed. All very neat, very tidy. When I arrive Mr Orton is on the phone, giving Sheila Ballantine, the leading actress in *Loot*, instructions as to how to reach his house. It is extremely easy to find but he gave me complicated directions also. He tells her he must ring off, as he is being interviewed for the *International Review*. She replies that she has never heard of it, but that it sounds very grand. He puts down the phone, then dons a purple tie, saying he couldn't possibly be interviewed not wearing a tie. The tape recorder is set up, and Joe Orton settles into an armchair close to it.

GORDON: May we talk first about what I would call, or rather what the critics call, art theatre as opposed to commercial theatre. Two of the most interesting plays put on in London in recent months, to my mind, have been your *Loot* and Charles Dyer's *Staircase*. It incensed me, particularly in the case of *Staircase*, that so many of the critics said that this was a commercial play, intending the word in a derogatory, dismissive sense; and adding that the play would not have been performed by a subsidized company but for the fact that it gave two strong parts to two of the company's stars.

ORTON: I gather that *Staircase* was offered to several commercial managements, all of whom turned it down. I don't see any reason why it shouldn't have been put on in the commercial theatre. Anyway, I think this whole thing of commercial and subsidized theatre is ridiculous. There are only good plays and bad plays. I got the same thing on *Entertaining Mr Sloane* – people were always saying 'Oh, it's just a commercial play.' It always infuriated me, because it wasn't; there isn't such a thing. It was a good play or a bad play.

GORDON: Why is it, do you think, that so many critics and directors – and audiences, for that matter – insist on categorizing plays in these two ways, quite falsely?

ORTON: I really don't know. It's quite a snob thing, of course. When you're put on at one of the subsidized theatres, you do get an enormous snob audience. I think people like to feel they're being entertained and also being cultural at the same time.

GORDON: Do you set out to write a certain kind of play? The three plays of yours that have been produced in London all deal with the same types of characters, from a particular segment of society. Are you conscious of this?

ORTON: In actual fact, the 'class' of my plays is going up all the time! *The Ruffian on the Stair* began by being pretty grotty and criminal; *Sloane* moved up slightly, since the characters were lower-middle class. (Lower-middle class nihilism, I was told.) *Loot* has moved up one rung more because it's now a woman who leaves £19,000 including her bonds and jewels. I'm sure you can – though I don't know that I can, yet – write about very upper class people and make them as interesting as lower class people. I think *people* are interesting. I was very pleased that *The Times* in its first review of *Loot* said that if you can attribute a serious purpose to the play – and of course you can – it was a plea against compartmentalization. This pleased me very much as I've always been against compartmentalization. What I wanted to do in *Sloane* was to break down all the sexual compartments that people have. It didn't entirely succeed because it's very difficult to persuade directors and actors to do what you want. When *Sloane* had been running for a while, it had got into compartments, so that Madge was the nympho, Peter was the queer and Dudley was the psycho. Which wasn't what I wanted and which wasn't what I intended at all, but people *will* put things into compartments. It's very bad in class, in sex, in anything.

GORDON: Which brings us straight on to taste. Many people have said that *Loot* is in exceedingly bad taste. Are you aware of such a thing as good taste or bad taste?

ORTON: No. You see, the kind of people who always go on about whether a thing is in good taste invariably have very bad taste. I think the English have the worst taste of any people on earth. No, I don't think there's such a thing as good taste and bad taste. Some things *offend* me, but they're rather odd things. For instance, those translations of Aristophanes by Dudley Fitts. I think they're extremely bad. They sicken me, but this is just *my* thing. They obviously don't offend a lot of people.

GORDON: It's interesting how in *Loot* a number of people are offended in that so much of the action is centred round a coffin.

ORTON: I never understand why, because if you're absolutely practical – and I hope I am – a coffin is only a box. One calls it a coffin and once you've called it a coffin it immediately has all sorts of associations. In *Sloane* I wrote a man who was interested in boys and liked having sex with boys. I wanted him played as if he was the most ordinary man in the world, and not as if the moment you wanted sex with boys you had to put on earrings and scent. This is very bad, and I hope that now homosexuality is allowed, people aren't going to continue doing the conventional portraits there have been in the past. I think that the portrait of the queer in Peter Shaffer's *Black Comedy* is very funny, but it's an awfully conventional portrait. It's compartmentalization again. Audiences love it, of course, because they're safe. But one shouldn't pander to audiences.

GORDON: That's the great thing about *Staircase*. You don't notice that the play is about two queers, you notice it's about two people.

ORTON: Two *people*, exactly!

GORDON: Who happen to love one another. But apparently when the production opened in Brighton for a week prior to its London premiere, audiences were outraged that their Paul Scofield (he evidently comes from Brighton) should have been subjected to such a role. They saw the characters as queers, and were shocked. It didn't occur to them they were people, human beings.

ORTON: Yes, it's very odd. Of course on this subject the English are for ever striving to be great liberals. I notice that even the great champion of liberalism, *The Observer*, always refers to homosexuals as queers. They would never actually refer to coloured people as niggers. Even in quite serious articles they call people queers. If someone had written a play about West Indians *The Observer* would never say 'So-and-so plays the nigger.' That I think is interesting.

GORDON: Before we switched on the tape recorder, you mentioned 'schools of playwrights'. Do you think that today there are such things?

ORTON: No, I don't think so. Playwrights, like people, are very individual. The fact that all sorts of things are written at a certain period immediately puts you into a school. You can talk about the Elizabethan and Jacobean playwrights, but they were all quite different. I think that if any plays survive from the 50s and 60s then their authors will be put into a school, but only because they were writing at about the same time.

GORDON: But I'd have thought that you almost more than any other playwright today have avoided being categorized along with other of your contemporaries?

ORTON: Yes, probably. I think that's because the people I admire aren't particularly modern. I admire Voltaire. Aristophanes, I read him in prose translations. I prefer these because they're literal. You don't get anybody coming between you and the playwright. I'm very conscious of what's gone before. I like Lucian and the classical writers, and I suppose that's what gives my writing a difference, an old fashioned classical education! Which I never received, but I gave myself one, reading them all in English, for I have so little Latin and less Greek.

GORDON: Do you admire particularly any playwright today?

ORTON: Beckett. And Pinter.

GORDON: Do you have 'an ultimate aim' as a playwright?

ORTON: I'd like to write a play as good as *The Importance of Being Earnest*.

GORDON: You admire Wilde?

ORTON: Yes. I admire his work, not his life. It was an appalling life.

GORDON: Your plays and his have, I think, certain affinities, mainly of style and artificiality of language. I wonder if there's anything significant in that two of his plays are having all star revivals in London at the moment?

ORTON: No. I think that's the tail end of the reaction in the theatre which I hope we're finished with now. After the so-called dirty plays controversy the English have one of their periodic fits of morality, and I think we're seeing the end of it. We saw all those dreary Shaw revivals, and the dreary Wilde revivals, and I hope we've seen the end of it with *Staircase* and *Loot* !

GORDON: Both *Staircase* and *Loot* are highly moral plays.

ORTON: I hope so. I was quite serious saying in the programme that I'm a puritan. I'm not sure that the word puritan is right but I think one can write only from that kind of standpoint. I would hate to see themes like those of *Staircase* or *Loot* done by people who . . . I don't know, it's rather pompous to say by people who haven't got talent as we have, but I would hate to see it done at the Whitehall with the kind of writing they have there, because I don't think much of Whitehall farces.

GORDON: When watching *Loot* I had an uneasy feeling that you were extremely shocked by what you were writing about.

ORTON: No, this is quite wrong. That's like the woman who said that I only wrote about the police because I had a terrible time in prison. But in actual fact I did not have a terrible time in prison. I had a wonderful time and wouldn't have missed it for the world. It's a curious society, a pyramid, and I suddenly saw how comforting it is to be in a pyramidical society, like Ancient Egypt must have been. I don't think you'd get any plays like, say, *Loot* from it, but certainly as far as living's concerned it's very comfortable. I wouldn't particularly like to do it indefinitely but it was most interesting. I certainly have nothing against the police. They're a necessary evil.

GORDON: Can we talk about the reason why you went to prison?

ORTON: Yes, libraries and library books. The thing that put me in a rage about librarians was that when I went to quite a big library in Islington and asked for Gibbon's *Decline and Fall of the Roman Empire* they told me they hadn't a copy of it. They could get it for me, but they hadn't one on their shelves. This didn't start it off, but it was symptomatic of the whole thing. I was enraged that there were so many rubbishy novels and rubbishy books. It reminded me of the phrase in the Bible: 'Of the making of books, there is no end,' because there isn't. Libraries might as well not exist; they've got endless shelves for rubbish and hardly any space for good books.

GORDON: Isn't this *you* deciding upon what is good, what is bad? Personal taste?

ORTON: Yes, I suppose so. But you can always say when some things are rubbish and some things aren't. I can obviously say Gibbon isn't. He said a very funny thing about books: When the Arabs took Alexandria they used the contents of the library to provide fuel for the baths and Gibbon thought that probably the books were doing more good being so used than they were when being read.

GORDON: Perhaps that's the birth date of auto-destructive art. Didn't you deface photographs in library books?

ORTON: Yes. I did things like pasting a picture of a female nude over a book of etiquette, over the picture of the author who, I think, was Lady Lewisham. I did other things, very strange things. There was the business when I got the biography of Sir Bernard Spilsbury and there was an illustration which said: 'The remains discovered in the cellar at number 23 Rosedown Road.' I pasted over the illustration, which was a very dreary one of a lot of earth, David's picture of Marat dead in his bath. It was in black and white. I left the original caption underneath, so that it really did look like what it said, 'The remains discovered in the cellar at number 23 Rosedown Road.' This picture of the corpse in the bath had quite an effect on people who opened the book. I used to write false blurbs on the inside of Gollancz books because I discovered that Gollancz books had blank yellow flaps and I used to type false blurbs on the insides. My blurbs were mildly obscene. Even at the trial they said they were only mildly obscene. When I put the plastic covers back over the jackets you couldn't tell that the blurbs weren't printed. I used to stand in corners after I'd smuggled the doctored books back into the library and then watch people read them. It was very funny, very interesting. There was a biography of Sybil Thorndike in which there was a picture of her locked up in a cell as Nurse Edith Cavell. I cut the caption from another picture and pasted it under the picture, so that it read: 'During the war I received many strange requests.' One of the interesting things at the trial was that the greatest outrage, the one for which I think I was sent to prison, was that I had stuck a monkey's face in the middle of a rose, on the cover of something called *Collins Book of Roses*. It was a very beautiful yellow rose. What I had done was held up as the depth of iniquity for which I should probably have been birched. They won't ever do that so they just sent me to prison for six months.

GORDON: Was it the only time someone has been sent to prison for defacing library books?

ORTON: I think so, but there has been a lot of it all over the country.

GORDON: How old are you?

ORTON: Thirty-three.

GORDON: What did you start life doing?

ORTON: I had an ordinary sort of schooling. I didn't get the eleven plus. I left school when I was sixteen, and went into an office. I had a number of jobs because I kept getting the sack. When I was eighteen I went to RADA, where I did a couple of years. I went into rep. – I didn't think much of rep. even in those days – I met someone recently who knew me in rep. and they said I was always moaning, even in rep., how awful the theatre was. This was in 1953. I gave it up after four months and came back to London later on and did nothing . . . got jobs . . . got a job at Cadbury's unloading things in the warehouse; and I used to write. I was writing novels then. Of course before 1956 it was very difficult to think what you could write in a play. After then I was writing plays and novels. None of the novels were success-ful, none of the plays were put on. I was really occupying myself with these library books. It used to be a full time job. I would stagger home from libraries with books which I'd borrowed and also stolen, and then I used to go back with them a couple of times a day. After I'd been in prison I wrote *The Ruffian*, which the BBC accepted, though it didn't come on until *Entertaining Mr Sloane* had opened.

GORDON: Are you writing a new play?

ORTON: I've just finished a one act play. I'm having a rest at the moment, doing all my reading.

GORDON: You're able to live off your plays?

ORTON: Oh, yes! I was on National Assistance when *Sloane* started. They were going to send me to a rehabilitation centre and I said, look, I'm having a play put on, and they said, well, we'll give you a respite then for a few months. So when *Sloane* came on I received a note saying 'We see your play has appeared, so presumably you don't want to receive National Assistance any more.' Which was actually nonsense, because I'd only had the £100 advance. Anyway, it did so well I didn't have to work at anything else or have National Assistance. I couldn't work at anything else anyway. I was pretty useless at everything except writing. It takes me a long time to write plays. The one act play I've just finished – mid November – I began in July. It doesn't just come out of my head as it appears to do. I've made about five versions of it. What I usually do is cut because I find cutting is the real thing. An awful lot of plays you could make much more brilliant by cutting, only there isn't anything there to cut. If you haven't a story and a plot you can't cut. I do all that myself, then polish and probably rewrite.

•

LESTER PIGGOTT
Interviewed by Kenneth Harris
The Observer, 7 June 1970

Lester Keith Piggott, the jockey and trainer, was born in 1935 into a racing family and married the daughter of a trainer. He has been champion jockey eleven times, including an unbroken spell from 1964 to 1971. Throughout his career he has regularly ridden over 100 winners a year. He has won the Derby nine times, the St Leger eight, the Oaks six, the 2,000 Guineas four times, and the 1,000 Guineas twice. He has also ridden in France and has won the Prix de l'Arc de Triomphe three times. He was convicted and imprisoned for tax evasion in 1987. He had his first Derby winner at the age of nineteen and he was thirty-five at the time of this interview. Kenneth Harris had several talks with him at his home in Newmarket, sometimes before and sometimes after races – 'the most memorable day being that on which he rode Nijinsky to success in the 1970 2,000 Guineas'.

Kenneth Harris (b. 1919) was educated at the High School for Boys, Trowbridge, Wiltshire, and at Wadham College, Oxford, where he read history. After the Second World War he travelled to Washington as a member of the Oxford debating team, along with Anthony Wedgwood-Benn (later Tony Benn) and Edward Boyle (later Lord Boyle). He joined *The Observer* as its Washington correspondent and was 'asked to do bits and pieces on radio and TV'. In 1953 he returned to the UK and began to conduct interviews for the BBC and ITV – which he reckons to have been a good discipline for his later print interviews. His first print interview was with the philosopher, Bertrand Russell. He visited Russell for two days, took not a single note, then produced 5,000 words of questions and answers. On reading the manuscript, Russell made five small corrections and agreed to let the interview be published posthumously because he felt he owed David Astor a debt of gratitude, as Astor had publicized his views on the atom bomb.

As a young child of about eight, Harris began to show an aptitude for remembering what he had read. It was artless and unselfconscious, he says today. Then, he remembers, at school he was good at a classroom exercise called 'Reading and Re-telling'. After the Russell encounter, he produced many in-depth interviews for *The Observer*. His technique was almost always the same. In the early days, he never used a tape recorder and never took notes. After the interview, he would 'go to the loo or to the top of a bus and write it out from the beginning, not pausing for a moment to get it right. Sometimes I would have to wait a day, and I often woke up and remembered things in the middle of the night. I tried to make it as spontaneous as possible.' The result was always sent to the subject for approval.

He saw the Archbishop of Canterbury, Dr Geoffrey Fisher, for two sessions of two hours each and subsequently produced an 8,000-word article. When Fisher saw it, he was vastly impressed by Harris's powers of recall, particularly as the subject matter had included some fairly abstruse theological discussion. Fisher wrote to Astor suggesting that this man Harris was the devil, he had such a prodigious memory. Later, Harris began to use a tape recorder and reckons that today he would have difficulty reproducing several thousand words of conversation from memory. Apart from having a powerful memory, Harris adopts what he prefers to call a 'village idiot' approach. 'My ignorance, not my knowledge, has got me my success as an interviewer. I am näive, curious, but I don't have much knowledge.'

HARRIS: Well, here you are, Mr Piggott, some saying you are the greatest jockey riding today, some saying the greatest jockey of the generation, and some saying the greatest jockey ever. How did you come to be a jockey in the first place?

PIGGOTT: Born into it.

HARRIS: Did you ever want to do anything else?

PIGGOTT: No.

HARRIS: If you had your time over again would you like to be a jockey again?

PIGGOTT: Yes.

HARRIS: Supposing you were reborn and *had* to grow up into a different career what would you choose?

PIGGOTT: Motor-car racing.

HARRIS: Why?

PIGGOTT: Excitement.

HARRIS: You remind me of the late Lord Attlee, Mr Piggott: you answer questions as if you were filling in an application for a driving licence. Let me put you some more general questions and try to get you to expand. And if I put up my hand, like this, will you take it that I'm asking you to, so to speak, go off the bit? For instance: What is the particular kind of excitement about motor-car racing that appeals to you?

PIGGOTT: You go as fast as you dare: you get hurt if you lose control: you're competing with other people: you're doing it to win.

HARRIS: And to make money?

PIGGOTT: Most of us would be doing it whether there was money or no money. Some of the best trainers are very wealthy men – they don't have to do anything for money. But they work at it as if they were broke. I'd be in racing if I had to pay to be in racing. It's life to me. I don't know another kind of life.

I do well out of racing. I know plenty of people who lived for racing who haven't done as well. Racing cost them a lot. It's not a game you go into, as an owner, to make money; you find too many people who've lost out to make you think that. I love it, but I do well out of it. And I try to earn as much as I can.

One day I shall stop being a jockey and be a trainer. But even if I didn't have one eye on that, I'd be riding as much as I could. You get into it. It gets into you. It's a way of life. It's a rhythm. It's day in, day out; you wouldn't know what else to do if you stopped. I never really want a holiday. Now and again I feel a bit tired, so I just stop riding for a few days. That's all the holiday I want. All the fun I want is in the game.

HARRIS: You say you were born into racing. Could you tell me about your family? Did you have a happy or unhappy childhood?

PIGGOTT: I come from racing families on both sides. My mother is a Rickaby. My uncle won the 1,000 Guineas four times; the only time I won it was this year. I was beginning to wonder if I'd ever win it.

Funny how some races get away from you. Gordon Richards didn't win the Derby till he was forty-nine: the year before he retired. My father's father was a jockey. Jumping. He won the Grand National three times. I think it's harder to do that than win the Derby three times. My father was a jumping jockey, and then he became a trainer.

Yes, I had a happy childhood. I didn't like school much, though – I was born near Wantage and I went to St Alfred's School there. I was slow at lessons: a dunce. They said my reactions were slow. I think I'd have been quicker if I'd seen the point of it. Every day I wanted to get back to the horses. I'd been riding since I was four. There were only two things I understood outside the family: horses, and races. I didn't really know what school was for, except that you had to go to it.

I was deaf too, in one ear. I wouldn't have liked to have to teach me. I'm not so deaf now, and I lip-read, and I watch people's faces; they're more expressive than horses' faces, but not so reliable. But even now if somebody says something when I'm not looking directly at them I may not hear. So sometimes people think I'm rude. Sometimes they think I'm disagreeing when I'm not. Sometimes they think I'm agreeing when I'm not, which is worse.

Nobody knows how I got deaf. And nobody could do anything about it. But it's much better now than it was when I was a boy. Being a bit deaf, you did live on your own a bit. It made you a bit shy. But it had its good points: you got on with things, and did them your own way, and you didn't rely on praise or blame because half the time you never heard it.

You asked about my parents. They're both alive. My father taught me everything I know about racing. He's different from me – he's easy-going, enjoys life, gives out a lot. But when it came to riding, racing, or generally being with horses, I was his pupil, not his son. Except that he'd never have done for a pupil what he did for his son.

He was a small trainer – he only had a few horses, so he could keep an eye on everybody and everything that was going on. If I slouched in the saddle, or had my hands too high or let a horse go too fast, he'd see it, and be on to me. He never let me know I was any good. He didn't believe in it. A taskmaster. I think it's the best way. I knew he knew his stuff, and I tried to please him because I knew he knew his stuff. I wanted to be good and I was ready to take it from him.

He's just the same today. One year, after I had ridden 200 winners, I went to see him, and I said: 'I've ridden 200 winners this year.' He said: 'What about the ones you should have won on?'

HARRIS: Has any jockey influenced your riding?

PIGGOTT: No, if you're as tall as I am – 5 ft 7 in. – you've got to work out your own method. Most jockeys are small men. There weren't any models for tall jockeys like me in my time. Gordon Richards was small even as jockeys go: he could do eight stone without effort.

There's an advantage in being tall, big: I think it's my main one. A horse responds to a good weight on its back – live weight – not dead weight – lead, under the saddle – to make up the right scale. When a biggish jockey gets up, the chances are that the horse feels – well, the authority. Not always. There is a great American jockey, Shoemaker, and he's only seven stone. And Gordon Richards again – eight stone. If you've got a good length of leg, you can communicate more with the horse, squeeze him with your knees, control him generally – show him you are there.

There's the other side, the disadvantages: I've got to earn my living in a pretty strenuous game working at about 1½ stone below my natural weight. Some people exaggerate how I live: I don't starve, and I don't live on cigars and the *Financial Times*, and I don't drive to every race meeting in a rubber suit. But you can't eat and drink what might come naturally to you.

If I'm riding at eight stone six, I have a boiled egg and a bit of toast for breakfast. If I have to do eight stone five that day, I'll give up the egg. I have a sandwich in the jockeys' room after I've finished riding, and I'll always have a meal at night. You lose the habit of eating, really – the less you have, up to a point, the less you want.

You were asking me about influences. Susan's a great influence on me. She's almost like my manager. She's a trainer's daughter, and she rides well, and if I can't hear somebody on a long-distance telephone call, Susan talks. Sometimes she persuades me to do things I don't want to. Like this interview, because she says it'll do me good to do something I don't normally do. And the two girls influence me – you know, Maureen and Tracy. If I'm getting a bit serious about something they come in, and one of them's bound to say something that makes me laugh.

You ask about being influenced by other jockeys. Race-riding changes with the years. Not all that much: you've always got a leg each side of the horse, but things do change. For instance, we go much faster in the first two furlongs than they did fifteen years ago. It doesn't do to model yourself on your predecessors.

Another disadvantage about being big is style. Style is how you look. If you're small, it doesn't matter so much how you look, there isn't so much of you to be seen. And your legs don't take up so much room. If you're big, you can be seen better, and there's less horse showing.

It's difficult for me to look stylish because I like to ride short. People ask me why I ride with my bottom in the air. Well, I've got to put it somewhere.

HARRIS: One of the things often said of you is that you're a tremendously 'strong' jockey. What does 'strength' mean? Is it the kind of strength that bends iron bars?

PIGGOTT: Well, you need muscular strength to hold a horse that's pulling for his head, a big horse and a real puller, on his way down to the post. And if a horse is big and broad, and he's lazy, and he needs to be squeezed and kicked along to keep him exerting himself, a small, light jockey can't do it so well. But when you talk about a jockey being 'strong', or being able to ride a strong finish, it's a bit different.

It's like this: a lot depends on the horse's balance. If he loses balance, he loses speed and direction, and that might cost him the race – he'll lose his position, or just get passed in the last fifty yards. Part of a jockey's job is to get his horse running balanced, and keep him balanced, and this means you've got to be balanced yourself all the time to fit in with the horse.

The horse has his own centre of gravity just behind his shoulders. The jockey has a centre of gravity. But the jockey can shift his, and the horse can't. At every stride the horse's centre of gravity is shifting in relation to the jockey's. Getting a horse balanced means keeping your balance, every stride, every second, to suit his.

Where strength comes in is that to keep doing this all the time without throwing yourself about in the saddle needs a lot of muscle control – you've got to be holding yourself as still as you can while you're making the right movements. The more control you have of your body, the fewer movements you have to make – but the more muscular effort you need: you need more strength to stand still on one leg than to walk down the street.

No, I don't say it's the strength that bends iron bars. It's the strength of an acrobat on a tightrope. Or of a juggler.

In the finish of the race as well as keeping your horse balanced you've got to be doing things with him. You've got to be encouraging the horse – moving your hands forward when his head goes forward, squeezing him with your knees, urging him on with your heels, flourishing your whip, maybe giving him a crack, and all this without throwing him off balance, which means doing all these things and not letting yourself be thrown around in the saddle.

In a tight finish a strong jockey may seem to be doing nothing in the saddle except throwing his hands forward – that's all you'll see, but the horse is going flat out, and still going straight. In the same finish a 'weaker' jockey will be throwing himself about in the saddle, and his horse will be rolling about off balance. Keeping the horse balanced in that last hundred yards, and making him put it all in, can take a lot out of a jockey. It's got to be there to start with.

Weight and length come into it again. If a jockey is strong, and he's good, I reckon live weight is better than dead weight. If all of the weight the horse is carrying is live, and the jockey can put it in the right place at every stride, the horse runs freer than he would if part of the weight is in a fixed place, in a bag on his back.

HARRIS: What other attributes must a jockey have?

PIGGOTT: A jockey has got to make horses want to run for him. Sometimes a horse and a jockey won't hit it off.

Then, you've got to have judgement – can you get through that gap or not? Is the pace too slow? Is it so slow that if I poach a lead of four lengths here, three furlongs out, I can hang on and win by a neck? And you've got to do your homework – find out as much as you can about the other horses, so that when you see one in front of you, you can guess what he can do.

Sometimes you can work out tactics in advance, but sometimes you've got to change them. Sometimes they don't come off. You've got to keep thinking about racing all the time – it's no good starting to think about a race just before you get up on the horse's back. That's one thing about not wanting to talk very much – I get time to read about racing, and to listen, and to think.

HARRIS: What trainers and jockeys stand out in your mind?

PIGGOTT: It's hard to compare trainers of today and the past. I wonder if some of the older ones could cope with today. All the paper work. Trade union hours for boys. Racing abroad. High costs. Training used to be for gentlemen. Now you've got to be a businessman as well. And a diplomat.

Keeping a horse in training is very expensive. Some of the owners want quick returns. A trainer needs character to stand up to them and say, 'Your horse isn't ready.' Or, 'He's not as good as you think he is.'

You asked about jockeys. It's hard to sort out British jockeys – different ages, and so on.

Abroad, I think the best is Yves St-Martin. We're supposed to be great enemies. He is supposed to have brought me down once. But you were in my house for lunch on 2,000 Guineas day, Mr Harris: who were the other three having lunch?

HARRIS: Mick Bartholomew, Freddie Head and Yves St-Martin. You say St-Martin is good. What makes him good?

PIGGOTT: He does the right thing at the right time. It sounds very obvious, but that's all it's about, really: getting your horse to do the right thing everywhere, and knowing what's going on.

HARRIS: What do you think of some of the courses you've ridden on?

PIGGOTT: York is the best course: Newmarket the easiest to ride. Straight. But it's hardest on the horses, no bends to take a breather. Sandown gives you the best viewing, and it's a very fair test of a horse – some bends and a tough uphill finish.

The hardest British courses to ride are Ascot and Epsom. Ascot's got a very short run in. So you can't afford to be too far back, which means you must have a horse that can stay with the leaders. It's not easy to come from behind and win at Ascot.

Epsom is a very difficult course. There's a curve in the course early on, a kind of bulge more than a curve, so you have to go fast to get a good forward position by the time you get to that curve, or horses crossing to it from your right will cut you off and pen you in. Then down the hill to Tattenham Corner, which is a race in itself; there's nothing like it anywhere else in the world.

Then there's Tattenham Corner itself, where horses may be almost falling over each other and trying to turn at the same time. Then the straight, where the ground slopes very sharply into the rails. It takes a good horse to get round Epsom.

There's another trouble about the Derby: it's a big social occasion. A lot of owners want to be represented even if it means running a poor-class horse. They often get to the front by the top of the hill going down to the Corner and then start coming back to you. Some years I've ridden in the Derby half the horses shouldn't have been in the race. That's the good thing about races like Laurel Park International: entries have got to be invited.

But in a way Longchamp, Paris, is the most difficult course I know. There's no theory of riding it. It's not the terrain – it's flat. Nor the bends – there's only one. The mile and a half, their equivalent of the Derby distance, is a very long elongated U-shape. They go very fast in the Arc, the first few furlongs. So you've got to have a horse that can go with them.

At Ascot you'd better be pretty well forward to have a chance. Usually goes for Epsom, too. And Sandown. But at Longchamp they can be last coming to the straight and win. They come from anywhere. There's no recipe for riding that course.

HARRIS: Well, you certainly rode the Derby course all right on Nijinsky.

PIGGOTT: You're only as good as your last race. I've ridden some losers since Nijinsky.

HARRIS: What horses stand out in your mind, Mr Piggott, when you look back?

PIGGOTT: There's the ones you remember because of what happened to you on them, and the ones you remember for themselves. When I was younger I used to remember more about what happened than about the horse – like my first winner when I was twelve; and the Derby when I was eighteen. As you get older, you remember more the horses.

When I was a kid I used to think more about the winning. I was racing against the top jockeys, all much older, some twice my age: some older than that. I had to compete on the same terms. Now I've got much more interested in horses, their character. It's partly getting older. And having children and watching them grow up makes you more interested in individuals and personality. It's difficult to look back and compare horses – memory isn't that good. The last great one you rode is easier to remember than the first one. I ride six hundred horses a year, and since I've been a freelance I ride a lot of top-class horses in France, Germany and Italy. So to make comparisons isn't fair to the horse.

Crepello was a great horse. He won the 2,000 Guineas and the Derby. He won the Derby copybook; he did what I wanted. I didn't have to ask for anything.

Sir Ivor, in 1968, was a grand horse. He was good-tempered, friendly, easy to ride if he knew what he was supposed to do. He didn't win the Eclipse, which he should have done; he would have beaten Royal Palace over that distance, mile and a quarter, but he'd run in the Irish Derby just before, and the going was very firm. When the time came for him to accelerate, he could not. He couldn't give of his best.

Park Top is a great mare. Great character. She knows what she's supposed to do and she loves it. When I get up on her, she cocks an ear, like saying, 'Come on, then, let's get on with it.' She goes down to the start as easy as you like – doesn't pull, doesn't sweat, she knows what it's all about. She goes into the gate as if she was going into church, and she comes out as if hell were after her. She knows more about racing than I do.

You've got to be interested in the character of a horse if you want to ride winners, if for no other reason. You've got to know what they can do and how they want to do it.

You know these Ribot horses? Mr Engelhard has raced a lot of them. With some of them you have to leave them to themselves in the early stages of a race, even if they lose ground. Then, when you feel they've settled down, you can get to work on them. It's not that they're dishonest horses; it's just that they like to do things their own way. You can't push them. You know that if they're not left to do it their own way, early on, they won't do it at all.

People watching from the stands don't always appreciate this. They see you sitting still on the horse at half way, looking as if you're not doing anything, and losing ground. They wonder what you think you're doing. Then the horse gets down to it and starts to race, you push him out, he gets beaten a neck; and the people in the stand say: 'If he pushed a bit more at half way, he'd have won by a length.' And they might add a few snide comments. But you can't be explaining this kind of thing all the time: you'd have no time to race.

Take Ribocco. He was good enough to finish third in the Arc de Triomphe in 1967. But he just wouldn't go fast enough in the first six furlongs to hold his place. When he started to let me help him race there was a wall of horses in front of him. But he was flying at the finish and we only got beaten by a couple of necks.

HARRIS: Do you think we in this country have got anything to learn from racing overseas?

PIGGOTT: I don't think they can teach our breeders or our trainers or our jockeys much. We do pretty well wherever we go. You find British trainers and British jockeys winning their share of all the big races abroad. We win races in Germany, France, Italy, sometimes. Organization of racing seems better in some places. Stands, changing-rooms, bars, restaurants, and facilities abroad are pretty good, better than some of ours. But Ascot, Newmarket, Redcar and York take some beating.

Most of the big racing countries abroad have the Tote. We have bookmakers as well. I don't know if we ought to have a Tote monopoly, though: the public don't seem to want that. And Sunday racing – that's very popular in France, Germany and Italy. But I don't know if it would work here. You've got to have one day off for the stables.

I don't know, really, how much we could do here what they do abroad. A jockey only gets a part view of it all. But I think more money ought to get back into racing. A lot of money is involved in racing – especially in betting. There's a big tax nowadays. I think the Government ought to put more money back into racing. The prize money here is nothing like it is, say, in France. Over there it can be four and five times as much.

It's the small trainer that's affected. It's harder than ever for the small trainer to stay in the game in this country. And he's the backbone of racing. Perhaps I'm prejudiced because I'm a small trainer's son.

HARRIS: What about the public life aspect of racing?

PIGGOTT: Well, there isn't much time to do anything outside your actual racing, because racing means a long day, what with travel, and telephoning, and everything.

But I'm vice-president of the Jockey's Association, and I do as much as I can for that. I think it's a very good thing, and does a lot of good work. It's a kind of welfare society for jockeys, and the idea is partly to help one another, and partly to liaise with the authorities in British racing on anything that comes up, so that whoever has to give or take in any particular case, British racing gains as a whole.

HARRIS: How far do you think the discipline of having to keep your weight down to this unnatural level changes, perhaps detrimentally, your natural personality?

PIGGOTT: I don't think it does very much. I don't think I'd be very different from what I am now if I didn't have to keep thin. But it's hard to say. As soon as I grew up I had to watch my weight hard and I've done it ever since. So I don't really know if I'd be different if I started living normally.

Wasting depresses a lot of people – it's the way you're made. They say Fred Archer committed suicide because having to keep his weight down got his mind down as well – got him so depressed he couldn't go on living.

I'm lucky because, well, you might say I'm pretty quiet and restrained by nature. I've never been one for living it up. Some people work to earn enough money to have fun. I enjoy the work best of all. If you like racing more than anything else, it's easier to give up things. It's easier to keep up your regime, without breaking out, and the steadier you keep it up the easier it is to live with it.

I told you when you asked about motor-car racing that I liked to compete, that I liked to try and win – the winning isn't all that important, it's the *wanting* to win that matters. The competition. It's competing more than winning, if you see what I mean.

In keeping your weight down you're competing. You're competing with yourself. After a time it becomes a habit and you're in one long competition with yourself. And you only keep winning if you're trying to win all the time.

If I got on the scales one morning intending to be 8 st 4 lb and I was 8 st 6 lb, and I hadn't meant to be, even if I wasn't being asked to ride at 8 st 4 lb, I'd want to get those two pounds off. You've got to get what you started out to do. Otherwise you start getting beaten. The others start to beat you when you start being beaten by yourself.

HARRIS: You don't develop a feeling of resentment at having to subject yourself to the regime, a feeling that might erupt occasionally into ill-temper?

PIGGOTT: No. I don't resent it because I want it. And the life I lead is very good to me. I don't think I am ill-tempered. I think I'm very patient. Sometimes you read that I've told people to, well, to push off, but that's never because I'm hungry; it's because I'm angry.

Now and again I'm criticized unfairly, mis-reported; people say I did something which I didn't. I put up with as much of that as most people, and sometimes I say 'No'. For instance, I rode Sir Ivor in a race in Washington DC, two years ago, and I won. But some newspapermen – only some, I mean – criticized my riding. Unfairly, and they didn't really know the facts. Well, when I rode Karabas, last year, and won, they wanted to talk to me about it. But I didn't want to talk to them. I said so, too. And they didn't like me for it. I understood that. I didn't like them the year before.

I live and work in a tough world. I can be a decent human at 8 st 4 lb, but I can't be a saint even at 9 st 7 lb.

HARRIS: You mentioned you would like to train when you give up riding. Do jockeys make good trainers? There's a general impression they don't. What kind of trainer will you make?

PIGGOTT: Well, they haven't had much chance to try. Not on the flat. I told you it used to be a job for gentlemen. Jockeys often come from the slums. Trainers often come from the big houses. And some jockeys became trainers and failed, that's true. But there was Sir Jack Jarvis, who died last year. He'd been a jockey. And he was a great trainer. Today there's Sir Gordon Richards, Harry Wragg, Doug Smith, for instance.

What kind of a trainer will I make? It's like asking if Nijinsky would stay the Derby distance: you can talk about it, but you've got to wait and see. I'll have the patience. And I'll have the temperament. Some trainers can be very temperamental. But it's a great responsibility – what with owners, stewards, public and Press all around you. I've had so many ups and downs, and criticism, and nasty remarks, that I reckon I can take what comes as a trainer.

One advantage I have is that I can ride the horses myself. That's one of the most important things a jockey can do for a trainer – ride the horse at work for him, and tell him what the horse is like, whether he's coming on (or going back in condition) – especially at the beginning of the season, when he wants to know if the horse has improved since the season before, and if so by how many pounds. You know you count a horse's ability in pounds: a horse that's improved six pounds since last time out could beat himself by two lengths compared with last time, if you see what I mean.

Well, a lot of jockeys are very good at assessing horses in work, but some are better than others, and even with the best there's nothing so good as getting up on the horse yourself, if you're a trainer.

And Susan would be there. I told you she's a trainer's daughter. She'd like it better than me going all over the place every day. Susan could train horses all right herself. She'd hold her own with some men I know.

HARRIS: Could you answer some rather detailed questions for me? Sheer curiosity on my part. When you ride in a race, who supplies the colours, the silks, I mean?

PIGGOTT: The owner pays for them. They usually supply two or three sizes. The man who actually hands them out to you is the valet. He usually looks after about a dozen jockeys at a meeting. His job is to go ahead to where you're riding and see that your tack and your kit are there. If I go abroad for the day, say to Paris, I have another set of equipment which I leave there permanently.

HARRIS: By the way, I notice that you split the leather thong of your whip so that it's really two pieces instead of one. Is that because it'll hurt more?

PIGGOTT: No. It hurts less. But it makes more noise. The whip doesn't hurt a horse, unless you hit him in a certain place – and then instead of extending his stride he'd shorten it.

It's difficult to explain the use of the whip except to people who've used it. Even a thoroughbred has got a pretty tough hide. And the whip is very rarely used as a punishment. It's used as a stimulus. If a horse looks like he's being hurt, the stewards have the jockey up.

HARRIS: You mentioned going abroad – how do you react to foreign travel?

PIGGOTT: It makes a change. Sharpens you up. Especially when you're in full training, making your lowest weight and feeling a bit hungry, travelling, catching the plane, riding on a different course is a bit of a distraction. That's where being a freelance comes in – you can go off abroad when you're offered a good ride.

HARRIS: Why do some horses race in white sheepskin nosebands, instead of the ordinary leather?

PIGGOTT: We don't use them as much as we used to. Some horses race with their heads up, and that causes them not to go as fast as they could. If you put that band of wool below his eyes he has to put his head down more to see properly over the top.

HARRIS: I always think of you as a tremendously fit and healthy man. Do you ever get ill – have a cold, for instance?

PIGGOTT: Only too often. I carry on riding and hope the damn thing will go away.

HARRIS: One last question of detail. Tell me: why is it generally accepted that big horses don't gallop down hills or round bends, aren't generally so manoeuvrable as small ones?

PIGGOTT: Because it's generally true. In the first place you can often put a small horse where there isn't room to put a big one – a gap between two other horses, or on the rails. That's obvious, isn't it? Then, because your size and strength is greater relative to the small horse, you can get a small horse to respond quickly to what you want him to do – accelerate, or slow, bear this way or that way. He's handier. But the other thing is that if a horse is bigger than average the chances are that his build isn't as equally proportioned as a small horse's is – there'll be a bit of imbalance about his size. So he might tend to get off balance coming down a hill, or if you try to move too fast on him, or going a bend.

HARRIS: Two last questions then: Horses and Men. What strikes you about them most looking back at them over the years?

PIGGOTT: There's two sides to a horse. In the natural state his speed is what keeps him alive – if there's danger, he runs. But he lives in a herd and even when he's running away from danger he doesn't like to be first: he likes to be in the middle of the herd. So in racing, in one way you're taking the horse back to his nature, and in another you're training him and riding him to be something different from what nature intended.

That's what makes all racehorses interesting to deal with. I think it's what gives them their character. Because horses *are* very interesting. There's no two alike. And of course nature taught a horse to run, but not to be ridden. So there's the relationship between the horse and the man on his back.

HARRIS: And what about human nature?

PIGGOTT: Well, people on their own are different from people in crowds. People on their own are all right, but in crowds something comes over them. They just want to be on the winner.

You ride a damn good race and get beaten a short head when you thought you'd be lucky to get within three lengths of the leader, and you may get booed. You make a mistake in the race, get shut in, or your horse does something silly, or you're unlucky, and you win by a short head when you should have won by a length and a half – and they clap. It's not your riding. It's whether they win or lose.

Well, I want to win, too. But I don't pay much attention, whether they clap, or whether they don't. I think you only pay attention if you care about what people think of you. And you only care if you think a lot about yourself. I don't think about myself much. I think about racing. I don't brood about how I look to other people. I ride as well as I can, and they can clap or boo – it's all the same to me.

HARRIS: Is that why even when you've won a big race you come in with a face like marble?

PIGGOTT: It's got something to do with it.

HARRIS: But I've noticed, very occasionally, that if you've won a really great race, like the Derby, in fine style, there is the ghost of a smile on your face as you enter the winner's enclosure. What are you thinking about then?

PIGGOTT: About Dad saying 'What about the times you didn't win?'

●

MARGARET THATCHER

Interviewed by Terry Coleman
The Guardian, 2 November 1971

Margaret Thatcher (b. 1925), the English politician, was the first woman to be prime minister of the UK. She was born in Grantham, Lincolnshire, where her father was a grocer and a local alderman. She was elected to parliament as a Conservative in 1959 and entered the cabinet in 1970 as Secretary of State for Education. She replaced Edward Heath as leader of the Conservative Party in 1975, after Heath had lost two successive elections. In the 1980s she dominated British politics and exerted considerable influence internationally as a champion of free market economies, privatization and tough defence policies. This interview gives one of the earliest glimpses of her particular brand of conviction politics.

Terry Francis Frank Coleman (b. 1931) was educated at fourteen schools and obtained a law degree at London. After cutting his journalistic teeth as a reporter on the *Poole Herald* and as a sub-editor on the *Sunday Mercury* and *Birmingham Post*, he joined *The Guardian*. From 1961 to 1970 he was a reporter, then arts correspondent, and from 1970 to 1974 he was chief feature writer. After a two-year spell with the *Daily Mail*, he returned to *The Guardian* as special correspondent, specializing in political interviews. Among many celebrities, he has interviewed seven British prime ministers: Eden, Macmillan, Douglas-Home, Wilson, Heath, Callaghan and Thatcher.

The capital and most valuable virtue of most Conservatives is their conservatism, which often shows as a conservatism of manner, a kind of moderation, an urbane self-assurance that everything will be all right if only you leave it alone. This is most attractive. It also gives some substance to the idea that Conservatives are above the fight, and that only the beastly Socialists drag politics into politics.

This moderation is an incalculable asset, but not one possessed by Mrs Margaret Thatcher, the present Conservative Secretary for Education and Science. She is an evangelist, and sets about her busily evangelizing. She will say I have got her all wrong, and so I may have. This is only one man's opinion, and I have formed it on my own and not, as she may suspect, after secret discussions with the corps of Fleet Street education correspondents, whom she dislikes. I only know our own education man, and he is in South America.

Well, I met Mrs Thatcher the other day in her room at the House of Commons and we talked for rather under an hour. Knowing that I came from *The Guardian* she must have mistaken me for some kind of radical, to be led into the True Faith. This was rather fun. We sat one at each end of a sofa, and she said: 'The object of the exercise is what?' I said I should like to write a profile, based on an interview. She said oh dear, those things always came out awfully artificial. Since I know this to be sometimes true, and since I have written my fair share of profiles which for one reason or another have missed the point, I just mumbled something placatory and asked whether her father's grocery shop at Grantham had been a great big one.

She said it was not big, just a family grocer's, where some people paid by account and others, having drawn their 10s pensions at the subpost office attached, paid in cash. They also sold tobacco, sweets, and fruit, and she got to know a good cross-section of the community. She sometimes served behind the counter in the post office.

She was a capable girl, won a bursary from grammar school to Somerville where she read chemistry, and worked as a research chemist for British

Xylonite and then for J. Lyons. I said I did not know what xylonite was or what it was for, and she said I wouldn't. Often they made a new and beautiful plastic and then sat round wondering what use there was for it. At Lyons she did pure research, which had very little to do with what a cake looked like.

Then she read for the Bar. She had always been interested in law since she used to watch her father in court when he was mayor and a magistrate. She used to have lunch with the Recorder. So she became a barrister and practised at the Revenue Bar. She also married the director of an oil company and had twins, one boy, one girl, who are now eighteen. She also became MP for Finchley in 1959. I think it is probably unfair to say she is the same age as the Queen, since you would not say of a man that he was the same age as the Duke of Edinburgh, but there it is. Since last year she has been Minister of Education, and has had lots of abuse thrown at her.

'Mm,' she says, 'an unjustified amount, I might say. However, I usually think that epithets signify more about the author than about the subject. Do they not?'

Several times in the course of the conversation she used this kind of rhetorical question, in this archaic form, with the *not* stuck at the end. Do they not? Is it not? Only barristers don't say isn't.

I suggested that any Tory Minister of Education, unless he is a Butler, is going to have to put up with a lot of criticism because so many people in education, particularly in the unions, will be out of sympathy with the Right. She replied that it has sometimes struck her that more people are interested in education for reasons of egalitarianism than for reasons of education.

But surely, in England, education had traditionally been part of the egalitarian process? Hadn't it been Disraeli who said in 1867, when the franchise was widened, that we must educate our masters?

'Of course you must,' she said. 'No one quarrels with that for one moment.' But one should educate children taking account of differences in ability, and not with the idea of producing all the same. And it was perfectly right that one should be able to choose to send one's children to independent schools.

I agree with this, and said so. I think it would be an intolerable interference with liberty to close independent schools. So there was nothing between us, but she made her point again, that it was educationally wrong to demand that 'everyone-shall-have-the-same'. She stressed each word. No one demanded this of housing. People could live in different kinds of houses.

Yes, I said, but that was another matter. Living in a big house was pleasant but the sort of house one lived in didn't affect one's whole life prospects, as education did.

'Oh,' she said, very quietly now, 'but it does. Look how wrong you are.' Living in a council house was different, was it not, from living in Bishop's Avenue. She explained that Bishop's Avenue was wealthy. You could spend your money on better houses, or on a good Savile Row suit, or on sending your children to the continent every vacation, so was it wrong to buy a different education? Mr and Mrs Thatcher sent their son to Harrow.

I was busy murmuring of course it wasn't wrong, and yes she was right, and something or other about us all agreeing on equality of opportunity. Exactly, she said. By then I was anxious to put forward an idea with which she could agree, so I said of course if you gave children equality of opportunity, then you gave them what amounted to an opportunity to prove themselves unequal.

'I wouldn't quarrel with one word of that,' she said. 'How do you think I got where I am?' Both she and Ted Heath had floated to the top. Anxious to get Mrs Thatcher in competition with her leader, I suggested she had had a better raft to float up from: hadn't his mother been a maidservant?

She said her own mother had been a dressmaker and had served in the shop. I said yes, but her father had become mayor. She asked what that mattered.

So we went on to the topic of educational journalists. She said they were there, and she had to cope with them. They didn't always give her credit where credit was due, but that, she thought, was part of journalism. They had 'put far more on to the milk thing', and not given her credit for getting a lot of extra money for primary schools. This would give more children more opportunity, and was far more important than knocking off free milk for those who did not have a medical need for it.

Well, she had introduced the topic of milk, though if she hadn't I should have. But why had she knocked off milk? She explained that she had to economize, but she was also determined to give a better education. So she looked around for economies which would do the least damage, and decided to stop free milk for the over-sevens and to put up the price of meals, which were due to go up anyway.

But could she have picked anything which would have made so small a saving at the cost of so much condemnation? Look, she said, Labour had put up the price of school meals by half, and nobody had squealed; the education correspondents hadn't given them absolute hell, oh no.

Well . . .

'WAIT a minute,' she said, and she was now advancing on me across the sofa. I waited. Labour, she said, had knocked off milk from secondary schools, and no one told them they mustn't do that because *some* children went to school without breakfast and that therefore they must supply milk free to the whole lot.

Very well, I said, but hadn't she now got herself an unworkable piece of legislation in the Education (Milk) Act? The local authorities were forbidden to give free milk to children, but some were ignoring this, and Manchester was putting in a dash of cocoa to make the drink not milk within the meaning of the Act. What was she going to do? Prosecute?

She said I would have to wait until the Act settled down. I was asking her something that was difficult, and to say something she must not say at the moment. But there was always the discretionary penny rate which councils could spend on anything they chose, though if they spent it on milk there would be less for the disabled.

Yes, but if councils just ignored her, would there be any councillors surcharged for improper spending? Look, she said, just wait and see. Surcharging was not a matter for her but for the District Auditor. When I suggested that the auditor wasn't going to have much discretion in the matter, was he, she said that I was trying to draw her into something into which she could not be drawn. As far as the ordinary public was concerned, a lot of the problem would go, except insofar as it was politically kept alive, if milk were offered for sale in schools, and it wasn't her fault that it was not. She had paid for hers as a schoolchild.

'But this one little decision,' I began . . .

'My dear,' she reasoned.

Had it really been worth all the fuss it had caused? She said it was if she got £9 millions out of it, enough to build 75 new primary schools.

Well, she had said in the Commons that she resented the suggestion that some mothers were not able to look after the nutritional needs of their children. Surely, inevitably, there were some who couldn't? She thought the vast majority could. It was wrong that, because of a small incapable minority, you should be expected to provide for the vast capable majority. 'And that,' she said, 'seems to me to be the false argument. Because if that is the case, then you're going to take children away from their mothers practically at birth and say, because a few are incapable of providing, THE STATE must provide free everything, not merely providing it but seeing that it goes down their throats.'

I thought this didn't seem to follow at all, and asked her if it wasn't a bit harsh. 'No, no,' she said. 'It isn't.'

Now, I asked, it had been said that she was necessarily a long way in her circumstances (a Minister herself and the wife of an oilman), and therefore in her understanding, from a poor woman with children. Was this fair? – 'No.'

Why not? Because, she said, she had known what it was like to have to stretch her money. She had started work when she came down from Oxford at about £8 10s a week.

Yes, but she had never in her life been poor? 'It depends what you mean by poor. It so happens we've always had access to food. Obviously, being a grocery store.'

But wasn't there *some* substance in the suggestion that she was distant from a poor mother? She evidently thought not, and I must say it seems to me she could safely have admitted to some difficulty of understanding. If you won't admit that understanding someone very different from yourself may be difficult, you aren't exactly helping yourself to achieve that understanding.

'Now,' she said, 'why do you go for me much more than you went for my predecessors? Why, why? Why are you doing it?'

I didn't think I was. I would do the same for any Labour Minister. And I hadn't the heart to tell Mrs Thatcher that at a primary school near where I live the little children have a new chant which goes:

> Mrs Thatcher,
> Mrs Thatcher,
> Milk snatcher.

I suppose it's something that they know her name. Not many Ministers of Education can have been familiar topics of conversation among eight- and nine-year-olds.

So I asked if she really thought I was going for her, and she said I was, and that I ought to ask myself why. I said she was defending herself pretty vigorously.

I asked how much longer she could let me have. She said ten minutes, that I had asked her very little about education, and that this was wrong. She had expanded education, and neither I nor anyone else would give her any credit for it.

I asked her about a Bible which had been presented to her recently, and she said she was a Christian and prayed when she had need of it. This was part of her background and upbringing and it would be very difficult to cut herself off from it. I said most people did, meaning that most people forgot their Christianity, but she took me to mean that most people cut themselves off from their origins, and remarked that this was where we all got her wrong. She said her beginnings were just as much a part of her as what she is now. She didn't think I could know what it was like to have the sort of beginnings she had.

A little later she said: 'You're getting a totally false impression of me. Because you're taking such selective subjects. I know, and it will come out wholly artificial. And this is just exactly how all the others come out. They come out devoid of flesh and blood, full of artifice, full of cynicism, full of the epithets of their writers.'

She said she was an ordinary woman, fundamentally interested in education, but that I was trying to veer my way, as so many correspondents did, towards saying this was the typical middle-class Tory woman who had never known anything else and didn't know what it was like. But she could go back to almost any standard of living, having been through most. She was living in a small house and was desperately trying to sell her other, large one. She had a second-hand Viva, four years old. She did not spend money on furs.

So, I said, she had little hope that what I wrote would be fair? 'No,' she said. We were both jolly and relaxed about this. We laughed a bit, and she said she didn't see how I could write anything fair after so short a time with her. I said well, if she had a day free ... She didn't seem to think that would work either. *Panorama* had taken three days and her opinion of their programme was not high.

I said she might be right, but wasn't she perhaps being a bit too cynical herself?

'Well, is it because I have seen what I have done being totally disregarded, and seeing the other played up?'

But not disregarded by everybody, surely?

'No, no, no,' she said. 'I can go round to an old people's meeting. What do they say? "You stick to your guns, Margaret."'

●

ARTHUR MILLER

Interviewed by Josh Greenfeld
The New York Times Magazine, 13 February 1972

Arthur Miller, the American playwright, was born in 1915 in New York City. He won the Pulitzer prize for his most famous play, *Death of a Salesman*, in 1949. Another play, *The Crucible* (1953), about the persecution of witches in seventeenth-century Salem, had contemporary resonance when first performed, coming as it did at the high-water mark of Senator Joseph McCarthy's anti-Communist witch-hunt, and it continues to resonate with other forms of political persecution. Miller himself was the victim of the McCarthyites and has remained active in opposing censorship internationally. He has always been faithful to the theatre, despite his one film script for *The Misfits*, which starred his wife, Marilyn Monroe. They divorced in 1961, a year before Monroe committed suicide. His plays are frequently revived.

Josh Greenfeld was born just outside Boston, Massachusetts, in 1928, but was brought up in Brooklyn, New York, where he first met Arthur Miller (they shared a play-writing teacher). For many years he combined the writing of plays for the theatre with freelance journalism, in particular interviews and profiles. Among the celebrities he interviewed were boxers Floyd Patterson and Sugar Ray Robinson for *The Reporter*, film director Cecil B. DeMille for the men's magazine *Saga*, and Truman Capote for *The New York Times Magazine*. Other interview subjects included Marlon Brando, Mayor John

Lindsay of New York, and Sidney Poitier. In 1972 he moved to Los Angeles and devoted his energies to writing TV movie and feature film screenplays. He co-wrote the Oscar-winning film *Harry and Tonto* (with its director Paul Mazursky). He has written three novels and also three books about his autistic son.

The voice on the phone traveled across years, tripped over geographies. The diction was cosmopolitan New York, but the accents, every bit as glottal and guttural as my own, were native Brooklyn. 'We've just postponed the production of my new play till next fall,' it was saying, 'so my schedule has lots of openings these days. Like I'll be home tomorrow and Friday. And this is the best place for us to talk – no interruptions or distractions. Can you possibly make it tomorrow?'

'Hold on,' I said. 'Let me ask my wife.' Then: 'OK Tomorrow's fine.' 'Now let me check with my wife.' After a moment it came back on the line. 'Tomorrow's OK. She has a bewildered expression, but OK. And why don't you have lunch here? It'll probably be right off the kitchen table because that's how we eat lunch around here.'

'Fine,' I replied, and hung up. In the living room, my wife asked, 'Where are you going tomorrow?'

'To Connecticut,' I said. 'To see Arthur Miller.'

'Oh,' she said, and returned to her reading.

Arthur Miller is no longer the supercelebrity seen running around with Monroe, being harassed by the House Un-American Activities Committee or misfitting around Nevada. The media long ago went on their trendy way, and Miller has become one of those rare celebrity writers who has gracefully made the transition from the limelight back to the desk lamp. His recently completed play, *The Creation of the World and Other Business*, which he subtitled 'a catastrophic comedy', is his fourth drama in the last eight years.

Such industry casts Miller, at the still-youthful age of fifty-six, in the unlikely role of a relic. He is an almost solitary survivor of that nostalgic era when the theater, not the TV talk show or new journalism, was the glamorous spot for the writer. The rest of the playwrighting stars of the forties and fifties have all but vanished into Hollywood, academia, publishing, death or some other dramatic silence.

And Miller's past is as active as his present. He will be represented in New York this season with a revival by the Lincoln Center Repertory Company of *The Crucible* (1953). His 1950 adaptation of Ibsen's *An Enemy of the People* has been the hit of the Madrid season, and *Incident at Vichy* (1964) opened in Paris last autumn. *After the Fall* (1963) and *A View From the Bridge* (1955) remain theatrical fixtures on both sides of the Iron Curtain. *The Price* (1968), his last Broadway play, and *Death of a Salesman* (1949), his most enduring one, have received major treatment as TV-network specials in recent years, and *A Memory of Two Mondays* (1955) was produced last year on NET.

Before driving out to Connecticut, I reviewed Miller's work and the facts of his life that inform his plays. Born Jewish; Urban; Middle class; Father a gruff entrepreneur. Mother more sensitive and culturally attuned. Family physically dislocated and emotionally traumatized by the Depression. As a young man in the thirties, worked in an auto-parts warehouse. Then off to college, emerging with a socialist fervor and a strong sense of moral rectitude. Joined – or fellow traveled – with leftist political groups. Later virulently – and then more compassionately – attacked former associates who informed and gave names to Congressional investigating committees. Married three times: a straight Midwestern woman, a neurotic show-business beauty and finally a refugee from the Nazi holocaust.

A few details round out the real-life Miller. A younger sister and an older brother. From his first marriage a daughter, twenty-four, married to a sculptor, living in Manhattan, and a son, twenty-six, married and making film commercials in Oregon. No grandchildren, but a young daughter, aged nine, from his third marriage, to the Austrian-born photographer Inge Morath.

But it is the ghost of Marilyn Monroe that still lingers, a hovering distraction in one's considerations – biographical and otherwise – of Miller. It is simply easier to recall that he was once a partner in an attempt at the great American dream marriage with her than to remember that he may actually have succeeded in writing the great American play, *Death of a Salesman*. So one must consciously try to keep the Monroe ghost in perspective to treat Miller with the proper respect. One must resolutely remind oneself that attention must be paid to him on his own terms for his own work.

Yet after turning off Route I-84 and heading north through cannon-ball-on-the-lawn and antique-shop country toward Miller's Roxbury farm I could not help but slow down as I recalled that a European correspondent, racing to cover a Miller-Monroe happening, was once killed in a crash on these roads.

Miller's farmhouse stands just a few feet from the road – less to plow out when it snows – but surveys acres of spectacular hills and a pond for swimming and ice skating. I parked my car and walked through an open garage containing a solitary Volkswagen onto a terrace behind the house, where a barking dog was announcing my arrival. Miller came toward me, wearing an open-collared shirt, slacks and high work shoes. Beneath his receding silver-gray hair, his face was still reminiscent of an unbearded Jewish Lincoln.

He greeted me, and as I paused to take in the view, which he seemed to see for the first time himself, he mused: 'You look at all this and you wonder why people are so screwed up.'

'Because they don't have it,' I said, and he laughed. 'How many acres do you have?'

'About 350,' he said, and then added quickly and apologetically: 'But don't forget I first began buying land up here almost two dozen years ago. I was just down the road then. I added on little by little. And then you could buy land for a song. Not like now.'

Miller's wife appeared, slender and intense in blue jeans and a polo shirt, and Miller introduced us.

'When would you like to have lunch?' she asked.

I shrugged, and Miller replied, 'Let me show him around the place first.' As he guided me down a gentle slope I asked whether he worked any of the land.

'I have a neighbor, and I let him graze his dairy stock here in exchange for the use of some of his heavier equipment when I need it. And I have a nursery where I grow some trees that I sell. And we have a garden that keeps our cold cellar full of fruits and vegetables all winter long. But let me show you what I'm doing here.'

He ushered me into the barn, which contained a studio-guest room completed years earlier and a carpentry shop with every manner of woodworking tool. Now contractors were installing a darkroom and a studio shaped like a ship's prow for Mrs Miller and an alternate studio-guest room for Miller.

'Now I'll show you where I work,' he said, and we walked past the terrace up a small knoll to a frame cabin covered with natural shakes. It was furnished with a desk and typewriter, a few chairs, a simple cot and bookshelves. Snapshots of his wife and daughter were pinned to the wall. There was no clutter on the desk; it looked almost too neat to be a writer's work area. Miller slumped into a chair behind the desk. 'See,' he said, 'I've got everything I need here and no telephone.'

How does he heat the cabin?

'I've got that,' he said, pointing to a fireplace, 'and I can use electricity. But it costs a fortune. That's why I'm thinking of moving into the barn.'

What does he use for a toilet? He pointed out the open door and laughed at the city boy's question.

We began to get reacquainted, bringing one another up to date on family blessings and mishaps. Having been a public man for so long, Miller is still guarded and wary. And, like so many theatrical people and politicians, he manages to combine extreme shyness with a bold sense of self, an almost excessive immodesty.

'You're putting on a little weight,' I remarked.

'No,' Miller replied, patting his thin-man's paunch and stretching his long legs, 'I just don't stand straight. But if I started working around here' – with a wave he took in the whole farm – 'it'd go away in a day. Which I'm going to do.'

Does he write every day?

'Every day. Sometimes seven days a week. I get up every morning about 7 o'clock, and I'm here by 8.30, and I work until – it depends on the day. Some days I can barely get up here. Some days I'm out by 10.30, 11 – just can't write much. And some days, once I get going, I can work eight hours – longer than that, around the clock. That's the beauty of this setup. I can set my own pace, go the way I want. If I get on a hot writing period there's nothing else I have to do.'

How much of his writing does he ultimately use and how much does he discard?

'Depends on the play,' Miller said, picking up his pipe and leaning forward to fill it. 'This new play I've only thrown away about seventy-five pages. The playscript ends up maybe 140 pages. So it's nothing. But normally – sometimes – given all the revision I would make I'd write maybe 2,000 pages.' He lit the pipe and exhaled. 'I always work on a typewriter, plus three or four notebooks.'

What does he use the notebooks for?

'Attempts at scenes. Organizing things. Developing them. I'll write a whole act sometimes and use only one scene, or a whole scene and use just one line. See, I'm discovering it, making up my own story. I think at the typewriter.

'But sometimes also there's another way of working: getting it all out in one burst. That's happened, too. This new one I did in about six weeks. *Salesman* was that way, too. Boom! One burst and it was done. But *After the Fall* took me over a year and still many months.'

Once a play is finished what does he do?

'I write a play for myself, so if I like it we do it.'

As simple as that?

'Yes, I go to Bob Whitehead (the producer) and say, "Let's do it." And we do it. There's an audience for my plays. They're there. They buy tickets and they come. For which I'm very grateful.'

Even without a star, is a Miller play certain to attract theater parties?

'Oh sure,' he said, and sucked on his pipe. 'More than any show apart from maybe a musical.'

What is the next step in the life of a play?

'Well, we decide on a director. Bob has his ideas, and I have my ideas, and we walk around and finally put them together and decide.'

What about serving as his own director?

'I never want to. I did it on *The Price* because I had to. We came to a disagreement with the director, and there simply wasn't time for any alternative but for me to direct. But ordinarily I don't want to direct. I'm not interested in it that much. To be a director you've got to know all the actors available, ideally speaking; you've got to be a theater person in the sense that you like to go to the theater often, which I don't. Never have.

'And you can't think of directing as a chore, but rather as a means of creation. To me, directing is all after the fact. And I hate to put myself through it. Just the sheer proposition, for example, of going through months of listening to my own lines endlessly repeated is a prospect I just hate. And if you're directing you have to be there at rehearsals all the time. Oh, I come in part of every day and whenever something has been changed. But I don't want to be a director.

'Also, even though this rarely happens, I always hope the director will think of something marvelous that I haven't thought of, in terms of staging, in terms of decor or something. And a good director does have an approach to actors, especially American actors, which I basically don't have. He knows how to communicate with them on a less-than-verbal level. Which is what they respond to best.'

Who is an ideal director for his work? What about Kazan, for example?

'Oh, Kazan's a marvelous director. He's also made his mistakes. Everybody does. But he's wonderful with actors, and he's superbly organized. I'm working with Harold Clurman now, and he has tremendous points. For one thing he's been in the theater for forty-five years, and I think he's the best critic there is. Of me and everybody else.'

Miller rose and stretched his long frame. 'Come on,' he said, 'let's eat.' He patted his stomach. 'It's my lousy posture. I never could stand up straight. But pretty soon I'll work it off.'

The Miller living room, separated from the terrace by sliding glass doors, exudes a comfortable feeling of Continental clutter. There are books and magazines piled atop a glass coffee table. End tables in a Spanish motif. Walls adorned with foreign theater posters proclaiming Miller productions. Inge Morath photographs of Russia. A mock marriage license by Saul Steinberg, the cartoonist. There are Eames chairs and an antique rocker, a modern rug, old figurines, Mexican candlesticks. Plant life is everywhere.

We lunched not in the kitchen but in a cheerful, traditional dining room. Mrs Miller unobtrusively served excellent tacos with beer, pears and Brie for dessert and good coffee. Somehow a box of Mallomars materialized at Miller's elbow, and he nibbled on them while discussing what he termed 'the crap-game aspect of playwrighting':

'Suppose you open the wrong night. When there's a big new event you're dead; it doesn't matter what kind of a play you had. If everybody has his head on Page 1, then it doesn't matter what's on Page 47.

'And nowadays, even before you open, there's the problem of casting. Used to be almost every good actor was in New York and available. But now the theater has become a fifth wheel for actors, too – something for them to consider when they're not doing a movie, or not in a television series or they're over the hill in movies, which is something I don't care about because that does not mean they're really over the hill as actors. But anyway, you make out a list of, say, thirty actors, and there're two you really care about. Well, the likelihood is you can't get those two actors for reasons that have nothing to do with the play – or anything. So you just have to wait, which is what I decided to do with my new play.'

Given the theatrical realities, then, does it pay to go on writing plays?

'Absolutely not. It doesn't make any sense. You've got to be obsessed and stupefied with the glory of the medium. Because if you look at it objectively it's absolutely senseless.'

Why does he do it?

'I love it. I just love it,' said Miller, dipping into the Mallomar box. 'I love the stage. And perforce I'm doing it for myself.'

How does he manage financially?

'Well, my plays are done all over the world. I've made my living basically for many years now on domestic and foreign amateur and semiprofessional productions. And of course I've had plays on almost every two or three years in New York. And I'm assured of productions in Paris, London, Italy, all over Germany. That's what makes it possible for me to go on.'

Is he fixed financially for the rest of his life?

'Yeah. Maybe not for the rest of my life, but for a long time. I wouldn't need too much more. I own this house and don't have to pay any rent – just the taxes and I have a roof over my head. And I could always do journalism if I had to.'

When did he last face financial pressures?

'In the middle or late fifties, I guess.'

Wasn't that the period in which critics consider him to have been essentially barren – those years with Marilyn Monroe?

'Barren?' said Miller, shaking his head. 'That's when I did *The Misfits*. And I started to do a movie for the New York City Youth Board, but they knocked me out of the box with a big red-baiting campaign. Barren? That whole period I never had an empty day.' He shook his head again.

'Anyway, that's all gone. Thank God. And I have more to do now than I have time to do it in. Besides the new play, I have another one almost finished and another one that I'm beginning to see in a form I can manage.'

Mrs Miller answered the telephone in the living room and we soon heard her speaking Russian. 'She's terrific,' her husband said. 'After we came back from Russia a few years ago she decided to learn Russian. And she did it.'

'What are your feelings,' it suddenly occurred to me to ask, 'about Women's Liberation?'

'I think a lot of it is terrific,' Miller replied. 'I think a lot of it should have been said a long time ago. But, like everything here, it gets said in hysteria. And I'm sure the media are the cause of that. You get tired of saying even a truth. It's as if there always has to be something new, so they create its perversion. I can't take seriously some of the idiocy that comes out of it. On the other hand, I'm sure if I talked to some people about it they could easily convince me to the contrary.'

I mentioned that he had not prepared lunch, though he probably could have.

'I could have,' Miller conceded, 'but Inge loves to. She wouldn't let me prepare lunch. My wife can cook in about eight languages, and I can only make chops, chicken and steak.' He resolutely pushed the Mallomar box away.

'I've tried, but it doesn't come out. I lived alone here once. I tried to cook and I had all the cookbooks and it was terrible. You have to have a certain talent.'

Inge came in, a camera bag slung over her shoulder. 'I'll be out photographing,' she told Miller, 'but I'll be back in time to take you to pick up your car. They called before to say it was ready.'

I asked what kind of car he has.

'A Mercedes 280 SEL.'

'It's a good car.'

'Yeah, but I've been having troubles with it. But one thing I'll say, they take care of it. And when it's running it gets me into the city in two hours.'

Does he get into the city often?

'Not as much as I used to. I can go a couple of weeks now without going in. And I don't miss it. I used to keep a place at the Hotel Chelsea, but I found that I was using it less and less. It was just a stop for me, and there were so many whores and pimps around, arguing all the time, I hated to bring my wife there. So I gave it up. Now when I stay over in town I stay with friends. I have enough friends with big houses and kids grown up and gone so there's room.'

Does he go to the theater at all?

'Oh, I always go to see Pinter. And I go Off-Broadway to see some of the black playwrights like Gordone and that other fellow, Bullins, who I think are close to having some real vitality. Because they're writing about something. Their work isn't simply an exercise in some fashionable kind of pique. So I'm glad they're on.'

Does he regret the absence of practicing playwrights of his own generation?

'Sure. It's always better when there are more plays that are interesting because then people assume there is something in theater, after all. But now I think there is a critical judgment – if you can call it that – that nothing good could possibly happen in the theater. And that *a priori* assumption is ridiculous. But I guess it makes it easier to be a critic under such circumstances.'

Assumptions aside, isn't the theater dead anyway?

'No,' said Miller, shaking his head emphatically. 'There's been a displacement, but not a destruction. New York City fell apart. How can you expect a theater to exist in a jungle like that? There is no community, or even a facsimile of one. There isn't even enough community to safeguard a pedestrian, so how can you expect a theater to go on there?' He leaned forward across the table.

'Look. The middle class has always supported the theater. And the middle class has fled New York City. But when you say, "Therefore the theater is dead," it isn't so. Not true. Is Macy's dead? What's happened to Macy's? They went to the suburbs. Is the wholesale and retail clothing business dead? No. They simply registered the change in population.

'So what we've been living through, really, is a transformation in the population. It comes to New York to make its money, and it gets out as fast as it can. And New York is stuck with a theater district and purely extraneous crap, such as negotiations with unions and real-estate people, that were formed in an entirely different social era.

'But that doesn't mean the form of the theater is dead. Not at all. I showed my new play to my son. He read it, and it appealed to him very deeply. But that's not the point. His reaction was interesting. "My God," he said. "What a thing, and to do it all with just words." You see, his attitude – and that of his friends – that the theater is dead simply masks the fact that they've never discovered it. They were born into TV and into a time when theater didn't amount to anything. It remains to be discovered, you know.

'And I think it's going to come back. Maybe not tomorrow or next year, but I have the feeling – not the feeling, the knowledge – that the day will come when theater again will surmount everything for the simple reason that it is an irreducible simplicity. It's a man up there facing other men. Somehow or other this always has to be possible. It takes less means than anything else we have, including painting. You don't need a machine. You don't need lenses. You don't need lights. You need a board and an actor. That's all you need; you don't need anything else. Except a certain amount of quiet, which is sometimes difficult to find.'

Miller smiled and stood up. 'Come on,' he said, 'let's go outside and get some fresh air. It's too beautiful a day to waste in here.'

We sat on the terrace, looking out at the rolling hills, and began to talk away the afternoon. I asked which contemporary novelists he liked. Miller lit his pipe and considered. 'I don't read many novels,' he said. 'I mean, I start to read a lot of novels, but I never finish them. I read Bellow's last book, *Mr Sammler's Planet*, but I like everything he writes. He still has a joy in writing, which is the first thing necessary. I love Roth's work, too, for that same reason. He seems to have fun doing it.'

Some critics, I pointed out, see a growing Jewishness or a more explicit Jewishness in Miller's work.

'I don't think that's so,' he said, shaking his head. 'I'm not aware of it. That novel I wrote in '45, *Focus*, is about a Jew and anti-Semitism and so forth. So if I've had a preoccupation it goes way back. And I suppose my new play is Jewish in the sense that it is the Old Testament. But I don't see Jewishness really as something emerging.'

What does he see emerging in his work?

'I can't see or predict the future. But I think my plays are getting more and more mythological; the people are becoming less and less psychological. Like, in the new play they're actually mythological. I mean, there's God and Lucifer and Adam and Eve and Cain and Abel. And perhaps it isn't as obvious to others as it is to me that the characters in all my other plays are also mythological. In *Incident at Vichy*, for example, I was not attempting to delineate psychological types. In fact, I did everything to strip the characters of any such thing. The characters were functions of the society, and I wasn't interested in whether they had any itches or not.'

Was he saying that he was becoming less naturalistic and more symbolic?

'Yes,' Miller answered, puffing on his pipe. 'I think ultimately, if you live long enough, that's the way it ends up anyway. I think you see patterns finally. Earlier on in life the individual overwhelms your vision. But then when you see three, five, thirty variations of the individual there seems to be an archetype lurking in the background. Consciously, though, I'm still trying and I've always tried to put people up there on the stage. And it's quite obvious they're all projections of me, same as with any other writer. But I don't think I can write until I see some mythos. I don't think I could ever generate the energy to do a whole play just to tell a story about some psychologically interesting folks. I mean, the most psychological of my characters was probably Willy Loman. And I've become aware now that I was dealing with something much more there than Willy Loman, the tactile quality of the experience of that one particular character.'

I commented on the irony that Miller is best known for realism while he sees abstraction as the thread that runs through his work.

'Yes,' he said, 'but you see, before *All My Sons* I had written thirteen plays, none of which is realistic and none of which got me anywhere. So I decided at the age of twenty-nine that I wasn't going to waste my life in this thing. I already had one child, and I couldn't see myself going on writing play after play and getting absolutely nowhere. I sat down and decided to write a play about which nobody could say to me, as they had with all the other plays, "What does this mean?" or "I don't understand that" or some such thing. And I spent two years writing that play, just to see if I could do it that way. Because I was working in a realistic theater, which didn't know anything else. But that doesn't mean I was ever at bottom simply a realistic playwright.'

What would he have done if *All My Sons* hadn't been successful?

'I don't know.' He took the pipe out of his mouth and stared at it. 'I probably would have gone on anyway. But maybe not, because I'm capable of doing a lot of things.'

Such as?

'Work of various kinds, like to be a carpenter. A good carpenter today makes more than 95 per cent of the members of the Authors Guild and gets a month's vacation, too – don't forget that. Eight dollars an hour – that's $64 a day. That's what they get here. God knows what they get down in the city.'

Would he have considered being a novelist?

'Somehow, a book has always been sort of remote to me. It doesn't offer the same kick that comes from the direct experience of a confrontation with an audience. And when it comes to writing I think my talent has always been fundamentally and essentially for the drama. I've never been comfortable writing in any other way. You see, I know I can do in three pages of dialogue what would take me endless pages of words. I know I can do what would be like a 2,000-page novel in less than two-and-a-half hours on a stage.

'There's also a dramatic structure which I find endlessly fascinating. I love to vary and reform it. And I love acting when I write. I mean, I'm the whole cast, I play all the parts. And that's not in a book. And I love real actors, too. I love to sit there and change one line and see an explosion happen that wouldn't have happened if the line hadn't been changed.

'So maybe I never could have gotten out of this playwriting thing anyway. Perhaps it's always been just too embedded in my head. I mean, I had opportunities to go to Hollywood way back before *All My Sons* was produced. You've got to remember in those days Hollywood was making a picture every Monday morning, there were hundreds of pictures made every year. It was a going, glamorous, prestigious place with all kinds of high-paying jobs for writers compared to Broadway, which even in those times was regarded as dying and on its way out.' Miller chuckled.

'You didn't even have to have written a play in those days. You just had to call yourself a playwright. And there was this Colonel Joy – that was his name, Colonel Joy – who came from 20th-Century Fox, and he'd carry playwrights out to the Coast in boxcars. Once everybody I knew, with practically no exceptions, vanished from the haunts of New York City overnight. I don't want to mention any names. But I know two guys I really thought were talented playwrights, and they never wrote anything else again. And I knew one fellow who had a remarkable play almost finished. He never got to finish it. In fact, whenever I would get out there in later years I would see him. And one day he said a frightful thing to me, quite seriously: "What's your next assignment?" I said, "I'm writing a play now." He said, "For whom?" I said, "Well, I'm just writing a play, and then I'll see for whom." "Oh," he said, "you mean you're doing it on spec."

'That's the story. He'd been living out there a long time. And I think after a certain length of time out there one loses one's independence, the feeling that one somehow has the right to invest one's time and life and talent the way one wants to.'

I suggested that we turn to politics briefly, and Miller snapped: 'I hate politics.'

'OK,' I said, 'then we'll talk about your Puritanism.' Miller raised his eyebrows and pursed his lips. 'Clurman says that in your younger days you were much more Puritan, much more sure of yourself, than you are now. Do you feel there's any validity in that?'

'I was a Puritan and unsure of myself,' Miller laughed. 'What Puritan is ever sure of himself ?'

'Do you feel more sure of yourself now?'

'Well, I know certain things that I feel more confidence about. As I've said it's purely an awareness of repetition. I know I can more or less rely on patterns, and to that degree I have more certainty than I did. But "Puritanism" doesn't quite relate to what's happened to me and my work. I'd say, rather, that early on the emphasis was on writing as legislating, as though the world were to be ordered by the implications in my work. Later, in emphasis, "what is" overtook "what ought to be".'

Which, I said, brought us back to politics.

'Look,' replied Miller, leaning forward and putting his pipe on an end table, 'when I said, "I hate politics" that doesn't mean I turn my back on politics. You can't; politics is something like tying your shoes or making a living. And, God help us, I know our fate is political. Yet I also think politics now is becoming less and less connected to what's really going on. It's never been so true as it is now that it hardly matters which party is in.'

Doesn't it matter that the Democrats lost and the Republicans won in 1968?

'Nixon's irritating,' Miller replied, 'but, don't you see, in a way that's good. Because he strips it bare. You're under no misapprehension as to what's going on. You don't get the illusion a very nice man is making a mistake and wish he only knew better.'

Who is Miller, a McCarthy delegate at the '68 Democratic convention, going to support in '72?

'There isn't a candidate except McGovern who I think makes any difference. And McGovern I don't think has a prayer – just because he makes a difference. You see, what's happening – and it's been happening for thirty years – is that we've become a corporate state. It has become the function of the state to make it possible for immense corporations to carry on their activities, and everything else is incidental. There are always conflicts between the corporations and between the Government and the corporations, but fundamentally what we have is a socialism of the individual corporations of a corporate socialism.'

Then are the militants the only ones presenting alternatives?

'No,' said Miller with a shudder, 'because they haven't arrived at any libertarian alternatives. The only alternative they've presented, if you dig beneath the rhetoric and verbiage, is really another kind of authoritarian socialism. I mean, even the rhetoric is intolerant and authoritarian and tyrannical. The real argument with this system is that it prevents a man from flowering freely. So why the hell should I get excited about a rhetoric that wants to supplant an oppressive ideology with a suppressive one? It doesn't make any sense. This is not 1932, when there were still possibilities of having illusions about the Soviet Union. I mean, then a man could say – as I did, and as I believed, and I'm not ashamed I did because then you had to if you had any brains in your head – that rationally the Socialist idea in the Soviet Union made much more sense than anything that was happening here; people were on breadlines and guys with degrees were lucky if they could get jobs selling ties at Macy's or delivering the mail. Really, it was tough stuff.'

What is his political stance now?

'Well,' said Miller, tapping his pipe against his hand, 'everybody's got some kind of a disembodied or confused anger, but I think somebody – and I know this sounds corny – has got to take the part of liberty and freedom. For example, when I became president of International PEN in 1965 I was amazed to discover the number of writers in jail in the free world as well as the Socialist bloc. Whenever I would start talking about this people would say, "You've got to have writers in jail, that goes with the territory," or "You can't have a revolution without scrambling the eggs." But I think the human being has got to be the center of any ideologies going at the moment. I mean, people aren't thinking that way any more. They're all power dealers, redistributing powers, so it always winds up the same thing all over again.'

Miller paused and let out a long sigh. 'Maybe that's the fate,' he said. 'Maybe we're doomed. But my particular job as I see it is not to let myself get into that whole bit.'

Hasn't he done that in the past?

'Oh sure. I believed the same thing years ago – that if you're going to have revolution in a country you've got to put the whole middle class in jail. It seemed very logical, intellectually sound. But that was before I started meeting some of the people who were in jails and some of the people who were putting them in jails.'

How does he find his children politically?

'I think they're disengaged now. And how can you blame them? Under what banner are they going to get excited? I think one good thing about that generation is that they've been in and out of it quickly, and they didn't get burned up too badly. After all, they were disappointed in a Eugene McCarthy, say, but that's just a pimple on the nose. They weren't made to pay the price the way my generation did. Many of us were slaughtered as a result of this, both intellectually and worse – our hearts were torn out. Because it was a slower process. You had to go through the war in Spain, the Second World War, the Nazi time, the reconstruction of Europe and the rest of it. It was a question of twenty years; the disillusionment now is a question of twenty months.'

Inge returned and warned Miller that he would have to be leaving soon. I said I had only one or two more questions to ask. The first was what he thinks his literary reputation is now.

'I have no idea,' he replied.

Some people think his work has gone steadily downhill since *Salesman*.

'I don't see it that way. I've had the problem of coming out of Broadway, which was our only professional theater. And some critics could never accept the proposition that the product of a commercial establishment could have anything to do with art. It was simply not permissible. This was before a review was ever written. If there was any public attraction to your work that was conclusive proof it couldn't possibly have any worth.

'Now,' he laughed, 'a Mary McCarthy can get ruined by *The Group*. So, you see, this irony proceeds remorselessly to the bitter end. Consequently, you have to end up smiling at the whole thing. It's just a game, an illusion in a little room.'

What about his reputation in the future?

'That's impossible to answer. I mean, when I was first coming up O'Neill was considered like old-fashioned jive talk – "Twenty-three skidoo." And look at him now. Or the other way around – take Hemingway. Given the real impact that man had on letters fifteen, twenty years ago, it would have been hard to believe that nothing but a sneer would now greet the mention of his name.'

Miller looked off at the hills for a moment. 'Therefore,' he concluded, 'you can't hang any value on a current estimate. You can only pick up a thing and relate yourself to it and say, "I believe in this. It meets some quality of reality that I recognize. It moves me this way. It moves me that way." And to hell with everything else.'

He rose, we said our goodby[e]s and he loped off toward the Volkswagen that would take him to retrieve his Mercedes.

●

BETTE DAVIS

Interviewed by Rex Reed
New York Daily News, 12 October 1975

Bette Davis (1908–89), the American actress, was born in Massachusetts and attended the John Murray Anderson school. After doing repertory and summer stock, she was screen-tested and signed by Warner Brothers, making her first film in 1931. Over the next decade-and-a-half she was a major box-office draw and during the course of a long career she received ten Academy Award nominations, winning Oscars for *Dangerous* (1935) and *Jezebel* (1938).

Rex Reed was born in Texas in 1938 and educated at Louisiana State University. After graduating, he worked as a film critic for *Holiday* magazine and *Woman's Wear Daily*, and as a music critic for *Stereo Review*. He later became a syndicated columnist for the *Chicago Tribune-New York Daily News Syndicate*, and a film critic for the *New York Daily News* and *Vogue*. His interviews have appeared in *The New York Times, Esquire, Gentleman's Quarterly*, and *Ladies' Home Journal*, and have been collected in several books.

Davis was annoyed that Reed had included her remark about the Burtons avoiding paying taxes by becoming Swiss residents (she thought Elizabeth Taylor might be offended). Ava Gardner, the subject of Reed's most frequently republished interview, hated the way she appeared in print, though she did not dispute the accuracy of the piece. She would not allow Reed to take notes, so he had to keep going to the bathroom to scribble down her best lines and the rest he reproduced from memory. Following Reed's interview with Governor Lester Maddox of Georgia, Maddox never gave another interview while in public office, so damaging did he reckon the result. Among many other interviews, Reed's 1971 encounter with Tennessee Williams (too long for inclusion in this anthology) stands as a classic of the genre.

San Francisco – They come and go in their sarongs and skates and sapphire sunglasses, but there is only one queen of the silver screen. She always was, still is, and always will be. She clawed her way to the top, and the nails are still sharp. 'I was never, repeat *never*, a movie star on a level with Joan Crawford,' seethes Bette Davis. 'I was more like Katharine Hepburn and others who came from the theater because we could act.'

Nostrils flare, eyes dilate like targets on a rifle range, and each word and gesture is emphasized by a blast of cigarette smoke that makes her look like she's walking in a cumulus cloud. It is 4 p.m. on a cool, sunny afternoon in San Francisco, and Bette Davis has a day off from shooting her eighty-fifth film, *Burnt Offerings*. It's one of those Gothic horrors about a family being driven to insanity and death by a spooky old house. Karen Black and Oliver Reed are the young couple, and Bette is the aunt. It is being directed entirely on location by a newcomer from TV, Dan Curtis.

The legendary Mother Goddam who brought Warner Brothers to both its zenith and its knees paces the living room of her Victorian hotel suite like a caged jaguar.

'I feel like I've spent the past six weeks in jail. I brought my own coffee pot and my own picture frames from Connecticut to remind me of home, but I can't *wait* to get out of here! I love San Francisco because all the theater scenes in *All About Eve* were shot here, and it has always brought me luck. It's the great city of the future, even if it is right in the middle of a fault and they're expecting another earthquake any minute.

'But I hate locations. You work six days a week from 6 a.m. till 6 p.m., and it costs a fortune in food, hotel rooms, and transportation bills. The conditions are horrible, the money is tight and everything is total chaos. This film has been amateur night in Dixie. I said I'd never make another horror film after *Baby Jane*, and here I am in the biggest horror of them *all*!

'They've got a new way of making movies today, and it *stinks*! I've been in this business for forty-five years, and in all that time they haven't learned a goddam thing. They still make all the same mistakes – it's waste, waste, waste. This is a penny-wise, pound-foolish industry. My curse is that I've always been a perfectionist, and that doesn't exist anymore.

'The director's daughter on this film committed suicide and we had to shut down a week. Then the cameraman was fired because we couldn't see one thing on the screen, the rushes were so dark. That cost us two weeks of retakes. Karen Black showed up six months pregnant, so they had to remake her clothes because they didn't fit. She changes her makeup in the middle of a scene so nothing matches on the screen, she sleeps all day, never goes to rushes to see what she looks like, and you can't hear one bloody thing she says on the set. When I made movies, you could hear me in a tunnel! Oliver Reed comes piling into the hotel at 5 a.m., and he's on the set at six with the hangover of the world. He fell down a mountainside the other night playing bagpipes!

'He lives right across the hall. I called up the hotel manager and had six locks installed on my door. I never had a drink on a set in my life, and I never will – I'd drop dead before I did that to a company with money this tight.

'I just spent the last two days writhing and dying and looking like the wrath of God, and I planned the hair, the aging, the lines under the eyes, the falls on the floor – I spent weeks working out the movements for my death scene. They all think I'm crazy to work so hard. At six o'clock last night after dying all day I was so exhausted I couldn't move, and my makeup man wasn't even there to take my makeup off. He was out in the front yard playing cricket! I tell you, my kind of professionalism is *dead*!'

She pours coffee, she raises a window, she brushes off her hand, she lowers the window, she drops cigarette ashes all over her starched white denim hostess gown, she adjusts the solitaire game on the card table, she takes the phone off the receiver, she spots a bald man down by the swimming pool who looks like her third husband and lets out a roar, she slashes lipstick across her mouth like iodine, she empties ten ashtrays overflowing with butts – she is like a locomotive, puffing and smoldering through the room. It is clear to see why the small black-and-white movie screen was too small to hold her energy. She overpowers the room the way she spilled out from the edges of the screen. She is bigger than life.

'I argue with audiences on this point,' she snarls. 'The greatest thrill for me today is not movies, but traveling around the world with my one-woman evening of film clips and conversation. At the end, I invite questions from the audience, and somebody always says, "You were better than the movies you made," and somebody else says, "The thing I remember most is that you smoked in every movie – long after the film is forgotten, we still remember you smoking," and I say, "You forget about all the heroines I played. I did not smoke in every movie. I played schoolteachers and housewives, too."

'But something I have had to face is they did not want to see me as a middle-aged schoolteacher. Their image of me was a *bitch*! So if I played bitches, or certain types of women who were nervous or angry or full of energy, I worked with cigarettes as props. If you're a woman who smokes, you can't just smoke one in the first scene and never be seen smoking again in the whole movie! You've gotta *stream* it out of your mouth and blow it all over the *screen*!'

One doesn't exactly interview Bette Davis. One just sits back, coughs while the smoke screen builds into a tornado and lets her do all the talking. She's been through all the wars, carried all the flags, and earned the right to say anything she bloody well pleases. She is strong and tough; she is coy and flirtatious; she is crisp as lettuce and warm as cocoa. She is a million things to a million people, but she is not now and never has been a phony or a bore.

'I'm like a cat,' she grins. 'Throw me up in the air, and I'll always land on my feet. I spent my whole goddam life saying, "Why should I apologize for being bright?" and I'm not stopping now. Bogart and I walked out of Warner Brothers sixteen times, but we survived. When horror movies came in, I did them instead of staying home like the other broads. When talk shows came in, I hated them, but I did them. When Warner Brothers sold its first batch of movies to TV twenty something years ago, sixty-five of them were *mine*, and I didn't get one penny in residuals. But I can't beef because millions of people today have seen those movies and I kept my whole career alive.

'I started in 1930 and made eighty-five movies, and now I've had it. I have no drive anymore. I'll never be poor, but I'll never be rich, either. Still, I wouldn't go to Switzerland and rob this country blind like the Burtons did. I couldn't sleep for the guilt. If we'd had the same lobby the gun-control lobby has, we'd be running the country, but actors are the most lily-hearted people who ever drew breath.

'So I am up to my ears in taxes and debts, and that's why I come out of my house in Connecticut every few years and work. I can hole up just so long, then I gotta get out and stir things up again. It's half for income, and half for *me*.'

Last year, she shattered her fans by closing in Philadelphia in a musical version of her film hit *The Corn Is Green*. The musical, which was bound for Broadway with millions of advance tickets already sold in anticipation of her return to the stage, was called *Miss Moffitt*. She becomes enraged when she talks about it.

'It was a mistake. The audiences stood up cheering and screaming every night, but I knew it wasn't what they wanted. They wanted me to be a bitch, not a middle-aged schoolteacher. The songs were wonderful, I sang them and I was good at it, but it was nothing but hell. I had to carry the burden of the rewrites, and I spent three weeks in a hospital in traction from the nerves and tension. The monkey on your back when you're carrying a show is wicked.

'Joshua Logan finished me off in two weeks. He was terrified of the critics and started changing things on opening night in Philly. I had one year on the road to do those changes, but I couldn't work twelve hours a day and play a different show at night. They wanted me to learn forty pages in four days! I had to get my health back before I could concentrate on that kind of work. So we closed it down. I will never go near the stage again as long as I live!'

Now she's concentrating on her one-woman show, which has toured America and is now heading for four weeks of sold-out one-nighters in England, Wales, Scotland, Ireland, and the London Palladium. 'When I started, I was scared, but now I love it. Nobody will ever know what that love and applause mean to me. Move on, never get repetitious, learn how to handle the audience – those are the things I believe in. I always walk out and say "What a dump!" and that brings down the house. Then they know it's not going to be a pompous evening; it's going to be a ball!

'They've asked me everything. One woman asked me which of my four husbands was my favorite, and I said without blinking an eye, "Obviously I had no favorite since I dumped them all!" The worst question was: "What would you do if President Nixon came to your house for dinner?" I thought for a second and said, "I'd do just like Baby Jane, and serve him a dead *rat!*"'

It's sad to see a woman with history for a middle name reduced to making movies with wall-eyed Karen Black, but on the day of her big death scene forty journalists showed up on the set. Bette roared at the publicity girl: 'I won't see them. Tell them to interview Karen Black. She's the star!' Not one journalist wanted to interview anyone but Bette Davis.

'I rest my case,' she sighs. 'I'm the nicest goddam dame who ever lived, but they made me the monster of the earth. They tried to blackmail me, they tried to run me out of Hollywood, they tried to ruin me, but I outfoxed them all. I made money and earned respect from the public and that's what makes a star. These kids today haven't got a chance.

'When I made *Dark Victory*, Jack Warner said, "Who wants to see some dame go blind and die?" But they let me do it because I wanted it so much. They paid for three sound stages with that one. Now actors have become inconsequential. Directors are the stars, and that to me is sad. There are no roles, no stars, and no excitement left on the screen.'

The last of a dying breed, she's already got her funeral plot bought and paid for at Forest Lawn. 'It's the final irony,' she shrieks. 'From where I'll be buried, you can look right down and *spit* on Warner Brothers!' Don't hold your breath. She's sixty-seven, but I'm taking bets. Bette Davis will bury us all.

•

JIMMY HOFFA
Interviewed by Jerry Stanecki
Playboy, December 1975

Jimmy Hoffa (1913–75) was born James Riddle in Indiana. He was a grocery warehouseman when he joined the Teamsters' Union in 1931. He worked his way up to the top of the organization and was elected president in 1957. That year the Teamsters were thrown out of the American Federation of Labour and Congress of Industrial Organizations for refusing to subscribe to its code of ethics. Hoffa was investigated by attorney-general Robert F. Kennedy and eventually imprisoned in 1967 for attempting to bribe a federal court jury. President Nixon commuted his sentence in 1971 and he was paroled in return for agreeing to resign from leadership of the Teamsters. This interview, Hoffa's last, was conducted by Jerry Stanecki, an investigative reporter with Detroit's WXYZ radio station. It is particularly memorable because of Hoffa's apparent obsession with the subject of death – he disappeared on 30 July 1975, five weeks after the final interview session, and ever since it has been believed that he was kidnapped and murdered. The timing of publication and the curious nature of Hoffa's remarks meant that *Playboy* had a tremendous scoop on their hands – indeed, the edition set a record at that time for the most copies ever sold. *Playboy*'s editor, G. Barry Golson, suggested Elvis Presley as Stanecki's next interview subject for the magazine. Arrangements for this were being made when Presley died and Stanecki was relieved that he had not obtained the interview, otherwise future subjects might have thought of him as a jinx.

From 1969 to 1973 Stanecki worked as an investigative reporter in Oklahoma City. His work there led to the indictment and conviction on bribery and kickback charges of Governor David Hall. In 1973 he joined ABC News in Detroit, working as a radio and TV reporter, later joining the local CBS television station. He has won four Emmys, the United Press award for outstanding individual reporter (three years in a row), and the Associated Press best individual reporter award for his coverage of the disappearance of Jimmy Hoffa.

The bumper sticker read: WHERE'S JIMMY HOFFA? CALL 313-962-7297. It was on an old flatbed truck on the John C. Lodge Freeway in Detroit. Thousands of similar bumper stickers on cars and trucks across the country asked the question: what happened to the 'little guy' who wheeled and dealed with money, words and clubs from the streets of Detroit to the huge white monument of a building known as Teamster International Headquarters in Washington?

Hoffa has been missing since 30 July 1975. His family last saw him when he reportedly left his home to attend a meeting with alleged mobster Anthony 'Tony Jack' Giacalone, former Teamster vice-president Anthony 'Tony Pro' Provenzano – a New Jersey man with alleged Mafia ties – and Leonard Schultz, a labor consultant and reputedly a key associate of Giacalone's. Supposedly, the meeting was arranged to mend fences after Hoffa and Tony Pro had a falling out while both were serving time at the Federal penitentiary in Lewisburg, Pennsylvania.

At 2.30 p.m., Jimmy called his wife, Josephine, and asked, 'Has Tony Giacolone called?'

At 3.30 p.m., Hoffa called longtime friend Louis Linteau, who runs an airline-limousine service in Pontiac: 'Tony Jack didn't show, goddamn it. I'm coming out there.'

Two witnesses placed Hoffa in front of the Machus Red Fox restaurant in Bloomfield Township, Michigan, around the time of the call to Linteau.

Hoffa has not been heard from since.

Interviewer Jerry Stanecki, an investigative journalist for WXYZ Radio in Detroit, reports:

'I first met Jimmy about two years ago. His wife and son had been tossed out of their Teamster jobs – Jimmy, Jr, a lawyer, as counsel, Jo as head of the women's political-action group. Newspapers were filled with speculation about a deepening Hoffa–Fitzsimmons rift. Most of the reports suggested that Hoffa himself had planted the speculation in the press. It was only after I called the manager of the condominium Jimmy owns in Florida and asked her to knock on his door with a request that he call me that I learned Hoffa hadn't talked with any reporters. "I said no such a goddamn thing," he told me.

'Apparently, he was impressed with the idea that I had gone to the trouble of finding him and getting his side of the story. From then on, Jimmy was available to me. He checked me out to see if I could be trusted, of course. And apparently I *could* be trusted. Often during the past two years I have gotten calls from Teamster officials, saying, "Jimmy says you're OK. Here's what's going on."

'I saw him many times and talked with him on the phone literally hundreds of times. Hoffa, a man who hated the press, seemed to consider me a friend.

'Jimmy lived in a modest lake-front home in Lake Orion, about forty miles from Detroit. It sits on four acres of land that is neatly trimmed and decorated with statues of deer. He installed a teeter-totter and a merry-go-round for his grandchildren, to whom he was obviously devoted.

'When I arrived at his home to begin the "Playboy Interview", Hoffa was dressed in work pants, blue shirt and chukka boots. He was feeling good. It was a warm, sunny May day. We walked first to the lake in front of his house, where he had been raking leaves and sticks from the swimming area. Back at the house, he offered me some coffee and we walked to his new kitchen. There we sat down and began to talk.'

*

PLAYBOY: You're sixty-two this year. Have you mellowed any?

HOFFA: Oh, I wouldn't say mellowed. I'd just say I got more common sense now than I had before. I used to take anybody on. Now I select who I take on.

PLAYBOY: How wealthy are you?

HOFFA: I think I'll be able to eat and live comfortable for the rest of my life. But so far as what I have . . . let it speak for itself. It's been in the press.

PLAYBOY: Are you a millionaire?

HOFFA: I would say.

PLAYBOY: We heard that you and Jimmy, Jr, got into a discussion on money and you commented, 'How many men can come up with two million cash immediately?'

HOFFA: I would say, exactly right. I'll put it to you this way: I just read an article the other day where they estimate that there's less than one half of one per cent of people who can lay their hands on $50,000 liquid cash overnight.

PLAYBOY: So you're comfortable. What else are you living for?

HOFFA: For the sake of living. I enjoy every minute of it, good, bad or indifferent. I enjoy life every day – and I'm looking forward to spending that life as part of the labor movement.

PLAYBOY: OK, let's get into that. By the terms of your release from prison, you've been banned from participating in the labor movement until 1980, and you're appealing that in the courts. If the courts ruled in your favor and you got your position back as president of the Teamsters, what would be your first priority?

HOFFA: Restructure the union back the way it was when I was there and reinstitute the trade divisions. Likewise, I'd reinstitute some additional organizers for the purpose of having master contracts. There's no other way unions can survive, except with master contracts – whether it's the building trades, retail clerks, meatcutters or anybody else. We need a common expiration date for the contracts of *all* unions.

PLAYBOY: That would virtually give you the power to bring the entire economy to a halt.

HOFFA: Well, corporations have it. The oil cartel, the lumber cartel, the steel cartel – they're all exactly the same.

PLAYBOY: But they're not united, the way you want the unions to be.

HOFFA: Of course they're united. There isn't a damned thing that happens in one of those industries that doesn't conform to what industry leaders decide together. The only thing they don't discuss collectively – at least openly – is prices. But as far as everything else goes, you'll find they have a master organization, a master contract. Put it to you this way: so far as power is concerned, does anybody believe the premiums of insurance companies are almost all uniform by accident? Is it an accident that if the price of gasoline goes up in one company, all the other prices go up the same rate in a matter of weeks?

PLAYBOY: Still, giving one man control over union contracts with a common expiration date isn't something the Congress would look upon very favorably.

HOFFA: The Congress of the United States wants to be judge, jury and prosecutor over what's good for the American people. And they think anyone who has a bloc of votes is dangerous. Truth is, everything the Congress has touched has been a failure. Can't show me one progressive thing they've did that didn't turn out a failure.

PLAYBOY: Have the Teamsters gone to hell since you were forced out?

HOFFA: Well, they haven't advanced. There are no master contracts, other than the ones I left them. The organizing campaigns and the joint councils of the local unions have deteriorated. And the morale of the local officers, the organizers, is at an all-time low, from what I hear. Even the members feel uncomfortable they don't have someone steerin' the ship. The leaders are too busy on the golf course, flyin' around in seven jet airplanes they own. Why the hell do they own *seven*? Most corporations don't own that many.

PLAYBOY: Do you blame the present head of the Teamsters, Frank Fitzsimmons?

HOFFA: Fitzsimmons has failed. He has failed in every promise he made to the union convention. He can't show one single thing that he said he would do that he did. Can't show one thing. Not one.

PLAYBOY: How did you and Fitzsimmons split?

HOFFA: Well, as far as I'm concerned, when I found out that Fitzsimmons, uh, lied when he said he'd been talking confidentially to John Mitchell about getting me out of prison.

PLAYBOY: Let's backtrack a bit. At first you thought Fitzsimmons was doing everything he could to get you out of prison?

HOFFA: During the whole time I was in prison, Fitzsimmons kept tellin' everybody – my son, my lawyers, all the union representatives – 'Now, don't do anything, you'll rock the boat. I'm taking care of it with Mitchell.' Well, when Mitchell later gave his deposition, he said the first time Fitzsimmons ever talked to him about me was in June 1971. I'd been in jail five years. It was when I'd already resigned and given Fitzsimmons the green light to become president. Then I found out that he'd fired Edward Bennett Williams as Teamsters' counsel and replaced him with Charles Colson. And when I found out there was a restriction on my parole until 1980, it didn't take a ton of bricks to fall on me to put two and two together – that he'd been lyin' all along.

PLAYBOY: You said Fitzsimmons kept saying he was going to work on Mitchell. Meaning what?

HOFFA: He claimed to all and any that he was responsible for getting me a rehearing on my parole and that Mitchell was going to take executive action to get me out of prison. As I said, when Mitchell gave his deposition later on, he said, 'I talked to Fitzsimmons about Hoffa, among other things, in June 1971.' Well, what a flat lie Fitzsimmons had been tellin' everyone in the union – for a period of almost five years!

PLAYBOY: How was Fitzsimmons going to persuade Mitchell?

HOFFA: I suppose by using his alleged influence with Nixon and by using his, uh, political arm to support the Republican Party.

PLAYBOY: With campaign contributions?

HOFFA: I don't know about that. I suppose he said he'd give him $14,000 [a publicly disclosed campaign contribution], which is a lot of nonsense. But the truth of the matter is he never did anything. I also found out from Dean that he didn't even *know* Fitzsimmons and he was sitting right outside Nixon's door.

PLAYBOY: John Dean?

HOFFA: Yeah. And it'd be damned funny that anyone could go in and out of the White House without knowing John Dean. In any case, what Colson did was wait until the President was coming in or out of his office, then introduce him: 'Mr President, this is Frank Fitzsimmons.' 'Hello, how are ya?' Then Colson would take him up to have dinner in the Senate Building.

Well, that's a hell of a big deal. Anybody must be out of their mind if they're head of the Teamsters Union and can be brushed off that way. In any case, John Dean testified that he and Colson had discussed the 1980 restriction and what with Colson already having the offer from the Teamsters to become general counsel, it all adds up to ... it *leads* me to believe that Fitzsimmons deliberately double-crossed, uh, the membership, the convention, my lawyers and myself. And that's it. So I don't wanna do business with a double-crosser ... or a liar.

PLAYBOY: If Fitzsimmons, Colson and Dean were working against you, how *did* you finally get a parole?

HOFFA: It came about because over 1,500,000 signatures were sent to the President of the United States. It came about by hundreds of thousands of letters going to the Attorney General and the President. Since Nixon was facing an election, in my opinion he didn't want to have to face all those people. So he met with Mitchell, according to Mitchell's affidavit, and they discussed the release of one James R. Hoffa. And it was agreed I would be released before Christmas 1971.

Immediately after that, when the recommendation was sent out, Dean intercepted it. Dean testified, or implied, that he and Mitchell talked about inserting the 1980 restriction into the recommendation at that time. Mitchell denies this.

PLAYBOY: So the original recommendation made by Mitchell and President Nixon did not have the 1980 restriction.

HOFFA: It did not. Furthermore, Dean called in Colson and [Presidential aide] Clark Mollenhoff and they decided on the restriction without talking to the Attorney General or the President and rewrote the recommendation, keeping it confidential even from everyone else at the White House – until fourteen minutes after I was out of jail. They were convinced that if I knew the 1980 restriction was there, I wouldn't have accepted.

PLAYBOY: But the President *did* sign the order, didn't he?

HOFFA: Aw, sure. Along with 212 other ones. But I'm sure the President didn't think Mitchell had changed what they'd agreed upon. And I'm sure he didn't read through 212 commutations and pardons.

PLAYBOY: How about you? You read it, didn't you?

HOFFA: I *couldn't* read it! I wasn't there. Wasn't anything I signed.

PLAYBOY: And your attorneys?

HOFFA: *Nobody* knew! Fourteen minutes after I'd gotten out of jail, they announced the restriction to the warden, to my attorneys, to the public. I found out about it hours later on the news. When I went to see the head of the parole board after the holidays, *he* didn't know about it. Nobody had informed him. He had to call Washington to find out what they were talking about and it wasn't until 14 January 1972 that I received notification of the restriction in the mail. And I refused to sign it.

PLAYBOY: There was no hint, no suggestion before you left prison?

HOFFA: I had asked the warden specifically, was there any restriction other than the one banning me from union activity until March 1973 [when Hoffa would have been released anyway]? He called Washington and said, 'No.'

PLAYBOY: But you signed *something* to get out of Lewisburg, didn't you?

HOFFA: Commutation. Read every word of it. Being suspicious-minded as I am concerning public people. I asked the warden to call Washington and find out if that's all there was. He came back and said that was all there was to it.

PLAYBOY: And you blame whom?

HOFFA: In my opinion, Dean, Mollenhoff, Colson and Fitzsimmons.

PLAYBOY: So there was a conspiracy to keep Hoffa out of the union?

HOFFA: I would say, uh, there certainly was an understanding of, uh, everyone of 'em getting a piece of the pie they wanted. And they used Dean to get the pie.

PLAYBOY: Straight question: Was there any *financial* deal made with Nixon to get you out of prison?

HOFFA: Fitzsimmons says no. He says he only gave him $14,000.

PLAYBOY: So there was no offer of what might be called a bribe?

HOFFA: Absolutely not. Positively not. I did not.

[At this point, there was an interruption and Hoffa walked over to the window of his kitchen. The tape recorder was turned off, but, by mutual agreement, the conversation remained on the record. The interviewer asked: 'Come on, Jimmy, was *any* money paid to Richard Nixon to get you out of prison?'

Hoffa turned from the window and said, 'Yaaaaa.'

The interviewer asked, 'How much?'

The reply, deadly serious, came after a long pause: 'You don't *wanna* know.'

A week later, with the tape recorder turned on, the interviewer reminded Hoffa of this exchange. Hoffa denied saying 'any such goddamned thing'.]

PLAYBOY: But you had no one approach Nixon and say, 'Look, $100,000 goes into your campaign . . .'?

HOFFA: I had nobody go there. If anybody went there, it was without my knowledge – even though there *is* a statement floating around that Allen Dorfman [a special consultant to the Teamsters' largest health-and-welfare fund] said at his trial in New York that he had a receipt signed by Mitchell for a large sum of money – as a contribution.

PLAYBOY: How large was the sum supposed to be?

HOFFA: Now, that's never been proven. Mitchell denied it under oath. What the hell's the name of the other guy – Stans? Yeah, Stans. He denied it, too.

PLAYBOY: Is this Dorfman a friend of yours?

HOFFA: A hundred per cent.

PLAYBOY: Isn't he the man you set up in business through your Chicago contacts back in the fifties?

HOFFA: No. Nobody set him up in business at all. Allen Dorfman submitted a sealed bid for the insurance. And by unanimous vote of the trustees, he became the agent for the insurance company.

PLAYBOY: But didn't you control the trustees at the time?

HOFFA: I spoke my piece in favor of Dorfman. Of course I did.

PLAYBOY: All right. Besides Fitzsimmons, it seems as if Colson were the one person who stood to gain most by the 1980 restriction. When did he go on the Teamsters' payroll?

HOFFA: Within months of the time I got out of prison. He certainly didn't command, by reputation, the retainer he got. Certainly didn't do that.

PLAYBOY: How much did he get from the Teamsters?

HOFFA: All told, probably in the neighborhood of $300,000 a year.

PLAYBOY: What qualifications did Colson have to be a Teamsters lawyer?

HOFFA: Well, he had a shingle.

PLAYBOY: So it was a deal?

HOFFA: In my opinion.

PLAYBOY: Jimmy, what *about* Frank Fitzsimmons?

HOFFA: Well, what the hell about him? I already said he's a double-crosser. And that's all there is to it.

PLAYBOY: You said –

HOFFA: A man I took off the truck! Made him an officer in the union, saw that he had more than one suit for the first time in his life, that he lived in a decent home, had an expense account! Kept raising him through the ranks of labor! And when I went to jail, he took over the presidency and then he became power hungry. He accepted the belief that he was a great labor leader and came about doing what he did in the 1980 restriction. In my opinion.

PLAYBOY: Why did he come to believe he was a great labor leader?

HOFFA: How the hell do I know? Look at some of the Congressmen and Senators we got. They couldn't spell rat backward, they couldn't make a living!

They get elected and, for Chrissakes, they're on TV, yakking around, telling you how to run the world, and they can't even run their own life! Same thing with him. People look in the mirror too often. They grow by inches – sideways and down – but they don't grow. Their heads get fatter, but they don't get any more sense than they had before. I just think Fitzsimmons has gone completely power nuts, that's all. Someone took him up to the top of the mountain. Showed him the valley, and he bought the valley. But he forgot the membership and he forgot the officers and forgot his responsibility to the oath he took for office.

PLAYBOY: Will Fitzsimmons be in office through 1980?

HOFFA: I don't think Fitzsimmons will run in 1976.

PLAYBOY: Why?

HOFFA: Well, the best evidence is he's building a home at La Costa. With his golfing and parading around all over the country in his jet, I don't think he'll be a candidate.

PLAYBOY: You were the one who extended the first loan to develop La Costa, somewhere around $10,000,000, isn't that right?

HOFFA: Somewhere around there, yeah. Been a long time ago.

PLAYBOY: How did it start?

HOFFA: Well, Moe Dalitz was the major owner of the Desert Inn. We loaned him money, he paid it back. When he wanted to go into the La Costa enterprise, real estate was booming at the time. And it couldn't go wrong. *That* real estate's a good buy today!

PLAYBOY: Was Meyer Lansky part of that?

HOFFA: Meyer Lansky had no more to do with Moe Dalitz than you had, in my opinion.

PLAYBOY: Aren't you and Lansky good friends?

HOFFA: I know him.

PLAYBOY: Ever do business with him?

HOFFA: Nope. Never asked me to. My opinion, he's *another* victim of harassment!

PLAYBOY: Then you don't think he's a member of organized crime? .

HOFFA: I don't believe there is any organized crime, period. Don't believe it. Never believed it. I've said it for the last forty years. *Hoover* said it! Supposed to be the greatest law-enforcement man in America, with the means to find out. He said there was no Mafia, no so-called organized crime.

PLAYBOY: No Mafia?

HOFFA: That's what *he* said. That's what Hoover said.

PLAYBOY: But in 1958, during the McClellan hearings, it was said that you knew more dangerous criminals than Dave Beck.

HOFFA: Ah-ha! That's a different question! I don't deny the fact that I know, I think, what's going on in most of the big cities of the United States. And that means knowing the people, uh, who are in the big cities. I'm no different than the banks, no different than insurance companies, no different than the politicians. You're a damned fool not to be informed what makes a city run when you're tryin' to do business in the city.

PLAYBOY: What about people like Lansky and Frank Costello?

HOFFA: What about 'em?

PLAYBOY: The McClellan Committee said that they were organized-crime members, members of the Mafia.

HOFFA: Yeah, yeah, sure. They said I was associated with the Mafia. They said Dorfman was part of the Mafia. And it's a complete, 100 per cent lie. They know it. Everybody else knows it. So it's easy to say, 'Well, he's a Mafia member, 'cause he got an Italian name.' Once in a while they say, for a man like Lansky, who's a Jew, 'Oh, well, he was accepted.'

PLAYBOY: How about Paul 'The Waiter' Ricca?

HOFFA: What about him? Jesus Christ Almighty! He was in Chicago for ninety-nine years and a day and if they thought he was so much involved in organized crime, why the hell didn't they arrest him? Hell of a note that the FBI, and the Congress, and the newspapers and everybody else says So-and-So's part of the Mafia; So-and-So-s doing this . . . Why don't they arrest him? Why the hell don't they put him on trial? What the hell they doing? Keeping him alive, like a mummy, so they can keep writing about him?

PLAYBOY: So where is Ricca now?

HOFFA: Dead! [Pause] Dead! Why the hell – What are you talking about all these people?

PLAYBOY: What about Johnny Dio?

HOFFA: Friend of mine. No question about that.

PLAYBOY: Member of organized crime?

HOFFA: Like *you* are.

PLAYBOY: Member of the Mafia?

HOFFA: Like *you* are.

PLAYBOY: Wasn't he convicted of extortion?

HOFFA: Ah-ha! That's a different question. I know Johnny's case. I know what Johnny's in jail for. Don't agree with it. Trying to help him get out. Should be out. Our association's trying to help him get out. And he's a victim of newspaper publicity, just like I was. [Pause] Damned funny, though! All these people are supposed to have millions and millions of dollars. Can't afford to hire lawyers. [Pause] Damned funny. I saw some of the biggest ones that there was supposed to be, in prison. And their wives were on welfare and they didn't have enough money to come down and visit 'em. And yet they keep talking about the millions they got.

PLAYBOY: Like who?

HOFFA: Well, I don't care to mention their names and embarrass them. But I seen 'em. They're there. [Pause] Damned funny. I know people in town *here*, right in Detroit, say they're part of the Mafia! Well, Christ! They ain't making a living! How come, if they're part of the Mafia, they're not making a living?

PLAYBOY: Care to be specific?

HOFFA: No, I don't want to ... everybody knows who they are ... the police department knows, the prosecutor's office knows, the media knows ...

PLAYBOY: What about Tony Giacalone?

HOFFA: Giacalone! Giacalone! Giacalone's a businessman!

PLAYBOY: Didn't he have dealings with La Costa?

HOFFA: La Costa! What the hell's *he* got to do with La Costa?

PLAYBOY: You mean he had no involvement at all?

HOFFA: Record speaks for itself. Got nothin' more to do with La Costa than *you* have. May have *visited* it – went to the spa or to one of the golf tournaments down there, 'cause he's a golfer. Why, he's got as much to do with La Costa as *you* have!

PLAYBOY: But Giacalone was named as a member of organized crime by a Senate committee back in –

HOFFA: What the hell has that got to do with it? I appeared in front of the same committee and they lied about me! They lied about Giacalone! They never proved it! And if they *had* such a charge, why in the hell didn't they charge everybody with conspiracy and go to court?

PLAYBOY: Conspiracy's hard to prove; it's almost *impossible* to prove.

HOFFA: Like *hell*! The easiest crime in the world to prove. Anybody indicted for a conspiracy, a lawyer will tell you it's the easiest crime the Government can prove. And that's why they put it on the books as conspiracy. The mere fact that you meet with somebody, or the fact that circumstantial evidence is involved. ... What the hell're you talking about? It's the easiest crime in the book to prove. That's why they use conspiracy.

PLAYBOY: As far as conspiracies go, you've always believed that the Government was out to 'get Hoffa', haven't you?

HOFFA: Of course. First, Bobby Kennedy wanted to use the Teamsters as a vehicle to get the Kennedy name out front with something that was probably the greatest thriller that ever appeared on TV [the televised McClellan hearings]. And when he couldn't bull me, when he couldn't take over the Teamsters, why, it became a vendetta between he and I. And he used $12,000,000 in Government money to convict me. Who the hell ever heard of the Kennedys before the McClellan Committee? They were nobody. A bootlegger, the old man. Common, ordinary bootlegger.

PLAYBOY: Have you ever wire-tapped anybody?

HOFFA: I've hired people to secure information for me where they could possibly secure it.

PLAYBOY: Did they secure it by wire-tapping?

HOFFA: I didn't ask them. Not interested.

PLAYBOY: Did you ever tap Bobby Kennedy?

HOFFA: If they did, I don't know. But I *received* information on Kennedy. How they got it, none of my business. Wouldn't wanna know it.

PLAYBOY: Did you tap any FBI agents?

HOFFA: No. *I* didn't tap 'em. Somebody else . . . uh, Bernie Spindel [a freelance electronics expert] set up a monitoring system in Chattanooga and took information outta the air from three of the FBI radio channels. We found out the FBI was violating the law; they were surveiling my lawyers and my witnesses. We also proved they were attempting to get information which was tantamount to interfering with justice. And then we submitted the transcripts to the judge, Frank Wilson. He opened the envelope, then charged we had tricked him and he had a fit. The next batch we handed him, Wilson wouldn't open; I think it's because among the transcripts was one of him making a telephone communication to Bobby Kennedy – and that was in the middle of the trial.

PLAYBOY: So then you had issued orders to tap Wilson's phone?

HOFFA: No. It's not a question of tapping Wilson's phone.

PLAYBOY: Kennedy's phone, then?

HOFFA: No. Taken out of the air.

PLAYBOY: Bullshit! You can't just take phone conversations 'out of the air'.

HOFFA: Don't tell *me* it's bullshit! Don't tell me what they can do. I have the proof! Frank Wilson finally admitted he *did* talk to Bobby Kennedy during the trial, although he said he was talking about hiring clerks for overtime typing. But it took forty-five minutes to do it! [Judge Wilson says that at no time did he communicate with Kennedy.]

As to taking out of the air, Bernie did it with about a ton of equipment he brought down with him. We gave him a suite and set it all up and, being the best expert in the United States, he just reached out with his communication system and took it out of the air. Right outta the air, everything that was going on. They knew it could be done. They do it every day in the week.

PLAYBOY: There's a story that you ordered Marilyn Monroe's phone tapped –

HOFFA: That's the silliest thing I ever read in my life.

PLAYBOY: And that the tapes are still supposed to be in existence.

HOFFA: Aw, that's a lotta crap! I never said no such thing. I read that stupid statement in that stupid book. And, uh, the 'Mailer' who wrote that book. I think his name was –

PLAYBOY: Norman Mailer.

HOFFA: The stupidest thing I ever read in my life. He admitted he hardly interviewed anybody, that all he did was gather information other people had wrote and did a book on it. [It was not Mailer's *Marilyn* that contained the allegation Hoffa referred to, but *The Life and Curious Death of Marilyn Monroe*, by Robert F. Slatzer.] And I understand right now he's in the process of writing a book on me. When he does, I'm gonna sue him. Very simple.

PLAYBOY: What if Mailer called and asked to interview you?

HOFFA: Wouldn't talk to him, under no circumstances. I think he must be some kind of nut.

PLAYBOY: All right, what about the allegations about the Marilyn Monroe tapes?

HOFFA: Marilyn Monroe? I never knew she *existed* with Bobby Kennedy. If I did, I would've told him about it in open hearing. I already *had* a tape on Bobby Kennedy and Jack Kennedy, which was so filthy and so nasty – given to me by a girl – that even though my people encouraged me to do it, I wouldn't do it. I put it away and said the hell with it. Forget about it.

PLAYBOY: What was on the tape?

HOFFA: Oh, their association with this young lady and what they had did, and so forth. I got rid of the tape. I wouldn't put up with it. [Pause] Pure nonsense.

PLAYBOY: You didn't feel you had a way to get back at Bobby?

HOFFA: I would not embarrass his wife and family.

PLAYBOY: Well, you've mentioned it now.

HOFFA: Let it be at that. Let it stay that way. I'm not talkin' about what's dirty and nasty. Maybe some people wouldn't think it. I did.

PLAYBOY: Who was the girl?

HOFFA: I'm not sayin' that. [Pause] *I* know.

PLAYBOY: All right. Did you ever threaten to kill Bobby Kennedy?

HOFFA: Nope. Another lie.

PLAYBOY: What about killing people?

HOFFA: Self-preservation's a big word.

PLAYBOY: Have you ever exercised your need for self-preservation?

HOFFA: Never had to.

PLAYBOY: You've never killed anybody?

HOFFA: Never had to exercise the self-preservation. But I'm certainly not going to let someone kill *me*.

PLAYBOY: Have you ever *ordered* anybody to be killed?

HOFFA: [Pause] Mmm, nope.

PLAYBOY: Killing isn't the way to solve a problem?

HOFFA: No, I don't think it solves anything. It just creates a few more problems – the FBI, the local police, newspapers. [Pause] Kill 'em by propaganda. Kill 'em by votes. But not *physically* kill 'em.

PLAYBOY: How about busting heads?

HOFFA: Nothin' wrong with that, if they're in your way, uh, tryin' to break a strike or tryin' to destroy the union. Nothin' wrong with that, in my opinion.

PLAYBOY: You *do* have a reputation for busting heads that goes way back.

HOFFA: Survival of the fittest, my friend. What do you think industry does? What do you think the police do? Police broke our heads every day of the week in 1932. Ford Motors? They cracked heads all *over* the lot. Unless you were able to take care of yourself, they'd crack your head where it'd kill you. I survived.

PLAYBOY: Have you ever hired any bodyguards?

HOFFA: Never. Don't need 'em. Don't need 'em. They're in your way.

PLAYBOY: But not everybody loves Jimmy Hoffa.

HOFFA: I'm not interested in what everybody does. You got a bodyguard, you become careless, and if you look at all the gangsters that were *killed* with bodyguards, you'll know they went to sleep. I don't *care* to go to *sleep*.

PLAYBOY: What do you mean, gangsters?

HOFFA: People who allegedly were, uh, involved in bank robberies and other kind of illegal enterprises individually. They had bodyguards. How about the question of Roosevelt? He had all *kind* of bodyguards down in Florida, didn't he? Little guy pops up nobody ever heard of. He starts shooting. He killed the mayor [Anton Cermak of Chicago], didn't he? Well, what do you want? What do you want? Bodyguards make you go to sleep and I don't care to go to sleep. The only guy who needs a bodyguard is a liar, a cheat, a guy who betrays friendship. I don't do any of them. What the hell do you need a bodyguard for?

PLAYBOY: So you're not afraid of anything?

HOFFA: What the hell am I gonna be afraid of? I'm sixty-two years old. I should've been dead maybe twenty-five years ago. Lived three lives. Well, what am I gonna be afraid of? Never was afraid in my life and don't intend to start tomorrow. Who's gonna bother me? *They* do? Well, then I'll do somethin' about *that*.

PLAYBOY: You'll do what, exactly?

HOFFA: Whatever I have to do.

PLAYBOY: What do you mean?

HOFFA: Just whatever I have to do to eliminate somebody bothers me . . . I'll do whatever I *have* to do.

PLAYBOY: Such as killing them?

HOFFA: Well, if they try to kill *me* and I'm in the position to take away their gun, or whatever they hell they're using against me. If they get shot, that's their trouble. It ain't mine. Hell, if I had people try to kill me, I survived it. Didn't have no bodyguard, but I survived the . . . the *threat* of being killed, the *attempt* to be killed. I'm still here. 'Cause I keep my eyes open – drive my own car, go where I wanna go, never need no bodyguard. I don't cheat nobody. I don't lie about nobody. I don't frame nobody. I don't talk bad about people. If I do, I tell 'em. So what the hell's people gonna try to kill *me* for?

PLAYBOY: OK. How's your private life? Do you get out much, to restaurants, that sort of thing?

HOFFA: Eh. Once in a while. Very seldom. Now, when we go out, arm and a leg. What the hell're you gonna do? Number one, I don't like the crowds. Number two, I don't like the prices. Number three, I don't like the service. So what the hell am I gonna go out for? Why should Josephine get dressed up for two hours? The hell with it. It's getting to the point where a guy with four kids, his old lady and himself has got to spend $70 a week for groceries.

PLAYBOY: What's the most important thing in your life right now?

HOFFA: Oh, my family. No question about *that*.

PLAYBOY: For years you feuded with the Kennedys, one of the most powerful families in the country. What did you think, personally, of Bobby Kennedy?

HOFFA: He was a creep!

PLAYBOY: And John Kennedy?

HOFFA: Creep!

PLAYBOY: How about Teddy?

HOFFA: Well, I've known a hell of a lot of brothers in my life. Two, three, four to a family, the majority of 'em no good. And maybe one of 'em outta the lot, you couldn't *find* a better guy. Who the hell knows? Just because you're brothers, it doesn't mean you're the same type. Don't mean that. Don't mean that at all.

Ted Kennedy I hardly know. But I know people who've known him since the day he was born. Our people in Boston've known him. And they say he's different from all two of the others. They say he likes a good time and that he would be the kind of guy who would gather around him a lot of people who wouldn't go to work for any other Administration. I suppose they mean professors and what have you – I have no faith in 'em. So that's all I know about the guy. He never made any statement concerning me that I know of – even when it was fashionable. Of course, he can get in . . . any time he wants it, he's got it.

PLAYBOY: You mean the Presidency? You think he's going to run?

HOFFA: Oh, just as sure as you and I are here. Just as sure as you and I are here. It'll be a draft at the convention.

PLAYBOY: How much do you think Chappaquiddick will hurt him?

HOFFA: Aw, Christ! Fifty per cent of the marriages are in divorces. And when you talk about morality, it went out the window. How the hell's that gonna hurt him? He's sure as hell gonna get the old people, the welfare people, the Puerto Ricans, blacks, Mexicans. He'll get the majority of those. No question of that in *my* mind. How the hell could he lose?

Unless – there's only one thing that could kill him and very well kill *all* Democrats. They got the House and the Senate now. If they keep fiddlin' around and not doing anything except quarreling with each other, very well, the American people could say, 'Now, the hell with ya', and vote Republican. That's the way *I* see it. I don't see it no other way.

PLAYBOY: Why did Kennedy say he wouldn't run?

HOFFA: Get the heat off Chappaquiddick for eighteen months. What the hell, they were banging him on the head with every kind of article, TV report, what have you. But you notice the very minute he said, 'I'm not gonna run', it stopped. So he was smart.

PLAYBOY: Don't you think Chappaquiddick will have to be resolved at some point?

HOFFA: Phhht! He wasn't found guilty of no crime. What's he supposed to do? They didn't find him *guilty*!

PLAYBOY: If Teddy runs and gets elected, do you think he'll be killed?

HOFFA: Naw. I don't think – You just don't kill – What the hell! I don't think anybody's so cold-blooded that he'd shoot a guy because he's a Kennedy.

PLAYBOY: There was at least one publicized attempt on *your* life, wasn't there? In 1962, during your trial on charges of illegal kickbacks, a man walked into the courtroom and shot you from behind.

HOFFA: Yeah, don't know his goddamned name. I forgot it now. It's a matter of record. [It was Warren Swanson, a deranged drifter.] But everyone was searched that went in and out of the courtroom. How the hell did he get in with a gun? . . . I'm sure the marshal didn't overlook *him*. And he walked in with a gun, after everybody's been searched! Like Martin Luther King. You're suspcious but you can't prove it.

PLAYBOY: The man had a pellet gun, right?

HOFFA: Which would go through a two-by-four. Kill you just as sure as a .22.

PLAYBOY: What's your version of what happened?

HOFFA: Well, I looked and I *seen* him. I ducked down, come up, broke his jaw, took his gun away from him. The marshals were behind the file cabinets, same as the Government lawyers, my lawyers, same as the judge. They all came pouncing out after it was all over. I got the guy knocked out and this marshal comes out with a blackjack and hits the poor bastard! I said, 'Ya dumb bastard! Get outta here! The guy's knocked out already!'

PLAYBOY: How about the attempt on George Wallace?

HOFFA: Who the hell *knows*? They got a file on every kook there is.

PLAYBOY: And John Kennedy? Why do you think he was killed?

HOFFA: Who the hell knows what deals he had? That he didn't keep? Who knows?

PLAYBOY: Do you think Oswald did it?

HOFFA: Aw, who the hell knows? I saw that simulation of the assassination on TV, which made more sense to me than the Warren Report did. I'll be goddamned. You tell me a guy can figure out how to be there at the right moment, the right time, with a rifle – and hit a guy, you're a good man. I don't see how you do it. I see guys shooting at deer and I see *cracks shots* shooting the deer. By God, *they* miss 'em. And a deer's about like a moving car. Ain't much difference.

PLAYBOY: Why did Jack Ruby kill Oswald, in your opinion?

HOFFA: That's the $64 question. Nobody'll ever figure that out. A fanatic, maybe. Who the hell knows?

PLAYBOY: What do you think of the conspiracy theories of that former district attorney in New Orleans, Jim Garrison? Is he just a kook?

HOFFA: No, sirree! Jim Garrison's a smart man . . . Goddamned smart attorney . . . Anybody think *he's a* a kook is a kook themselves.

PLAYBOY: All right, back to the Bobby Kennedy assassination. You don't think Nixon had anything to do with it, do you?

HOFFA: Hell, no. Hell, no. He ain't that kind of guy.

PLAYBOY: So it was Sirhan acting alone?

HOFFA: Well, I handle guns all my life. Here's a kid that went out and got a gun. Not much practice with the damned gun. And I would question whether he was cold-blooded enough to be able to pop up and shoot the guy without someone . . . helping him. I just read about another guy, a ballistics guy, who said there was another type of bullet. Who the hell knows? *Who the hell knows?*

PLAYBOY: Do you think we'll ever know about all these killings?

HOFFA: Well, I watched the damned TV the other night, that *Police Story* and *S.W.A.T.* They killed more goddamned people than you got hair on your *head!* [Pause] Goddamned movies, TV! Kills forty-nine guys a night, for Chrissake – on Monday and Tuesday night! Forty-nine guys they kill! So who the hell knows what you can do? There was a nut on TV last night, just started *killing* people. Nobody knew why the goddamned fool killed people. Then they finally catch him . . . kill *him*. So he's dead. *He* can't tell why he killed 'em. People go off their rocker. Who can tell?

●

WILLIAM BURROUGHS

Interviewed by Duncan Fallowell
Time Out, 24–30 September 1982

William Seward Burroughs, the American writer, was born into a wealthy Mississippi family in 1914 and educated at Harvard. After graduating in 1936 he travelled in Europe, returning to New York where he worked as a detective, a pest exterminator, and a bartender. He became a heroin addict in 1944 and his first book, *Junkie: Confessions of an Unredeemed Drug Addict*, was published in 1953. This was followed in 1959 by *The Naked Lunch*, the book which gained him an international reputation as an exponent of the 'beat' movement. His later works have been more experimental and have borrowed techniques from other art forms, such as music and film. He has lived in Mexico (where he accidentally killed his wife in a shooting), Tangier, London, and Paris, though he now lives in Kansas for reasons that are explained in this interview.

Duncan Fallowell was born in Harrow, Middlesex, in 1948. On coming down from Oxford in 1970, he wrote to *The Spectator* offering his services as a pop columnist. Since then, he has always been a freelance writer. His first book was a biography of April Ashley, the transsexual, and he has written two novels and a travel book. Among those he has interviewed are: Kirk Douglas, Germaine Greer, Gabriel Garcia Márquez, Graham Greene, Nadine Gordimer, Divine, A. J. P. Taylor, Sir John Betjeman, R. D. Laing, Peter O'Toole, Arthur Koestler, and James Brown.

It's a very hot day. Grandparents' Day in the United States.

'Did you read this about a professor at Gainesville, Florida?' asks Mr Burroughs. 'Murdered by three gay boys. They had a smother party – *the head of the forty-one-year-old bachelor was wrapped in canvas, with sheets, a pillow and a bag of ice tied over his face so there was no chance he could breathe.* Dumb jerks. I hate criminals. They're stupid! One of the three, a very good-looking boy, he's going to get his arse fucked off in prison, then beaten up, then fucked, then beaten – '

'Excuse me.' It's Wayne, the plumber, who props himself in the doorway in paint-spattered denim. 'Will that be all, Bill?'

'I guess so, Wayne,' says Mr Burroughs, twitching wildly about the mouth. 'Are you going out to John's? I've got to go out there and fetch my .45 automatic.'

'No, I'm going to take a shower and get back to you guys and talk about getting this place secure with some door and window locks.'

'Yeah. Big ones.'

William Burroughs – ex-drug fiend, cat lover, America's most something writer – has moved house. He's been in the new one three days but the hot water doesn't work. The flat in New York (which was the shower-and-locker-room floor of a converted YMCA building, complete with latrines) has been turned over to a friend. Burroughs then moved to a stone farmhouse a few miles outside Lawrence, Kansas – 'Very convenient for shooting. I blasted my sculptures there, shotguns blasting sheets of plywood which produces very innaresting splitting. Then I sign 'em.'

Now he has moved into this small one-floor weatherboard house on the edge of Lawrence itself. Last night he was woken up – 'I'm a *very* light sleeper' – by a possum eating the cat's food on the back porch. 'I may have to shoot it with my air rifle. Did you know that in the old days, air guns had to be pumped up by an assistant before they could be used? I say, Carruthers, some ruffians are approaching – where is my pump boy?'

'Have you met your neighbours?'

Burroughs convulses violently – is it laughter or a cry for help? 'Not really,' he says, jabbing an electric cattle prod in the air. 'I spoke to the woman next door – over the fence. I asked her if there'd been any burglars round here. And she said no. And I said good, let's keep it that way. I haven't seen her since then. I'm getting some *real* locks put on the doors – anyone could pick these silly little things with a fucking paperclip.'

He speaks in a low drawl which is at first almost incomprehensible but which reveals elegant characteristics when you tune in. It comes out of a long lugubrious mask of a face criss-crossed round the eyes by creases which resemble the markings of a clown. Burroughs's basic facial expression is one of infinite disappointment.

He grew up in St Louis. The countryside in this part of Kansas is geographically similar. It is almost coming home after long absences in Central and South

America, North Africa and Europe. 'But I've never been further east than Athens – I was married first time in the American consulate in Athens.'

What about father? 'He was very distant. He knew about my addictions to hard drugs – his brother was a morphine addict. It was just about the only thing which ran in the family. About the homosexual stuff – sex in any shape or form embarrassed him acutely,' and Burroughs begins furiously polishing the table with a dirty rag.

'Contrary to a rumour put out by Jack Kerouac, I was never rich. My parents gave me an allowance of 200 dollars a month. I couldn't have written my books without it. All this about millions from the Burroughs Adding Machine is nonsense. It never came my way. Now half my income is produced by these public readings – and you don't just pick up any old thing and start reading it. I rehearse. Usually I concentrate on the comic stuff – like where the captain of the sinking ship gets up in women's clothes and rushes into the first lifeboat. You mustn't go on too long. At that poetry festival out on the beach near Rome – this eighty-one-year-old poet got sand thrown at him by 10,000 people and well, I said that's not going to happen to me and we did three minutes. We had some trouble one night and Yevtushenko refused to go on.'

D.F.: What's Yevtushenko like?

W.B.: He's charming. He's a great performer and performed in English eventually in front of the Italians and just wowed them. The actual content of the poem didn't sound so great but he put it across. McLuhan's 'the medium is the message'.

D.F.: I disagree with McLuhan on that. There is something called the core of meaning.

W.B.: Oh, good heavens, yes. McLuhan also said we're all travelling at the speed of light. What the hell does that mean? I don't know and I don't think he did.

D.F.: Perhaps he meant that light is travelling at the speed of people.

W.B.: Well, if we were travelling at the speed of light we wouldn't age.

D.F.: But we wouldn't have mass either. This is one of the problems of advanced space technology – people disappear.

W.B.: That's no obstacle.

D.F.: Well . . . do you speak any foreign languages fluently?

W.B.: No. I come as close to being at home with Spanish as any other – three years in Mexico and about five years in Tangier where Spanish is a second language. I'd like to take refuge in Bernard Shaw – he who is at home in his own language will never be at home in any other. But that's not true. Joyce was a brilliant linguist. And some very stupid people too can make good linguists, just sort of smack it out at the airport. English is very useful. You can do more with it than with almost any other language. French is a very poor language for any sort of verbal experimentation. You can hardly cut up French.

Burroughs is happy to be no longer living in New York. 'It isn't true that I spent my time there going to parties with Andy Warhol. I hate parties, I hardly know Mick Jagger, I don't know those pop people – well, I know Chris Stein and Blondie – they visited me out here and we had a very pleasant afternoon shooting guns and fooling around – he's into guns and knives and stuff.'

But why Lawrence of all places?

'My assistant, James Grauerholz, lives here. I have a doctor here, a lawyer, someone to look after the cat when I'm away, very little crime here – although James had some things stolen out of his car the other day, some tear gas cartridges and stuff. And I hear the Indian college down the road can be dangerous. I must look into that. They have a bad reaction to alcohol, Indians do.'

'You've never wanted to live in California?'

'Hell, no.'

'What's wrong with it?'

'Everything's wrong with it! They have the most ridiculous guns and weapons laws in the country.' He is twitching up against one of the walls at the moment, then slowly zig-zags across to an ancient air-conditioning device in the middle of a bare wall. He turns it on and the ensuing racket almost drowns out the conversation. 'On the West Coast it's a misdemeanour to carry a gun but a felony if you carry a knife and you have to go on a course before you can carry a tear gas gun which is a lot of nonsense.'

In 1951 Burroughs accidentally killed his second wife with a pistol in Mexico City but it didn't put him off. 'It isn't a question of the gun,' he says, piling sugar into a cup of tea, 'it's a question of carelessness.' The couple were looning around, playing William Tell with a glass on her head – he shot at it and missed. 'We were together about five years. She was very intuitive, one of the more intelligent people I've known.' But not sufficiently intuitive and intelligent, it seems, to have avoided this death, a curious amalgam of whimsy and tragedy. At the time she was a confirmed alcoholic and amphetamine addict. Burroughs himself was into all sorts of substances, including the exotic *yage* (pronounced 'yah-hay') from Amazonia.

D.F.: How did marriage square with your homosexuality?

W.B.: When I was younger I wasn't exclusively homosexual.

D.F.: So when did you realize you preferred boys to girls?

W.B.: Oh, when I was thirteen or fourteen.

D.F.: What is your relationship with your son these days?

W.B.: He's dead.

D.F.: Oh . . . how did that happen?

W.B.: He had cirrhosis of the liver and had a liver transplant and lived about five years after the transplant. After a transplant the anti-rejection drugs they give you have very bad side effects. It makes people self-righteous. You are dealing with the whole immunity mechanism – if you reduce the body's ability to reject, you get a paranoid reaction. The person, feeling himself to be vulnerable, will react with self-righteousness and terrible rigidity of character.

D.F.: His book *Speed* was quite successful.

W.B.: I hate speed. I hate anything that makes me chew the carpet.

He walks round the room in ever-decreasing circles and eventually reaches a point of introspection. Silent thoughts for a while.

'This is an excellent cup of tea – very English.'

'Glad you like it,' he says. 'Well, I lived in London for ten years, five of them behind Fortnum & Mason. But when I left London I was never more glad to get out of a place in my entire life!'

'Did you use the Piccadilly boys?'

'Certainly. Who wouldn't? I like boys eighteen to twenty-five. I can go as low as fifteen, perhaps fourteen in exceptional circumstances. Wordsworth was mad about little girls. Have you read the Lucy poems? Outrageous!'

Victor Bockris has transcribed an encounter between Burroughs and Andy Warhol.

BOCKRIS: The English are very odd sexually.

WARHOL: They're really odd, but they're so sophisticated, that's why . . .

BURROUGHS: They like to be beaten with rulers and hairbrushes.

BOCKRIS: I think the English . . .

WARHOL: . . . are the sexiest people.

BOCKRIS: Did you ever have any really good sex in England?

WARHOL: Oh yeah, the best.

BURROUGHS: Yeeesss . . .

Bill says, 'I notice circumcision is on the wane in Europe. Is this wise? Most American boys are still circumcised. Virtually all the uncircumcised boys in my high school were Roman Catholics – this goes back to the old days when they wanted to distinguish themselves from the Arabs in Spain and places. I'm circumcised myself. I like boys who are circumcised. When my son came along the doctor said do you want him circumcised? and I said sure, let's have it off, it's a very sanitary thing. Hum, then everything got so expensive in London and went downhill fast – this was in the 70s. When I got to New York everything was a helluva lot cheaper – it hasn't necessarily stayed that way. And in New York there's this violence problem which I rather like. It kinda tones you up to sort through your weapons before you go out visiting friends. I carry the lot there – except a gun of course.'

'Guns are illegal in New York?'

'Good God, are they ever! And they always were,' he adds, picking a crust of uncertain origin off his dark green nylon trousers. Burroughs's body is painfully thin but very much alive. Indeed he never stops moving about. Even if he's standing still some part of him will be twitching, curling, jerking. 'A mandatory gaol sentence of a year if you're caught with a gun in New York. My dear, incarceration in an overcrowded zoo! In New York they're absolute . . . animals. I don't like prison and always get myself bailed out. But Kansas is very much gun territory.'

Writers are often chameleons. They can partake of their surroundings without surrendering any essential part of the self. Burroughs has this. In London he is the Harvard avant-garde writer, in Tangier a junkie, in Paris a beat, in New York a member of café society, and in Lawrence, Kansas, he becomes coloured by the old-fashioned frontiersman down on the homestead.

As yet there is hardly any furniture in the house. Could this be that impossible thing, an American home without a television? 'Well, there's an old black & white out the back. I occasionally flick it on if I'm passing – it might produce some synchronicity.' A few magazines lie about on the shiny wood floor. *Guns, Guns & Arms, Warriors, Science Digest*. And a few paperbacks – *The Mask of Apollo, The Silva Mind Control Method* . . . 'I read a lot of horror,' he says, opening another packet of Player's Navy Cut. He chain smokes them except when, in the evening, one might be displaced by the occasional joint. 'I especially like medical horror.'

After studying English Literature at Harvard, Burroughs studied medicine briefly in Vienna just before the Second World War – 'coz there's no way I could have got into an American medical school. Have you read *Brain*? It's by the guy that wrote *Coma*. And *Fever*. Titles are very important. I like those ones in the *Reader's Digest* – "Thank God for my Heart Attack". And "My Eyes Have a Cold Nose" by some writer who went blind,' and we both collapse into choked laughter like muzzled hyenas.

'They don't give you nightmares?'

'There's a recurring nightmare where I'm attacked by a giant centipede, sometimes a cross between a centipede and a scorpion. In the typical centipede nightmare it suddenly rushes me and fastens on to my leg. Then I wake up kicking the bedclothes off – ugh, centipedes! I have to kill 'em.'

'Have you worked out the origin of this phobia?'

'It's not a phobia! I can't think of anybody who would have a good word to say for centipedes. Generally I don't have nightmares but dreams. I keep a note-pad handy. Maybe 40 per cent of my material comes from dreams – sets and characters. There's no line between the dream world and the actual world. But of course, if you get to the point where you find it difficult to cross the road then you should see a doctor. Ugh, that's a fly! I can't stand a fly that alights anywhere near me. Wait a minute.' He pushes his chair back with a screech.

'Do you have a spray?'

'Sure I got sprays, but this isn't a spray case.' Burroughs, whose gait is a combination of shuffle and hop, takes himself out to the kitchen, scratching his thin grey arms which look like two broken pencils, and returns grinning with a large orange plastic swat.

'Where was I?' he wonders, sitting down again, swat erect. 'Yes, from the evolutionary point of view, dreams are very important. Man is an artefact designed for space conditions – and I don't mean going up in, as it were, an aqualung which is all we've done so far. The evolution from land into space is equivalent to the evolution from water on to land and will involve biologic alterations quite as drastic.' Thwack! Missed it . . .

'From where you are sitting, what do you think it'll be like?'

The gristle green needlepoint eyes scan the environment with a measure of fatigue tinged with disgust. 'I'm sitting in time. The transition to space is the escape from time, it's immortality even – because my definition of time is that which runs out. You got water creatures looking up at the land – can they conceive what it's like to live up there? Hardly. The fear of falling means nothing to a fish.' Thwack! . . . 'The key to what space is like is to be found in dreams.'

'Interesting.'

'Ha. Gore Vidal said he never heard me say anything interesting. But I have no interest in being interesting. It's what you say to those writers who send you unreadable stuff – very innaresting.'

'Have you ever heard Gore Vidal say anything interesting?'

'He was once asked if he believed in corporal punishment and he said yes, between consenting adults. Dreams are a biological necessity. If animals are deprived of REM sleep they eventually die. This is the clue. One of the big barriers to getting into space is weight. But we have at hand the model of a much lighter body, the dream or astral body which is almost, probably not completely, weightless. Of course very little research is going on in this direction at the present time. You see, man is designed for a purpose. This is the flaw in all utopias – no purpose. How dull it is to rust unburnished, not to shine in use. You know where that's from? *Ulysses.*'

'I didn't know that Joyce –'

'By Tennyson.' Thwack! Got 'im.

D.F.: You're pretty expert at this now.

W.B.: Oh, my dear, I've been in training ever since I was old enough to pick up a fly swatter. In other words, what we call happiness is a by-product of function. Happiness isn't sitting on your arse some place. Would you care for a drink? I can only drink Coca-Cola and vodka. But I always drink them simultaneously.

D.F.: Are you alone in this dream theory?

W.B.: Maybe Governor Jerry Brown will be up there. He believes the future of the race is in space. That's the only thing I agree with him on – he's a gun control person.

D.F.: You're pretty gun crazy.

W.B.: I don't think crazy is quite the word. I just *like* guns. Some people like butterflies, some people like . . . knife collections are very popular, you know. For me to be justified in shooting someone, he has to be using what is legally known as *deadly force*. The deadly force hasn't come at me yet, and I don't expect it will, but it doesn't do any good to be wise after the event.

D.F.: What don't you like?

W.B.: I don't like centipedes and I don't like flies. Flies are dangerous, they can lay eggs in your ear, then the larvae hatch out and eat into the brain and kill people. If you are ever in the South Seas and see a tiny blue octopus on the beach, don't pick it up – they bite and everyone who's been bitten by the blue ring octopus has been dead within the hour. There's no antidote. I'm going to do a book of things you mustn't do. It gets very cold in Kansas in winter. If it's 16 below zero and there's a slight wind, say 30 mph, that makes it the equivalent of 60 below. My dear, several people round here in the winter popped out to collect their mail and a little wind came up and poop, they never came back.

But today the temperature is in the mid 80s in the heart of America and the crickets whirr like a Lancashire mill. We are in the garden now and Burroughs is dancing slowly along the perimeter of his property, waving the long, pink cattle prod.

W.B.: It packs 5,000 volts. Enough to make any trespasser apologize. It works best if there's a little water around – perhaps you should spit on em first!

D.F.: Are you healthy? I mean physically.

W.B.: Very healthy. I've never had a major illness in my life. I used to do martial arts, judo, but this bit of jumping up six feet into the air and kicking your opponent in the back of the head, my arthritis gets in the way. I go walking round Lawrence.

D.F.: Is there a conflict in you between the writer and the man of action?

W.B.: This is an artificial dichotomy, although Hemingway's determination to act out the least interesting facets of his own character posed serious limitations on his writing.

D.F.: This conflict – is this why he committed suicide?

W.B.: Oh, he was out of his head. I was convinced he suffered organic brain damage when he had that crash and had to butt his way out of the plane. The best thing he ever wrote was *The Snows of Kilimanjaro*, a story about death which he had a particular feeling for. He could smell it on others.

D.F.: Have you ever wanted to commit suicide?

W.B.: Never. I can't see that suicide is bettering one's position at all.

D.F.: Do you believe in an afterlife?

W.B.: Certainly. I never doubted the possibility of an afterlife, nor the existence of gods –

D.F.: But an afterlife presupposes –

W.B.: Hold on – wait a minute – I'm quoting from *The Place of Dead Roads*, a book of mine. *Kim never doubted the possibility of an afterlife nor the existence of gods. He thought that immortality was the only goal worth fighting for and he knew it was not something you just automatically get from believing some rubbish or other like Christianity or Islam. It was something you had to work and fight for like everything else in this life or another.* I do feel that Christianity is the most virulent spiritual poison ever administered to a disaster-prone planet. It is parasitic, fastens on to people, and the essence of evil is parasitism.

D.F.: So what is your function as a writer?

'The function of all art,' he shouts from the other side of the garden as he crawls playfully on all fours round a tree after the cat, 'and by that I include creative scientific thought, is to make people aware of what they know and don't know they know, coz you can't tell anybody anything that they don't know already on some level.'

'Do you cry easily, Bill?'

'Not easily – but I do cry. It's not necessarily a question of getting upset – it's something that hits you, something that moves you. I cried not so long ago.'

'Is loneliness ever a problem?'

'No, it isn't. I gave a course in creative writing at New York City College. I don't believe it can be taught. But I said there are certain prerequisites. One, you have to be able to spend hours at a typewriter in solitude – if you can't, forget about being a writer.

'What are the other prerequisites?'

'A lot of reading. I think it was T. S. Eliot who said that if someone has a pretentious literary style it's usually because they haven't read enough books.'

Bill talks very well, for hours, then on through the next day. Why is Kansas a dry state? Why is Lawrence called the Paris of the Plains? Where do you get your vice in a place like this? What indeed is the Plains sensibility?

'Good God, these aren't the Plains! The Plains are 300 miles west of here – the most goddam desolate country I've ever seen, not a tree in any direction. The Plains sensibility must be whatever lunacy causes people to carry on living there.'

James Grauerholz, future tender of the shrine, arrives in gold-rimmed spectacles to take us to dinner. Burroughs produces a large shopping bag and starts to fill it with weaponry.

'With these books of yours, the strange worlds and weird sex and so on, you must get a lot of people just turning up on the doorstep making horrible suggestions.'

'It's not something I encourage. But I'm prepared,' he says, clanking the shopping bag. 'Some people call it paranoia – but I say a paranoiac is a man in possession of all the facts. Was Pasolini paranoid? That kid murdered Pasolini from behind with a plank with nails sticking out of it. The nails penetrated his skull. I have heard from various people that this kid was hired by a right-wing group.'

It's getting dark outside. Magnificent sheets of shocking pink lightning light up patches of the sky and tornadoes are forecast over the next few days.

'Look at this, my favourite, my Charter Arms 2″ Barrel Undercover .38 Special – I'd like to see some dumb fucker with a bag of ice get past that! And look at this,' he says, pulling on a jacket of blue-based tartan in some synthetic material. 'I got it from the Thrift Shop. They're the Salvation Army places. Eight dollars, pretty good, eh? I enjoy a bargain.' And donning the famously unalluring spectacles, plonking a pork pie hat on his head, he selects a stout walking stick, picks up the clanking shopping bag, and moves keenly into the outside world.

●

MAE WEST

Interviewed by Charlotte Chandler
The Ultimate Seduction, 1984

Mae West (1893–1980), the American actress, was born in Brooklyn, New York. She started out in vaudeville as an impersonator and singer, and she first performed on Broadway in 1911. She wrote and starred in the plays *Sex* (1926) and *Diamond Lil* (1928) before entering films in her forties. *Diamond Lil* was filmed as *She Done Him Wrong* (1933) and West's screen persona emphasized her delight in sexual innuendo. She made ten films between 1932 and 1943, and returned to the screen for a cameo role in the film version of Gore Vidal's *Myra Breckinridge* (1970). She was noted for her wit.

Charlotte Chandler is an only child and was born in California, and at the age of nineteen she gave up telling people her age. She started writing as a child, for children's and poetry magazines, and she has always been a freelance. Her first major article, an interview with Juan Perón, was bought by *Playboy*. Her next assignment for *Playboy* was to obtain an interview with Groucho Marx, who was famous for turning down interviews. 'I asked Groucho if he would do the *Playboy* interview with me. He said, "*Life* magazine just offered me $10,000, and I told them I wouldn't do it for $20,000. And I wouldn't do it with you for $30,000." Then, he asked me if I'd like to come over so he could tell me "no" in person. I went right over. Groucho showed me his "Marxabilia" collection, invited me to dinner, and spent the rest of the evening talking about his long career in show-business. About 11 o'clock, he said, "Why aren't you writing?" That's when I knew I was doing the interview .'

After publication of the interview, Groucho suggested that Chandler write a book about him. The result was *Hello, I Must Be Going* (1978), which was based on interviews with Groucho (one conducted by Woody Allen in Chandler's presence) and his friends. Groucho also spurred Chandler into writing a book about 'all those famous people' she had met. The book was called *The Ultimate Seduction* ('The passions that motivate you may change, but it is your work in life that is the ultimate seduction') and contained long interviews with Federico Fellini, Henry Moore, Henry Fonda, Alfred Hitchcock, Juan Perón, Mae West and Tennessee Williams, and shorter interviews with Picasso, Charlie Chaplin and Frank Sinatra. *Confessions of a Nightingale*, a one-man show based on Chandler's conversations with Tennessee Williams, played for a year in Los Angeles.

Mae West held out her hand to me. As I took it, I scratched my palm on one of her diamond rings. Noticing what had happened, she commented in a matter-of-fact tone, 'They're old-cut, very sharp. That's the best kind.'

All of her fingers were covered with diamonds. She wore a diamond necklace, diamond bracelets, and a diamond anklet. These, she explained, were just her 'daytime diamonds'. Holding out her hands so I could examine them, she said, 'Look, they're all real. They were given to me by admirers.' Her gaze settled on my own unadorned hands. 'Oh, my, you poor kid! You don't have any!'

For a moment she regarded me silently with amazement and pity. Then she brightened. 'But you have some at home?'

I shook my head.

Her look of deep sympathy returned. She studied me for a moment, then said encouragingly, 'You *could*, honey. But you've gotta try, and you've gotta know *how* to try. There's nothing better in life than diamonds.'

'Maybe that's what one has to believe in order to get them,' I said.

'You're right,' she said. 'You put your finger on it. Everything's in the mind. That's where it all starts. Knowing what you want is the first step toward getting it.' She held out her hands for both of us to admire. 'These diamonds here – they're my friends. Aren't they beautiful? The only thing more important is health.'

I found myself aware of a distracting sound – something like the fluttering of the wings of little birds. Trying not to appear inattentive to what she was saying, I could not resist glancing around the room. But I saw no birdcages. The sound continued at frequent intervals. Only after Mae had been speaking for a while did I realize that it was the sound of her heavily mascaraed, multilayered false eyelashes brushing her cheeks whenever she blinked.

Mae West had been giving no interviews at all. Whenever she answered her telephone, which was rarely, she would pretend to be the maid. Mae already knew all the people she ever wanted to know, especially in light of the many hours she felt compelled to spend on her hair, makeup, and dress before she could see anyone. Her face was nearly hidden by its mask of makeup, but her throat and décolletage revealed strikingly fair, soft, and youthful skin. I had cost her three hours, as I was told more than once, but it would have been double that if I had been a man. If she were going to see anyone at all, a man would have been preferable any day, and especially any night.

'They always sent a man,' she told me, not specifying who 'they' were. 'I considered spending my time with girls a waste of time, so I didn't mingle with any.' The only exceptions were her beloved mother and her sister, Beverly. Men were the ones doing the interesting things, and they were the ones who had the power to enable her to do them.

For Mae West, Hollywood had real unreality, and that was the way she liked it. To the end, she nobly resisted any assault on her fairy-tale castle. The apartment in Hollywood's Ravenswood was truly an extension of Mae West, not only reflecting her, but also enhancing her and probably inspiring her. She had put a great deal of herself into it, and in return got a great deal back. The furniture was upholstered in eggshell-white silk and satin, and appeared virginal, as if it had just been moved in for my visit. Actually, the white and gold furnishings had been there since the early thirties when Mae first arrived, with time out only for reupholstering or cleaning.

There were none of the ubiquitous house plants. 'Plants use up too much oxygen,' Mae explained erroneously, but with certainty. The apartment was cool because, as she said, 'It's good for the furniture and the complexion. I like the air filtered and moving.'

I wondered how her apartment was maintained in such pristine condition, wishing that the answer would be something I could apply to my own, but knowing instinctively that the sorcery could not be transferred. It seemed somehow natural that Mae West's furniture would not get dirty. Magic has a certain fragility; any answer would only spoil the illusion.

Once Mae had achieved perfection by her own standards, she hated any change. She had never forgotten the life of the stock company and vaudeville when she had no control over her environment. 'I did enough traveling when I was very young, so I didn't need to do that anymore. I got it out of my system. I have everything I want right here.' She said she never wanted to have to move.

Mae West's apartment was a home for her and by her which reflected not some noted interior decorator but Mae herself. The accumulation of memorabilia, gifts from fans, and treasured family souvenirs indicated that the private Mae West was a more sentimental person than her public character pretended to be. The celebrations of herself on display throughout the apartment – the nude marble statues and oil paintings in 'classical' style of Mae West at the moment of her greatest success – evinced no false modesty. They also signified that in her mid-eighties she was not afraid to be in competition with her younger self. She was still optimistic and had future plans and ambitions.

Whenever Mae interjected one of her celebrated epigrams or aphorisms to make a point, she would change from a serious tone to the sultry flippancy of Diamond Lil. Sometimes she would break up long words into several syllables, pausing between the syllables to create an exaggerated sensual effect. As she spoke, her sculpted platinum hair would swing as in a shampoo commercial, but without a wind machine to blow it. She frequently tossed her head and the movement of her hair would punctuate her comments.

Always the mistress of illusion, Mae wore long dresses or flared-bottom pants designed to cover her stiltlike shoes. Her shoes had the highest heels I had ever seen, and the heels seemed higher than the shoes were long. Just looking at them made my feet hurt. They reminded me of the heels on Carmen Miranda's platform shoes I had seen exhibited at the museum in Rio de Janeiro. Edith Head speculated that it was the height of those heels that had caused Mae West's famous suggestive walk. In those shoes it was the only way she *could* walk! They were so heavy it was actually difficult for her to rise from a chair. I asked Mae how she thought men would do if they had to live their lives in high heels.

'They wouldn't make it,' she answered. 'They'd be wiped out.'

Perhaps she didn't like to give interviews to women because she couldn't act her part. With a woman she had to reveal a lot more of the private person. Mae West had to be there herself; she couldn't just send Diamond Lil. She pointed out that although she was Diamond Lil, Lil was not Mae because there was more to Mae West. Public and personal success are two different things. It was easier for Lil to be happy than it was for Mae. For Lil, happiness was sex. For Mae, it was work.

Mae gave me a hard look and said there was something she had to tell me before we really 'got into it'.

'If you want to smoke,' she said, 'you'll have to leave the room and go out into the hall. We don't keep any ashtrays here. I don't let anyone smoke in my presence. I don't breathe it, and I don't want it getting into the furniture. Let me know when you want to go out into the hall.'

I assured her that this wouldn't be necessary because I didn't smoke and never had. Her approving look indicated that I had passed an important test.

MAE WEST: Then you'll keep your soft skin. That's how I kept mine. I always use baby oil. Baby oil's good for the whole body. But the secret is it has to be warm, and you have to have a man put it on you – all over.

I can smell you're telling the truth about smoking, because if you smoked, your clothes and hair would smell from it, especially your hair. You know, I never liked being touched by a man who smoked.

*

Her next query had the same tone of entrapment as the smoking suggestion. She asked me if I wanted to have a drink. I declined. She said it was a good thing because she didn't have any liquor.

MAE WEST: My mother was a health nut and my father an athlete. I never understood drinking. It isn't good for your health or your looks, and it cuts down on what you are. I never wanted to cut down on what I am.

I was indefatigable. I never knew exactly why. I always had this extraordinary energy that I had to do something with. They only just found out that I had a double thyroid. Always had it, but I didn't know it. Maybe that's always been the source of my energy, especially my sex energy. When they told me I had a double thyroid, they wanted to take one away, but I wasn't doing that. I don't believe in tampering.

I: Differences the world considers odd or eccentric may actually be a person's good fortune, but there are always those who value conformity over individuality.

MAE WEST: Individuality is everything – individuality and enthusiasm.

I: I think enthusiasm is a big factor in energy. There's nothing more tiring than things going wrong – discouragement and disappointment.

MAE WEST: I could hardly wait for life. I wanted to run toward it with open arms.

Is that scarf because you're cold, or do you have something to hide? [*I take it off*] That's better. Now, if you'd unbutton a few buttons . . . Men like it if you show them a thing or two. I dress for women and undress for men.

Mae loved clothes and was a collector of them. Her perfectly kept gowns were not just stored but seemed to have a life of their own, rather like a row of headless ladies standing there waiting for a party to rescue them from their boredom. The feathered boas and lacy peignoirs looked as though they had stories to tell if I could have interviewed them, but they were forever keeping all confidences. Mae's final fashion show was for her best and favorite audience – herself, alone.

When she encouraged me to try on some of the clothes, I was hesitant, but she persuaded me to model a black peignoir. 'Doesn't it make you feel sexy?' she asked. Her words were barely spoken when she looked at me in disgust. I had put it on over my blouse and skirt. 'You can't get the feeling like *that*,' she explained. 'You have to be naked underneath.'

MAE WEST: When I was making a film, I would stand during the whole shooting – five, six, seven hours a day – so I wouldn't wrinkle my dress. I even stood to eat. They'd say to me, 'Mae, aren't you tired?' But I didn't let myself get tired. I'd say to myself, 'Do I want to look my best for my public that expects it of me? Or would I rather sit down?' That ain't no choice.

First impressions are what count. I was always careful about the first dress I wore onstage or in a picture. It's like when you arrive at a party. That's the important moment. That's when people take a real look at you, size you up, and if they're impressed, that's how they think of you and remember you. If your makeup fades a little and you get a few creases in your dress later and you look a little tired, that isn't what they remember.

I: What would you do if you didn't make the best first impression on a man?

MAE WEST: Get a different man. I'd figure there was something wrong with him.

See that gold lion under my piano? A fan sent it to me. They send me gifts all the time. I have some women fans, too. I added the costumes to my shows to get the women. The women came to see my clothes, and the men came to see *me*. Clothes are important to a woman because a woman feels sexier in a black nightgown with lace.

I: It seems to me that elegant nightgowns are of more interest to women than to men.

MAE WEST: Well, I never needed clothes to make *me* feel sexy. I felt that way all the time, and that's the kind of thing men can tell. The nearness of an attractive man kept me in a constant state of sensual unrest.

I: You summed it up at the end of *I'm No Angel* when Cary Grant asked you, 'What are you thinking about?' and you answered, 'The same thing you are.'

MAE WEST: That's very exciting for a man. When men sense a woman is ready for sex, they're ready right away. Men are simpler than women that way. It's the way they're made – very uncomplicated. When men came to see me, I had to try to calm them down a little first.

I: It was probably the scenario in their minds on the way over here that did that.

MAE WEST: Yeah, calming them down wasn't easy. [*Sighing*] I had a lot of great love affairs.

I: I almost had dinner with you the last time you were at Groucho's house. Elliott Gould was there, and he told me about that evening.

MAE WEST: Elliott's a bear of a man. I've always loved bears. Say, you know what I just thought of? I remember my first sex dream. It was with a bear. I guess I was about ten, maybe younger. He came through the door standing up – a giant male bear. I never had the dream again. It worried me for a long time. I really haven't thought about this for years. I never told anyone. I learned later that the bear is a symbol of sex.

I: Maybe it has something to do with 'bare'.

MAE WEST: Sex and work have been the only two things in my life.

I: But in reverse order of importance . . .

MAE WEST: Yeah. If I ever had to choose between sex and my work, it was always my work I'd choose. I'm glad I didn't ever have to choose between them for more than a week at a time, though. Since I was grown up, I've never been without either for more than a week.

I: What's 'grown up'?

MAE WEST: Thirteen. I was active before that, but it wasn't on a regular basis. Before that, I was finding my way.

I: Didn't you ever have any trouble finding a man?

MAE WEST: [*Puzzled*] What do you mean?

I: I mean one you really liked.

MAE WEST: I never had any trouble. They always found me. I could always find something to like about every man. Well, *almost* every man.

Paul Novak, Mae's friend who lived with her and who had opened the door for me, came in from the kitchen carrying a tray with glasses and bottles of mineral water. Each glass had on it a different illustration of a glamorously costumed Mae.

MAE WEST: Would you like some mineral water? It's all we drink here. I even take my bath in mineral water. You know, I never had a cold.

I: To what do you attribute that?

MAE WEST: My mind. I made up my mind. People don't understand its power. [*Touching her forehead*] Everything's right here. Everybody's busy thinking about what's in other people's heads. It's your own you've gotta live with.

I: So much of what seems to be happening to us, I suppose, is only happening in our minds, and it's really our perception of it that makes us happy or unhappy.

MAE WEST: Imagination can make you happier. People don't have to use their minds to torture themselves. I think you've gotta take as good care of your mind as you do of your body. Just like you put oil on your body and take bubble baths to keep it soft and in good shape, you don't want to clutter up your mind with negative thoughts and bad news.

Paul asked me how I had managed to get through the Ravenswood's protective lobby and up in the elevator without even being announced. I said that I had asked for him, assuming that strangers gave Mae West's name but knowing his name would be the password.

Mae kept looking at the gift-wrapped box from Krön I had set down on the table. 'What's that?' she asked with childlike enthusiasm.

'George Cukor told me you have a passion for chocolates,' I explained.

'I do have a passion,' she said. 'What kind of chocolates are they?'

'One is made very healthy, with hardly any sugar. It has prunes and dried apricots inside because I was told you like healthy things. The other is a cream truffle.'

Opening the first box, Mae almost destroyed the contents in her haste to get inside. Then she voraciously attacked the second box, nearly mashing a few creams. It was only after she had both boxes open that she made her choice. As if fearing someone might take the box away from her, she snatched two chocolate truffles.

'I like my pleasure,' she said, composing herself and holding out the box to

me. 'You can have one, too, honey.' She never let go of the box. Not wishing
to deprive her, I selected one chocolate-covered apricot and began to eat it.

'You have nice manners,' Mae said. 'You eat like a lady. When I was a little
girl, I watched myself in the mirror while I ate so I'd do it right. Some people
chew like cows chewing their cud.' Then she took the box away, as if she
thought I was going to be too much of a lady and eat another piece. Mae
indulged in one more and was reaching for a fourth when Paul firmly took the
box away from her. She looked petulant, but not displeased.

MAE WEST: I like my men to be men. You know, my mother never let me
have any chocolate when I was a child. She said it was bad for my teeth. I have
every one of them.

PAUL NOVAK: [*To Mae*] Do you want anything else?

MAE WEST: [*Suggestively*] Maybe later . . . [*To me, as Paul leaves the room*] That's
a nice pair of shoulders, isn't it? Did you see those biceps? [*Crashing sound of glass
from the kitchen*] I hope he didn't hurt anything . . . important. Paul's handsome,
and he's a wonderful man. He never tries to change me. Men always liked me
because I wasn't like any other woman they'd ever known. They'd all say to
me, 'I never knew a woman like you, Mae,' because I was unique. But you
know what was funny – when a man was courting me, he'd want to put a
diamond on my finger, and as soon as he thought he had me, he wanted to put
an apron around my waist. I didn't want any diamond handcuffs. I had my
career to think about, and any man who wanted me to be less than I was, I
didn't need.

You're sure you don't smoke?

I: I never have.

MAE WEST: The next time you come, I'm gonna give *you* some chocolate.
Have you ever eaten Ragtime chocolate?

I: I don't even know what it is.

MAE WEST: Hardly anyone does anymore. I know the last place in America
that still makes it, and it's not far from here.

I want to show you my mother's picture. Isn't she beautiful?

I: She's lovely.

MAE WEST: She was soft and feminine, completely the opposite from my
father. My father was called 'Battling Jack'. He was a real man. He'd fought in
the ring and on the streets. He had a stable, but later he was a detective. I
remember sitting outside his office, playing with my doll and watching the
people. Then, when they left, I'd go in and give him my opinion of them. I was
always right. He'd say, 'How could Mae know so much about people?' I judged
people that way all my life. If I didn't like you when you came in, I would've
told you to go.

My mother lost a baby girl just before me. My sister only lived a few months,
so I was her whole world. She treated me like a jewel. She never even used
a bad tone with me. She did everything I wanted. If I saw a doll, she got me

the doll I wanted. Once we went to a store, and there were a hundred dolls. Everyone thought all the dolls looked alike. The one I wanted was on the highest shelf no one could reach. They had to go and get a ladder and someone to climb the ladder. It drew a crowd. Everyone in the store thought I just wanted that one because I was difficult. But I wanted her because she had a mauve dress. I don't know where that color went. It used to be real big. I was four years old, but I knew I only wanted that one. They didn't see the difference. If you see the difference and other people don't, they think you're just being difficult. I always knew what I wanted. My mother never questioned it. She made them get a ladder and get me the one I wanted.

    i: Do you know where that doll is now?
    MAE WEST: No. I wish I did. Maybe the doll's with my mother.
    I was an only child for a long time. I was lucky that way. I had a sister and a brother, but they came along later, and it wasn't the same for them. I had my mother alone for the first five years. My sister and brother had to share her with each other and with me. By the time they came, I didn't need so much from her anymore. I was never jealous of my sister and brother. In my whole life, I've never envied anyone. I was too busy thinking about myself.
    My mother wanted to be an actress. She finally got that through me. She always came to see me. She had a box seat. I took her out on the stage with me for a curtain call before she died. That really made me happy, that I could give her that. On a New Year's night, I was playing with Harry Richman. Everyone came onstage, and I brought her out. She loved it. She lit up. I threw the audience a kiss, and she did, too.
    The hardest thing that happened to me in my life was when my mother died. I cried. I never got over it.

On the white piano Mae had pictures in old silver frames of her parents. 'I lost a lot of pictures when the basement flooded,' she told me. 'It was terrible. I lost a part of me.'
    MAE WEST: The success I had on the stage was worth it for my mother to come out and take that bow with me. And all the money I made, it was worth everything, because it paid for the most important thing I ever bought. My mother loved hats, and I saw this hat which was the most wonderful hat in the world. She had a black dress with lace sleeves, long tight-fitted lace sleeves, and black lace up around the neck. One day in New York I saw this hat, and right away I knew it was made for my mother, and that she could wear it with her favorite black lace dress. It was mauve.
    I can see that hat in my mind just as clear today as I did the day I was holding it in my hand in the store. It was turned up on one side so you'd be able to see her blond hair. The crowning touch was the feather, the greatest ostrich feather you ever saw. The hat cost eighty-five dollars, which was really a

lot then. I'd never seen a hat that expensive before. But I knew I had to have it for my mother. I didn't hesitate a second. I would have bought it whatever it cost.

I took it home, and I couldn't wait for any special occasion. I just rushed in the door and gave it to her. She couldn't wait either. She put it right on and kept it on for a long time. She just didn't want to take it off at all, she loved it so much, just the way I knew she would. It was worth everything – that look of pleasure on her face. That's what money's for, when it's really worth something – to buy someone you love so much happiness. That meant more than any diamonds.

I always loved hats just the way my mother loved hats. I loved buying them. I still have just about all of them I ever bought. I can go into the bedroom and try them on by myself all afternoon and be happy. I own more than anyone could wear, but show me a great hat and I can always make room. The funny thing is I live in California where nobody wears them, and many of my hats have never been out of my bedroom. Some people thought I ought to see a psychiatrist, but why spoil a good thing?

I: I believe the more things we have in life that give us pleasure and make our lives richer, the better off we are.

MAE WEST: My mother used to massage me with baby oil after my bath as a child. It's my earliest memory. Nothing ever felt more wonderful than that. I was always more like my father than like my mother, more like a man. My mother took wonderful care of me, but as I grew up, it was like I became her mother and she was my child. I wanted to take care of her and spoil her the way she had done for me.

My mother always started out talking to me with, 'Dear, would you please do this,' or she'd say, 'Would you do this for mother.' She had beautiful manners. Mother knew I could never be forced. Even a wrong tone of voice upset me terribly. I've never liked arguments. They ruin making love.

I always knew when I came offstage my mother would be there waiting for me, holding my favorite little fur muff. My mother is so much a part of my life, I didn't know how I could go on without her. Later, I realized that as long as I live, she lives.

When I was a little girl, my father built me a small stage in the basement of our Brooklyn brownstone. It was all white with a beautiful white curtain. White was always my color. My father wasn't as sure as my mother about me going on the stage so young. He thought maybe I could wait till I was eight. But I couldn't. He said, 'Let her have a chance, and we'll see how she does. But if she gets stage fright, she'll have to wait till she's older.' Can you imagine? Sometimes even one of your own parents doesn't know you. Stage fright! I didn't know the meaning of the word. Still don't.

My mother didn't listen to my father. She knew I could do anything I wanted. As a child I had perfect confidence. Maybe that's why I wasn't ever afraid of anything. Earthquakes don't bother me. I was always happy on boats. It never bothered me that I couldn't swim.

Once when I was a little girl at the beach, I heard someone screaming. There was this little girl drowning. There wasn't anyone else around, so I just jumped in and pulled her out, and got her back to shore. I didn't think about it before I did it because there wasn't any time. Afterwards my father was really angry. 'How could that child have done it when she couldn't swim?' he asked my mother. 'You gotta watch Mae. You never know what she's gonna do.' It was the only time I ever heard him raise his voice to her.

I'd always admired lions. Lions are so beautiful. When I'd go to a new city, I'd go to the zoo just to see the lions. I'd stand outside their cages and have this fantasy:

I'd be in there with them, and they'd be doing just what I wanted them to do, surrendering to me. I would totally command them. I had this tremendous passion for it and no fear. I knew the lions would recognize me and wouldn't hurt me. I'd always wanted to be a lion tamer. It was a kind of dream of mine. *I'm No Angel* was a circus picture, and through being an actress I really got to do it. I didn't use a double.

They weren't gonna let me do it. The professional lion tamer couldn't be there because, just before, a lion had attacked him, and he had to be taken to the hospital. I told them I wasn't gonna wear the fur cape they had for me. I just didn't like it. But it was a good thing. Maybe the lions wouldn't have liked the fur. There had been some dogs near the fur, and they might have smelled them. The lions were wonderful. They were nervous, though, probably because of what had happened just before, but I wasn't. I was thrilled. I was able to stand my ground and dominate those big male lions.

When I came out of the cage, everyone applauded. I didn't ever have to go back because I'd done it.

I: Very few of us have the opportunity to live out our fantasies. An actress may have that opportunity.

MAE WEST: Being an actress and a writer both – that's the best thing you could be in life because you can be anyone you want to be. You just write yourself the part, and then you play it. That way you can skip the dull stuff. And when you get tired, you can be somebody else.

Say, do you want to know about my first love affair? It was when I was five. I made my debut in Brooklyn at the Royal Theater. I fell in love on that stage. It was my first love affair with my audience, and it's lasted all my life. That was the only one that ever really counted. No man could equal that. I could hardly wait to be on the stage – in the warm glow of the lights. Even then I knew that's when I'd really be alive. I heard the applause, applause just for me, and I knew they really liked me, and I knew then there wasn't any other place I ever wanted to be. I've never been more secure than when I'm onstage. I had to have the spotlight more than anything else, shining full on me. I ached for it, the spotlight, which was like the strongest man's arms around me, like an ermine coat.

As a child I was always imagining my name up in lights. I would fall asleep at night seeing my name up there in lights. I used to sit and practice my autograph for hours. I'd try one way and then another until I got it just right. I'm the one who changed my name from May to Mae. It looked better to me that way when I was a little girl signing the autographs. Besides, I didn't like that 'y' hanging down below the line. I don't like anything downbeat.

I always changed things in my parts. When I was eight years old, I would see a piece of business that could be added. Sometimes I'd add lines of my own. I always got my way. I was always putting fresh things in my act to keep my own interest. If you don't keep your own interest, it shows. I used to write myself extra material so I could do fresh stuff for my encores. You gotta believe in yourself. I knew the theater was my destiny, and I always worked hard. That's all I wanted, to work. I didn't want a life of dull routine.

I: Who were the performers who influenced you when you were beginning your career?

MAE WEST: Nobody influenced me. I've always just been myself.

I: And you got to be more yourself as you went along.

MAE WEST: Maybe so. I created Diamond Lil. She was one of the great characters of all times. I respected Groucho and the Marx Brothers because they were funny, but what I admired most was they created their own characters. Chaplin was a really great artist who also created his own character.

My education was the theater. I saw Billie Burke and Tyrone Power, the father. Bert Williams was my favorite when I was a child, and I wanted to meet him. One night my father came home and said, 'Mae, I have a big surprise for you. Bert Williams is here. I've brought him home to have dinner with you.' I rushed in, looked at this man, and screamed, 'It's not! It's not!' I went up to my room and cried. I was terribly upset. My mother told me my father wanted to go up to me, but Bert Williams stopped him. He said, 'I'll do it.' He stood outside my door and started to sing. Then I knew and came right out of my room, and we all had dinner.

Do you know why I didn't recognize him? He was too light. He was a black man, but he was too light, so onstage he wore blackface. He was a great star, but they used to make him use a separate entrance. He died a long time ago, before I came to Hollywood.

I cried because I couldn't bear the thought that my father had lied to me. I never cried again except when my mother died. I had no other reason to cry. I got everything I wanted.

I: Was there ever something you wanted a lot and didn't get?

MAE WEST: No. Some women know how to get what they want. Others don't. I've always known how.

I: How what?

MAE WEST: If you gotta ask, that's bad. You know, honey, you're one who *doesn't* know how. You're missing something. You haven't got wiles, woman's wiles. Am I right?

I: Probably. I've always believed that pretending only gets you what you *don't* want. As a woman who *does* know how to get what she wants, what advice would you give to the ones who don't?

MAE WEST: I couldn't give advice to a woman unless I knew her, and I don't know any.

This room makes me feel rich. I always liked nice things around me. Money does that. People judge you by the value you put on yourself – in show business, in sex, in life. But in my first show I didn't even sign a contract. The show was a tremendous success, and people said to me, 'Now you can hold 'em up and get plenty.' I didn't care. I just wanted to be the star of a hit show.

I: Did you prefer being on the stage or making films?

MAE WEST: I liked both. It was nice to have the live audience, but the films are so important. We can look at them now. All those people who weren't even born when the films were being made are my fans now. My pictures are on television just about every night. I hope you've been watching. I haven't changed, have I? [*She doesn't wait for my answer*] Men were always most of my audience. They got to the box office first! [*Laughs*] But seriously, I used to wonder about it. We put a lot of beautiful clothes into the shows so we'd have the fashion to attract the women. Even when I was doing the nightclub act, there were still a lot more men in the audience. But some of the men brought wives, so I decided to ask the women why they were there. 'It's for our husbands.' So there it was.

I've stayed in demand because I never gave 'em too much. I've always left 'em wanting more. Today television is the fastest way to finish yourself off. Now you don't see great people like there used to be in the world.

I: Giants are in short supply.

MAE WEST: Too many people see you for nothing. They're always wanting me to be on those talk shows, but I don't go. Television's okay for people who've got something to sell. I don't need to.

I: Of what in your career are you proudest?

MAE WEST: I saved Paramount Pictures. They were selling out. The Paramount theaters would've been finished. But my pictures made so much money for them, they were able to stay in business during the thirties. They oughta have a statue of me. At least a bust. Miss Bette Davis didn't save Warner Brothers. Miss Joan Crawford didn't save any studios. Paramount oughta have put up a statue of me.

I: [*Indicating a nude statue of Mae West in her living room*] Like that?

MAE WEST: No. One of Diamond Lil in a beautiful dress. After my picture about Diamond Lil, sex was more out in the open. I'm proud of that because I always believed that sex was nothing to be ashamed of. I didn't see love as a sin. Overwhelming desire is wonderful.

I: Do you think sex is better with love?

MAE WEST: Honey, sex with love is the greatest thing in life. But sex without love – that's not so bad either. Sex is the best exercise for developing everything. It's very good for the complexion and the circulation. Keeps it all moving along. I've always had the skin of a little girl. Go ahead, touch it. [*I touch her skin*] That's all real. I didn't ever have to lift *anything*. Never go out in the sun. I never did. It'll ruin your complexion. You have nice skin, too.

I: Thank you.

MAE WEST: Don't thank me. I didn't do it. You're just lucky.

I: Lucky is the best thing to be.

MAE WEST: Timing is very important in life. And in sex. Life and sex are a lot alike, don't you think?

I: Life is discovery of the unknown, and I suppose sex is the discovery of the unknown in another person.

MAE WEST: We oughta know everything about ourselves, but it's better not to know everything about each other. Each of us oughta draw up a private, a very private, accounting of our sexual needs. Sex isn't common, to be handed around like a box of chocolates. First sex meetings are very special. The first time with each man is important. I remember one who did it the first time for fifteen hours.

I: Do you remember when you first thought about sex?

MAE WEST: I can't remember when I didn't. I was curious about the boys and what they had that I didn't. I always played with boys. They used to gather 'round me. They called me 'Peaches'. I liked to see how each one kissed. A man's kiss is his signature.

At twelve I'd kiss all the boys at parties. I liked comparing their techniques. But kissing and all that stuff, that's all we did. I liked to feel their muscles.

I always liked having a lot of men around. On a rainy night it's like having more than one book to choose from, only better. Men's thoughts and ambitions were like mine. If you were out in the world doing interesting things, it would be men you'd meet. It was a man's world, and you'd be with men because men were the ones doing things.

I found one man who had beautiful hair, another had great muscles, and another one . . . umm. I didn't see why I should deprive myself of anything, so a lot of men was better for me than just one man. That way I could enjoy what was great about each one, but I wasn't tied to him. I didn't have to waste any time worrying about what he didn't have and trying to change him.

All of my ideas about women are what men's ideas are about women because all I know is what men told me. I never mingled with too many women. Men were so surprised by me, I knew there must be a lot of women out there doing it badly. Or maybe not doing it bad enough. Women spend too much of their lives saying no. Most women are used to practicing no, they get to stay home and wash their hair on Saturday night. They expect a man to answer all their problems for them. There's nothing better than a man's shoulder to lean on, but you don't want to lean too hard.

I: It always seemed to me it's difficult being a man. So much is expected from a man. With women, the problem is often just the opposite – not enough is expected.

MAE WEST: You've gotta help your man, to put him at his ease. He's gotta be relaxed to get excited.

I: It's like trust and lust. Trust has to precede lust.

MAE WEST: Yeah. I made my man feel like a hero as long as it lasted. Then I was always the one who said good-bye. A few times I was drawn to falling in love, but I didn't let myself fall. I made an effort, and I cut it off. I know why they call it 'falling'. I never let that happen to me.

When I was very young, there'd be all these boys hanging around, and I'd start to think I liked one of them better than the others. Well, my mother wouldn't say anything much against him, but if she saw me liking one too much for my own good, she would point out some little flaw he had, like big ears that stuck out or something. Then I'd see it right away. So I'd like another one, and she'd just mention lightly some little fault he had. That gave me the idea early, which was very important – there wasn't just one.

I never could understand women who would almost die over one man. It wasn't what he had but what qualities they gave him in their own minds. I never wanted anyone to have power like that over me. All the wrong man is, is a bad habit. When you get rid of one, you don't want to waste any time getting another, so you don't sit around moping. When you mope, your mouth turns down; it puts lines in your face. There isn't any man in the world worth getting lines over. I felt it could mean the loss of my identity. That kind of all-consuming love threatened me. And you can't tell who's going to give you the most fun. You never know in advance what any man's physical capacities are going to be. He doesn't even know himself what he might be capable of. Until he finds the right inspiration – the right woman. Too many women wait around depending on men to bring them happiness. I didn't depend on men for mine. I knew how to handle men: Handle them a lot. I have a code though: No drinking, no smoking, and no married men. There are enough men to go around. I never needed to take away another woman's man. Women tell themselves that there's only one man in the world they want. Men are really all alike.

I: Men are all alike except the one who's different.

MAE WEST: But you gotta watch out for men who are heels. A heel is a completely selfish man. He can be clever. He knows how to say just enough of what you want to hear, and to do just enough of what you want, to give you hope. Then when he wants to disappear, he just does. But he comes back after a while just to test his power. He only likes conquest because he's really only making love to himself. The heel likes to keep you waiting for his phone call. You know, a lot of women think, 'I'll be the one it'll be different with. I'm the one he'll change for.' But they're always wrong. While they last, heels can be a lot of fun. I prefer a forty-ripened man, a man who's been around. Of course, there's fun in teaching a young man. He's so thrilled when he learns what he's capable of.

I've heard men say that they were afraid of the responsibility with a girl who was a virgin. But I always thought that initiating a virgin man was a privilege. A certain lack of expertise can have its own kind of charm, and they learn fast. Women don't like a man with *too* much experience. If he's too experienced, too good at what he does, they know how he arrived at his well-practiced techniques. It's fun to be able to teach a man something. Don't you think so?

I: I find it more interesting to play tennis with a better player.

MAE WEST: My best lover was a Frenchman who would pick me up in his car after *Diamond Lil* and take me over to the other theater to rehearse *Pleasure Man*. One Saturday night we were at it till four the next afternoon. A dozen rubber things. Twenty-two times. I was sorta tired. Like I always said, 'It's not the men in my life, it's the life in my men.'

I: What kind of 'life' do you look for in a man?

MAE WEST: Fire. A man can be short and dumpy and getting bald, but if he has fire, women will like him.

I: What if he's tall and slim with plenty of hair?

MAE WEST: That's no problem. But even if he hasn't got fire, maybe you can be the one to light it. A man who could only do it once or twice a night suddenly finds he's got more talent than he knew, and he could do it twelve times. But after that, the same man couldn't ever do it like that with anybody else.

I: Do you think it might be in the head rather than the bed?

MAE WEST: I don't think about it. Thinking spoils the fun, like talking.

I: Don't you think talking can actually enhance making love, if it's the right conversation? It seems that conversation between two people and making love are really quite similar.

MAE WEST: You can talk it all away. The talk of love shouldn't ever be put down on paper, either. It looks silly.

I: I suppose that's because other people's sex seems funny, but not one's own.

MAE WEST: Sex can be funny, but men take it pretty seriously. The most terrible thing you can do to a man is to laugh at him.

I: Who were some of the men you've known who had that fire you mentioned?

MAE WEST: John Barrymore wasn't so bad. I wouldn't have minded playing with him. In a movie, that is.

I: You mean you'd rather have had him as a leading man in a film than as a lover in real life?

MAE WEST: If I'd had to make the choice, yeah. Because movies are forever, and sex doesn't last.

I: You don't think sex and passion *can* last a long time?

MAE WEST: No. Not for the same two people together. What happens is, you might get to be friends, and you could keep that. But being good friends isn't good for sex.

I: If excitement and security don't go together, that could be a problem in marriage.

MAE WEST: Well, I'm not married. I could've married a lot of people, but I was busy.

I: Besides John Barrymore, what other men had that fire?

MAE WEST: Cary Grant. I heard him before I saw him, talking in the alley outside my dressing room at Paramount. Then I went out to take a look, and I liked what I saw. I liked his voice first, but I saw right away that the rest of him measured up. They didn't want him for my second picture, but I insisted. In my second picture he got to dress up, and he got noticed.

I: I gather that most of the men with whom you've had affairs were not performers.

MAE WEST: You weren't in the bedroom with us, honey. With me, they were *all* good performers. But actors don't make good lovers. A man who's just thinking about himself can't be much of a lover.

I: Jean Renoir told me that he always felt a woman who was an actress was more of a woman, while a man who was an actor was less of a man.

MAE WEST: I always liked a strong man, and not many actors seemed that way to me. I liked boxers, wrestlers, body builders. My father was a weight lifter, and he taught me how to use the weights. I taught myself how to use the lifters. Feeling biceps always excited me. Have you felt any good biceps lately?

I: Not today.

MAE WEST: Maybe tonight.

I: Is there a kind of atmosphere or situation that you found conducive to good sex?

MAE WEST: There's something about love under pressure – stolen moments. There's something about knowing you can't get all you want that makes for greater passion.

I: You were married once . . .

MAE WEST: It was a secret marriage. I wish it had been a secret from me. I didn't know it then, but I wasn't the marrying kind. I was asked why did I get married at seventeen. I certainly can't remember now. I guess it was just this physical thing. I always took marriage very seriously. It just wasn't for me. I don't believe in being married and not keeping the contract. And I never fooled around with a married man if I knew he was married. Once one fooled me, and as soon as I found out, I told him to get out. I've never taken a man away from a woman – even in a play.

I: You once said, 'Men are easy to get but hard to keep.' What do you think women should do to keep their men?

MAE WEST: You have to keep your eye on the balls. If you don't take good care of your man, someone else will.

I: Do you ever feel you missed something by not having children?

MAE WEST: Maybe, but I knew I didn't want children. When I was a little girl, I wanted a doll. But I knew that a doll wasn't a baby. You can just put your dolly away when you don't feel like playing that game anymore. Maybe if I missed something, that was it – having a baby. But I don't think I was meant to be a mother. I respect those who make the sacrifice. Motherhood's a full-time career. I already had a career. I didn't think I could do both things right. And they never persuaded me that men don't have the more fun part of having babies. The pill made women feel freer. I didn't need anything to make me feel free. The kind of guy a woman oughta like is one who wouldn't let her take the pill and take a chance on hurting her health.

I: How do you find these times different for women?

MAE WEST: These are vulgar times. I wouldn't discuss my sex life even with my sister. It wouldn't be proper.

I: What do you find vulgar?

MAE WEST: Four-letter words. I'm no puritan, but I don't like bad language. You know, I was always a lady.

I: What's a 'lady'?

MAE WEST: I never said anything vulgar or used rough language, and I never made a beeline for anyone else's man. I never did anything that hurt other people.

I: Do you think that being a lady means something different now from what it did?

MAE WEST: You'd know better about what it is now than I would.

I: One thing that's changed is talking about it as a value. You were a lady or you weren't anything. You were a good girl or a bad girl.

MAE WEST: I was a bad girl with a good heart.

I: You defined lady for yourself. Now, I think, one of the differences is that more girls are defining it for themselves. It used to be that a lady did what other people *said* a lady did. She dressed according to a certain style. Her demeanor was in keeping with a more formalized code of behavior, and she was supposed to want only certain things. The rules were totally prescribed and not open to question. Now there seems to be a less objective definition and a more subjective one, with more women defining it for themselves.

MAE WEST: It used to be a woman was a lady because of what she held back. She was a lady because she didn't give it away unless she had the right contract and everybody said, 'I do', first.

I: That presupposed that she was only giving and not getting, with marriage being all she had to gain.

MAE WEST: I don't think things have changed so much. The rules used to be made by men for men. The rules are a little different, but it's still a man's world, with men making the rules that suit them best.

I: Which time do you think was better for women?

MAE WEST: I think it was better then. The way it is now is really a lot better for men. Now a woman's *expected* to do it, and the man doesn't even have to court her. The woman used to be a bigger prize. She could do what she wanted, but she didn't advertise. I never understood the kind of woman who could write a book and tell who was in her bed. That's selling it. Why would a woman do that?

I: Notches on her garter belt, I guess, though it's pantyhose now.

MAE WEST: I didn't see why marriage and divorce, and marriage again and divorce again was better than two unmarried people making love. I never believed some things were all right for a man and not for a woman. It didn't seem right to me that in a marriage the woman is married all the time and the man only some of the time – when he chooses. I was about six when I noticed that. You've gotta have plenty of self-esteem, nerve, and be bold in life. I've been liberated all my life. I always did what I wanted to do.

I: That's quite a definition of Women's Lib! That would be a lot of liberty for a man.

MAE WEST: Men and women aren't the same. Men worry about what they haven't got, and women *know* what they haven't got.

I: Do you see advantages to being a woman?

MAE WEST: In lovemaking, men run down, but a woman can just go on. Men are a lot better off in life, but not better off than me. No man ever had a better life than I did.

I: [*Indicating a picture of a monkey on the wall*] Who is he?

MAE WEST: One of my best friends, Boogie. But that monkey isn't really my Boogie. He doesn't even look like him. Boogie never ate a grape without peeling it first, and he ate a lot of grapes. He was fastidious. That's where I got my line in *I'm No Angel*. You know, when I say to my maid, 'Peel me a grape.' I loved him. When I was at Paramount I had a dog. My dog loved me so much that when I left him at home, he followed me all the way to Paramount. Of course, I never had any trouble finding men to love me.

I: Perhaps it's more important and even more difficult to find someone *to* love.

MAE WEST: I miss George [Raft]. There was a thing between me and him after *Night After Night*. We stayed friends. That's a real man. I never liked sissies.

I: Who were the directors with whom you liked working?

MAE WEST: Leo McCarey was good, but I was really always the director.

Nobody could tell me how to be me. George [Cukor] was the only director I ever wanted to work with. I never worked with him. He's the biggest and the greatest. There's still time.

I: He told me he went to see *The Drag* in New Jersey.

MAE WEST: *The Drag* was a landmark in treating homosexuality. I did a drag ball in it that caused a sensation. People came from all over the country. They paid scalpers as much as a hundred dollars for a ticket.

The difference between the greatest directors and the ordinary director is that the greatest makes *you* create. It isn't that he tells you exactly what you should do. That would cramp my style. I wouldn't let them hurt my films. They're good pictures. I'd rather watch myself than anyone else. I feel sorry for people who aren't proud of what they do.

I: What do you think about as you're watching?

MAE WEST: It's just like I'm there in them, and then is now. I relive it every time. There was never anyone like me. You know, the female impersonators really like to do me. Some of them are pretty good, but they never fool me.

I: They don't fool me either.

MAE WEST: I'm glad to hear you say that. I used to worry people would be fooled and think it was me.

I: Only striking originality lends itself to imitation.

MAE WEST: They could only do that because I was an original. I didn't understand then what films meant, every new generation rediscovering you. When I first came out here, I didn't understand how important Hollywood was going to be. I always held Hollywood at arm's length – like a would-be lover you can't exactly trust.

I: Do you find Hollywood greatly changed now?

MAE WEST: The star system's gone. I was a real star. The star is someone who has a love affair with her audience. They want to know everything about you, but they can't because you have mystery and romance.

I: There is a delicate balance between access and magic.

MAE WEST: I didn't go out to restaurants and places as much as I might have liked to because who wants to pay money to see someone who's always there for free? These days they're telling every detail of the sex act. Well, I don't think people want to know everything about other people's love lives. I think the two-dimensional figure is more lovable. I think two-dimensional with illusion beats three-dimensional. Valentino had great star quality. When he died, thousands of women wept at his funeral. That's star quality. Now me, I fill a need. If everybody had the most stimulating sex life and the greatest romance, maybe they'd have been less interested in Mae West, and they wouldn't care so much about stars in films.

Garbo was a star, too. Garbo always conducted herself right. She was a real professional. I admired her. She didn't let other people make her live her life the way they wanted her to live it. She had style; she was her own person. She was the only star I wanted to meet I hadn't met, so George [Cukor] arranged for us to meet. He gave a dinner for me and invited her, and she wanted to meet me, too. I kissed her on the cheek. I felt like we knew each other because we were the biggest stars in the world. She didn't say much. She had a wonderful voice and was just the way I thought she would be.

I: Being a celebrity opens up a relatively closed world of famous and, one hopes, interesting people. Was there someone you wanted to meet whom you didn't meet?

MAE WEST: Amelia Earhart. I thought it would be fun to fly, and the sky was a man's world. She was never afraid and she was smart. Brains are an asset – if you hide them. Men think a gal with good lines is better than one with a good line. But if you've got some brains in reserve, people can't use you.

I: Did you feel that people used you?

MAE WEST: *I* did the using. Like we were talking about, a lot of women thought they were giving something away every time a man had some pleasure. I did it for my own pleasure. So why should I begrudge the man having some fun, too?

I: Are there any ways you feel you're different from the public image of Mae West?

MAE WEST: I'm glad you asked that. When people think you're funny, they start to laugh at everything you say. There was a lot of serious reflection in what I said. I hoped you're going to show me that way. You know, my head was always working. And I was always writing.

I: I know you're especially proud of your writing.

MAE WEST: The secret of it is to keep everything moving. Don't let the audience think of the dishes. Once you lose an audience for a moment, it's so hard to get them back. You've gotta milk an audience. You need to have some lines they can take away and remember, like songs they go away humming. I'd have everything in my mind before I'd start to write, so I wouldn't have to stop. I'd imagine it all first, then I'd just write it down. I'd be living it while I was writing it. I never read much because I was too busy living.

Do you type or write longhand?

I: I write longhand.

MAE WEST: That's the only way I could do it. They offered to teach me to type when I was in prison. Did you know I was in prison?

I: Yes. But you weren't an ordinary prisoner.

MAE WEST: I was never an ordinary anything. I had to stand trial because of my show, *Sex*. They said I could pay the fine, but I decided it would be more interesting to go to prison. I was always fascinated by prisons and mental institutions. They told me I had to wear the prison clothes, but I said I was bringing my own underwear. I wore my silk underwear the whole time. It was ten days.

I wanted to help the girls there, but I couldn't do much. A lot of them had made just one mistake. They all wanted to meet me. They admired me, and they weren't jealous. What I wrote was ahead of its time, and I took other chances of going to jail with what I put on stage.

I: How do you feel about censorship?

MAE WEST: I *believe* in censorship! If a picture of mine didn't get an 'X' rating, I'd be insulted. Don't forget, dear – I *invented* censorship. Imagine censors that wouldn't let you sit in a man's lap. I've been in more laps than a napkin! They'd get all bothered by a harmless little line like 'Is that a gun in your pocket or are you just glad to see me?'

I had my tricks for handling the censors. I'd write some lines I knew they would take out so the others could stay in. You had to let them earn their money. You might say I created the Hays Office. They had to do it because of me. I'm a kind of godmother to the Motion Picture Code. Now they use nudity and talking dirty to take the place of a good story and good characters. I didn't have to take off my clothes. Men imagined what was under them.

I: A man's imagination is a woman's best friend.

MAE WEST: Do you know what question I'm asked the most? About the mirrors on my bedroom ceiling. I say, 'I like to see how I'm doin'.' I've never been able to sleep with anyone. I like to have my own bed. I need a lot of room. I don't know if the bed's made, but you can go look at my bedroom.

As in the living room, everything in the bedroom was white. The perfectly made bed was covered with a white satin spread. The mirrored vanity wore a white ruffled skirt and held a queen's ransom of crystal and silver perfume bottles, porcelain powder boxes, and pots of makeup. The white rug looked as if it had known only bare feet. The white drapes were drawn in secrecy. The room and its occupant of half a century were clearly symbiotic as well as sybaritic.

I returned to the living room.

MAE WEST: Did you like what you saw?

I: I did. I appreciate your inviting me to see it. It's one of the most famous bedrooms in the world.

MAE WEST: *The* most famous.

Are you gonna get a mirror on *your* ceiling? [*Not waiting for my answer*] But it isn't any good when you see your reflection alone. What did you think of my bed?

I: I thought what an interview *it* might give!

MAE WEST: I wish I could've shown you my beach house. But I sold it. I miss it. I had murals of naked men on the walls. Great art. Nudity in art isn't sex, it's art. I never lost any money in art or real estate. Real estate and diamonds, those are the best investments. I always put my money into my own projects, something I was doing or something I could see. Money is sexy for men, but people don't find it feminine for a woman to talk about it. So, you don't have to talk about it, just have it. The real security is yourself. You know you can do it, and they can't ever take that away from you.

I: Do you think money buys happiness?

MAE WEST: No, but money is a great love potion for an affair. It buys a good bed in a nice bedroom with clean linens and time to enjoy it all. If you have money, you don't have to worry about it, and worrying spoils your looks.

Are you doing this whole book about me?

I: No, there are other people in it, too.

MAE WEST: I don't usually like to share. What are you calling your book?

I: Do you have a suggestion?

MAE WEST: [After thinking for a moment] You could call the book 'Mae West and others'. That's 'others' with a small 'o', and I want to be the first. Being first is important in life.

I: For you, what's the most important thing in life?

MAE WEST: Getting what you want. My career is everything. Always was. I never changed. Inside, I feel like the same little girl I was. But it was the way I grew up outside that men liked.

I: What else do you think men like in a woman besides physical beauty?

MAE WEST: That's what men care about, except in their wives. Men admire devotion in their wives, beauty in other women. What do you think?

I: It seems to me that for the world a woman is the way she looks, and a man is what he does.

MAE WEST: A man should take as good care of his body as a woman does. I liked physically strong men who could fight over me. I didn't incite them. They just did it and I couldn't stop them.

I: These men seem to be quite a lot like your father, as you've described him.

MAE WEST: I never thought about it, but it's true. I remember once a man looked the wrong way at my mother, and my father took care of him. My mother said, 'You shouldn't have done that,' but she was really pleased.

When my mother died, just living was hard, but going onstage, that was terrible. Then when I was able to do it, working made it easier. [Indicating the photo of her mother on the piano] I didn't want her buried underground. I bought a family place above ground for her. I cried for days and couldn't stop crying. It was the only time I cried. They thought my heart was going to give out. It's the only time I was ever depressed. I always have too much to do to be depressed. I don't believe in depression. Wipe it out! You've got to replace a bad thought with a good one. Happiness is a habit, a good habit. People get depressed because they are bored. I don't get bored because I know how to go into the unknown. I can just sit here and go off into the world of my own thoughts. I could always make up a story. If I wanted to be anyone besides Mae West, I just wrote a story and played the part. I always liked Catherine the Great. She was great. Maybe I was her in another life. After my mother, I never needed another person.

I: Do you feel you deliberately tried not to need another person so you wouldn't feel such pain again?

MAE WEST: Yeah. I knew I couldn't go through that again. When I was a child, I could always talk things over with my mother. Even after she died, in my thoughts I'd be talking with her. I knew her so well that I knew what she'd tell me.

What have you got there?

I: A camera. I was hoping . . .

MAE WEST: I don't have my picture taken with other women. I never like to see myself in a picture, except surrounded by men. I only keep the best pictures of myself, you know. You should always keep the best picture of yourself in your own head. You should have beautiful pictures of yourself all around to look at. Throw away the bad ones. When you don't look your best, you shouldn't even look at yourself in the mirror. You should put on your most beautiful wrapper and all your makeup, and you should wear a wig if your hair doesn't look right. If you don't think you're wonderful, why should anyone else? You should look your best for yourself when you're alone.

I: *Especially* when you're alone.

MAE WEST: Yeah, you can't afford not to look good alone or you'll stay alone. I don't usually go on talking so much.

I: 'Too much of a good thing can be wonderful.'

Now that you aren't working as much, how is your life different?

MAE WEST: I'm lazier. I was always scribbling. Whenever I got an idea, in bed or in a restaurant, I'd write it down on a napkin or a little piece of paper. I saw you scribbling on that little bit of paper, and it reminded me of me.

You know, honey, I see something men must like about you: You're a brilliant listener!

I: It's easy. I've had a wonderful time.

MAE WEST: Do you know my idea of a wonderful time? Sex and chop suey.

I: Together?

MAE WEST: No, not at the same time. The chop suey tastes better after. Chop suey restaurants stay open late, and if they close, you can always go the next night. Chop suey, sex, and my career. My work was the most fun. Sex was second best. I didn't want it when I was working. I wanted to save my sexual energy to put into my work. You've gotta conserve your sex energy in order to do your work. It's the same energy. When I started to write or did a picture, I stopped all my sex activities. Sex divides your mind.

The sex drive is behind everything creative we do. The stronger the sex drive, the stronger the desire to create. When an architect designs a building, he puts his sex drive into creating that building. People who want one thing more want everything more. It's part of the same drive. But there are moments to slow down. I don't like a man that's in a hurry. 'I like a guy what takes his time.'

I: Perhaps men could be divided into two kinds – those who take their watches off, and those who leave them on.

MAE WEST: Say – I like that. You know, maybe you *could* learn, honey. [*I gather up my things to leave*]

Don't forget your baby oil. But remember what I told you: It's gotta be warm, and you've gotta have a man put it on – all over.

Mae apologized for not being able to drive me to my hotel. 'Paul could've given you a lift, but we don't have the Dusenberg anymore.'

I said I understood.

Just as I was leaving, she called me back.

'Honey, there's something I want to tell you before you go,' she said, reaching out and clutching my arm. 'You know, my diamonds I told you all those men gave me? I wanted you to know – I bought some of them myself.'

●

GALINA VISHNEVSKAYA
Interviewed by George Urban
Encounter, December 1986 and January 1987

Galina Vishnevskaya, the Russian soprano, was a member of the Bolshoi Opera company and married the internationally acclaimed cellist Mstislav Rostropovich. Both of them were stripped of their Soviet citizenship in 1978 because of their avowal of dissident opinions. Galina Vishnevskaya's memoirs had been published in both the United States and Britain a couple of years before she gave this interview, which was published in the monthly magazine *Encounter*. I have chosen excerpts from this wide-ranging interview.

George Urban, the journalist and historian, conducted several interviews for *Encounter* during the 1980s, in particular with commentators on Soviet and East European affairs such as Milovan Djilas, Vladimir Bukovsky, and Leszek Kolakowski; US diplomats such as Averell Harriman, Jeane Kirkpatrick and Zbigniew Brezinski; and intellectuals such as Eugene V. Rostow and Daniel Bell. A graduate of Budapest University, Urban worked for the BBC during the 1950s and subsequently for Radio Free Europe. A collection of some of his interviews was published in Britain in 1985 under the title *Can the Soviet System Survive Reform?*

There are many instances in Russian memoirs, yours and others, where ordinary people behave with great callousness towards the victims of persecution. When the NKVD's van arrives to collect some family for deportation, the neighbours look on and nod in approval.

Pasternak, on receiving the Nobel Prize, is reviled and condemned by the authorities, but the Moscow writers at once follow suit, denouncing him as a 'Judas', a 'mercenary scribbler', 'an enemy and betrayer of his own people', and the like. Your own father, having served ten years in Stalin's camps under Article 58, comes out and promptly denounces you at the Bolshoi for having failed to report that you knew why he had been arrested. As you write in your memoirs: 'Of course he hoped that I would be kicked out of the Bolshoi. But Papa had miscalculated: times had changed. He died of lung cancer two years later, one more moral monster spawned by the Soviet régime.' Reading your accounts of Soviet indifference, I was chillingly reminded of Pastor Martin Niemöller's account of public indifference under another dictatorship:

> *When they came for the Jews, I was not a Jew,*
> *so I did not protest;*
> *When they came for the Communists, I was not a Communist,*
> *so I did not protest;*
> *When they came for the trade unionists, I was not a trade unionist,*
> *so I did not protest;*
> *When they came for me, there was nobody left to protest.*

GALINA: It is not exactly that most people approved of what was going on under Stalin, but they were malicious and indifferent. They saw what was happening and said: 'Well, that's how things are – I'm having a bad time, why shouldn't you have a bad time too?' It's terrible.

Let me tell you a story which has done the rounds in Russia.

An Italian, an Englishman, a Frenchman and a Russian are summoned by God.

'You may pronounce one wish for your people and it will be fulfilled,' God says.

The Italian says: 'My wish is that the Italians should be the best singers in the world.'

The Englishman says: 'I want my people to be the best horsemen in the world.'

The Frenchman says: 'I want my nation to have the most beautiful women in the world.'

'And what about you?' God says to the Russian.

'I want my neighbour Vasily's mare to drop dead.'

That encapsulates it to perfection.

Is this appalling attitude an expression of straightforward envy inspired by poverty and deprivation (as left-wing sociologists tend to believe) or is it part of the culture – perhaps both?

GALINA: Well, Russian serfdom is only 120-odd years behind us, and the habits of serfdom seem to die hard. This is, I must confess, not a very satisfactory explanation because in the USA slavery ended later than serfdom did in Russia, and yet in America you have a flourishing democracy, with the black community not a bit behind the whites in their demands for a fuller and more and more egalitarian democracy. But I feel this attitude of malicious envy is rooted in serfdom which has now been reinforced by Communist ideology. Life in a Communist society, with its permanent restrictions, deprivations and bottlenecks, is a rat-race.

Let me put it to you that the vessels of spiritual escape in Soviet society – the holy fools of our day – may very well be people like yourself: artists, especially musicians, who can say things through their pianos and singing and painting that no one else can. The wordless media have a great advantage here over books and poems. Their 'message' is more difficult to identify and it is, therefore, harder to dictate to their authors.

One excellent example of this is mentioned in your book: the Soviet government's hesitation to allow Shostakovich's Fifth Symphony to be performed. The Leningrad Party 'aktiv' which scrutinized the symphony for ideological rectitude first felt that the symphony was 'pessimistic' and 'un-Soviet'. They lectured Shostakovich on how to write music. But Shostakovich had to save his symphony. As you tell us. 'He tried to deceive them in the most rudimentary way, and succeeded! All he had to do was use other words to describe the huge complex of human passions and suffering that is so apparent in his music – he described his music to the Party as joyous and optimistic *– and the entire pack dashed off, satisfied.' What I am suggesting is that in a totalitarian society it is people like yourself who are most likely to be the symbols of dissent from orthodoxy – 'holy fools', if you like: 'liberation musicians'.*

GALINA: Here I agree with you entirely. I felt to be that symbol with great intensity when I sang Leonora in Beethoven's *Fidelio* – the very first time it was put on the stage in the Soviet Union. I wasn't at first quite conscious of that symbol in the sense in which you have just expressed it, but as the rehearsals went on I realized more and more distinctly that this was a 'liberation-opera' and it was really about us in Soviet society.

Of course, I knew from the beginning that *Fidelio* was about freedom, honour and love, but it grew on me only gradually that the words I was singing about freedom, the conquest of injustice and oppression were directly addressed to my audiences, and that I was the person entrusted by the music to impart them. My God, it was an unforgettable experience.

There I was, like Jeanne d'Arc, standing on the stage of the world, calling on the people to release those unjustly imprisoned and punish the wicked. It was a moment that changed my life.

There is that memorable scene in the first Act of Fidelio *where Rocco, at Leonora's urging, allows the prisoners to come out of their dungeon. Emaciated and in rags, and blinded by the sun to which their eyes had become unaccustomed, they stumble out and sing Beethoven's famous prayer to light and liberty 'O welche Lust in freier Luft'. What did you feel when you saw them approaching?*

GALINA: I had my back turned to the audience even though I had an aria coming, but I simply could not take my eyes off this devastating spectacle of human suffering. I felt that it was I personally who had brought them out from prison and was leading them and the public on to liberty. I was overwhelmed.

This was in March 1954, a year after the death of Stalin — after the death of the man about whom the Soviet people had been made to sing:

> *O Great Stalin, O leader of the peoples,*
> *Thou who brought man to birth, . . .*
> *Thou who makes the spring to bloom,*
> *Thou who makes vibrate the chords of music.*

Did the Soviet audiences realize that Fidelio *was about their fate — about the fate of their brothers and sisters who had been in the camps by the million and were just beginning to be released if they were lucky enough to have survived?*

GALINA: No, they did not. Shostakovich and his friends, of course, did; but the public just didn't get the message. Why didn't they get it? Well, in Moscow the sort of people who go to the Bolshoi are not your men and women of culture. They tended to be people who had business in Moscow and felt it was good form to be seen at the Bolshoi, or men and women who were given tickets *ex officio* and were more or less sent to the opera. They went for the ambience and the spectacle, or out of a sense of duty, but were often quite irritated by the music which they didn't understand.

I find it a little hard to believe that the public could have been so insensitive. Didn't they know what was happening around them? Could they have missed the meaning of your aria: 'Zur Freiheit, zur Freiheit ins himmlische Reich'?

GALINA: They didn't make the connection. Some felt such things happened in Spain or in Germany, not in the Soviet Union. They didn't identify with Leonora or Florestan.

In 1978, under the late Karl Boehm, I saw one of the great performances of Fidelio *at the Munich opera. Boehm appended this observation to the programme: 'Und mit dem Fidelio hat er [Beethoven] nicht für irgendeine Freiheit, sondern fur die persönliche Freiheit des Menschen gekämpft.' (With* Fidelio *Beethoven fought not for any kind of freedom, but for man's personal freedom.) I fail to see how this could have been lost on your average Soviet audience. If they missed that, what did they understand?*

GALINA: Quite. As you say, in 1954 there was hardly a Soviet family that had not lost one or several of its members in the Gulag. And yet our audiences did not make the connection. But it wasn't only the people who didn't feel *Fidelio's* sharp relevance to the state of society in Stalin's Russia, but the Party and the Government didn't either.

Throughout the long period of preparation and rehearsal the authorities never showed the slightest sign of realizing that we were about to stage an opera deeply subversive of the Soviet system. In Russia operatic productions go through various stages of censorship. At each stage the message, the decor, the diction, and so on are examined for political suitability. *Fidelio* passed every stage of censorship. No one felt that Beethoven was addressing the oppressed masses of the Soviet Union.

But, surely, you did?

GALINA: I first felt the message to be coming out of the music only. I didn't take in the plot or relate it to Stalin's Russia. But the music spoke for itself. That started me on my journey. The relevance of the libretto to our situation emerged as we went on rehearsing.

Did the other singers and musicians feel that they were performing 'dissident' music?

GALINA: By the time it came to the first night, most of them felt that this was a daring enterprise. After all, *Fidelio* had never been performed in Russia or the Soviet Union, and here we were, one year after the great leader's death, putting it on the stage with our best talents. But they didn't think we were in danger, and we weren't, because the people's finer senses had been too dulled and they were too downtrodden to pick up what Beethoven was saying.

You will recall how Wilhelm Furtwängler attracted some formidable criticism because he conducted Fidelio *in Hitler's Berlin during World War II and sometimes in the presence of Nazi dignitaries. It was said that he and his musicians were mocking Beethoven's music by the sheer act of performing it in that environment. After 1945 Furtwängler and his friends defended themselves by saying that it was precisely in that environment that* Fidelio *had to be performed – those who could hear understood the message. What I'm saying is that* Fidelio *was a litmus-test for many Germans, especially in the German emigration. It does not seem to have been one in the Soviet Union, or in the Russian emigration.*

GALINA: No, it wasn't. But there was another and quite mundane factor which accounts for the indifference. The Soviet audiences did not, as I say, much like the music – they found it heavy going. They were used to Moscow's staple fare: *Aida, Rigoletto, La Traviata, Boris Godunov, Eugene Onegin, Pique Dame.* Even Mozart was a stranger. *Fidelio* bored them. It's all very sad.

The Moscow correspondent of the Neue Zürcher Zeitung *reported recently (20 June 1986) that the death of individual Soviet soldiers in Afghanistan, though keenly felt by their families, was causing no national unrest and was not even registering in the minds of people as an 'issue'. 'There is in Russia no social fabric, no collective consciousness that would create spontaneous reactions of the kind the leadership would have to fear. The ability to abstract from individual suffering and to ascribe it to overall causes is just not there.' Isn't this inability to abstract from individual misfortune our best clue to your audiences' failure to react to* Fidelio?

GALINA: I would agree. Individual people in Russia do react, and react very strongly, to their losses in Afghanistan, but you are right in saying they regard them as an act of God and will leave it at that.

But there is another slight puzzle. You started rehearsing Fidelio *while Stalin was still alive. Clearly, the authorities did not expect that it would attract his displeasure. Why didn't they? As we know from Shostakovich and others, Stalin was extremely suspicious of*

Hamlet *and* Macbeth. *'Stalin could stand neither of these plays,' Shostakovich observed.*
'. . . A criminal ruler – what could attract the leader and teacher in that theme?'
Didn't considerations of this kind enter the minds of the cultural apparat *when the*
decision to mount Fidelio *was made?*

GALINA: There was a report in Moscow that Stalin admired Beethoven the
way he admired everything spectacular and exalted. That may have given
encouragement to the cultural *apparat*. But I don't believe the rumour was true.
Stalin was too much of a primitive. My personal feeling is that he could tell
what a straight *play* was about – a dithering prince of Denmark or a
tearful King Lear were clearly not to his taste – but he was less sure about
music.

But one can think of another explanation. A believing Communist audience
could have persuaded itself that *Fidelio* was about the Liberation of Man as
envisaged by Lenin. By the same token, your fascist audiences in Berlin during
the War could easily have thought that *Fidelio* was about the liberation of, shall
we say, Europe from Bolshevik or plutocratic oppression – and *wept*. Either
must have been pretty difficult to believe, but there is no limit to the perversion
of the human mind and to wishful thinking.

You relate in your memoirs that at one stage in your early life at the Bolshoi the KGB
tried to enlist you as an informer. You went along to the extent of not rejecting the KGB
outright, but when the first opportunity of freeing yourself from this connection came up in
the shape of an admiring Marshal Bulganin, you grabbed it and sent the KGB men
packing.

GALINA: I did.

In so doing you must have realized that accepting the KGB connection would have been
an unbearable limitation on your freedom. You were a child of Soviet society and had no
model of freedom you could emulate; yet you had an instinctive understanding of what was
right and what was wrong, what was freedom and what was unfreedom.

GALINA: Not quite. I could recognize *treachery*. I knew that it was wrong to
spy on my fellow musicians (because that is what the KGB wanted me to do).
You can be an unfree person and yet recognize treachery.

Whether you can or cannot is a moot point; I will not press you. But surely when you
asked Bulganin to stop the KGB you must have responded to the voice of some moral
indignation in your soul for which there were no models in Soviet society? Indeed, it
was Communist Party policy 'that every citizen of the USSR be an NKVD agent',
as Mikoyan put it in 1937, commemorating the 20th anniversary of the Cheka *secret*
police.

GALINA: Yes, I was led by moral revulsion. To resist treachery, baseness,
duplicity – these are God's instructions. You don't have to learn them.

But doesn't your yearning for freedom also come self-evidently from the inner recesses of
your mind – without models and without 'instruction'?

GALINA: I don't think so. The Ten Commandments are one thing; freedom
is another. Freedom can be negative.

Perhaps we should think of two different kinds of freedom: freedom from and freedom to. The first is, I think, easy to recognize: 'I am free from imprisonment.' The second is more tricky: 'I am free to emigrate to Australia . . . I am free to reject my heritage; I am free to support Solidarity, and so on.'

GALINA: I accept that. It is the second that was beyond my understanding while I lived in the Soviet Union. I have had to live in England, France, and the US for twelve years to comprehend the meaning of real freedom – the freedom of choice. That is perhaps why I have now lost every vestige of homesickness. In Russia my 'free' life was limited to life on the stage of the theatre. Real life began when my cue came up and I began to sing. Off-stage I was *playing* at life, not living it. Here in the West I can live a rounded life as a free person, on-stage, off-stage.

You said your realization of the meaning of freedom was gradual.

GALINA: Yes, we first left the USSR with the intention of staying abroad for three years, perhaps four or five. Rostropovich and I felt that the Kremlin let us go because we had become a nuisance on account of the Solzhenitsyn affair. We thought that during the years of our absence something might change in the Soviet government's attitude to us; but we had every intention of going back. We lived, therefore, in the consciousness that we would return – which kept me worried. The prospect of re-entering the Soviet system was paralysing.

In 1978, however, we were deprived of our citizenship. A terrible weight I had carried all my life was suddenly lifted. I felt I was being born again. The Moloch had released me. At last I was free!

You had, as you tell us in your book, a curious contretemps with one of Lenin's heirs, Nikolai Alexandrovich Bulganin, Marshal of the Soviet Union and Prime Minister at the time. He was, not to put too fine a point on it, strongly attracted by your charm and your singing and tried to win your favours. Unfortunately for the Prime Minister, you had just married Slava Rostropovich. His advances did not make very good progress, yet neither you nor Rostropovich could afford to be discourteous or uncooperative. This is not the place to reveal the whole story; I am interested in the 'patrimonial' side of Bulganin's courting of you.

GALINA: Bulganin was very upset because I had just been snatched from under his nose by an unknown cellist, a man much younger than himself. His courting was crude and passionate. He would send me his adjutants with carloads of flowers. The invitations to dine with him privately would pour in; he would telephone to urge me to sing at some reception or other, or would get the Minister of Culture to persuade me if he couldn't.

How did you meet the Chairman of the Council of Ministers?

GALINA: I met Bulganin in Belgrade when he, Khrushchev, Mikoyan and others made their 'trip of Canossa' to pacify Tito. It is the custom of the Soviet leadership to add some attractive singers, actresses, or dancers to their own dour company. So I was summoned to join the party and asked to dine with Tito, his wife (whom I was made to toast), and the entire Soviet delegation.

That's where I met Bulganin. He was a portly man with an avuncular air and a ready smile about him, looking like everyone's idea of a great Czarist general (which he imagined himself to be). The very next day the first flowers arrived, and I knew I would have to do some clever manoeuvring to avoid trouble.

You were becoming a member of a charmed circle and stayed there throughout your Soviet career. Was the circle charming, too?

GALINA: I had known these men only from the posters we had to carry, from the press and television where they had been displayed as supermen. Wisdom, virtue, foresight, a caring concern for the good of the people, revolutionary vigilance and suchlike were riveted to their names in the popular imagination. In reality I found them to be a closely-knit circle of ordinary power-conscious men of crude manners and sparse education, with a worm's-eye-view of the larger world, and unspeakable conceit. They were at the apex of the Mafia and they didn't make much of an attempt to conceal it. Also, most of them (and their wives) were very ugly to look at.

To answer your question: their charm was not immediately obvious, but their power was, and so was their addiction to alcohol. The number of times I had to sing to the chomping jaws of our drunken leaders is too many to remember. When I finally refused to comply with any more of Bulganin's invitations, I told him quite openly that I was tired of the gossip, that buffooning before his inebriated chums disgusted me, and that I found the whole experience humiliating. But that, of course, didn't put off the Prime Minister.

What fascinates me most in your story is that Bulganin tried to treat you as part of his baronial estate. He was the great feudal lord who retained a kind of ius primae noctis, a right of the first night, vis-à-vis the women of his choosing. Wasn't this Imperial Russia all over again?

GALINA: Had Bulganin's passion for me arisen a few years earlier, neither Rostropovich nor I would have escaped. Without Stalin at the helm things were made a little more difficult for him. But Nikolai Aleksandrovich was openly hankering after the days when men like Beria could hunt down the women they wanted and have them delivered by the security police. In his many alcoholic stupors Bulganin related to us with relish and a good deal of envy Beria's amorous adventures. I think he did look upon me as his property – one that had been temporarily rented but would be available again. Could he evict the tenant?

Did it occur to you that he might have really loved you?

GALINA: It did, and I think he might have. Certainly the scenes that occurred between Bulganin and Rostropovich on the theme of who-loved-me-more and who-should-have-me belonged to a comedy; but Bulganin's feelings may well have been genuine.

I don't think we can improve on the description that you've given us in your memoirs of how these extraordinary threesomes actually happened.

'N.A. drank a lot, and he made Slava drink. But Slava didn't need to be persuaded; he drank out of sheer wrath.

When they would both get tipsy, the old man would stare at me like a bull and start in on Slava.

'Yes, you beat me to it.'

'It looks that way.'

"And do you love her?"

"Very much, Nikolai Aleksandrovich."

"No. Tell me, how can you love her? You're just a boy! Can you really understand what love is? Now, I love her. She's my swan song. But, all right, all right! Let's wait. I know how to wait – I've had my training."

I would sit there between them and listen. He didn't acknowledge that Slava had any right to me. Every drinking bout ended with an explanation to my husband of how much he loved me and that anything I asked for I could have.'

In a totalitarian system it is no small thing to be so passionately courted by a power-holder. Had you not been just married, might you have succumbed to Bulganin?

GALINA: Perhaps I might. As I say in my book, the temptation to be a Czarina to the Communist Czar would not have been all that easy to resist. I must be entirely honest: I'm not going to say, 'Oh, it couldn't possibly have happened', because it might have . . .

Did you find Bulganin attractive?

GALINA: Czars are never unattractive. If you look at a portrait of the Sun King, Louis XIV, he was an absolute nightmare. Nevertheless he had great success with women. Power is a magnet.

Didn't Bulganin's declarations of love give you some small satisfaction – one of the Olympians, a Communist Prime Minister, prostrating himself at your feet?

GALINA: Let me put it this way: Bulganin's fervour did not in any way offend me.

Nikolai Aleksandrovich had the reputation of being an intellectual sort of Marshal. Was he?

GALINA: In comparison with his cronies in the Party and Government he wasn't quite so barbaric. He had slightly better manners and a slightly more lucid mind.

Soviet society takes great pride in 'Communist morality', which is Victorian and rather prissy by our standards. I find it surprising that the man who was Prime Minister in that society should have pressed his case quite so blatantly in front of your husband.

GALINA: Ah, but he was the Chairman of the Council of Ministers! He was our master and the rest of us were serfs. That was his basic attitude to Slava and myself. We were, in fact, lucky that we didn't live in Stalin's time. Beria used to have his girls' hands tied behind their backs – and on to the bed. Without any question: under Stalin my husband would have been sent to the Gulag or handed to the executioner.

Was Khrushchev aware of Bulganin's infatuation?

GALINA: Of course.

What was his attitude to it all?

GALINA: Khrushchev was a cunning and vulgar peasant. He would smirk and enjoy the story.

He didn't come up to you and say: 'Galina Pavlovna, you have a duty to Socialism'?

GALINA: No, he didn't. I saw Khrushchev only very occasionally.

You said the leadership were very close-knit and power-conscious . . .

GALINA: That is putting it mildly. They were drunk on power and highly arrogant about it.

No revolutionary 'humility' in the style of Lenin?

GALINA: None, if indeed Lenin himself ever had such humility.

A few years ago I was attending a concert in the Kennedy Center in Washington with Rostropovich conducting. In the foyer in the interval I saw Zbigniew Brzezinski, whom I had met a year earlier when Carter was President and Brzezinski his personal National Security Adviser. I walked past Brzezinski but didn't go up to him because I thought I had really nothing to say to him. Then suddenly I heard Brzezinski call out: 'Hello, Galina! How are you? Don't you remember me?'

I was thunderstruck. Did *I* remember one of the most powerful men in the United States of America? And how could this still powerful man be so informal as to call out to me in a public foyer within the earshot of all and sundry: 'Don't you remember me?'

This was as though, shall we say, Marshal Ogarkov or Mikhail Suslov had had the humility of thinking that he was an ordinary mortal whose image was not graven in perpetuity on the minds of all who had ever seen him. It just could not have happened in Moscow. Our leaders took it for granted that anyone who had ever had the honour of meeting them would remember them all their lives and do obeisance to them if they were fortunate enough to see them again.

Stalin once made the famous remark that Communists were 'special people', but probably he didn't quite mean it in the sense in which you have depicted the Soviet ruling class.

GALINA: They are indeed 'special people'. Seventy years ago they occupied our land and have kept electing and re-electing themselves ever since. Their images are our new icons, their wishes our commands. They are 'special' in the way all history's tyrants were special to the people who were unlucky enough to fall into their hands.

Anyone who has read your memoirs is, I think, tempted to agree with Virginia Woolf that it is hard for a West European reader to identify with Russian life and the Russian character. She observed in one of her finest essays, 'The Russian Point of View', that there is 'a cloud which broods above the whole of Russian literature'. In Chekhov, there is too much bewildering inactivity, in Dostoevsky too much 'soul', with its 'violent diseases and raging fevers', and in Tolstoy too much questioning of the meaning of 'life'. 'We find [she writes about Tolstoy] always at the centre of all the brilliant and flashing petals of the flower this scorpion "why live?" . . .' We are both enthralled and repelled; the landscape is breathtaking but alien to us.

Your book struck me with a similar force of enthralling strangeness. Yours is no fiction, and one should, I know, apply a different yardstick to it. But the common reader cannot quite do that. He reads you as a testimony to the most cruel period in Russian history, but also as history that might have taken a different turn had Russian 'soul' and 'life' not stamped it with their signatures. Your characters suffer from appalling luck; when they go down they die miserably of alcoholism or starvation; an air of doom envelops them and their families the moment they appear in our sights, and we pray that they be spared the tragedies we witnessed on earlier pages.

And where the air is less heavily laden, we marvel at strange and scandalous happenings. Who is that woman accepting a $400 bribe from the hands of Galina Vishnevskaya? Why, it is the Minister of Culture of the Soviet Union. Who is that man dropping dead at the rehearsal of Shostakovich's symphony dedicated to the theme of death? Why, it is Pavel Ivanovich Apostolov, Shostakovich's ideological watchdog and tormentor. Who is in that strange collection of singers who denounce Vishnevskaya and Rostropovich to the Central Committee for betraying the trust of the Soviet state and people? Why, they are Galina's favourite protégée Elena Obraztsova, and her Bolshoi friends, Atlantov and Nestorenko . . . One could go on. Such amazing images flit past our mental screen in bewildering succession and we are left wondering: Are they real? Are they the portents of yet stranger things to follow?

GALINA: Your gentle mockery is well taken. I have no objection to your parallel with Dostoevsky and Tolstoy; if you accuse me of having written about the same country and the same people Dostoevsky and Tolstoy had written about – to that I plead guilty. But my story is sadly real and very different from the sort of reality that inspired nineteenth-century fiction. Life under the Czars may have been hard and even beastly, but no one expected Tchaikovsky to write cantatas to glorify the deeds of the Czar and no one told him to make public denunciations of his fellow composers on pain of losing his livelihood. *Absolutism* is one thing, *totalitarianism* another – and that is my theme. The figures alone show the difference. According to respectable calculations, between the 1917 Revolution and the death of Stalin the Soviet authorities slaughtered, starved, beat or tortured to death or otherwise killed some 40 million of our own people. This is more than twice Russia's losses in the Second World War. Nothing like that happened in the nineteenth century.

Now, when your whole country is one festering wound, your individual men and women will bleed from a thousand wounds too. They will die of starvation, they will eat the flesh of fellow prisoners, they will betray their kith and kin for three square metres of living space; they will even write film music to the glory of Stalin (as Shostakovich had to).

And don't forget another thing: the Soviet Union is an enormous empire. It is the stage on which hundreds of nations, languages and civilizations clash and mingle. The conflicts in culture and perception are legion and the nervous energy they generate stupendous. Therefore it isn't (as you suggest) that the Russian people are unduly sensitive and metaphysical – although, for all I know, they may be that too – but that Soviet activism, superimposed on the permanent drama of the conflict of nations and civilizations, leaves the ordinary man in a state of breathless bewilderment.

Imagine the whole of Europe run by a single government, from a single centre, under a single ideology. Imagine the problems you would have to deal with as between Frenchmen and Serbs, or Englishmen and Spaniards, between Mediterranean and Germanic attitudes to work and timekeeping. That's the kind of permanent turmoil you have in the Soviet Union.

Let me, therefore, say that your slight incredulity is a sign that even sophisticated people in the West are not quite able to make the imaginative leap to understand what goes on under Soviet rule.

Don't misunderstand me. Personally I find the Russian inclination to use almost any human problem as a departure for profound questioning most congenial. It betrays a serious bent of mind, and the courage to face that great emptiness which is often the result of our quest for final answers.

GALINA: This was more true of our writers and thinkers in the last century than it is today. Our 'talking classes' today have more pressing preoccupations, such as finding a decent roof above their heads.

Nor did I seriously think for a moment that Soviet life wasn't exactly as you painted it. Indeed, I believe it is paradoxically the intolerance of the Soviet system that has caused an important spiritual element to be injected into Western thinking, for which we must, by way of felix culpa, be grateful to both Russia and Communism.

Pope John Paul II is said to have remarked not so long ago that the Church does not need intellectuals but witnesses, and to the extent that it does need intellectuals it needs them only as witnesses. It is, I would suggest, the great merit of many of those Russian writers and artists who fled or were expelled from the Soviet Union that they are such witnesses – whether they are Christians, Jews, Muslims, or agnostics. They have brought back to us the authentic voice of suffering and the cry for deliverance at a time when our own culture raises them only hesitantly (or not at all). When Solzhenitsyn arrived in Western Europe he was first celebrated not only as a great writer but as a seer and a prophet.

GALINA: I hope you are right, but I am not absolutely convinced. The truth about the Soviet system had been told in volume after volume by the most authentic witnesses much before Solzhenitsyn. There has *never* been any excuse for a lack of knowledge. The question has always been whether people in the Western countries were ready to take in the truth that was reaching them from the East, and to do something about it. And there you may be right in hinting that Solzhenitsyn may have played a vital part, because he is not only an inspired chronicler of the history of Communism in the Soviet Union, but also a tormentor of the Western conscience for having done so little to oppose Communism as a menace to mankind.

I regard my own small role in the same sort of light. Now that I live in the West I feel it to be my duty to tell people what is really happening under Soviet rule. Anyone who has read my book cannot possibly say 'I didn't know', or 'I don't believe it'. All Russians in the West have that duty, and I go on telling the truth about Communism to whoever happens to come my way: friends, the bus-conductor, the girl who serves me in the grocer's shop, my gardener. Let them all know – there must be no excuse left for anyone saying, 'We weren't told . . .' That much we certainly ought to have learned from the silence which surrounded Hitler's extermination of the Jews.

Talking about silence, there is a scene in your book which left me with a lasting impression.

Solzhenitsyn's wife, Alya, came to say goodbye as she was about to join her husband in Switzerland. More than a month had passed since Solzhenitsyn had been deported by the KGB. Alya Solzhenitsyn had assumed that your house was bugged, so she brought a blackboard and you proceeded to talk to one another by writing questions and answers on it, erasing the words as soon as they had been put down.

GALINA: Alya wanted to know whether we too were planning to go West – and at the time we were not. Little did we suspect that Solzhenitsyn's deportation and his reception in the West would soon make it impossible for us too to go on living in Russia.

But wasn't this a scene of pungent symbolism – you, Rostropovich, Alya, and through her Alexander Solzhenitsyn, trying to communicate with one another on a blackboard, in silence? I was reminded of Beethoven's deafness – and I could not help remembering your vibrant impersonation of Leonora, in Fidelio.

GALINA: Yes, we were all of us what you might call people of 'the word' and 'the voice'. Sound was our medium. Yet there we were, sitting in complete silence, like conspirators, trying to make ourselves understood in sign-language, and through chalk-marks on a blackboard.

Our voices had been strangled, first in public and finally in the privacy of my kitchen, too. If I were to make a film about our lives in the Soviet Union, this would be its final scene . . .

●

PAUL JOHNSON
Interviewed by Richard Stengel
SPY, June 1992

Paul Bede Johnson was born in 1928 and educated at Stonyhurst and Magdalen College, Oxford. He was assistant executive editor of *Réalités* from 1952 until 1955, when he joined the staff of *The New Statesman*. He edited the latter from 1965 to 1970. In 1976 *The New Statesman* published a famous article by Johnson, 'Farewell to Labour', in which he announced his disillusionment with socialism and trade unionism. He subsequently became one of the most fervent apologists for Thatcherism. Apart from his prolific journalism, he has published several historical books, including *A History of the Modern World from 1917 to the 1980s* (1983) (published in America as *Modern Times*), *A History of the Jews* (1987), and *The Birth of the Modern: world society 1815–30* (1991).

Richard Stengel was born in New York City in 1955. He was educated at Princeton and gained a Rhodes Scholarship to Christchurch, Oxford, where he wrote a thesis on expatriate American writers. He was on the staff of *Time* magazine from 1982 to 1988 and has contributed articles to *The New York Times*, *The New Republic*, *Vanity Fair* and *Esquire*. In 1990 he published *January Sun*, a non-fiction book about the lives of three families in a South African town, and he is currently collaborating with Nelson Mandela on his memoirs. The interview with Paul Johnson was originally intended for *Time*, but when the meeting went awry because of Johnson's curious condition, Stengel abandoned the assignment. He described the episode at a dinner party in the company of Kurt Anderson, the then editor of *SPY* magazine, who invited him to write up the experience of this 'foiled' interview.

'Come round to the house at four-thirty,' Paul Johnson said in his confident, donnish voice over the telephone.

I had persuaded an American magazine to send me to London to interview the great Paul Johnson: the magisterial Anglo-Saxon man of letters, the modern Macaulay, the contemporary Carlyle, the author of *Modern Times*, *A History of the Jews*, *Intellectuals* and, most recently, *The Birth of the Modern*, a man of towering intellect and equally lofty moral standards. This month HarperCollins is reissuing paperbacks of his best-known works.

Modern Times, which many consider his masterwork, is a bible for contemporary conservatives. Richard Nixon once called it his favorite book. Dan Quayle lugged it around with him as an intellectual prop during the first several years of his vice presidency. In the Iran-Contra hearings, Oliver North admiringly testified that CIA Director William Casey had read a massive book at one sitting – a book, Ollie recalled, by Paul Johnson. It was *Modern Times*.

By all accounts, Johnson is a family man and a devout Catholic. A man who has acted on his principles as an informal adviser to Margaret Thatcher, to Rupert Murdoch, to former Secretary of State George Shultz. Ultimately, Johnson is a moralist who writes history, a man who sees the narrative of human events as a set of moral choices. He is a man of principle, a man who has written that there is no excuse for improper behavior. He is also a man who loathes the press, once noting that 'most journalists are scoundrels. They should all be locked up.'

I arrived at Johnson's Bayswater townhouse at precisely four-thirty. I had decided to wear something tweedy, thinking that my rumpled sport coat would put him at ease, make him imagine that we were engaged in some sort of Oxford tutorial.

He met me at the door. He wore a salmon-colored tie. 'Do you have a photographer with you?' he asked as I entered his musty, antique-filled house. Actually, no, I said. 'Ah, well.' He closed the door behind me and said, 'Marigold was terribly disappointed not to be here to meet you.' Marigold is his wife. He ushered me into a book-lined den. 'I'm off to make some tea. You take tea, don't you – or *coffee*?' he said, rather ominously. Tea was fine, I replied.

A plate of chocolate-covered biscuits sat on the table. I took my place on a lumpy couch, figuring that Johnson would prefer to sit in the thronelike wing chair opposite me. He returned a few minutes later with the tea and then leaned back in the chair, eyeing me suspiciously. He made no move to pour the tea. I asked him if he would like some. He nodded.

'Are you married?' he asked me.

'No,' I said.

'Don't like *women*, then?' he said loudly, giving me a fishy stare.

'Well,' I said, 'I think perhaps I like them a little too much.'

'Why would you want to interview a chap like me?' he said irritably.

This was the moment for flattery. I told him that he was the great popular contemporary historian and a man of international stature. Besides, I said, I knew he was writing a history of the United States.

'Yes, I'm fascinated by America, I'm trying to find out what America is *about*, you see. What do *you* think America is about?' he said, looking straight at me.

It was a rather broad question. I said I wasn't sure what America was *about*, but that I suspected America was on the decline.

'Yes,' he said. 'I'd like to find out what America is *about*.'

I then told him that if he didn't mind, I'd turn on my tape recorder and begin the interview. What follows is the transcript.

*

RICHARD STENGEL: In *Modern Times*, you talk about moral relativism and how it has existed in the twentieth century. What examples of moral relativism do you see now on the world scene?

PAUL JOHNSON: [*Eight-second pause, during which time he scratches his chin.*] Don't know.

R.S.: Um . . . [*Seven-second pause.*] Certainly not on the same scale, perhaps, as the examples that you used before, but do you see any, uh . . .

JOHNSON: No.

R.S.: No? [*Six-second pause.*] Um . . . uh . . . One of the issues that you have written about is, uh, biological determinism. Do you think that – now that we're finding out more about genetic inheritances – the idea of morality is becoming less, uh, important and more a function of biology?

JOHNSON: [*Twenty-seven-second pause, during which time he rubs his face and eyes and then closes them.*] Don't know.

R.S.: Okay . . . [*Laughs nervously.*] Are these questions not up your alley?

JOHNSON: [*Eyes closed*] Don't know.

R.S.: [*Staccato*] Do you think Reaganomics caused the recession in the United States?

JOHNSON: [*Quickly*] Very unlikely.

R.S.: Um . . . [*Six-second pause.*] Very unlikely, but perhaps the speed with which money was spent and borrowed and the way the debt increased – don't you think that might have something to do with –

JOHNSON: Unlikely.

R.S.: What do you think has caused the recession?

JOHNSON: [*Slightly belligerent tone*] Don't know.

R.S.: [*Laughs nervously.*]

JOHNSON: [*Also laughs.*]

R.S.: Um . . . [*Eleven-second pause.*] One of the things that you've mentioned as being of great importance in the twentieth century is the failure of religious belief to disappear. How do you account for that, and do you see some of the excesses of religion going on now?

JOHNSON: [*Five-second pause.*] Don't know.

I turned off my recorder. His *Don't knows* had become progressively more churlish. His two *Unlikelys* had dripped with scorn.

I paused for several seconds after the last *Don't know* and then said, 'But what about the recent elections of fundamentalist Muslims in Algeria, and the situation in Iran – aren't those negative examples of the persistence of religion?'

He stood up and, without looking at me, rumbled out of the room. Five minutes passed. Perhaps he had trundled off to the bathroom? I stood and strolled around the room. I listened for running water. After ten minutes I walked into the hallway and peeked about. No sign of him.

After fifteen minutes I stood in the hallway and called out, 'Hello! Hellooo?'

I walked halfway up the stairs and looked around: nothing. I walked halfway down the stairs: nothing. Again, 'Hello?' Nothing. I returned to the den. After half an hour I put on my coat. I walked out into the hall, called out 'Goodbye!' and then shut the front door behind me.

I looked back at the house as I walked away. All the lights were out, and I didn't see any movement of the curtains. I went to a nearby pub and, half an hour later, called his house. The answering machine picked up, with Marigold Johnson's plummy voice on it. I left a message.

On the plane back, I leafed through the final chapter of *Intellectuals* and came across the following passage: 'I think I detect today a certain public skepticism when intellectuals stand up to preach to us, a growing tendency among ordinary people to dispute the right of academics, writers and philosophers, eminent though they may be, to tell us how to behave and conduct our affairs. The belief seems to be spreading that intellectuals are no wiser as mentors, or worthier as exemplars, than the witch doctors or priests of old. I share that skepticism.' So do I.

●

BIBLIOGRAPHY

Books

Ayerst, David, *Guardian: Biography of a Newspaper*, London, Collins, 1973.

Banks, Elizabeth L., *The Autobiography of a 'Newspaper Girl'*, London, Methuen, 1902.

Barnes [Crosland], Susan, *Behind the Image: Profiles*, London, Jonathan Cape, 1974.

Barry, Alyce (ed.) *Interviews: Djuna Barnes*, Washington, DC, Sun & Moon Press, 1985.

Barry, Alyce (ed.), *Djuna Barnes's New York*, Washington, DC, Sun & Moon Press, 1989.

Bell, Edward Price, *Creed of the Klansmen*, Chicago, published as a pamphlet by the Chicago Daily News, 1924.

Bell, Edward Price, *Major Interviewing: Its Principles and its Functions*, Chicago, published as a pamphlet by the Chicago Daily News Co., 15 January 1927.

Blathwayt, Raymond, *Interviews*, London, A.W. Hall, 1893.

Blathwayt, Raymond, *Through Life and Round the World, Being the Story of My Life*, London, George Allen & Unwin, 1917.

Blathwayt, Raymond, *The Tapestry of Life*, London, George Allen & Unwin, 1924.

Bleyer, Willard Grosvenor, *Newspaper Writing and Editing*, Boston, Houghton Mifflin, 1913.

Blowitz, Henri de, *My Memoirs*, London, Edward Arnold, 1903.

Boardman, Harry, *The Glory of Parliament* (ed. Francis Boyd), London, George Allen & Unwin, 1960.

Bohlke, Brent (ed.), *Willa Cather in Person: Interviews, Speeches, and Letters*, Lincoln, University of Nebraska Press, 1981.

Boswell, Young (pseud. of Harold Stark), *People You Know*, New York, Boni & Liveright, 1924.

Brady, John, *The Craft of Interviewing*, Cincinnati, Writer's Digest, 1976.

Brandon, Henry, *Conversations with Henry Brandon*, London, André Deutsch, 1966.

Breit, Harvey, *The Writer Observed*, London, Alvin Redman, 1957.

Brendon, Piers, *The Life and Death of the Press Barons*, London, Martin Secker & Warburg, 1982.

Brian, Denis, *Murderers and Other Friendly People: The Public and Private Worlds of Interviewers*, New York, McGraw-Hill, 1973.

Bruccoli, Matthew J., and Bryer, Jackson R. (eds.), *F. Scott Fitzgerald In His Own Time: A Miscellany*, Kent State University Press, 1971.

Bruccoli, Matthew J., and Bryer, Jackson R. (eds.), *Conversations with Ernest Hemingway*, Jackson, University Press of Mississippi, 1986.

Burnham, Lord, *Peterborough Court: The Story of The Daily Telegraph*, London, Cassell & Co., 1955.

Chandler, Charlotte, *Hello, I Must be Going: Groucho & His Friends*, Garden City, NY, Doubleday, 1978.

Chandler, Charlotte, *The Ultimate Seduction*, Garden City, NY, Doubleday, 1984.

Clarke, Gerald, *Truman Capote*, London, Hamish Hamilton, 1988.

Chesterton, G.K, *What I Saw in America*, London, Hodder & Stoughton, 1923.

Cockburn, Claud, *In Time of Trouble*, London, Rupert Hart-Davis, 1956.

Cohen, Morton N. (ed.), *Lewis Carroll: Interviews and Recollections*, London, Macmillan, 1989.

Coleman, Terry, *The Only True History*, London, Hutchinson, 1969.

Coleman, Terry, *The Scented Brawl*, London, Hamish Hamilton, 1978.

Coleman, Terry, *Movers and Shakers*, London, André Deutsch, 1987 (with an introduction by Alistair Cooke on 'The Art of Interviewing').

Coleridge, Nicholas and Quinn, Stephen (eds.), *The Sixties in Queen*, London, Ebury Press, 1987.

Cook, Edward T., *Edmund Garrett, a Memoir*, London, Edward Arnold, 1909.

Cooper-Clark, Diana, *Interviews with Contemporary Novelists*, London, Macmillan, 1986.

Crosland, Susan, *Looking Out, Looking In: Profile and a Self Portrait*, London, Weidenfeld & Nicolson, 1987.

Cunliffe, J.W., and Lomer, Gerhard R. (eds.), *Writing of Today: Models of Journalistic Prose*, New York, The Century Co., 1926.

Dawson, John, *Practical Journalism*, London, L. Upcott Gill, 1885.

Devlin, Albert J. (ed.), *Conversations with Tennessee Williams*, Jackson, University Press of Mississippi, 1986.

Diehl, Digby, *Supertalk*, Garden City, NY, Doubleday, 1974.

Driberg, Tom, *Ruling Passions*, London, Jonathan Cape, 1977.

Fallaci, Oriana, *The Egotists: Sixteen Amazing Interviews*, Chicago, Henry Regnery, 1968.

Fallaci, Oriana, *Interview With History*, Boston, Houghton Mifflin, 1976.

Foster, Ernest, *An Editor's Chair: A Record of Experiences and Happenings*, London, Everett & Co., 1909.

Giles, Frank, *A Prince of Journalists: The Life and Times of Henri Stefan Opper de Blowitz*, London, Faber and Faber, 1962.

Gilliatt, Penelope, *Three-Quarter Face: Reports and Reflections*, New York, Coward, McCann & Geoghegan, 1980.

Golson, G. Barry, (ed.), *The Playboy Interview*, New York, Playboy Press, 1981.

Golson, G. Barry (ed.), *The Playboy Interviews with John Lennon and Yoko Ono* (conducted by David Sheff), Sevenoaks, New English Library, 1982.

Golson, G. Barry (ed.), *The Playboy Interview II*, New York, Putnam, 1983.

Grobel, Lawrence, *Conversations with Capote*, New York, New American Library, 1985.

Hammerton, J.A., *Stevensoniana*, London, Grant Richards, 1903.

Harris, Kenneth, *Conversations*, London, Hodder & Stoughton, 1967.

Harris, Kenneth, *Kenneth Harris Talking To*, London, Weidenfeld & Nicolson, 1971.

Haultain, Arnold (ed.), *A Selection from Goldwin Smith's Correspondence*, London, T. Werner Laurie, 1913.

Hayes, Harold (ed.), *Smiling Through the Apocalypse: Esquire's History of the Sixties*, New York, McCall Publishing Co., 1969.

Higham, Charles, *Celebrity Circus*, New York, Delacorte, 1979.

Higham, Charles, and Greenberg, Joel (eds.), *The Celluloid Muse: Hollywood Directors Speak*, London, Angus & Robertson, 1969.

Hill, A.F., *Secrets of the Sanctum, an Inside View of an Editor's Life*, Philadelphia, Claxton, Remsen & Haffelfinger, 1875.

Hirshton, Stanley P., *Lion of the Lord: A Biography of the Mormon Leader Brigham Young*, London, J. M. Dent, 1971.

Holmes, Charles, *The Clocks of Columbus: The Literary Career of James Thurber*, London, Secker & Warburg, 1973.

How, Harry, *Illustrated Interviews*, London, G. Newnes, 1893.

How to Write for the Magazines (by '£600 a year from it'), London, Grant Richards, 1900.

Huber, Jack, and Diggins, Dean, *Interviewing America's Top Interviewers*, New York, Birch Lane Press, 1991.

Hyde, H. Montgomery, *Baldwin: The Unexpected Prime Minister*, London, Hart-Davis, MacGibbon, 1973.

Inge, M. Thomas (ed.), *Truman Capote: Conversations*, Jackson, University Press of Mississippi, 1987.

Juergens, George, *Joseph Pulitzer and the New York World*, Princeton, Princeton University Press, 1966.

Kelley, Kitty, *His Way: The Unauthorized Biography of Frank Sinatra*, New York, Bantam Press, 1986.

Kingsmill, Hugh, *Frank Harris*, London, Jonathan Cape, 1932.

Kipling, Rudyard, *From Sea to Sea: Letters of Travel*, New York, Doubleday & McClure, 1899.

Kobler, John, *Capone: The Life and World of Al Capone*, London, Michael Joseph, 1972.

Kunitz, S. J. and Haycraft, H., *Twentieth Century Authors*, New York, H. W. Wilson, 1942; and Supplement, 1955.

Leacock, Stephen, *My Discovery of England*, New York, Dodd, Mead, 1922.

Lennon, Michael, J. (ed.), *Conversations with Norman Mailer*, Jackson, University Press of Mississippi, 1988.

Liebling, A.J., *The Best of A.J. Liebling*, London, Methuen, 1965.

Ludwig, Emil, *Talks With Mussolini*, London, George Allen & Unwin, 1933.

Ludwig, Emil, *Leaders of Europe*, London, Ivor Nicholson & Watson, 1934.

Lyons, Eugene, *Assignment in Utopia*, London, George G. Harrap, 1937.

Malcolm, Janet, *The Journalist and the Murderer*, London, Bloomsbury, 1991.

Marcosson, Issac F., *Adventures in Interviewing*, New York, John Lane, 1919.

Martin, Thornton (Pete), *Pete Martin Calls On . . .*, New York, Simon & Schuster, 1962.

McClellan, David, *Karl Marx: Interviews and Recollections*, London, Macmillan, 1981.

McCrindle, Joseph (ed.), *Behind the Scenes: Theater and Film Interviews from The Transatlantic Review*, New York, Holt Rinehart & Winston, 1971.

Meriwether, James B., and Millgate, Michael (eds.), *Lion in the Garden: Interviews with William Faulkner 1926–1962*, New York, Random House, 1968.

Metcalfe, Philip, *1933*, New York, The Permanent Press, 1988.

Milne, James, *A Window in Fleet Street*, London, Constable, 1921.

Minney, R.J., *The Journalist*, London, Geoffrey Bles, 1931.

Morgan, Louise, *Writers at Work*, London, Chatto & Windus, 1931.

Morgan, Thomas B., *Self-Creations: Thirteen Impersonalities*, New York, Holt & Rinehart, 1969.

Morrison, Stanley, *The English Newspaper*, Cambridge, Cambridge University Press, 1932.

Mott, Frank Luther, *American Journalism, A History of Newspapers in the United States through 250 Years, 1690 to 1940*, New York, Macmillan, 1941.

Mott, Frank Luther, *A History of American Magazines, 1885–1905*, Cambridge, Harvard University Press, 1957.

Newquist, Roy, *Counterpoint*, Chicago, Rand McNally, 1964.

Newquist, Roy, *Showcase*, New York, William Morrow and Co., 1966.

Newquist, Roy, *Conversations*, Chicago, Rand McNally, 1967.

Newquist, Roy, *A Special Kind of Magic*, Chicago, Rand McNally, 1967.

Newquist, Roy, *Conversations with Joan Crawford*, Secaucus, NJ, Citadel Press, 1980.

Nichols, Beverley, *Are They the Same at Home?*, London, Jonathan Cape, 1927.

Plimpton, George (ed.), *Writers at Work. The Paris Review Interviews, Second Series*, New York, Viking Press, 1963.

Plimpton, George (ed.), *Writers at Work. The Paris Review Interviews, Third Series*, New York, Viking Press, 1967.

Plimpton, George (ed.), *Writers at Work. The Paris Review Interviews, Fourth Series*, New York, Viking Press, 1976.

Plimpton, George (ed.), *Writers at Work. The Paris Review Interviews, Fifth Series*, New York, Viking Press, 1981.

Plimpton, George (ed.), *Writers at Work. The Paris Review Interviews, Sixth Series*, New York, Viking Press, 1984.

Pound, Reginald, *Mirror of the Century: The Strand Magazine*, London, William Heinemann, 1966.

Probst, Leonard, *Off Camera: Leveling about themselves*, New York, Stein Day, 1975.

Reed, Rex, *Do You Sleep in the Nude?*, London, W.H. Allen, 1969.

Reed, Rex, *People Are Crazy Here*, New York, Delacorte, 1974.

Reed, Rex, *Valentines and Vitriol*, New York, Delacorte, 1977.

Reed, Rex, *Travolta to Keaton*, New York, William Morrow and Co., 1979.

Robertson, J.W., *The Story of the Pall Mall Gazette*, London, Oxford University Press, 1950.

Robertson, J.W., *The Life and Death of a Newspaper*, London, Methuen, 1952.

Robertson, J.W., *'We' and Me*, London, W.H. Allen, 1956.

Roudané, Matthew C., *Conversations with Arthur Miller*, Jackson, University Press of Mississippi, 1987.

Salmon, Lucy Maynard, *The Newspaper and the Historian*, New York, Oxford University Press, 1923.

Shaw, Gerald, *Some Beginnings: The Cape Times (1876–1910)*, London, Oxford University Press, 1975.

Shenker, Israel, *Words and Their Masters*, Garden City, NY, Doubleday, 1974.

Schults, R.L., *Crusader in Babylon: W.T. Stead and the Pall Mall Gazette*, Lincoln, University of Nebraska Press, 1972.

Shulman, Edwin L., *Practical Journalism: A Complete Manual of the Best Newspaper Methods*, New York & London, D. Appleton, 1903.

Spencer, M. Lyle, *News Writing: The Gathering, Handling and Writing of News Stories*, Boston, D.C. Heath & Co., 1917.

Springfield, Lincoln, *Some Piquant People*, London, T. Fisher Unwin, 1924.

Urban, George, *Can the Soviet System Survive Reform?*, London, John Spiers, 1989.

Van Gelder, Robert, *Writers and Writing*, New York, Charles Scribner's Sons, 1946.

Vanderbilt, Jr, Cornelius, *Farewell to Fifth Avenue*, New York, Simon and Schuster, 1935.

Vanderbilt, Jr, Cornelius, *Man of the World: My Life on Five Continents*, New York, Crown Publishing, 1959.

Viereck, George Sylvester, *Glimpses of the Great*, London, Duckworth, 1930.

Vrana, Stan A., *Interviews and Conversations with 20th Century Authors Writing in English: An Index*, Metuchen, NJ, Scarecrow Press, 1982.

Vrana, Stan A., *Interviews and Conversations with 20th Century Authors Writing in English: An Index, Series II*, Metuchen, NJ, Scarecrow Press, 1986.

Vrana, Stan A., *Interviews and Conversations with 20th Century Authors Writing in English: An Index, Series III*, Metuchen, NJ, Scarecrow Press, 1990.

Wells, H.G., *Experiments in Autobiography*, London, Victor Gollancz, Cresset Press, 1934.

Whyte, Frederick, *The Life of W.T. Stead*, 2 vols., London, Jonathan Cape, 1925.

Zolotow, Maurice, *It Takes All Kinds*, London, W.H. Allen, 1953.

Periodicals

'An Interviewer Interviewed', *Lippincott's Magazine,* November 1891.

'Are Interviewers a Blessing or a Curse?', by the Interviewed (Mrs Lynn Linton, Barry Pain, W.T. Stead, John Strange Winter, and W.L. Alden), *The Idler*, December 1895.

'Are Interviewers a Blessing or a Curse?' by the Interviewers (Raymond Blathwayt, Miss M.A. Belloc, Frederick Dolman, Miss Friederichs, and G.B. Burgin), *The Idler*, January 1896.

Frank Banfield, 'Interviewing in Practice', *National Review*, November 1895.

Kenton Bird, 'Impertinent, Inaccurate, Superficial . . . Has the Interview Had Its Day?', *Journalism Studies Review*, July 1980.

Kenton Bird, 'Who Conducted the First Interview? – And Was it the Start of a Downward Trend?', *Journalism Studies Review*, July 1979.

Raymond Blathwayt, 'The Editor of "Great Thoughts": A Character Sketch and an Interview', *Great Thoughts*, 1909.

Raymond Blathwayt, 'The Ethics of the Higher Journalism: An Interview with the Proprietor of "Great Thoughts"', *Great Thoughts*, 17 July 1892.

Raymond Blathwayt, 'My "Great Thoughts" Interviews', *Great Thoughts*, 1903.

Frank A. Burr, 'The Art of Interviewing', *Lippincott's Magazine*, September 1890.

'Character Sketch: Mr T.P. O'Connor, MP', *The Review of Reviews*, 1902.

'An Experiment in Journalism: A Talk with Mr William Hill, of the "Westminster Gazette",' *The Young Man*, November 1903.

Hulda Friederichs, 'Difficulties and Delights of Interviewing', *The English Illustrated Magazine*, February 1893.

Jim A. Hart, 'The McCullagh–Johnson Interviews: A Closer Look', *Journalism Quarterly*, Spring 1968.

Joyce Kilmer, 'The American Interviewer', *The New Witness*, 10 January 1918.

John B. Lane, 'Confessions of an Interviewer', *The Pall Mall Magazine*, December 1893.

Melvin J. Lasky, 'The Art of the Interview', *Encounter*, March 1989.

Arthur H. Lawrence, 'Christmas . . . Then, and Now: Mr George R. Sims at Home', *The Idler*, December 1897.

'Literature and Journalism: A Talk with Sir Wemyss Reid', *Great Thoughts*, 5 April, 1902.

Gertrude Lynch, 'Interviewed and Interviewer: Certain Celebrities as the Reporter Sees Them', *The Saturday Evening Post*, 18 March 1905.

'Mark Twain, A Conglomerate Interview, Personally Conducted by Luke Sharp', *The Idler*, February 1892.

C.E. Moreland, 'The Art of Interviewing: A Chat with Mr Raymond Blathwayt', *Great Thoughts*, 11 June 1892.

Gunnar Nilsson, 'The Origin of the Interview', *Journalism Quarterly*, Winter 1971.

Evelyn March Phillips, 'The New Journalism', *New Review*, August 1895.

George Turnbull, 'Some Notes on the History of the Interview', *Journalism Quarterly*, September 1936.